G000113256

THE NATIONAL

HANDBOOK

for members and visitors

March 2005 to February 2006

The National Trust is a registered charity
and is independent of government

© 2005 The National Trust

Editor: Pamela Smith
Editorial assistance: Cindy Edler, Penny Shapland
Production: Lorna Simmonds
Project Manager: Margaret Willes
Art Direction: Neil Eastell
Customer Care: Alex Youel
Designed by Mike Blacker (4254)
Database development: Roger Shapland
Maps: ©Maps in Minutes™ 2004. ©Crown Copyright, Ordnance
    Survey & Ordnance Survey Northern Ireland 2004 Permit No.
    NI 1675 & ©Government of Ireland, Ordnance Survey Ireland.
Print managed by Astron
Printed by Benhamgoodheadprint Ltd., Colchester, England
Printed on Matussiere & Forest VGreen Silk made from 100 per cent
post-consumer waste

ISBN 0 7078-0399-3

Photographic Acknowledgments

All photographs are taken from the National Trust Photographic
Library, with the exception of: p.5, photograph by Ian
Berry/Magnum Photographers; p.6 (above) & p.7 (above),
photographs by Val Corbett/Country Life Picture Library;
p.293 NT/Andrew Montgomery; and p.382 Edward Chambré
Hardman Collection/NTPL

National Trust Photographic Library photographers:
Matthew Antrobus; Bill Batten; Andrew Besley; John Boothroyd;
Andrew Butler; Mike Caldwell; Martin Charles; Colin Clarke;
Peter Cook; Joe Cornish; Derek Croucher; John Darley;
Rod J. Edwards; Andreas von Einsiedel; Derek Forss; Roy Fox;
Geoffrey Frosh; Jonathan Gibson; Dennis Gilbert; David Hall;
John Hammond; Paul Harris; Roger Hickman; Andrew Lawson;
David Levenson; Nadia Mackenzie; Leo Mason; Nick Meers;
John Miller; Andrew Montgomery; James Mortimer; David Noton;
Alasdair Ogilvie; Stephen Robson; David Sellman;
Neil Campbell-Sharp; Ian Shaw; David Tarn; Martin Trelawny;
Rupert Truman; Paul Wakefield; Chris Warren; Ian West;
Mike Williams; Jennie Woodcock; George Wright

Front cover: Lindisfarne Castle on Holy Island, Northumberland
Inside front cover: Detail of stained glass with William Morris's
motto at Red House, Bexleyheath, south-east London
Title page: Llyn Gwynant on the Hafod y Llan Estate, Snowdonia,
Gwynedd
Left: Detail of the dining room at Wallington, Northumberland
Contents page: (top) A statue in the garden at Buscot Park,
Oxfordshire; (middle) The dining room at Chartwell, Kent; (bottom)
Yockenthwaite Top Farm in Langstrothdale, Yorkshire
Page 25: Tulips at Sissinghurst Castle, Kent
Back cover: The Courtyard in the Back to Backs, Birmingham

Contents

General information

Highlights for 2005	4
How to use this Handbook	8
What's new	10
About the National Trust	10
Area Maps	11
National Trust Membership	372
Making the most of your visits	375
Conservation and Access	382
Holidays with the National Trust	384
Making contact	386
How you can help the National Trust	388
County Index	389
Property & General Index	395

Places to visit

South West	26
South & South East	106
London	166
East of England	178
East Midlands	210
West Midlands	234
North West	262
Yorkshire	294
North East	314
Wales	330
Northern Ireland	354

Sea dogs and Pagodas

In 2005 Britain is celebrating a 'Year of the Sea'. On 21 October 1805, Admiral Nelson died at the very moment of victory in the Battle of Trafalgar. The bicentenary is commemorated by a series of events throughout Britain under the banner of SeaBritain 2005.

The National Trust owns more than 700 miles of diverse coastline around England, Wales and Northern Ireland, including iconic sites such as the Giant's Causeway (a World Heritage Site) and the spectacular White Cliffs of Dover in Kent.

There are also many marine and naval associations with National Trust houses. On his return from his circumnavigation of the world, Sir Francis Drake was a national hero in search of a suitable house. In 1580 he bought Buckland Abbey in Devon from his sea dog rival, Sir Richard Grenville, and from the converted medieval abbey planned his attack on the Spanish Armada.

'The Wizard Earl', Henry Percy, 9th Earl of Northumberland, a portrait by Anthony Van Dyck, now hanging in the Square Dining Room, Petworth House, West Sussex

Another sea dog, Sir Walter Raleigh, shared his imprisonment in the Tower of London with Henry Percy, 9th Earl of Northumberland, after the latter was sentenced to life for his alleged complicity in the Gunpowder Plot of 1605. Raleigh is believed to have presented the earliest surviving English globe, made in 1592, to Northumberland, and it is still to be seen at his home, Petworth in Sussex. The 9th Earl's reputation as a scientist, astrologer, alchemist – and addiction to tobacco? – earned him the soubriquet of the 'Wizard Earl'.

Centuries later, in the dark days of the Second World War and the Cold War years that followed, the east coast of England saw a very different kind of activity from that of the Elizabethan adventurers. On a bleak shingle spit in Suffolk owned by the Ministry of Defence, history was made with vital research into radar along with the development of experimental weapons. But now Orford Ness is a wonderful National Trust nature reserve where the silent

The pagodas at Orford Ness, Suffolk

Please remember – your membership card is always needed for free admission

National Trust Wardens at Strangford Lough, County Down, by Magnum photographer Ian Berry

presence of those obsolete MoD buildings – the pagodas - fascinates visitors.

In celebration of SeaBritain 2005 the National Trust's Photographic Library is joining with photographers from the renowned photo-journalism agency, Magnum, to produce a major exhibition of images of the coast, reflecting the wide range of the Trust's coastal properties and activities. The exhibition will be launched at the National Maritime Museum in Greenwich on 23 March and continues to 8 January 2006. Other venues are the Gallery at Trelissick in Cornwall, the Lowry in Salford and the Waterfront in Belfast.
(See **www.nationaltrust.org.uk** for details.)

Everyone is welcome to take part in SeaBritain and find out about our maritime past, present and future, perhaps by visiting a favourite stretch of coastline or a property with maritime connections, or by helping with a beach clean or other voluntary activity. A wide variety of special events will be happening at locations throughout England, Wales and Northern Ireland. Some of them are mentioned in the entries to specific properties in this Handbook, but others are being organised as we go to press, so do check when you are planning a visit, or look at the National Trust's website.

part of

For further information check our website www.nationaltrust.org.uk

Philippa Hodkinson, gardener-in-charge at Lindisfarne Castle. She has tracked down many of the cultivars specified by Gertrude Jekyll

Take in the view

A survey undertaken on the National Trust's behalf last year asked people 'what do you really want out of the countryside? What do you value about it in your everyday life?' The results suggested that for at least 80 per cent of us, visiting the countryside is vital, the essential counterbalance to the stressful pressures of daily life. 'Peace and quiet', 'getting close to nature' and 'a sense of

freedom' came at the top of the list, along with fresh air and exercise.

The Trust has recently purchased a large area of open country on the outskirts of Belfast, including Divis and the Black Mountain, which till now could be easily seen from the city but not so easily explored. A series of new paths is being developed, which will give access to the hills, from where breathtaking views can be taken across the city and Belfast Lough, and on a clear day to the Mourne Mountains, Strangford Lough and even to Scotland.

Arts & Crafts in the garden

In March this year the Victoria & Albert Museum in London is putting on the latest of its blockbuster design style exhibitions – 'International Arts & Crafts'. In last year's Handbook we celebrated the Trust's recent acquisition of William Morris' Red House in Bexleyheath, the first and probably the most influential Arts & Crafts home. The Trust also looks after some wonderful Arts & Crafts

The view from Divis Mountain, County Down

Please remember – your membership card is always needed for free admission

The walled garden, Lindisfarne Castle, looking towards the North Sea

gardens, including two designed by Gertrude Jekyll. When Edwin Lutyens was asked in 1903 to convert the Tudor blockhouse, Lindisfarne Castle in Northumberland (see the Handbook cover), he called upon his friend Miss Jekyll to design the jewel-like garden. This little gem can so easily be missed, surrounded by stone walls in the midst of a windswept crag. It is being lovingly restored and cared for by one of the Trust's army of gardeners, along with the invaluable help of volunteers – and the castle still benefits from regular supplies of sweet

peas cut from the garden to adorn the rather surprisingly cosy interiors.

The second Jekyll garden is located at the other end of England, at Barrington Court in Somerset. By the time this garden was laid out, Gertrude Jekyll was a very old lady, and almost blind, so plans were submitted to her by the tenant, Colonel Lyle, with biscuit boxes of garden soil to guide her choice of plants.

The structure and style of Barrington epitomises the Arts & Crafts garden, with a series of outdoor rooms. This approach to garden design was noted by the architect Charles Paget Wade when writing about his own Arts & Crafts garden at Snowshill Manor in Gloucestershire: 'A garden is an extension of the house … a delightful garden can be made in which flowers play a very small part, by using effects of light and shade, vistas, steps to changing levels, terraces, walls, fountains, running water, an old well head or a statue in the right place.'

Whether you are fascinated by gardens or by houses, be they grand mansions or Modernist masterpieces such as The Homewood in Surrey, whether you like to be outdoors beside the sea or in the countryside, there is in 2005 a vast range of marvellous places to visit and enjoy.

The garden at Snowshill Manor, Gloucestershire

The Handbook gives details of how you can visit National Trust properties, including opening arrangements for the period from March 2005 to the end of February 2006 inclusive, admission charges and available facilities. Property entries are arranged by area (see map on page 11) and are ordered alphabetically within each area. Maps for each area appear on pages 12 to 24, and these show properties with a charge for entry, together with a selection of coast and countryside places mentioned in each introduction. Maps also show main population centres.

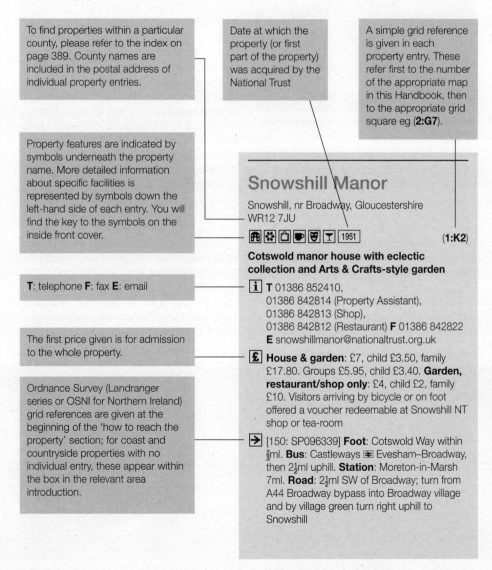

To find properties within a particular county, please refer to the index on page 389. County names are included in the postal address of individual property entries.

Date at which the property (or first part of the property) was acquired by the National Trust

A simple grid reference is given in each property entry. These refer first to the number of the appropriate map in this Handbook, then to the appropriate grid square eg (**2:G7**).

Property features are indicated by symbols underneath the property name. More detailed information about specific facilities is represented by symbols down the left-hand side of each entry. You will find the key to the symbols on the inside front cover.

T: telephone **F**: fax **E**: email

The first price given is for admission to the whole property.

Ordnance Survey (Landranger series or OSNI for Northern Ireland) grid references are given at the beginning of the 'how to reach the property' section; for coast and countryside properties with no individual entry, these appear within the box in the relevant area introduction.

Snowshill Manor

Snowshill, nr Broadway, Gloucestershire WR12 7JU

⌂ ❀ ⌂ ● ☻ ☂ 1951   (**1:K2**)

Cotswold manor house with eclectic collection and Arts & Crafts-style garden

ℹ **T** 01386 852410,
01386 842814 (Property Assistant),
01386 842813 (Shop),
01386 842812 (Restaurant) **F** 01386 842822
E snowshillmanor@nationaltrust.org.uk

£ **House & garden**: £7, child £3.50, family £17.80. Groups £5.95, child £3.40. **Garden, restaurant/shop only**: £4, child £2, family £10. Visitors arriving by bicycle or on foot offered a voucher redeemable at Snowshill NT shop or tea-room

→ [150: SP096339] **Foot**: Cotswold Way within ⅔ml. **Bus**: Castleways ≋ Evesham–Broadway, then 2½ml uphill. **Station**: Moreton-in-Marsh 7ml. **Road**: 2½ml SW of Broadway; turn from A44 Broadway bypass into Broadway village and by village green turn right uphill to Snowshill

Please remember – your membership card is always needed for free admission

Opening arrangements

The information is given in table format, intended to show at a glance when properties or parts of properties are open and when they are closed.

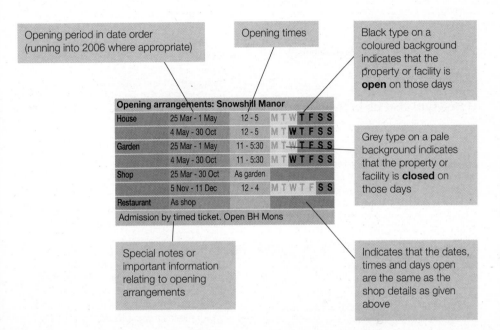

Opening period in date order (running into 2006 where appropriate)

Opening times

Black type on a coloured background indicates that the property or facility is **open** on those days

Grey type on a pale background indicates that the property or facility is **closed** on those days

Opening arrangements: Snowshill Manor

House	25 Mar - 1 May	12 - 5	M	T	W	**T**	**F**	**S**	**S**
	4 May - 30 Oct	12 - 5	M	T	**W**	**T**	**F**	**S**	**S**
Garden	25 Mar - 1 May	11 - 5:30	M	T	W	**T**	**F**	**S**	**S**
	4 May - 30 Oct	11 - 5:30	M	T	**W**	**T**	**F**	**S**	**S**
Shop	25 Mar - 30 Oct	As garden							
	5 Nov - 11 Dec	12 - 4	M	T	W	T	F	**S**	**S**
Restaurant	As shop								

Admission by timed ticket. Open BH Mons

Special notes or important information relating to opening arrangements

Indicates that the dates, times and days open are the same as the shop details as given above

Please note the following points about this year's Handbook:

- areas are shown in hectares (1ha = 2.47 acres) with the acres equivalent in brackets. Short distances are shown in yards (1 yard = 0.91m); longer distances are measured in miles (ml). Heights are shown in metres (m).

- although opening times and arrangements vary considerably from place to place and from year to year, most houses will be open during the period 1 April to 31 October inclusive, usually on three or more days per week between about noon and 5pm.

  Please note that, unless otherwise stated in the property entry, last admission is 30 minutes before the stated closing time.

- we make every effort to ensure that property opening times and available facilities are as published, but very occasionally it is essential to change these at short notice. Always check the current Handbook for details and, if making a special journey, please telephone in advance for confirmation. You can also check our website on **www.nationaltrust.org.uk**.

- when telephoning a property, please remember that we can provide a better service if you call on a weekday morning, on a day when the property is open. Alternatively, call our Membership Department on 0870 458 4000, seven days a week (9–5.30 Monday to Friday, 9–4 at weekends and bank holidays).

For further information check our website www.nationaltrust.org.uk

Properties open less often

This new feature, to be found at the end of each area section of the Handbook, lists those often fascinating National Trust properties (many tenanted) which are open significantly less often than the majority. Visits to some can be made by prior arrangement only.

Full details, including how to get there and access arrangements, are on our website **www.nationaltrust.org.uk** or obtainable from the Membership Department, tel. 0870 458 4000.

Come and visit us in Swindon

Summer 2005 will see the opening of Heelis, the Trust's new central office in Swindon, which will bring four existing central offices from London, Swindon, Westbury and Cirencester under one roof. A National Trust café and shop will be open to the public; parking (pay & display) is available in the Outlet Shopping Centre car park opposite the building. The name of the building was chosen to honour one of the Trust's greatest supporters and benefactors. Better known to millions through her children's books as Beatrix Potter, to the National Trust she was Mrs Heelis, donor of Hill Top and the Monk Coniston Estate, a huge area of fell and farmland in the beautiful Lake District.

You will find Heelis next to the Steam Museum on the Great Western Railway Works Heritage Site. (Kemble Drive, Swindon SN2 2NA. Tel. 0870 242 6620). The café and shop are open (from August) from 11am to 5pm every day.

New look website

The new National Trust website has been designed to be even more user-friendly and accessible for everybody. With improved mapping, page layout and new content on all our regions, planning visits to our properties and checking our events has never been simpler. **www.nationaltrust.org.uk**

The National Trust:

- is a registered charity, founded in 1895, to look after places of historic interest or natural beauty permanently for the benefit of the nation across England, Wales and Northern Ireland

- is independent of government and receives no direct state grant or subsidy for its general work

- is one of Europe's leading conservation bodies, protecting through ownership, management and covenants over 250,000 hectares (620,797 acres) of land of outstanding natural beauty and over 700 miles of coastline

- is dependent on the support of its 3.4 million members and its visitors, volunteers, partners and benefactors

- is responsible for historic buildings dating from the Middle Ages to modern times, ancient monuments, gardens, landscape parks and farmland leased to over 1500 tenant farmers.

- has the unique statutory power to declare land inalienable – such land cannot be voluntarily sold, mortgaged or compulsorily purchased against the Trust's wishes without special parliamentary procedure. This special power means that protection by the Trust is for ever

- spends all its income on the care and maintenance of the land and buildings in its protection, but cannot meet the cost of all its obligations – four in every five of its historic houses run at a loss – and is always in need of financial support.

The National Trust's core purpose is:

- to look after special places for ever, for everyone.

Our strategic aims are to:

- show leadership in the regeneration of the countryside

- deepen understanding of our cultural heritage

- put education and lifelong learning at the heart of everything we do

Please remember – your membership card is always needed for free admission

This key shows how England, Wales and Northern Ireland are divided into eleven areas for the purposes of this Handbook, and displayed on seven maps. The maps show those properties which have individual entries as well as most of those which are mentioned briefly in the area Coast & Countryside introductions.

In order to help with general orientation, the maps show main roads and population centres. However, the plotting of each site serves only as a guide to its location. (Full-scale maps can be purchased from National Trust shops.) Please note that some countryside properties, eg. those in the Lake District, cover many thousands of hectares. In such cases the symbol is placed centrally as an indication of general location.

KEY:

Map 1	South West
Map 2	South and South East
	London
Map 3	East of England
	East Midlands
Map 4	Wales
	West Midlands
Map 5	Yorkshire
	North West (S)
Map 6	North West (N)
	North East
Map 7	Northern Ireland

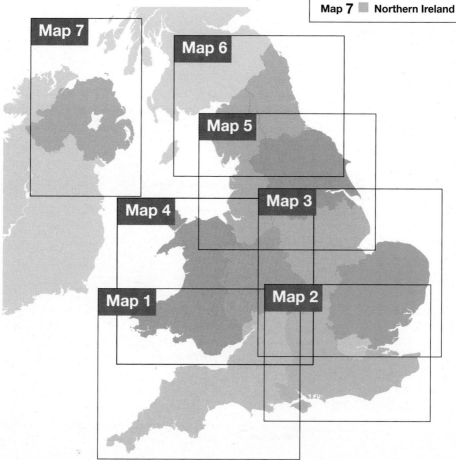

Map 1

- ▦ South West
- ▲ Buildings & gardens
- ■ Coast & countryside

0   10   20 Miles
0 10 20 30 Km

© MAPS IN MINUTES™ 2004

Map 2

South and South East

London

▲ Buildings & gardens

■ Coast & countryside

| 0 | | 10 | | 20 Miles |
| 0 | 10 | 20 | 30 Km |

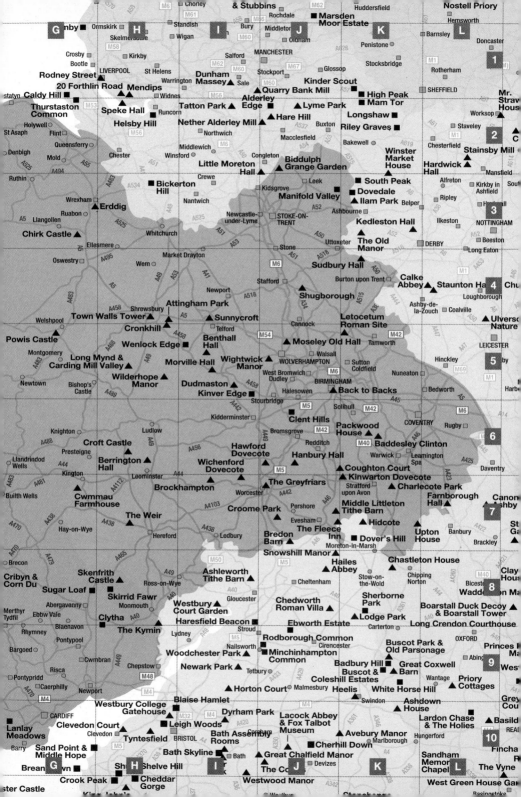

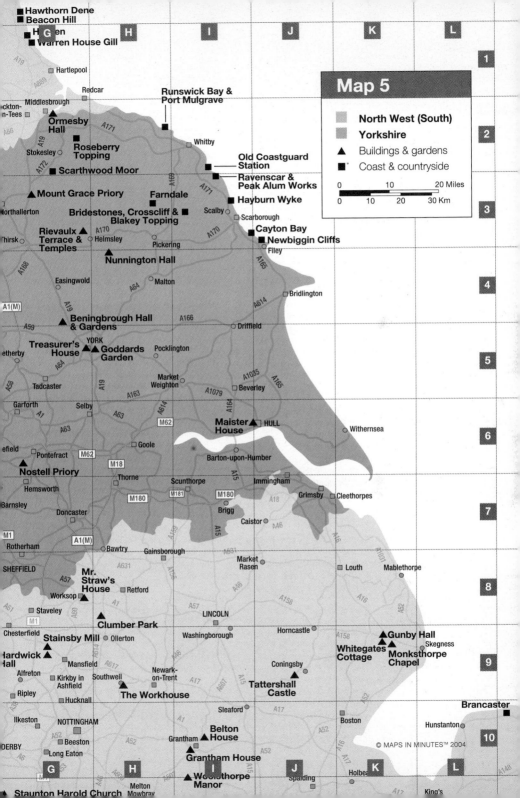

■ Hawthorn Dene
■ Beacon Hill
■ H en
■ Warren House Gill

G **H** **I** **J** **K** **L**

1

Hartlepool

A19

Redcar

Middlesbrough
ckton-
n-Tees
A66

Runswick Bay &
Port Mulgrave

Whitby

2

▲ Ormesby
Hall

A171

Stokesley
■ Roseberry
Topping

A172

■ Scarthwood Moor

Old Coastguard
Station

A169

Ravenscar &
Peak Alum Works

Map 5

North West (South)
Yorkshire
▲ Buildings & gardens
■ Coast & countryside

0   10   20 Miles
0   10   20   30 Km

▲ Mount Grace Priory

▲ Farndale

A171

■ Hayburn Wyke

3

Northallerton

■ Bridestones, Crosscliff &
Blakey Topping

Scalby

□ Scarborough

Rievaulx ▲
Terrace &
Temples

A170

Helmsley

A170

Pickering

■ Cayton Bay
■ Newbiggin Cliffs

Thirsk
○

○

Filey

▲ Nunnington Hall

A165

4

A168

Easingwold

○ Malton

A64

□ Bridlington

A19

A614

A1(M)

A59

▲ Beningbrough Hall
& Gardens

A166

□ Driffield

etherby

Treasurer's
House

YORK

▲▲ Goddards
Garden

□ Pocklington

5

A64

A19

Market
Weighton

A1035

A165

Tadcaster

A163

A1079

○ Beverley

Garforth
□

Selby

A63

A194

A1

M62

□ Goole

□

Maister ▲
House

HULL

6

A63

efield
□ Pontefract

M62

M18

Barton-upon-Humber

○ Withernsea

▲ Nostell Priory

Thorne

□

A15

Immingham

■ Hemsworth

Scunthorpe
□

M180

M181   M180

Grimsby
□ Cleethorpes

7

Barnsley

Doncaster

Brigg

A18

M1

A1(M)

□ Bawtry

Caistor ○

AA6

Rotherham
□

Gainsborough

A631

A15

Market
Rasen ○

□ Louth

Mablethorpe

SHEFFIELD

A57

Mr.
Straw's
House

A631

A46

A16

A101

8

Worksop □

Retford
□

A57

LINCOLN
□

A158

Horncastle ○

A158

▲ Gunby Hall

A52

▲ Staveley

A1

Washingborough
○

Whitegates
Cottage

▲ Monksthorpe
Chapel

Skegness

M1

▲ Clumber Park

□ Ollerton

A46

Coningsby

9

Chesterfield

▲ Stainsby Mill

Mansfield

A617

Newark-
on-Trent

▲ Tattershall
Castle

Hardwick ▲
Hall

Alfreton

Kirkby in
Ashfield

Southwell

A17

A607

□ Ripley

Hucknall

The Workhouse

Sleaford ○

A17

□ Boston

Brancaster ■

Ilkeston

NOTTINGHAM

A1

A52

▲ Belton
House

Grantham

A52

Hunstanton ○

10

DERBY

A52

Beeston

Long Eaton

A6

▲ Grantham House

Holbea

A148

▲ Woolsthorpe
Manor

Spalding
○

King's

G **H** **I** **J** **K** **L**

© MAPS IN MINUTES™ 2004

Staunton Harold Church

Melton
Mowbray

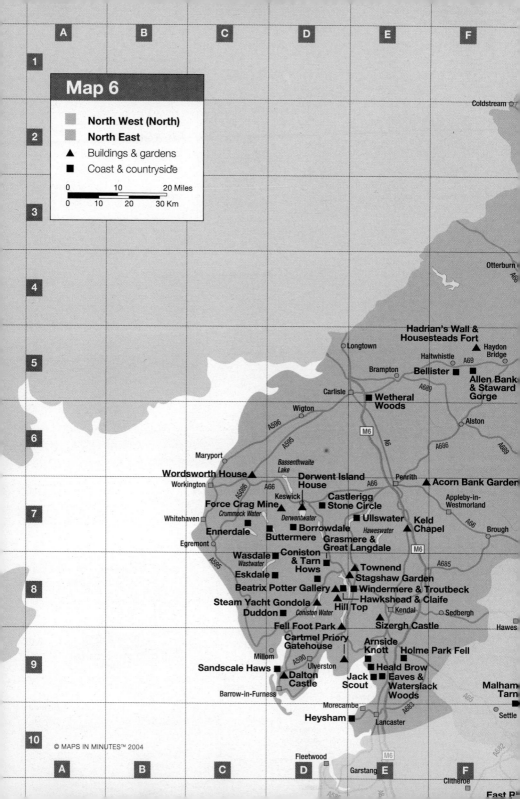

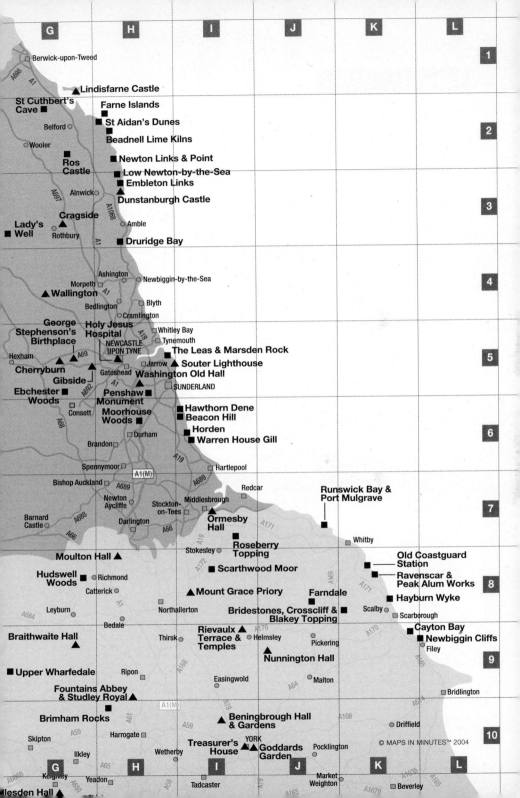

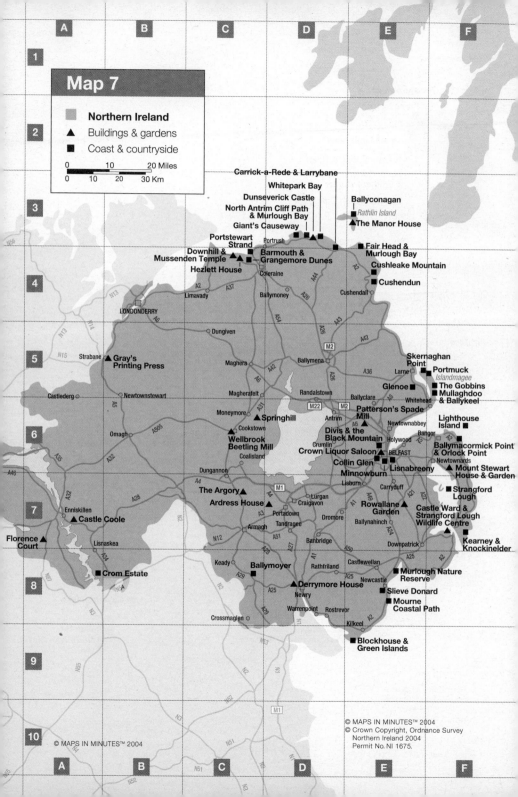

South West South & South East
London East of England
East Midlands West Midlands
North West Yorkshire North East
Wales Northern Ireland

In the far west of the area, the Trust's holdings in Cornwall amount to 9900ha (over 24,500 acres), including 161 miles of one of Europe's most spectacular coastlines (57 per cent of the total Cornish coast). There are magnificent walks throughout the county, many with breathtaking views. On the north coast, notable stretches include five miles either side of **Crackington Haven**, much of **Boscastle** and the **Valency Valley**, **The Rumps** and **Pentire** headlands, **Holywell Bay** and the **Kelseys**, **Wheal Coates** and **Chapel Porth**, **North Cliffs** and **Godrevy**, and considerable stretches of the Penwith coast including **Zennor Head** and **Cape Cornwall**. On the south coast, Trust land includes **Porthcurno**, **Logan Rock** and **Penberth**, **Loe Pool** and **Gunwalloe**, **Kynance Cove** and **Lizard Point**, key stretches of the Helford, Fal and Fowey estuaries, **Nare Head**, **The Dodman** and **The Gribbin**, and most of the coast from Polruan to Looe. Significant inland estates include **Godolphin**, **Lanhydrock**, **Ethy** and **Cotehele**. For further details, see the in-depth coast and countryside guides listed on page 31.

In neighbouring Devon, the Trust protects 111 miles of coast (55 per cent of the total Devon coast), including **Foreland Point**, **Countisbury**, the wooded valleys of

Watersmeet and the beautiful stretch between **Woody Bay** and Combe Martin on the Exmoor coast. The Trust also protects much of the coastal land between Ilfracombe and Croyde, including **Morte** and **Baggy Points**, between which extends a superb beach. At Bideford Bay, there are fine walks on the remote coastline between **Abbotsham**, **Portledge** and **Buck's Mills**, and also further west at **Brownsham** and **East Titchberry**, **Hartland** and **South Hole**.

South Devon has an equally interesting coastline. From **Bolt Tail** to **Overbeck's** near Salcombe run six miles of rugged Trust-owned cliffland, crossed by the coastal footpath, which dips to give access to safe bathing at **Soar Mill Cove** and **Starehole Bay**.

The area between **Portlemouth Down** and **Prawle Point** offers low cliffs with walks, views and sandy coves. The cliffs become more impressive again towards **Gammon Head** to the east.

The River Dart is a famous beauty spot, and the Trust protects several woods along the estuary, as well as coast on either side of the mouth at **Little Dartmouth** and between **Kingswear** and Southdown Cliff, near Brixham. To the east the Trust owns three miles of coastline between **Salcombe Hill**, Sidmouth and **Branscombe**.

St Michael's Mount, Cornwall

Previous page: Wheal Coates engine house perched above the sea at St Agnes, Cornwall

The Trust also owns extensive areas in and around the Dartmoor National Park, including fine walking country in the Teign Gorge, between **Whiddon Deer Park** and **Fingle Bridge**, below **Castle Drogo**. Downstream are the spectacular hanging oak-woods at **Steps Bridge**. To the south, on the fringe of the National Park, is **Parke Estate**, with delightful walks along the River Bovey. Near Buckfast are **Holne Woods** and **Hembury Woods**, in which there is an Iron Age hill-fort. Further west are **Hentor**, **Willings Walls** and **Trowlesworthy Warren**, on which there are also many archaeological sites, and the **Dewerstone**, a popular area for climbers. Nearer to Plymouth lie **Plym Bridge Woods**, interesting for their industrial archaeology.

The Dorset coast offers equally splendid walking opportunities. In total the Trust protects over 15 miles of Dorset coastline, most within the East Devon World Heritage Site and, including the highest cliff in southern England, **Golden Cap**. From here there are breathtaking views along the coast to Portland Bill. To the east is **Cogden Beach**, where the dramatic Chesil Beach starts. At **Spyway Farm** in Purbeck there are information panels about the area and access to the sea at **Dancing Ledge**, while to the north lies **Studland National Nature Reserve**, noted for its rare birds, unspoilt heathland and glorious beach. Between **Corfe Castle** and Wareham is **Hartland Moor**, another National Nature Reserve, home to all species of Britain's rarest reptiles. Adjacent to the moor is an area of 160ha (400 acres) of former farmland which is being restored to lowland heath by the Trust.

Inland Dorset boasts some of England's classic landscapes, with rolling chalk downland and hidden valleys. This is an area rich in archaeological remains, such as those at **Hod Hill** and **Turnworth Down**, near Blandford, and **Pilsdon Pen**, **Lamberts Castle** and **Coney's Castle** near Bridport, as well as the famous ancient figure of the **Cerne Giant**, cut into the chalk near Cerne Abbas. The **Fontmell Down Estate** south of Shaftesbury includes **Melbury Beacon** and botanically rich chalk grassland at **Melbury Down**, from where there are magnificent views across the Blackmore Vale.

The prehistoric heritage of Wiltshire is celebrated worldwide. Apart from the **Stonehenge Historic Landscape** and **Avebury**, the Trust also owns Iron Age hill-forts at **Figsbury Ring** near Salisbury, **Cherhill Down** near Calne and **Cley Hill** near Warminster. These sites are also important for nature conservation and all give fine views over

Pentire Head, Cornwall

the surrounding countryside, as does **Pepperbox Hill** and its 17th-century folly overlooking Salisbury, and **Win Green Hill**, the highest point of Cranborne Chase.

The extensive areas of unimproved chalk downland in Wiltshire are home to many rare plants, among them clustered bell flower, early gentian and many orchids. Insects include butterflies such as the adonis blue and marsh fritillary. In May the downs are covered in cowslips and the skylark sings high overhead. The Trust is grazing the sites, often with traditional breeds, to control scrub and coarse grasses, in favour of the grassland species, which constitute one of the richest habitats on earth.

To the north, the Cotswolds offer excellent walking, superb views and some of the most charming villages to be found anywhere in England, including Sherborne and Bibury which has **Arlington Row**, described by William Morris as the most beautiful village in England. The natural limestone amphitheatre at **Dover's Hill** is the venue for the annual Cotswold 'Olympick Games' and at the other end of the escarpment **Haresfield Beacon**, the site of a prehistoric hill-fort, offers magnificent views across to Wales. The **Ebworth Estate** near Painswick has many delightful waymarked walks through protected beech-woods rich in wildlife, as well as a daytime conference centre (tel. 01452 814213 for details).

Near Stroud are **Minchinhampton** and **Rodborough Commons**, an area of nationally important limestone grassland forming a steep-sided open plateau with a wide variety of wild flowers and butterflies. Minchinhampton Common has many interesting archaeological features, and there are breathtaking views from the southern side of Rodborough Common.

On the shores of the Bristol Channel near Weston-super-Mare there are fine coastal walks at **Sand Point** and **Middle Hope**. To the west is **Brean Down**, the site of a Roman temple, Iron Age hill-fort and other archaeological features. Nearby are **Crook Peak**, **Wavering Down** and **Shute Shelve Hill**, a limestone landscape with heath, scrub and woodland rich in wildlife. Inland, the Trust owns some dramatic parts of the Quantocks, including **Beacon** and

Old Light, Lundy, Devon

Bicknoller Hills, east of Williton. The **Wellington Monument** has stood as a pinnacle on the highest point of the **Blackdown Hills** since 1817. Built as a tribute to the Duke of Wellington's military achievements at the Battle of Waterloo, the monument is surrounded by grassland and woodland. Access to the top of the monument is limited and supervised by volunteers. Further east are **Glastonbury Tor** and **Walton** and **Collard Hills**, overlooking the remote expanse of the Somerset Levels. Further west, between Minehead and Porlock, the diverse landscape of the **Holnicote Estate** extends south from the Bristol Channel through farmland and ancient woodland to the high moorland of Exmoor.

The **Bath Skyline** is a beautifully diverse green area around the World Heritage City of Bath, encompassing an Iron Age hill-fort, medieval and Roman settlements, and 18th-century follies. The tranquil ancient woodlands and patchworks of small meadows are all rich in wildlife. From here there are spectacular views of Bath and perfect places to picnic, fly a kite, or simply enjoy this unique landscape.

Highlights for Visitors with Disabilities ...

In Cornwall there are accessible viewpoints at many coastal properties such as **Bodigga Cliff** near Looe, **Nare Head** and **St Anthony Head**. Estate walks at **Lanhydrock**, alongside the River Fowey, and at **Godolphin** are suitable for wheelchair users. In Devon the upgraded path from **Salcombe Hill** car park gives magnificent views over Sidmouth; **Plym Bridge Woods** has gates fitted with RADAR locks and a wheelchair-accessible fishing platform. There is access at **Hartland Moor** along Hartland Way to an adapted bird hide. In Dorset, a gentle slope gives easy access from the car park down to the shingle beach at **Burton Bradstock**; a summer boardwalk leads onto the beach at **Studland**, and **Stonebarrow Hill** at Golden Cap has marvellous views (and an adapted WC). Nearby **Langdon Hill Wood** has a circular forest route suitable for powered vehicles (access either via kissing-gates or gates with RADAR locks). Two easy access trails have been created on the Holnicote Estate in Somerset, at **North Hill** and at **Webbers Post**, offering fine views over moorland, woodland and coast. **Leigh Woods** in Bristol has an all-ability trail (see below). In the Cotswolds in Gloucestershire the viewpoint at **Dover's Hill** is wheelchair-accessible. From **Haresfield Beacon** there is access onto Short Wood where superb views can be enjoyed from extensive grasslands.

... and for Families

The **Heddon Valley** in north Devon is especially recommended for children, with bridges and stepping stones along the river, meadows full of flowers and easy walks which start from the NT shop and information centre. **Plym Bridge Woods** is excellent for family walks and cycle rides and a good educational site for groups of all ages. **Leigh Woods**, in Bristol, is ideal for families out on a walk, especially those with pushchairs who can use the all-ability purple trail which begins and ends at the Forestry Commission car park (no charge). The woods offer wonderful nature walks and diverse events throughout the year. Tel. 0117 973 1645 for details. Conegar Capers on the **Kingston Lacy Estate** is a woodland play area for children aged 5–13. **Dyrham Park** offers three parkland walks for families to discover stunning views, hidden history, magnificent trees and secret wildlife.

Further Information

Please contact the Membership Department, PO Box 39, Warrington WA5 7WD. Tel. 0870 458 4000. Email: enquiries@thenationaltrust.org.uk

The *Coast of Cornwall* series of 22 detailed map-guides, priced £1 each, covers the Trust's extensive coastal ownership and is available from NT shops in the county or by post from the shop at Lanhydrock, Bodmin PL30 5AD, tel. 01208 265952. 1 Bude to Morwenstow; 2 Crackington Haven; 3 Boscastle; 4 Tintagel; 5 Polzeath to Port Quin; 6 Trevose to Watergate Bay inc. Bedruthan Steps (not NT); 7 Crantock to Holywell Bay; 8 St Agnes & Chapel Porth; 9 Godrevy to Portreath; 10 West Penwith: St Ives to Pendeen; 11 West Penwith: Levant to Penberth; 12 Loe Pool and Mount's Bay; 13 The Lizard, West Coast: Gunwalloe Church Cove to Kynance; 14 The Lizard: Kynance, Lizard Point & Bass Point; 15 The Lizard, East Coast: Landewednack to St Keverne; 16 The Helford River; 17 Trelissick woodland walk; 18/19 The Roseland & St Anthony Head; 20 Nare Head & the Dodman; 21 Fowey; 22 East Cornwall: Polruan to Whitsand Bay.

Tamworth pigs foraging in the woods, Woodchester Park, Gloucestershire

OS Grid Reference

OS grid references for main properties with no individual entry (OS Landranger map series numbers given in brackets)

Abbotsham	[190] SS410277	Stonebarrow	[193] SY383934
Arlington Row	[163] SP115066	Haresfield Beacon	[162] SO820089
Ashclyst Forest	[192] SX999994	Hartland Moor	[195] SY963854
Bath Skyline	[172] ST777630	Hembury Woods	[202] SX726685
Beacon & Bicknoller Hills	[181] ST124397	Hentor	[202] SX595653
Bodigga Cliff	[201] SX273542	Hod Hill	[194] ST857107
Bolt Tail	[202] SX666398	Holne Woods	[202] SX712708
Botallack Count House	[203] SW365332	Holnicote Estate:	
Burton Bradstock	[194] SY492888	North Hill	[181] SS911476
Cerne Giant	[194] ST666016	Webbers Post	[181] SS903439
Cherhill Down	[173] SU046694	Kingswear	[202] SX885510
Cley Hill	[183] ST838443	Lamberts Castle	[193] SY366988
Cogden Beach	[194] SY503883	Leigh Woods	[172] ST555730
Collard Hill	[182] ST485345	Minchinhampton	[162] SO850010
Coney's Castle	[193] SY372975	Morte Point	[180] SS443457
Crook Peak	[182] ST387558	Nare Head	[204] SW918373
Damage Cliffs	[180] SS470465	Parke Estate	[191] SX805785
Dancing Ledge	[195] SY998769	Pepperbox Hill	[184] SU212248
Dewerstone	[201] SX539638	Pilsdon Pen	[193] ST414012
Dover's Hill	[151] SP137397	Plym Bridge Woods	[201] SX525587
Ebworth Estate	[163] SO890097	Portlemouth Down	[202] SX740375
Figsbury Ring	[184] SU193338	Rodborough Common	[162] SO850038
Fingle Bridge	[191] SX743898	Sand Point	[182] ST330660
Fontmell &		Sherborne Park	[163] SP162138
Melbury Downs	[183] ST885187	Spyway Farm	[195] SY998778
Foreland Point	[180] SS754523	Steps Bridge	[202] SX802883
Golden Cap:		Walton Hill	[182] ST474348
Langdon Hill	[193] SY413931	Wellington Monument	[180] SS137173
		Whiddon Deer Park	[191] SX725894
		Win Green Hill	[184] ST925206
		Woody Bay	[180] SS675487

Farmland near Tivington, Holnicote Estate, Somerset

Full-colour walks leaflets on coast and countryside properties in Devon are available, priced £1 each, from NT shops in the county or by post from the shop at Arlington Court, Barnstaple EX31 4LP, tel. 01271 851111. They include West Exmoor Coast, Watersmeet & Countisbury, Arlington, Killerton, Dartmouth, Salcombe, Castle Drogo and the Teign Valley, Bideford Bay to Welcombe Mouth, Wembury and Ayrmer Cove, and Ilfracombe to Croyde.

Walks leaflets for the Wessex area are obtainable from individual properties. Titles include Bath Skyline, Leigh Woods, Cheddar Gorge & Crook Peak, Golden Cap (detailing walks from Stonebarrow and Langdon Hill), Kingston Lacy Estate, Isle of Purbeck (five walks), The Cerne Giant and Dorset Hill-forts, Holnicote Estate (eight walks) and Stourhead Estate. Also available from local NT properties and shops are free leaflets on Wildlife and Places to Visit in Dorset, Somerset and Wiltshire & South Gloucestershire.

A La Ronde

Summer Lane, Exmouth, Devon EX8 5BD

🏠 📷 ☕ 🖼 1991   (1:G7)

Quirky 18th-century house with fascinating interior decoration and collections

This unique 16-sided house was built on the instructions of two spinster cousins, Jane and Mary Parminter, on their return from a grand tour of Europe. Completed c.1796, the house contains many objects brought back by the Parminters. The interior includes a feather frieze and shell-encrusted gallery which, due to its fragility, can only be viewed on closed-circuit television.

⭐ The size of the property allows for only a small number of visitors in at a time, so it is essential (as always) to contact the custodian in advance of a group visit

ℹ **T** 01395 265514, 01395 255918 (Shop), 01395 255912 (Tea-room)

£ £4.50, child £2.20

Opening arrangements: A La Ronde									
House	21 Mar - 31 Oct	11 - 5:30	M	T	W	T	F	S	S
Shop	21 Mar - 31 Oct	10:30 - 5:45	M	T	W	T	F	S	S
Tea-room	21 Mar - 31 Oct	10:30 - 5	M	T	W	T	F	S	S

♿ **Building**: Level entrance. Ground floor has narrow doorways, small rooms. Lower ground floor has small step and narrow doors. **WCs**: Adapted WC. **Shop**: Level entrance. **Refreshments**: Step to entrance

👁 Braille guide

🏠 NT shop. Plant sales

☕ Tea-room (NT-approved concession)

👶 Hip-carrying infant seats for loan

🎯 Children's quiz/trail. Adult study days

➡ [192: SY004834] **Foot**: South West Coast Path within ⅜ml. **Bus**: Stagecoach in Devon 57 Exeter–Exmouth to within ¼ml. **Station**: Lympstone Village (U) 1¼ml; Exmouth 2ml. **Road**: 2ml N of Exmouth on A376

🅿 Free parking. Parking for one coach only

NT properties nearby
Branscombe, Killerton

Diamond-shaped windows at A la Ronde, Devon

Antony

Torpoint, Plymouth, Cornwall PL11 2QA

🏠 🚂 ✿ ♿ 🏛 📷 ☕ 🛡 🚶 1961   (1:E8)

Superb early 18th-century mansion set in parkland and fine gardens

The house, containing collections of paintings, furniture and textiles, and home of the Carew family for almost 600 years, is faced in silvery-grey Pentewan stone, flanked by colonnaded wings of mellow brick. The grounds were landscaped by Repton and include the formal garden with the National Collection of Day Lilies and fine summer borders. The woodland garden (owned privately by the Carew Pole Garden Trust) has an outstanding display of rhododendrons, azaleas, camellias and magnolias, and surrounding woods provide delightful walks. Also of note are the 18th-century dovecote and 1789 Bath Pond House.

ℹ **T** 01752 812191 **F** 01752 815724
E antony@nationaltrust.org.uk

Opening arrangements: Antony

House	28 Mar	1:30 - 5:30	M	T	W	T	F	S	S
	29 Mar - 26 May	1:30 - 5:30	M	T	W	T	F	S	S
	31 May - 28 Aug	1:30 - 5:30	M	T	W	T	F	S	S
	30 Aug - 27 Oct	1:30 - 5:30	M	T	W	T	F	S	S
Shop	As house								
Restaurant	As house	12:30 - 5:30							
Woodland gdn	1 Mar - 30 Oct	11 - 5:30	M	T	W	T	F	S	S

Open BH Mons. Last admission 45mins before closing. Bath Pond House can only be seen by written application to the Property Manager, on days house is open

£ £5, child £2.50, family £12.50, family (one adult) £7.50. Groups £4.30, child £2.10. **Antony garden only**: £2.60. **Woodland garden (not NT)***: £4, child free. **Woodland garden season ticket**: £20. **Combined garden-only ticket**: £4.20, child £2.10. Groups £3.50. *NT members free only on days when house is open

Drop-off point. **Building**: Steps to entrance. Alternative accessible entrance. Photograph album. **WCs**: Adapted WC.

Grounds: Accessible route map.
Shop: Ramped entrance.
Refreshments: Ramped entrance

Braille guide

Restaurant (NT-approved concession) in east wing. Children's menu

Near car park

Baby-changing facilities. Baby back-carriers admitted. Hip-carrying infant seats for loan

Children's quiz/trail

[201: SX418564] **Cycle**: NCN27 2ml. **Ferry**: Torpoint 2ml. **Bus**: First 80/1 from Plymouth (passing close ≣ Plymouth), alight Great Park Estate, ¼ml. **Station**: Plymouth 6ml via vehicle ferry. **Road**: 6ml W of Plymouth via Torpoint car ferry, 2ml NW of Torpoint, N of A374, 16ml SE of Liskeard, 15ml E of Looe

P Free parking, 120yds

NT properties nearby
Cotehele, Saltram

The Chintz Bedroom, Antony, Cornwall

Arlington Court

Arlington, nr Barnstaple, Devon EX31 4LP

[icons] 1949
(1:F5)

Intimate and intriguing Regency house with interesting collections, set in extensive estate

Nestling in the thickly wooded valley of the River Yeo lies the 1125ha (2700 acre) Arlington Court estate. At its centre stands the home of Miss Rosalie Chichester, who lived here for 84 years until 1949. Crowded with treasures amassed from her travels, the house contains model ships, tapestry, pewter and shells. In the basement, from May to September, visitors can view Devon's largest colony of Lesser Horseshoe bats via the 'batcam'. The stable block houses one of the best collections of 19th-century horse-drawn vehicles in the country and offers carriage rides around the grounds. The 12ha (30 acre) gardens are largely informal but include a small Victorian garden with conservatory and ornamental pond, leading to a partially restored walled kitchen garden. Wonderful walks take in

Please see the area introductions for details of coast & countryside properties

Opening arrangements: Arlington Court

House	20 Mar - 30 Oct	11 - 5	M	T	W	T	F	S	S
Carriage Coll'n	As house								
Gardens	20 Mar - 30 Oct	10:30 - 5	M	T	W	T	F	S	S
	1 Jul - 31 Aug	10:30 - 5	M	T	W	T	F	S	S
Bat cave	As gardens								
Shop/tea-room	20 Mar - 30 Oct	As gardens							
Shop/tea-room	4 Nov - 18 Dec	11 - 4	M	T	W	T	F	S	S

Whole property open Sats of BH weekends; other Sats in Jul & Aug only gardens, bat cave, shop & tea-room open. Carriage rides available most days, tel. to check. Light refreshments only 4 Nov–18 Dec. Grounds open dawn–dusk 1 Nov–Mar 2006

historic parkland grazed by Jacob sheep and Shetland ponies, leafy woodlands and a lake with heronry and bird hide.

What's new in 2005 SeaBritain events exploring the unusual ship collection and the Chichesters' exciting maritime history

i **T** 01271 850296, 01271 851115 (Shop), 01271 851110 (Tea-room) **F** 01271 851108 **E** arlingtoncourt@nationaltrust.org.uk

£ £6.50, child £3.20, family £16.20, family (one adult) £9.70. Groups £5.50. **Gardens & carriage collection only**: £4.20, child £2.10. **Sats Jul & Aug (gardens & bat cave only)**: £2.60, child £1.30

⬇ Separate designated parking, 200yds. On arrival please visit Visitor Reception next to the designated parking. **Building**: Many steps to entrance. Alternative accessible entrance. Entrance to carriage collection is level. 2 wheelchairs. Ground floor accessible. Many stairs with handrail to other floors. There are stairs to the hay loft in the carriage collection. Seating available. Photograph album. **WCs**: Adapted WC. **Grounds**: Partly accessible, loose gravel paths, slopes. Accessible route map. 2 single-seater PMV. **Shop**: Level entrance. **Refreshments**: Level entrance

👐 Braille guide and large-print guide. Sensory list. Handling collection

📷 NT shop. Plant sales

🍴 Old Kitchen Tea-room (licensed). Serves hot and cold meals and picnic food. Children's menu

👶 Baby-changing facilities. Front-carrying baby slings and hip-carrying infant seats for loan. Children's play area

🏫 Suitable for school groups. Education room/centre. Family guide. Children's quiz/trail

🐕 On short leads in gardens, grounds and carriage collection only

→ [180: SS611405] **Bus**: First 309 Barnstaple–Lynton (passing close ≋ Barnstaple). **Station**: Barnstaple 8ml. **Road**: 8ml NE of Barnstaple on A39. Use A399 from South Molton if travelling from the south

P Free parking, 150yds. Coaches access car park at 2nd entrance. An area will be marked off if prior warning is given

NT properties nearby
Dunster Castle, Knightshayes Court, North Devon Coastline, Watersmeet House

Ashleworth Tithe Barn

Ashleworth, Gloucestershire

🏠 1956   (1:J2)

15th-century tithe barn

The barn, with its immense stone-tiled roof, is picturesquely located on the banks of the River Severn.

⭐ No WC

i **T** 01452 814213 **F** 01452 810055 **E** ashleworth@nationaltrust.org.uk

£ £1

→ [162: SO818252] **Bus**: Swanbrook 51 Gloucester–Tewkesbury (passing close ≋ Gloucester), alight Ashleworth ¼ml. **Station**: Gloucester 7ml. **Road**: 6ml N of Gloucester, 1¼ml E of Hartpury (A417), on W bank of Severn, SE of Ashleworth

P Parking (not NT) on the roadside

NT properties nearby
Bredon Barn, May Hill, Westbury Court Garden

Opening arrangements: Ashleworth Tithe Barn

	1 Apr - 31 Oct	9 - 6	M	T	W	T	F	S	S

Closes dusk if earlier. Other times by appointment

Unless indicated, last admission is always 30mins before closing time

Avebury

nr Marlborough, Wiltshire SN8 1RF

 1943 (1:K4)

World-famous stone circle at the heart of a prehistoric landscape

The stone circle, Avebury, Wiltshire

One of the most important megalithic monuments in Europe is spread over a vast area at Avebury, much of it under Trust protection. The great stone circle, encompassing part of the village of Avebury, is enclosed by a ditch and external bank and approached by an avenue of stones. Many of the stones were re-erected in the 1930s by the archaeologist Alexander Keiller. The site museum, including an exhibition in the 17th-century thatched threshing barn, presents the archaeological story. Finds from the site and interactive and audio-visual displays are used to tell the story of the monuments and the people who have helped to reveal their past. Nearby, Windmill Hill was once the site of an important Neolithic settlement and has several well-preserved Bronze Age burial mounds. West of Avebury, the Iron Age earthwork of Oldbury Castle crowns Cherhill Down, along with the conspicuous Lansdowne Monument. With the spectacular folds of Calstone Coombes, this area of open downland provides wonderful walking opportunities.

[i] **T** 01672 539250, 01672 539384 (Shop), 01672 539514 (Restaurant)
F 01672 538038
E avebury@nationaltrust.org.uk

[£] **Alexander Keiller Museum inc. Barn Gallery**: £4.20, child £2.10, family £10.50, family (one adult) £7.50. Groups £3.60, child £1.80. Reduced rate when arriving by public transport or cycle. EH members free. Stone circle free

[🚶] *Walking around Avebury* guide features six local walks; obtainable from property (£2.50 plus 50p p&p)

[♿] Separate designated parking, 200yds. Drop-off point. **Building**: 2 museum galleries accessible. Ramped entrance. **WCs**: Adapted WC. **Grounds**: Only parts of the circle accessible. **Shop**: Level entrance. **Refreshments**: Level entrance

[🔊] Induction loop in audio-visual presentation

[♿] Braille guide and large-print guide. Handling collection

[🛍] In Granary. Also museum shop sells books on archaeology

[🍽] The Circle Restaurant (licensed). Serves vegetarian lunches and teas, specialising in vegan and gluten-free dishes, using organic and local products. Children's menu

[🪑] Picnic area by barn

[👶] Baby-changing facilities. Pushchairs and baby back-carriers admitted

[🏫] Suitable for school groups. Education room/centre

[🐕] On leads in stone circle

[🚴] Ridgeway National Trail and NCN4 and 45 go through property and are shared with walkers

[→] [173: SU102699] **Foot**: Ridgeway National Trail. **Cycle**: NCN4 and 45. **Bus**: Stagecoach in Swindon/First 49 Swindon–Trowbridge; Thamesdown 48/A, 49A from Marlborough; Wilts & Dorset 5, 6 Salisbury–Swindon. All

Opening arrangements: Avebury										
Stone circle	All year		M	T	W	T	F	S	S
Museum	1 Apr - 31 Oct	10 - 6	M	T	W	T	F	S	S
	1 Nov - 31 Mar 06	10 - 4	M	T	W	T	F	S	S
Shop	1 Apr - 31 Oct	10 - 6	M	T	W	T	F	S	S
	1 Nov - 31 Mar 06	11 - 4	M	T	W	T	F	S	S
Restaurant	As museum								

Closes dusk if earlier. Closed 24–26 Dec

There are special events at most Trust properties; please telephone 0870 458 4000 for details

pass close ⛁ Swindon. **Station**: Pewsey 10ml; Swindon 11ml. **Road**: 6ml W of Marlborough, 1ml N of the Bath road (A4) on A4361 and B4003

P Parking, 500yds, £1 (pay & display). Located off A4361. EH members free. Parking during the Summer Solstice 18–23 June will be very limited. Tel. Estate office before travelling

NT properties nearby
Lacock

Avebury Manor & Garden

nr Marlborough, Wiltshire SN8 1RF

 1991   **(1:K4)**

16th-century manor house with lovely Edwardian garden

A much-altered house of monastic origin, the present buildings date from the early 16th century, with notable Queen Anne alterations and Edwardian renovation. The garden was completely redesigned in the early 20th century by Colonel and Mrs Jenner. The topiary and other formal gardens are contained within walls and ancient clipped box, creating numerous 'rooms'. Some features may be survivals of the original priory precinct.

⭐ The manor house is occupied and furnished by private leaseholders, who open a part of it to visitors. Owing to restricted space guided tours operate and ticket numbers are limited. Tours

run every 40 minutes from 2, last tour 4.40. Following periods of prolonged wet weather it may be necessary to close the house and garden. No smoking in house or garden

i **T** 01672 539250 (Avebury Estate office)
F 01672 538038 (Avebury Estate office)
E avebury@nationaltrust.org.uk

£ £3.90, child £2. **Garden only**: £3, child £1.50. Groups £2.55, child £1.30

⫪ To house only

♿ Separate designated parking, 300yds. Drop-off point. **Building**: Step to entrance, ramp available. Stairs to other floors. **WCs**: Adapted WC. **Grounds**: Accessible route

◈ Braille guide and large-print guide

⫪ House not suitable for young children

→ [173: SU100699] As Avebury

P Parking, 600yds, £1 (pay & display). Located off A4361. EH members free. Parking during the Summer Solstice 18–23 June will be very limited. Tel. Estate office before travelling

NT properties nearby
Lacock

Opening arrangements: Avebury Manor									
House	27 Mar - 31 Oct	2 - 4:40	**M**	**T**	W	T	F	S	**S**
Garden	25 Mar - 31 Oct	11 - 5:30	**M**	**T**	W	T	F	**S**	**S**
Admission by timed ticket and guided tour (max. 12 per tour). Last admission to house 4.40; to garden 5 or dusk if earlier									

Barrington Court

Barrington, nr Ilminster, Somerset TA19 0NQ

🏠 🐾 ✢ 🗋 🍴 🍽 1907 (1:16)

Jekyll-inspired garden, working kitchen garden and Tudor manor house

The enchanting formal garden, influenced by Gertrude Jekyll, is laid out in a series of walled rooms, including the White Garden, the Rose and Iris Garden and the Lily Garden. The working kitchen garden has espaliered apple, pear and plum trees trained along high stone walls. The Tudor manor house was restored in the 1920s by the Lyle family. It is let to Stuart Interiors as showrooms with antique furniture for sale, thereby offering NT visitors a different kind of visit.

ℹ️ **T** 01460 241938, 01460 242614 (Infoline), 0870 240 4068 (Box office), 01460 243127 (Shop), 01460 249332 (Plant sales), 01460 243129 (Restaurant)
F 01460 243133
E barringtoncourt@nationaltrust.org.uk

£ £6, child £3, family £14.50. Groups £5.10

🎪 Programme of events, inc. varied selection for families. Send s.a.e. for details

Opening arrangements: Barrington Court			M	T	W	T	F	S	S
House/garden	3 Mar - 20 Mar	11 - 4:30				**T**	**F**	**S**	**S**
	21 Mar - 30 Sep	11 - 5:30	**M**	**T**		**T**	**F**	**S**	**S**
	1 Oct - 30 Oct	11 - 4:30				**T**	**F**	**S**	**S**
Restaurant	3 Mar - 20 Mar	11 - 4				**T**	**F**	**S**	**S**
	21 Mar - 30 Sep	12 - 3	**M**	**T**		**T**	**F**		
	26 Mar - 25 Sep	12 - 5						**S**	**S**
	1 Oct - 30 Oct	11 - 4				**T**	**F**	**S**	**S**
Beagles Café	5 Mar - 20 Mar	10:30 - 4						**S**	**S**
	21 Mar - 30 Sep	10:30 - 5	**M**			**T**	**F**	**S**	**S**
	1 Oct - 30 Oct	10:30 - 4						**S**	**S**
Shop	As house/gdn								

21 March–30 Sept: restaurant open for lunches only weekdays, for lunches and teas weekends. Café may be closed in poor weather (March & Oct) but restaurant will be open

♿ Designated parking in main car park. Drop-off point. **Building**: Step to entrance. 2 wheelchairs, booking essential. Ground floor accessible. Many stairs to other floors. Seating available. **WCs**: Adapted WC. **Grounds**: Partly accessible, uneven paths. Accessible route map. 1 single-seater PMV, booking essential. **Shop**: Level entrance. **Refreshments**: Level entrance

👁 Large-print guide. Touchable objects and interesting scents

🗋 NT shop. Plants and kitchen garden produce

🍽 Strode House Restaurant (licensed). Available for functions and Christmas lunches (booking essential). Children's menu. Beagles café

🅰 In designated area near car park

👶 Baby-changing facilities. Pushchairs and baby back-carriers admitted

🎒 Suitable for school groups. Children's quiz/trail

➡️ [193: ST396182] **Cycle**: NCN30. **Bus**: First 630, 632/3 Martock–Taunton (passing close ➹ Taunton). **Station**: Crewkerne 7ml. **Road**: In Barrington village, 5ml NE of Ilminster, on B3168. Signposted from A358 (Ilminster–Taunton) or A303 (Hayes End roundabout)

P Free parking, 30yds

NT properties nearby
Fyne Court, Lytes Cary Manor, Montacute House, Tintinhull Garden, Treasurer's House

Statue in the kitchen garden, Barrington Court, Somerset

Please note: groups must book in advance with the property

Bath Assembly Rooms

Bennett Street, Bath, Bath & NE Somerset
BA1 2QH

🏛 🏠 💼 🔔 ⑂ 1931   **(1:J4)**

**Elegant public rooms at the heart of
fashionable 18th-century Bath life**

Designed by John Wood the Younger in 1769, at
a time when Bath and its spa were becoming
fashionable among polite society, the Assembly
Rooms were both a meeting place and a venue
for public functions. Bombed in 1942, they were
subsequently restored and are now let to Bath &
North East Somerset Council, which has its
Museum of Costume on the lower ground floor.

What's new in 2005 Family activities every Wed
in summer hols

ℹ️ **T** 01225 477752 **F** 01225 428184

£ Admission free. Admission charge to Museum
of Costume (inc. NT members)

👟 When Rooms not in use for booked functions

🎧 7 languages

🎭 Programme of events, inc. 'behind the
scenes' events in August

♿ Parking nearby for disabled badge holders
only. Parking in city centre car parks. Nearest
Charlotte St. Drop-off point. **Building**: Level
entrance. 1 wheelchair, booking essential.
Ground floor accessible. Stairs to other floors,
lift available. Seating available. **WCs**: Adapted
WC. **Grounds**: Fully accessible. Small formal
garden used as a café in the summer.
Shop: Level entrance. **Refreshments**: Level
entrance. Large-print menu

👂 Sign interpreter by arrangement. Audioguide
T-function for hearing-aid users

👁 Sensory list

Opening arrangements: Bath Assembly Rooms			
Rooms	1 Mar - 31 Oct	11 - 6	**M T W T F S S**
	1 Nov - 28 Feb 06	11 - 5	**M T W T F S S**
Shop	As rooms		

Last admission 1hr before closing. Closed when in use
for booked functions and 25/26 Dec. Access is
guaranteed in Aug, but at other times visitors should
tel. in advance

💼 Assembly Rooms Café (not NT) in card room
and formal garden. Open daily all year,
available when rooms not in use for booked
functions; tel. 01225 444477 for reservations

🚼 Baby-changing facilities. Pushchairs admitted

🏫 Suitable for school groups. Hands-on activities

➡️ [156: ST749653] **Cycle**: NCN4 ¼ml.
Bus: From ≋ Bath Spa and surrounding
areas. **Station**: Bath Spa ¾ml. **Road**: N of
Milsom Street, E of the Circus

P Parking (not NT) (pay & display), charge inc.
NT members. Street parking very limited, park
& ride recommended

NT properties nearby
The Courts Garden, Dyrham Park, Great Chalfield
Manor, Lacock, Leigh Woods, Prior Park,
Tyntesfield, Westbury College Gatehouse,
Westwood Manor

Blaise Hamlet

Henbury, nr Bristol

🏛 1943   **(1:I4)**

Nine rustic cottages around a green

The hamlet of nine different Picturesque cottages
was designed by John Nash in 1809 for Quaker
banker and philanthropist John Harford, to
accommodate Blaise Estate pensioners.

⭐ No WC

ℹ️ **T** 01225 833977 (Property Manager)

£ Admission free. Access to green only;
cottages not open. Please respect tenants'
privacy

♿ Four steps into the Hamlet, otherwise flat path

🚼 Pushchairs admitted

➡️ [172: ST559789] **Cycle**: NCN4 ¾ml. **Bus**: First
1 from ≋ Bristol Temple Meads; also 43 from
city centre. **Station**: Sea Mills 3ml; Filton
Abbey Wood 3½ml. **Road**: 4ml N of central
Bristol. Entrance on Hallen Road, W of
Henbury village, just N of Weston Road
(B4057)

Opening arrangements: Blaise Hamlet	
All year	**M T W T F S S**

P No parking on site. Not suitable for coaches. Car parking on Hallen Road

NT properties nearby
Bath Assembly Rooms, Clevedon Court, Dyrham Park, Horton Court, Leigh Woods, Prior Park, Tyntesfield, Westbury College Gatehouse

---

Boscastle

Cornwall

 1955   **(1:D7)**

Picturesque harbour and village on the north Cornish coast

Much of the land in and around Boscastle is owned by the Trust, including the cliffs of Penally Point and Willapark which guard the sinuous harbour entrance, Forrabury Stitches, high above the village and divided into ancient 'stitchmeal' cultivation plots, and large areas of woodland and meadow in the lovely Valency Valley.

i **T** 01840 250353 (Shop/Info centre), 01288 331372 (Area Warden's office), 01208 863046 (Property Manager's office) **E** boscastle@nationaltrust.org.uk

Ⓙ Occasional guided walks (possibly later in season)

Ⓧ NT *Coast of Cornwall* leaflet 3 includes map and details of circular walks and information on local history, geology and wildlife

Ⓞ Shop and information centre should be open from Easter

→ [190: SX097914] **Bus**: Western Greyhound 524 and 594 Bude–Truro. **Road**: 5ml N of Camelford, 3ml NE of Tintagel on B3263

NT properties nearby
Tintagel Old Post Office

Opening arrangements: Boscastle

Reconstruction work at Boscastle has been in progress since the floods of 16 August 2004. Boscastle is welcoming visitors in 2005, but if you are looking for any specific facilities, eg car parking, adapted WCs for disabled visitors, please contact the Tintagel or Camelford Tourist Information Centres (tel. 01840 779084 or 212954) or visit the Boscastle page of the NT website

---

Bradley

Newton Abbot, Devon TQ12 6BN

Ⓗ Ⓣ Ⓢ 1938   **(1:G8)**

Small medieval manor house set in woodland and meadows

Given to the National Trust in 1938 by Mrs A. H. Woolner, the house, which has a fine east front and chapel, is still lived in and managed by her family.

★ No refreshments. No WC

i **T** 01626 354513 **E** greenway@nationaltrust.org.uk

£ £3.50, child £1.75

Ⓖ Separate designated parking, 30yds. At the house, directions from car park attendant. **Building**: Step to entrance. Ground floor has steps. Chapel door too narrow for wheelchairs. Stairs with handrail to other floors. Seating available. Photograph album. **Grounds**: Partly accessible. Accessible route map

Ⓑ Braille guide and large-print guide. Touchable objects

Ⓐ In meadow adjoining car park

Ⓚ Hip-carrying infant seats for loan

Ⓜ Suitable for school groups

Ⓨ Only in meadows and woodland surrounding manor

→ [202: SX848709] **Foot**: Within easy walking distance of town along Totnes Road. **Bus**: Stagecoach in Devon X64, Country Bus 176/7, Duchy 189 from Newton Abbot (passing close ≆ Newton Abbot). **Station**: Newton Abbot 1½ml. **Road**: Drive gate (with small lodge) is ½ml from town centre on Totnes road (A381)

P Free parking, 400yds. Not suitable for coaches

NT properties nearby
Coleton Fishacre, Compton Castle, Greenway

Opening arrangements: Bradley

	5 Apr - 29 Sep	2 - 5	M	**T**	**W**	**T**	F	S	S

30 Sept–31 Oct open weekdays by prior appointment only. Tel. at least one day in advance during office hours

---

Please remember – your membership card is always needed for free admission

Branscombe – The Old Bakery, Manor Mill & Forge

Branscombe, Seaton, Devon EX12 3DB

🏠 ⚒ 🛠 🍴 🎨 💷 | 1965 | (1:H7)

Charming vernacular buildings with mill and forge restored to working order

The Old Bakery is a stone-built and partially rendered building beneath thatch, which at the time of its closure as a business in 1987 was the last traditional working bakery in Devon. The old baking equipment has been preserved in the baking room and the rest of the building now serves as a tea-room. The water-powered Manor Mill probably supplied the flour for the bakery. The forge is open daily and the blacksmith sells the ironwork he produces.

⭐ WCs at bakery and village hall

ℹ️ **T** 01297 680333 (Old Bakery – Tenant), 01392 881691 (Manor Mill – Regional office), 01297 680481 (Forge – Tenant)

💷 **Manor Mill only**: £2, child £1

🚶 Branscombe walks leaflet available

♿ **Building**: Steep slope to first floor. Stairs to other floors. **WCs**: Adapted WC. **Grounds**: Partly accessible, reasonably level hard paths to sea

🍴 Tea-room (NT-approved concession)

👶 Pushchairs and baby back-carriers admitted

🏫 Suitable for school groups. Live interpretation. Family guide

🐕 On leads and only in garden and Old Bakery information room

➡️ [192: SY198887 – 150880] **Foot**: South West Coast Path within ⅜ml. **Cycle**: Public bridleway from Great Seaside to Beer gives shared access for cyclists. **Bus**: Axe Valley 899 Sidmouth–Lyme Regis (connections from 🚂 Axminster or Honiton). **Station**: Honiton 8ml. **Road**: In Branscombe village, off A3052

🅿️ Free parking. Small NT car park adjacent to Forge, also car park adjacent to village hall; donations in well

Opening arrangements: Branscombe

Old Bakery	31 Mar - 30 Oct	11 - 5	M	T	**W**	**T**	**F**	**S**	**S**
Manor Mill	3 Apr - 26 Jun	2 - 5	M	T	W	T	**F**	**S**	**S**
	3 Jul - 28 Aug	2 - 5	M	T	**W**	T	**F**	**S**	**S**
	4 Sep - 30 Oct	2 - 5	M	T	W	T	**F**	**S**	**S**
Forge	-		**M**	**T**	**W**	**T**	**F**	**S**	**S**

Forge: tel. for details of opening times

NT properties nearby

A La Ronde, Loughwood Meeting House, Shute Barton

Brean Down

Brean, North Somerset

🏠 🎨 💷 🚶 | 1954 | (1:H4)

Promontory of land with dramatic cliffs and Victorian fort

Brean Down, rich in wildlife and history, is one of the most striking landmarks of the Somerset coastline, extending 1½ml into the Bristol Channel. At its most seaward point a Palmerston Fort, built in 1865 and then re-armed in the Second World War, provides a unique insight into Brean's past.

What's new in 2005 New programme of guided walks

⭐ The cliffs are extremely steep. Please stay on the main paths, keep dogs on leads and wear suitable footwear. The beach (not NT) can be dangerous – watch out for soft sand and fast incoming tides. The Fort and Down are reached by a steep climb from the car park. On most Sat and Sun afternoons from Easter to end Sept, volunteers open officers' quarters and gun magazines for visitors. Also open Mon, Wed & Fri during school holidays. Groups guided on request. No WC

ℹ️ **T** 01934 844518 (North Somerset office)

🚶 Circular walks leaflet

♿ Brean Down has steep steps and a steep single-track road. The road is a public footpath, therefore no private drivers allowed. Contact in advance. **Building**: Ramped

Opening arrangements: Brean Down

	All year		**M**	**T**	**W**	**T**	**F**	**S**	**S**

entrance. Brean Fort has gravel courtyard, underground gun magazines accessed by steep stairs. **WCs**: Adapted WC. **Refreshments**: Steps to entrance. Ground-level seating available outside

☕ Brean Down Cove Café (not NT) by car park

🏛 Suitable for school groups. Hands-on activities. Small exhibition about Down and Fort in room opposite café entrance

🐕 On leads at all times. The cliffs are steep and at least one dog is lost over the cliffs every month

→ [182: ST290590] **Bus**: First 102,112 Highbridge–Weston-super-Mare (passing close ≋ Highbridge and close ≋ Weston-super-Mare), alight Brean, 1¾ml. **Station**: Highbridge 8½ml. **Road**: Between Weston-super-Mare and Burnham-on-Sea about 8ml from exit 22 of M5

P Parking, 200yds. NT members must display cards. Situated at Brean Down café at the bottom of Brean Down. The higher Down is a steep climb from the car park and the Fort is approx 1½ml further

NT properties nearby
Cheddar Cliffs, Clevedon Court, Crook Peak, Wavering Down & Shute Shelve Hill, Sand Point, Tyntesfield

---

Bredon Barn

Bredon, nr Tewkesbury, Worcestershire

🏚 1951   (1:J2)

Large medieval threshing barn

The 14th-century barn is beautifully constructed of local Cotswold stone and noted for its dramatic aisled interior and unusual stone chimney cowling.

❌ No WC

ℹ **T** 01985 843600 (Regional office), 01451 844257 (Warden) **E** bredonbarn@nationaltrust.org.uk

Opening arrangements: Bredon Barn										
	31 Mar - 27 Nov	10 - 6	M	T	**W**	T	F	**S**	**S**

Closes dusk if earlier. At other times by appointment only

£ £1

♿ **Building**: Level entrance. Uneven surfaces, some visitors may require assistance from their companion

🏛 Information panels

→ [150: SO919369] **Bus**: First 540/5 Evesham–Cheltenham (passing ≋ Evesham). **Station**: Pershore (U) 8½ml. **Road**: 3ml NE of Tewkesbury, just N of B4080

P Parking. Access difficult – tight corners and narrow lane. NT sign set back from road

NT properties nearby
Ashleworth Tithe Barn, Croome Park, Hailes Abbey, Snowshill Manor

---

Brownsea Island

Poole, Dorset BH13 7EE

🚻 ♿ 🏛 🌳 ⌂ ☕ 🏕 1962   (1:K7)

Atmospheric island of heath and woodland with wide variety of wildlife

The island is dramatically located at the entrance to Poole harbour, offering spectacular views across to Studland and the Purbeck Hills. Its varied and colourful history includes use as a coastguard station, Victorian pottery, Edwardian country estate, daffodil farm and as a decoy to protect Poole in the Second World War. In 1907 it was the site of Baden-Powell's experimental camp from which Scouting and Guiding evolved. Home to important populations of red squirrel and seabirds, the island provides a safe and relaxing place for walks and picnics, ideal for families to explore.

What's new in 2005 Red squirrel walks; SeaBritain self-led and guided walks; free live music monthly

Opening arrangements: Brownsea Island										
Island	12 Mar - 22 Jul	10 - 5	**M**	**T**	**W**	**T**	**F**	**S**	**S**
	23 Jul - 2 Sep	10 - 6	**M**	**T**	**W**	**T**	**F**	**S**	**S**
	3 Sep - 30 Sep	10 - 5	**M**	**T**	**W**	**T**	**F**	**S**	**S**
	1 Oct - 30 Oct	10 - 4	**M**	**T**	**W**	**T**	**F**	**S**	**S**
Shop	As island									
Coffee shop	As island									
At other times by appointment										

Please see the area introductions for details of coast & countryside properties

★ Part of the island is leased as a nature reserve to Dorset Wildlife Trust (tel. 01202 709445 for information). Brownsea Castle is not open to the public

ℹ️ **T** 01202 707744,
01202 700244 (Coffee Shop),
0870 240 4068 (Box office),
01202 700852 (Shop)
F 01202 701635
E brownseaisland@nationaltrust.org.uk

£ £4.20, child £2, family £10.40, family (one adult) £6.20. Groups £3.60, child £1.70, group visits outside normal hours £3

🔑 Guided tours. Group tours by arrangement. Dorset Wildlife Trust self-guided nature trail and other tours

😃 Programme of events, inc. open-air theatre. Family activity days

🚶 Walks for all abilities: woodland, heath, shoreline and clifftop. Self-guided trail leaflets

♿ Island tracks are rough in places. Trailer trails for disabled visitors on certain days and for group visits (booking essential). Wheelchair users are advised to contact ferry operators for information. **Building**: Steps to entrance. Alternative accessible entrance. 4 wheelchairs, booking essential. Seating available. **WCs**: Adapted WC. **Grounds**: Partly accessible. Accessible route map. Staff-driven multi-seater vehicle, booking essential. **Shop**: Level entrance. **Refreshments**: Level entrance

♲ Braille guide

☕ Coffee shop near landing quay. Children's lunch boxes. Sweet shop near landing quay, selling sweets, ice cream and cold drinks

👶 Baby-changing facilities. Pushchairs and baby back-carriers admitted. 10 all-terrain baby buggies for loan (booking advisable)

🏫 Suitable for school groups. Education room/centre. Hands-on activities. Children's guide. Children's quiz/trail. Adult study days

➡️ [195: SZ032878] In Poole Harbour.
Ferry: Half-hourly boat service (not NT) from Poole Quay and Sandbanks. Also service from Bournemouth and Swanage. Visitors can land from their own boats at W end of the island. **Bus**: Wilts & Dorset 150

Bournemouth–Swanage, alight Sandbanks; 152 Poole Quay–Sandbanks. Yellow Buses 30 Poole Quay–Boscombe (passes ≋ Poole), also 12 Christchurch Quay–Sandbanks, June–Sept only; also from surrounding areas to Poole bridge, few mins walk.
Station: Poole ½ml to Poole Quay; Branksome or Parkstone, both 3½ml to Sandbanks

NT properties nearby
Corfe Castle, Kingston Lacy, Studland Beach

Buckland Abbey

Yelverton, Devon PL20 6EY

🏠 🚗 ✝ ✵ 🔄 🍴 💧 🍷 | 1948 | (1:F8)

700-year-old building with fine 16th-century great hall, associated with Elizabethan seafarers Drake and Grenville

Tucked away in its own secluded valley above the River Tavy, Buckland was originally a small but influential Cistercian monastery. The house, incorporating the remains of the 13th-century abbey church, has rich associations with Sir Francis Drake and his seafaring rival, Sir Richard Grenville, containing much interesting

Drake's Drum in the Drake Gallery, Buckland Abbey, Devon

memorabilia from their time. There are exhibitions on Buckland's history as well as a magnificent monastic barn, herb garden, delightful estate walks and craft workshops. Recent developments include new interpretive exhibitions and displays, a hand-crafted plasterwork ceiling in the Drake Chamber and the creation of an Elizabethan garden.

What's new in 2005 Quilting and embroidery exhibition in September on SeaBritain theme

★ The Abbey is presented in association with Plymouth City Museum

[i] **T** 01822 853607, 01822 853706 (Shop), 01822 855024 (Restaurant) **F** 01822 855448 **E** bucklandabbey@nationaltrust.org.uk

[£] £6, child £3, family £15, family (one adult) £9. Groups £4.60, child £2.30. **Grounds only**: £3.20, child £1.60. Reduced rate when arriving by public transport or cycle. Winter admission (1 Nov to 18 March): reduced price for house; grounds free

[†] Pre-booked guided tours may be available for groups during normal opening hours

[⚑] Programme of events, inc. 'Kids Galore', Elizabethan Experience, Christmas Craft Fair, Abbey decorated for Christmas, family activities

[†] Four waymarked walks through woodland and farmland, map available from reception

[♿] Property on steep slopes. Separate designated parking, 150yds. Transfer available. **Building**: Ramped entrance. 2 wheelchairs. Ground floor has steps. Stairs to other floors. 119 steps on normal visitor route. One other floor accessible via different door. Seating available. Audio visual/video, computer, interpretation material from inaccessible floors is available. **WCs**: Adapted WC. **Grounds**: Partly accessible, slopes. Accessible route map. Staff-driven multi-seater vehicle. **Shop**: Wooden lip to doorway. **Refreshments**: Level entrance. Wooden lip to doorway, split-level restaurant, only top half accessible

[♪] Induction loop in reception. Subtitled version of introductory film available on request

[♨] Braille guide and large-print guide. Sensory list. Handling collection

Opening arrangements: Buckland Abbey

			M	T	W	T	F	S	S
House & Estate	12 Feb - 13 Mar	2 - 5						**S**	**S**
	19 Mar - 30 Oct	10:30 - 5:30	**M**	**T**	**W**		**F**	**S**	**S**
	5 Nov - 27 Nov	2 - 5						**S**	**S**
	3 Dec - 18 Dec	11 - 5						**S**	**S**
	18 Feb - 26 Feb 06	2 - 5						**S**	**S**
Shop	12 Feb - 13 Mar	12:30 - 5						**S**	**S**
	19 Mar - 30 Oct	10:30 - 5:30	**M**	**T**	**W**		**F**	**S**	**S**
	4 Nov - 16 Dec	12 - 4					**F**		
	5 Nov - 27 Nov	12:30 - 5						**S**	**S**
	3 Dec - 18 Dec	11 - 5						**S**	**S**
	18 Feb - 26 Feb 06	2 - 5						**S**	**S**
Restaurant	As shop								

Admission by timed ticket at busy times. Last admission 45mins before closing

[🛍] NT shop. Independent craft workshops, usually open as Abbey. Tel. woodturner 01364 631585, countryside artist 01752 783291. Plant sales

[🍴] Restaurant/tea-room (licensed) in reception building. Restricted menu Nov to March. Open Dec for booked Christmas lunches. Children's menu

[🚻] In car park and quarry orchard

[👶] Baby-changing and feeding facilities. Front-carrying baby slings and hip-carrying infant seats for loan. Parent and baby room

[🏫] Suitable for school groups. Education room/centre. Hands-on activities. Children's quiz/trail. Occasional watercolour workshops and live interpretation. Tel. for details

[🐕] On leads and only in car park; dog posts in shade

[→] [201: SX487667] **Cycle**: NCN27 2ml. **Bus**: Plymouth Citybus 55 from Yelverton (with connections from [≣] Plymouth) Mon–Sat; First 48 from Plymouth Suns. **Station**: Bere Alston (U), 4½ml. **Road**: 6ml S of Tavistock, 11ml N of Plymouth: turn off A386 ¼ml S of Yelverton

[P] Free parking, 150yds

NT properties nearby
Antony, Castle Drogo, Cotehele, Lydford Gorge, Plym Estate, Saltram

There are special events at most Trust properties; please telephone 0870 458 4000 for details

Carnewas & Bedruthan Steps

nr Bedruthan, St Eval, Wadebridge, Cornwall
PL27 7UW

 1930 (1:C8)

Dramatic coastline with views over massive rock stacks

This is one of the most popular destinations on the Cornish coast because of the spectacular clifftop view of rocks stretching into the distance across the sweep of Bedruthan beach (not NT). There are magnificent walks along the coast path between Carnewas and Park Head. The Trust has rebuilt the cliff staircase down to the beach, but it is **unsafe to bathe at any time** and visitors need to be aware of the risk of being cut off by the tide.

★ WC not always available

ℹ️ T 01841 540540 (Area Warden), 01208 863046 (Property Manager), 01637 860563 (Shop), 01637 860701 (Tearoom)

🏃 Occasional guided walks

🚶 NT *Coast of Cornwall* leaflet 6 includes maps and details of circular walks and information on local history, geology and wildlife

♿ **WCs**: Adapted WC. **Shop**: Level entrance. **Refreshments**: Level entrance

🏪 Shop and information centre

☕ Tea-room and garden (NT-approved concession) in Carnewas car park overlooking Bedruthan Steps

🎯 Children's quiz/trail

Opening arrangements: Carnewas & Bedruthan			M	T	W	T	F	S	S
	All year		M	T	W	T	F	S	S
Shop/info	23 Mar - 30 Apr	11 - 5	M	T	W	T	F	S	S
	1 May - 30 Sep	10:30 - 5:30	M	T	W	T	F	S	S
	1 Oct - 30 Oct	11 - 5	M	T	W	T	F	S	S
Tea-room	12 Feb - 21 Mar	11 - 5	M	T	W	T	F	S	S
	22 Mar - 30 Oct	10:30 - 5:30	M	T	W	T	F	S	S

Cliff staircase closed 1 Nov to 28 Feb 2006. Tea-room: limited opening in winter. Tel 01637 860701 or 01841 540554 to check times

Bedruthan Steps and Park Head looking from Carnewas, Cornwall

➡️ [200: SW849692] **Foot**: ⅔ml of South West Coast Path on property. **Bus**: Western Greyhound 556 from ⮕ Newquay–Padstow. **Station**: Newquay 7ml. **Road**: Just off B3276 from Newquay to Padstow, 6ml SW of Padstow

🅿️ Parking. Seasonal charge

NT properties nearby
Trerice

Castle Drogo

Drewsteignton, nr Exeter, Devon EX6 6PB

🏰 1974 (1:F7)

The 'last castle to be built in England', dramatically situated above the Teign Gorge

This granite fortress, commanding panoramic views of Dartmoor, was built between 1910 and 1930 for the self-made millionaire Julius Drewe, and is one of the most remarkable works of Sir Edwin Lutyens. The interior combines the grandeur of a medieval castle with the comfort of the 20th century. The terraced formal garden

Opening arrangements: Castle Drogo			M	T	W	T	F	S	S
Castle	18 Mar - 30 Oct	11 - 5	M	T	W	T	F	S	S
	31 Oct - 6 Nov	11 - 4	M	T	W	T	F	S	S
Garden	All year	10:30 - 5:30	M	T	W	T·	F	S	S
Shop	18 Mar - 6 Nov	10:30 - 5:30	M	T	W	T	F	S	S
	11 Nov - 18 Dec	11 - 4	M	T	W	T	F	S	S
Castle tea-room	18 Mar - 30 Oct	12 - 5	M	T	W	T	F	S	S
Tea-room	18 Mar - 6 Nov	10:30 - 5:30	M	T	W	T	F	S	S
	11 Nov - 18 Dec	11 - 4	M	T	W	T	F	S	S

Closes dusk if earlier. Castle also open 5, 6, 12 & 13 March, Sat & Sun, tel. for details. Castle Tea-room: Dec open for booked Christmas lunches and dinners

has an established rhododendron and magnolia collection, spring bulbs, summer and autumn . flowering herbaceous borders, rose garden, shrub garden and circular croquet lawn. There are delightful varied walks through the River Teign Gorge.

What's new in 2005 30th anniversary of castle opening to the public. Special events throughout the year

The main stairs at Castle Drogo, Devon

[i] **T** 01647 433306, 01647 433563 (Shop), 01647 432629 (Catering) **F** 01647 433186 **E** castledrogo@nationaltrust.org.uk

[£] £6.50, child £3.20, family £16.20, family (one adult) £9.70. Groups £5.50, child £2.70. **Garden & grounds only**: £4, child £2. Groups £3.40, child £1.70. Reduced rate when arriving by public transport or cycle. Croquet lawn normally open June–Sept; equipment hire from visitor reception

[K] Occasional guided walks on estate

[U] March–December

[i] Walks leaflet

[&] Designated parking in main car park, 400yds. Transfer available. Drop-off point. **Building**: Ramped entrance. 2 wheelchairs. Hall and library accessible, steps up to drawing room. Many stairs to other floors. Seating available. **WCs**: Adapted WC. **Grounds**: Partly accessible, steep slopes, some steps. Accessible route map. Level routes to rose garden and scented garden. **Shop**: Level entrance. **Refreshments**: Ramped entrance. Large-print menu

[&] Braille guide and large-print guide. Sensory list

[🛍] NT shop. Plant sales

[🍴] Castle tea-room in castle. Children's menu. Tea-room at visitor centre. Children's menu

[🏕] Picnic area adjacent to car park

[👶] Baby-changing facilities. Baby back-carriers admitted. Hip-carrying infant seats for loan. Children's play area

[🏫] Suitable for school groups. Live interpretation. Family guide. Children's guide. Children's quiz/trail

[🐕] On leads and only in car park and on estate walks

[→] [191: SX721900] **Foot**: Two Moors Way. **Bus**: First 173 Exeter–Newton Abbot (passing ⟐ Exeter Central); Carmel 174, First 179 from ⟐ Okehampton, Suns only. **Station**: Yeoford (U) 8ml. **Road**: 5ml S of A30 Exeter–Okehampton. Take A382 Whiddon Down–Moretonhampstead road; turn off at Sandy Park

[P] Free parking, 400yds. Coaches must be no bigger than 43-seater or 10m x 2.39m. Tight corners and narrow lanes. All coaches must be booked. Limited space available

NT properties nearby
Finch Foundry, Fingle Bridge, Lydford Gorge, Parke Estate, Steps Bridge

Please note: groups must book in advance with the property

Chedworth Roman Villa

Yanworth, nr Cheltenham, Gloucestershire
GL54 3LJ

🏛 🖱 ♿ 🎫 1924   **(1:K2)**

Remains of one of the largest Romano-British villas in the country

Over a mile of walls survives and there are several fine mosaics, two bathhouses, hypocausts, a water-shrine and latrine. Set in a wooded Cotswold combe, the site was excavated in 1864 and still has a Victorian atmosphere. The museum houses objects from the villa and a 15-minute audio-visual presentation gives visitors an insight into the history of this fascinating place.

What's new in 2005 Family activity packs

[i] **T** 01242 890256,
01242 890904 (Learning),
01242 890908 (Shop)
F 01242 890909
E chedworth@nationaltrust.org.uk

[£] £5, child £2.50, family £12.50. **Audio tour**: £1.20, child 80p

[🎫] For booked groups only; £16 for schools, £32 for others. Max. 30 people per guide

[🎭] Programme of events, inc. living history

[♿] Separate designated parking, 10yds. Disabled parking by entrance. Drop-off point. **Building**: Ramped entrance with handrail. 1 wheelchair. Poor access to main features of site, steps to all mosaics and museum. **WCs**: Adapted WC. **Shop**: Ramped entrance

[🔊] Induction loop in audioguide and AV presentation

[🏫] Open for school groups outside normal hours

[☕] Limited range of refreshments on sale in shop

[👶] Baby-changing facilities. Pushchairs and baby back-carriers admitted. Activities for children in school holidays

[🎒] Suitable for school groups. Education room/centre. Live interpretation. Hands-on activities. Children's guide. Children's quiz/trail. Family activity packs. Adult study days

Opening arrangements: Chedworth Roman Villa										
Villa	1 Mar - 24 Mar	11 - 4	M	**T**	**W**	**T**	**F**	**S**	**S**
	25 Mar - 30 Oct	10 - 5	M	**T**	**W**	**T**	**F**	**S**	**S**
	1 Nov - 13 Nov	10 - 4	M	**T**	**W**	**T**	**F**	**S**	**S**
Shop	As villa								

Open BH Mons. Shop and reception close at advertised time – visitors already on the property are allowed up to 30 mins to finish their visit

[➔] [163: SP053135] **Bus**: Cotswold Lion from Cirencester (tel 01451 862000 for details). **Station**: Cheltenham Spa 14ml. **Road**: 3ml NW of Fossebridge on Cirencester–Northleach road (A429); approach from A429 via Yanworth or from A436 via Withington (coaches must approach from Fossebridge)

[P] Free parking

NT properties nearby
Lodge Park & Sherborne Estate, Snowshill Manor

The Church House

Widecombe in the Moor, Newton Abbot, Devon
TQ13 7TA

🏠 🖱 ♿ 🎫 1933   **(1:F7)**

Fine two-storey granite building dating from 1537

Originally a brewhouse, this former village school is now leased as a village hall. The adjacent Sexton's Cottage is a NT shop and Dartmoor National Park information point.

[⭐] No WC. Nearest in public car park

[i] **T/F** 01364 621321

[£] Admission free. Donations welcome

[♿] 100yds. Drop-off point. **Building**: Ramped entrance. Ground floor accessible. Stairs to other floors. Seating available. **Grounds**: Fully accessible. **Shop**: Ramped entrance

[📖] Braille guide

Opening arrangements: The Church House									
Shop	10 Feb - 24 Dec	10:30 -	**M**	**T**	**W**	**T**	**F**	**S**	**S**

Open to visitors when not in use as the village hall. Closing time of shop/information centre is dependent on the weather

Parking in National Trust car parks is free for members

🚼 Pushchairs admitted

➡ [191: SX718768] In centre of Dartmoor, N of Ashburton, W of Bovey Tracey. **Bus**: First 170/2 Newton Abbot–Totnes/Tavistock, Carmel 174 from Okehampton. All Suns only, June–Sept only, but 172 runs daily July & Aug

P Parking (not NT), 100yds (pay & display)

NT properties nearby
Hembury Woods, Holne Woods, Parke Estate

Clevedon Court

Tickenham Road, Clevedon, North Somerset BS21 6QU

🏠 ♿ 1961   (1:I4)

Outstanding 14th-century manor house and 18th-century terraced garden

The house was built by Sir John de Clevedon in c.1320, incorporating parts of a massive 13th-century tower and great hall. Much of the original building is still evident. Altered and added to by the Elizabethans, it has been home to the Elton family since 1709. The house contains many striking Eltonware pots and vases and a fascinating collection of Nailsea glass. There is also a beautiful terraced garden.

⭐ The Elton family open and manage the property for the National Trust

ℹ **T** 01275 872257 (Administrator)
F 0871 433 9294

£ £5, child £2.50

♿ Drop-off point. **Building**: Steps to entrance. Photograph album. **Grounds**: Steps with handrails to terraces

👁 Braille guide and large-print guide

🎒 Suitable for school groups. Children's guide. Children's quiz/trail

➡ [172: ST423716] **Bus**: First 364, 662/3 from Bristol (passing ☒ Nailsea & Backwell). **Station**: Yatton 3ml. **Road**: 1½ml E of

Clevedon, on Bristol road (B3130), signposted from M5 exit 20

P Free parking, 50yds. Unsuitable for trailer caravans or motor caravans. Some parking 100yds E of entrance in cul-de-sac

NT properties nearby
Blaise Hamlet, Brean Down, Dyrham Park, Horton Court, Leigh Woods, Tyntesfield, Westbury College Gatehouse

Clouds Hill

Wareham, Dorset BH20 7NQ

🏠 📷 1937   (1:J7)

The rural retreat of T. E. Lawrence

T. E. Lawrence ('Lawrence of Arabia') bought this tiny isolated brick and tile cottage in 1925. The austere rooms are much as he left them and reflect his complex personality and close links with the Middle East. An exhibition details Lawrence's extraordinary life.

⭐ No WC

ℹ **T** 01929 405616 (Custodian)

£ £3.50. No reduction for children

📖 Leaflet – 'The Lawrence Trail'

♿ **Building**: Doorways approx 2ft wide, rooms are very small with limited space for visitors. Exhibition accessible in separate room. Audio visual/video. Walking frame available

👁 Braille guide

📷 T. E. Lawrence books on sale

🎒 Suitable for school groups

➡ [194: SY824909] **Bus**: First 101–4, 107 from ☒ Wool, alight Bovington, 1¼ml. **Station**: Wool 3½ml; Moreton (U) 3½ml. **Road**: 9ml E of Dorchester, 1¼ml E of Waddock crossroads (B3390), 4ml S of A35 Poole–Dorchester road, 1ml N of Bovington Camp

Opening arrangements: Clevedon Court								
27 Mar – 29 Sep	2 – 5	M	T	**W**	**T**	F	**S**	**S**
Open BH Mons. Car park and gardens open at 1								

Opening arrangements: Clouds Hill								
18 Mar – 30 Oct	12 – 5	M	T	W	**T**	**F**	**S**	**S**
Open BH Mons. Closes at dusk if earlier than 5; no electric light								

Please remember – your membership card is always needed for free admission

P Free parking, 30yds. No coaches (only minibuses). No trailer caravans

NT properties nearby
Brownsea Island, Corfe Castle, Hardy Monument, Hardy's Cottage, Kingston Lacy, Max Gate

---

Coleridge Cottage

35 Lime Street, Nether Stowey, Bridgwater, Somerset TA5 1NQ

🏠 1909   **(1:H5)**

Home of the poet Samuel Taylor Coleridge

Coleridge lived in the cottage for three years from 1797, and there are mementoes of the poet on display. It was here that he wrote *The Rime of the Ancient Mariner*, part of *Christabel*, *Frost at Midnight* and *Kubla Khan*.

⭐ No WC. Nearest WC at village library 300yds.

ℹ **T** 01278 732662

£ £3.20, child £1.60

🏃 Can be arranged by appointment

♿ Contact in advance. **Building**: Steps to entrance

👁 Braille guide and large-print guide

🏫 Suitable for school groups

➡ [181: ST191399] **Bus**: First 15/A, 915, 927 Bridgwater–Minehead (passing close ≋) Bridgwater). **Station**: Bridgwater 8ml. **Road**: At W end of Nether Stowey, on S side of A39, 8ml W of Bridgwater

P Parking (not NT), 500yds. Coach parking available by arrangement

NT properties nearby
Dunster Castle, Fyne Court, Holnicote Estate

Opening arrangements: Coleridge Cottage									
1 Apr - 25 Sep	2 - 5	M	T	W	T	F	S	S
Open BH Mons									

Coleton Fishacre

Coleton, Kingswear, Dartmouth, Devon TQ6 0EQ

🏠 ✳ 📐 📷 1982   **(1:G8)**

Arts & Crafts-style house with elegant Art Deco-influenced interior, set amid gardens in a spectacular coastal setting

Built in a stream-fed valley on a beautiful stretch of the NT-protected South Devon coastline, the house was designed in 1925 for Rupert and Lady Dorothy D'Oyly Carte, who created its luxuriant garden. This has year-round interest with a wide variety of rare and exotic plants, water features and a gazebo with fine views.

ℹ **T** 01803 752466, 01803 753012 (Shop), 01803 753013 (Tea-room)
F 01803 753017
E coletonfishacre@nationaltrust.org.uk

£ £5.50, child £2.75, family £13.75, family (one adult) £8.25. Groups £4.70. **Garden only**: £4.40, child £2.10. Groups £3.70

🏃 Free 1-hour guided walk every Fri at 2:15. Others by arrangement or as advertised

🎭 Programme of events. Tel. for details

🚶 Coastal walks on the surrounding Dart and Start Bay estate. Walks booklet for sale

♿ Designated parking in main car park, 20yds. Drop-off point. **Building**: Ramped entrance. 3 wheelchairs, booking essential. Ground floor accessible. Seating available. Photograph album. **WCs**: Adapted WC. **Grounds**: Partly accessible, steep slopes, grass paths. Accessible route map. Upper paths reasonably flat. **Shop**: Level entrance. **Refreshments**: Level entrance

👁 Braille guide. Interesting scents

📷 Small selection of gifts, postcards and books. Unusual shrubs and herbaceous plants

Opening arrangements: Coleton Fishacre									
Garden	5 Mar - 20 Mar	11 - 5	M	T	W	T	F	**S**	**S**
	23 Mar - 30 Oct	10:30 - 5:30	M	T	**W**	**T**	**F**	**S**	**S**
House	23 Mar - 30 Oct	11 - 4:30	M	T	**W**	**T**	**F**	**S**	**S**
Tea-room	5 Mar - 20 Mar	11 - 5	M	T	W	T	F	**S**	**S**
	23 Mar - 30 Oct	10:30 - 5	M	T	**W**	**T**	**F**	**S**	**S**
Open BH Mons									

Coleton Fishacre, Devon

☕ Tea-room (NT-approved concession). Limited indoor seating in wet weather. Credit cards not accepted. Children's menu

🎋 Picnics in car park area only; tables provided

🧍 Baby-changing facilities. Hip-carrying infant seats for loan

📖 Children's quiz/trail

🐾 On surrounding NT land only, on leads

➡ [202: SX910508] **Foot**: South West Coast Path within ⅔ml. **Bus**: Stagecoach in Devon 120 Paignton–Kingswear; otherwise Stagecoach in Devon 22/4 Brixham–Kingswear (with connections from ☒ Paignton). On all, alight ¾ml SW of Hillhead, 1½ml walk to garden. **Station**: Paignton 8ml; Kingswear (Paignton & Dartmouth Rly) 2¼ml by footpath, 2¾ml by road. **Road**: 3ml from Kingswear; take Lower Ferry road, turn off at toll house (take care in narrow lanes). Narrow entrance and drive

🅿 Free parking, 20yds. Coaches must book

NT properties nearby
Bradley, Compton Castle, Dart Estuary, Greenway

Compton Castle

Marldon, Paignton, Devon TQ3 1TA

🖼 ✛ ✿ ▢ 1951 (1:G8)

Dramatic fortified manor house

Built between the 14th and 16th centuries, the castle has been home to the Gilbert family for most of the last 600 years. Sir Humphrey Gilbert (1539–1583) was coloniser of Newfoundland and half-brother to Sir Walter Raleigh. Within the curtain wall can be seen the old kitchen with spiral staircase to the guard room, reconstructed great hall, solar and chapel. There is also a lovely rose garden and knot garden.

⭐ Compton Castle is occupied and administered by Mr & Mrs G E Gilbert

ℹ **T/F** 01803 875740 (Answerphone)
E greenway@nationaltrust.org.uk

£ £3.50, child £1.75. Groups £3, child £1.50

Opening arrangements: Compton Castle			M	T	W	T	F	S	S
4 Apr - 27 Oct	10-12.15, 2-5		**M**	**T**	**W**	**T**	F	S	S
Open BH Mons 10–12.15, 2–5									

Please see the area introductions for details of coast & countryside properties

♿ Drop-off point. **Building**: Steps to entrance, ramp available. Ground floor has steps. Spiral staircases to other floors. Seating available. Photograph album. Access to the Solar is by a spiral staircase only.
WCs: Ambulant disabled access in ladies.
Grounds: Steps to rose garden.
Refreshments: Castle Barton, not NT, is not wheelchair accessible, set up a very steep hill and with steps

♪ Braille guide and large-print guide

📷 Guidebooks, postcards and slides only

🍴 Refreshments at Castle Barton restaurant (not NT) from 10am (tel. 01803 873314)

🅿 In car park

👶 Baby-changing and feeding facilities. Baby back-carriers admitted. Front-carrying baby slings and toddlers' reins for loan

🎒 Suitable for school groups. Children's guide. Children's quiz/trail

🐕 On leads in car park

➔ [202: SX865648] **Bus**: Stagecoach Devon 7 ≅ Paignton–Marldon; First 111 Dartmouth–Torquay (passing ≅ Totnes); 66 Brixham–Torquay. On all alight Marldon, 1½ml.
Station: Torquay 5ml. Newton Abbot 6ml.
Road: At Compton, 5ml W of Torquay, 1½ml N of Marldon. Signposted off A380 to Marldon (not suitable for coaches) or turn south from A381 Totnes road at Ipplepen–2ml to Compton

Corfe Castle, Dorset

🅿 Free parking, 30yds. Additional parking at Castle Barton opposite entrance, 100yds. Access for coaches via Ipplepen, not Marldon. Coaches may park at bus turning area opposite, 125yds

NT properties nearby
Bradley, Coleton Fishacre, Greenway

Corfe Castle

The Square, Corfe Castle, Wareham, Dorset
BH20 5EZ

🏰📷🍴🅿 1982 **(1:K7)**

Thousand-year-old castle rising above the Isle of Purbeck

One of Britain's most majestic ruins, the castle controlled the gateway through the Purbeck Hills and has been an important stronghold since the time of William the Conqueror. Defended during the Civil War by the ardent and virtuous Lady Bankes, the castle fell to treachery from within, and was substantially destroyed afterwards by the Parliamentarians. Many fine Norman and Early English features remain.

ℹ **T** 01929 481294, 01929 480609 (Learning), 01929 480921 (Shop), 01929 481332 (Tearoom) **F** 01929 477067
E corfecastle@nationaltrust.org.uk

£ £5, child £2.50, family £12.50, family (one adult) £7.50. Groups £4.30, child £2.10. Paying visitors arriving by public transport offered a reduction on production of a valid bus or train ticket. NT members arriving by public transport offered a voucher redeemable at the NT shop or tea-room in Corfe Castle (offer open until Dec 2005). Discounted Corfe Castle/Swanage Steam Railway joint tickets available from Swanage Steam Railway (tel. 01929 425800)

🎭 Guided tours of castle often available during opening hours, April to Oct. Private groups by arrangement

🎭 Programme of events, inc. living history, archaeology weekend, traditional crafts, outdoor theatre, school holiday activities

🚶 Corfe Common walks leaflet from NT shop

Unless indicated, last admission is always 30mins before closing time

Opening arrangements: Corfe Castle

Castle	1 Mar - 31 Mar	10 - 5	M T W T F S S
	1 Apr - 30 Sep	10 - 6	M T W T F S S
	1 Oct - 31 Oct	10 - 5	M T W T F S S
	1 Nov - 28 Feb 06	10 - 4	M T W T F S S
Shop	As castle		
Tea-room	1 Mar - 31 Mar	10 - 5	M T W T F S S
	1 Apr - 30 Sep	10 - 5:30	M T W T F S S
	1 Oct - 31 Oct	10 - 5	M T W T F S S
	1 Nov - 28 Feb 06	10 - 4	M T W T F S S

Closed 25, 26 Dec. Tea-room closed two weeks in Jan 2006 for internal repair and decoration, tel. for details. High winds may cause closure of parts of grounds

♿ Drop-off point. **Building**: Access to Outer Bailey only for wheelchair users. **WCs**: Adapted WC. **Grounds**: steep slopes, uneven paths. **Shop**: Ramped entrance. **Refreshments**: Level entrance. Tea-room garden accessible via side gate

💭 Braille guide and large-print guide. Sensory list. Handling collection

▣ In village square

🕶 Traditional tea-room (licensed). Children's menu

🚼 Baby-changing facilities. Pushchairs and baby back-carriers admitted. Baby back-carriers for loan. Children must be accompanied by an adult within the castle

■ Suitable for school groups. Education room/centre. Hands-on activities. Children's guide. Children's quiz/trail. Interactive exhibition

🐶 On leads only

→ [195: SY959824] **Bus**: Wilts & Dorset 142/3/4 Poole–Swanage (passing ▣ Wareham). **Station**: Wareham 4½ml. Corfe Castle (Swanage Steam Railway) a few mins walk (park & ride from Norden Station). **Road**: On A351 Wareham–Swanage road

Ⓟ Free parking. Car- & coach-parking is at Castle View off A351 (10 mins walk to castle); also at Norden park & ride (20 mins walk to castle) and West St (not NT)

NT properties nearby
Brownsea Island, Clouds Hill, Studland Beach

Cornish Mines & Engines

Pool, nr Redruth, Cornwall TR15 3NP

♻ ▣ 🕶 1967 (1:C9)

Impressive beam engines and industrial heritage discovery centre

Cornwall's engine houses are dramatic reminders of the time when the county was a powerhouse of tin, copper and china clay mining. These two great beam engines were used for pumping water (from a depth of over 550m) and for winding men and ore up and down. The engines were originally powered by high-pressure steam, introduced by the local engineer Richard Trevithick. Today one is rotated by electricity. The site also includes the Industrial Discovery Centre at East Pool, which provides an overview of Cornwall's industrial heritage and incorporates a fascinating audio-visual presentation.

⭐ Trevithick Cottage is nearby at Penponds and is open April to Oct, Wed 2–5, free of charge (donations welcome)

ⓘ **T** 01209 315027

Engine houses for the Botallack Mine, St Just, Cornwall

Opening arrangements: Cornish Mines & Engines

Centre/shop	23 Mar - 30 Oct	11 - 5	**M T W T F** S S

Nov to March 2006 by arrangement only; for details or to arrange group visits at any time of year please tel.

£ £5, child £2.50, family £12.50, family (one adult) £7.50. Groups £4.30

Building: Ramped entrance. Stairs to other floors. Audio visual/video. Michell's Engine House ground floor only. **Shop**: Level entrance

Braille guide and large-print guide. Sensory list

Pushchairs admitted

Suitable for school groups. Children's quiz/trail

→ [203: SW672415] **Cycle**: NCN3 ½ml.
Bus: From surrounding areas (some passing Redruth). **Station**: Redruth 2ml; Camborne 2ml. **Road**: At Pool, 2ml W of Redruth on either side of A3047 midway between Redruth and Camborne. Site is sign-posted from A30 'Camborne East' junction

P Free parking (not NT). Main car park is shared with Safeway superstore

NT properties nearby
Glendurgan Garden, Godolphin Estate, Godrevy, Trelissick Garden

Cotehele

St Dominick, nr Saltash, Cornwall PL12 6TA

1947

(1:E8)

Medieval house with superb collections of textiles, armour and furniture, set in extensive grounds

At the heart of this riverside estate sits the granite and slatestone house of Cotehele, built mainly between 1485 and 1627 and a home of the Edgcumbe family for centuries. Intimate chambers feature large Tudor fireplaces and rich hangings. Outside, the formal gardens overlook the richly planted valley garden below, with medieval dovecote, stewpond and Victorian summer house, and 18th-century tower above. At the Quay interesting old buildings house the

A doorway at Cotehele, Cornwall

Edgcumbe Arms tea-room and an outstation of the National Maritime Museum. The restored Tamar sailing barge *Shamrock* is moored alongside. A network of footpaths throughout the estate provides a variety of riverside and woodland walks with nature conservation and industrial archaeology interest.

What's new in 2005 New information about the historic development of the house following recent architectural survey

★ There is no electric light, so visitors should avoid dull days

i **T** 01579 351346, 01579 352739 (Infoline), 01579 352713 (Shop), 01579 352711 (Restaurant), 01579 352717 (Tea-room) **F** 01579 351222 **E** cotehele@nationaltrust.org.uk

Opening arrangements: Cotehele

House	19 Mar - 29 Sep	11 - 5	**M T W T** F S S
	1 Oct - 31 Oct	11 - 4:30	**M T W T** F S S
Garden	All year	10.30 - dusk	**M T W T F S S**
Shop	12 Feb - 18 Mar	11 - 4	**M T W T F S S**
	19 Mar - 30 Sep	11 - 5	**M T W T F S S**
	1 Oct - 31 Oct	11 - 4:30	**M T W T F S S**
Restaurant	As house		
Edgcumbe Arms	As house		

Open Good Fri. Shop & Restaurant: Nov & Dec Christmas opening, tel. for details. Edgcumbe Arms closes at dusk if earlier than 5. Light refreshments available 12 Feb–18 Mar, 11–4, and on Fridays from 19 Mar–31 Oct, 11–5 (4:30 Oct)

£ £7.40, child £3.70, family £18.50, family (one adult) £11.10. Groups £6.40. **Garden & mill only**: £4.40, child £2.20, family £11, family (family one adult) £6.60. Reduced rate when arriving by public transport or cycle

🚶 Estate walks leaflet available

♿ Separate designated parking. Drop-off point. **Building**: Ramped entrance. 2 wheelchairs. Ground floor accessible. Stairs with handrail to other floors. Seating available. Audio visual/video, photograph album. **WCs**: Adapted WC. **Shop**: Steps to entrance. Ramp available at alternative entrance. **Refreshments**: Level entrance

🔊 Induction loop in reception and introductory film room

✍ Braille guide. Sensory list

🛍 NT shop. Plant sales

🍴 Barn Restaurant (licensed). Children's menu. Edgcumbe Arms tea-room on Cotehele Quay

👶 Baby-changing and feeding facilities. Hip-carrying infant seats for loan. Children's buggy route available for the garden

🏫 Suitable for school groups. Education room/centre. Children's guide. Children's quiz/trail

🐕 Under close control on woodland walks

➔ [201: SX422685] **Cycle**: NCN27 8ml. Hilly route from Tavistock to Cotehele. **Ferry**: Calstock can be reached from

The mill at Cotehele, Cornwall

Plymouth by water (contact Plymouth Boat Cruises Ltd, tel. 01752 822797) and from Calstock local river passenger ferry operates during summer subject to tides, tel. 01822 833331: **Bus**: First 79 Callington–Tavistock (passing ≅ Gunnislake). **Station**: Calstock (U), 1½ml (signposted from station). **Road**: On W bank of the Tamar, 1ml W of Calstock by steep footpath (6ml by road), 8ml SW of Tavistock, 14ml from Plymouth via Saltash Bridge; 2ml E of St Dominick, 4ml from Gunnislake (turn at St Ann's Chapel). Coaches only by prior arrangement

P Free parking. Parking charge on quay

NT properties nearby
Antony, Buckland Abbey, Lydford Gorge, Saltram

Cotehele Mill

See main Cotehele entry

🚫 🚽 ♿ 🚶 1947   **(1:E8)**

Restored working watermill and agricultural workshops

Tucked away in dense woodland, the mill is a fine reminder of the recent past when corn was ground here for the local community. Flour is produced regularly and is available for sale. Nearby, a range of outbuildings containing a collection of blacksmiths', carpenters', wheelwrights' and saddlers' tools is presented as workshops, giving an insight into the working lives of local craftsmen.

ℹ **T** 01579 350606,
01579 351346 (Booking)
E cotehele@nationaltrust.org.uk

£ £4.40, child £2.20, family £11, family (one adult) £6.60. Also admits to Cotehele garden, 1ml away

♿ Main visitor reception by house can make arrangements for extra parking. Drop-off point. **Building**: Steps to entrance. Cartshed, wheelwright's and blacksmith's workshops and cider press accessible. Level steps up to mill, saddler's and carpenter's workshops. Stairs with handrail to other floors. Photograph album. **WCs**: Adapted WC. **Grounds**: Partly accessible

Please note: groups must book in advance with the property

Opening arrangements: Cotehele Mill		M	T	W	T	F	S	S
19 Mar - 30 Jun	1 - 5:30	M	T	W	T	F	S	S
1 Jul - 31 Aug	1 - 6	M	T	W	T	F	S	S
1 Sep - 29 Sep	1 - 5:30	M	T	W	T	F	S	S
1 Oct - 31 Oct	1 - 4:30	M	T	W	T	F	S	S
Open Good Fri								

Opening arrangements: The Courts Garden		M	T	W	T	F	S	S
19 Mar - 16 Oct	11 - 5:30	M	T	W	T	F	S	S
Tea-room	As garden							
Out of season by appointment only								

Sensory list. Handling collection

Pushchairs admitted

Suitable for school groups. Children's quiz/trail

Under close control on woodland walk to mill. Dogs not allowed in mill buildings

→ [201: SX417682] See main Cotehele entry

P There is no parking at the mill except by prior arrangement for visitors with disabilities. All other visitors must park at Cotehele Quay and walk ⅓ml through the woods. Do not forget your membership card!

The Courts Garden

Holt, nr Bradford-on-Avon, Wiltshire BA14 6RR

[1943] (1:J4)

Delightful English country garden

An example of the English style at its best, the garden is full of charm and variety. There are many interesting plants and an imaginative use of colour, with surrounding topiary, ornaments and water features. The garden is complemented by an arboretum with natural planting of spring bulbs, a kitchen garden and orchard.

What's new in 2005 Tea-room, WC

★ Please, no tripods or easels without prior consent. No ball games or picnics

i **T** 01225 782875 (opening hours), 01225 782340 (other times) **E** courtsgarden@nationaltrust.org.uk

£ £4.80, child £2.40, family (2 adults & 2 children) £12.20. Groups £4.20, child £2.10. Guided tours £2 extra per person

By appointment at an additional charge

Drop-off point. **WCs**: Adapted WC. **Grounds**: Partly accessible. 1 wheelchair. **Refreshments**: Ramped entrance

Braille guide and large-print guide. Interesting scents

Tea-room (NT-approved concession) on ground floor of house

Pushchairs and baby back-carriers admitted

Suitable for school groups. Children's quiz/trail. Adult study days

The lily pond in The Courts Garden, Wiltshire

→ [173: ST861618] **Cycle**: NCN4 1¼ml.
Bus: First 237 Trowbridge–Melksham
(passing close ⭤ Trowbridge).
Station: Bradford-on-Avon 2½ml; Trowbridge
3ml. **Road**: 3ml SW of Melksham, 2½ml E of
Bradford-on-Avon, on S side of B3107.
Follow signs to Holt

P Free parking (not NT), 80yds. Parking in village
hall car park opposite (not for coaches)

NT properties nearby
Dyrham Park, Great Chalfield Manor, Lacock,
Westwood Manor

Dunster Castle

Dunster, nr Minehead, Somerset TA24 6SL

🏰 ✣ 🕭 🗈 🎧 1976 **(1:G5)**

Ancient castle with fine interiors and sub-tropical gardens

Dramatically sited on a wooded hill, a castle has
existed here since at least Norman times. The
13th-century gatehouse survives, and the
present building was remodelled in 1868–72 by
Antony Salvin for the Luttrell family, who lived
here for 600 years. The fine oak staircase and
plasterwork of the 17th-century house he
adapted can still be seen. A sheltered terrace to
the south is home to palms, subtropical plants,
a variety of citrus trees, and the National
Collection of Strawberry Trees *(Arbutus)*. There
is a pleasant walk beside the River Avill.

What's new in 2005 Series of SeaBritain events

⭐ Major roof repairs will be undertaken in 2005.
Property open as normal. Access to one or
two rooms may be restricted. Tel. for details

i **T** 01643 821314,
01643 823004 (Infoline),
01643 821626 (Shop)
F 01643 823000
E dunstercastle@nationaltrust.org.uk

£ £7.20, child £3.60, family £17.80. Groups
£6.10. **Garden & park only**: £3.90, child
£1.70, family £9.50

ⓘ Tel. for details of out of hours guided tours of
house and/or attics and basements

🛡 Programme of events. Tel. for details

♿ Property on steep slope. Designated parking
in main car park. Wheelchair-accessible
transfer. Drop-off point. **Building**: Many steps
to entrance. 2 wheelchairs. Ground floor has
steps into conservatory and billiard room.
Stairs to other floors, stairclimber available.
Seating available. Please tel. in advance to
check availability of stairclimber and mobility
vehicles. **WCs**: Adapted WC.
Grounds: Partly accessible. Accessible route
map. Steep paths. 1 single-seater PMV.
Shop: Level entrance. Cobbled floor

👆 Braille guide and large-print guide. Sensory
list. Handling collection

🛍 NT shop. Plant sales

🅿 In picnic area adjacent to car park

🚼 Baby-changing facilities. Baby back-carriers
admitted. Front-carrying baby slings for loan.
Buggy park. Colouring sheets. Activity days

▦ Suitable for school groups. Education
room/centre. Live interpretation. Children's
guide. Children's quiz/trail. Adult study days

🐕 On leads and only in park

→ [181: SS995435] **Bus**: First 28, 38, 300, 928
Taunton–Minehead (passing ⭤ Taunton),
alight Dunster Steep, ½ml. **Station**: Dunster
(W Somerset Steam Rly) 1ml. **Road**: In
Dunster, 3ml SE of Minehead. NT car park
approached direct from A39

P Free parking, 300yds. Steep climb to castle,
NT vehicle transfer available

NT properties nearby
Arlington Court, Coleridge Cottage, Dunster
Watermill, Holnicote Estate, Knightshayes Court

Opening arrangements: Dunster Castle										
Castle	19 Mar - 30 Oct	11 - 5	M	T	W	T	F	S	S
	31 Oct - 6 Nov	11 - 4	M	T	W	T	F	S	S
Garden & park	1 Jan - 18 Mar	11 - 4	M	T	W	T	F	S	S
	19 Mar - 30 Oct	10 - 5	M	T	W	T	F	S	S
	31 Oct - 31 Dec	11 - 4	M	T	W	T	F	S	S
Shop	19 Mar - 30 Oct	10 - 5	M	T	W	T	F	S	S
	31 Oct - 8 Jan 06	11 - 4	M	T	W	T	F	S	S
	1 Feb - 18 Mar 06	11 - 4	M	T	W	T	F	S	S

Open Good Fri castle 11–5. garden, park & shop 10–5.
Garden, park & shop closed 25/26 Dec

Please remember – your membership card is always needed for free admission

Windows in Conygar Tower, Dunster Castle, Somerset

£ £2.50, child £1.50, family £6.25, senior citizens £2 (inc. NT members)

🏃 For groups by arrangement

♿ **Building**: Level entrance. Ground floor accessible. Stairs to other floors. **Shop**: Level entrance. **Refreshments**: Many steps to entrance

🏷 Selling mill flour, muesli & souvenirs (not NT)

☕ Riverside Tea-room (not NT)

👶 Baby back-carriers admitted

🎭 Suitable for school groups

➡ [181: SS995435] On River Avill, beneath Castle Tor. **Foot**: Approach via Mill Lane or Castle Gardens. **Bus**: As Dunster Castle

P Parking (not NT), 500yds

NT properties nearby
Arlington Court, Coleridge Cottage, Dunster Castle, Holnicote Estate

Dunster Working Watermill

Mill Lane, Dunster, nr Minehead, Somerset
TA24 6SW

 1976   (1:G5)

Fully-restored watermill

Built on the site of a mill mentioned in the Domesday Survey of 1086, the present mill dates from the 18th century and was restored to working order in 1979.

⭐ The mill is a private business and all visitors inc. NT members pay the admission charge

ℹ **T** 01643 821759

Opening arrangements: Dunster Watermill										
Mill	2 Apr - 30 Jun	11 - 4:45	M	T	W	T	F	S	S
	1 Jul - 30 Sep	11 - 4:45	M	T	W	T	F	S	S
	1 Oct - 6 Nov	11 - 4:45	M	T	W	T	F	S	S
Tea-room	As Mill	10:30 - 4:45							
Open Good Fri										

Dyrham Park

Dyrham, nr Chippenham, Gloucestershire
SN14 8ER

🏛 ✝ 🌸 🍎 🏷 ☕ 🎧 1961   (1:J4)

Spectacular late 17th-century mansion, garden and deer park

Dyrham Park is a beautiful baroque country house set in 110ha (274 acres) of garden and parkland, designed by Talman for William Blathwayt, Secretary at War during the reign of William III. As a consquence of Blathwayt's royal connections and influential uncle, Thomas Povey, the house was to become a showcase for his taste in Dutch decorative arts. The collection includes delftware, paintings and furniture; later 18th-century additions include furniture by Gillow and Linnell. Amongst the restored Victorian domestic rooms are kitchens, tenants' hall and delft-tiled dairy.

⭐ Due to the fragile nature of their contents, some rooms have very low light levels

ℹ **T** 0117 9372501, 0117 9371342 (Shop), 0117 9371344 (Restaurant)
F 0117 9371353
E dyrhampark@nationaltrust.org.uk

East front, Dyrham Park, Gloucestershire

£ £8.80, child £4.35, family £21.75. **Garden and park only**: £3.40, child £1.70, family £7.75. **Park only (on days when house and garden closed)**: £2.25, child £1.10

🕴 Park, garden and house walks and talks held on weekdays during the season (not Good Fri or BH Mons)

😃 Flower festivals April & Sept. Tel. for details

♿ Designated parking in main car park, 10yds. Wheelchair-accessible transfer. **Building**: Many steps to entrance. Alternative accessible entrance. No electric wheelchairs admitted to house due to fragile floors, manual wheelchairs can access house. 3 wheelchairs. Domestic rooms accessible via separate entrance. Stairs to other floors. **WCs**: Adapted WC. **Grounds**: Accessible route. Some slopes, cobbled courtyard and gravel paths. **Shop**: Ramped entrance. **Refreshments**: Ramped entrance

👓 Braille guide and large-print guide

🛍 NT shop. Small selection of plants

🍴 Courtyard Tea-room (licensed) at main house. Children's menu. Kiosk (NT-approved concession) in top car park, open during busy periods

🪑 Groups (15+) please tel. in advance. No barbecues

🚼 Baby-changing facilities. Front-carrying baby slings and hip-carrying infant seats for loan

🎒 Suitable for school groups. Education room/centre. Family activity packs. Children's guidebook illustrated by member of the Blathwayt family. Guide leaflets to the house in several languages

🐕 Only in dog-walking area

➔ [172: ST743757] **Foot**: Cotswold Way passes property. **Cycle**: Avon and Wiltshire cycleways. **Bus**: Special link (X56) 🚇 Bath Spa into Dyrham. Tel. property for details. **Station**: Bath Spa 8ml. **Road**: 8ml N of Bath, 12ml E of Bristol; approached from Bath–Stroud road (A46), 2ml S of Tormarton interchange with M4, exit 18

P Free parking, 500yds

Opening arrangements: Dyrham Park										
House	18 Mar - 30 Oct	12 - 4	M	T	W	T	F	S	S
Garden	18 Mar - 30 Oct	11 - 5	M	T	W	T	F	S	S
Park	All year	11 - 5	M	T	W	T	F	S	S
Shop	18 Mar - 30 Oct	11 - 5	M	T	W	T	F	S	S
Tea-room	18 Mar - 30 Oct	11 - 5	M	T	W	T	F	S	S

Admission by timed ticket to house may operate on BH Suns & Mons. Open BH Mons and Good Fri 11-5. Last admission 45mins before closing. Shop and tea-room open weekends until 18 Dec

NT properties nearby
Bath Assembly Rooms, Clevedon Court, Lacock, Leigh Woods, Newark Park, Prior Park, Tyntesfield

Please see the area introductions for details of coast & countryside properties

Finch Foundry

Stocklepath, Okehampton, Devon EX20 2NW

🖼 🔧 🏠 🍴 🧍 🎭 🧍 1994   **(1:F7)**

Fascinating 19th-century water-powered forge in working order

In its heyday the foundry produced agricultural and mining hand tools. Regular demonstrations throughout the day show the three waterwheels driving the huge tilt hammer and grindstone.

⭐ Due to essential maintenance the machinery will not be in operation after 30 September 2005. The foundry bulding and garden will remain open as usual and guided tours will be extended to explain the conservation work being done

ℹ️ **T** 01837 840046

💷 £3.50, child £1.75

♿ Drop-off point. **Building**: Steps to entrance with handrail. Ground floor has uneven floors. 12 external stone steps to other floors. **WCs**: Adapted WC. **Shop**: Level entrance. **Refreshments**: Level entrance

👐 Braille guide. Sensory list. Handling collection. Volunteers will explain history of foundry

🏠 NT shop. Plant sales

☕ Tea-room

👶 Baby back-carriers admitted

🏫 Suitable for school groups. Children's quiz/trail

🐕 Dogs welcome in all areas except tea-room and foundry during demonstrations

➡️ [191: SX641940] In the centre of Stocklepath village. **Bus**: First X9, 171/9 Exeter–Bude, passing 🚉 Exeter St David's. **Station**: Okehampton (Sun, Jun–Sept only) 4½ml. **Road**: 4ml E of Okehampton off A30

🅿️ Free parking. Access is narrow

NT properties nearby
Castle Drogo, Lydford Gorge

Opening arrangements: Finch Foundry					
Foundry	21 Mar - 31 Oct	11 - 5:30	**M** T **W T F S S**		
Tea-room/shop	As Foundry				

Fyne Court

Broomfield, Bridgwater, Somerset TA5 2EQ

🖼 🏊 🧍 🏠 🎋 🎭 🧍 1967   **(1:H5)**

Nature reserve and visitor centre

Formerly the pleasure grounds of the now partly demolished home of the pioneer electrician Andrew Crosse (1784–1855), this nature reserve is the headquarters of the Somerset Wildlife Trust and a visitor centre for the Quantocks.

⭐ Only visitor centre and grounds open to visitors; buildings contain offices of the Wildlife Trust. 8ha (20-acre) reserve managed by Somerset Wildlife Trust, remainder of estate by NT

ℹ️ **T** 01823 451587 (Somerset Wildlife Trust), 01823 451814 (NT Warden)

💷 Admission free

♿ Drop-off point. **WCs**: Adapted WC. **Grounds**: Partly accessible. Accessible route map. All-ability trail. **Shop**: Ramped entrance

🏠 Not NT. Plant sales

👶 Pushchairs and baby back-carriers admitted

🏫 Suitable for school groups. Children's quiz/trail

➡️ [182: ST222321] 6ml N of Taunton; 6ml SW of Bridgwater. **Foot**: Linked to Quantock 'Greenway'. **Station**: Taunton 6ml; Bridgwater 6ml

🅿️ Parking (not NT), 150yds, 50p, charge inc. NT members

NT properties nearby
Beacon & Bicknoller Hills, Coleridge Cottage, Dunster Castle, Holnicote Estate

Opening arrangements: Fyne Court			
1 Apr - 31 Oct	9 - 6	**M T W T F S S**	
1 Nov - 31 Mar 06	9 - 5	**M T W T F S S**	

Opens 10am Sat and Sun. Closes dusk if earlier. Shop: Easter to Sept, daily 2–5. Tel. for winter opening times

Unless indicated, last admission is always 30mins before closing time

Glastonbury Tor

nr Glastonbury, Somerset

✛ ♨ 1933 (1:I5)

Prominent hill overlooking the Isle of Avalon, Glastonbury and the Somerset Levels

The dramatic and evocative Tor dominates the surrounding countryside and offers spectacular views over Somerset, Dorset and Wiltshire. At the summit of this very steep hill an excavation has revealed the plans of two superimposed churches of St Michael, of which only the 15th-century tower remains.

★ No WC

ℹ️ **T** 01985 843600 (Regional office), 01934 844518 (N Somerset office) **F** 01934 845100

£ Admission free. Donations welcome. Information leaflet (50p) available from N Somerset office (please add 50p for p&p)

🚶 Public footpaths across the Tor

♿ Blue badge holders can park on double yellow lines at Moneybox field entrance at top of Wellhouse Lane. Tor is 158m high; entrance to Moneybox field wheelchair-friendly but slope rapidly becomes steep. Steps, rails and seat only on part of route

👆 Braille guide

🅿 In Moneybox field, Fairfield and Tor field – all are on the main footpath. Cattle and sheep may be grazing

🐕 On leads only

The fishing hamlet of Durgan, just below Glendurgan Garden, Cornwall. Two of the buildings are now National Trust holiday cottages

Opening arrangements: Glastonbury Tor								
All year		M	T	W	T	F	S	S

➔ [182/183: ST512386] **Foot**: Short walk from the town centre, eastwards along A361. **Bus**: First 29, 929 from ⇌ Taunton, 376/7, 976/7 from ⇌ Bristol Temple Meads, 377, 977 from Yeovil. All pass within ½ml of the Tor **Cycle**: NCN3. **Road**: Signposted from Glastonbury town centre, from where seasonal park & ride (not NT) operates

🅿 No parking on site (except for orange or blue badge holders). Please use council-run park & ride from centre of Glastonbury from April to Sept, or park in free car park at Somerset Rural Life Museum, Abbey Farm, Glastonbury. Tel. 01458 831197 to confirm times available. Lower entrance to the Tor is approx. ½ml from museum car park

NT properties nearby
Collard Hill, Ivythorn & Walton Hills, Lytes Cary Manor, Stourhead

Glendurgan Garden

Mawnan Smith, nr Falmouth, Cornwall TR11 5JZ

✿ 🏛 🏠 ♨ 1962 (1:C9)

Superb subtropical garden with year-round interest

This valley garden of great beauty was created in the 1820s and developed over many years by the Fox family. Running down to the tiny village of Durgan and its beach, the garden has many fine trees and rare and exotic plants, with outstanding spring displays of magnolias and camellias. In their season glorious displays of wild flowers carpet the valley slopes. The laurel maze, dating from 1833, puzzles young and old. An original cob and thatch schoolroom has been reconstructed. The house is privately occupied.

Opening arrangements: Glendurgan Garden									
Garden	12 Feb - 29 Oct	10:30 - 5:30	M	T	W	T	F	S	S
Shop	As garden								
Tea-room	As garden								
Open BH Mons. Closed Good Fri. Last admission 1hr before closing									

There are special events at most Trust properties; please telephone 0870 458 4000 for details

What's new in 2005 Link from Durgan beach to Helford village by ferry

ℹ️ **T** 01326 250906 (Opening hours only), 01872 862090 (Property Manager's office), 01326 250247 (Tea-room) **F** 01872 865808 **E** glendurgan@nationaltrust.org.uk

💷 £4.50, child £2.20, family £11.20, family (one adult) £6.70. Groups £3.80. Reduced rate when arriving by public transport or cycle

🚶 *Coast of Cornwall* leaflet 16 (Helford River)

♿ Separate designated parking. **WCs**: Adapted WC. Small ramp. **Grounds**: Steep paths but viewing point accessible. **Shop**: Ramped entrance. **Refreshments**: Level entrance

🔊 Induction loop in reception

👆 Braille guide

🛍️ NT shop. Plant sales

☕ Tea-room (NT-approved concession)

👶 Baby-changing facilities. Pushchairs and baby back-carriers admitted. Giant's Stride (a pole with ropes to swing from) and maze

🏫 Suitable for school groups. Children's guide

➡️ [204: SW772277] **Foot**: South West Coast Path within ⅞ml. **Ferry**: Service links Helford village, Helford Passage, Trebah beach and Durgan beach (for Glendurgan). Tel. 01326 250770/250749. **Bus**: Truronian T4/8 from Falmouth (passing close ≋ Penmere). **Station**: Penmere (U) 4ml. **Road**: 4ml SW of Falmouth, ½ml SW of Mawnan Smith, on road to Helford Passage

🅿️ Free parking. Car park gates locked at 5:30

NT properties nearby
Trelissick Garden

The Godolphin Estate

Godolphin Count House, Godolphin Cross, Helston, Cornwall TR13 9RE

🏠 ⚙️ 🔧 ☕ 💷 🅰️ 2000   **(1:C9)**

Historic landscape offering extensive walks with fine views

The Trust acquired this ancient estate of 222ha (555 acres) in 2000; improvements to public access continue to be made. From Godolphin Hill there are wonderful views over west Cornwall. More than 400 recorded archaeological features range from Bronze Age enclosures to dramatic 19th-century mine buildings.

⭐ **GODOLPHIN HOUSE AND GARDENS ARE NOT OWNED BY THE NATIONAL TRUST** but are open to the public on certain days between Easter and end Sept. Group tours by arrangement. Free access to restaurant, plant sales, shop and WC during house opening hours. For house use NT car park

ℹ️ **T** 01736 762479 (NT Warden), 01736 763194 (House and garden – not NT) **F** 01736 763689 **E** godolphin@nationaltrust.org.uk

💷 Admission free to estate. For house admission charges tel. house and garden no.

🚶 Occasional guided walks

🎭 Programme of events. Tel. for details

🚶 Estate walks leaflet available

♿ One level surfaced path, approx. 400yds

☕ Refreshments (not NT) at Godolphin House when open, and nearby at Godolphin Cross

👶 Pushchairs admitted

🏫 Suitable for school groups. Education room/centre. WC for booked groups only. Bookings and information, tel. Warden

🐕 Welcome on leads and under control, on estate only

➡️ [203: SW599321] **Bus**: First 39 Camborne–Helston (passing close ≋ Camborne). **Station**: St Erth 5ml. **Road**: From Helston take A394 to Sithney Common, turn right onto B3302 and follow signs. From Hayle take B3302 through Leedstown. From the west, take B3280 through Goldsithney

🅿️ Free parking. Coach access from Townshend village

NT properties nearby
Glendurgan Garden, The Lizard, St Michael's Mount, Trelissick Garden, Trengwainton Garden

Opening arrangements: Godolphin Estate			
Estate	All year		**M T W T F S S**

Godrevy

Gwithian, nr Hayle, Cornwall

 1939   (1:B9)

High cliffs and sheltered coves with sandy beaches

The Trust owns all the coastline from Godrevy to Navax Point. The main beach below the summer car park connects to Gwithian Beach, forming an impressive sweep of unbroken sand around the edge of St Ives bay. Away from the bustle of the beach the coastal grasslands and heathland are rich with wild flowers and provide open access for miles of walking. Seals are a common sight and guillemot, razorbill, fulmar and cormorant breed on the cliffs.

⭐ Please be aware of cliff edges, unstable cliffs and the state of the tide, and keep children supervised. WC not always available

ℹ **T** 01872 552412 (Area Warden), 01736 754510 (Car park hut), 01872 862945 (Countryside Manager)

📖 NT *Coast of Cornwall* leaflet 9 includes details of walks

♿ **WCs**: Adapted WC

🍦 Ice-cream van. Godrevy Café (NT-approved concession) (licensed). Open main season and weekends/holidays all year. Tel. 01736 757999

🏫 Suitable for school groups

🐕 Seasonal restriction on dogs on beach, Easter to end Sept

➡ [203: SW582430] **Bus**: First X14 Truro–🚉 St Ives (passing 🚉 Truro, 🚉 Redruth and 🚉 Hayle), alight Loggans Way, then 2¼ml. **Station**: Hayle 5ml. **Road**: Just off the B3301 N of Gwithian village

🅿 Parking, £2.50

NT properties nearby
Cornish Mines & Engines, Godolphin Estate, St Michael's Mount, Trengwainton Garden

Opening arrangements: Godrevy							
All year	M	T	W	T	F	S	S

Great Chalfield Manor

nr Melksham, Wiltshire SN12 8NH

🏛 ✚ 🌸 1943   (1:J4)

Charming 15th-century manor house and garden

Completed in 1480, the manor house is enhanced by a moat and gatehouse and has beautiful oriel windows and a great hall. The house and garden were restored c.1905–11 by Major R. Fuller, whose family live here and manage the property. The garden, designed by Alfred Parsons to complement the manor, has been replanted.

ℹ **T** 01225 782239
F 01225 783379

£ £4.60, child £2.30, family (2 adults & 2 children) £11.80. Groups £4.20, child £2.10

🎫 Admission by guided tour

🌱 Garden open outside normal times for spring flowers, under National Gardens Scheme. Charity plant fair Sun 1 May. Charges apply, inc. NT members. Tel. for details

♿ Designated parking in main car park. Drop-off point. **Building**: Steps to entrance. 1 wheelchair. Ground floor has steps to dining room and hall. Stairs to other floors. Photograph album. Seats available in garden adjoining manor. **WCs**: Adapted WC. **Grounds**: Partly accessible. Ramp from forecourt allows access to parts of garden

♿ Braille guide

🪑 Hip-carrying infant seats for loan

🏫 Suitable for school groups

➡ [173: ST860631] **Foot**: Pleasant 1ml walk by public footpath from car park opposite The

Opening arrangements: Great Chalfield Manor							
3 Apr - 30 Oct	M	T	W	T	F	S	S

Admission by guided tour. Tues-Thur: tours at 11.30, 12.15, 2.15, 3 & 3.45. Sun: open 2-5 only. The tours take 45min and numbers are limited to 25. Visitors arriving during a tour can visit the adjoining parish church and garden first. Group visits are welcome on Fri & Sat (not BHols) by written arrangement with the tenant Mrs Robert Floyd. Charge applies

Courts Garden (NT), Holt. **Cycle**: NCN4. On the Wiltshire Cycleway. **Bus**: First 237 Trowbridge–Melksham (passing close ⚏ Trowbridge), alight Holt, 1ml. **Station**: Bradford-on-Avon, 3ml: Chippenham 10ml. **Road**: 3ml SW of Melksham off B3107 via Broughton Gifford Common (sign for Atworth, take care in narrow lane). Coaches must approach from N (via Broughton Gifford); lanes from S too narrow

[P] Free parking on grass verge outside manor gates, 100yds

NT properties nearby
The Courts Garden, Dyrham Park, Lacock, Westwood Manor

Greenway

Greenway Road, Galmpton, nr Brixham, Devon TQ5 0ES

 2000   **(1:G8)**

Glorious woodland garden on the banks of the Dart estuary

Renowned for rare half-hardy plants underplanted with native wild flowers, Greenway has an atmosphere of wildness and timelessness, a true 'secret' garden of peace and tranquillity with wonderful views, set within an extensive estate and associated with many fascinating characters.

What's new in 2005 Newly replanted top garden herbaceous border

⭐ To protect the amenities of local people living on the roads leading to Greenway, the Trust is required to restrict the number of visitors' vehicles admitted to the property. Visitors are encouraged to travel by 'green ways' to Greenway. All those (both members and non-members) intending to arrive by car/mini-coach (max 25-seaters) must book a parking space before arriving at this property.

Opening arrangements: Greenway										
Garden	2 Mar - 8 Oct	10:30 - 5	M	T	W	T	F	S	S
Shop/café	As garden									

Barn Gallery: open as garden, showing modern contemporary art by local artists

Car bookings can easily be made on day of visit, please tel. 01803 842382. Some paths in the garden are very steep. Visitors who have difficulty in walking up hills should tel. for advice. All visitors should wear walking shoes

[i] **T** 01803 842382 (Infoline), 01803 661903 (Restaurant)
F 01803 661900
E greenway@nationaltrust.org.uk

[£] £4.50, child £2.20. Groups £3.75.
Visitors arriving by 'green ways': £3.75, child £1.90

[🚶] 'Meet the Gardener' guided walks, £1.50pp – Fri 2pm; booking essential, numbers limited. Estate walks

[🎭] Programme of events, inc. lectures and workshops in the Barn Gallery, garden days

[🚶] Walks through the estate link with the Dart Valley Trail, Dartmouth/Kingswear/Greenway Quay circular walk; Torbay Dart Link and Village Walk to Galmpton

[♿] Separate designated parking, 100yds.
WCs: Adapted WC. **Grounds**: Partly accessible. Accessible route map. Some steep and slippery paths so access may be difficult for some visitors. Limited access for PMV access. **Shop**: Level entrance. **Refreshments**: Ramped entrance with handrail. Large-print menu. Ramp to upstairs of Barn gallery. Separate parking to main disabled car park

[👁] Braille guide and large-print guide

[🏪] NT shop. Plant sales

[☕] Licensed café. Serves home-made light meals, locally produced organic and vegetarian food. Children's menu

[🎡] In parkland adjacent to car park

[👶] Baby-changing facilities. Pushchairs and baby back-carriers admitted

[▮] Children's quiz/trail. Adult study days

[🐕] On leads on main drive to visitor reception and café courtyard only (not in garden). Dog park in shade outside reception, water available. Walks on the estate, on leads when farm animals present

Please note: groups must book in advance with the property

→ [202: SX876548] **Foot**: Dart Valley Trail from Kingswear or Dartmouth. Torbay Dart Link from Brixham. Village Walk from Galmpton. **Ferry**: Enjoy a cruise on the River Dart from Dartmouth (use Dartmouth Park & Ride, bus service every 15 mins, please allow at least 4 hours' parking). Riverlink service from pontoon adjacent to Station Restaurant, tel. 01803 834488. Dittisham Ferry from North Steps, tel. 01803 833206. Ferries available for individuals, groups and charters. NB there is a steep walk uphill (800yds) from Greenway Quay to the garden. Allow 1½hrs to visit garden. **Station**: Paignton 4½ml, Churston (Paignton & Dartmouth Steam Rly) 2ml. **Road**: There are no parking spaces on the narrow country lanes leading to Greenway. No brown signs; follow signs for Greenway Ferry

P Free parking, 550yds. All cars must book parking space. Mini coaches (25-seat max.) only

NT properties nearby
Bradley, Coleton Fishacre, Compton Castle, Dart Estuary, Overbeck's Museum & Garden

£ £3.20, child £1.60, concessions £2.40. (Correct at time of going to press). NT members charged admission on special event days and for audio tour

& **Building**: Ramped entrance. Tape guides. **WCs**: One purpose-built WC available

Braille guide. Sensory list

EH shop in museum

Ice cream and soft drinks

Baby-changing facilities

Suitable for school groups

On leads and only in grounds

→ [150: SP050300] **Foot**: Cotswold Way within ⅝ml. **Bus**: Castleways from Cheltenham, alight Didbrook, 1¼ml, or more frequent to Greet, 1¾ml by footpath. **Station**: Cheltenham 10ml. **Road**: 2ml NE of Winchcombe, 1ml E of Broadway road (B4632, originally A46)

P Free parking (not NT)

NT properties nearby
Hidcote Manor Garden, Snowshill Manor

Hailes Abbey

nr Winchcombe, Cheltenham, Gloucestershire
GL54 5PB

✝ 🏠 🍺 🎧 🎭 🎭 1937   **(1:K2)**

13th-century Cistercian abbey

Founded in 1246 and once a celebrated pilgrimage site, the abbey now lies in ruins. Remains of the dramatic cloister arches survive and there is a small museum.

⭐ Hailes Abbey is financed, managed and maintained by English Heritage. For further information tel. 0117 975 0700 (EH regional office) or visit www.english-heritage.org.uk/hailes

ⓘ **T** 01242 602398
E customers@english-heritage.org.uk

Opening arrangements: Hailes Abbey			
Site & museum	1 Apr - 30 Jun	10 - 5	**M T W T F S S**
	1 Jul - 31 Aug	10 - 6	**M T W T F S S**
	1 Sep - 30 Sep	10 - 5	**M T W T F S S**
	1 Oct - 31 Oct	10 - 4	**M T W T F S S**

Hardy's Cottage

Higher Bockhampton, nr Dorchester, Dorset
DT2 8QJ

🏠 ❄ 🏠 1948   **(1:J7)**

Birthplace of novelist and poet Thomas Hardy

Thomas Hardy was born in 1840 in this small cob and thatch cottage and from here he would walk to school every day in Dorchester, three miles away. It was built by his great-grandfather and is little altered since the family left. The interior has been furnished by the NT (see also Max Gate). His early novels *Under the Greenwood Tree* and *Far from the Madding Crowd* were written here. It has a charming cottage garden.

What's new in 2005 Start of major project to refurbish the cottage

⭐ No WC

ⓘ **T** 01305 262366 (Custodian)

£ £3. No reduction for children

Please remember – your membership card is always needed for free admission

Opening arrangements: Hardy's Cottage			
18 Mar - 31 Oct	11 - 5	**M** T W **T F S S**	
Closes dusk if earlier than 5			

[&] Drop-off point. **Building**: Step to entrance. Seating available. **Grounds**: Accessible route

[Braille] Braille guide and large-print guide

[Shop] Thomas Hardy's books, postcards and other items for sale

[School] Suitable for school groups

[→] [194: SY728925] **Bus**: Wilts & Dorset X84, 184–6 Weymouth–Salisbury, 187–9 Poole–Dorchester (all pass [≋] Dorchester South & close Dorchester West), alight Bockhampton Lane, ½ml. **Station**: Dorchester South 4ml; Dorchester West (U) 4ml. **Road**: 3ml NE of Dorchester, ½ml S of A35. From Kingston Maurward roundabout follow signs to Stinsford and Higher Bockhampton

[P] Free parking (not NT). Not suitable for coaches. Cottage is 10 min walk through woods or lane from car park. Drop-off point by prior arrangement with Custodian

NT properties nearby
Clouds Hill, Hardy Monument, Max Gate

Heddon Valley Shop

Heddon Valley, Parracombe, Barnstaple, Devon
EX31 4PY

[icons] 1963   (1:F5)

Information centre and gift shop set in a spectacular NT-owned wooded valley on the West Exmoor coast

The area offers many beautiful coastal and woodland walks.

[i] **T/F** 01598 763402, 01598 763306 (Warden)

[K] See local listings for programme of guided walks on the surrounding coastal estate. Walks leaflet from shop

Opening arrangements: Heddon Valley Shop			
Shop/centre	19 Mar - 4 Nov	11 - 5	**M T W T F S S**
	1 Jun - 30 Sep	10:30 - 5:30	**M T W T F S S**
	5 Nov - 18 Dec	11 - 4	M T W T F **S S**

[&] Drop-off point. **Shop**: Level entrance

[Ice-cream] Ice-cream kiosk in shop

[School] Suitable for school groups (Heddon Valley). Tel. Warden

[→] [180: SS655481] **Foot**: South West Coast Path within ⅔ml. **Bus**: First 309, 310 Barnstaple–Lynton (passing close [≋] Barnstaple), alight just N of Parracombe, then 2ml. **Road**: Halfway between Combe Martin and Lynton, off A39 at Hunters Inn

[P] Parking, 50yds. Donations welcome

NT properties nearby
Arlington Court, Dunster Castle, Watersmeet House

Hidcote Manor Garden

Hidcote Bartrim, nr Chipping Campden, Gloucestershire GL55 6LR

[icons] 1947   (1:K1)

Celebrated 20th-century garden in the beautiful North Cotswolds

One of England's great gardens, Hidcote was designed and created in the Arts & Crafts style by the horticulturist Major Lawrence Johnston. It is arranged as a series of outdoor rooms, each with a different character and separated by walls and hedges of many different species. The garden is famous for its rare shrubs and trees, outstanding herbaceous borders and unusual plant species from all over the world. The varied styles of the outdoor rooms peak at different times of year, making for an interesting visit at any time.

Opening arrangements: Hidcote Manor Garden			
Garden	19 Mar - 2 Oct	10:30 - 6	**M T W** T **S S**
	3 Oct - 30 Oct	10:30 - 5	**M T W** T **S S**
Shop/restaurant	19 Mar - 30 Oct	10:30 - 5	**M T W** T **S S**
Shop	4 Nov - 18 Dec	12 - 4	M T W T **F S S**
Restaurant	5 Nov - 18 Dec	12 - 4	M T W T F **S S**
Tea-bar	19 Mar - 2 Oct	10:30 - 5	**M T W** T **S S**
Plant centre	As tea-bar		
Open Good Fri 10:30-6. Last admission 1hr before closing			

The Pillar Garden, Hidcote Manor, Gloucestershire

⭐ As the number of groups is limited per day, group leaders should check with property before booking transport. On BHols and fine weekends garden is least crowded after 3pm

ℹ️ **T** 01386 438333,
01386 438703 (Catering office)
F 01386 438817
E hidcote@nationaltrust.org.uk

💷 £6.60, child £3.30, family £16.10. Groups £5.90, child £2.65

♿ Designated parking in main car park, 20yds. Limited number of designated parking bays available. Entrance via gravelled courtyard and car park. Drop-off point. **Building**: Ramped entrance. 1 wheelchair. **WCs**: Adapted WC. **Grounds**: Partly accessible. Accessible route map. Some informal stone paved paths and steps. Wheelchair access possible to one-third of gardens only. Some visitors may require assistance from their companion. 2 single-seater PMV. **Shop**: Ramped entrance with handrail. **Refreshments**: Steps to entrance. Level entrance via office door

♨️ Braille guide. Interesting scents

🏠 NT shop. Plant sales

🍽️ Garden Restaurant (licensed) close to visitor reception. Children's menu. Thatched Tea-Bar close to car park

👶 Baby-changing facilities. Hip-carrying infant seats for loan. Limited access for pushchairs and prams

🎒 Children's quiz/trail

➡️ [151: SP176429] **Cycle**: NCN5 1¼ml. No cycle parking. **Bus**: Hedgehog H4 Wed only from Moreton-in-Marsh.
Station: Honeybourne (U) 4½ml. **Road**: 4ml NE of Chipping Campden, 1ml E of B4632 (originally A46), off B4081. Coaches are not permitted through Chipping Campden High Street

🅿️ Free parking, 100yds

NT properties nearby
Charlecote Park, Chastleton House, Dover's Hill, The Fleece Inn, Snowshill Manor, Upton House

Please see the area introductions for details of coast & countryside properties

Holnicote Estate

Selworthy, Minehead, Somerset TA24 8TJ

🏠 ✚ 🏖 🎔 🏚 🐾 | 1932 | (1:G5)

Diverse landscape of moor, woods, farms and coast, rich in wildlife

The Holnicote Estate covers 5042ha (12,500 acres) of Exmoor National Park and includes the high tors of Dunkery and Selworthy Beacons, with breathtaking views in all directions. Its traditional cottages and farms are grouped in and around the villages and hamlets, which include Selworthy, Allerford, Bossington, Horner and Luccombe. The Estate also covers 4ml of coastline between Porlock Bay and Minehead, where the South West Peninsula Coast Path begins. There are over 100ml of footpaths to enjoy through the fields, woods, moors and villages. The area is noted for its diversity of wildlife and many rare species can be found in the Horner and Dunkery National Nature Reserve.

i **T** 01643 862452, 01643 862745 (Shop)
F 01643 863011
E holnicote@nationaltrust.org.uk

Programme of events. Tel. for details

Holnicote walks pack and leaflets available from estate office and shop/info centre

Easy access trail at North Hill (SS911477) and Webbers Post (SS903439). Adapted bird hide (SS907463). Contact in advance. **WCs**: Adapted WC. Located at Bossington and Horner car parks. **Shop**: Steps to entrance. Steep slopes to information centre/shop

Small shop at information centre

Suitable for school groups. Education room/centre. Hands-on activities. Adult study days. Piles Mill Study Centre available for school groups, adult learning and exhibitions

On Porlock family cycle route. Also waymarked adventurous mountain-bike trail. Tel. for details

Opening arrangements: Holnicote Estate				
Estate	All year		**M T W T F S S**
Info centre	19 Mar - 29 Apr	11 - 4	**M T W T F S S**
	30 Apr - 2 Oct	10 - 5	**M T W T F S S**
	3 Oct - 30 Oct	11 - 4	**M T W T F S S**

➔ [181: SS920469] **Foot**: 3¾ml of South West Coast Path on property. **Bus**: First 38, 300, Minehead–Porlock, alight Holnicote, then ½ml. **Station**: Minehead (West Somerset Rly) 5ml. **Road**: Off A39 Minehead–Porlock, 3ml W of Minehead

P Free parking. Large car parks with WCs at Selworthy, Bossington, Horner and Allerford. Others at North Hill, Dunkery, Webbers Post

NT properties nearby
Arlington Court, Beacon & Bicknoller Hills, Coleridge Cottage, Dunster Castle, Fyne Court, Knightshayes Court, Watersmeet House

Killerton

Broadclyst, Exeter, Devon EX5 3LE

🏠 🏠 ✚ 🏛 ✿ ♣ 🏖 🏚 ♥ ☕ | 1944 | (1:G7)

Fine 18th-century house with costume collection, hillside garden and estate

Built for the Acland family in 1778, the house is furnished as a comfortable home. The Paulise de Bush collection of 18th- to 20th-century costume is displayed in period rooms. There is an introductory exhibition in the stable courtyard, a substantial Victorian laundry and interesting chapel. The garden was created in the 1770s by John Veitch, one of the greatest nurserymen and landscape designers of his day. It features rhododendrons, magnolias, herbaceous borders and rare trees, as well as an ice house and early 19th-century rustic-style summer house known as The Bear's Hut. The surrounding parkland and woods offer a number of beautiful circular walks giving access to the 2500ha (6100 acre) estate, and there is also a discovery centre offering varied activities.

What's new in 2005 Costume exhibition – 'Officer and Gentleman, Dandies, Swells & Mods' – dashing and flamboyant men's (and ladies') wear from 18th to early 20th century

⭐ Garden open every day of the year

i **T** 01392 881345 (House & events),
01392 881912 (Shop),
01392 882081 (Restaurant)
F 01392 883112
E killerton@nationaltrust.org.uk

Unless indicated, last admission is always 30mins before closing time

£ £6.50, child £3.20, family £16.20, family (one adult) £9.70. Groups £5.50, child £2.70. **Garden and park only**: £5, child £2.50. Groups £4.30, child £2. Reduced rate when arriving by public transport or cycle. Garden and park: reduced rate Nov to Feb

Ⓘ Introductory talks on house and garden by arrangement

Ⓘ Programme of events, inc. open-air concerts. Tel. for details

Ⓘ Walks leaflet available for park and nearby Ashclyst forest

Ⓘ Separate designated parking. Wheelchair-accessible transfer. Drop-off point. **Building**: Steps to entrance, ramp available. 4 wheelchairs. Ground floor accessible. Many stairs to other floors. Costume collection main exhibition on first floor. Photograph album. **WCs**: Adapted WC. **Grounds**: loose gravel paths, steep slopes. Accessible route map. Staff-driven multi-seater vehicle. **Shop**: Steps to entrance, lift available. Use entrance by plants. Split level in shop with steep steps. **Refreshments**: Level entrance. Large-print menu. Stable block: cobbled access to tea-

The Corridor, looking towards the original front door at Killerton House, Devon

room (steps between servery and seating area). Restaurant can be accessed through house or outside

Ⓘ Braille guide and large-print guide. Sensory list

Ⓘ NT shop. Selection of quality peat-free plants grown on the property

Ⓘ Garden Restaurant (licensed). Children's menu. Orchard Tea-room in stable block. Children's menu

Ⓘ In park and picnic area

Ⓘ Baby-changing and feeding facilities. Pushchairs and baby back-carriers admitted. Hip-carrying infant seats for loan. Children's play area. Family activities and discovery centre open in school holidays

Ⓘ Suitable for school groups. Education room/centre. Live interpretation. Children's guide. Children's quiz/trail

Ⓘ On leads and only in park; shaded parking in overflow car park

Ⓘ New cycle track to Broadclyst opening in 2005

Opening arrangements: Killerton										
House	16 Mar - 31 Jul	11 - 5:30	M	T	W	T	F	S	S
	1 Aug - 31 Aug	11 - 5:30	M	T	W	T	F	S	S
	1 Sep - 30 Sep	11 - 5:30	M	T	W	T	F	S	S
	1 Oct - 30 Oct	11 - 5:30	M	T	W	T	F	S	S
	11 Dec - 23 Dec	2 - 4	M	T	W	T	F	S	S
Park & garden	All year	10:30-dusk	M	T	W	T	F	S	S
Shop/plants	1 Mar - 31 Oct	11 - 5:30	M	T	W	T	F	S	S
	3 Nov - 27 Nov	11 - 5	M	T	W	T	F	S	S
	1 Dec - 24 Dec	11 - 5	M	T	W	T	F	S	S
Restaurant	As house	12 - 5							
Tea-room	1 Mar - 31 Oct	10:30 - 5:30	M	T	W	T	F	S	S
	1 Mar - 31 Oct	10:30 - 4:30	M	T	W	T	F	S	S
	3 Nov - 27 Nov	11 - 4	M	T	W	T	F	S	S
	1 Dec - 24 Dec	11 - 4	M	T	W	T	F	S	S

In the summer there may be events in the park or garden, please pick up a leaflet. House open Mon 24 Oct (in half-term week). House open afternoons for part of Dec, tel. for details; also for tea-room, shop, plant sales and opening times in Jan & Feb 2006. In winter shop and tea-room may not open in bad weather. Restaurant open on selected dates in Dec for Christmas lunches, booking essential

There are special events at most Trust properties; please telephone 0870 458 4000 for details

➡ [192: SS973001] **Cycle**: NCN52.
Bus: Stagecoach in Devon 1/B Exeter–▤
Tiverton Parkway (passing close ▤ Exeter
Central) to the house on summer Suns,
otherwise alight Killerton Turn ¾ml.
Station: Pinhoe (U), not Sun, 4½ml; Whimple
(U), 6ml; Exeter Central & St David's, both
7ml. **Road**: Off Exeter–Cullompton road
(B3181, formerly A38); from M5 northbound,
exit 30 via Pinhoe and Broadclyst; from M5
southbound, exit 28

Ⓟ Free parking

NT properties nearby
Budlake Old Post Office Room, Clyston Mill,
Knightshayes Court, Marker's Cottage

Killerton: Budlake Old Post Office Room

Broadclyst, Exeter, Devon EX5 3LW

🏠 1944 (1:G7)

Charming example of a 1950s Post Office Room with cottage garden

This small thatched cottage housed the village
post office. Outside are a wash-house, double-
seated privy and chicken house.

✖ No refreshments or WCs. Nearest WCs at
Killerton. Footpath to Kilerton along old
carriage drive

ⓘ **T** 01392 881690

£ £2, child £1

♿ Parking outside post office. **Building**: Level
entrance. **Grounds**: Fully accessible.
Accessible route. Gentle slopes in garden.
Bench seating available

👁 Large-print guide. Interesting scents

👶 Baby back-carriers admitted

🐕 In garden on leads, not in Post Office Room

➡ [192: SS973001] As for Killerton, just past
bridge over M5. **Cycle**: NCN27

Ⓟ Limited parking on site, 10yds. Not suitable for
coaches. Ample parking at Killerton 800yds

NT properties nearby
Clyston Mill, Killerton, Knightshayes Court,
Marker's Cottage

Killerton: Clyston Mill

Broadclyst, Exeter, Devon EX5 3EW

✖ ⓘ 1944 (1:G7)

Water-powered grain mill in working order

Believed to date from the early 19th century, the
mill is in an idyllic setting by the River Clyst.

What's new in 2005 Special milling afternoons
2nd Sun each month, April–Oct inc.

✖ No refreshments or WCs. Nearest WCs in
village car park

ⓘ **T** 01392 462425,
01392 881345 (Killerton House)

£ £2, child £1. **Joint ticket with Marker's
Cottage**: £3.50, child £1.75. Small groups
welcome by arrangement

♿ Limited parking for disabled visitors.
Building: Level entrance. Mill on three floors
with steep staircase. **Refreshments**: Picnic
area accessible

🍴 In the orchard

👶 Pushchairs and baby back-carriers admitted.
Children need to be supervised – mill on three
floors

▦ Suitable for school groups. Children's quiz/trail

➡ [192: SX981973] **Bus**: As for Killerton, but
shorter distance to stations. **Road**: Off
Exeter–Cullompton Road (B3181) in village of
Broadclyst. Park in village car park, walk
towards church and follow signs through
churchyard

Ⓟ Free parking (not NT), 450yds. Not suitable for
coaches

NT properties nearby
Budlake Old Post Office Room, Killerton,
Knightshayes Court, Marker's Cottage

Opening arrangements: Budlake Old PO Room									
27 Mar - 31 Oct	2 - 5	**M**	**T**	W	T	F	S	**S**

Opening arrangements: Clyston Mill									
27 Mar - 31 Oct	2 - 5	**M**	**T**	W	T	F	S	**S**

Killerton: Marker's Cottage

Broadclyst, Exeter, Devon EX5 3HR

🏠 🗺 1944   (1:G7)

Thatched medieval cob house with interesting interior

Constructed of cob (a mixture of clay and straw), the house contains a cross-passage screen decorated with painted decorative 'grotesque' work and a landscape scene with St Andrew. In the garden is a cob summer house.

ℹ️ **T** 01392 461546,
01392 881345 (Killerton House)

£ £2, child £1. **Joint ticket with Clyston Mill**: £3.50, child £1.75. Not suitable for groups

♿ Drop-off point. **Building**: Steps to entrance with handrail. Alternative accessible entrance

➜ [192: SX985973] **Bus**: As for Killerton, but bus services pass the property and distance shorter to stations. **Road**: In village of Broadclyst. Park in village car park. Leaving car park by vehicle entrance, turn left, then right and turn right on to Townend. Marker's Cottage is second cottage on left

P Free parking (not NT), 250yds

NT properties nearby
Budlake Old Post Office Room, Clyston Mill, Killerton, Knightshayes Court

Opening arrangements: Marker's Cottage			M	T	W	T	F	S	S
27 Mar - 31 Oct	2 - 5		**M**	**T**	W	T	F	S	**S**

King John's Hunting Lodge

The Square, Axbridge, Somerset BS26 2AP

🏠 1968   (1:I5)

Wool-merchant's house of c.1500

The early Tudor timber-framed house was extensively restored in 1971.

⭐ The property is run as a local history museum by Axbridge and District Museum Trust, in co-operation with Sedgemoor District Council, Somerset County Museums Service and Axbridge Archaeological and Local History Society

ℹ️ **T** 01934 732012

£ Admission free. Donations welcome

🚶 Occasional tours of historic Axbridge start from the museum

♿ **Building**: Step to entrance. Alternative accessible entrance. Ground floor accessible. Steep, spiral staircase to other floors

📢 Hearing loop at reception

➜ [182: ST431545] In the Square, on corner of High Street. **Bus**: First 126, 826 Weston-super-Mare–Wells (passing close ≋ Weston-super-Mare). **Station**: Worle (U) 8ml

P Parking (not NT), 100yds

NT properties nearby
Cheddar Cliffs, Clevedon Court, Prior Park, Tyntesfield

Opening arrangements: Hunting Lodge			M	T	W	T	F	S	S
1 Apr - 30 Sep	1 - 4		**M**	**T**	**W**	**T**	**F**	**S**	**S**

Oct 05–March 06: open first Sat of month to coincide with farmers' market, 10-4. Open during History Week in Oct. Tel. for details

Kingston Lacy

Wimborne Minster, Dorset BH21 4EA

🏠 🏛 ❖ ♠ 🎫 🏠 🍴 🎭 🍽 1982   (1:K7)

Elegant country mansion with important collections, set in attractive formal gardens and extensive parkland

Home of the Bankes family for over 300 years, having replaced the ruined family seat at Corfe Castle, this 17th-century house was radically altered in the 19th century by Sir Charles Barry. The house contains the outstanding collection of paintings and other works of art accumulated by William Bankes. It is famous for its dramatic Spanish Room, with walls hung in magnificent gilded leather, and collection of Egyptian

Please note: groups must book in advance with the property

The drawing room, looking towards the library,
Kingston Lacy, Dorset

artefacts. The house and garden are set in a
wooded park with waymarked walks and a fine
herd of North Devon cattle. The surrounding
working estate of over 3200ha (8000 acres), with
its rich diversity of flora and fauna, is crossed by
many paths (leaflet available from reception) and
dominated by the Iron Age hill-fort of Badbury
Rings. The botanically rich Rings are managed
by grazing and dogs are not permitted.

⭐ Point-to-point races are held at Badbury
Rings on 26 Feb, 26 March & 16 April and on
these days a charge is made for car-parking

ℹ️ **T** 01202 883402, 01202 880413 (Infoline),
01202 842913 (Sat & Sun 11–5 Visitor
reception), 01202 840630 (Wardens/gardeners),
0870 240 4068 (Box office),
01202 841424 (Shop),
01202 889242 (Restaurant) **F** 01202 882402
E kingstonlacy@nationaltrust.org.uk

£ £8, child £4, family £20. Groups £6.80, child
£3.40. **Park & garden only**: £4, child £2,
family £10

🚶 For groups of 15+. Booking essential. Guided
walks of park and wider estate with
Countryside Wardens (see Events leaflet)

🚶 Estate walks leaflet from property

♿ Designated parking in main car park, 30yds.
Visitor reception at top of moderate slope.
Transfer available. **Building**: Steps to
entrance with handrail. Ground floor has
steps. 4 steps internally. Stairs with handrail to
other floors. Seating available. 2 extra access
days for disabled visitors; tel. property for
details. **WCs**: Adapted WC. **Grounds**: loose
gravel paths. 4 wheelchairs. 1 single-seater
PMV, booking essential. **Shop**: Ramped
entrance. **Refreshments**: Level entrance.
Large-print menu

📻 Induction loop in reception, shop, restaurant

👁 Braille guide and large-print guide. Sensory
list

🛍 NT shop. Plant sales

🍴 Stables Restaurant (licensed) in courtyard and
stables. Limited menu on Mon and Tues when
house is closed. Alcohol only served with knife
and fork meals. Function room. Sunday
roasts. Christmas lunches. Children's menu

🪧 In designated picnic areas only

👶 Baby-changing facilities. Front-carrying baby
slings and hip-carrying infant seats for loan.
Children's play area

🏫 Suitable for school groups. Education
room/centre. Hands-on activities. Children's
guide. Adult study days

🐕 On leads and only in park and on woodland
walks

🚲 22ml of public bridleway with shared access
for cyclists on the estate (but not the park)

Opening arrangements: Kingston Lacy										
House	18 Mar - 30 Oct	11 - 5	M	T	**W**	**T**	**F**	**S**	**S**
Garden & park	18 Mar - 30 Oct	10:30 - 6	**M**	**T**	**W**	**T**	**F**	**S**	**S**
	4 Nov - 18 Dec	10:30 - 4	M	T	W	T	**F**	**S**	**S**
	4 Feb - 18 Mar 06	10:30 - 4	M	T	W	T	F	**S**	**S**
	13 Feb - 17 Feb 06	10:30 - 4	**M**	**T**	**W**	**T**	**F**	S	S
Shop	18 Mar - 30 Oct	10:30 - 5:30	**M**	**T**	**W**	**T**	**F**	**S**	**S**
	4 Nov - 18 Dec	10:30 - 4	M	T	W	T	**F**	**S**	**S**
Restaurant	As shop								

Admission by timed ticket to house may operate on
BH Suns & Mons. Open BH Mons. Last admission 1hr
before closing. Special snowdrop days in Jan/Feb: for
details tel. infoline. Due to concert on Sat 2 Jul, house
& shop will close at 4, restaurant & grounds at 4:30

→ [195: ST980019] **Bus**: Wilts & Dorset 132/3, 182/3 from Bournemouth, Poole (passing ≥ Bournemouth & close ≥ Poole), alight Wimborne Square 2½ml. **Station**: Poole 8½ml. **Road**: On B3082 Blandford–Wimborne road, 1½ml W of Wimborne Minster

P Free parking. Charge at Badbury Rings on point-to-point race days

NT properties nearby
Brownsea Island, Corfe Castle, Hardy's Cottage, Max Gate, Mompesson House, White Mill

Opening arrangements: Knightshayes Court

House	23 Mar - 29 Sep	11 - 5:30	M	T	W	T		S	S
	1 Oct - 30 Oct	11 - 4	M	T	W	T		S	S
Garden	4 Mar - 20 Mar	11 - 4	M	T	W	T	F	S	S
	23 Mar - 30 Oct	11 - 5:30	M	T	W	T	F	S	S
Shop	4 Mar - 13 Mar	11 - 4	M	T	W	T	F	S	S
	18 Mar - 30 Oct	11 - 5	M	T	W	T	F	S	S
	3 Nov - 18 Dec	11 - 4	M	T	W	T	F	S	S
	19 Dec - 20 Dec	11 - 4	M	T	W	T	F	S	S
Restaurant	As shop								

Open Good Fri. The new walled garden project is open as main garden above

Knightshayes Court

Bolham, Tiverton, Devon EX16 7RQ

🏠 ❄ ♠ 🗄 🖤 🎧 🖗 🍽 ⏰ 1973   **(1:G6)**

Victorian country house with richly decorated interiors and fine garden

Begun in 1869, Knightshayes is a rare survival of the work of designer William Burges. The interiors combine medieval romanticism with lavish Victorian decoration, and the smoking and billiard rooms, elegant boudoir and drawing room all give an atmospheric insight into the grand country house life which revolved around the Heathcoat-Amory family. A recently opened room shows original Burges designs, including furniture and wall-paintings. The celebrated garden features a water lily pool and topiary, specimen trees, rare shrubs and delightful seasonal colours. Attractive woodland walks lead through the grounds.

What's new in 2005 The Victorian walled garden: its design and purpose make it one of the Trust's most exciting current projects

ℹ️ **T** 01884 254665,
01884 257381 (Visitor reception),
01884 243464 (Plant centre),
01884 259010 (Shop),
01884 259416 (Restaurant) **F** 01884 243050
E knightshayes@nationaltrust.org.uk

£ £6.50, child £3.20, family £16.20, family (one adult) £9.70. Groups £5.50, child £2.70. **Park & garden only**: £5, child £2.50. Groups £4.30, child £2.20

📕 Guided tours of house and garden for groups by arrangement

🚶 Parkland leaflet at reception (free)

♿ Separate designated parking. Please show membership card at reception before parking by house. Drop-off point. **Building**: Ramped entrance. 3 wheelchairs. Ground floor accessible. Stairs to other floors. Lift available for visitors able to stand. Seating available. Audio visual/video. **WCs**: Adapted WC. **Grounds**: Partly accessible, slopes. Accessible route map. **Shop**: Level entrance. **Refreshments**: Level entrance. Large-print menu

👁 Braille guide. Sensory list. Handling collection

🛍 Gift shop. Well-stocked plant centre with many unusual plants

🍴 Stable Restaurant (licensed). In Oct opening hours may vary, although light refreshments are always available during opening hours. Children's menu

⛺ Picnic area in car park and parkland

👶 Baby-changing facilities. Pushchairs and baby back-carriers admitted. Front-carrying baby slings for loan

🏫 Suitable for school groups. Education room/centre. Hands-on activities. Children's guide. Children's quiz/trail. Adult study days

🐕 Welcome on leads in facilities areas, woodland and park

→ [181: SS960151] **Cycle**: NCN3. **Bus**: First 398 Tiverton–Minehead, alight Bolham, then ¾ml. Otherwise Stagecoach in Devon 1 from ≥ Tiverton Parkway; 55/A/B Exeter–Tiverton (passing close ≥ Exeter Central), alighting Tiverton 1¾ml. **Station**: Tiverton Parkway 8ml.

Please remember – your membership card is always needed for free admission

Road: 2ml N of Tiverton; turn right off Tiverton–Bampton road (A396) at Bolham; 7ml from M5 exit 27 (A361)

P Free parking, 400yds

NT properties nearby
Budlake Old Post Office Room, Clyston Mill, Killerton, Marker's Cottage

Lacock Abbey, Fox Talbot Museum & Village

Lacock, nr Chippenham, Wiltshire SN15 2LG

 1944   (1:J4)

The medieval cloisters, Lacock Abbey, Wiltshire

Country house created out of a medieval abbey, the home of a pioneer of photography

Founded in 1232 and converted into a country house c.1540, the fine medieval cloisters, sacristy, chapter house and monastic rooms of the Abbey have survived largely intact. The handsome 16th-century stable courtyard has half-timbered gables, a clockhouse, brewery and bakehouse. The naturalistic woodland garden has a fine display of spring flowers and magnificent trees. There is an intimate Victorian rose garden with 18th-century summer house. A 'botanic' garden including unusual plant varieties has been developed over the last few years. The Photographic Museum commemorates the achievements of a former resident of the Abbey, William Henry Fox Talbot (1800–77), inventor of the negative/positive photographic process, whose descendants gave the Abbey and village to the Trust in 1944. The village, which dates from the 13th century and has many limewashed half-timbered and stone houses, was used as a location in the TV and film productions of *Pride and Prejudice, Moll Flanders* and *Emma*. The Abbey also featured in the recent *Harry Potter* films.

What's new in 2005 'Botanic' garden: first phase of greenhouse reconstruction

★ Children's playground opposite Fox Talbot Museum maintained by Lacock Parish Council, not by NT

i **T** 01249 730459 (Visitor Reception), 01249 730227 (Abbey Tel/Fax), 01249 730176 (Museum), 01249 730141 (Learning), 0870 240 4068 (Box office), 01249 730302 (Shop)
F 01249 730501 (Estate office)

£ **Abbey, museum, cloisters & grounds**: £7.40, child £3.70, family (2 adults & 2 children) £18.90. Groups £6.60, child £3.30. **Garden, cloisters & museum**: £4.60, child £2.30, family £11.80. Groups £4.20, child £2.10. **Abbey, cloisters & grounds**: £6, child £3, family £15.30. Groups £5.40, child £2.70. **Museum (winter)**: £3.20, child £1.60, family £8.20. Groups £2.80, child £1.40

⚡ By arrangement. Tel./fax property for details

⚑ Programme of events (book via Box office). Garden open outside normal opening times for spring flowers under National Gardens Scheme. Charges apply, inc. NT members

Opening arrangements: Lacock Abbey											
Museum	26 Feb - 30 Oct	11 - 5:30	M	T	W	T	F	S	S
Cloisters	As museum								
Grounds	As museum								
Abbey	19 Mar - 30 Oct	1 - 5:30	M	T	W	T	F	S	S
High St shop	2 Jan - 18 Mar	11 - 4	M	T	W	T	F	S	S
	19 Mar - 30 Oct	10 - 5:30	M	T	W	T	F	S	S
	31 Oct - 31 Dec	11 - 4	M	T	W	T	F	S	S

Museum, Abbey & grounds closed Good Fri, but High St shop open. Museum (only) open winter weekends (11–4), but closed 25 Dec to 2 Jan 06 inc. High St shop closed 25, 26 Dec & 1 Jan 06

⟨♿⟩ Separate designated parking, 100yds. Limited parking in Abbey courtyard, by arrangement. Otherwise reserved spaces in nearby Red Lion car park. Drop-off point. **Building**: Many steps to entrance. 4 wheelchairs. 3 sets of steps in Abbey. Ramped access to abbey cloisters, largely accessible. Ground floor of museum fully accessible. Stairs to other floors. Museum has non-wheelchair stairlift. Seating available. Photograph album. **WCs**: Adapted WC. **Grounds**: Partly accessible. Accessible route map. Steep drops and open water around grounds. 1 single-seater PMV. **Shop**: Ramped entrance with handrail

⟨◉⟩ Braille guide and large-print guide. Audio guide

⟨🏠⟩ In village. Also Museum shop selling photographic books, films and postcards (open times as Museum)

⟨🍴⟩ Tea-rooms, pubs, restaurant and bakery in the village. (Most owned by NT but leased and managed by tenants.)

⟨⛱⟩ Picnic area in the pound, opposite Fox Talbot Museum

⟨👶⟩ Baby-changing facilities. Baby back-carriers admitted. Hip-carrying infant seats for loan. Baby-changing facilities in Abbey WCs and Red Lion car park WCs. Children's play area (not NT) in village playing field (opposite Museum). No pushchairs in Abbey but can be left in hall

⟨🏫⟩ Suitable for school groups. Education room/centre. Live interpretation. Hands-on activities. Children's guide. Children's quiz/trail

⟨➜⟩ [173: ST919684] **Cycle**: NCN4 1ml. **Bus**: First 234 Chippenham–Frome (passing ⧉ Melksham, close ⧉ Chippenham and close ⧉ Trowbridge), Hatts 73 Melksham–Corsham. **Station**: Melksham 3ml. Chippenham 3½ml. **Road**: 3ml S of Chippenham, just E of A350; signposted to car park

⟨P⟩ Free parking, 220yds

NT properties nearby
The Courts Garden, Dyrham Park, Great Chalfield Manor, Prior Park, Westwood Manor

Lanhydrock

Bodmin, Cornwall PL30 5AD

⟨🏛 ✚ ❀ ♠ ⛽ 🏠 💼 🎭 ⛱ 🍴 ♿⟩ 1953   (1:D8)

Magnificent late Victorian country house with extensive servants' quarters, gardens and wooded estate

One of the most fascinating and complete late 19th-century houses in England, Lanhydrock is full of period atmosphere. Although the gatehouse and north wing (with magnificent 32yd-long gallery with plaster ceiling) survive from the 17th century, the rest of the house was rebuilt following a disastrous fire in 1881. The new house featured the latest in contemporary living, including central heating. The garden has a stunning collection of magnolias, rhododendrons and camellias, and offers fine colours right through into autumn. All this is set in a glorious estate of 364ha (900 acres) of woods and parkland running down to the River Fowey, with an extensive network of footpaths.

⟨★⟩ 50 rooms are open to visitors, who should allow at least 2 hours to tour the house. Secure locker system for large bags. Church (adjacent to house): service every Sun 9.45

⟨i⟩ **T** 01208 265950,
01208 265211 (Countryside office),
01208 265952 (Shop),
01208 265951 (Restaurant) **F** 01208 265959
E lanhydrock@nationaltrust.org.uk

Opening arrangements: Lanhydrock										
House	19 Mar - 30 Sep	11 - 5:30	M	T	W	T	F	S	S
	1 Oct - 30 Oct	11 - 5	M	T	W	T	F	S	S
Garden	All year	10 - 6	M	T	W	T	F	S	S
Shop & plants	12 Feb - 18 Mar	11 - 4	M	T	W	T	F	S	S
	19 Mar - 30 Sep	11 - 5:30	M	T	W	T	F	S	S
	1 Oct - 30 Oct	11 - 5	M	T	W	T	F	S	S
Shop only	31 Oct - 24 Dec	11 - 4	M	T	W	T	F	S	S
	27 Dec - 31 Dec	11 - 4	M	T	W	T	F	S	S
	7 Jan - 18 Feb 06	11 - 4	M	T	W	T	F	S	S
Refreshments	12 Feb - 18 Mar	11 - 4	M	T	W	T	F	S	S
	19 Mar - 30 Sep	10:30 - 5:30	M	T	W	T	F	S	S
	1 Oct - 30 Oct	10:30 - 5	M	T	W	T	F	S	S
	31 Oct - 24 Dec	11 - 4	M	T	W	T	F	S	S
	27 Dec - 31 Dec	11 - 4	M	T	W	T	F	S	S
	7 Jan - 18 Feb 06	11 - 4	M	T	W	T	F	S	S
Open BH Mons									

Please see the area introductions for details of coast & countryside properties

The dairy at Lanhydrock, Cornwall

£ £7.90, child £3.95, family £19.75, family (one adult) £11.85. Groups £6.90, child £3.45. **Garden & grounds only**: £4.40, child £2.20. Reduced rate when arriving by public transport or cycle

Estate walks leaflet available

Separate designated parking. Drop-off point. **Building**: Alternative accessible entrance. 4 wheelchairs. 3 steps down to billiard room. Stairs to other floors, lift available. Seating available. Photograph album. **WCs**: Adapted WC. **Grounds**: Partly accessible. Accessible route map. 2 single-seater PMV, booking essential. **Shop**: Step to entrance, ramp available. **Refreshments**: Ramped entrance

Induction loop in reception

Braille guide and large-print guide. Sensory list

NT shop. Plant sales in car park

Licensed restaurant in main house. Children's menu. Stables tea-room in harness block

Baby-changing and feeding facilities. Front-carrying baby slings and hip-carrying infant seats for loan. Children's play area. Pushchair loan for use in grounds

Suitable for school groups. Education room/centre. Live interpretation. Hands-on activities. Children's quiz/trail. Organised children's activities in school holidays

On leads and only in park and woods

→ [200: SX088636] **Cycle**: NCN3. **Bus**: Western Greyhound 555 ⬛ St Austell–Padstow, DAC Coaches 269 St Austell–Callington. **Station**: Bodmin Parkway 1¾ml via original carriage-drive to house, signposted in station car park; 3ml by road. **Road**: 2½ml SE of Bodmin. Follow signposts from either A30, A38 Bodmin–Liskeard or take B3268 off A390 at Lostwithiel

P Free parking, 600yds

NT properties nearby
Trerice

Lawrence House

9 Castle Street, Launceston, Cornwall PL15 8BA

🏠 🏚 1964   (1:E7)

Typical Georgian town house

Built in 1753, Lawrence House was given to the Trust to help preserve the character of the street. It is now leased to Launceston Town Council and in use as a local museum and civic centre.

i **T** 01566 773277 (Hon. Curator), 01566 773693 (Town Clerk)

£ Admission free. Donations welcome

Building: Steps to entrance, ramp available. Ground floor accessible. Stairs with handrail to other floors. Limited access for disabled visitors. Photograph album. **WCs**: Adapted WC

Braille guide

Small shop open as museum

Pushchairs admitted

Suitable for school groups. Hands-on activities

→ [201: SX330848] **Bus**: First X8, 76 from Plymouth (passing ⬛ Plymouth); First X10 from ⬛ Exeter St Davids–Newquay

P Parking (not NT) (pay & display)

NT properties nearby
Cotehele

Opening arrangements: Lawrence House								
18 Apr - 30 Sep	10:30 - 4:30	**M**	**T**	**W**	**T**	**F**	S	S

Open evenings, weekends all year by appointment for groups or individuals for study

Unless indicated, last admission is always 30mins before closing time

Levant Mine & Beam Engine

Trewellard, Pendeen, nr St Just, Cornwall
TR19 7SX

 **1967** (1:B9)

Working steam-powered beam engine

In its tiny engine house perched on the cliff edge, the famous Levant beam engine is steaming again after sixty idle years. The sight, sounds and smells of this 165-year-old engine conjure up the feel of Cornwall's industrial past. A short underground tour takes the visitor from the miners' dry to the man engine shaft via a spiral staircase. Also on view are the winding and pumping shafts, and the newly restored electric winding engine. Half a mile along the cliff is Geevor mine (not NT) and a mining museum, and in the other direction is the Botallack Count House (NT) with information on the history of the St Just coastal area.

What's new in 2005 Model pumping engine working on compressed air

★ WC not always available. Portaloo; otherwise nearest WC at Geevor mine ½ml

ⓘ **T** 01736 786156,
01736 796993 (Penwith countryside office)
F 01736 794390

£ £5, child £2.50, family £12.50, family (one adult) £7.50. Groups £4.30. Reduced rate when arriving by public transport or cycle. Stewarded by NT staff and volunteers and volunteer members of the Trevithick Society. NT members are invited to contribute to the cost of the project

ⓚ Self-guided tour leaflet available

Opening arrangements: Levant Beam Engine										
Steaming	4 Mar - 18 Mar	11 - 5	M	T	W	T	**F**	S	S
	25 Mar - 27 May	11 - 5	M	**T**	W	T	**F**	S	S
	1 Jun - 30 Jun	11 - 5	M	T	**W**	**T**	**F**	S	**S**
	1 Jul - 30 Sep	11 - 5	M	**T**	**W**	**T**	**F**	S	**S**
	4 Oct - 21 Oct	11 - 5	M	**T**	W	T	**F**	S	S
	25 Oct - 28 Oct	11 - 5	M	**T**	**W**	T	**F**	S	S
Not steaming	4 Nov - 24 Feb 06	11 - 4	M	T	W	T	**F**	S	S
Open BH Suns & Mons 11–5									

& Separate designated parking, 50yds. Wheelchair access path on slope. **Building**: Ramped entrance. Alternative accessible entrance. Access available to first floor and external workings only. Audio visual/video. **WCs**: Nearest WC at Geevor mine, ½mile. **Shop**: Many steps to entrance

Braille guide. Sensory list

Small outlet for industrial/mining artefacts

Nearest refreshments (not NT) available at Geevor mine or Pendeen village

Pushchairs and baby back-carriers admitted

Suitable for school groups. Live interpretation

→ [203: SW368346] **Foot**: South West Coast Path passes entrance. **Bus**: First 17/A from Penzance. **Station**: Penzance 7ml. **Road**: 1ml W of Pendeen, on B3306 St Just–St Ives road

P Free parking, 100yds. Limited parking for coaches at Geevor mine, ½ml walk to Levant mine

NT properties nearby
Botallack Count House, St Michael's Mount, Trengwainton Garden

The Lizard and Kynance Cove

Cornwall

1935 (1:C10)

Dramatic and historic stretch of Cornish coast

The Lizard is the most southerly point of mainland Britain and the turning point of one of the busiest shipping lanes in the world. The coastline on either side offers dramatic cliff walks, masses of rare wild flowers and fascinating geological features. The area played a key role in the history of modern communications. Marconi's historic wireless experiments on The Lizard in

Opening arrangements: The Lizard	
All year	M T W T F S S
Tel. for opening times of Lizard Wireless Station and Marconi Centre	

There are special events at most Trust properties; please telephone 0870 458 4000 for details

1901 are celebrated at the restored **Lizard Wireless Station**, Bass Point, and the **Marconi Centre** at Poldhu. Two miles north of Lizard Point lies Kynance Cove – white sand, turquoise water and islands of multi-coloured serpentine rock with stacks and arches hidden amongst the towering cliffs – long considered one of the most beautiful places in Cornwall.

i **T** 01326 561407 (SW Cornwall Office), 01326 290384 (Lizard Wireless Station), 01326 241656 (Marconi Centre) **F** 01326 562882 **E** lizard@nationaltrust.org.uk

⚑ Occasional guided walks

⚐ NT *Coast of Cornwall* leaflet 14 includes maps and details of circular walks and information on local history, geology and wildlife

♿ Surfaced paths to viewpoints overlooking Kynance and Lizard Point approx. 180yds. **WCs**: Adapted WC

Kynance Cove, The Lizard, Cornwall

☕ Café (NT-approved concession) at Kynance Cove beach. Ice-cream van at Kynance car park in the season. Café on Lizard Point (not NT)

👶 Baby-changing facilities at Lizard Point car park WC and Kynance Cove WC

▦ Suitable for school groups

🐕 Dogs welcome, but seasonal bans on some beaches including Kynance

➜ [203: SW688133] **Foot**: 3¾ml of South West Coast Path on property. **Bus**: Truronian T3 Helston–Kynance Cove, June–Oct only (with connections from ▇ Redruth; otherwise T1 Perranporth–Lizard (passing ▇ Truro), then to Kynance Cove 1½ml; to Lizard Point 1ml. **Road**: From Helston, A3083 to Lizard town

P Car parks at Kynance and The Lizard. Free parking in Lizard town, from where a footpath leads to Lizard Point. No caravans or trailers

NT properties nearby
Glendurgan Garden, Godolphin Estate, St Michael's Mount

Lodge Park & Sherborne Estate

Sherborne, nr Cheltenham, Gloucestershire GL54 3PP

🏛🌳♨💬🦌👤🔔🍴 1983   (1:K2)

Rare 17th-century grandstand and Cotswold country estate

Situated on the picturesque Sherborne Estate in the Cotswolds, **Lodge Park** was created in 1634 by John 'Crump' Dutton. Inspired by his passion for gambling and banqueting, it is a unique survival of what would have been called a grandstand, with its deer course and park. It was the home of Charles Dutton, 7th Lord Sherborne, until 1983 when he bequeathed his family's estate to the National Trust. The interior of the grandstand has been reconstructed to its original form, and was the first project undertaken by the Trust that relied totally on archaeological evidence. The park behind was designed by Charles Bridgeman in 1725. The

Opening arrangements: Lodge Park & Sherborne									
Grandstand	18 Mar - 30 Oct	11 - 4	**M**	T	W	T	**F**	**S**	**S**
Deer Park	As grandstand								
Sherborne Est	All year		**M**	**T**	**W**	**T**	**F**	**S**	**S**
Please note the grandstand closes at 3 on Sat and will close at 1.30 on Sat 11 June									

Sherborne Estate is 1650ha (4000 acres) of rolling countryside with views down to the River Windrush. Much of the village of Sherborne is owned by the Trust, including the post office and shop, school and social club. There are walks for all ages around the estate, which includes the restored and working water meadows.

What's new in 2005 Additional sculptures on trail

[i] **T** 01451 844130 (Lodge Park), 01451 844257 (Estate office)
F 01451 844131 (Lodge Park)
E lodgepark@nationaltrust.org.uk

[£] **Grandstand**: £4.50, child £2.20, family £11. Estate free

[🚶] Out of hours guided tours and walks can be arranged

[♿] Separate designated parking, 50yds. Drop-off point. **Building**: Steps to entrance, ramp available. Audio visual/video, photograph album. **WCs**: Adapted WC

[👋] Braille guide

[📷] Post office & shop in Sherborne village sells ice cream and soft drinks. Open all year round but closed all day Wed, Sun and Sat pm. Social club (licensed) open Sun 12–2. Shop and social club not managed by NT

[🗺] Picnic tables provided at Lodge Park

[👶] Pushchairs admitted

[🎦] Children's quiz/trail. Introductory video shown at regular intervals throughout the day

[🐕] Under close control

[→] [163: SP146123] **Bus**: Swanbrook 53 Oxford–Gloucester (passing ⟰ Gloucester and close ⟰ Oxford). 1ml walk to Lodge Park from bus stop. **Road**: 3ml E of Northleach; approach from A40 only

[P] Parking, for estate walks [163:SP158143] and water meadows [163:SP175154]. Donation of £1 welcome

NT properties nearby
Chastleton House, Chedworth Roman Villa, Hidcote Manor Garden, Snowshill Manor

---

Loughwood Meeting House

Dalwood, Axminster, Devon EX13 7DU

[✚] | 1969 | (**1:H7**)

17th-century Baptist meeting house

Around 1653 the Baptist congregation of the nearby village of Kilmington constructed this simple building dug into the hillside.
They attended services here at the risk of imprisonment or transportation. The interior was fitted in the early 18th century.

[★] No WC

[i] **T** 01392 881691 (Regional office)
F 01392 881954

[£] Admission free. Donations welcome. Not suitable for groups

[♿] Steep slope from the car park.
Building: Level entrance. Stairs to other floors

[👶] Pushchairs and baby back-carriers admitted

[■] Family guide

[→] [192/193: SY253993] **Bus**: Stagecoach in Devon 380 Axminster–Exeter (passing close ⟰ Axminster). **Station**: Axminster 2½ml. **Road**: 4ml W of Axminster; turn right on Axminster–Honiton road (A35), 1ml S of Dalwood, 1ml NW of Kilmington

[P] Free parking, 20yds. Not suitable for coaches. Very narrow country lanes

NT properties nearby
Branscombe, Shute Barton

Opening arrangements: Loughwood Meeting House							
All year	**M**	**T**	**W**	**T**	**F**	**S**	**S**

Please note: groups must book in advance with the property

Lundy

Bristol Channel, Devon EX39 2LY

🏠 🐕 ✝ 🏰 🔧 🍴 ⛵ 🚹 👶 📷 🖼

👶 〒 1969   **(1:D5)**

Unspoilt island, home to a fascinating array of wildlife amidst dramatic scenery

Undisturbed by cars, the island encompasses a small village with an inn and Victorian church, and the 13th-century Marisco Castle. Of interest to nature-lovers are the variety of migratory seabirds, heathland and grassland habitat and the Lundy ponies. Designated the first Marine Conservation Area, Lundy offers opportunites for diving and seal watching.

⭐ The island is financed, administered and maintained by the Landmark Trust. Holiday cottages available to rent, tel. Infoline for details

ℹ️ **T** 01237 431831 (Warden),
01271 863636 (Infoline)
F 01237 477779
E info@lundyisland.co.uk

£ **NT members**: £25, child £12.50. **Non-NT members**: £28, child £14. Entrance fee included in fare for ferry passengers, or £3.50 per person for those arriving by other means. Discount for NT members applies when booking in advance and arriving by ferry (day trips only)

🚶 Walks with the Warden

♿ Some level areas and some slopes. Transfer available. Drop-off point. **Building**: Steps to entrance. Stairs to other floors.
Grounds: Limited by boat trip to Island.
Shop: Ramped entrance.
Refreshments: Level entrance

🛍 Shop selling the famous Lundy stamps, souvenirs and postcards, plus general supplies and groceries

🍴 Marisco Tavern (not NT) (licensed) in the village. Children's menu

Opening arrangements: Lundy		
1 Apr - 31 Oct		M T W T F S S

Helicopter service from Hartland Point 1 Nov–31 March, Mon & Fri only, for visitors staying on the island

👶 Baby-changing facilities. Pushchairs admitted

🖼 Suitable for school groups. Education room/centre. Live interpretation. Hands-on activities. Shore rambles

➡️ [180: SS130450] In the Bristol Channel 11ml N of Hartland Point, 25ml W of Ilfracombe, 30ml S of Tenby. **Cycle**: NCN31 (Bideford). **Ferry**: Sea passages from Bideford or Ilfracombe according to tides up to 4 days a week. Tel. infoline for details. **Bus**: Frequent services from 🚉 Barnstaple to Bideford or Ilfracombe. **Station**: Barnstaple: 8½ml to Bideford, 12ml to Ilfracombe

P Public parking at Bideford or Ilfracombe for ferries (pay & display)

NT properties nearby
Arlington Court, North Devon Coastline

Lydford Gorge

The Stables, Lydford Gorge, Lydford, nr Okehampton, Devon EX20 4BH

⛵ 🛍 🍴 🍴 🖼 👕 👶 1947   **(1:F7)**

Spectacular river gorge and waterfall

This famous gorge is 1½miles long and can be viewed from a circular walk, which starts high above the river and passes through attractive oak woods before dropping down to the dramatic 30m-high White Lady waterfall. The path then proceeds along an enchanting riverside walk through the steeply sided ravine, scooped out by the River Lyd as it plunges into a series of whirlpools, including the thrilling Devil's Cauldron.

Opening arrangements: Lydford Gorge			
Gorge	23 Mar - 30 Sep	10 - 5:30	M T W T F S S
	1 Oct - 30 Oct	10 - 4	M T W T F S S
Waterfall only	31 Oct - 31 Mar 06	10:30 - 3	M T W T F S S
Tea-room	23 Mar - 30 Sep	10:30 - 5	M T W T F S S
	1 Oct - 30 Oct	10:30 - 4	M T W T F S S
Shop	23 Mar - 30 Oct	As gorge	M T W T F S S
Christmas Shop	4 Nov - 18 Dec	11 - 3:30	M T W T F S S

31 Oct to 31 March access is from waterfall entrance to waterfall only

Parking in National Trust car parks is free for members

The Main Walk through Lambhole Wood, Lydford Gorge, Devon

⭐ The walk is arduous in places; visitors should wear stout footwear. Unsuitable for visitors with heart complaints or walking difficulties and very young children

ℹ️ **T** 01822 820320, 01822 820441 (Shop), 01822 822004 (Tea-room) **F** 01822 822000 **E** lydfordgorge@nationaltrust.org.uk

💷 £4.50, child £2.20. Groups £3.80, child £1.90. Reduced rate when arriving by public transport or cycle

♿ Separate designated parking, 5yds. **WCs**: Adapted WC. **Grounds**: Fully accessible. Accessible route map. Accessible walk accessed from waterfall entrance only. Easy access path. Seats every 50yds. ½ml path with wheelchair-accessible bird hide. **Shop**: Level entrance. Some parking on hard surface. **Refreshments**: Ramped entrance

🔊 Induction loop at both entrances

👓 Braille guide and large-print guide. Seats are numbered with raised numerals. Tapping rail

🛍️ Shop and information at main entrance. Small shop at waterfall entrance. Plant sales

🍽️ Lydford Gorge Tea-room at main entrance to gorge. Specialises in home-made cakes, etc. using local produce. Children's menu

👶 Baby-changing and feeding facilities. Baby back-carriers admitted. Front-carrying baby slings and hip-carrying infant seats for loan. Children's play area. Unsuitable for pushchairs due to terrain and width of some paths

🏫 Suitable for school groups. Children's guide

🐕 On leads only

➡️ [191/201: SX509845] **Foot**: As road directions or via Blackdown Moor from Mary Tavy. **Cycle**: NCN27 & 31. Property is close to three cycle routes: Devon Coast to Coast, West Devon Way and Plym Valley. **Bus**: First 86 Plymouth–Barnstaple (most passing ⛴ Plymouth); 187 ⛴ Gunnislake–⛴ Okehampton, Sun, June to Sept only; bus stop at main entrance and waterfall entrance to gorge. **Road**: Halfway between Okehampton and Tavistock, 1ml W off A386 opposite Dartmoor Inn; main entrance at W end of Lydford village; waterfall entrance near Manor Farm

🅿️ Free parking, 10yds

NT properties nearby
Buckland Abbey, Castle Drogo, Cotehele, Finch Foundry

Lytes Cary Manor

nr Charlton Mackrell, Somerton, Somerset
TA11 7HU

🏠✝️🌼🎣🏡🎦 1949 (1:16)

Intimate manor house with walled gardens and estate

The house with its 14th-century chapel and 15th-century Great Hall was much added to in the 16th century. In the 20th century it was rescued from dereliction by Sir Walter Jenner who refurnished the interiors in period style. At the same time the garden was laid out in a series of rooms with many contrasts, topiary, mixed borders and a herbal border based on the famous 16th-century Lytes Herbal, which can be seen in the house. Several walks through the

Opening arrangements: Lytes Cary Manor				M	T	W	T	F	S	S
23 Mar - 30 Oct	11 - 5			M	T	**W**	T	**F**	**S**	**S**

Open BH Mons. Closes dusk if earlier than 5

Please remember – your membership card is always needed for free admission

wider estate show many features typical of farmed lowland England, including ancient hedges, rare arable weeds and farmland birds.

★ Parts of Lytes Cary Manor may be under repair

ℹ️ **T** 01458 224471
E lytescarymanor@nationaltrust.org.uk

£ £5, child £2. **Garden only**: £3, child £1

🏃 Available by prior arrangement

🚶 Guided walks. Details from property

♿ **Building**: 1 wheelchair. Ground floor accessible. Seating available. **WCs**: Adapted WC. **Grounds**: Partly accessible, uneven paths. Accessible route

👁️ Braille guide. Interesting scents

🎒 Children's quiz/trail

🐕 On leads and only in car park and on river walk

➡️ [183: ST529269] **Bus**: First 376/7 Bristol–Yeovil (passing ➡️ Bristol Temple Meads); 54/A Taunton–Yeovil (passing close ➡️ Taunton). Both pass within ¾ml ➡️ Yeovil Pen Mill. On both, alight Kingsdon, 1ml. **Station**: Yeovil Pen Mill 8½ml; Castle Cary 9ml; Yeovil Junction 10ml. **Road**: Signposted from Podimore roundabout at junction of A303, A37 take A372

🅿️ Free parking. Small coaches by prior arrangement only (up to 7.5m, max 30 people)

NT properties nearby
Barrington Court, Montacute House, Priest's House, Stembridge Tower Mill, Tintinhull Garden, Treasurer's House

Max Gate

Alington Avenue, Dorchester, Dorset DT1 2AA

🏠 ❄️ 🏃 1940 (1:J7)

Home of novelist and poet Thomas Hardy

Thomas Hardy designed and lived in this house from 1885 till his death in 1928. Here he wrote *Tess of the d'Urbervilles, Jude the Obscure* and *The Mayor of Casterbridge*, as well as much of his poetry. The house contains several pieces of his furniture.

★ No WC

ℹ️ **T** 01305 262538 **F** 01305 250978

£ £2.75, child £1.50

♿ **Building**: Steps to entrance with handrail. Ground floor accessible. Photograph album

👁️ Braille guide and large-print guide

🎒 Suitable for school groups. See opening arrangements (below)

➡️ [194: SY704899] **Bus**: Coach House Travel 4 from town centre. **Station**: Dorchester South 1ml; Dorchester West (U) 1ml. **Road**: 1ml E of Dorchester. From Dorchester follow A352 Wareham road to roundabout named Max Gate (at junction of A35 Dorchester bypass). Turn left and left again into cul-de-sac outside the house

🅿️ Free parking (not NT), 50yds

NT properties nearby
Cerne Giant, Clouds Hill, Hardy Monument, Hardy's Cottage

Opening arrangements: Max Gate								
20 Mar - 28 Sep	2 - 5	**M**	T	**W**	T	F	S	**S**

Only hall, dining and drawing rooms and garden open. Private visits, tours and seminars by schools, colleges and literary societies, at other times, by appointment with the tenants, Mr and Mrs Andrew Leah

Mompesson House

The Close, Salisbury, Wiltshire SP1 2EL

🏠 ❄️ 🍴 🍵 1952 (1:K6)

Elegant and spacious 18th-century house in the Cathedral Close

The house, featured in the award-winning film *Sense and Sensibility*, has magnificent plasterwork and a fine oak staircase. As well as pieces of good-quality period furniture, the house contains the Turnbull Collection of 18th-century drinking glasses. Outside, the delightful walled garden has a pergola and traditional herbaceous borders.

What's new in 2005 'The Illuminated Page' – an exhibition of wood engravings, including work by Gwen Raverat, Gertrude Hermes, John Farley, John Nash, Eric Ravilious, Agnes Miller Parker and Edward Bawden

---

For general and membership enquiries, please telephone 0870 458 4000

Opening arrangements: Mompesson House										
House	19 Mar - 30 Oct	11 - 5	**M**	**T**	**W**	T	F	**S**	**S**	
Garden	As house									
Tea-room	As house									
Open Good Fri										

i **T** 01722 335659, 01722 420980 (Infoline)
F 01722 321559
E mompessonhouse@nationaltrust.org.uk

£ £4.20, child £2.10, family £10.40. Groups £3.70. **Garden only**: 90p. Reduced rate when arriving by public transport

Ⓚ Special openings for groups by arrangement

♿ Drop-off point. **Building**: Steps to entrance. Alternative accessible entrance. Ground floor has steps, ramp available. Stairs to other floors. Seating available. Photograph album. **WCs**: Adapted WC. **Grounds**: Partly accessible. **Refreshments**: Step to entrance

Ⓑ Braille guide and large-print guide. Sensory list

The chimneypiece in the Library at Mompesson House, Salisbury, Wiltshire

◌ NT shop 2 mins walk, in High Street, tel. 01722 331884

▣ Tea-room

♟ Pushchairs and baby back-carriers admitted. Front-carrying baby slings and hip-carrying infant seats for loan

▣ Suitable for school groups. Children's guide

→ [184: SU142297] On N side of Choristers' Green in the Cathedral Close, near High Street Gate. **Bus**: From surrounding areas. **Station**: Salisbury ½ml

P Parking (not NT) in city centre, 260yds (pay & display). Coach-parking in central car park. Coach drop off-point 100yds at St Ann's Gate

NT properties nearby
Mottisfont Abbey, Pepperbox Hill, Philipps House & Dinton Park, Stourhead

Montacute House

Montacute, Somerset TA15 6XP

▥ ✿ ♠ ◌ ▣ ▼ 1931 (1:16)

Magnificent Elizabethan stone-built house, with fine collections, garden and park

Built in the late 16th century for Sir Edward Phelips, Montacute glitters with many windows and is adorned with elegant chimneys, carved parapets and other Renaissance features, including contemporary plasterwork, chimneypieces and heraldic glass. The splendid staterooms are full of fine 17th- and 18th-century furniture. Montacute House is a regional partner with the National Portrait Gallery and displays on permanent loan over 50 Tudor and Elizabethan portraits in the Long Gallery, the longest of its type in England. There are also fine textiles, including 17th- and 18th-century samplers from the Goodhart Collection. The formal garden includes mixed borders, old roses and interesting topiary and is surrounded by a landscape park. The wider estate encompasses St Michael's Hill, site of a Norman castle, topped with an accessible 18th-century lookout tower.

What's new in 2005 Farmers' markets, family garden trail, SeaBritain events

Please see the area introductions for details of coast & countryside properties

The garden at Montacute House, Somerset

T 01935 823289, 0870 240 4068 (Box office), 01935 824575 (Shop), 01935 826294 (Restaurant)
F 01935 826921
E montacute@nationaltrust.org.uk

£ £7.40, child £3.70, family £17. Groups £6.30, child £3.10. **Garden only: 18 Mar–30 Oct**: £3.90, child £1.80. **Garden only: 2 Nov–Mar 2006**: £2, child £1

Guided tours for groups by arrangement as well as out-of-hours tours. Contact Visitor Services Manager for details

Programme of events. Tel. for details

Many walks in park and estate to enjoy. Leaflet available

Separate designated parking, 40yds. **Building**: Alternative accessible entrance. 3 wheelchairs. Great Hall fully accessible – other 3 ground floor rooms leading off 2 steps. Many stone steps to other floors. Seating available. Interpretation in Great Hall. **WCs**: Adapted WC.
Grounds: Accessible route. 1 single-seater PMV, booking essential. **Shop**: Level entrance. **Refreshments**: Level entrance

Braille guide and large-print guide. Sensory list

NT shop. Plant sales

Licensed restaurant available for private bookings. Christmas lunches served Suns in Dec, booking recommended. Café

In 2 designated picnic areas in gardens

Opening arrangements: Montacute House										
House	18 Mar - 30 Oct	11 - 5	**M**	T	**W**	**T**	**F**	**S**	**S**	
Garden	1 Jan - 17 Mar	11 - 4	M	T	**W**	**T**	**F**	**S**	**S**	
	18 Mar - 30 Oct	11 - 6	**M**	T	**W**	**T**	**F**	**S**	**S**	
	2 Nov - 18 Mar 06	11 - 4	M	T	**W**	**T**	**F**	**S**	**S**	
Shop	2 Mar - 17 Mar	11 - 4	M	T	**W**	**T**	**F**	**S**	**S**	
	18 Mar - 30 Oct	11 - 5:30	**M**	T	**W**	**T**	**F**	**S**	**S**	
	2 Nov - 18 Dec	11 - 4	M	T	**W**	**T**	**F**	**S**	**S**	
Restaurant	6 Mar - 13 Mar	11 - 4	M	T	W	T	F	S	**S**	
	18 Mar - 30 Oct	12 - 5	**M**	T	**W**	**T**	**F**	**S**	**S**	
	6 Nov - 18 Dec	11 - 4	M	T	W	T	F	S	**S**	
Café	4 Mar - 13 Mar	11 - 4	M	T	W	T	**F**	**S**	**S**	
	18 Mar - 30 Oct	11 - 5:30	**M**	T	**W**	**T**	**F**	**S**	**S**	
	4 Nov - 18 Dec	11 - 4	M	T	W	T	**F**	**S**	**S**	

Restaurant closed 2–3 and at 2 on Mons (except BHols). Park and Estate unlimited opening

Unless indicated, last admission is always 30mins before closing time

[👶] Baby-changing facilities. Pushchairs and baby back-carriers admitted. Children's play area. Family picnic area where children can run and play ball games, etc.

[■] Suitable for school groups. Live interpretation. Children's guide. Children's quiz/trail. Family activity packs

[🐕] On leads and only in park; some shaded parking

[→] [183/193: ST499172] **Foot**: Leyland Trail and Monarch Trail both pass through Montacute Park. **Cycle**: NCN30. Passes Montacute Village. **Bus**: Safeway 681 Yeovil Bus Station–South Petherton/Crewkerne. **Station**: Yeovil Pen Mill 5½ml; Yeovil Junction 7ml (bus to Yeovil Bus Station); Crewkerne 7ml. **Road**: In Montacute village, 4ml W of Yeovil, on S side of A3088, 3ml E of A303; signposted

[P] Free parking. Limited parking for coaches

NT properties nearby
Barrington Court, Lytes Cary Manor, Priest's House, Stourhead, Tintinhull Garden, Treasurer's House

Newark Park

Ozleworth, Wotton-under-Edge, Gloucestershire GL12 7PZ

[🏠][✿][♠][♞][⛩][🎭] [1949]   (1:J3)

Tudor hunting lodge

This unusual and atmospheric property was built c.1550 as a hunting lodge and added to in the 1790s. It stands high on the edge of a 40ft cliff with outstanding views.

What's new in 2005 New woodland walk

[★] The property is lived in and has an interesting and warm atmosphere. In addition to the April–Oct visiting season, the garden is also open 3 weekends in early spring for the wonderful display of snowdrops

[i] **T/F** 01453 842644 (Visitor Services Manager) **E** newarkpark@nationaltrust.org.uk

[£] £4.70, child £2.30, family £12

[🧍] Leaflet available

[♿] Drop-off point. **Building**: Ramped entrance. Ground floor accessible. Stairs to other floors. Seating available. **Grounds**: Partly accessible

[👶] Baby back-carriers admitted. Pushchairs on ground floor only

[■] Suitable for school groups. Family guide. Children's quiz/trail

[🐕] On leads in grounds only

[→] [172: ST786934] **Foot**: Cotswold Way passes property. **Bus**: First 309, 310 Bristol–Dursley, alight Wotton-under-Edge, 1¾ml. Frequent services link [≣] Bristol Temple Meads with the bus station. **Station**: Stroud 10ml. **Road**: 1¼ml E of Wotton-under-Edge, 1¾ml S of junction of A4135 & B4058, follow signs for Ozleworth. House signposted from main road

[P] Free parking, 100yds. Coaches by prior arrangement only

NT properties nearby
Chedworth Roman Villa, Dyrham Park, Horton Court, Lodge Park & Sherborne Estate, Prior Park, Woodchester Park

Opening arrangements: Newark Park										
House & garden	6 Apr - 26 May	11 - 5	M	T	**W**	**T**	F	S	S
	1 Jun - 30 Oct	11 - 5	M	T	**W**	**T**	F	**S**	**S**
Garden only	4 Feb - 19 Feb 06	11 - 5	M	T	W	T	F	**S**	**S**
Open BH Mons and Good Fri. Closes dusk if earlier. Also open Easter Sat & Sun 11-5										

The Old Mill

Wembury Beach, Wembury, Devon PL9 0HP

[🏠][⛱][💧][🧍] [1939]   (1:F9)

Former mill house

A café is housed in the building, which stands on a small beach near the Yealm estuary.

[★] WC not always available

Opening arrangements: The Old Mill									
28 Mar - 30 Oct	10:30 - 5	**M**	**T**	**W**	**T**	**F**	**S**	**S**
5 Nov - 18 Dec	12 - 4	M	T	W	T	F	**S**	**S**
26 Dec - 1 Jan 06	12 - 4	**M**	**T**	**W**	**T**	**F**	**S**	**S**
May close early in bad weather, or at dusk, if earlier than 5. Also open daily in Feb half-term week									

There are special events at most Trust properties; please telephone 0870 458 4000 for details

ℹ️ **T** 01752 862314 (Tea-room),
01548 810197 (Area Warden)

💷 Admission free

🕴 Regular guided rock pool rambles and other marine-related events are led by the Devon Wildlife Trust wardens from Wembury Marine Centre (open Easter to end Sept), for details tel. 01752 862538

🍽 Café (NT-approved concession)

🐕 On beach, 1 Oct to 31 March only

➡️ [201: SX517484] **Foot**: South West Coast Path within ⅜ml. **Bus**: First 48 from ➡️ Plymouth, then ½ml. **Station**: Plymouth 10ml. **Road**: At Wembury, off A379 E of Plymouth

🅿️ Parking. Seasonal charge

NT properties nearby
Overbeck's Museum & Garden, Saltram

Overbeck's Museum & Garden

Sharpitor, Salcombe, Devon TQ8 8LW

 1937   (1:F9)

Elegant Edwardian house with diverse collections and luxuriant garden

The scientist Otto Overbeck lived here from 1928 to 1937 and the Museum containing his collections of curios and nautical artefacts has an intimate atmosphere. Some of Overbeck's inventions are on show, including the intriguing 'rejuvenator' machine. The house is set in 2¾ha (7 acres) of beautiful exotic gardens with spectacular views over the Salcombe estuary. It enjoys a sheltered microclimate and so is home to many rare plants.

⭐ Youth hostel on site (tel. 01548 842856). WC not available when museum is closed

ℹ️ **T** 01548 842893, 01548 845013 (Shop), 01548 845014 (Tea-room) **F** 01548 845020 **E** overbecks@nationaltrust.org.uk

💷 £5, child £2.50, family £12.50, family (one adult) £7.50. **Garden only**: £4.50, child £2.25

🕴 By arrangement, outside normal opening hours

♿ Separate designated parking, 20yds. Drop-off point. **Building**: Alternative accessible entrance. 1 wheelchair. Ground floor accessible. No access to other floors. Seating available. Photograph album. **Grounds**: Partly accessible. Accessible route map. Steep gravel paths to main building. Some visitors may require assistance from their companion. **Shop**: Level entrance. **Refreshments**: Level entrance

👓 Braille guide. Sensory list. Handling collection

🏪 NT shop. Plant sales

🍽 Tea-room in museum building. Children's menu

🚼 Baby-changing facilities. Pushchairs and baby back-carriers admitted. Single pushchairs only

🏫 Suitable for school groups. Children's quiz/trail. Secret room with dolls, toys and other collections; ghost hunt for children

🐕 Only on coastal walks from car park

➡️ [202: SX728374] **Foot**: South West Coast Path within ⅜ml. **Ferry**: From Salcombe to South Sands, then 20 mins strenuous walk (uphill). **Bus**: Stagecoach in Devon X64, Tally Ho! 164, 606 from ➡️ Totnes; also 92 from ➡️ Plymouth. On all alight Salcombe, 1½ml. **Road**: 1½ml SW of Salcombe, signposted from Malborough and Salcombe (narrow approach road). Roads leading to Overbeck's are steep and single track and not suitable for coaches over 25 seats or large vehicles

🅿️ Parking, 150yds, £3.50 (refunded on admission)

NT properties nearby
Coleton Fishacre, Greenway, Saltram

Opening arrangements: Overbeck's										
Museum	23 Mar - 17 Jul	11 - 5:30	M	T	W	T	F	S	S
	18 Jul - 28 Aug	11 - 5:30	M	T	W	T	F	S	S
	29 Aug - 30 Sep	11 - 5:30	M	T	W	T	F	S	S
	2 Oct - 27 Oct	11 - 5	M	T	W	T	F	S	S
Garden	All year	10 - 6	M	T	W	T	F	S	S
Shop	As museum								
Plant sales	As museum								
Tea-room	As museum	11:30 - 4:15							

Last admission 15mins before closing. Closed Good Fri. Open Easter Sat. Garden closes dusk, if earlier than 6

Penrose Estate: Gunwalloe and Loe Pool

nr Helston, Cornwall TR13 8GT

 1974 **(1:C10)**

Wooded country around Cornwall's largest natural lake and dramatic coastal scenery

At the heart of the Penrose Estate lies Loe Pool, a freshwater lake which meets the sea at the dramatic shingle bank of Loe Bar. Surrounding the Pool is a mix of rich farmland and woodland through which there are many paths, including the 5-mile circuit of the Pool itself. At Gunwalloe, two sandy coves lie either side of the 14th-century church (not NT) and the valley reedbed provides a haven for bird life.

[i] **T** 01326 561407 (SW Cornwall Office)
F 01326 562882
E southwestcornwall@nationaltrust.org.uk

[🚶] Occasional guided walks

[🚶] NT *Coast of Cornwall* leaflet 12 includes maps, details of walks and information on local history and wildlife

[♿] Rough but level path from Helston to adapted bird hide over Loe Pool approx. 2mls. Level access to edge of beach at Gunwalloe 150yds

[🍴] Gunwalloe Beach Café (not NT)

[🏫] Suitable for school groups

[🐕] Dogs welcome, but seasonal bans on one beach at Gunwalloe and must be on leads in landscaped park at Penrose

[→] [203: SW639259 – Penrose car park. 203: SW660208 – Gunwalloe car park] **Foot:** SW Coast Path goes through property. **Bus:** First 2/2A, 7 ⊞ Penzance–Falmouth to Porthleven. **Station:** Camborne 10ml to Porthleven. **Road:** Penrose Estate: 2ml SW of Helston on B3304 turn left, signposted Loe Bar, and left to car park. Gunwalloe: take A3083 from Helston and turn right 1ml past main RNAS Culdrose entrance

Opening arrangements: Penrose Estate		
All year		**M T W T F S S**

[P] Parking at Gunwalloe. Charge applies April–Oct. Free parking at various sites around Penrose

NT properties nearby
Glendurgan Garden, Godolphin Estate, The Lizard

Philipps House & Dinton Park

Dinton, Salisbury, Wiltshire SP3 5HH

[🏠][♣] 1943 **(1:K5)**

Early 19th-century neo-Grecian house

Designed by Jeffry Wyatville for William Wyndham, the house was completed in 1820. The principal rooms on the ground floor are open to visitors and contain fine Regency furniture. Both the house and the surrounding landscape park have recently been restored.

[★] No WC

[i] **T** 01722 716663

[£] £3

[🚶] Various walks around the park start from the car park; leaflet from property (when open), or from the village shop/post office or NT shop in Salisbury

[♿] **Building:** Ramped entrance. **Grounds:** Access limited, but good views of the lake from main access point from St Mary's Road car park

[📖] Braille guide

[🐕] In park only

[→] [184: SU004319] **Bus:** Wilts & Dorset 25 from Salisbury (passing ⊞ Salisbury & Tisbury). **Station:** Tisbury 5ml. **Road:** 9ml W of Salisbury, on N side of B3089; in Dinton take St Mary's Road at crossroads. Park in car park opposite cricket ground. House entrance 200yds further on left

[P] Free parking. Visitors to house only should park at house. Visitors to park should at all times use St Mary's Road car park, from where walks begin

Opening arrangements: Philipps House			
	19 Mar - 29 Oct	10 - 1	M T W T F **S S**
	21 Mar - 31 Oct	1 - 5	**M** T W T F S S
Park	All year		**M T W T F S S**

Please note: groups must book in advance with the property

NT properties nearby
Little Clarendon, Mompesson House, Stonehenge Historic Landscape, Stourhead

NT properties nearby
Barrington Court, Lytes Cary Manor, Montacute House, Stembridge Tower Mill, Tintinhull Garden, Treasurer's House

Opening arrangements: Priest's House									
27 Mar - 26 Sep	2 - 6	**M**	T	W	T	F	S	**S**	

Priest's House

Muchelney, Langport, Somerset TA10 0DQ

 1911 (1:I6)

Late medieval hall house in a picturesque village

The house was built by Muchelney Abbey in 1308 for the parish priest and has been little altered since the hall was divided in the early 17th century. Interesting features include the Gothic doorway, beautiful double-height tracery windows and a massive 15th-century stone fireplace. The house is occupied and furnished by tenants. Nearby Muchelney Abbey (EH, not NT) can also be visited.

⭐ No WC

ℹ️ **T** 01458 253771 (Tenant)

£ £3, child £1.50. Not suitable for groups

♿ **Building**: Steps to entrance. Ground floor accessible

📖 Braille guide

➡️ [193: ST429250] Muchelney is on the South Somerset cycle trail. **Bus**: First 54/A Yeovil Bus Station–Taunton (passing close ≷ Taunton and within ¾ml ≷ Yeovil Pen Mill), alight Huish Episcopi, 1ml. **Road**: 1ml S of Langport

🅿️ No parking on site. Not suitable for coaches

Prior Park Landscape Garden

Ralph Allen Drive, Bath, Bath & NE Somerset BA2 6BD

 1993 (1:J4)

Beautiful and intimate 18th-century landscape garden

Created by local entrepreneur and philanthropist Ralph Allen with advice from both the pioneer of landscape gardens the poet Alexander Pope and 'Capability' Brown, the garden is set in a sweeping valley with magnificent views of the City of Bath. The many interesting features include a Palladian bridge and three lakes. The Wilderness Project, the final phase of the restoration of this sustainably managed garden, will reinstate the Serpentine Lake, Gothic Temple, Grass Cabinet and Mrs Allen's Grotto. A 5-minute walk from the garden leads on to the **Bath Skyline**, a 6-mile circular walk around the city which encompasses woodlands, meadows, an Iron Age hill-fort, Roman settlements, 18th-century follies and spectacular views.

The Palladian bridge, Prior Park, Bath, Somerset

What's new in 2005 Children's activity packs. Completion of the Summer-house restoration

⭐ Prior Park College, a co-educational school, operates from the mansion (not NT)

ℹ️ **T** 01225 833422, 09001 335242 (Infoline) **E** priorpark@nationaltrust.org.uk

£ £4, child £2, family (2 adults & 2 children) £10

🏃 Guided tours for groups by arrangement

🚶 Bath Skyline walk leaflet and map available free from Prior Park visitor reception and NT website

♿ Separate designated parking. Drop-off point. **WCs**: Adapted WC. **Grounds**: Partly accessible, steep slopes. Level path to viewpoint over Bath

👓 Braille guide and large-print guide

☕ Refreshments available Fri/Sat/Sun/BH Mons April–Sept (not NT)

👶 Baby-changing facilities. Pushchairs and baby back-carriers admitted. Hip-carrying infant seats for loan

🏫 Suitable for school groups. Live interpretation. Hands-on activities. Children's quiz/trail. Children's activity packs. Adult study days

🎄 Welcome Nov–Feb inclusive

➡️ [172: ST760633] Prior Park is a green tourism site; there is no parking for cars, but public transport runs regularly (every 20 mins) to and from the park. Please tel. for leaflet or download from the website. **Foot**: Kennet & Avon canal path ¾ml. Avon Walkway (garden is 30 min uphill walk). **Cycle**: NCN4 ¾ml. **Bus**: First 2,4 ⬛ Bath–Combe Down. Park & ride services to town centre from Odd Down (daily) and Bath University (Sats). **Please note that park & ride services do not go direct to the garden.** Skyline Tour open-top tour bus runs every hour to the garden (11–5, all year). Pick up from railway station and Abbey. Half price to NT members. **Station**: Bath Spa 1¼ml

Opening arrangements: Prior Park

		M	T	W	T	F	S	S
6 Feb - 28 Nov	11 - 5:30	M	T	W	T	F	S	S
2 Dec - 29 Jan 06	11 - dusk	M	T	W	T	F	S	S

Last admission 1hr before closing. Closed 25, 26 Dec & 1 Jan. Closes dusk if earlier than 5:30

P No parking on site

NT properties nearby
Bath Assembly Rooms, Clevedon Court, The Courts Garden, Dyrham Park, Great Chalfield Manor, Lacock, Tyntesfield, Westwood Manor

---

St Anthony Head

Cornwall

🦀 ⚓ 🏛️ 1959 (1:C9)

Headland with fine views over Falmouth Bay

At the southernmost tip of the Roseland peninsula, St Anthony Head overlooks the spectacular entrance to one of the world's largest natural harbours – Carrick Roads and the Fal estuary. The starting point for a number of excellent coastal and sheltered creekside walks, the Head also bears newly revealed remains of a century of defensive fortifications.

ℹ️ **T** 01872 862945 (Fal countryside office), 01872 580509 (Area Warden) **F** 01872 865619

🚶 NT *Coast of Cornwall* leaflet 18/19 includes maps and details of circular walks and information about local history, geology and wildlife

♿ **WCs**: Adapted WC. **Grounds**: Partly accessible. Wheelchair access to viewing points. Accessible footpath to adapted bird hide. One steep but tarmacked section

🏫 Suitable for school groups. Adult study days

➡️ [204: SW847313] **Ferry**: Falmouth to St Mawes foot ferry (all year, but no Sun service in winter); St Mawes to Place (1ml from St Anthony Head along coast path), daily in summer only. **Bus**: First 50 Truro–St Mawes, alight St Mawes for ferry to Place, or alight Portscatho, then 3ml. **Station**: Penmere, via ferry to St Mawes then to Place, 6ml. **Road**: S of St Mawes off A3078

P Parking

NT properties nearby
Trelissick Garden

Opening arrangements: St Anthony Head

	M	T	W	T	F	S	S
All year	M	T	W	T	F	S	S

Please remember – your membership card is always needed for free admission

St Michael's Mount

Marazion, nr Penzance, Cornwall TR17 0EF

🏰 🏠 ✚ 🖼 🏛 💺 🍷 1954   **(1:B9)**

Rocky island crowned by medieval church and castle, home to a living community

This iconic island rises gracefully to the church and castle at its summit. Accessible on foot at low tide across a causeway, at other times it is reached by a short evocative boat trip. The oldest surviving buildings date from the 12th century, when a Benedictine priory was founded here. Following the English Civil War, the island was acquired by the St Aubyn family, who still live in the castle. In the intervening years many additions and alterations were made to convert it for use as a mansion house. Fascinating rooms from different eras include the mid-18th-century Gothick-style Blue Drawing Room.

⭐ Sensible shoes are advisable, as causeway and paths are cobbled and uneven. Steep climb to castle. Unsuitable for prams and pushchairs. Passages in the castle are narrow, so some delays may occur at the height of the season. Dogs are not permitted on Marazion beach from Easter to Oct, so it is not possible to bring dogs to the island during this time

ℹ️ **T** 01736 710507,
01736 710265 (Tide information only),
01736 711067 (Shop),
01736 710748 (Restaurant) **F** 01736 719930
E godolphin@manor-office.co.uk

💷 £5.50, child £2.75, family £13.75, family (one adult) £8.25. Groups (20+) £5. **Garden (not NT)**: £3

Opening arrangements: St Michael's Mount									
Castle	21 Mar - 31 Oct	10:30 - 5:30	M	T	W	T	F	S	S
Shop	As castle								
Restaurant	21 Mar - 31 Oct	10 - 5	M	T	W	T	F	S	S

Last admission 4.45 on the island. Sufficient time should be allowed for travel from the mainland. Nov to end March: open when tides and weather favourable. Private garden (not NT): open weekdays in May & June; Thur & Fri July–Oct. Garden open some evenings – see local press. Island shop and café (not NT): open as restaurant

🎭 Church services at 11.15am Suns, Whitsun–end Sept, Good Fri, Easter Sun and Christmas. Concert in Sept. Local bands play beside harbour, most days July & Aug. Garden evenings, with supper

♿ Contact in advance. Designated parking in both main car parks (not NT) 800yds.
Building: Access over uneven causeway or by motor boat. Climb to castle steep and uneven. Many surfaces cobbled. **Grounds**: terraces. **Refreshments**: Many steps to entrance with handrail

👁 Braille guide

🛍 NT shop. Island shop (not NT). Plant sales

🍴 The Sail Loft Restaurant (licensed). Children's menu. Island café (not NT) (licensed)

👶 Baby-changing facilities. Hip-carrying infant seats for loan

🎒 Suitable for school groups. Children's quiz/trail

➡️ [203: SW515298] **Foot**: South West Coast Path within ⅔ml. **Cycle**: NCN3 ¾ml.
Bus: First 2, 2A/B Penzance–Helston; 17A Penzance–St Ives, 3 Penzance–Camborne. All pass ▣ Penzance. **Station**: Penzance 3ml.
Road: ½ml S of A394 at Marazion, from where there is access on foot over the causeway at low tide or, during summer months only, by ferry at high tide, if weather conditions favourable

🅿️ Public car parks in Marazion on the mainland opposite St Michael's Mount (not NT)

NT properties nearby
Godolphin Estate, Trengwainton Garden

Saltram

Plympton, Plymouth, Devon PL7 1UH

🏰 🏠 ✨ 🍷 🏛 💺 🚪 🕺 🍷 1957   **(1:F8)**

Magnificent Georgian house with Adam interiors, gardens and landscaped parkland

Saltram stands high above the River Plym in a rolling and wooded landscaped park that now provides precious green space on the outskirts of Plymouth. The house, with its magnificent decoration and original contents, was largely created between the 1740s and 1820s by three

West front, Saltram, Devon

generations of the Parker family. It features some of Robert Adam's finest rooms, exquisite plasterwork ceilings, original Chinese wallpapers and an exceptional collection of paintings, including many by Sir Joshua Reynolds and Angelica Kauffmann. The gardens are predominantly 19th-century and contain an Orangery and several follies, as well as beautiful shrubberies and imposing specimen trees.

What's new in 2005 A new restaurant opens in July. Corporate and special functions welcome

T 01752 333500, 01752 348671 (Warden), 01752 333503 (Booking), 01752 330034 (Shop), 01752 347852 (Gallery) **F** 01752 336474 **E** saltram@nationaltrust.org.uk

£7, child £3.50, family £17.50, family (one adult) £10.50. Groups £5.90, group visits outside normal hours £15. **Garden only:** £3.50, child £1.80. Reduced rate when arriving by public transport or cycle (on house ticket)

House: Connoisseur tours outside normal open times – Tues, Wed or Thur mornings in Sept and Oct. Booking essential. Grounds: guided walks. Tel. for details

Programme of events, inc. Plant Fair, Summer Jazz Picnic, Hallowe'en Night, theatre performances and craft fairs. Tel. for details

Separate designated parking, 50yds. Drop-off point. **Building:** Ramped entrance. 3 wheelchairs, booking essential. One or more stairs to Dining Room, Great Kitchen or children's activity rooms. Stairs to other floors. Small lift available for those who can transfer from wheelchair to seat in lift. Please tel. in advance. **WCs:** Adapted WC. **Grounds:** Accessible route map. **Shop:** Level entrance. Over cobbled area. **Refreshments:** Level entrance. Large-print menu

Braille guide. Interesting scents. Sensory tour being developed

Shop at the stables. Art Gallery selling local arts and crafts. Plant sales

Licensed tea-room at the stables. New restaurant to open July. Tel. for details. Separate room for groups. Children's menu

Baby-changing facilities. Due to construction work the play area will unfortunately be out of use until Aug

Suitable for school groups. Education room/ centre. Hands-on activities. Children's guide. Children's quiz/trail. Adult study days (contact House & Collections Manager to arrange)

Please see the area introductions for details of coast & countryside properties

🎯 On leads on designated paths only, not in garden or grazed area of park

🚲 Many good cycle tracks in the parkland, part of NCN27

➔ [201: SX520557] **Foot**: South West Coast Path within 4ml. **Cycle**: NCN27.
Bus: Plymouth Citybus 19/A/B, 20–2, 51 from Plymouth, alight Plymouth Road–Plympton Bypass jct, then $\frac{3}{4}$ml by footpath. **Station**: Plymouth $3\frac{1}{4}$ml. **Road**: $3\frac{1}{2}$ml E of Plymouth city centre. Travelling south (from Exeter): leave A38, 3ml N of Plymouth. Exit is signed Plymouth City Centre/Plympton/Kingsbridge. At roundabout take centre lane, then 3rd exit for Plympton. Take right-hand lane and follow brown signs. Travelling north (from Liskeard): leave A38 at Plympton exit. At roundabout take first exit for Plympton, then as above

🅿 Free parking, 50yds

NT properties nearby
Antony, Buckland Abbey, Cotehele, Overbeck's Museum & Garden, Wembury Bay and Yealm Estuary

Opening arrangements: Saltram										
House	23 Mar - 29 Sep	12 - 4:30	M	T	W	T		S	S	
	1 Oct - 30 Oct	11:30 - 3:30	M	T	W	T		S	S	
Garden & gallery	23 Mar - 29 Sep	11 - 5	M	T	W	T		S	S	
	1 Oct - 22 Dec	11 - 4	M	T	W	T		S	S	
	7 Jan - 29 Jan 06	11 - 4	M	T	W	T		S	S	
	1 Feb - 28 Feb 06	11 - 4	M	T	W	T		S	S	
Tea-room	23 Mar - 14 Jul	11 - 5	M	T	W	T		S	S	
New restaurant	16 Jul - 30 Sep	11 - 5	M	T	W	T	F	S	S	
	1 Oct - 22 Dec	11 - 4	M	T	W	T		S	S	
	7 Jan - 29 Jan 06	11 - 4	M	T	W	T		S	S	
	1 Feb - 28 Feb 06	11 - 4	M	T	W	T		S	S	
Shop	23 Mar - 14 Jul	11 - 5	M	T	W	T		S	S	
	16 Jul - 30 Sep	11 - 5	M	T	W	T	F	S	S	
	1 Oct - 22 Dec	11 - 4	M	T	W	T		S	S	
	3 Jan - 31 Jan 06	11 - 4	M	T	W	T	F	S	S	
Park	All year	Dawn-dusk	M	T	W	T	F	S	S	
	4 Feb - 26 Feb 06	11 - 4	M	T	W	T		S	S	

Admission by timed ticket. Open BH Mons as above and Good Fri. Closed 23 Dec to 2 Jan 06 inclusive. NGS days Suns 3 April & 15 May: on these days NT members will be asked to pay to enter the garden – proceeds to the National Gardens Scheme

Snowshill Manor

Snowshill, nr Broadway, Gloucestershire WR12 7JU

 1951   **(1:K2)**

Cotswold manor house with eclectic collection and Arts & Crafts-style garden

Snowshill Manor contains Charles Paget Wade's extraordinary collection of craftmanship and design, including musical instruments, clocks, toys, bicycles, weavers' and spinners' tools and Japanese armour. Run on organic principles, the intimate garden is laid out as a series of outdoor rooms, with terraces and ponds, and wonderful views across the Cotswold countryside.

⭐ As a result of ongoing conservation work to the collection some objects may not be available at all times. Tel. for details. Photography only by written arrangement. The Snowshill costume collection is housed at Berrington Hall in Herefordshire and can be viewed there, by appointment only (tel. 01568 613720, email berrington@nationaltrust.org.uk)

ℹ **T** 01386 852410,
01386 842814 (Property Assistant),
01386 842813 (Shop),
01386 842812 (Restaurant) **F** 01386 842822
E snowshillmanor@nationaltrust.org.uk

£ **House & garden**: £7, child £3.50, family £17.80. Groups £5.95, child £3.40. **Garden, restaurant/shop only**: £4, child £2, family £10. Visitors arriving by bicycle or on foot offered a voucher redeemable at Snowshill NT shop or tea-room

♿ Contact in advance. Designated parking in main car park. House and garden are 500yds from car park along undulating path. Transfer available. 2 wheelchairs. **Building**: Steps to

Opening arrangements: Snowshill Manor									
House	25 Mar - 1 May	12 - 5	M	T	W	T	F	S	S
	4 May - 30 Oct	12 - 5	M	T	W	T	F	S	S
Garden	25 Mar - 1 May	11 - 5:30	M	T	W	T	F	S	S
	4 May - 30 Oct	11 - 5:30	M	T	W	T	F	S	S
Shop	25 Mar - 30 Oct	As garden							
	5 Nov - 11 Dec	12 - 4	M	T	W	T	F	S	S
Restaurant	As shop								

Admission by timed ticket. Open BH Mons

Unless indicated, last admission is always 30mins before closing time

Some of the nautical objects on display in Admiral at Snowshill Manor, Gloucestershire

entrance. Ground floor has steps. Stairs to other floors. Floors uneven. Seating available. Audio visual/video, photograph album. Visitor centre accessible. **WCs**: Adapted WC. **Grounds**: Partly accessible, terraces. Limited access to top area only. **Shop**: Level entrance. **Refreshments**: Level entrance

Braille guide and large-print guide. Sensory list. Handling collection

NT shop. Plant sales

Licensed restaurant. Children's menu

Baby-changing and feeding facilities. Pushchairs admitted. Front-carrying baby slings and hip-carrying infant seats for loan

Children's quiz/trail. Family activity packs

[150: SP096339] **Foot**: Cotswold Way within ⅔ml. **Bus**: Castleways ➡ Evesham–Broadway, then 2½ml uphill. **Station**: Moreton-in-Marsh 7ml. **Road**: 2½ml SW of Broadway; turn from A44 Broadway bypass into Broadway village and by village green turn right uphill to Snowshill

Parking, 500yds. Walk from car park along undulating country path. Transfer available

NT properties nearby
Chastleton House, Chedworth Roman Villa, Hidcote Manor Garden, Lodge Park & Sherborne Estate

Stoke-sub-Hamdon Priory

North Street, Stoke-sub-Hamdon, Somerset TA4 6QP

[🏠] [1946]   (1:I6)

14th/15th-century farm buildings, formerly a priests' residence

The priests who lived here served the Chapel of St Nicholas (now destroyed). The Great Hall is open to visitors.

⭐ No WC

[i] **T** 01985 843600 (Regional office)

[£] Admission free. Not suitable for groups

[&] **Building**: Floors all stone and at different levels throughout the area. **Grounds**: Partly accessible, some steps, undulating terrain

[→] [193: ST473175] **Bus**: Safeway 681 Yeovil Bus Station–South Petherton/Crewkerne (passing within ¾ml ➡ Yeovil Pen Mill). **Station**: Crewkerne or Yeovil Pen Mill, both 7ml. **Road**: Between A303 and A3088. 2ml W of Montacute between Yeovil and Ilminster

[P] No parking on site. Not suitable for coaches

NT properties nearby
Barrington Court, Lytes Cary Manor, Montacute House, Priest's House, Stembridge Tower Mill, Tintinhull Garden, Treasurer's House

Opening arrangements: Stoke-sub-Hamdon Priory		
27 Mar - 31 Oct	10 - 6	**M T W T F S S**
Closes dusk if earlier. Only Great Hall open		

Stonehenge Historic Landscape

3/4 Stonehenge Cottages, Kings Barrows, Amesbury, Wiltshire SP4 7DD

[🏛][♿][🚶][🚶] [1927]   (1:K5)

Ancient ceremonial landscape with many archaeological features

The Trust owns 850ha (2100 acres) of downland surrounding the famous monument, including The Avenue, King Barrows Ridge, Normanton

There are special events at most Trust properties; please telephone 0870 458 4000 for details

Down Barrows and the Cursus, variously interpreted as an ancient racecourse or processional way. The Trust is now managing this historic landscape, which forms approximately one-third of the Stonehenge World Heritage Site, to conserve archaeology, increase access and balance the needs of modern agricultural practice with nature conservation. Recent additions to the estate include Durrington Walls, and the Lesser Cursus on Greenlands Farm. Leaflets on recommended walks and archaeology are obtainable from the estate office.

What's new in 2005 Education programme and series of guided walks. Tel. estate office for details

⭐ The stone circle is owned and administered by English Heritage. All grassland areas on the estate are designated NT open access and are open to everyone, but on foot only. Camping is not permitted anywhere on the estate. Please observe the NT byelaws

[i] **T** 01980 623108 (Visitor centre EH), 01980 664780 (Estate office NT)

[∩] For the stone circle only. Available from the English Heritage shop

[&] The historic landscape is open countryside, much of which is rough undulating terrain

[📢] Interesting sounds

[📷] EH shop adjacent to the monument

[🎦] An education programme and facility is planned for 2005

[🐕] Under close control at all times; not on archaeological walks

[🚲] An annual Avebury to Stonehenge World Heritage cycle event takes place in Avebury. Tel. estate office for details

[→] [184: SU120420] **Bus:** Wilts & Dorset 3 ▣ Salisbury–Stonehenge. **Station:** Salisbury 9½ml. **Road:** Monument 2ml W of Amesbury, at junction of A303 & A344/A360

[P] Parking (not NT), 50yds. NT members must display cards. A charge may apply over the peak period June–Oct

Opening arrangements: Stonehenge Landscape
Tel. EH visitor centre for details. NT land north of visitor centre open at all times, but parts may be closed at the Summer Solstice (21 June) for up to 2 days

NT properties nearby
Avebury, Little Clarendon, Mompesson House, Philipps House & Dinton Park, Stourhead

---

Stourhead

Stourhead Estate Office, Stourton, Warminster, Wiltshire BA12 6QD

[🏠][🏛️][✿][♠][⚑][♟][☕][📷][🍴][▲][T] 1946   (1:J5)

Celebrated 18th-century landscape garden and Palladian mansion

An outstanding example of the English landscape style, this splendid garden was designed by Henry Hoare II and laid out between 1741 and 1780. Classical temples, including the Pantheon and Temple of Apollo, are set around the central lake at the end of a series of vistas, which change as the visitor moves around the paths and through the magnificent mature woodland with its extensive collection of exotic trees. Built in the 1720s the mansion was home to the Hoare family, owners of Britain's only independent private bank surviving to the present. The magnificent interior includes an outstanding Regency library, an extensive picture collection and furniture by Chippendale the Younger. King Alfred's Tower, an intriguing red-brick folly built in 1772 by Henry Flitcroft, is almost 50m high and gives breathtaking views over the estate. Much of the estate woodland and downland is managed for nature conservation and there are two interesting Iron Age hill-forts, Whitesheet Hill and Park Hill Camp.

What's new in 2005 Licensed for civil weddings. Farm shop

⭐ Due to external decoration work there may be some disruption to visitor route and opening times at the house during June & July. If intending to visit the house, please tel. shortly before, to confirm current arrangements.

[i] **T** 01747 841152,
01747 842030 (Visitor reception),
01747 842012/01747 842018 (Learning),
0870 240 4068 (Box office),
01747 842040 (Shop),
01747 840747 (Gallery),
01747 842006 (Restaurant) **F** 01747 842005
E stourhead@nationaltrust.org.uk

For further information check our website www.nationaltrust.org.uk

£ **Garden & house**: £9.90, child £4.80, family £23.50. Groups £9.40. **Garden or house**: £5.80, child £3.20, family £14.20. Groups £5.10. **Garden only 1 Nov to end Feb 06**: £4.30, child £2.10, family £10.50. Groups £4.10. **King Alfred's Tower**: £2.15, child £1.10, family £5.20. Groups £1.90

ℹ️ Group tours of house and garden by arrangement. Tel. for Group Information leaflet

🎪 Programme of events. Tel. for details

🚶 5 waymarked walks across estate – information in leaflet 'Stourhead Walks for all Seasons'

♿ Separate designated parking. Transfer available in main season to house and garden entrances. **Building**: Many steps to entrance. 1 wheelchair. All showrooms on one level. **WCs**: Adapted WC. **Grounds**: Partly accessible. Accessible route map. $1\frac{1}{4}$ml path around lake is accessible to wheelchair users, but is steep in places. 5 wheelchairs. 2 multi-seater PMV. **Shop**: Level entrance. **Refreshments**: Level entrance

👁️ Braille guide and large-print guide. Sensory list

🛍️ NT shop. Plant sales

☕ Licensed restaurant. Children's menu. Private dining room max 50, must be booked. Ice cream in Spread Eagle courtyard available on fine days during the summer. Spread Eagle Inn, open all year, weekend and midweek breaks available (tel. 01747 840587)

Opening arrangements: Stourhead										
Garden	All year	9 - 7	M	T	W	T	F	S	S
House	18 Mar - 31 Oct	11 - 5	M	T	W	T	F	S	S
Tower	18 Mar - 31 Oct	12 - 5	M	T	W	T	F	S	S
Restaurant	1 Mar - 31 Mar	10 - 5	M	T	W	T	F	S	S
	1 Apr - 30 Sep	10 - 5:30	M	T	W	T	F	S	S
	1 Oct - 31 Oct	10 - 5	M	T	W	T	F	S	S
	1 Nov - 28 Feb 06	10:30 - 4	M	T	W	T	F	S	S
Shop	1 Mar - 31 Mar	10 - 5	M	T	W	T	F	S	S
	1 Apr - 30 Sep	10 - 6	M	T	W	T	F	S	S
	1 Oct - 31 Oct	10 - 5	M	T	W	T	F	S	S
	1 Nov - 28 Feb 06	10:30 - 4	M	T	W	T	F	S	S

Garden, house and tower close dusk if earlier. In March & Oct last admission to house and tower 4pm (closing 4:30pm), otherwise 30 mins before closing. Restaurant & shop closed 25 Dec

🏕️ Throughout landscape garden and estate in addition to designated picnic areas

👶 Baby-changing facilities. Hip-carrying infant seat for loan in house

🏫 Suitable for school groups. Education room/centre. Hands-on activities. Children's guide. Children's quiz/trail. Family activity packs. Adult study days

🐕 Landscape garden: between 1 Nov and 18 Mar only, on short fixed leads. Estate: under close control at any time of year on estate outside landscape garden. Not admitted to King Alfred's Tower or house

🚲 Some access across estate on bridleways

The Temple of Flora, Stourhead, Wiltshire

Please note: groups must book in advance with the property

→ [183: ST780340] **Cycle**: Wiltshire cycleway runs through estate. **Bus**: South West Coaches 80 Frome to Stourhead (Sat only); otherwise First 58/A ⊞ Shaftesbury–Yeovil, some to Stourhead, but on others alight Zeals, 1¼ml. **Station**: Gillingham 6¼ml; Bruton (U) 7ml. **Road**: At Stourton, off B3092, 3ml NW of Mere (A303), 8ml S of Frome (A361). King Alfred's Tower: 3½ml by road from Stourhead House

P Free parking, 400yds. Transfer by buggy, throughout main season only, to house and garden entrances. King Alfred's Tower: designated parking 50yds

NT properties nearby
Barrington Court, Lytes Cary Manor, Mompesson House, Montacute House, Tintinhull Garden

---

Studland Beach & Nature Reserve

Countryside Office, Studland, Swanage, Dorset BH19 3AX

 1982   (1:K7)

Vast area of sandy beaches and heathland

Fine beaches stretch continuously for 3 miles from South Haven Point to the chalk cliffs of Handfast Point and Old Harry Rocks, and include Shell Bay and a designated naturist area. The heathland behind the beach is a National Nature Reserve, a haven for many rare birds and other forms of wildlife. There are several footpaths, two nature trails and bird hides at Little Sea. Studland Beach is just one highlight of the 3200ha (8000-acre) Purbeck Estate cared for by the National Trust.

Opening arrangements: Studland Beach											
Beach	All year		**M**	**T**	**W**	**T**	**F**	**S**	**S**
Shop/café	1 Mar - 20 Mar	10 - 4	**M**	**T**	**W**	**T**	**F**	**S**	**S**
	21 Mar - 2 Oct	10 - 5	**M**	**T**	**W**	**T**	**F**	**S**	**S**
	3 Oct - 28 Feb 06	10 - 4	**M**	**T**	**W**	**T**	**F**	**S**	**S**

Shop and café open hours may be longer in fine weather and shorter in poor weather. Visitor centre, shop and café closed 25 Dec. **Car parks can be very full in peak season**

⭐ WCs at Knoll and Middle Beach. Shell Bay WCs are environmentally friendly and self-composting

ℹ **T** 01929 450259 (Estate office), 01929 480609 (Learning), 01929 450500 (Shop), 01929 450305 (Restaurant) **E** studlandbeach@nationaltrust.org.uk

£ Boat launching: charge applies. No powered craft over 20hp permitted. For information on boat launching, horse permits and beach hut hire, tel. Estate office

Guided tours of nature reserve by wardens

Programme of events, inc. family, winter and evening events. Tel. for details

Purbeck walks leaflets obtainable from NT shop

♿ Separate designated parking, 30yds from Knoll Beach visitor centre. **WCs**: Adapted WC. **Grounds**: Wheelchairs and pushchairs suitable for beach use available for loan. **Shop**: Ramped entrance. **Refreshments**: Ramped entrance

Located at Knoll Beach visitor centre and seasonally at Middle Beach. NT range and beach products

Beach café (NT-approved concession) at Knoll Beach visitor centre. Children's menu. Licensed café (NT-approved concession) at Middle Beach, small takeaway at South Beach. Fish restaurant (not NT) (licensed) at Shell Bay

Designated barbecue area at all beaches; barbecues must be extinguished by 8pm

Baby-changing facilities at all beach WCs. Beach pushchairs available for loan from Knoll visitor centre. Play table in café

Suitable for school groups. Education room/centre. Adult study days

Only on main beaches from first Mon in Sept to last Fri in June (must be on leads from 1 May to 30 Sept). Last Sat in June to first Sun in Sept inclusive: prohibited from Knoll and Middle beaches; permitted on Shell Bay and South beaches. No fouling of the beaches. Dogs permitted all year on nature reserve and Estate footpaths

Parking in National Trust car parks is free for members

🚴 Cycling on bridleways across the Purbeck Estate

→ [195: SZ036835] **Foot**: 5ml of South West Coast Path on property. **Bus**: Wilts & Dorset 150 Bournemouth–Swanage (passing ✉) Branksome) to Shell Bay & Studland. Also 152 Poole–Sandbanks (passing close ✉) Parkstone); Yellow Buses 12 Christchurch Quay–Sandbanks, summer only then vehicle ferry from Sandbanks to Shell Bay.
Station: Branksome or Parkstone, both 3½ml to Shell Bay or 6ml to Studland via vehicle ferry

🅿 Car parks at Shell Bay and South Beach (open 9am–11pm), The Knoll & Middle Beach (open 9am–8pm). Prices vary through the season

NT properties nearby
Brownsea Island, Clouds Hill, Corfe Castle, Hardy's Cottage, Kingston Lacy, Max Gate

Tintagel Old Post Office

Fore Street, Tintagel, Cornwall PL34 0DB

🏠 ✳ 📷 1903 (1:D7)

One of the Trust's most delightful medieval buildings, enhanced by a cottage garden

A rare survival of Cornish domestic architecture of its time, this diminutive 14th-century yeoman farm house is well furnished with local oak pieces. One room was used in the 19th century as the letter-receiving office for the district and is now restored to show how it looked and functioned then.

⭐ WC in car park opposite (not NT)

🛈 **T** 01840 770024 **F** 01840 779021
E tintageloldpo@nationaltrust.org.uk

£ £2.50, child £1.20, family £6.20, family (one adult) £3.60. Groups (10+) £2.10

The Post Room in the Old Post Office, Tintagel, Cornwall

Please remember – your membership card is always needed for free admission

🚶 **Building**: Step to entrance, ramp available. Ground floor has uneven floors. Stairs to other floors. Seating available. Virtual tour is usually available, tel. first. **Grounds**: Partly accessible, some steps. **Shop**: Steps to entrance

📳 Induction loop in shop

👁 Braille guide and large-print guide. Sensory list

👶 Hip-carrying infant seats for loan. Pushchairs, rucksacks and backpacks can be left at entrance

🏫 Suitable for school groups. Children's quiz/trail

➔ [200: SX056884] In centre of village. **Foot**: South West Coast Path within ⅔ml. **Bus**: Western Greyhound 524 Bude–Wadebridge, 594 Bude–Truro (with connections on 555 at Wadebridge from ⊠ Bodmin Parkway)

🅿 Numerous pay & display car parks in village (not NT)

NT properties nearby
Boscastle

Opening arrangements: Tintagel Old Post Office									
23 Mar - 30 Sep	11 - 5:30	M	T	W	T	F	S	S	
1 Oct - 30 Oct	11 - 4	M	T	W	T	F°	S	S	
Last admission 15mins before closing									

Tintinhull Garden

Farm Street, Tintinhull, Yeovil, Somerset
BA22 8PZ

✂ 🍴 1953   (1:I6)

Delightful formal garden

Created last century around a 17th-century manor house, the garden features small pools, varied borders and secluded lawns, all neatly enclosed within walls and clipped hedges. There is also an attractive kitchen garden.

What's new in 2005 Video cams to bird boxes

ℹ **T** 01935 822545,
01935 826357 (Visitor reception),
01935 827707 (Tea-room)
F 01935 826357
E tintinhull@nationaltrust.org.uk

💷 £4.50, child £2.20

📖 Book in advance with the Gardener

🚶 Separate designated parking, 5yds. Drop-off point. **Building**: Level entrance. 1 wheelchair

👁 Braille guide and large-print guide. Interesting scents

☕ Tea-room in courtyard. Light refreshments only

🅰 In field above car park

👶 Pushchairs and baby back-carriers admitted

🏫 Suitable for school groups

➔ [183: ST503198] **Bus**: First 52 Yeovil Bus Station–Martock (passing within ⅔ml ⊠ Yeovil Pen Mill). **Station**: Yeovil Pen Mill 5½ml; Yeovil Junction 7ml (bus to Yeovil Bus Station). **Road**: 5ml NW of Yeovil, ½ml S of A303, on E outskirts of Tintinhull. Follow road signs to Tintinhull village

🅿 Free parking, 150yds

NT properties nearby
Barrington Court, Lytes Cary Manor, Montacute House, Priest's House, Stembridge Tower Mill, Treasurer's House

Opening arrangements: Tintinhull Garden								
	23 Mar - 1 Oct	11 - 5	M	T	W	T	F	S	S
Tea-room	As garden	11 - 4:30						
Open BH Mons								

Treasurer's House

Martock, Somerset TA12 6JL

🏠 1971   (1:I6)

Small medieval house

The Great Hall was completed in 1293 and the solar block, with an interesting wall painting, is even earlier. There is also a kitchen added in the 15th century.

⭐ The house is occupied by tenants. Only the medieval hall, wall painting and kitchen are shown to visitors. No WC

ℹ **T** 01935 825801 (Tenant)

💷 £2.70, child £1.60. Not suitable for groups

♿ **Building**: Steps to entrance. **Grounds**: Partly accessible, some steps, uneven paths

➔ [193: ST462191] **Bus**: First 52 Yeovil Bus Station–Martock (passing within ¾ml ⚏ Yeovil Pen Mill). **Station**: Crewkerne 7½ml; Yeovil Pen Mill 8ml. **Road**: Opposite church in middle of village; 1ml NW of A303 between Ilminster and Ilchester

P Free parking (not NT), 400yds. Not suitable for coaches. Parking limited and unsuitable for trailer caravans

NT properties nearby
Barrington Court, Lytes Cary Manor, Montacute House, Priest's House, Stembridge Tower Mill, Tintinhull Garden

Opening arrangements: Treasurer's House									
27 Mar - 27 Sep	2 - 5	**M**	T	W	T	F	S	**S**	

Trelissick Garden

Feock, nr Truro, Cornwall TR3 6QL

⑩⑨⑦⑧ 1955   **(1:C9)**

Tranquil garden set on many levels, containing a superb collection of tender and exotic plants

Beautifully positioned at the head of the Fal estuary, the estate commands panoramic views over the area and has extensive park and woodland walks beside the river. At its heart is the garden, which has year-round colour, with the display of spring blossom being particularly delightful. The house is not open, but there is an art and craft gallery, shop, plants for sale, restaurant, café and a fine Georgian stable block.

Opening arrangements: Trelissick Garden									
Garden	12 Feb - 30 Oct	10:30 - 5:30	**M**	**T**	**W**	**T**	**F**	**S**	**S**
	31 Oct - 23 Dec	11 - 4	**M**	**T**	**W**	**T**	**F**	**S**	**S**
	27 Dec - 1 Jan 06	12 - 4	M	**T**	**W**	**T**	**F**	**S**	**S**
	5 Jan - 12 Feb 06	11 - 4	M	T	W	**T**	**F**	**S**	**S**
	13 Feb - 28 Feb 06	10:30 - 5:30	**M**	**T**	**W**	**T**	**F**	**S**	**S**
Woodland walks	All year		**M**	**T**	**W**	**T**	**F**	**S**	**S**
Shop/gallery	As garden								
Restaurant	As garden								
Closes dusk if earlier									

What's new in 2005 Fal River Links partnership ferries to new Trelissick landing stage from Falmouth, Truro and St Mawes. SeaBritain: NT/Magnum photography exhibition in Trelissick Gallery 30 July–4 Sept

★ Copeland China Collection, by courtesy of Mr & Mrs William Copeland, open every Thursday in March, April, May, June and September at 2pm for guided tour. Booking recommended, tel. 01872 862248. Joint ticket for garden and China Collection £7.80, NT members £3.50

i **T** 01872 862090,
01872 865515 (Shop),
01872 864084 (Gallery),
01872 863486 (Restaurant)
F 01872 865808
E trelissick@nationaltrust.org.uk

£ £5, child £2.50, family £12.50, family (one adult) £7.50. Groups £4.30. Reduced rate when arriving by public transport or cycle •

🎭 Programme of events, inc. theatrical, musical and winter events

🚶 NT *Coast of Cornwall* leaflet 17 – Trelissick woodland walks

♿ Separate designated parking, 30yds. **WCs**: Adapted WC. **Grounds**: Partly accessible. Accessible route. 1 single-seater PMV, booking essential. **Shop**: Level entrance. **Refreshments**: Level entrance. Barn restaurant on ground floor, courtyard tea-room on 1st floor.

👂 Induction loop in reception

👁 Braille guide and large-print guide. Interesting scents

🛍 Shop, art gallery, Cornwall Crafts Association craft gallery. Plant sales

☕ Trelissick Barn Restaurant (licensed). Last orders 30mins before closing. Children's menu. Courtyard tea-room on 1st floor. Ice-cream kiosk in courtyard, limited opening

🚼 Baby-changing facilities. Pushchairs and baby back-carriers admitted

🏫 Suitable for school groups. Education room/centre. Children's guide. Family activity packs

🐕 On leads in park and on woodland walks only

Please see the area introductions for details of coast & countryside properties

The Truro River viewed from the garden at Trelissick, Cornwall

→ [204: SW837396 – Car park] **Cycle**: NCN3. **Ferry**: Link from Falmouth, Truro and St Mawes. Enterprise boats 01326 374241, K&S Cruisers 01326 211056, Newman's Cruises/Tolverne Ferries 01872 580309. **Bus**: Truronian T16 from Truro (passing close ⇌ Truro). **Station**: Truro 5ml; Perranwell (U), 4ml. **Road**: 4ml S of Truro, on B3289 above King Harry Ferry

P Parking, 50yds, £3 (refunded on admission)

NT properties nearby
Glendurgan Garden, Trerice

Trengwainton Garden

Madron, nr Penzance, Cornwall TR20 8RZ

❀ ◻ 🍴 ⛱ 1961   (1:B9)

Sheltered garden with an abundance of exotic trees and shrubs

Intimate and closely linked to the picturesque stream running through its valley, the garden leads up to a terrace and summer houses with splendid views across Mount's Bay to The Lizard. The walled gardens contain many rare and unusual species which are difficult to grow in the open anywhere else in the country.

ℹ **T** 01736 363148, 01736 362297 (Shop), 01736 331717 (Tea-room) **F** 01736 367762 **E** trengwainton@nationaltrust.org.uk

£ £4.50, child £2.20, family £11.20, family (one adult) £6.70. Groups £3.80. Reduced rate when arriving by public transport, cycle or on foot

🦮 Throughout the open season

🚶 By arrangement with Head Gardener

♿ Separate designated parking, 100yds. Drop-off point. **Building**: 2 wheelchairs, booking essential. **WCs**: Adapted WC. **Grounds**: Accessible route map. Approx. 75% of the garden accessible to wheelchair users. Some visitors may require assistance from their companion. **Shop**: Level entrance. **Refreshments**: Steps to entrance with handrail, ramp available

🛍 NT shop. Plant sales

☕ Tea-room (NT-approved concession) adjacent to car park. Children's menu

👶 Baby-changing facilities. Pushchairs and baby back-carriers admitted

Opening arrangements: Trengwainton Garden										
	13 Feb - 31 Mar	10 - 5	**M**	**T**	**W**	**T**	F	S	**S**
	1 Apr - 30 Sep	10 - 5:30	**M**	**T**	**W**	**T**	F	S	**S**
	3 Oct - 30 Oct	10 - 5	**M**	**T**	**W**	**T**	F	S	**S**
Tea-room	As garden								

Open Good Fri. Last admission 1hr before closing. Tea-room – last admission ¼ hour before closing. For details of special pre-Christmas opening (shop, tea-room and most of garden), tel. shop

Unless indicated, last admission is always 30mins before closing time

⬛ Suitable for school groups. Children's quiz/trail

🐾 On leads only and not in tea-room garden

➡ [203: SW445315] **Foot**: Footpath to the property from Penzance via Heamoor.
Cycle: NCN3 2½ml. **Bus**: First 17/B St Ives–St Just (passing ⊠ Penzance).
Station: Penzance 2ml.
Road: 2ml NW of Penzance, ½ml W of Heamoor off Penzance–Morvah road (B3312), ½ml off St Just road (A3071)

P Free parking, 150yds

NT properties nearby
Godolphin Estate, Levant Beam Engine, St Michael's Mount

Trerice

Kestle Mill, nr Newquay, Cornwall TR8 4PG

🏠❀🗂📷🎭🔔▲🍷 1953   **(1:C8)**

Elizabethan manor house with fine interiors and delightful garden

Set in a beautiful secluded spot, the house contains fine fireplaces, plaster ceilings, oak and walnut furniture, interesting clocks, needlework and Stuart portraits. The highlight of the interior is the magnificent Great Chamber with its splendid barrel ceiling. The garden has some unusual plants and an orchard with old varieties of fruit trees. In the hayloft behind the Great Barn is an exhibition on the history of the lawnmower. Visitors are welcome to play 'Kayles' (Cornish skittles) on the parade ground.

What's new in 2005 Brass rubbing (£1); Christmas opening: hall traditionally decorated, shop and light refreshments available

i **T** 01637 875404 (Property office),
01637 879216 (Shop),
01637 879434 (Restaurant)
F 01637 879300
E trerice@nationaltrust.org.uk

£ £5.50, child £2.75, family £13.75, family (one adult) £8.25. Groups £4.70. Reduced rate when arriving by public transport or cycle. Please show valid bus or rail ticket

♿ Separate designated parking, 300yds. Drop-off point. **Building**: Level entrance. 2 wheelchairs, booking essential. Ground floor has steps, ramp available. Wheelchair access to first floor, via side door on to terrace. **WCs**: Adapted WC. **Grounds**: Fully accessible. Accessible route map.
Shop: Level entrance.
Refreshments: Ramped entrance

👁 Braille guide and large-print guide. Sensory list

🛍 NT shop. Plant sales

🍽 Licensed restaurant in Great Barn. Children's menu. Licensed tea-garden

🍴 In orchard, top lawn and parade ground

👶 Baby-changing facilities. Front-carrying baby slings and hip-carrying infant seats for loan

⬛ Suitable for school groups. Hands-on activities. Children's quiz/trail

🐾 On leads and only in car park. Trees provide shade in car park

➡ [200: SW841585] **Cycle**: NCN32.
Bus: Western Greyhound 526 Newquay–St Austell/Heligan, alight Kestle Mill, ¾ml.
Station: Quintrell Downs (U), 1½ml. **Road**: 3ml SE of Newquay via A392 and A3058 signed from Quintrell Downs (turn right at Kestle Mill), or signed from A30 at Summercourt via A3058

P Free parking, 300yds. Coach access only via Kestle Mill 1ml

NT properties nearby
Carnewas & Bedruthan Steps, Cornish Mines & Engines, Lanhydrock, Trelissick Garden

Opening arrangements: Trerice									
House	20 Mar - 25 Jul	11 - 5:30	M	T	W	T	F	S	S
	26 Jul - 30 Aug	11 - 5:30	M	T	W	T	F	S	S
	31 Aug - 30 Sep	11 - 5:30	M	T	W	T	F	S	S
	2 Oct - 30 Oct	11 - 5	M	T	W	T	F	S	S
Shop	As house								
Restaurant	As house								

Restaurant: last serving 5 (4.30 in March & Oct).
Decorated hall and shop open, light refreshments available 3 & 4, 10 & 11, 17 & 18 Dec, 11–3

East front, Trerice, Cornwall

Tyntesfield

Wraxall, North Somerset BS48 1NT

 2002 (1:14)

Spectacular Victorian country house and estate

Situated on a ridge overlooking the beautiful Land Yeo Valley, Tyntesfield was inspired and remodelled by John Norton in 1864 for William Gibbs, a successful merchant. The mansion is an extraordinary Gothic Revival extravaganza bristling with towers and turrets. It survives intact with an unrivalled collection of Victorian decorative arts, an insight into life below stairs and a sumptuously decorated private chapel. Its surrounding 200ha (500 acres) of land include formal gardens and a wonderful walled kitchen garden. Tyntesfield was saved for the nation by the National Trust in June 2002 with funding from the National Heritage Memorial Fund, other heritage partners and a £3 million public appeal.

Opening arrangements: Tyntesfield

Tel. infoline for details

⭐ The project at Tyntesfield is still in the early stages of development and visitors should expect to see conservation and building work going on during open hours. Facilities on site will also be very basic. It is a very exciting project with new discoveries being found all the time from exquisite ladies' evening gloves to rare wild orchids.

Following two successful years of guided tours, we are aiming to increase public access to the Tyntesfield Project in 2005. Although restrictions will still be in place it is likely that the property will be open for three days per week at most. At the time of going to print, planning permission is being sought for a temporary car park and facilities, therefore access arrangements are still to be confirmed. **Visitors are asked to call the property infoline, or visit the website for updates**

ℹ️ **T** 0870 458 4500 (Infoline)

💷 Tel. infoline for details. High demand for group visits. Booking essential

🎭 Programme of events

For further information check our website www.nationaltrust.org.uk

♿ Separate designated parking. **Building**: Level access to ground floor of house and parts of garden. Access to chapel via very steep spiral staircase or very steep loose gravel path, contact in advance. **Grounds**: some steps, terraces

📶 Induction loop in reception

✍ Large-print guide. Touchable objects

🚼 Baby-changing facilities. Hip-carrying infant seats for loan

🎯 Children's quiz/trail

→ [172: SO506716] **Bus**: First 354 Bristol–Nailsea. **Station**: Nailsea & Backwell 3½ml

NT properties nearby
Blaise Hamlet, Clevedon Court, Dyrham Park, Leigh Woods, Prior Park

---

Watersmeet House

Watersmeet Road, Lynmouth, Devon EX35 6NT

🏠 🍽 🎫 📷 💼 1996   **(1:F5)**

19th-century former fishing lodge in a picturesque setting

Built c.1832 in a valley at the confluence of the East Lyn and Hoar Oak Water, the house now serves as a NT shop, with refreshments and information. The site has been a tea-garden since 1901 and is the focal point for several beautiful walks.

⭐ Property in deep gorge

ℹ **T** 01598 753348 (Catering Manager), 01598 763306 (Warden), 01271 850887 (Property Manager), 01598 752648 (Shop)

£ Admission free

🎯 See local listings for programme of guided walks on Watersmeet Estate

🚶 Walks leaflet from shop

♿ Parking by arrangement with Catering Manager. Drop-off point. **Building**: Steps to entrance. **WCs**: Adapted WC

📷 Tea-garden

🚼 Baby-changing facilities

Opening arrangements: Watersmeet House

19 Mar - 30 Sep	10:30 - 5:30		M	T	W	T	F	S	S
1 Oct - 30 Oct	10:30 - 4:30		M	T	W	T	F	S	S

🎯 Children's quiz/trail

→ [180: SS744487] **Foot**: South West Coast Path within ⅝ml. **Bus**: First 309, 310 Barnstaple–Lynmouth (passing close ⦿ Barnstaple), 300 Minehead–Ilfracombe. On both, alight Lynmouth, then walk through NT gorge. **Road**: 1½ml E of Lynmouth, in valley on E side of Lynmouth–Barnstaple road (A39)

🅿 Parking (not NT), 500yds (pay & display). Free car parks at Combepark, Hillsford Bridge and Countisbury

NT properties nearby
Arlington Court, Dunster Castle, Heddon Valley Shop, Holnicote Estate

---

Westbury Court Garden

Westbury-on-Severn, Gloucestershire GL14 1PD

🌻 📷 💼 🎓 1967   **(1:J2)**

Dutch water garden – a rare and beautiful survival

Originally laid out in 1696–1705, this is the only restored Dutch water garden in the country. It was the National Trust's first garden restoration, undertaken in 1971, and is planted with species dating from before 1700.

What's new in 2005 Recreated 17th-century rabbit warren

ℹ **T/F** 01452 760461 **E** westburycourt@nationaltrust.org.uk

£ £3.75, child £1.85

🎯 Garden tours 11 May, 8 June, 13 July & 10 Aug

🎮 Programme of events, inc. Easter trails 25–28 March. Apple Days 22 & 23 Oct

Opening arrangements: Westbury Court Garden

		M	T	W	T	F	S	S
2 Mar - 30 Jun	10 - 5	M	T	W	T	F	S	S
1 Jul - 31 Aug	10 - 5	M	T	W	T	F	S	S
1 Sep - 30 Oct	10 - 5	M	T	W	T	F	S	S

Open BH Mons. Open other times of year by appointment

Please note: groups must book in advance with the property

The parterre,
Westbury Court
Garden,
Gloucestershire

🦽 Drop-off point. **WCs**: Adapted WC.
Grounds: Partly accessible, some steps.
Accessible route. 24 steps up to tall pavilion,
3 steps up to summer house. Wheelchair
users are not able to do full circuit of garden
and have to double back ¾ of the way round

👓 Braille guide. Sensory list

☕ Coffee machine. Hot and cold drinks

👤 Pushchairs and baby back-carriers admitted

📷 Family guide. Children's quiz/trail

➡ [162: SO718138] **Foot**: River Severn footpath
runs from garden to river. **Bus**: Stagecoach in
South Wales/Duke's 73 ⊠
Gloucester–Newport (passing close ⊠
Newport); Stagecoach in Wye & Dean 31 ⊠
Gloucester–Coleford. **Station**: Gloucester
9ml. **Road**: 9ml SW of Gloucester on A48

Ⓟ Free parking, 3yds

NT properties nearby
Ashleworth Tithe Barn, Haresfield Beacon

Westwood Manor

Bradford-on-Avon, Wiltshire BA15 2AF

🏠 ❄ 1960   (1:J4)

15th-century stone manor house

The house was altered in the early 17th century
and has late Gothic and Jacobean windows and
fine plasterwork. There is a modern topiary
garden.

⭐ Westwood Manor is administered for the
National Trust by the tenant. No WC

ℹ **T** 01225 863374 **F** 01225 867316

💷 £4.60, child £2.30, family (2 adults & 2
children) £11.80

🦽 Drop-off point. **Building**: Steps to garden
then level access to ground floor. Ground floor
has 2 steps down to King's room

👓 Braille guide and large-print guide

👤 Hip-carrying infant seats for loan. House
unsuitable for under 5s

📷 Children's quiz/trail

➡ [173: ST812590] **Cycle**: NCN4 ¾ml.
Bus: First 94, Bodmans 96 ⊠ Bath–Trowbridge
(passing close ⊠ Trowbridge).
Station: Avoncliff (U), 1ml; Bradford-on-Avon
1½ml. **Road**: 1½ml SW of Bradford-on-Avon, in
Westwood village, beside the church; village
signposted off Bradford-on-Avon to Rode
road (B3109)

Ⓟ Free parking, 90yds

NT properties nearby
The Courts Garden, Dyrham Park, Great Chalfield
Manor, Lacock

Opening arrangements: Westwood Manor									
27 Mar - 28 Sep	2 - 5	M	**T**	**W**	T	F	S	**S**

Groups at other times by written application with s.a.e.
to the tenant

Woodchester Park

The Ebworth Centre, Ebworth Estate, The Camp,
Stroud, Gloucestershire GL6 7ES

♿ ♨ 1994   **(1:J3)**

Beautiful secluded Cotswold valley

The valley contains a 'lost garden' – the remains
of an 18th- and 19th-century landscape park
with a chain of five lakes, fringed by woodland
pasture. An unfinished Victorian mansion (not
NT), is open to the public on specified days from
Easter to October. There are waymarked trails
(steep and strenuous in places) through
delightful scenery.

⭐ Woodchester mansion is not NT; for details,
contact the Woodchester Mansion Trust, tel.
01453 861541. WC not always available

ℹ️ **T** 01452 814213 **F** 01452 810055
E woodchesterpark@nationaltrust.org.uk

🚶 By appointment

🚶 Contact warden for details

🐕 Under strict control, on leads where
requested

➡️ [162: SO797012] **Foot**: Cotswold Way within
⅔ml. **Station**: Stroud 5ml. **Road**: 4ml SW of
Stroud off B4066 Stroud–Dursley road

🅿️ Parking, £1 (pay & display). Accessible from
Nympsfield road, 300yds from junction with
B4066. Last admission to car park 1hr before
park closes

NT properties nearby
Ebworth Estate, Haresfield Beacon,
Minchinhampton Common, Newark Park,
Rodborough Common

Opening arrangements: Woodchester Park					
Park	1 May - 30 Sep	9 - 8	**M T W T F S S**
	1 Oct - 30 Apr 06	9 - 5	**M T W T F S S**

Properties open less often

This section includes National Trust
properties, often tenanted, which are open
two days a week or less (plus Bank
Holidays in some cases). Visits to some
must be made by prior arrangement and
where this applies admission prices are not
shown (please ask when making contact).
**Full details are on our website
www.nationaltrust.org.uk
or obtainable from the Membership
Department, tel. 0870 458 4000.**

Hardy Monument

Black Down, Portesham, Dorset   **(1:I7)**
Monument to Vice-Admiral Hardy, Flag-Captain
of HMS Victory at Trafalgar, with views to the sea.

⭐ No WC

ℹ️ **T** 01297 561900 (West Dorset office)
F 01297 561901

£ £1. No reduction for children

Opening arrangements: Hardy Monument			
2 Apr - 25 Sep	11 - 5	M T W T F **S S**

Open BH Mons 11-5. May close in bad weather.
Staffed by volunteers. Numbers at the top of the
monument are limited. Children must be accompanied
by an adult

Horton Court

Horton, nr Chipping Sodbury, South
Gloucestershire BS37 6QR   **(1:J3)**
Remains of a 12th-century rectory with Norman
hall and early Renaissance decoration.

⭐ No WC

ℹ️ **T** 01179 372501

£ £2.20, child £1.10, family (2 adults & 2
children) £5.60. Unsuitable for coach groups

Opening arrangements: Horton Court			
19 Mar - 29 Oct	2 - 6	M T **W** T F **S** S

Closes dusk if earlier. Other times by written
appointment with tenant

Please remember – your membership card is always needed for free admission

Little Clarendon

Dinton, Salisbury, Wiltshire SP3 5DZ   (1:K5)
Late 15th-century stone house, with three oak-furnished rooms on show.

⭐ No WC

ℹ️ T 01985 843600 (Regional Office)

Opening arrangements: Little Clarendon
Open Mon 28 Mar, 2 May, 30 May, 29 Aug, 2–5

Little Fleece Bookshop

Painswick, Gloucestershire GL6 6QQ
Closed in 2005. Tel. 01452 814213 for further information.

Shute Barton

Shute, nr Axminster, Devon EX13 7PT   (1:H7)
One of the most important surviving non-fortified manor houses of the Middle Ages, with later architectural features.

⭐ No WC

ℹ️ T 01297 34692 (Tenant)

£ £2.50, child £1.20

Opening arrangements: Shute Barton

		M	T	W	T	F	S	S
2 Apr - 29 Oct	2 - 5:30	M	T	**W**	T	F	**S**	S

Admission by guided tour. The house is tenanted; there is visitor access to most parts of the interior

Stembridge Tower Mill

High Ham, Somerset TA10 9DJ   (1:I5)
The last remaining thatched windmill in England, overlooking the Somerset Levels.

⭐ No WC

ℹ️ T 01458 250818

£ £2.30, child £1.20

Opening arrangements: Stembridge Tower Mill

		M	T	W	T	F	S	S
27 Mar - 26 Sep	2 - 5	**M**	T	W	T	F	**S**	**S**

Coach and school groups at other times by arrangement with the tenant

West Pennard Court Barn

West Pennard, nr Glastonbury, Somerset   (1:I5)
15th-century barn with unusual roof.

⭐ Access by key only – see opening arrangements. One floor of the barn is of compacted earth and the surroundings are pastures grazed by cows. In winter the ground is wet and soft - suitable footwear advised. No WC

ℹ️ T 01985 843600 (Regional office), 01458 850212 (Keyholder Mr P. H. Green)

Opening arrangements: West Pennard Court Barn
Admission by appointment. Access by key, to be collected by arrangement with Mr P. H. Green, Court Barn Farm, West Bradley, Somerset, tel. 01458 850212

Westbury College Gatehouse

College Road, Westbury-on-Trym, Bristol   (1:I4)
15th-century gatehouse of the College of Priests.

⭐ Access by key only – see opening arrangements (below). No WC

ℹ️ T 01225 833977

Opening arrangements: Westbury Gatehouse
Access by key, to be collected by appointment with the Vicar, The Vicarage, 44 Eastfield Road, Westbury-on-Trym, Bristol BS9 4AG, tel. 0117 962 1536/0117 950 8644

White Mill

Sturminster Marshall, nr Wimborne, Dorset BH21 4BX   (1:K7)
Corn mill with original wooden machinery in a peaceful riverside setting.

⭐ No WC. Nearest at the mill house

ℹ️ T 01258 858051 F 01258 858389

£ £3, child £2

Opening arrangements: White Mill

		M	T	W	T	F	S	S
26 Mar - 30 Oct	12 - 5	M	T	W	T	**F**	**S**	**S**

Admission by guided tour. Open BH Mons 12–5, last tours 4pm

South West **South & South East**
London East of England
East Midlands West Midlands
North West Yorkshire North East
Wales Northern Ireland

Although this is one of England's most densely populated and urbanised areas, it includes some remarkably extensive and beautiful open spaces, as well as miles of dramatic coastline. The fact that so much has survived is due largely to the work of the National Trust, which over many decades has acquired and protected land threatened by development and insensitive use.

The Trust owns many properties within easy reach of everyone in London and the South East, including most of the delightful village of **Chiddingstone** in Kent, complete with cobbled streets and the famous Chiding Stone, from which it takes its name. The Trust's founder, Octavia Hill, knew this area well, and a woodland is named after her at **Toys Hill**, from where there are magnificent views.

One of the South East's most mysterious areas is Romney Marsh, still peaceful and relatively inaccessible. Here the Trust owns 3¼ miles of the **Royal Military Canal**, between Appledore and Warehorne. There are pleasant walks along the banks of the canal, which was built in 1804–7 as a defence against Napoleonic invasion.

The **White Cliffs of Dover** need no introduction. Information about this fascinating area can be found in the **Saga Gateway to the White Cliffs Visitor Centre**, which provides access to miles of outstanding coastline and walking country, as well as the chance to visit the lighthouse at **South Foreland**. Recent years have seen much development in this part of Kent

due to the Channel Tunnel, but man's presence has been felt here for many thousands of years – at **Coldrum Long Barrow**, near Trottiscliffe, the Trust owns a Neolithic burial chamber, in which skeletal remains have been found.

Along the Sussex coast Trust-owned land on the white cliffs of the **Seven Sisters**, including **Birling Gap** and **Crowlink**, offers delightful walks over open downland with spectacular coastal views. **Chyngton Farm**, on the estuary of the meandering River Cuckmere, and **Frog Firle Farm** inland near Alfriston, are both in classic South Downs country, rich in natural history.

East Head offers a mile of unspoilt sandy beach and dunes at the entrance to Chichester Harbour. Access is through the West Wittering Estate. West along the South Downs Way are important areas of downland, such as **Devil's Dyke** and **Harting Down**. Both are rich in downland flora and fauna, and reward those who leave the beaten track. Also with all-round spectacular views is the country's second largest Iron Age hill-fort, **Cissbury Ring**, north of Worthing. The **Slindon Estate** offers a picturesque flint village and walks in ancient woodland, parkland and downland.

The Trust cares for seventeen miles of beautiful coastline on the Isle of Wight and nine per cent of countryside, including the major downland areas – **Ventnor, St Catherine's, Bembridge and Culver, Afton, Brook, Compton** and **Mottistone** – as well as **The**

Previous page: Detail of the statue by Oscar Nemon of Sir Winston and Lady Churchill at Chartwell, Kent
Below: Oast house at Outridge Farm, Toys Hill, Kent

Cycling along Edburton Escarpment at Devil's Dyke, West Sussex

Needles Headland with the **Old Battery**, overlooking the famous stacks of rock. From here there are excellent walks to enjoy as far as **Tennyson Down**, where the great poet once strolled. The ancient port of Newtown, with its **Old Town Hall** and important nature reserve, is also an interesting place to visit.

In Hampshire, **Stockbridge Common Down**, 60ha (150 acres) of chalk grassland, has a superb butterfly population and excellent views, and nearby **Stockbridge Common Marsh** is easily accessible from Stockbridge High Street. Above the village of Hambledon lies **Speltham Down**, again with fine views. Along the banks of the River Hamble stretches the **Curbridge Nature Reserve**, a delightful area of ancient woodland.

The West Weald includes several large expanses of rare lowland heath. **Black Down**, probably the most wooded of these, is the highest point in Sussex, and over the border in Surrey there are large expanses of heathland at **Frensham** and **Hindhead**, including the dramatic **Devil's Punch Bowl**. The issues involved in the management of heathland and its associated wildlife are interpreted at the **Witley Centre**. In Hampshire, there is further rolling heath at **Ludshott** and hammer ponds at **Waggoners Wells**, while **Selborne Hill and**

Common were made famous by the 18th-century naturalist Gilbert White. The Trust also cares for some 1200ha (3000 acres) in the magnificent New Forest, including **Hale Purlieu** and **Bramshaw Commons**, and the recently acquired **Ibsley** and **Rockford Commons**, which offer excellent walking.

The Surrey Hills, rising to **Reigate Hill**, **Box Hill** and **Leith Hill** at their highest point, provide a picturesque backdrop to some of the Trust's classic country estates. This is idyllic countryside, offering a variety of walks with breathtaking views. Running for nearly 20 miles between Godalming and Weybridge are the **River Wey Navigations**, dating back to the 17th century and once part of London's lost route to the sea. Information on this important waterway is available at **Dapdune Wharf** in Guildford.

The Chilterns offer some of the finest scenery in southern England and from their highest point, **Coombe Hill**, there are spectacular views over three counties. To the south-west lies another notable beauty spot, **Watlington Hill**, 210 metres high and celebrated for its chalk-loving flora and fine yew forest. There are some beautiful villages in this area, including **West Wycombe** and **Bradenham**, which both serve as ideal centres for good walking through typical Chiltern beech-woods. Exploration on foot is also the best way to enjoy the steep heather-clad slopes of the **Finchampstead Ridges** near Wokingham, overlooking the River Blackwater and a haven for wildlife and naturalists alike.

Hertfordshire offers superb opportunities for outdoor recreation in beautiful and varied landscapes. The **Ashridge Estate** has many miles of footpaths giving superb views over the Chilterns and providing access over the area's magnificent woodland, commons, farmland and chalk downland, all of which are home to many species of interesting birds and plants.

Further west, in Oxfordshire, the **Buscot and Coleshill Estates** offer wide expanses of unspoilt countryside, including **Badbury Hill**, with splendid views over the upper Thames valley. Buscot and Coleshill are both attractive villages built of Cotswold stone, and there is a popular picnic area at **Buscot Weir**. Not far from here is **White Horse Hill**, with its famous horse cut into the chalk escarpment. The hill is crowned by the Bronze Age hill-fort of **Uffington Castle** and nearby is **Dragon Hill**, where St George allegedly slew the beast. The Ridgeway Path gives good access to these sites.

Regional Highlights for Visitors with Disabilities ...
Particularly recommended are The Old Brick & Tile Works at **Pinkney's Green**, a nature reserve near Maidenhead with specially adapted paths and viewing platforms, and a tapping rail (access by RADAR key). **St Helen's Duver**, Isle of Wight, has a level shingle walk suitable for accompanied wheelchair users, and an accessible holiday cottage.

... and for Families
Plenty of space to run around and play at **Box Hill**, with open heathland at **Headley Common** close by, **Leith Hill**, **Polesden Lacey**, **Coombe Hill**, the **White Cliffs of Dover** and the **Seven Sisters**. **Devil's Dyke** and the **Witley Centre** offer a wide range of activities for children and school groups. The **Saga**

Gateway to the White Cliffs Visitor Centre and spectacular **Bodiam Castle** have much to offer families on a day out. The interactive exhibits and boat trip at **Dapdune Wharf** are always popular with the under 10s.

Further information
Please contact the Membership Department, PO Box 39, Warrington WA5 7WD. Tel. 0870 458 4000. Email: enquiries@thenationaltrust.org.uk

There is a *Stroll the South Downs* walks leaflet pack covering East and West Sussex properties, available from the NT Slindon office (tel. 01243 814554), a North Downs Countryside Pack, available from Box Hill shop (tel. 01306 888793) and West Weald countryside leaflets, available from the Witley Centre (tel. 01428 683207). A *Walks & Places to Visit on the Isle of Wight* leaflet can be obtained free of charge, from the NT IoW office (tel. 01983 741020). A book of *Walks Around the Wey and Godalming Navigations* is available from Dapdune Wharf or Thames Lock (tel. 01483 561389).

OS Grid Reference

OS grid references for main properties with no individual entry (OS Landranger map series numbers given in brackets)

Afton	[196] SZ350858	Frog Firle Farm	[199] TQ517012
Badbury Hill	[163] SU250940	Hale Purlieu	[184] SU200180
Birling Gap	[199] TV554960	Hindhead area	[186] SU891358
Black Down	[186] SU922308	Ibsley &	
Bramshaw Commons	[184] SU297178	Rockford Commons	[184] SU175095
Brook	[196] SZ395851	Ludshott Common	[186] SU835358
Buscot Weir	[163] SU230976	Pinkney's Green	[175] SU860825
Chiddingstone	[188] TQ501451	Reigate Hill	[187] TQ262522
Cissbury Ring	[198] TQ130078	Royal Military Canal	[189] TQ958292
Coldrum Long Barrow	[188] TQ654607	St Catherine's	[196] SZ495785
Compton	[196] SZ376850	St Helen's Duver	[196] SZ637891
Coombe Hill	[165] SP849066	Selborne	[186] SU742335
Crowlink	[199] TV544975	Seven Sisters	[199] TV549978
Culver	[196] SZ636855	Speltham Down	[196] SU645148
Curbridge	[196] SU528117	Stockbridge Marsh	[185] SU357348
Devil's Dyke	[186] TQ260110	Stockbridge Down	[185] SU375347
Dragon Hill	[174] SU293866	Tennyson Down	[196] SZ325853
East Head	[197] SZ766990	Toys Hill	[188] TQ465517
F'hampstead Ridges	[175] SU808634	Ventnor	[196] SZ563784
Frensham Common	[186] SU859419	Waggoners Wells	[186] SU862343
		Watlington Hill	[175] SU709935
		White Horse Hill, Uffington Castle & Dragon Hill	[163] SU301866

Alfriston Clergy House

The Tye, Alfriston, Polegate, East Sussex
BN26 5TL

🏠 ❁ 🖻 🍴 🎭 🎭 [1896]　　　　　　(2:H8)

Medieval thatched cottage and picturesque garden

This 14th-century thatched Wealden 'hall house' was the first building to be acquired by the National Trust in 1896. It has an unusual chalk and sour milk floor and its pretty cottage garden is in an idyllic setting beside Alfriston's parish church, with views across the meandering River Cuckmere.

★ Conservation in action: Alfriston Clergy House will be rethatched during the autumn, which will involve some scaffolding. No WC. WCs in main village car park

ℹ️ **T** 01323 870001, 01323 871443 (Shop)
F 01323 871318
E alfriston@nationaltrust.org.uk

Opening arrangements: Alfriston Clergy House									
House	5 Mar - 20 Mar	11 - 4	M	T	W	T	F	S	S
	26 Mar - 31 Oct	10 - 5	M	T	W	T	F	S	S
	2 Nov - 18 Dec	11 - 4	M	T	W	T	F	S	S
Shop	As house								
Open Good Fri									

£ £3.10, child £1.55, family £7.75. Groups £2.65. Guided tour £1 extra (inc. NT members)

♿ Drop-off point at garden gates or front entrance. **Building**: Steps to entrance. Very narrow corridors and small rooms. Ground floor has steps. Photograph album. **Grounds**: loose gravel paths, slopes, some steps, grass paths. Some visitors may require assistance from their companion. **Shop**: Step to entrance

♨ Braille guide and large-print guide. Sensory list

🎁 Selling local crafts

🚼 Pushchairs and baby back-carriers admitted

🎞 Suitable for school groups. Children's quiz/trail

➜ [189: TQ521029] **Foot**: South Downs Way within ⅔ml. **Cycle**: NCN2. **Bus**: RDH 125 from Lewes, Renown 126 from Eastbourne & Seaford (pass close ≋ Lewes and Seaford), Cuckmere Valley Rambler bus, weekends only from ≋ Berwick. **Station**: Berwick (U) 2½ml. **Road**: 4ml NE of Seaford, just E of B2108, in Alfriston village, adjoining The Tye and St Andrew's Church

🅿 Parking (not NT) at other end of village, 500yds

NT properties nearby
Bateman's, Frog Firle Farm, Monk's House, Sheffield Park Garden

The herb garden, Alfriston Clergy House, East Sussex

Ascott

Wing, nr Leighton Buzzard, Buckinghamshire
LU7 0PS

🏛 ❄ 1949   (2:E3)

**Jacobean house remodelled in the 19th
century, with superb collections and gardens**

Originally a half-timbered farmhouse, Ascott
was bought in 1876 by the de Rothschild family
and considerably transformed and enlarged. It
now houses a quite exceptional collection of
fine paintings, Oriental porcelain and English
and French furniture. The extensive gardens are
a mixture of the formal and natural, containing
specimen trees and shrubs, as well as a
herbaceous walk, lily pond, Dutch garden and
remarkable topiary sundial.

ℹ️ **T** 01296 688242 **F** 01296 681904
E info@ascottestate.co.uk

£ £6.50, child £3.25. **Garden only**: £4, child
£2. NT members will be asked to pay on
2 National Gardens Scheme days

♿ Drop-off point. **Building**: Step to entrance,
ramp available. 3 wheelchairs, booking
essential. **WCs**: Adapted WC.
Grounds: Accessible route

👁 Braille guide and large-print guide

🐕 On leads and only in car park

➡️ [165: SP891230] **Bus**: Arriva X15
Aylesbury–Milton Keynes (passing close
🚉 Aylesbury & Leighton Buzzard).
Station: Leighton Buzzard 2ml. **Road**: ½ml E
of Wing, 2ml SW of Leighton Buzzard, on
S side of A418

P Free parking, 220yds

NT properties nearby
Ashridge Estate, Claydon House

Opening arrangements: Ascott										
House & garden	15 Mar - 30 Apr	2 - 6	M	T	W	T	F	S	S
	3 May - 28 Jul	2 - 6	M	T	W	T	F	S	S
	2 Aug - 31 Aug	2 - 6	M	T	W	T	F	S	S

Last admission 1hr before closing. Garden only open
in aid of NGS on Mons 2 May and 29 Aug (NT
members pay on these days)

Ashdown House

Lambourn, Newbury, Berkshire RG17 8RE

🏛 ❄ 🖼 👤 1956   (2:C5)

**17th-century house perched on the Berkshire
Downs**

This extraordinary Dutch-style house is famous
for its association with Elizabeth of Bohemia
('The Winter Queen'), Charles I's sister, to whom
the house was 'consecrated'. The interior has
an impressive great staircase rising from hall to
attic, and important paintings contemporary
with the house. There are spectacular views
from the roof over the formal parterre, lawns and
surrounding countryside, as well as beautiful
walks in neighbouring Ashdown Woods. Nearby
Weathercock Hill and Alfred's Castle, an Iron
Age defended settlement where in 871 King
Alfred is rumoured to have defeated the Danes,
offer fine walking country.

What's new in 2005 The house will be
undergoing extensive stonework repairs and will
be scaffolded for much of the season

★ Visitor access in the house is to staircase (100
steps) and roof only. No WC

ℹ️ **T** 01793 762209 (Coleshill Estate Office)
E ashdownhouse@nationaltrust.org.uk

£ £2.30. **Woodland**: Free

♿ Access to roof via 100 steps

🅰 Picnic area by car park

🐕 On leads and only in woodland

➡️ [174: SU282820] **Bus**: Thamesdown 47
Swindon–Lambourn, with connections from
Newbury (passing close 🚉 Swindon &
Newbury). **Road**: 2½ml S of Ashbury, 3½ml N
of Lambourn, on W side of B4000

P Free parking, 250yds

NT properties nearby
Avebury, Buscot Park, Great Coxwell Barn, White
Horse Hill, Uffington Castle & Dragon Hill

Opening arrangements: Ashdown House										
House/garden	2 Apr - 29 Oct	2 - 5	M	T	W	T	F	S	S
Woodland	All year	Daylight	M	T	W	T	F	S	S

Admission by guided tour to house at 2.15, 3.15 &
4.15. Numbers limited

Please see the area introductions for details of coast & countryside properties

Ashridge Estate

Visitor Centre, Moneybury Hill, Ringshall,
Berkhamsted, Hertfordshire HP4 1LX

 1926 (2:F3)

Vast area of open downland and woods

This magnificent and varied estate runs across
the borders of Herts and Bucks, along the main
ridge of the Chiltern Hills. There are 2000ha
(5000 acres) of woodlands, commons and chalk
downland supporting a rich variety of wildlife
and offering splendid walks through outstanding
scenery. The focal point of the area is the
Monument, erected in 1832 to the Duke of
Bridgewater. There are also splendid views from
Ivinghoe Beacon, accessible from Steps Hill.

What's new in 2005 Buses run to Monument
Drive

★ WC not always available

ℹ **T** 01442 851227, 01494 755557 (Infoline),
01442 842716 (Riding warden),
01494 755572 (Box office),
0788 4315 101 (Tea-room) **F** 01442 850000
E ashridge@nationaltrust.org.uk

£ **Monument**: £1.30, child 60p. **Countryside**:
Free. Donations welcome. Riding permits from
riding warden, tel. for details

🚶 Programme of guided walks all year

🎪 Programme of events, inc. workshops and
activity days for children and adults. Send
s.a.e. for details

🚶 Extensive network of paths. Information about
self-guided walks available from the shop

♿ Separate designated parking, 25yds.
Building: Visitor centre fully accessible. 1
wheelchair. Audio visual/video. **WCs**: Adapted
WC. **Grounds**: Partly accessible. Accessible
route map. 4ml of surfaced routes for use by
wheelchairs and PMV. 5 single-seater PMV, 3
multi-seater PMV, booking essential.
Shop: Level entrance. **Refreshments**: Level
entrance

👓 Sensory list. Handling collection

🍴 Licensed tea-room (NT-approved concession)
in visitor centre. Children's menu

Opening arrangements: Ashridge Estate

Estate			M	T	W	T	F	S	S
Estate	All year		**M**	**T**	**W**	**T**	**F**	**S**	**S**
Visitor Centre	21 Mar - 9 Dec	1 - 5	**M**	**T**	**W**	**T**	**F**	S	S
	19 Mar - 11 Dec	12 - 5	M	T	W	T	F	**S**	**S**
Monument	19 Mar - 30 Oct	12 - 5	M	T	W	T	F	**S**	**S**
Shop	As centre								
Tea-room	1 Jan - 11 Dec	12 - 5	M	**T**	**W**	**T**	**F**	**S**	**S**

Open BH Mons and Good Fri 12–5. Monument also
Mon–Fri by arrangement, weather permitting. Shop
closes dusk if earlier than 5

🚼 Baby-changing facilities. Pushchairs and baby
back-carriers admitted

🎒 Suitable for school groups. Education
room/centre. Hands-on activities. Family
activity packs. Adult study days

🐾 Under close control

🚲 Short stretch of permitted cycle path and 9ml
of bridleways giving cyclists shared access

➡️ [181: SP970131] **Foot**: 2¾ml of The Ridgeway
on property. **Bus**: Monument: Arriva 30/31
≋ Tring, alight Aldbury, ½ml. Beacon: Arriva 61
Aylesbury–Luton (passing close ≋ Aylesbury
and Luton); Chiltern Rambler 327 from Tring
to Monument and Beacon, Suns May–Sept
only. **Station**: Monument: Tring 1¾ml; Beacon:
Cheddington 3½ml. **Road**: Between
Berkhamsted and Northchurch, and Ringshall
and Dagnall, just off B4506

🅿 Free parking, 50yds

NT properties nearby
Dunstable Downs, Pitstone Windmill, Shaw's
Corner, Whipsnade Tree Cathedral

Basildon Park

Lower Basildon, Reading, Berkshire RG8 9NR

🏠 ❄ 🌰 🏠 🍴 🔔 ☂ 1978 (2:D5)

**18th-century country house set in extensive
parkland**

This beautiful Palladian mansion was built in
1776–83 by John Carr for Francis Sykes, who
had made his fortune in India. The interior is
notable for its original delicate plasterwork and
elegant staircase, as well as for the unusual
Octagon Room. The house fell on hard times in
the early part of the last century, but was

Unless indicated, last admission is always 30mins before closing time

The Octagon Room, Basildon Park, Berkshire

rescued by Lord and Lady Iliffe, who restored it and filled it with fine pictures and furniture. The early 19th-century pleasure grounds are currently being restored, and there are waymarked trails through the parkland. From the top of Streatley Hill two miles away access can be gained to The Holies, Lough Down and Lardon Chase, an outstanding area of downland and woodland with many beautiful walks and breathtaking views.

i **T** 0118 984 3040, 01494 755558 (Infoline), 01494 755572 (Box office), 0118 976 7363 (Shop), 0118 976 7365 (Restaurant)
F 0118 976 7370
E basildonpark@nationaltrust.org.uk

£ £5, child £2.50, family £12.50. Groups £3.70.
Park & garden only: £2.40, child £1.20, family £6

Special tours by arrangement; guided walks

Programme of events. For details send s.a.e. marked 'Events' to Box office, P.O.Box 180, High Wycombe, Bucks HP14 4XT

Leaflet with details of waymarked trails

Designated parking 20yds from ticket office. Transfer available. Please enquire on arrival. **Building**: Ramped entrance with handrail. 3 wheelchairs. Ground floor has steps, ramp available. Many stairs with handrail to other floors. Seating available. Photograph album. **WCs**: Adapted WC. **Grounds**: Partly accessible. Loose gravel paths around pleasure grounds. **Shop**: Level entrance. **Refreshments**: Ramped entrance

Induction loop in reception, shop, restaurant

Braille guide and large-print guide. Sensory list

Licensed restaurant. Children's menu

Picnics in grounds except on main lawns near house

Baby-changing facilities. Front-carrying baby slings and hip-carrying infant seats for loan

There are special events at most Trust properties; please telephone 0870 458 4000 for details

Opening arrangements: Basildon Park										
House	23 Mar - 30 Oct	1 - 5:30	M	T	**W**	**T**	**F**	**S**	**S**
Shop	23 Mar - 30 Oct	11 - 5:30	M	T	**W**	**T**	**F**	**S**	**S**
	2 Nov - 18 Dec	12 - 4	M	T	**W**	**T**	**F**	**S**	**S**
Restaurant	As house	11 - 5:30	M	T	**W**	**T**	**F**	**S**	**S**
Grounds	As house	11 - 5:30	M	T	**W**	**T**	**F**	**S**	**S**

Open BH Mons. Property closes at 4 on 19, 20 & 21 Aug for firework concerts (last entry 3.30)

🎒 Suitable for school groups. Children's guide. Children's quiz/trail

🐕 On leads and only in park, woodland and grounds, not on main lawns near house

➔ [175: SU611782] **Bus**: Thames Travel 132 Wallingford–Reading (passes ☰ Goring & Streatley). **Station**: Pangbourne 2½ml; Goring & Streatley 3ml.
Road: Between Pangbourne and Streatley, 7ml NW of Reading, on W side of A329; leave M4 at exit 12 and follow brown NT signs to Pangbourne. From A34 take Oxford ring road and leave at Henley/Reading junction, then turn right at roundabout for Wallingford bypass, cross over river and take first left onto A329

🅿 Free parking, 400yds

NT properties nearby
Greys Court, Lardon Chase, The Vyne

Bateman's

Burwash, Etchingham, East Sussex TN19 7DS

 1940   (2:H7)

Jacobean house, home of Rudyard Kipling

The interior of this beautiful 17th-century house, Rudyard Kipling's home from 1902 to 1936, reflects the author's strong associations with the East. There are many oriental rugs and artefacts, and most of the rooms – including his book-lined study – are much as Kipling left them. The delightful grounds run down to the small River Dudwell with its watermill, and contain roses, wild flowers, fruit and herbs. Kipling's Rolls-Royce is also on display.

⭐ The garden, tea-room and shop remain open after the house has closed in October

ℹ **T** 01435 882302, 01435 883769 (Tea-room)
F 01435 882811
E batemans@nationaltrust.org.uk

£ £5.90, child £2.95, family £14.75. Groups £4.90, child £2.45. Free entry to garden in Nov & Dec

♿ Designated parking in main car park, 20yds. Drop-off point. **Building**: Step to entrance. 2 wheelchairs, booking essential. Ground floor has steps. Many stairs with handrail to other floors. Seating available. Virtual tour. **WCs**: Adapted WC. **Grounds**: Partly accessible. Accessible route map. **Shop**: Steps to entrance. **Refreshments**: Step to entrance

🔊 Induction loop in reception, shop, restaurant

👁 Braille guide and large-print guide. Sensory list

🍴 Mulberry Tea-room (licensed) in the garden. Children's menu

🧺 In picnic area in copse adjacent to car park

🚼 Baby-changing facilities. Front-carrying baby slings and hip-carrying infant seats for loan

🎒 Children's guide. Children's quiz/trail

🐕 On leads and only in car park; dog crèche

➔ [199: TQ671238] **Bus**: Stagecoach in the South Downs/Renown 318 Uckfield–☰ Etchingham. **Station**: Etchingham 3ml.
Road: ½ml S of Burwash. A265 W from Burwash, first turning on left; or N from B2096 Heathfield to Battle road at Woods Corner

🅿 Free parking, 30yds. Coaches: tight left turn into first bay

NT properties nearby
Bodiam Castle, Scotney Castle, Sissinghurst Castle Garden

Opening arrangements: Bateman's										
House	19 Mar - 30 Oct	11 - 5	**M**	**T**	**W**	T	**F**	**S**	**S**
Garden	5 Mar - 13 Mar	11 - 4	M	T	W	T	**F**	**S**	**S**
	19 Mar - 30 Oct	11 - 5	**M**	**T**	**W**	T	**F**	**S**	**S**
	2 Nov - 23 Dec	11 - 4	M	T	**W**	**T**	**F**	**S**	**S**
Tea-room	As garden								
Shop	5 Mar - 13 Mar	11 - 4	M	T	W	T	**F**	**S**	**S**
	19 Mar - 30 Oct	11 - 5:30	**M**	**T**	**W**	T	**F**	**S**	**S**
	2 Nov - 23 Dec	11 - 4	M	T	**W**	**T**	**F**	**S**	**S**

Open Good Fri 11–5. The mill grinds corn most Weds and Sats at 2

Bembridge Windmill

High Street, Bembridge, Isle of Wight PO35 5SQ

✖ 🏠 🍴 1961   **(2:D9)**

Grade I listed windmill

Built *c*.1700 and still with its original wooden machinery, the windmill is the only one surviving on the Island.

⭐ No WC

ℹ️ **T** 01983 873945

£ £2, child £1, family £6. All school groups are conducted by a NT guide; special charge applies

🏃 Conducted school groups and special visits March to end Oct (but not July or Aug), by written appointment

🚶 The Windmill is the starting point for the Culver trail

♿ Drop-off point. **Building**: Steps to entrance

👁️ Braille guide. Sensory list

🏠 Small shop in kiosk

🍴 Kiosk. Tea, coffee and ice cream

🏫 Suitable for school groups. Children's quiz/trail

➡️ [196: SZ639874] **Ferry**: Ryde (Wightlink Ltd) 6ml (tel. 0870 582 7744); E Cowes (Red Funnel) 13ml (tel. 0870 444 8898). **Bus**: Southern Vectis 1 Cowes–Sandown (passing 🚂 Ryde Esplanade). Alight Bembridge village, then ½ml. **Station**: Brading (U) 2ml by footpath. **Road**: ½ml S of Bembridge on B3395

🅿️ Free parking in lay-by, 100yds

NT properties nearby
Brighstone Shop & Museum, Mottistone Manor Garden, The Needles Old Battery, Old Town Hall, Newtown

Opening arrangements: Bembridge Windmill											
Mill	21 Mar - 30 Jun	10 - 5	**M**	**T**	**W**	**T**	**F**	S	S
	1 Jul - 31 Aug	10 - 5	**M**	**T**	**W**	**T**	**F**	S	S
	1 Sep - 30 Oct	10 - 5	**M**	**T**	**W**	**T**	**F**	S	S
Shop	As Mill								
Closes dusk if earlier. Open Easter Sat									

Bodiam Castle

Bodiam, nr Robertsbridge, East Sussex TN32 5UA

🏰 🍴 🏠 🍴 🌳 👁️ 🍴 1926   **(2:I7)**

Perfect example of a late medieval moated castle

One of the most famous and evocative castles in Britain, Bodiam was built in 1385, as both a defence and a comfortable home. The exterior is virtually complete and the ramparts rise dramatically above the moat. Enough of the interior survives to give an impression of castle life. There are spiral staircases and battlements to explore and wonderful views of the Rother Valley from the top of the towers.

What's new in 2005 New interpretation brings to life the fascinating story of the castle and its inhabitants

⭐ Bodiam Castle is often used by education groups in term time. The only WC is located in the car park, 400yds from the castle entrance

ℹ️ **T** 01580 830436, 01580 830212 (Shop), 01580 830074 (Tea-room) **F** 01580 830398 **E** bodiamcastle@nationaltrust.org.uk

£ £4.40, child £2.20, family £11. Groups £3.75, child £1.90. Reduced rate when arriving by public transport or for visitors arriving via Kent and East Sussex Steam Railway; stations at Tenterden and Northiam

🏃 By arrangement

♿ Path from main car park is uneven grass and shingle track. Alternative access along private road for easier route, tel. Property Manager in advance. Drop-off point. **Building**: Level entrance. 1 wheelchair. Stairs to other floors. Photograph album. **WCs**: Adapted WC. **Grounds**: Partly accessible. Accessible route map. Some visitors may require assistance particularly when ground is muddy. **Shop**: Ramped entrance. **Refreshments**: Level entrance. Large-print menu

👁️ Braille guide and large-print guide. Sensory list. Handling collection. Video with soundtrack in castle

Please note: groups must book in advance with the property

Opening arrangements: Bodiam Castle

Castle	7 Feb - 30 Oct	10 - 6	**M** **T** **W** **T** **F** **S** **S**
	5 Nov - 12 Feb 06	10 - 4	M T W T F **S** **S**
	13 Feb - 28 Feb 06	10 - 6	**M** **T** **W** **T** **F** **S** **S**
Shop	7 Feb - 30 Oct	10 - 5	**M** **T** **W** **T** **F** **S** **S**
	2 Nov - 23 Dec	10 - 4	M **T** **W** **T** **F** **S** **S**
	7 Jan - 12 Feb 06	10 - 4	M T W T F **S** **S**
	13 Feb - 28 Feb 06	10 - 5	**M** **T** **W** **T** **F** **S** **S**
Tea-room	As shop		

Last admission 1hr before closing. Castle closes dusk
if earlier than stated. Closed 24 Dec–6 Jan

Wharf Tea-room. Pre-book for private room
with waitress service. Children's menu.
Special meals available for coeliacs and
vegetarians; dairy-free cakes available.
Function room

Baby-changing facilities. Pushchairs and baby
back-carriers admitted

Suitable for school groups. Education
room/centre. Hands-on activities. Family
guide. Children's guide. Children's quiz/trail.
'Bat Pack' Discovery Fun Pack for young
children. Live interpretation on specific dates.
Tel. for details

On leads and only in grounds

Bodiam Castle, East Sussex

→ [199: TQ785256] **Foot**: Located on the
Sussex Border path. **Ferry**: Bodiam Ferry
from Newenden Bridge (A28). **Bus**: Arriva 254
Tunbridge Wells–Hastings (passing
Wadhurst). **Station**: Wadhurst 12ml,
(Robertsbridge 5ml – no bus link), Bodiam
(Kent & E Sussex Steam Rly) ¼ml. **Road**: 3ml
S of Hawkhurst, 3ml E of A21 Hurst Green

P Parking, 400yds, £2 (pay & display).
Coaches £5

NT properties nearby
Bateman's, Scotney Castle, Sissinghurst Castle
Garden, Smallhythe Place

Box Hill

The Old Fort, Box Hill Road, Box Hill, Tadworth,
Surrey KT20 7LB

 1914 (2:F6)

**Woodland and open down with wonderful
views**

An outstanding area of woodland and chalk
downland, Box Hill has long been famous as a
destination for day-trippers from London.
Surprisingly extensive, it has much to offer the
rambler and naturalist with many beautiful walks

and views towards the South Downs. On the summit there is an information centre, shop, servery and a fort dating from the 1890s (access to exterior only).

What's new in 2005 Resurfaced walk from information centre to viewpoint

[i] **T** 01306 885502 (Head Warden), 01306 742809 (Learning), 01306 888793 (Shop) **F** 01306 875030 **E** boxhill@nationaltrust.org.uk

[£] Countryside free

[🏃] Guided walks throughout the year. Groups by arrangement with the Warden

[♥] Programme of events, inc. Discovery Days in spring and autumn half-terms and special Christmas shopping day 9 Dec, when all welcome, especially visitors with disabilities

[🏃] Short walk, nature walk and long walk self-guided trails with leaflets

[♿] South scarp is very steep. Accessible paths to viewpoint and along short length of North Downs Way. Separate designated parking, 30yds. **Building**: Level entrance. 1 wheelchair. **WCs**: Adapted WC

[👁] Braille guide. Sensory list. Handling collection

[🍴] Servery. For snacks and hot and cold drinks. Ice-cream kiosk (not NT) in East car park

[🚫] No barbecues

[👶] Baby-changing facilities. Pushchairs admitted

[🏫] Suitable for school groups. Education room/centre. Children's quiz/trail. Series of Box Hill books: *Box, Archaeology, Orchids, Bats* and *Butterflies*

[🐕] Under close control (where sheep grazing)

[→] [187: TQ171519] **Foot**: 1ml of North Downs Way from Stepping Stones to South Scarp; 1ml of Thames Down link footpath at Mickleham Downs; 1ml from Dorking station (½ml from Box Hill station). Many rights of way lead to Box Hill summit. **Bus**: Centra 516 ⊞ Leatherhead–Dorking (bus goes to the top of the hill). **Station**: Box Hill & West Humble ½ml. **Road**: 1ml N of Dorking, 2½ml S of Leatherhead on A24

Opening arrangements: Box Hill

			M T W T F S S
	All year		**M T W T F S S**
Servery	All year	11 - 5	**M T W T F S S**
Shop/info centre	All year	11 - 5	**M T W T F S S**

Shop, information centre & servery closed 25, 26 Dec & 1 Jan; close dusk if earlier than 5; close later than 5 in summer, weather permitting

[P] Parking, £2 (pay & display). NT members must display cards. Annual car park pass available from information centre or North Downs office tel. 01372 220642. Coaches must not use zig-zag road from Burford Bridge on W side of hill as weight restriction applies, but should approach from E side of hill B2032 or B2033; car/coach parks at summit

NT properties nearby
Headley Heath, Leith Hill, Polesden Lacey, Ranmore Common

Bradenham Village

nr High Wycombe, Buckinghamshire

[🏠][👥][🏃] [1956] (2:E4)

Picturesque village in the Chiltern hills

The church and 17th-century manor house (not open) provide an impressive backdrop to the sloping village green. The manor was once the home of Isaac D'Israeli, father of Benjamin Disraeli, who lived nearby at Hughenden Manor. A network of paths provides easy access for walkers to explore the delightful surrounding countryside, which includes hills, farmlands and classic Chilterns beech-woods.

[i] **T** 01494 528051 (Regional office)

[→] [165: SU825970] **Bus**: Carousel/Z&S International 321/2 High Wycombe–⊞ Princes Risborough. **Station**: Saunderton 1ml. **Road**: 4ml NW of High Wycombe, off A4010

[P] Parking at the village green

NT properties nearby
Hughenden Manor, West Wycombe Park

Opening arrangements: Bradenham

		M T W T F S S
	All year	**M T W T F S S**

Brighstone Shop & Museum

North Street, Brighstone, Isle of Wight PO30 4AX

🐇 🏠 [1989]   (2:D9)

Row of attractive thatched cottages

The traditional cottages contain a National Trust shop and Village Museum (run by Brighstone Museum Trust), depicting village life in the late 19th century.

⭐ Nearest WC in public car park 100yds

ℹ️ **T** 01983 740689

£ Admission free

🚶 Numerous walks to the coast, Mottistone Estate and Brighstone Forest

♿ **Building**: Step to entrance. **Shop**: Step to entrance

📷 Large range of books for walkers and cyclists

👶 Pushchairs admitted

➡️ [196: SZ428828] **Ferry**: Yarmouth (Wightlink Ltd) 8ml (tel. 0870 582 7744); E Cowes (Red Funnel) 12ml (tel. 0870 444 8898).
Bus: Southern Vectis 7B Newport–Alum Bay.
Road: Next to post office, just off B3399 in Brighstone

P Free parking (not NT), 100yds

NT properties nearby
Bembridge Windmill, Mottistone Manor Garden, The Needles Old Battery, Old Town Hall, Newtown

Opening arrangements: Brighstone		
4 Jan - 24 Mar	10 - 1	**M T W T F S** S
25 Mar - 28 May	10 - 4	**M T W T F S** S
29 May - 30 Oct	12 - 5	M T W T F S **S**
30 May - 29 Oct	10 - 5	**M T W T F S** S
31 Oct - 24 Dec	10 - 4	**M T W T F S** S
28 Dec - 31 Dec	10 - 4	M T **W T F S** S
Closed 25–27 Dec inc. and 1 Jan		

The Buscot & Coleshill Estates

Coleshill Estate Office, Coleshill, Swindon, Wiltshire SN6 7PT

🐇 ⚒️ ✿ 🍴 👶 🍽️ 🏠 [1956]   (2:C4)

Traditional agricultural estates encompassing villages, farms and woodland

On the western border of Oxfordshire in the heart of the Thames Valley, the Buscot & Coleshill Estates are made up of 3035ha (7500 acres) that include the attractive villages of Buscot and Coleshill, with surrounding woodland and farmland. The vernacular stone cottages in Coleshill village, along with the Home Farm buildings, are an integral part of a well-planned 19th-century model farm. A network of footpaths criss-crosses the Estates. Main visitor sites include Buscot House and garden, the Buscot Weir field adjacent to the Thames, the Iron Age hill-fort at Badbury Clump and the 13th-century monastic Great Coxwell Barn.

What's new in 2005 Coleshill Mill, which ceased working in the 1920s, is being restored to working order – open on certain days throughout 2005. Tel. for details

ℹ️ **T** 01793 762209 (Estate office)
   F 01793 861110
   E buscot@nationaltrust.org.uk

£ Admission free

🚶 Guided tours throughout the year and on request for groups

🎭 Programme of events, inc. Open Day in September, village open gardens and guided walks

🚶 Walks leaflet available from Coleshill estate office

🍽️ Tea-room (not NT) in Buscot village shop

🏫 Suitable for school groups. Education room/centre

🐕 On leads

Opening arrangements: The Buscot & Coleshill Estates		
Estate	All year	**M T W T F S S**

For general and membership enquiries, please telephone 0870 458 4000

→ **Cycle**: NCN45 10ml. Regional Route 40: Oxfordshire Cycleway. **Bus**: Stagecoach in Swindon 7 Swindon–Highworth (passing close ₴ Swindon), alight Highworth then 2ml walk. **Station**: Swindon 10ml. **Road**: Coleshill village on B4019 between Faringdon and Highworth. Buscot village on A417 between Faringdon and Lechlade

P Not suitable for coaches. Free car parks at Buscot village and Badbury Clump

NT properties nearby
Buscot Old Parsonage, Buscot Park, Great Coxwell Barn, White Horse Hill, Uffington Castle & Dragon Hill

Buscot Park

Estate Office, Buscot Park, Faringdon, Oxfordshire SN7 8BU

 1949 **(2:C4)**

Neo-classical mansion with fine art and furniture collection, set in landscaped grounds

The late 18th-century house contains the fine paintings and furniture of the Faringdon Collection Trust. The grounds include various avenue walks, an Italianate water garden, designed in the early 20th century by Harold Peto, and a large walled garden.

⭐ This property is administered on behalf of the National Trust by Lord Faringdon, and the contents of the house are owned by The Faringdon Collection Trust

ℹ **T** 0845 345 3387 (Infoline), 01367 240786 (Estate office), 01367 245705 (PYO produce)
F 01367 241794 **E** estbuscot@aol.com

Opening arrangements: Buscot Park										
House/grounds	25 Mar - 30 Sep	2 - 6	M	T	**W**	**T**	**F**	S	S
	See below	2 - 6	M	T	W	T	**F**	**S**	**S**
Grounds only	25 Mar - 30 Sep	2 - 6	**M**	**T**	W	T	F	S	S
Tea-room	25 Mar - 30 Sep	2:30 - 5:30	M	T	**W**	**T**	**F**	S	S

Open BH Mons. Last admission 1hr before closing. House & grounds also open 2–6 (tea-room 2.30–5.30) on weekends 26/27 Mar; 9/10, 23/24, 30 Apr/1 May; 14/15, 28/29 May; 11/12, 25/26 June; 9/10, 23/24 July; 13/14, 27/28 Aug; 10/11, 24/25 Sept

£ £6.50, child £3.25. **Grounds only**: £4.50, child £2.25

🚶 Extensive walks in grounds

♿ Drop-off point. **Building**: Many steps to entrance. For safety reasons, due to the width of the corridors, there is no wheeled vehicle access. Stairs with handrail to other floors. Computer. **WCs**: Adapted WC. **Grounds**: Partly accessible. Accessible route map. Due to steep gradients, gravel paths and distances, grounds are more suitable for PMVs. The garden also has terraces with steps. 1 wheelchair. 2 single-seater PMV, booking essential. **Refreshments**: Ramped entrance

👓 Braille guide and large-print guide. Information in all rooms

🛍 Occasional sales of plants surplus to garden requirements; pick-your-own soft fruit, vegetables and flowers in season

🍴 Licensed tea-room (not NT)

🧺 Only in picnic area by main car park

🚼 Baby-changing facilities. Hip-carrying infant seats for loan

🐕 Only in the paddock car park

→ [163: SU239973] **Bus**: Stagecoach in Oxford 64 Swindon–Carterton, Stagecoach in Swindon 74 Swindon–Fairford (both passing close ₴ Swindon). On both, alight Lechlade, 2¾ml walk. **Road**: Between Lechlade and Faringdon, on A417

P Free parking

NT properties nearby
The Buscot & Coleshill Estates, Buscot Old Parsonage, Great Coxwell Barn

Chartwell

Mapleton Road, Westerham, Kent TN16 1PS

🏠 ❄ 📷 🍴 1946 **(2:G6)**

Family home of Sir Winston Churchill

Bought by Sir Winston for its magnificent views over the Weald of Kent to Sussex, Chartwell was his home and the place from which he drew inspiration from 1924 until the end of his life. The rooms and gardens remain much as they

Please see the area introductions for details of coast & countryside properties

were when he lived here, with pictures, books, maps and personal mementoes strongly evoking the career and wide-ranging interests of this great statesman. The beautiful terraced gardens contain the lakes Sir Winston created, the water garden where he fed his fish, Lady Churchill's rose garden and the Golden Rose Walk, a Golden Wedding anniversary gift from their children. Many of Sir Winston's paintings can be seen in the garden studio.

What's new in 2005 *Churchill: Gifts to a Hero –* exhibition of gifts and artefacts from across the world

⭐ Car park open for countryside access throughout the year (except 25 Dec); programme of conservation work in some garden areas in 2005. WC available only when car park open

ℹ️ **T** 01732 868381, 01732 866368 (Infoline), 01732 867837 (Shop), 01732 863087 (Restaurant) **F** 01732 868193 **E** chartwell@nationaltrust.org.uk

£ £8, child £4, family £20. **Garden & studio only**: £4, child £2, family £10

𝕏 Private guided tours and special talks by arrangement. Group booking pack available on request

🎭 Programme of events, inc. lecture lunches, special tours, guided walks

🚶 Three waymarked walks

♿ Designated parking in main car park, 200yds. Chartwell is sited on side of a steep valley, access from the car park via slopes and steps. 5 wheelchairs. Special arrangements to park near the house can be made on request (not coaches). Drop-off point. **Building**: Steps to entrance with handrail, ramp available. Ground floor has steps. Stairs to other floors. Seating available. Photograph album, virtual tour. **WCs**: Adapted WC. **Grounds**: Partly accessible, slopes, grass paths. **Shop**: Level entrance. **Refreshments**: Ramped entrance. Large-print menu. Stairs to function room

🦮 Braille guide and large-print guide. Sensory list

🍷 With licence to sell alcohol

☕ Licensed restaurant in car park. Children's menu. Dispatch Box kiosk next to restaurant

🖼️ In field adjacent to car park with wonderful countryside views

👶 Baby-changing and feeding facilities. Front-carrying baby slings and hip-carrying infant seats for loan

👥 Suitable for school groups. Children's quiz/trail

🐕 On short leads in gardens

➡️ [188: TQ455515] **Foot**: Greensand Way passes through car park. **Bus**: Metrobus 246 from ⇌ Bromley North (passing ⇌ Bromley South); 401 from ⇌ Tunbridge Wells (passing ⇌ Sevenoaks). Both Suns only. Otherwise Metrobus 238 from Edenbridge (Wed only) or 236 Westerham–East Grinstead (passing ⇌ Edenbridge and ⇌ Edenbridge Town), Mon–Fri only, to within ½ml. **Station**: Edenbridge (U) 4ml, Edenbridge Town 4½ml, Sevenoaks 6½ml. **Road**: 2ml S of Westerham, fork left off B2026 after 1½ml; leave M25 at exit 5 or 6

Chartwell, Sir Winston Churchill's home in Kent

Opening arrangements: Chartwell										
House/garden	19 Mar - 3 Jul 03	11 - 5	M	T	**W**	**T**	**F**	**S**	**S**	
	5 Jul - 31 Aug	11 - 5	M	**T**	**W**	**T**	**F**	**S**	**S**	
	1 Sep - 30 Oct	11 - 5	M	T	**W**	**T**	**F**	**S**	**S**	
Restaurant	2 Mar - 18 Mar	10:30 - 4	M	T	**W**	**T**	**F**	**S**	**S**	
	19 Mar - 3 Jul	10:30 - 5	M	T	**W**	**T**	**F**	**S**	**S**	
	5 Jul - 31 Aug	10:30 - 5	M	**T**	**W**	**T**	**F**	**S**	**S**	
	1 Sep - 30 Oct	10:30 - 5	M	T	**W**	**T**	**F**	**S**	**S**	
	2 Nov - 23 Dec	10:30 - 4	M	T	**W**	**T**	**F**	**S**	**S**	
Shop	2 Mar - 18 Mar	11 - 4	M	T	**W**	**T**	**F**	**S**	**S**	
	19 Mar - 3 Jul	11 - 5:30	M	T	**W**	**T**	**F**	**S**	**S**	
	5 Jul - 31 Aug	11 - 5:30	M	**T**	**W**	**T**	**F**	**S**	**S**	
	1 Sep - 30 Oct	11 - 5:30	M	T	**W**	**T**	**F**	**S**	**S**	
	2 Nov - 23 Dec	11 - 4	M	T	**W**	**T**	**F**	**S**	**S**	
Car park	All year	9 - 5:30	**M**	**T**	**W**	**T**	**F**	**S**	**S**	

Admission by timed ticket which should be purchased immediately on arrival but cannot be pre-booked. Open BH Mons. Last admission 45mins before closing. Car park closes 5:30 or dusk if earlier and is closed on 25 Dec

P Free parking, 250yds. Year-round opening (except 25 Dec) for countryside access; gates locked at 5.30 or dusk if earlier. Coach park and disabled parking adjacent to main car park

NT properties nearby
Emmetts Garden, Ightham Mote, Knole, Quebec House, Toys Hill

Chastleton House

Chastleton, nr Moreton-in-Marsh, Oxfordshire GL56 0SU

| 🏠 | ❖ | 1991 |

(2:C3)

One of England's finest and most complete Jacobean houses

Chastleton House is filled not only with a mixture of rare and everyday objects, furniture and textiles collected since its completion in 1612, but also with the atmosphere of 400 years of continuous occupation by one family. The gardens have a typical Elizabethan and Jacobean layout with a ring of fascinating topiary at their heart and it was here in 1865 that the rules of modern croquet were codified. Since acquiring the property, the Trust has concentrated on conserving it rather than restoring it to a pristine state.

⭐ As Chastleton House is relatively fragile and the access roads are quiet and narrow, the maximum number of visitors is restricted to 175 a day. Admission is by timed ticket. Tickets can be reserved in advance by contacting the NT box office. No same day telephone bookings. Visitors not booked are admitted on first come, first served basis. Groups of 10 or more must book in advance. The largest vehicles that can be accommodated are 25-seater, 7.5m long minicoaches. There is no shop or tea-room

i **T/F** 01608 674355,
01494 755560 (Infoline),
01494 755585 (Box office)
E chastleton@nationaltrust.org.uk

£ £6, child £3, family £15

🚶 Out-of-hours guided 'Private View' Wed morning at 10, NT members £2.50, non-members £7.50; booking essential

♿ Separate designated parking, 30yds. Please enquire at main car park for directions. Drop-off point. **Building**: Many steps to entrance. 1 wheelchair. Stairs to other floors. Photograph album. **WCs**: Adapted WC

👁 Braille guide. Sensory list

🅿 In car park

👶 Pushchairs and baby back-carriers admitted. Hip-carrying infant seats for loan

🎒 Family activity packs

→ [163: SP248291] **Cycle**: Cycles can be hired from Country Lanes at Moreton-in-Marsh station, Easter to 30 Sept (tel. 01608 650065). **Station**: Moreton-in-Marsh 4ml. **Road**: 6ml from Stow-on-the-Wold. Approach only from A436 between A44 (W of Chipping Norton) and Stow

Opening arrangements: Chastleton House									
23 Mar - 1 Oct	1 - 5	M	T	**W**	**T**	**F**	**S**	S	
5 Oct - 29 Oct	1 - 4	M	T	**W**	**T**	**F**	**S**	S	

Admission by timed ticket – booking recommended. Last admission 1hr before closing. To book advance tickets tel. box office Mon to Fri 9.30–4 or write to NT box office, PO Box 180, High Wycombe, Bucks HP14 4XT

There are special events at most Trust properties; please telephone 0870 458 4000 for details

The east front of Chastleton House, Oxfordshire

P Free parking, 270yds. Return walk to car park includes a short but steep hill. Sensible shoes recommended

NT properties nearby
Hidcote Manor Garden, Lodge Park & Sherborne Estate, Snowshill Manor, Stowe Landscape Gardens, Upton House

Clandon Park

West Clandon, Guildford, Surrey GU4 7RQ

🏠 🐾 ❖ 🗋 💼 ♠ ⛃ 1956　　　　　　(2:F6)

Grand 18th-century Palladian mansion

Built c.1730 by the Venetian architect Giacomo Leoni, Clandon is notable for its magnificent two-storeyed Marble Hall. The house is filled with the superb collection of 18th-century furniture, porcelain, textiles and carpets acquired in the 1920s by the connoisseur Mrs David Gubbay, and also contains the Ivo Forde Meissen collection of Italian comedy figures and a series of Mortlake tapestries. The attractive gardens contain a parterre, grotto, sunken Dutch garden and a Maori meeting house with a fascinating history.

What's new in 2005 The Visitors' Room is open for reading and relaxation, and will also be the venue for special events. Tel. for details

★ The Queen's Royal Surrey Regiment Museum (tel. 01483 223419) is based at Clandon Park and open to visitors the same days as the house 12–5 (free entry)

i **T** 01483 222482,
01483 225971 (Infoline),
01483 224912 (Weddings/Functions),
01483 211412 (Shop),
01483 222502 (Restaurant)
F 01483 223479
E clandonpark@nationaltrust.org.uk

£ £6, child £3, family £15. Groups £5.
Combined ticket with Hatchlands Park:
£9, child £4.50, family £22.50

🚍 Booked coach groups welcome Tues, Wed & Thur and after 2 on Sun. Morning guided tours (extra charge) and introductory talks (free); booking essential for both

🎭 Programme of events, inc. concerts in the Marble Hall. Tel. for details

♿ Separate designated parking. Drop-off point. **Building**: Many steps to entrance with handrail, stairlift available. Booking advisable. 3 wheelchairs. Stairs to other floors. Seating available. **WCs**: Adapted WC. **Grounds**: Partly accessible, some steps, ramp available. **Shop**: Level entrance. **Refreshments**: Level entrance

👓 Braille guide and large-print guide. Sensory list

🍴 Licensed restaurant (not NT). Advance booking for lunch advisable on Sun, essential for December, for waitress service. Light refreshments and lunches also available on Sun. Children's menu

Opening arrangements: Clandon Park											
House	13 Mar - 30 Oct	11 - 5	M	**T**	**W**	**T**	F	**S**	**S**
Museum	13 Mar - 30 Oct	12 - 5	M	**T**	**W**	**T**	F	**S**	**S**
Garden	As house								
Shop	6 Mar	12 - 4	M	T	W	T	F	**S**	**S**
	13 Mar - 30 Oct	12 - 5	M	**T**	**W**	**T**	F	**S**	**S**
	1 Nov - 30 Nov	12 - 4	M	**T**	**W**	**T**	F	**S**	**S**
	1 Dec - 22 Dec	12 - 4	**M**	**T**	**W**	**T**	F	**S**	**S**
Restaurant	6 Mar	10:30 - 5:30	M	T	W	T	F	**S**	**S**
	13 Mar - 30 Nov	10:30 - 5:30	M	**T**	**W**	**T**	F	**S**	**S**
	1 Dec - 22 Dec	10:30 - 5:30	**M**	**T**	**W**	**T**	F	**S**	**S**
Open BH Mons, Good Fri and Easter Sat									

🅰 In grounds and gardens, tables in car park area

🧍 Baby-changing and feeding facilities. Front-carrying baby slings and hip-carrying infant seats for loan. Pushchairs allowed in house Tues, Wed & Thur

🖼 Children's quiz/trail

🐕 in car park area only, on leads

➡ [186: TQ042512] **Bus**: Countryliner 478/9, Guildford–Epsom (passing ≋ Leatherhead and close ≋ Guildford); 463 Guildford–≋ Woking (passing ≋ Clandon); Surrey Hills Explorer NT2 weekends April–Oct only from ≋ Dorking or Arriva 36/7 from close ≋ Guildford, alight Park Lane roundabout, then ½ml walk to west gate of park. **Station**: Clandon 1ml. **Road**: At West Clandon on A247, 3ml E of Guildford; if using A3 follow signposts to Ripley to join A247 via B2215

🅿 Free parking, 300yds

NT properties nearby
Box Hill, Claremont Landscape Garden, Hatchlands Park, Leith Hill, Polesden Lacey, River Wey and Dapdune Wharf

Claremont Landscape Garden

Portsmouth Road, Esher, Surrey KT10 9JG

❖ 🏠 🍴 🍸 1949   **(2:F6)**

One of the first and finest gardens of the English Landscape style

Claremont's creation and development involved some of the great names in garden history, including Sir John Vanbrugh, Charles Bridgeman, William Kent and 'Capability' Brown. The first gardens were begun c.1715 and later the delights of Claremont were famed throughout Europe. Since 1975 the Trust has been restoring this layout. The many features include a lake, island with pavilion, grotto, turf amphitheatre, viewpoints and vistas.

⭐ The house (Claremont Fancourt School) is not NT. Tel. 01372 467841 for details

ℹ **T** 01372 467806,
01372 469421 (Tea-room)
F 01372 464394
E claremont@nationaltrust.org.uk

The island temple of Belisle in Claremont Landscape Garden, Surrey

Please note: groups must book in advance with the property

Opening arrangements: Claremont

Garden	1 Apr - 28 Oct	10 - 6	**M**	**T**	**W**	**T**	**F**	S	S
	2 Apr - 30 Oct	10 - 7	M	T	W	T	F	**S**	**S**
	1 Nov - 31 Mar 06	10 - 5	M	**T**	**W**	**T**	**F**	**S**	**S**
Shop	1 Apr - 30 Oct	11 - 5	M	T	**W**	**T**	**F**	**S**	**S**
	2 Nov - 18 Dec	11 - 5	M	**T**	**W**	**T**	**F**	**S**	**S**
	15 Jan - 26 Mar 06	11 - 5	M	T	W	T	F	**S**	**S**
Tea-room	As shop								

Closes dusk if earlier. BH Mons closes at 7. Late night opening Sats 4, 11, 18, 25 June until 9; Nov to end March closes at sunset. Closed 25 Dec; and closes on major event days in July. Tel. for details. Belvedere Tower open first weekend each month April to Oct. Shop and tea-room close dusk if earlier than 5, and may close early in bad weather

£ £5, child £2.50, family £12.50. Groups £4.20, child £2.10. £1 tea-room voucher given if arriving by public transport (please present valid ticket) or cycle. No coaches on Sun or BHols.

Guided tours for booked groups (min. 15) £1 extra per person. Unbooked tours 1st and 3rd Sat, 2nd Wed and last Sun of each month from April to Oct, 2pm at entrance kiosk

Programme of events, inc. open-air concerts. Send s.a.e. for details

Designated parking in main car park, 10yds. **WCs**: Adapted WC. **Grounds**: Partly accessible, steep slopes. Accessible route map. **Shop**: Level entrance. **Refreshments**: Level entrance. Large-print menu

Braille guide and large-print guide. Interesting scents

Pierre's Kitchen. Children's menu

Accessible areas except outside tea-room

Baby-changing facilities. Pushchairs admitted

Suitable for school groups. Children's quiz/trail

On leads and only Nov to end March (under review)

→ [187: TQ128634] **Bus**: Tellings-Golden Miller 515 Kingston–Guildford (passing close Esher). **Station**: Esher 2ml; Hersham 2ml; Claygate 2ml. **Road**: On S edge of Esher, on E side of A307 (no access from Esher bypass)

P Free parking. Located at entrance

NT properties nearby
Clandon Park, Ham House, Hatchlands Park, The Homewood, Polesden Lacey, River Wey and Dapdune Wharf

Claydon House

Middle Claydon, nr Buckingham, Buckinghamshire MK18 2EY

🏠 ✝ 🍴 📷 🍽 1956 **(2:D3)**

House famous for its 18th-century rococo interiors

The extraordinary architecture of Claydon House includes extravagant rococo and chinoiserie decoration. Features of the house include the unique Chinese Room and parquetry Grand Stairs. In continuous occupation by the Verney family for over 380 years, the house has mementoes of their relation Florence Nightingale, who was a regular visitor.

What's new in 2005 Florence Nightingale's carriage on display

⭐ All Saints' Church (not NT) in the grounds is also open to the public. Evensong at 4pm: 15 May, 19 June, 17 July, 21 Aug

ℹ **T** 01296 730349, 01494 755561 (Infoline) **F** 01296 738511 **E** claydon@nationaltrust.org.uk

£ £5, child £2.50, family £12.50. Groups £4.20. **Garden only**: £1.10. (Guided tour 50p extra pp)

Programme of events. Tel. 01494 755572 for details or send s.a.e. to NT Box office, PO Box 180, High Wycombe, Bucks HP14 4XT

Half-price admission for visitors unable to climb stairs. Drop-off point. **Building**: Steps to entrance, ramp available. 2 wheelchairs, booking essential. Ground floor accessible. Seating available. Photograph album. **WCs**: Adapted WC. Ramped access. **Grounds**: Accessible route. **Refreshments**: Ramped entrance. Large-print menu

Braille guide. Sensory list. Handling collection

Parking in National Trust car parks is free for members

◨ Carriage House Restaurant (not NT) (licensed) **privately owned**. Tel. 01296 730004 for details. Open same days as house, 12–6. Picnic hampers available. Children's menu

▐ Baby-changing facilities. Front-carrying baby slings and hip-carrying infant seats for loan

▐ Suitable for school groups. Family guide. Children's guide. Children's quiz/trail

▐ On leads and only in park

➔ [165: SP720253] **Cycle**: NCN51. **Bus**: Red Rose 17 from Aylesbury (passing close ◉ Aylesbury). **Road**: In Middle Claydon 13ml NW of Aylesbury, 4ml SW of Winslow; signposted from A413 & A41 (M40 exit 9 12ml); entrance by N drive only

▐**P**▐ Free parking

NT properties nearby
Long Crendon Courthouse, Stowe Landscape Gardens, Waddesdon Manor

Opening arrangements: Claydon House										
House	26 Mar - 30 Oct	1 - 5	**M**	**T**	**W**	T	F	**S**	**S**
Grounds	As house									

Secondhand bookshop: 1–5. Leaflets available in French, German and Spanish. Pottery (not NT), open as house

The house and formal parterre, Cliveden, Buckinghamshire

Cliveden

Taplow, Maidenhead, Buckinghamshire SL6 0JA

▐🏠▐ ▐✿▐ ▐♦▐ ▐🗂▐ ▐◨▐ ▐1942▐   **(2:E5)**

Grade I listed garden, extensive woodlands and Italianate mansion

This spectacular estate overlooking the River Thames has a series of gardens, each with its own character, featuring topiary, statuary, water gardens, a formal parterre, Octagon temple, informal vistas, woodland and riverside walks. The present house, the third on the site, was built by Charles Barry for the Duke of Sutherland in 1851. Once the home of Nancy, Lady Astor, it is now let as an hotel and is open only on certain days.

What's new in 2005 The Tortoise Fountain and steps restored. New interpretation panels

⭐ No WC at woodlands

ℹ️ **T** 01628 605069, 01494 755562 (Infoline), 01628 665946 (Shop), 01628 661406 (Restaurant) **F** 01628 669461 **E** cliveden@nationaltrust.org.uk

💷 **Grounds**: £7, child £3.50, family £17.50. Groups £6. **Woodlands**: £3, child £1.50, family £7.50. House: £1 extra, child 50p. **Note**: Mooring charge on Cliveden Reach (£2 up to 4hrs; £6 per 24hrs, season ticket £30; inc. NT members) does not include entry fee to Cliveden. Tickets from River Warden. Mooring at suitable locations for more than ½ml downstream from Cliveden boathouse

🎭 Programme of events, inc. concerts, open-air theatre, children's theatre, throughout season

♿ Separate designated parking. Drop-off point. **Building**: Level entrance. 3 wheelchairs. Ground floor has steps, alternative route available. **WCs**: Adapted WC. **Grounds**: Accessible route map. 1 single-seater PMV, 3 multi-seater PMV, booking essential. **Shop**: Level entrance. **Refreshments**: Level entrance

🔊 Induction loop in reception and Film studio and house

👓 Braille guide and large-print guide. Sensory list

Please remember – your membership card is always needed for free admission

Opening arrangements: Cliveden

Estate & garden	16 Mar - 30 Oct	11 - 6	**M**	**T**	**W**	**T**	**F**	**S**	**S**
	31 Oct - 22 Dec	11 - 4	**M**	**T**	**W**	**T**	**F**	**S**	**S**
House (part)	3 Apr - 30 Oct	3 - 5:30	M	T	**W**	T	F	S	**S**
Restaurant	16 Mar - 30 Oct	11 - 5	**M**	**T**	**W**	**T**	**F**	**S**	**S**
	6 Nov - 18 Dec	11 - 3	M	T	W	T	F	**S**	**S**
Woodlands	1 Apr - 30 Oct	11 - 5:30	**M**	**T**	**W**	**T**	**F**	**S**	**S**
	31 Oct - 22 Dec	11 - 4	**M**	**T**	**W**	**T**	**F**	**S**	**S**
	3 Jan - 31 Mar 06	11 - 4	**M**	**T**	**W**	**T**	**F**	**S**	**S**
Octagon temple	As house									
Shop	16 Mar - 30 Oct	12 - 5:30	**M**	**T**	**W**	**T**	**F**	**S**	**S**
	31 Oct - 22 Dec	12 - 4	**M**	**T**	**W**	**T**	**F**	**S**	**S**

Admission to house is limited and by timed ticket obtainable from information kiosk only. Some areas of formal garden may be roped off when ground conditions bad

[icon] Licensed restaurant. Children's menu. Kiosk in main car park

[icon] Three picnic areas. No picnics or barbecues in formal gardens

[icon] Baby-changing facilities. All-terrain buggies for hire

[icon] Children's guide. Audio-visual guide in Gas Yard

[icon] Under close control and only in specified woodlands (not in formal gardens)

[icon] [175: SU915851] **Bus**: No bus service. **Station**: Bourne End 2ml; Taplow (not Sun) 2½ml; Burnham 3ml. **Road**: 2ml N of Taplow; leave M4 at exit 7 onto A4, or M40 at exit 4 onto A404 to Marlow and follow brown signs. Entrance by main gates opposite Feathers Inn

[icon] Parking

NT properties nearby
Greys Court, Hughenden Manor, West Wycombe Park

Emmetts Garden

Ide Hill, Sevenoaks, Kent TN14 6AY

[icons] 1965   (2:G6)

Charming Victorian garden with year-round interest

Influenced by William Robinson, this delightful informal garden – with the highest treetop in

Kent – was laid out in the late 19th century, with many exotic and rare trees and shrubs from across the world. While there are glorious shows of spring flowers and shrubs, a rose garden and rock garden, Emmetts is equally attractive for its spectacular views at all times and for its autumn colours.

[icon] The house is privately occupied and not open to visitors. WC only available when garden is open

[icon] **T** 01732 750367 (Head Gardener), 01732 751509 (Infoline), 01732 868381 (Chartwell office) (Booking) **F** 01732 750490 **E** emmetts@nationaltrust.org.uk

[icon] £4, child £1, family £9. Groups £3.50. **Adult ticket inc. guidebook**: £6.50

[icon] By prior arrangement. Group booking pack available

[icon] Programme of events, inc. family picnic days

[icon] Separate designated parking, 100yds. Wheelchair-accessible transfer. **WCs**: Adapted WC. **Grounds**: Partly accessible, steep slopes, uneven paths. Accessible route. Some doubling back required. **Caution: sheer drop at end of shrub garden**. **Shop**: Ramped entrance. **Refreshments**: Ramped entrance. Large-print menu

[icon] Braille guide and large-print guide. Interesting scents

[icon] NT shop. Plant sales

[icon] Stable tea-room in former stable block

[icon] In designated areas

[icon] Baby-changing facilities. Pushchairs and baby back-carriers admitted

[icon] Suitable for school groups. Children's quiz/trail

[icon] On short leads only

Opening arrangements: Emmetts Garden

Garden	19 Mar - 31 May	11 - 5	M	**T**	**W**	**T**	**F**	**S**	**S**
	1 Jun - 3 Jul	11 - 5	M	T	**W**	**T**	**F**	**S**	**S**
	6 Jul - 30 Oct	11 - 5	M	T	**W**	T	F	**S**	**S**
Shop	As garden									
Tea-room	As garden									
Open BH Mons. Last admission 45mins before closing										

→ [188: TQ477524] **Foot**: From Ide Hill (½ml). Weardale walk from Chartwell (3ml) – guide leaflet available. **Bus**: Kent Passenger Services 404 from ⇌ Sevenoaks, Mon–Fri only, alight Ide Hill, 1½ml. **Station**: Sevenoaks 4½ml; Penshurst (U) 5½ml. **Road**: 1½ml S of A25 on Sundridge to Ide Hill road, 1½ml N of Ide Hill off B2042, leave M25 at exit 5, then 4ml

P Free parking, 100yds

NT properties nearby
Chartwell, Ightham Mote, Knole, Quebec House, Toys Hill

Great Coxwell Barn

Great Coxwell, Faringdon, Oxfordshire

 1956
(2:C4)

13th-century stone barn

This large monastic barn has a stone-tiled roof and interesting timber structure.

★ No WC

i **T** 01793 762209 (Coleshill Estate office)
E greatcoxwellbarn@nationaltrust.org.uk

£ £1

⊛ Braille guide

▧ Suitable for school groups

🐾 On leads only

→ [163: SU269940] **Bus**: Stagecoach in Swindon 65/6 Swindon–Oxford (passing close ⇌ Swindon & passing ⇌ Oxford), alight Great Coxwell Turn, ¾ml. **Station**: Swindon 10ml. **Road**: 2ml SW of Faringdon between A420 and B4019

P Limited parking in roadside lay-by

NT properties nearby
Ashdown House, Buscot Park, Coleshill Estate, including Badbury Hill, White Horse Hill, Uffington Castle & Dragon Hill

Opening arrangements: Great Coxwell Barn								
All year	Early–dusk	**M**	**T**	**W**	**T**	**F**	**S**	**S**

Greys Court

Rotherfield Greys, Henley-on-Thames, Oxfordshire RG9 4PG

🏠 🏠 ✿ 🗄 ☕ 🍴 1969
(2:E5)

Intriguing house with a tranquil garden

This picturesque house, mainly Tudor in style, has a beautiful courtyard and one surviving tower dating from 1347. The house has an interesting history and was involved in Jacobean court intrigue. It has been the home of the Brunner family since the 1930s and the interior, with some outstanding 18th-century plasterwork, is still furnished as a family home. Outside are a Tudor wheelhouse, walled gardens full of old-fashioned roses and wisteria, an ornamental vegetable garden, maze and ice-house.

i **T** 01491 628529, 01494 755564 (Infoline), 01491 628145 (Gardens), 01494 755572 (Events) **F** 01491 628935
E greyscourt@nationaltrust.org.uk

£ £5.20, child £2.60, family £13. **Garden only**: £3.70, child £1.80, family £9.20. Free cup of tea for those arriving by public transport or cycle, and coach drivers

🎋 Gardens only

🎪 Programme of events. Tel. for details

🚶 Estate walk leaflet available at ticket kiosk

♿ Separate designated parking, 5yds. Drop-off point. **Building**: Steps to entrance with handrail, ramp available. 1 wheelchair, booking essential. Photograph album. **WCs**: Adapted WC. **Grounds**: Partly accessible, loose gravel paths, slopes. **Shop**: Steps to entrance. Spiral staircase. **Refreshments**: Steps to entrance, ramp available

⊛ Braille guide

🗄 Book and card shop

☕ Tea-room in Cromwellian stables

🅿 In car park only

🚼 Baby-changing facilities. Pushchairs in gardens only

▧ Children's quiz/trail

Please see the area introductions for details of coast & countryside properties

Opening arrangements: Greys Court										
House	28 Mar - 30 Sep	2 - 5	M	T	**W**	**T**	**F**	S	S
Garden	2 Mar - 23 Mar	2 - 5:30	M	T	**W**	T	**F**	S	S
	28 Mar - 30 Sep	2 - 5:30	M	**T**	**W**	**T**	**F**	S	S
	5 Oct - 26 Oct	2 - 5:30	M	T	**W**	T	**F**	S	S
Tea-room	As garden								

Open BH Mons (inc. 28 Mar): house 2–5, gardens & tea-room 2–5:30. House also open first Sat of the month 9 April–3 Sep, 2–5

🐕 On leads and only in car park and on footpaths around the estate

➔ [175: SU725834] **Bus**: White's 145 from Henley-on-Thames town hall (4 min. walk from ⊠ Henley-on-Thames). Alight Greys Green and follow signed footpath to Greys Court (approx ¼ml). **Station**: Henley-on-Thames 3ml. **Road**: W of Henley-on-Thames. From Nettlebed mini-roundabout on A4130 take B481 and property is signed to the left after approx 3ml. There is also a direct (unsigned) route from Henley-on-Thames town centre. Follow signs to Badgemore Golf Club towards Peppard, approx 3ml out of Henley

P Free parking, 220yds

NT properties nearby
Basildon Park, Cliveden, Hughenden Manor

Hatchlands Park

East Clandon, Guildford, Surrey GU4 7RT

 1945 (2:F6)

18th-century mansion with Adam interiors and collection of keyboard instruments, set in parkland

Built in the 1750s for Admiral Boscawen, hero of the Battle of Louisburg, Hatchlands is set in a beautiful 170ha (430-acre) Repton park, offering a variety of waymarked walks. The house contains the earliest recorded decorations in an English country house by Robert Adam, whose ceilings here appropriately feature nautical motifs. On display is the Cobbe Collection, the world's largest group of keyboard instruments associated with famous composers such as Purcell, J. C. Bach, Chopin, Mahler and Elgar.

Hatchlands House, Surrey. In the foreground is a statue of a classical boatman, an appropriate image for a house built by Admiral Boscawen

There is also a small garden by Gertrude Jekyll, flowering from late May to early July and a stunning bluebell wood in May.

What's new in 2005 New walks; dog walkers welcome in the parkland this year; Stable exhibition: *The People of Hatchlands*

ℹ️ **T** 01483 222482, 01483 225971 (Infoline), 01483 224523 (Shop), 01483 211120 (Restaurant) **F** 01483 223176 **E** hatchlands@nationaltrust.org.uk

£ £6, child £3, family £15. Groups £5. **Park walks only**: £3, child £1.50. **Combined ticket with Clandon Park**: £9, child £4.50, family £22.50

🎧 No guided tours, but audio tour of house and keyboard instruments for hire (Standard and Basic Language versions) £2 (inc. NT members)

🎭 Programme of events. Tel. for details. For Cobbe Collection Trust concerts tel. 01483 211474 or see www.cobbecollection.co.uk

♿ Designated parking in main car park, 300yds. Transfer available. **Building**: Ramped entrance. 3 wheelchairs. **WCs**: Adapted WC. **Grounds**: Partly accessible. Accessible route. **Shop**: Level entrance. **Refreshments**: Level entrance

♒ Braille guide. Sensory list

Unless indicated, last admission is always 30mins before closing time

Opening arrangements: Hatchlands Park										
House	27 Mar - 31 Jul	2 - 5:30	M	T	W	T	F	S	S	
	2 Aug - 31 Aug	2 - 5:30	M	T	W	T	F	S	S	
	1 Sep - 30 Oct	2 - 5:30	M	T	W	T	F	S	S	
Park walks	1 Apr - 30 Oct	11 - 6	M	T	W	T	F	S	S	
Shop	As house	1 - 5								
Restaurant	As house	11 - 5								
Open BH Mons										

🍽 Licensed restaurant (not NT). Busy for lunch on Wed concert days. Children's menu

🚼 Baby-changing facilities. Front-carrying baby slings and hip-carrying infant seats for loan

🎪 Children's quiz/trail

🐕 Dogs under close control welcome in specified parkland areas for this year

→ [187: TQ063516] **Bus**: Countryliner 478/9 Guildford–Epsom (passing ≋ Leatherhead and close ≋ Guildford); Surrey Hills Explorer NT2 weekends April–Oct only from ≋ Dorking. **Station**: Clandon 2ml, Horsley 2½ml. **Road**: E of East Clandon, N of A246 Guildford–Leatherhead road

P Free parking, 300yds

NT properties nearby
Box Hill, Clandon Park, Leith Hill, Polesden Lacey, River Wey and Dapdune Wharf

Hindhead Commons & The Devil's Punch Bowl Café

London Road, Hindhead, Surrey GU26 6AB

🏔 🍽 🐕 1906 (2:E7)

The gateway to the Surrey Hills, with fine views

Local people, visitors from further afield and those journeying along the A3 can all enjoy the stunning scenery of the Devil's Punch Bowl and Hindhead Commons from the viewpoint 50yds from the café.

ℹ️ **T** 01428 608771 **F** 01428 608767

🧍 Maps and local walks leaflets on sale

♿ Designated parking in main car park, 20yds. **WCs**: Adapted WC. **Refreshments**: Level entrance

🍽 Devil's Punch Bowl Café. Selection of hot and cold food available. Children's menu

🚼 Baby-changing facilities

→ [133: SU895356] Beside A3, at Hindhead, near crossroads with A287. **Bus**: Stagecoach in Hants & Surrey 18/19; 71 ≋ Haslemere–≋ Aldershot. **Station**: Haslemere 3ml

P Parking, £1.50 (pay & display). NT members must display cards. Charges apply after the first hour. No lorries. Coach parties by arrangement

NT properties nearby
Ludshott Common & Waggoners' Wells, Oakhurst Cottage, Winkworth Arboretum, The Witley Centre

Opening arrangements: Hindhead Commons									
Commons	All year		M	T	W	T	F	S	S
Café	1 Apr - 31 Oct	9 - 5	M	T	W	T	F	S	S
	1 Nov - 31 Mar 06	9 - 4	M	T	W	T	F	S	S
Café closes dusk if earlier. Closed 25, 26 Dec and 1 Jan									

Hinton Ampner Garden

Bramdean, nr Alresford, Hampshire SO24 0LA

🏠 ❖ 🍽 🧍 1986 (2:D7)

One of the great gardens of the 20th century

A masterpiece of design by Ralph Dutton, 8th and last Lord Sherborne, the 5ha (12-acre) garden unites a formal layout with varied and informal plantings in pastel shades. There are magnificent vistas over 32ha (80 acres) of parkland and rolling Hampshire countryside. The house, which is tenanted, contains Ralph Dutton's fine collection of Regency furniture, Italian paintings and hardstone items.

ℹ️ **T** 01962 771305 **F** 01962 793101
E hintonampner@nationaltrust.org.uk

£ £6, child £3. **Garden only**: £5, child £2.50

♿ Separate designated parking.
Building: Ramped entrance. 4 wheelchairs. Ground floor accessible. Seating available.

There are special events at most Trust properties; please telephone 0870 458 4000 for details

Opening arrangements: Hinton Ampner Garden

Garden	20 Mar	12 - 5	M	T	W	T	F	S	**S**
	26 Mar - 28 Sep	12 - 5	**M**	**T**	**W**	T	F	**S**	**S**
House	29 Mar - 27 Jul	1:30 - 5	M	**T**	**W**	T	F	S	S
	2 Aug - 31 Aug	1:30 - 5	M	**T**	**W**	T	F	**S**	**S**
	6 Sep - 28 Sep	1:30 - 5	M	**T**	**W**	T	F	S	S
Tea-room	As garden								

WCs: Adapted WC. **Grounds**: Fully accessible. Accessible route map. **Refreshments**: Ramped entrance

Braille guide and large-print guide. Sensory list

Small tea-room

In grass car park only

Baby-changing facilities. No baby-feeding facilities

Children's quiz/trail

→ [185: SU597275] **Bus**: Stagecoach in Hampshire 67 Winchester–Petersfield (passing close Winchester & passing Petersfield). **Station**: Winchester 9ml, Alresford (Mid-Hants Railway) 4ml. **Road**: On A272, 1ml W of Bramdean village, 8ml E of Winchester, leave M3 at exit 9 and follow signs to Petersfield

P Free parking. Special entrance for coaches. Map indicating where coaches can park will be sent with confirmation of booking

NT properties nearby
Mottisfont Abbey, Uppark, The Vyne, Winchester City Mill

Hughenden Manor

High Wycombe, Buckinghamshire HP14 4LA

 1947 (2:E4)

Home of the Victorian statesman Benjamin Disraeli

Queen Victoria's trusted prime minister Benjamin Disraeli lived here from 1848 until his death in 1881. Most of his furniture, books and pictures remain in this, his private retreat from the rigours of parliamentary life in London. There are beautiful walks through the surrounding park and woodland, and the garden is a recreation of the colourful design of Disraeli's wife, Mary Anne.

★ Certain rooms have little electric light. Visitors wishing to make a close study of the interior of the house should avoid dull days early and late in the season

i **T** 01494 755573, 01494 755565 (Infoline), 01494 755596 (Learning), 01494 755572 (Box office), 01494 755575 (Shop), 01494 755576 (Restaurant) **F** 01494 474284 **E** hughenden@nationaltrust.org.uk

£ £5, child £2.50, family £12.50. Groups £4.20, child £2.10, group visits outside normal hours £10. **Garden only**: £1.80, child 90p. **Park & woodland**: Free. Reduced rate when arriving by public transport

Guided and out-of-hours tours for booked groups on Wed, Thur & Fri only

Separate designated parking, 110yds. Drop-off point. **Building**: Level entrance. 3 wheelchairs. Stairs to other floors. Seating available. Photograph album. **WCs**: Adapted WC. **Grounds**: Partly accessible, loose gravel paths. Access to terrace for view of garden. Some visitors may require assistance from their companion. **Shop**: Level entrance. **Refreshments**: Level entrance

Braille guide and large-print guide. Sensory list

NT shop. Plant sales in stableyard

Licensed restaurant in stableyard. Also available for private bookings, Christmas lunches and winter events. Children's menu

In orchard

Opening arrangements: Hughenden Manor

House	5 Mar - 27 Mar	1 - 5	M	T	W	T	F	**S**	**S**
	30 Mar - 30 Oct	1 - 5	M	T	**W**	**T**	**F**	**S**	**S**
Garden	5 Mar - 27 Mar	12 - 5	M	T	W	T	F	**S**	**S**
	30 Mar - 30 Oct	12 - 5	M	T	**W**	**T**	F	**S**	**S**
Park	All year		**M**	**T**	**W**	**T**	**F**	**S**	**S**
Shop	5 Mar - 30 Oct	As garden							
	31 Oct - 18 Dec	11 - 4	**M**	**T**	**W**	**T**	**F**	**S**	**S**
Restaurant	5 Mar - 30 Oct	As garden							
	5 Nov - 18 Dec	11 - 4	M	T	W	T	F	**S**	**S**

Admission by timed ticket on Sun, BHols & other busy days. Open BH Mons and Good Fri [baby-changing] Baby-changing facilities. Front-carrying baby slings and hip-carrying infant seats for loan. All-terrain buggy for outdoors for loan

[school] Suitable for school groups. Education room/centre. Live interpretation. Hands-on activities. Children's guide

[dog] Under close control and only in park and woodland; shaded parking; dog rings in stable yard

➔ [165: SU866955] **Bus**: Arriva 323/4 High Wycombe–Aylesbury (passing close ⭢ High Wycombe). **Note**: Long and steep walk to house entrance. **Station**: High Wycombe 2ml. **Road**: 1½ml N of High Wycombe; on W side of the Great Missenden road (A4128)

P Free parking, 200yds. Parking space for only one coach; overflow car park 400yds

NT properties nearby
Bradenham, Claydon House, Cliveden, King's Head, Waddesdon Manor, West Wycombe Park

---

Ightham Mote

Ivy Hatch, Sevenoaks, Kent TN15 0NT

🏠✝️❄️🦅📷💼 1985   (2:H6)

Superb 14th-century moated manor house

Nestling in a sunken valley and dating from 1320, the house has features spanning many centuries. These include the Great Hall, Old Chapel, crypt, Tudor chapel with painted ceiling, drawing room with Jacobean fireplace, frieze and 18th-century wallpaper, and billiards room. The recently opened South West Quarter includes the apartment of Charles Henry Robinson, the American donor of the house. There is an extensive garden and interesting walks in the surrounding woodland. A comprehensive programme of repair begun in 1989 was completed in 2004 and is the subject of a 'Conservation in Action' exhibition in the ticket office.

What's new in 2005 20th anniversary of the acquisition of the property by the NT and completion of 15 years of conservation work. See NT website for events celebrating 'IM20'

ℹ️ **T** 01732 810378, 01732 811145 (Infoline), 01732 811203 (Shop), 01732 811314 (Restaurant) **F** 01732 811029 **E** ighthammote@nationaltrust.org.uk

£ £7, child £3.50, family £17.50. Groups £6, child £3

[talks] Free introductory talks. Regular garden tours. Booked special guided tours for groups of 15+ on open weekday mornings only

[events] Programme of events, inc. NGS Day and plant sale, 16 June. Tel. for details

[walks] Occasional guided walks. Estate walks leaflet obtainable from ticket office

Ightham Mote and gardens, Kent

Opening arrangements: Ightham Mote

House	18 Mar - 30 Oct	10:30 - 5:30	M	T	W	T	F	S	S
Garden	18 Mar - 30 Oct	10 - 5:30	M	T	W	T	F	S	S
Estate	All year	Dawn–dusk	M	T	W	T	F	S	S
Restaurant	3 Mar - 12 Mar	11 - 3	M	T	W	T	F	S	S
	18 Mar - 30 Oct	10 - 5:30	M	T	W	T	F	S	S
	3 Nov - 23 Dec	11 - 3	M	T	W	T	F	S	S
Shop	As restaurant								

'Putting the house to bed' 3 & 4 Nov. Tel for details. Restaurant open for occasional themed Fri and Sat evenings and for pre-booked functions. Please tel. for opening times of restaurant and shop outside normal property hours. Booking at restaurant advised in winter and evenings. Thur–Sat 3 Nov–23 Dec (also Suns in Dec): restaurant open for booked lunches

♿ Contact in advance. Separate designated parking, 10yds. 87yds to accessible entrance. Drop-off point. **Building**: Level entrance. Alternative accessible entrance. 3 wheelchairs. Ground floor has steps, ramp available. Stairs to other floors. Seating available. Photograph album, virtual tour. Conservation exhibition at ticket office accessible. **WCs**: Adapted WC. **Grounds**: Partly accessible, slopes, some cobbles. Accessible route map. **Shop**: Level entrance. Stairs to upper floor. **Refreshments**: Level entrance. Large-print menu

♻ Induction loop in restaurant

⚀ Braille guide and large-print guide. Sensory list

☕ Mote Restaurant (licensed). Children's menu. Tea-wagon in car park open on busy days

🗾 At picnic area in car park only

👶 Baby-changing facilities. Front-carrying baby slings and hip-carrying infant seats for loan

■ Suitable for school groups. Education room/centre. Family guide. Children's guide. Children's quiz/trail. Children's activity packs. Adult study days

🐶 Only on estate walks

🚲 On surrounding 223ha (550-acre) estate

→ [188: TQ584535] **Bus**: Kent Passenger Service 404 from ⏭ Sevenoaks, calls Wed only, or on other days alight Ivy Hatch, ¾ml; New Enterprise 222 ⏭ Tonbridge–Borough Green, alight Fairlawne, ½ml (footpath); otherwise Arriva 306/8 ⏭ Sevenoaks–Gravesend (passing ⏭ Borough Green), alight

Ightham Common, 1½ml. **Station**: Borough Green & Wrotham 3 ml; Hildenborough 4ml. **Road**: Exit 2 off M20 to Borough Green and A25, then follow brown signs. Exit 5 off M25 to A25 (follow Maidstone signs, not Sevenoaks)

P Free parking, 200yds

NT properties nearby
Chartwell, Knole, Old Soar Manor, Toys Hill

King's Head

King's Head Passage, Market Square, Aylesbury, Buckinghamshire HP20 2RW

🏠 🍺 🚶 ☕ 🍸 1925   **(2:E3)**

Ancient coaching inn

This restored and still operating inn dates from 1455 and is of particular interest for its architectural features from many eras, including a large stained-glass window, cobbled courtyard and timber framing.

What's new in 2005 Interpretation centre; bookshop & coffee shop in Great Hall; arts centre open by end of year

⭐ The King's Head has full conference facilities. Tel. for details or a brochure

ℹ **T** 01296 381501 (Office), 01296 718812 (Pub) **F** 01296 381502 **E** kingshead@nationaltrust.org.uk

£ **Tour**: £2.10. Tel. to book

🛡 Re-enactments; outdoor theatre; beer festivals

♿ **Building**: Steps to entrance. Ground floor accessible. Stairs to other floors. Seating available. **WCs**: Adapted WC. **Grounds**: Partly accessible, some cobbles, uneven paths. Some visitors may require assistance from their companion

⚀ Touchable objects and interesting sounds

👶 Baby-changing facilities. Pushchairs and baby back-carriers admitted

Opening arrangements: King's Head

All year	Licensing hrs	M	T	W	T	F	S	S

Closed BH Mons. Tours available Wed, Fri, Sat at 2

Parking in National Trust car parks is free for members

▥ Suitable for school groups. Education room/centre. Hands-on activities. Adult study days

➔ [165: SP818138] At top of Market square. Access through cobbled lane. **Bus**: from surrounding areas. **Station**: Aylesbury 400yds

P No parking on site. Car parks in town centre (not NT)

NT properties nearby
Boarstall Duck Decoy, Boarstall Tower, Claydon House, Long Crendon Courthouse, Waddesdon Manor

Knole

Sevenoaks, Kent TN15 0RP

▦ ❄ ♠ ⎙ ▣ 1946 　　　　　　　　　 (2:H6)

One of the great treasure houses of England, set in a magnificent deer park

Knole's fascinating historic links with kings, queens and the nobility, as well as its literary connections with Vita Sackville-West and Virginia Woolf, make this one of the most intriguing houses in England. Thirteen superb state rooms are laid out much the same as they were in the 17th century to impress visitors by the wealth and standing of those living there. The house includes rare furniture, paintings by Gainsborough, Van Dyck and Reynolds, as well as many 17th-century tapestries. Knole is set at the heart of the only remaining medieval deer park in Kent.

What's new in 2005 This year Lord Sackville has kindly agreed to open the family garden (10.5ha/26 acres) at Knole every Wednesday in the season. Exclusive guided tours of house for booked groups on Wednesday, Friday and Saturday, before opening to the public. Family days – first three Tuesdays of August

⭐ Please do not feed the deer; they can be dangerous. In order too protect Knole's fragile and rare textiles, light of all kinds is carefully controlled. This restricts opening hours of the showrooms – last entry 3.30pm

ℹ️ **T** 01732 462100, 01732 450608 (Infoline), 01732 467155 (Learning), 01732 743748 (Shop), 01732 741762 (Tea-room)
F 01732 465528
E knole@nationaltrust.org.uk

£ £6.40, child £3.20, family £16. Groups £5.50, child £2.75. **Garden (note limited opening)**: £2, child £1. Park free to pedestrians

🛡 Guided tours and private tours by prior arrangement

🎭 Programme of events, inc. concerts in the Great Hall, Easter trails

🚶 Deer park has pedestrian access all year round

♿ Separate designated parking, 30yds. Drop-off point. **Building**: Ramped entrance. 2 wheelchairs. Ground floor has steps. 1 step in Great Hall. Stairs with handrail to other floors. All showrooms (other than Great Hall) are on the first floor. Seating available. Virtual tour. **WCs**: Adapted WC. **Grounds**: Partly accessible, steep slopes. **Shop**: Ramped entrance. **Refreshments**: Level entrance. Large-print menu

📡 Induction loop in reception

👁 Braille guide and large-print guide. Sensory list

⎙ NT shop. Also open during events

▣ Brewhouse Tea-room. Children's menu

🚼 Baby-changing facilities. Front-carrying baby slings and hip-carrying infant seats for loan

▥ Suitable for school groups. Education room/centre. Hands-on activities. Children's quiz/trail. Family activity packs

🐕 On leads and only in park

🚲 Permits required – obtained through Knole Estates, Knole, Sevenoaks TN15 0RP

Opening arrangements: Knole										
House	19 Mar - 30 Oct	12 - 4	M	T	**W**	**T**	**F**	**S**	**S**
Shop	19 Mar - 30 Oct	10:30 - 5	M	T	**W**	**T**	**F**	**S**	**S**
Christmas shop	2 Nov - 18 Dec	11 - 4	M	T	**W**	**T**	**F**	**S**	**S**
Tea-room	As shop								
Garden	23 Mar - 26 Oct	11 - 4	M	T	**W**	T	F	S	S

Open BH Mons (house, shop and tea-room). Park: open daily for pedestrians. Vehicles admitted only when house is open. Garden: open by courtesy of Lord Sackville – please note limited opening

Please remember – your membership card is always needed for free admission

[188: TQ532543] **Bus**: From surrounding area to Sevenoaks, $\frac{3}{4}$ml walk. **Station**: Sevenoaks 1$\frac{1}{2}$ml. **Road**: Leave M25 at exit 5 (A21). Park entrance in Sevenoaks town centre off A225 Tonbridge Road (opposite St Nicholas' Church)

Parking, 60yds, £2.50. In the 'open season' park is open to vehicles from 10.15am. Park gates locked at 6pm. Park not accessible to vehicles on days when house is closed – parking available in nearby town centre

NT properties nearby

Chartwell, Emmetts Garden, Ightham Mote

Leith Hill

c/o Pond Cottage, Broadmoor, Dorking, Surrey RH5 6JZ

1923 **(2:F6)**

Woodland and open heath with Leith Hill Tower commanding extensive views

The highest point in south-east England, the hill is crowned by an 18th-century Gothic tower, with panoramic views northwards to London and the English Channel to the south. There are colourful displays of rhododendrons and bluebells in May and June. Rugged countryside provides exhilarating walking in woodland and over heathland and farmland.

What's new in 2005 New nature trail guide. New tables and benches at Tower picnic area. Etherley Farm campsite, tel. 01306 621423 for details

No WC

T 01306 711777, 01306 742809 (Learning), 01306 712434 (Tea-room)
F 01306 712153

Tower: £1, child 50p

Guided walks throughout the year. Groups by arrangement with the Warden

2 circular trails – guide available from dispenser £1

Building: Spiral stone staircase.
Grounds: Partly accessible. Accessible paths in Rhododendron Wood

Opening arrangements: Leith Hill			
Tower	18 Mar - 31 Jul	10 - 5	M T W T **F S S**
	3 Aug - 31 Aug	10 - 5	M T **W** T **F S S**
	2 Sep - 30 Oct	10 - 5	M T W T **F S S**
	5 Nov - 12 Nov	10 - 3:30	M T W T F **S S**
Wood & estate	All year		**M T W T F S S**
Open all BHols. Closed 25 Dec (Tower)			

Servery (not NT) at Leith Hill Tower. Light refreshments when tower open. May close early in bad weather

Picnic areas beside tower and in Rhododendron Wood

Suitable for school groups. Information room and telescope in the tower

On leads in Rhododendron Wood, not in tower

[187: TQ139432] **Foot**: Comprehensive network of rights of way including the Greensand Way National Trail. **Cycle**: Many rights of way lead to the tower. **Bus**: Arriva 21 Guildford–Dorking (passing close Guildford and passing Chilworth and Dorking), alight Holmbury St Mary, 2$\frac{1}{2}$ml. **Station**: Holmwood (U), not Sun, 2$\frac{1}{2}$ml; Dorking 5$\frac{1}{2}$ml. **Road**: 1ml SW of Coldharbour A29/B2126

Free parking in designated areas along road at foot of the hill, some steep gradients to the tower. No direct vehicle access to summit. Rhododendron Wood £2 per car.

NT properties nearby

Box Hill, Clandon Park, Hatchlands Park, Polesden Lacey, Ranmore Common

Tower at Leith Hill, Surrey

Long Crendon Courthouse

Long Crendon, Aylesbury, Buckinghamshire
HP18 9AN

[🏠 1900]   (2:D4)

Early 15th-century two-storeyed building

Set in an attractive village, this building with its timbered, whitewashed and tiled façade was probably first used as a wool store. It is a fine example of early timber frame construction. Manorial courts were held here from the reign of Henry V until Victorian times. The ground floor (now tenanted) was the village poor house.

⭐ No WC

ℹ️ **T** 01280 822850 (enquiries Mon–Fri)

💷 £1, child 50p

♿ **Building**: Steps to entrance

➔ [165: SP698091] **Bus**: Arriva 260/1, Aylesbury–Oxford (passing ➱ Haddenham & Thame Parkway). **Station**: Haddenham & Thame Parkway 2ml by footpath, 4ml by road. **Road**: 2ml N of Thame, via B4011, close to the church

🅿️ Limited on-street parking (not NT)

NT properties nearby
King's Head

Opening arrangements: Long Crendon Courthouse			M	T	W	T	F	S	S
Upper floor only	23 Mar - 28 Sep	2 - 6	M	T	**W**	T	F	S	S
	19 Mar - 25 Sep	11 - 6	M	T	W	T	F	**S**	**S**
Open BH Mons 11–6									

Mottisfont Abbey Garden, House & Estate

Mottisfont, nr Romsey, Hampshire SO51 0LP

[🏠 🏠 ❖ ⚓ 🏛 💷 🚩 🔺 🍽 1957]   (2:C7)

Historic and atmospheric riverside estate

Set amidst glorious countryside along the River Test, this 12th-century Augustinian priory was converted into a private house after the Dissolution of the Monasteries, and still retains the spring or 'font' from which its name is derived. The abbey contains a drawing room decorated by Rex Whistler and Derek Hill's 20th-century picture collection, but the key attraction is the grounds with magnificent trees, walled gardens and National Collection of Old-fashioned Roses, at their best in mid-June. The estate includes Mottisfont village and surrounding farmland and woods.

What's new in 2005 Special events and a small exhibition to celebrate the life of Rex Whistler

⭐ As the roses are renowned for their scent, please do not smoke in the walled garden during the rose season. To appreciate the roses evening viewing is recommended. On certain Sats some rooms in the house may not be open due to private functions

ℹ️ **T** 01794 340757, 01794 341220 (Infoline), 020 8332 6644 (Functions, inc. weddings), 01794 341901 (Shop)
F 01794 341492
E mottisfontabbey@nationaltrust.org.uk

💷 £7, child £3.50, family £17.50. Group discount, rate on application

🚶 7ml estate path (leaflet £1), access from main car park (open 9–6)

♿ Designated parking in main car park, 200yds. Transfer available. **Building**: Ramped entrance. 6 wheelchairs. Ground floor accessible. Audio visual/video, photograph album. **WCs**: Adapted WC. **Grounds**: Accessible route. Staff-driven multi-seater vehicle. **Shop**: Ramped entrance. **Refreshments**: Level entrance. Large-print menu

Opening arrangements: Mottisfont Abbey			M	T	W	T	F	S	S
Garden	5 Feb - 20 Mar	11 - 4	M	T	W	T	F	**S**	**S**
	21 Mar - 1 Jun	11 - 6	**M**	**T**	**W**	T	F	**S**	**S**
	4 Jun - 26 Jun	11 - 8:30	**M**	**T**	**W**	**T**	**F**	**S**	**S**
	27 Jun - 31 Aug	11 - 6	**M**	**T**	**W**	**T**	F	**S**	**S**
	3 Sep - 30 Oct	11 - 6	**M**	**T**	**W**	T	F	**S**	**S**
House	21 Mar - 1 Jun	11 - 5	**M**	**T**	**W**	T	F	**S**	**S**
	4 Jun - 26 Jun	11 - 5	**M**	**T**	**W**	**T**	**F**	**S**	**S**
	27 Jun - 31 Aug	11 - 5	**M**	**T**	**W**	**T**	F	**S**	**S**
	3 Sep - 30 Oct	11 - 5	**M**	**T**	**W**	T	F	**S**	**S**
Shop	As garden *								
Kitchen café	As house **	11 - 5							

Open Good Fri 11–5. Last admission 1hr before closing. * Shop not open 5 Feb–20 Mar. ** Kitchen café last orders 5pm

Please see the area introductions for details of coast & countryside properties

Rosa 'Constance Spry', part of the National Collection of Old-fashioned Roses at Mottisfont Abbey, Hampshire

Braille guide. Interesting scents

NT Shop. Secondhand bookshop. Plant sales

Kitchen Café (licensed) at E entrance to house. Children's menu. Kiosk outside rose garden available to meet demand

Not on formal lawns or in rose garden

Baby-changing facilities. Pushchairs admitted. Hip-carrying infant seats for loan

Children's quiz/trail. Children's activity packs. Presentations on film about the estate and rose garden

Only in car park on lead. Dogs welcome in Spearywell Wood and Great Copse under close supervision

[185: SU327270] In the Test Valley between Romsey and Stockbridge. **Foot**: Situated on Hampshire's long distance path, Testway. Clarendon Way passes 2ml to the N. **Cycle**: On Testway. **Station**: Dunbridge (U) ¾ml. **Road**: Signposted off A3057 Romsey to Stockbridge, 4½ml N of Romsey. Also signposted off B3087 Romsey to Broughton

Free parking

NT properties nearby
Hinton Ampner Garden, Mompesson House, Winchester City Mill

Mottistone Manor Garden

The Gardener, Manor Cottage, Hoxall Lane, Mottistone, Isle of Wight PO30 4ED

1965   (2:D9)

20th-century garden with views to the sea

The garden is noted for its colourful herbaceous borders, grassy terraces planted with fruit trees and its views. The 16th- and 17th-century manor house, which is tenanted, lies at the heart of the Mottistone Estate, which offers delightful walks between the Downs and the coast.

What's new in 2005 SeaBritain exhibition in the barn celebrating dramatic lifeboat rescues and local heroes

T 01983 741302

£3, child £1.50, family £7.50. Group discount

Programme of events, inc. open-air concerts

Many trails across surrounding estate

Designated parking in main car park. Drop-off point. **WCs**: Adapted WC. **Grounds**: steep slopes. Some visitors may require assistance from their companion. **Refreshments**: Level entrance

Plant sales

Tea-garden (NT-approved concession). Serving hot and cold snacks (covered area)

Baby-changing facilities. Pushchairs and baby back-carriers admitted

Children's quiz/trail

On leads only

[196: SZ406838] **Cycle**: On the 'Round the Island' cycle route. **Ferry**: Yarmouth (Wightlink Ltd) 6ml (tel. 0870 582 7744); E Cowes (Red Funnel) 12ml (tel. 0870 444 8898). **Bus**: Southern Vectis 7B Newport–Alum Bay. **Road**: At Mottistone, 2ml W of Brighstone on B3399

Free parking, 50yds

NT properties nearby
Brighstone Shop & Museum, Needles Old Battery

Opening arrangements: Mottistone Manor Garden									
Garden	20 Mar - 30 Oct	11 - 5:30	**M**	**T**	**W**	**T**	F	S	**S**

Closes dusk if earlier. House open Aug BH Mon only, 2–5.30. Guided tours for NT members on that day, 10–12

Unless indicated, last admission is always 30mins before closing time

The Needles Old Battery

West Highdown, Totland, Isle of Wight PO39 0JH

 1975 **(2:C9)**

Victorian gun battery perched on the tip of the Isle of Wight

The threat of a French invasion prompted the construction in 1862 of this spectacularly sited fort, which now contains exhibitions about the Battery's involvement in the First and Second World Wars and the Headland's intriguing past as a secret rocket testing site. The Battery retains two of its original gun barrels, and the laboratory and position-finding cells have been restored. A 60yd tunnel leads to dramatic views of The Needles rocks and the Dorset coastline beyond.

What's new in 2005 Exhibition depicting shipwrecks off The Needles rocks; Headland Visitor Point with refreshments kiosk and information on the NT's work on the Isle of Wight

★ No WC or seating for refreshments at the Headland Visitor Point. No vehicle access to · Battery (visitors with disabilities by arrangement). Many paths are steep and not suitable for people with walking difficulties. Access to the searchlight is by narrow spiral staircase, with further steps to tea-room and headland beyond the Battery

ℹ️ **T** 01983 754772, 01983 756473 (Needles Headland Visitor Point)

£ £3.80, child £1.90, family (2 adults and their children 5–17) £8.50

♿ Contact in advance. Designated parking in main car park. Parking space is limited. **Building**: Level entrance. Ground floor accessible. Seating available. Audio visual/video. **WCs**: Adapted WC. **Grounds**: Partly accessible, steep slopes, some steps, uneven paths. **Refreshments**: Many steps to entrance with handrail. Downstairs seating area

Opening arrangements: The Needles Old Battery										
Battery	20 Mar - 30 Jun	10:30 - 5	**M**	**T**	**W**	**T**	F	**S**	**S**	
	1 Jul - 31 Aug	10:30 - 5	**M**	**T**	**W**	**T**	**F**	**S**	**S**	
	1 Sep - 30 Oct	10:30 - 5	**M**	**T**	**W**	**T**	F	**S**	**S**	
Tea-room	As Battery	10:30 - 4:30								

Open Good Fri. Property closes in bad weather; tel. on day of visit to check

A war-time illustration at the Needles Old Battery, Isle of Wight

◈ Sensory list. Taped guide is available

☕ Tea-room. Spectacular views. Kiosk at Needles Headland. No seating available

👶 Baby-changing and feeding facilities. Pushchairs and baby back-carriers admitted

▥ Suitable for school groups. Children's activity packs. Children's exhibition on 'The Needles at War' and cartoon information boards explaining how the Battery functioned. From 1 April to 1 Nov (but not Aug) school groups can be conducted by a NT guide, by arrangement. Charge applies

🐕 On leads only

➜ [196: SZ300848] **Foot**: Access is on foot only – from Alum Bay 15 mins, High Down NT car park 45 mins, Freshwater Bay 1½hrs. **Ferry**: Yarmouth (Wightlink Ltd) 5ml (tel. 0870 582 7744); E Cowes (Red Funnel) 16ml (tel. 0870 444 8898). **Bus**: Southern Vectis 42 Yarmouth–Needles Battery, April to Oct only; otherwise any service to Alum Bay, then 1ml. **Road**: At Needles Headland, W of Freshwater Bay and Alum Bay (B3322)

🅿 No parking on site. Parking Alum Bay (not NT; minimum £3), or in Freshwater Bay (IOW Council) or Highdown car park (NT) and walk over Downs (or see bus services above)

NT properties nearby
Mottistone Manor Garden, Old Town Hall, Newtown, Tennyson Down

There are special events at most Trust properties; please telephone 0870 458 4000 for details

Nymans Garden

Handcross, nr Haywards Heath, West Sussex
RH17 6EB

🏠 ✄ 🍴 🏠 🍵 🕴 ⊤ 1954   (2:G7)

Great Sussex Weald garden with historic collection of plants

Developed in the 20th century by three generations of the Messel family, Nymans Garden still retains much of its distinctive family style in the historic collection of plants, shrubs and trees. This is reflected also in the surrounding estate, with its woodland walks and wild garden, and in the many rare and exotic species collected from overseas. The Messel family rooms are open during the main season and here too, in the library, drawing room and dining room, their creativity is much in evidence.

What's new in 2005 Interactive virtual tour of garden and estate, showing the garden in all seasons and with information on plants and history; tactile map

ℹ️ **T** 01444 400321 (General enquiries & wheelchair booking),
01444 405250 (Office),
01444 400157 (Shop),
01444 400161 (Restaurant)
F 01444 405254
E nymans@nationaltrust.org.uk

£ £6.70, child £3.30, family £16.70. Groups £5.70, child £2.80. **Joint ticket with same-day entry to Standen (Wed to Fri):** £10, child £5. **Winter weekends:** £3.30, child £1.60, family £8

🎭 Wed & Sat 11.30 & 2.15. Winter Sat 11.30. Please tel. office for confirmation

🎪 Programme of events, inc. lecture lunches, summer evening suppers & garden tours, Easter trail, croquet days, bat walk, 'Art in the Garden' days. Send s.a.e. for details

♿ Designated parking in main car park, 50yds. Drop-off point. **Building**: Steps to entrance. Alternative accessible entrance. 7 wheelchairs, booking essential. Ground floor has steps, ramp available. Virtual tour. **WCs**: Adapted WC. **Grounds**: Partly accessible, slopes. Accessible route map.

Opening arrangements: Nymans Garden										
Garden	16 Feb - 30 Oct	11 - 6	M	T	**W**	**T**	**F**	**S**	**S**
Garden (winter)	5 Nov - 12 Feb 06	11 - 4	M	T	W	T	F	**S**	**S**
House	16 Mar - 30 Oct	11 - 5	M	T	**W**	**T**	**F**	**S**	**S**
Shop	16 Feb - 27 Nov	11 - 6	M	T	**W**	**T**	**F**	**S**	**S**
Christmas shop	28 Nov - 24 Dec	11 - 4	**M**	**T**	**W**	**T**	**F**	**S**	**S**
Shop	7 Jan - 12 Feb 06	11 - 4	M	T	W	T	F	**S**	**S**
Restaurant	16 Feb - 27 Nov	11 - 5	M	T	**W**	**T**	**F**	**S**	**S**
	29 Nov - 23 Dec	11 - 4	M	**T**	**W**	**T**	**F**	**S**	**S**
	7 Jan - 12 Feb 06	11 - 4	M	T	W	T	F	**S**	**S**

Open BH Mons. We regret that on BHols and weekends in spring and summer admission may be restricted if garden is too full. Closed 25 & 31 Dec and 1 Jan 2006. Shop and garden close at dusk if earlier. In winter access to some areas is limited

Some doubling back required. Some visitors may require assistance from their companion. 1 single-seater PMV, booking essential.
Shop: Level entrance. **Refreshments**: Level entrance. Large-print menu

👁 Braille guide and large-print guide. Sensory list. Handling collection. Tactile map and audio guide

🏠 NT shop. Plant sales

☕ Licensed restaurant. Winter warmer specials Nov–end Feb. Christmas lunches Dec. Children's menu. Kiosk. Open weather permitting

⛱ In Pinetum area only

👶 Baby-changing facilities. Pushchairs and baby back-carriers admitted. Hip-carrying infant seats for loan

🏫 Suitable for school groups. Children's quiz/trail

🐕 Only in woods or car park. Must be on leads

➡️ [187: TQ265294] **Bus**: Metrobus 273 Brighton–Crawley, 271 Haywards Heath–Crawley. Both pass 🚃 Crawley.
Station: Balcombe 4½ml; Crawley 5½ml.
Road: On B2114 at Handcross, 4¼mi S of Crawley, just off London–Brighton M23/A23

P Free parking, 15yds. Space for 3 coaches only

NT properties nearby
Devil's Dyke & Saddlescombe Farm, Sheffield Park Garden, Standen, Wakehurst Place

For further information check our website www.nationaltrust.org.uk

Oakhurst Cottage

Hambledon, nr Godalming, Surrey GU8 4HF

🏚 1952   (2:F7)

Small 16th-century timber-framed cottage

Restored and furnished as a simple labourer's dwelling, the cottage contains fascinating artefacts reflecting four centuries of continuing occupation. The delightful garden contains typical Victorian plants.

⭐ No WC

ℹ️ **T** 01483 208477 (Winkworth Arboretum for bookings and information)
F 01483 208252
E oakhurstcottage@nationaltrust.org.uk

💷 £4, child £2. Price inc. guided tour. Schools and groups by arrangement any day or evening

🏃 All visits include a 45-min guided tour

♿ Contact in advance. Separate designated parking, 50yds. Drop-off point.
Building: Ground floor has steps. Many stairs with handrail to other floors. Photograph album. **Grounds**: Fully accessible

👆 Braille guide

🏛 Children's quiz/trail

➡️ [186: SU965380] **Bus**: Countryliner 503 from Godalming (Wed only); otherwise Stagecoach in Hants & Surrey 71 Guildford–Hindhead (passes close ⇌ Godalming), alight Lane End 1ml. **Station**: Witley 1½ml. **Road**: Off A283 between Wormley and Chiddingfold

🅿️ Parking (not NT), 200yds. (Outside post office)

NT properties nearby
Petworth, Winkworth Arboretum, The Witley Centre

Opening arrangements: Oakhurst Cottage								
23 Mar - 30 Oct	2 - 5	M	T	W	T	F	S	S

Admission by guided tour and appointment only. Open BH Mons 2–5. Please book at least 24 hours in advance

Old Soar Manor

Plaxtol, Borough Green, Kent TN15 0QX

🏚 1947   (2:H6)

Remains of a late 13th-century knight's dwelling

This is all that is left of the manor house of c.1290 which stood here until the 18th century. The solar chamber over a barrel-vaulted undercroft was once inhabited by a medieval knight.

⭐ No WC

ℹ️ **T** 01732 810378 (Ightham Mote), 01732 811145 (Infoline)

💷 Admission free. Not suitable for groups

🏛 Exhibition on Manor and surrounding areas

➡️ [188: TQ619541] **Bus**: New Enterprise 222 ⇌ Tonbridge–⇌ Borough Green; Kent Passenger Service 404 from ⇌ Sevenoaks. On both alight E end of Plaxtol, then ¾ml by footpath. **Station**: Borough Green & Wrotham 2½ml. **Road**: 2ml S of Borough Green (A25); approached via A227 and Plaxtol; narrow lane

🅿️ No parking on site. Not suitable for coaches

NT properties nearby
Chartwell, Ightham Mote, Knole, Toys Hill

Opening arrangements: Old Soar Manor								
2 Apr - 29 Sep	10 - 6	M	T	W	T	F	S	S

Old Town Hall, Newtown

c/o The Custodian, Ken Cottage, Upper Lane, Brighstone, Isle of Wight PO30 4AT

🏚 1933   (2:C9)

17th-century town hall with a fascinating history

The small, now tranquil, village of Newtown once sent two members to Parliament and the Town Hall was the setting for often turbulent elections. An exhibition depicts the exploits of 'Ferguson's Gang', an anonymous group of Trust benefactors in the 1920s and 1930s.

What's new in 2005 SeaBritain exhibition about the local salt and brick industry

Please note: groups must book in advance with the property

⭐ No WC. Nearest WC in car park

ℹ️ **T** 01983 531785

💷 £1.80, child 90p, family £4.50

📷 By written appointment

♿ **Building**: Many steps to entrance with handrail. Stairs to other floors. **WCs**: Adapted WC nearby

📖 Braille guide

👶 Baby back-carriers admitted. Pushchairs admitted if visitor numbers allow

🏫 Suitable for school groups

➡️ [196: SZ424905] **Ferry**: Yarmouth (Wightlink Ltd) 5ml (tel. 0870 582 7744); E Cowes (Red Funnel) 11ml (tel. 0870 444 8898). **Bus**: Southern Vectis 35, 47 from Newport; otherwise 7 Ryde Esplanade–Freshwater (passing Yarmouth Ferry Terminal), alight Barton's Corner, 1ml. **Road**: Newtown is between Newport and Yarmouth, 1ml N of A3054

🅿️ Free parking, 15yds. Not suitable for coaches

NT properties nearby
Brighstone Shop & Museum, Mottistone Manor Garden, The Needles Old Battery

Opening arrangements: Old Town Hall, Newtown								
20 Mar - 29 Jun	2 - 5	M	T	W	T	F	S	S
3 Jul - 31 Aug	2 - 5	M	T	W	T	F	S	S
4 Sep - 26 Oct	2 - 5	M	T	W	T	F	S	S
Open Good Fri and Easter Sat. Last admission 15mins before closing								

Petworth House & Park

Petworth, West Sussex GU28 0AE

🏛️🌳🏠💼🎧🎪🍽️ 1947   **(2:F7)**

Magnificent country house and park with an internationally important art collection

The vast late 17th-century mansion is set in a beautiful park, landscaped by 'Capability' Brown and immortalised in Turner's paintings. The house contains the Trust's finest and largest collection of pictures, with numerous works by Turner, Van Dyck, Reynolds and Blake, as well as ancient and neo-classical sculpture, fine

Family portraits and paintings by Turner in the Carved Room, Petworth, West Sussex

furniture and carvings by Grinling Gibbons. The Servants' Quarters contain fascinating kitchens (including a splendid copper *batterie de cuisine* of over 1000 pieces) and other service rooms. On weekdays additional rooms in the house are open to visitors by kind permission of Lord and Lady Egremont (see over).

What's new in 2005 Ten-minute 'Welcome to Petworth' introductory talks on the house and grounds on weekdays when house is open. The Estate Office, once central to the running of a great estate, opens to the public for the first time following extensive conservation work. Continued progress on the 'Capability' Brown-inspired Pleasure Ground redevelopment

ℹ️ **T** 01798 342207, 01798 343929 (Infoline), 01798 344975 (Shop/Restaurant), 01798 344976 (Learning) **F** 01798 342963 **E** petworth@nationaltrust.org.uk

💷 £7.50, child £4, family £19. Groups £6.50. **Pleasure Ground only**: £2, child £1

📷 Guided tours for groups and school visits by arrangement; tel. for details

📅 Programme of events, inc. open-air concerts, family events, lecture lunches, 'behind the scenes' tours and Christmas events. Send s.a.e. for details

Parking in National Trust car parks is free for members

Opening arrangements: Petworth			M	T	W	T	F	S	S
House	19 Mar - 30 Oct	11 - 5	M	T	W	T	F	S	S
Shop	5 Mar - 16 Mar	12 - 4	M	T	W	T	F	S	S
	19 Mar - 30 Oct	11 - 5	M	T	W	T*F		S	S
	2 Nov - 17 Dec	10 - 3:30	M	T	W	T	F	S	S
	18 Dec - 21 Dec	10 - 3:30	M	T	W	T	F	S	S
Restaurant	As shop								
Park	All year	8 - Dusk	M	T	W	T	F	S	S
Pleasure Grnd	5 Mar - 16 Mar	12 - 4	M	T	W	T	F	S	S
	19 Mar - 30 Oct	11 - 6	M	T	W	T	F	S	S
	2 Nov - 17 Dec	10 - 3:30	M	T	W	T	F	S	S

Open Good Fri. **Please note**: Extra rooms shown weekdays (but not BH Mons) as follows: Mon, White & Gold Room and White Library; Tues & Wed, three bedrooms on first floor. Park: closed afternoons of open-air concerts

[⟰] Pleasure Ground: spring bulbs guided walks 6 & 20 March, autumn guided walks in October; tours throughout the year

[♿] Designated parking in main car park, 800yds. Limited designated parking at Church Lodge entrance (next to Servants' Quarters). Initial slope from car park to house quite steep. Transfer available. Drop-off point. **Building**: Ramped entrance. 5 wheelchairs. Ground floor accessible. 7 steps to chapel. Stairs to other floors. Seating available. Photograph album, virtual tour. **WCs**: Adapted WC. **Grounds**: Partly accessible. Pleasure grounds gently undulating. Path surfaces good. **Shop**: Level entrance. **Refreshments**: Steps to entrance with handrail, lift available. Large-print menu

[🔊] Induction loop in reception

[♨] Braille guide and large-print guide. Sensory list

[🛍] NT shop. Plant sales

[🍽] Licensed restaurant. Mother"s Day lunches 6 March and Christmas lunches by arrangement. Children's menu

[🚼] Baby-changing facilities

[🏫] Suitable for school groups. Education room/centre. Hands-on activities. Children's quiz/trail. Family activity packs. Adult study days. Teachers' resource books, education service. Foreign language guides

[❌] Under close control and only in park (not in Pleasure Ground)

[→] [197: SU976218] **Bus**: Stagecoach in the South Downs 1 Worthing–Midhurst (passing ≣ Pulborough); Compass 76 Horsham–Petworth (passing ≣ Horsham). **Station**: Pulborough 5¼ml. **Road**: In centre of Petworth (A272/A283); car parks for house and park on A283; pedestrian access from Petworth town and from A272. No vehicles in park

[P] Free parking, 800yds. Coaches can drop off at Church Lodge entrance and park in main car park

NT properties nearby
Black Down, Oakhurst Cottage, Uppark, Winkworth Arboretum

Polesden Lacey

Great Bookham, nr Dorking, Surrey RH5 6BD

[🏠][✳][♣][📷][💷][📷][⟰] 1944 **(2:F6)**

House with opulent Edwardian interiors, set in beautiful downland countryside

In an exceptional setting on the North Downs this Regency house was extensively remodelled in 1906–9 by the Hon. Mrs Ronald Greville, a well-known Edwardian hostess. Her collection of fine paintings, furniture, porcelain and silver is displayed in the reception rooms and galleries, as it was at the time of her celebrated house parties. There are extensive grounds, a walled rose garden, lawns and landscape walks through part of the 560ha (1400-acre) estate. The future King George VI and Queen Elizabeth spent part of their honeymoon here in 1923.

What's new in 2005 Children's adventure trail and play area

[i] **T** 01372 452048, 01372 458203 (Infoline), 01372 457230 (Shop), 01372 456190 (Tearoom) **F** 01372 452023
E polesdenlacey@nationaltrust.org.uk

[£] £8, child £4, family £20. Groups £6.50. **Grounds only**: £5, child £2.50, family £12.50. Croquet lawns and equipment for hire from house (book in advance)

[𝐼] Tours of garden and grounds by volunteer guides on most days. Special tours of house for booked groups only at additional charge

---

Please remember – your membership card is always needed for free admission

Opening arrangements: Polesden Lacey

House	16 Mar - 6 Nov	11 - 5	M	T	**W**	**T**	**F**	**S**	**S**
Garden	All year	11 - 6	**M**	**T**	**W**	**T**	**F**	**S**	**S**
Shop	21 Mar - 6 Nov	11 - 5	**M**	**T**	**W**	**T**	**F**	**S**	**S**
	9 Nov - 4 Dec	11 - 3	M	T	**W**	**T**	**F**	**S**	**S**
	5 Dec - 23 Dec	11 - 3	**M**	**T**	**W**	**T**	**F**	**S**	**S**
	18 Jan - 22 Mar 06	11 - 3	M	T	**W**	**T**	**F**	**S**	**S**
Tea-room	As shop								

Open BH Mons 11 - 5. Garden: closes dusk if earlier

🎭 Programme of events, inc. summer open-air festival. Tel. for details

♿ Separate designated parking, 100yds. **Building**: Ramped entrance. 3 wheelchairs, booking essential. Ground floor accessible. Seating available. Photograph album. **WCs**: Adapted WC. **Grounds**: Partly accessible, loose gravel paths. Accessible route map. 2 single-seater PMV, booking essential. **Shop**: Level entrance. **Refreshments**: Ramped entrance

👆 Braille guide. Sensory list. Handling collection

🛍 NT shop. Plant sales

☕ Licensed tea-room. Limited menu on Mon & Tues in main season. Also in Jan–March & Nov–Dec. Booked Christmas lunches 7–9, 12–16 & 19–21 Dec

👶 Baby-changing facilities. Front-carrying baby slings and hip-carrying infant seats for loan. Children's play area

🖼 Children's quiz/trail. Children's activity packs

🐕 Under very close control in grounds and on landscape walks, not in formal gardens

🚲 Public bridleway alongside Polesden Lacey and across Ranmore Common gives shared access for cyclists

➔ [187: TQ136522] **Foot**: North Downs Way within ⅜ml. **Bus**: Surrey Hills Explorer NT1/2 weekends April–Oct only ➤ Dorking–Polesden Lacey; Countryliner 478 from Guildford, Mon–Fri, Aug only; otherwise Tellings-Golden Miller 465 ➤ Dorking–➤ Surbiton, alight near Gt Bookham, 1½ml. **Station**: Boxhill & Westhumble 2ml by scenic path through NT park. **Road**: 5ml NW of Dorking, 2ml S of Gt Bookham, off A246 Leatherhead–Guildford road

P Free parking, 200yds

NT properties nearby
Box Hill, Clandon Park, Hatchlands Park, River Wey and Dapdune Wharf

River Wey & Godalming Navigations and Dapdune Wharf

Navigations Office and Dapdune Wharf, Wharf Road, Guildford, Surrey GU1 4RR

🏠 ♿ 🛍 🎁 ☕ 🚻 ☕ 1964 **(2:F6)**

Tranquil waterway running for nearly twenty miles through the heart of Surrey

The Wey was one of the first British rivers to be made navigable, and opened to barge traffic in 1653. This 15½ml waterway linked Guildford to Weybridge on the Thames, and then to London. The Godalming Navigation, opened in 1764, enabled barges to work a further 4ml upriver. The visitor centre at Dapdune Wharf in Guildford tells the story of the Navigations and the people who lived and worked on them, through interactive exhibitions. Visitors can see where the huge Wey barges were built and climb aboard *Reliance*, one of the last to survive. Boat trips are available.

ℹ **T** 01483 561389 **F** 01483 531667
  E riverwey@nationaltrust.org.uk

£ **Dapdune Wharf**: £3.50, child £2, family £10. Groups £3, child £1.50. NT Education Group Members free. Sessions led by Education Officer and all resources available at £1 per child per session (minimum charge £40). Separate charge for river trips on electric launch trips subject to weather conditions. Charge applies to children over 1yr and NT members; max. 12 passengers. **Navigations**: the entire 19½ml towpath is open to walkers, with free moorings for visiting boats. Navigation licences (inc. all lock tolls) payable

Opening arrangements: River Wey & Dapdune Wharf

Wharf	19 Mar - 30 Oct	11 - 5	**M**	T	**W**		**T**	**F**	**S**	**S**

River trips 11–5 (conditions permitting). Access to towpath during daylight hours all year on all craft are issued for the year; visitor passes issued for up to 21 days. NT members have 10% reduction on production of current membership card for visitor passes only. There are insurance and safety requirements and restrictions on engine size to protect the property; check with Navigations Office in advance. Horse-drawn boat trips on narrow boat *Iona* (not NT) from Godalming Wharf (tel. 01483 414938); rowboats, punts, canoes and narrow boats at Farncombe Boat House (tel. 01483 421306); restaurant boats, excursion boats, rowboats and canoes at Guildford Boat House (tel. 01483 504494)

Booked guided tours of Dapdune Wharf for groups, also guided walks along the towpath

Programme of events. Tel. for details

Building: Ramped entrance at Dapdune Wharf. All areas accessible, some visitors may require assistance fom their companion. Computer. **WCs**: Adapted WC. **Shop**: Ramped entrance. **Refreshments**: Ramped entrance

Braille guide and large-print guide. Sensory list. Handling collection

Small shop run by volunteers at Dapdune

Small tea-room run by volunteers at Dapdune Wharf. Tea-room (not NT) at Farncombe Boat House. Tel. 01483 418769

Riverside picnic areas at Dapdune Wharf

Baby-changing facilities at Dapdune Wharf

Suitable for school groups. Education room/centre. Hands-on activities. Children's quiz/trail

On leads at Dapdune Wharf and within lock areas; elsewhere under control

Cyclists welcome, but the towpath is very narrow and cyclists are asked to give way to other users and to dismount in lock areas

[186: SU993502] **River**: Visiting craft can enter from the Thames at Shepperton or slipways at Guildford or Pyrford. Visitor moorings available at Dapdune Wharf and along towpath side of Navigations. **Foot**: North Downs Way crosses Navigations south of Guildford. **Bus**: Arriva 28 Guildford–Woking, Stagecoach Hants & Surrey 20 Guildford–Aldershot, Arriva 4 Guildford–Park Barn (Cricket ground, 100yds). **Station**: Addlestone, Byfleet & New Haw, Guildford, Farncombe & Godalming all close to the Navigations. **Road**: Dapdune Wharf is on Wharf Road to rear of Surrey County Cricket Ground, off Woodbridge Rd (A322), Guildford. Easy access from town centre on foot via towpath; tel. Navigations Office for details. Access to rest of Navigations from A3 & M25

Free parking at Dapdune Wharf, 10yds. Parking for the Navigations available in Godalming town centre, Catteshall Road bridge. Dapdune Wharf: Bowers Lane (Guildford), Send village, Newark Lane (B367), Pyrford Lock and New Haw Lock

NT properties nearby
Clandon Park, Claremont Landscape Garden, Hatchlands Park, Polesden Lacey, Shalford Mill, Winkworth Arboretum

Lock-keeper's cottage, River Wey Navigations, Surrey

Runnymede

c/o North Lodge, Windsor Road, Old Windsor,
Berkshire SL4 2JL

🏠📷💧🐾 1931   (2:F5)

Riverside site of the sealing of Magna Carta

Runnymede is an attractive area of riverside
meadows, grassland and broad-leaved
woodland, rich in flora and fauna, and part-
designated SSSI. It was on this site, in 1215,
that King John sealed Magna Carta, an event
commemorated by the American Bar Association
Memorial and John F. Kennedy Memorial. Also
here are the Fairhaven Lodges, designed by
Lutyens. On the opposite bank of the Thames
from Runnymede lies the important archaeological
site of Ankerwycke, an area of parkland acquired
by the National Trust in 1998, containing the
remains of the 12th-century St Mary's Priory and
the Ankerwycke Yew, a magnificent tree believed
to be over 2000 years old.

⭐ The information given below relates to the
Runnymede side of the river. WC only
available when tea-room car park is open

ℹ️ **T** 01784 432891, 01494 755572 (Box office),
01784 477110 (Tea-room) **F** 01784 479007
E runnymede@nationaltrust.org.uk

💷 Fishing: daytime fishing only by permit, all year
except 15 March to 15 June; day and season
tickets available from tea-room or river warden.
24-hr mooring, fees payable, inc. NT members

🏃 Programme of guided walks throughout the
year

📣 For event information tel. box office

🏃 Network of footpaths; map guide available

♿ Limited designated parking. **WCs**: Adapted
WC. **Refreshments**: Steps to entrance with
handrail

👁️ Braille guide

🏠 Small shop in tea-room

💧 Magna Carta Tea-room (not NT)

🚫 No barbecues

🚼 Pushchairs admitted

🚲 Cycling permitted on Thames Path

➡️ [176: TQ007720] **Foot**: 1¼ml of Thames Path
on property. **Cycle**: NCN4. **Bus**: Ankerwycke:
Ashford Coaches 305 Staines– 🚍 Wraysbury,
also First 60 🚍 Slough–🚍 Wraysbury, alight
Magna Carta Lane. Runnymede; 1¼ml from
Memorials: First 41 🚍 Egham–Old Windsor,
alight 'Bells of Ouzeley'. **Station**: Egham ⅓ml
from Runnymede, 1½ml from Memorials;
Wraysbury 1ml from Ankerwycke.
Road: Runnymede: on the Thames, 2ml W of
Runnymede Bridge, on S side of A308 (M25,
exit 13), 6ml E of Windsor. Ankerwycke: 3ml E
of Windsor, 2ml W of Staines off B376 Staines
to Wraysbury road, 1½ml from M25 (exit 13)

🅿️ Parking (pay & display). NT members must
display cards. Limited space for coaches on
hard-standing, grass surface car park closed
when wet

NT properties nearby
Claremont Landscape Garden, Cliveden, River
Wey and Dapdune Wharf

Opening arrangements: Runnymede							
All year			M	T W T F S S			
Grass riverside car park: April to 30 Sept daily when ground conditions allow, 9–7. Tea-room car park (hard-standing) April to 30 Sept, 8.30–7; Oct to 31 March, 8.30–5. Tea-room (not NT) May to end Sept: daily 8.30–5.30; Oct & Nov 9–4.30, Dec, Jan & Feb 9–4, March & April 9–5. Closed 24, 25 & 26 Dec. 1 Jan: open 11–3 (brunch menu only)							

Sandham Memorial Chapel

Harts Lane, Burghclere, nr Newbury, Hampshire
RG20 9JT

✝️📷 1947   (2:D6)

**Chapel containing Stanley Spencer's
visionary paintings**

This red-brick chapel was built in the 1920s to
house paintings by the artist Stanley Spencer,
inspired by his experiences in the First World
War. Influenced by Giotto's Arena Chapel in
Padua, Spencer took five years to complete
what is arguably his finest achievement. The
chapel is set amidst lawns and orchards with
views across Watership Down.

Unless indicated, last admission is always 30mins before closing time

⭐ As there is no lighting in the chapel, it is best to view the paintings on a bright day. No WC. Facilities nearby in pub

ℹ️ **T/F** 01635 278394
E sandham@nationaltrust.org.uk

£ £3, child £1.50

📻 Tel. for details

♿ **Building**: Steps to entrance. Alternative accessible entrance. **Grounds**: Fully accessible

👆 Braille guide and large-print guide

📖 Stanley Spencer books on sale

🍴 Refreshments 100yds away at Carpenter's Arms (not NT), 11–11. Tel. 01635 278251 *

🅰 On front lawn

👶 Pushchairs and baby back-carriers admitted

🎒 Suitable for school groups. Children's quiz/trail

🐕 On leads only

➡️ [174: SU463608] **Bus**: Cango C21/2 'demand-responsive' service from Newbury. Book on 0845 602 4135. **Station**: Newbury 4ml. **Road**: 4ml S of Newbury, ½ml E of A34

🅿️ Parking in lay-by opposite chapel, 100yds

NT properties nearby
Basildon Park, The Vyne

Opening arrangements: Sandham Memorial Chapel									
5 Mar - 20 Mar	11 - 4	M	T	W	T	F	S	S
23 Mar - 30 Oct	11 - 5	M	T	**W**	**T**	**F**	**S**	**S**
5 Nov - 27 Nov	11 - 4	M	T	W	T	F	**S**	**S**
Open BH Mons 11–5. Dec to Feb: by appointment only									

Scotney Castle Garden & Estate

Lamberhurst, Tunbridge Wells, Kent TN3 8JN

🎭 🛏 ❀ ♿ 🍴 📷 🎧 1970   **(2:H7)**

One of England's most romantic gardens, set in a beautiful wooded estate

Designed in the Picturesque style around the ruins of a 14th-century moated castle, the garden has spectacular displays of rhododendrons, azaleas and kalmia in May and June, wisteria and roses rambling over the ruins in summer, and trees and ferns providing rich colour in autumn. There are fine walks through the estate with its parkland, woodland, hop farm, and wonderful vistas and viewpoints.

ℹ️ **T** 01892 891081, 01892 893820 (Infoline), 01892 890912 (Shop) **F** 01892 890110
E scotneycastle@nationaltrust.org.uk

£ £4.80, child £2.40, family £12. Groups £4.20, child £2.10. **Estate walks**: Free

🎯 By arrangement, charges apply

📻 Programme of events. Tel. for details

📕 Estate walks guide on sale at garden entrance and shop

♿ Designated parking in main car park, 100yds. Drop-off point. **Building**: Step to entrance. 3 wheelchairs. Stairs to other floors. Photograph album. **WCs**: Adapted WC. **Grounds**: steep slopes. Accessible route map. Some visitors may require assistance from their companion. **Shop**: Level entrance

👆 Braille guide and large-print guide. Sensory list

📖 NT shop. Plant sales

🅰 In Walled Garden next to car park (no tea-room)

👶 Baby-changing facilities. Pushchairs admitted

🎒 Suitable for school groups. Children's quiz/trail

🐕 Welcome on leads on estate walks only

➡️ [188: TQ688353] **Foot**: Links to local footpath network. **Cycle**: NCN18 3ml. **Bus**: Coastal Coaches 256 Tunbridge Wells–Wadhurst (passing ➚ Tunbridge Wells), alight Lamberhurst Green, 1ml. **Station**: Wadhurst 5½ml. **Road**: 1ml S of Lamberhurst on A21

🅿️ Free parking, 130yds

NT properties nearby
Bateman's, Bodiam Castle, Sissinghurst Castle Garden

Opening arrangements: Scotney Castle									
Garden	5 Mar - 13 Mar	11 - 6	M	T	W	T	F	**S**	**S**
	18 Mar - 30 Oct	11 - 6	M	T	**W**	**T**	**F**	**S**	**S**
Old Castle	1 May - 25 Sep	11 - 6	M	T	**W**	**T**	**F**	**S**	**S**
Shop	As garden								
Estate walks	All year		**M**	**T**	**W**	**T**	**F**	**S**	**S**
Open BH Mons 11 - 6. Closed Good Fri. Last admission 1hr before closing. Closes dusk if earlier									

There are special events at most Trust properties; please telephone 0870 458 4000 for details

Autumn at Sheffield Park Garden, East Sussex

Sheffield Park Garden

Sheffield Park, East Sussex TN22 3QX

❀ ⬚ 💜 1954   **(2:G7)**

Internationally renowned landscape garden

This magnificent, informal landscape garden was laid out in the 18th century by 'Capability' Brown and further developed in the early years of the 20th century by its owner, Arthur G. Soames. The original four lakes form the centrepiece. There are dramatic shows of daffodils and bluebells in spring, and the rhododendrons, azaleas and stream garden are spectacular in early summer. Autumn brings stunning colours from the many rare trees and shrubs and winter walks can be enjoyed in this garden for all seasons.

What's new in 2005 Extended opening hours including Mondays in May and October

ℹ️ **T** 01825 790231,
01825 790302 (Booking for powered mobility vehicles), 01825 790655 (Shop)
F 01825 791264
E sheffieldpark@nationaltrust.org.uk

£ £5.50, child £2.75, family £13.75. Groups £4.70, child £2.35. Joint ticket with Bluebell Railway available. Individual RHS members free

🧍 Booked tours for groups of 10+, £1.50 per person (inc. NT members)

📅 Programme of events. Tel. for details

♿ Separate designated parking, 50yds. **Building**: Level entrance. 4 wheelchairs. **WCs**: Adapted WC. **Grounds**: Partly accessible, steep slopes. Accessible route map. 1 single-seater PMV, 2 multi-seater PMV, booking essential. **Shop**: Level entrance. **Refreshments**: Ramped entrance

♿ Braille guide and large-print guide. Interesting scents

⬚ NT shop. Plant sales

💜 Tea-room (not NT) adjoins NT car park

🔲 Picnic area adjoining car park

🧍 Baby-changing facilities. Pushchairs and baby back-carriers admitted. All-terrain pushchair and back carriers available

🔲 Children's quiz/trail. Family activity packs

🐕 On leads and only in car park

➡️ [198: TQ415240] **Bus**: Bluebell Rly link 473 from 🚉 East Grinstead to Kingscote, then train to Sheffield Park; RDH 121 from Lewes (passing close 🚉 Lewes); 246 from Uckfield (Mon–Fri only). **Station**: Sheffield Park (Bluebell preserved steam railway) 1ml; Uckfield 6ml; Haywards Heath 7ml. **Road**: Midway between East Grinstead and Lewes, 5ml NW of Uckfield, on E side of A275 (between A272 & A22)

P Free parking

NT properties nearby
Nymans Garden, Standen, Wakehurst Place

Opening arrangements: Sheffield Park Garden										
Garden	15 Feb - 30 Apr	10:30 - 6	M	T	W	T	F	S	S
	1 May - 31 May	10:30 - 6	M	T	W	T	F	S	S
	1 Jun - 30 Sep	10:30 - 6	M	T	W	T	F	S	S
	1 Oct - 31 Oct	10:30 - 6	M	T	W	T	F	S	S
	1 Nov - 22 Dec	10:30 - 4	M	T	W	T	F	S	S
	28 Dec - 1 Jan 06	10:30 - 4	M	T	W	T	F	S	S
	7 Jan - 12 Feb 06	10:30 - 4	M	T	W	T	F	S	S
Shop	As garden								

Open BH Mons. Last admission 1hr before closing. Closes dusk if earlier

Sissinghurst Castle Garden

Sissinghurst, nr Cranbrook, Kent TN17 2AB

 1967 (2:17)

One of the world's most celebrated gardens, the creation of Vita Sackville-West and her husband Sir Harold Nicolson

Developed around the surviving parts of an Elizabethan mansion with a central red-brick prospect tower, a series of small enclosed compartments, intimate in scale and romantic in atmosphere and including the renowned White Garden, provide outstanding design and colour through the season. The study, where Vita worked, and library are also open to visitors.

★ The library and Vita Sackville-West's study close each day at 5.30. Tower and library opening may be restricted early and late in the season. Please tel. to check details. No tripods or easels in the garden. Members are recommended to visit in the late afternoon to enjoy the garden at its quietest

The Lime Walk in spring, Sissinghurst Castle Garden, Kent

Opening arrangements: Sissinghurst										
Garden	19 Mar - 30 Oct	11 - 6:30	M	T	W	T	F	S	S
Shop	19 Mar - 30 Oct	11 - 5:30	M	T	W	T	F	S	S
	31 Oct - 20 Dec	10:30 - 4:30	M	T	W	T	F	S	S
Restaurant	19 Mar - 30 Oct	11 - 5:30	M	T	W	T	F	S	S
	31 Oct - 20 Dec	11 - 4	M	T	W	T	F	S	S

Garden, shop and restaurant open from 10 at weekends and BHols. Last admission 1 hr before closing or before dusk if earlier

ℹ️ **T** 01580 710700, 01580 710701 (Infoline), 01580 710703 (Shop), 01580 710704 (Restaurant) **F** 01580 710702 **E** sissinghurst@nationaltrust.org.uk

£ £7.50, child £3.50, family £18.50

🎭 Programme of events. Also painting and photography with easels/tripods on closed days. Tel. for details

🚶 Woodland & lake walks open all year. Free

♿ Separate designated parking, 115yds. Drop-off point. **Building**: Level entrance. 4 wheelchairs. Step to library. 70 steps in tower. Photograph album. **WCs**: Adapted WC. **Grounds**: Partly accessible, uneven paths, narrow paths. Accessible route map. Due to the nature of the garden, only 4 wheelchairs users can be accommodated at any one time, the garden is not suitable for PMVs. **Shop**: Level entrance. **Refreshments**: Level entrance

🔊 Induction loop in reception, shop and Lecture lunches

📖 Braille guide and large-print guide. Guides trained to assist visually impaired visitors may be available, contact in advance. Guidebook on tape, by arrangement

🍴 Licensed restaurant. Christmas menu 25 Nov–20 Dec. Lecture lunches during 3 weeks from 4 Nov

🚗 Welcome in designated area in car park and elsewhere on the estate, but not in garden

👶 Baby-changing facilities. Baby back-carriers admitted. Front-carrying baby slings and hip-carrying infant seats for loan. Back-carriers for loan. No pushchairs admitted, as paths are narrow and uneven. Ball games etc not allowed in garden

Please note: groups must book in advance with the property

■ Children's quiz/trail

🐕 Not in garden but welcome elsewhere on the estate

🚲 Local lanes and bridlepaths good for cycling

→ [188: TQ810380] **Bus**: Special link from ⇌ Staplehurst to Garden, Tue & Sun only, mid-May to 29 Aug (tel. property); otherwise Arriva 4/5 Maidstone-Hastings (passing ⇌ Staplehurst), alight Sissinghurst, 1¼ml (not Sun). **Station**: Staplehurst 5½ml. **Road**: 2ml NE of Cranbrook, 1ml E of Sissinghurst village (A262)

P Free parking, 315yds

NT properties nearby
Bateman's, Bodiam Castle, Scotney Castle, Smallhythe Place, Stoneacre

---

Smallhythe Place

Smallhythe, Tenterden, Kent TN30 7NG

 1939   (2:I7)

Ellen Terry's early 16th-century house and cottage gardens

The half-timbered house, built for the harbourmaster in the early 16th century when Smallhythe was a thriving shipbuilding yard, was the home of the Victorian actress Ellen Terry from 1899 to 1928 and contains her fascinating theatre collection. The cottage grounds include her rose garden, orchard, nuttery, a wonderful display of wild flowers and the Barn Theatre, which holds exhibitions and regular performances of plays, music and talks.

What's new in 2005 Barn Theatre events; SeaBritain activities

ℹ **T/F** 01580 762334
    E smallhytheplace@nationaltrust.org.uk

£ £4.25, child £1.90, family £10

🎭 Programme of events, inc. open-air theatre. Tel. for details

Opening arrangements: Smallhythe Place									
5 Mar - 20 Mar	11 - 5	M	T	W	T	F	S	S
26 Mar - 29 Oct	11 - 5	**M**	**T**	**W**	T	F	**S**	**S**

Open Good Fri. Last admission 4.30 or dusk if earlier

♿ **Building**: Steps to entrance. Ground floor has steps, uneven floors. Stairs to other floors. Photograph album. **Grounds**: Accessible route

👁 Braille guide and large-print guide. Sensory list

🍽 Refreshments available at Tenterden Vineyard Park (not NT), 500yds from property

🧒 Children must be accompanied by an adult

■ Children's quiz/trail. Exhibitions

→ [189: TQ893300] **Bus**: Coastal Coaches 312 ⇌ Rye–Tenterden. **Station**: Rye 8ml; Appledore 8ml; Headcorn 10ml. **Road**: 2ml S of Tenterden, on E side of the Rye road (B2082)

P Free parking, 50yds. Coaches park at Tenterden Vineyard Park

NT properties nearby
Bodiam Castle, Lamb House, Scotney Castle, Sissinghurst Castle Garden

---

South Foreland Lighthouse

The Front, St Margaret's Bay, Dover, Kent CT15 6HP

🏠 🔧 🚗 🏪 🔭 🧒 1989   (2:K6)

Fascinating and distinctive Victorian lighthouse

A striking landmark on the White Cliffs of Dover, this historic building was the site of Faraday's work in pioneering the use of electricity in lighthouses, and was the first to display an electrically powered signal. South Foreland was also used by Marconi for his successful wireless telegraphy experiments in 1898.

What's new in 2005 Restored mechanism powering the rotation of the optic; SeaBritain events May–October

ℹ **T** 01304 852463 (Lighthouse),
    01304 202756 (White Cliffs Visitor Centre)
    F 01304 205295
    E southforeland@nationaltrust.org.uk

£ **Lighthouse**: £2.40, child £1.20, family £6. Groups £2, child £1. Large groups can be

---

accommodated, but will be split into smaller tour groups of about 10, so there may be some waiting. No shelter available for more than 30 people

⟨i⟩ Guided tours for all visitors. Out-of-hours tours for booked groups only; guided walks to the lighthouse from the White Cliffs visitor centre, Apr–Oct.

⟨&⟩ Contact for directions to property.
Building: Steps to entrance. Ground floor accessible. Many stairs with handrail to other floors. Seating available. Photograph album.
Grounds: Partly accessible, loose gravel paths, steep slopes. **Shop**: Steps to entrance

⟨◉⟩ Braille guide and large-print guide. Sensory list

⟨⬤⟩ Bottled water and some confectionery available from shop

⟨🕴⟩ Pushchairs and baby back-carriers admitted. Pushchairs on ground floor (reception) only, due to stairs

⟨🏛⟩ Suitable for school groups. Children's quiz/trail. Group activity packs available

⟨🐕⟩ In the grounds

→ [179: TR359433] **No vehicular access.**
Foot: On public footpaths (Saxon Shoreway long-distance path) 2½ml from Dover, 1ml from St Margaret's. **Cycle**: NCN1 ½ml.
Bus: Stagecoach in E. Kent 90/1, 113 Dover–St Margarets (passing ⧫ Dover Priory), then ½ml. **Station**: Martin Mill 2½ml

⟨P⟩ No parking on site. Not suitable for coaches. Drivers must park at White Cliffs of Dover (NT) and walk along clifftops to lighthouse (approx. 2ml) or walk from St Margaret's village/bay (approx. 1ml)

NT properties nearby
The White Cliffs of Dover

Opening arrangements: South Foreland										
Lighthouse	3 Mar - 31 Oct	11 - 5:30	M	T	W	T	F	S	S
	21 Mar - 8 Apr	11 - 5:30	M	T	W	T	F	S	S
	30 May - 3 Jun	11 - 5:30	M	T	W	T	F	S	S
	18 Jul - 9 Sep	11 - 5:30	M	T	W	T	F	S	S
	24 Oct - 31 Oct	11 - 5:30	M	T	W	T	F	S	S
	11 Feb - 19 Feb 06	11 - 5:30	M	T	W	T	F	S	S

Admission by guided tour. Nov–Feb open by arrangement for booked groups

South Foreland Lighthouse, Kent

Standen

West Hoathly Road, East Grinstead, West Sussex RH19 4NE

⟨🏠⟩ ⟨❀⟩ ⟨⬤⟩ ⟨⬤⟩ ⟨⬤⟩ ⟨T⟩ 1973 (2:G7)

Arts & Crafts family home with Morris and Co. interiors, set in a hillside garden

Philip Webb, friend of William Morris, designed this family house in the 1890s. A showpiece of the Arts & Crafts Movement, it is decorated throughout with Morris carpets, fabrics and wallpapers, complemented by contemporary paintings, tapestries and furniture. The house retains its original electrical light fittings. The beautiful garden gives fine views over the Sussex countryside and there are delightful woodland walks set in the AONB of the High Weald.

What's new in 2005 Redecorated conservatory; Cook's Store open

⟨★⟩ Some exterior redecoration will take place during 2005

⟨i⟩ T 01342 323029, 01342 301795 (Restaurant)
F 01342 316424
E standen@nationaltrust.org.uk

⟨£⟩ £6.50, child £3.25, family £16. Groups (15) £5.50. **Garden only**: £3.90, child £1.90. Joint ticket with same day entry to Nymans Garden Wed to Fri £10

[⚡] Guided tours for groups Wed am. Tel. for details

[♨] Programme of events, inc. 'Behind the Scenes' 26 Jul. Tel. for details or send s.a.e for full listing

[⚘] Nature walks through the Standen estate

[♿] Designated parking in main car park, 100yds. Disabled drivers can park in courtyard. Drop-off point. **Building**: Step to entrance, ramp available. 5 wheelchairs. Ground floor accessible. Stairs to other floors. Seating available. Photograph album. Accessible exit through side door is different from main exit through shop. **WCs**: Adapted WC. **Grounds**: Partly accessible, slopes, some steps, grass paths. Accessible route map. Some visitors may require assistance from their companion. **Shop**: Level entrance. Alternative entrance available via door bell. **Refreshments**: Level entrance

[🔊] Induction loop in shop

[👓] Braille guide and large-print guide. Sensory list

[🛍] Shop specialises in Arts & Crafts Movement merchandise. Plant sales

[☕] The Barn Restaurant (licensed). Offers variety of hot and cold dishes. Nov to Dec limited menu. Reservation not possible. Children's menu

Arts & Crafts furniture in the dining room at Standen, West Sussex

Opening arrangements: Standen											
House	18 Mar - 30 Oct	11 - 5	M	T	**W**	**T**	**F**	**S**	**S**
Garden	18 Mar - 30 Oct	11 - 6	M	T	**W**	**T**	**F**	**S**	**S**
	5 Nov - 18 Dec	11 - 3	M	T	W	T	F	**S**	**S**
Shop	18 Mar - 30 Oct	11 - 5	M	T	**W**	**T**	**F**	**S**	**S**
	5 Nov - 18 Dec	11 - 3	M	T	W	T	F	**S**	**S**
Restaurant	As shop								

Open BH Mons 11–5. Property may close for short periods on BHols to avoid overcrowding

[⛱] In picnic site overlooking Weir Wood Reservoir

[👶] Baby-changing and feeding facilities. Front-carrying baby slings, hip-carrying infant seats and reins for loan. All-terrain child's buggy available for loan

[🎒] Suitable for school groups. Hands-on activities. Children's quiz/trail. Family activity packs. Adult study days. Arts & Crafts resource room

[🐕] On leads and only in lower car park; under close control on woodland walks (via lower car park)

[→] [187: TQ389356] **Cycle**: NCN21 1¼ml. **Bus**: Bluebell Rly link 473 from [≋] East Grinstead (tel. property for details); Metrobus 84 [≋] East Grinstead–Crawley (passing [≋] Three Bridges), alight at approach road just north of Saint Hill, or at Saint Hill, then ½ml by footpath. **Station**: E Grinstead 2ml; Kingscote (Bluebell Rly) 2ml. **Road**: 2ml S of East Grinstead, signposted from town centre and B2110 (Turners Hill Road)

[P] Free parking, 200yds

NT properties nearby
Nymans Garden, Sheffield Park Garden, Toys Hill, Wakehurst Place

Stowe Landscape Gardens

Buckingham, Buckinghamshire MK18 5EH

[🏠][✿][♣][🗄][☕][⛱][🔔][⛶] 1990   (2:D2)

Europe's most influential landscape gardens

Stowe is a 100ha (250-acre) work of art, both beautiful and full of meaning. With its ornamental lakes, glorious open spaces and wooded valleys, adorned by over 40 temples

The Palladian bridge, Cobham monument and Gothic Temple at Stowe Landscape Gardens, Buckinghamshire

and monuments, it is one of the supreme creations of the Georgian era and has inspired writers, artists and visitors for more than three centuries. Today Stowe can be enjoyed by all for its peace and tranquillity, as an unspoilt setting for a family picnic or for invigorating walks in the surrounding 304ha (750 acres) of parkland.

What's new in 2005 Newly restored monuments: Corinthian Arch, new column and statue of George II, not seen since the early 1800s. Continuing restoration: Stowe House roof

⭐ Visitors to the gardens should allow plenty of time because of the extensive areas to see. Stowe House is home to Stowe School, which is opened to the public by Stowe House Preservation Trust. Tel. 01280 818166 for opening times. The house is undergoing restoration, with the support of the Heritage Lottery Fund, and access may have to be restricted at times

ℹ️ **T** 01494 755568 (Infoline),
01280 822850 (Enquiries Mon–Fri),
01280 818825 (Reception weekends, BHols & powered mobility vehicle bookings),
01280 818809 (Weddings),
01280 818810 (Learning),
01494 755572 (Box office),
01280 821709 (Shop), 01280 815819 (Tea-room) **F** 01280 822437
E stowegarden@nationaltrust.org.uk

💷 **Gardens**: £5.80, child £2.90, family £14.50. Groups £4.90. **House (inc. NT members)**: £2, child £1. **House tours**: £3, child £1.50. House admission payable at NT reception. **House not NT**

🚶 Free guided tours in gardens most days. Tel. for details

🎭 Programme of events. Tel. for details

♿ Separate designated parking, 200yds. **WCs**: Adapted WC. Ambulant disabled/baby change facilities. **Grounds**: undulating terrain. Accessible route map. 2 multi-seater PMV, booking essential. **Shop**: Level entrance. **Refreshments**: Ramped entrance with handrail. Large-print menu

👓 Braille guide and large-print guide

☕ Temple Tea-rooms (licensed) 2 mins walk from Visitor Lodge. Kiosk next to Visitor Lodge. Light refreshments available through winter months

🚼 Baby-changing and feeding facilities. Pushchairs and baby back-carriers admitted

🎒 Suitable for school groups. Live interpretation. Hands-on activities. Children's quiz/trail. Family activity packs. Interpretation, learning and family days throughout the year. Tel. for details

🐕 On leads only

Opening arrangements: Stowe Landscape Gardens										
Gardens	2 Mar - 30 Oct	10 - 5:30	M	T	**W**	**T**	**F**	**S**	**S**
	5 Nov - 26 Feb 06	10 - 4	M	T	W	T	F	**S**	**S**
Shop	As gardens								
Tea-room	2 Mar - 30 Oct	10:30 - 5	M	T	**W**	**T**	**F**	**S**	**S**
	5 Nov - 26 Feb 06	10:30 - 4	M	T	W	T	F	**S**	**S**
Kiosk	2 Jun - 31 Aug	2 - 6	M	T	**W**	**T**	**F**	**S**	**S**

Open BH Mons. Last admission 1hr 30mins before closing. Gates locked at 5:30. Gardens closed Sat 28 May, 24 & 25 Dec

Please see the area introductions for details of coast & countryside properties

In park only

➔ [152: SP665366] **Foot**: 3ml from Buckingham along Stowe Avenue and through park.
Bus: Stagecoach Express X5 Cambridge–Oxford (passing ⊞ Milton Keynes Central & Bicester North); Jeffs 32 from Milton Keynes (passing close ⊞ Milton Keynes Central); Arriva 66 from Aylesbury (passing close ⊞ Aylesbury). On all, alight Buckingham, then 3ml. It is hoped to run a direct service from Bicester North station on summer Sats, connecting with the X5 at Buckingham Tesco. Tel. property for details.
Station: Bicester North 9ml. **Road**: 3ml NW of Buckingham via Stowe Avenue, off A422 Buckingham–Banbury road. Motorway access from M40 (exits 9 to 11) and M1 (exit 13 or 15a)

P Free parking, 200yds

NT properties nearby
Buckingham Chantry Chapel, Canons Ashby, Claydon House, King's Head, Waddesdon Manor

---

Uppark

South Harting, Petersfield, West Sussex
GU31 5QR

 1954 **(2:E8)**

Late 17th-century house in an impressive setting

The drama of the 1989 fire and restoration adds to the magic of this romantic house, which is set high on the South Downs with magnificent sweeping views to the sea. The elegant Georgian interior houses a famous Grand Tour collection that includes paintings, furniture and ceramics. An 18th-century dolls' house with original contents is one of the highlights. The complete servants' quarters in the basement are shown as they were in Victorian days when H. G. Wells' mother was housekeeper. The beautiful and peaceful garden is now fully restored in the early 19th-century Picturesque style, in a downland and woodland setting.

What's new in 2005 Large ball games area (bats and balls provided)

Opening arrangements: Uppark

House	20 Mar - 2 Oct	1 - 5	**M**	**T**	**W**	**T**	F	S	**S**
	3 Oct - 27 Oct	1 - 4	**M**	**T**	**W**	**T**	F	S	**S**
Grounds	20 Mar - 2 Oct	11 - 5:30	**M**	**T**	**W**	**T**	F	S	**S**
	3 Oct - 27 Oct	11 - 4:30	**M**	**T**	**W**	**T**	F	S	**S**
Exhibition	As grounds								
Shop	20 Mar - 2 Oct	11:30 - 5:30	**M**	**T**	**W**	**T**	F	S	**S**
	3 Oct - 27 Oct	11:30 - 4:30	**M**	**T**	**W**	**T**	F	S	**S**
Restaurant	As shop								

House opens 11 on BH Mons and 12 on BH Suns and Suns in August. Print room open 1st Mon of each month, times as house

★ To avoid congestion timed tickets are issued on arrival on BH Mons

i **T** 01730 825415, 01730 825857 (Infoline), 01730 825256 (Restaurant/Shop)
F 01730 825873
E uppark@nationaltrust.org.uk

£ £6, child £3, family £15. Groups £5

Booked group guided tours (Mon–Thur mornings) by arrangement. Garden History tour at 3, first Thur of month (Apr–Oct) and every Thur in July and Aug

Woodland walk

Designated parking in main car park, 300yds. Drop-off point. **Building**: Ramped entrance. 6 wheelchairs. Ground floor accessible. Many stairs with handrail to other floors. Lift to basement. Seating available. **WCs**: Adapted WC. **Grounds**: Accessible route map. **Shop**: Level entrance. **Refreshments**: Ramped entrance

Braille guide and large-print guide. Sensory list. Handling collection

NT shop. Plant sales

Licensed restaurant. Children's menu

Picnic areas near car park and woodland walk

Baby-changing facilities. Front-carrying baby slings and hip-carrying infant seats for loan. Children's play area. Pushchairs welcome Mon–Thur (not Suns or BHols)

Hands-on activities. Children's quiz/trail. Ball games

On leads and only in car park and on woodland walk (no shade in car park)

Unless indicated, last admission is always 30mins before closing time

→ [197: SU775177] **Foot**: South Downs Way within $\frac{2}{3}$ml. **Bus**: Stagecoach in Hampshire 54 ⊠ Petersfield–⊠ Chichester. **Station**: Petersfield 5$\frac{1}{2}$ml. **Road**: 5ml SE of Petersfield on B2146, 1$\frac{1}{2}$ml S of South Harting

P Free parking, 300yds

NT properties nearby
Harting Down & Beacon Hill, Hinton Ampner Garden, Petworth

The Vyne

Sherborne St John, Basingstoke, Hampshire
RG24 9HL

 1956 (**2:D6**)

16th-century house and estate reflecting changing styles and tastes over 500 years

Built in the early 16th century for Lord Sandys, Henry VIII's Lord Chamberlain, the house acquired a classical portico in the mid-17th century (the first of its kind in England) and contains a fascinating Tudor chapel with Renaissance glass, a Palladian staircase and a wealth of old panelling and fine furniture. The attractive grounds feature herbaceous borders and a wild garden, with lawns, lakes, one of the earliest summer-houses and woodland walks. A newly developed wetlands area attracts a diversity of wildlife.

What's new in 2005 Family woodpecker trail and living sculpture walk in the woodlands; display on recent research and family activity book about the Tudor Chapel; extra value days Mon–Wed. Tel. or visit website for details

Opening arrangements: The Vyne										
House	26 Mar - 30 Oct	11 - 5	M	T	W	T	F	**S**	**S**
	23 Mar - 26 Oct	1 - 5	**M**	**T**	**W**	T	F	S	S
Grounds	5 Feb - 20 Mar	11 - 5	M	T	W	T	F	**S**	**S**
	23 Mar - 30 Oct	11 - 5	**M**	**T**	**W**	T	F	S	S
	4 Feb - 26 Mar 06	11 - 5	M	T	W	T	F	**S**	**S**
Shop/restaurant	As grounds								
Shop/restaurant	3 Nov - 23 Dec	11 - 3	M	T	W	**T**	**F**	**S**	**S**

Open Good Fri 11–5 (including house). Special opening for groups, by appointment only, 23 March–26 Oct: Mon, Tue & Wed 11–1

The Oak Gallery, The Vyne, Hampshire

i **T** 01256 883858, 01256 881337 (Infoline), 01256 880039 (Shop/restaurant), 01494 755572 (Box office) **F** 01256 881720 **E** thevyne@nationaltrust.org.uk

£ £7, child £3.50, family £17.50. Groups £5.50. **Grounds only**: £4, child £2. Reduced rate when arriving by public transport or cycle (on house & grounds ticket)

Programme of events, inc. outdoor concerts and theatre, family events and lecture lunches

Woodland, parkland and wetland walks and trails

Separate designated parking. Transfer from visitor reception to summer house garden. **Building**: Level entrance. 6 wheelchairs. Ground floor accessible. Many stairs to other floors. Seating available. Photograph album. **WCs**: Adapted WC. **Grounds**: Partly accessible, steep slopes. Accessible route. **Shop**: Level entrance. **Refreshments**: Level entrance

Induction loop in reception and Guided tours

Braille guide and large-print guide. Sensory list

NT shop. Plant sales

Brewhouse (licensed) adjacent to house. Children's menu. Licensed kiosk in tea garden open at busy times

In car park and picnic field

There are special events at most Trust properties; please telephone 0870 458 4000 for details

Baby-changing and feeding facilities. Hip-carrying infant seats for loan

Suitable for school groups. Children's quiz/trail

On leads and only in car park and Morgaston Wood

→ [175/186: SU639576] **Cycle**: NCN23 1ml. **Bus**: Stagecoach in Hampshire 45 from Basingstoke (passing ⮕ Basingstoke). **Station**: Bramley 2½ml; Basingstoke 4ml. **Road**: 4ml N of Basingstoke between Bramley and Sherborne St John. From Basingstoke Ring Road A339, follow Basingstoke District Hospital signs until property signs are picked up. Follow A340 Aldermaston Road towards Tadley. Right turn into Morgaston Road. Right turn into car park

P Free parking, 40yds. 5–10 mins walk through gardens from visitor reception to house entrance

NT properties nearby
Basildon Park, Sandham Memorial Chapel, Selborne, West Green House Garden

---

Waddesdon Manor

Waddesdon, nr Aylesbury, Buckinghamshire
HP18 0JH

🐎 ♿ 🖼 🚼 📷 💷 🎋 🔔 🍴 | 1957 | **(2:D3)**

Magnificent house and grounds in the style of a 16th-century French château

Waddesdon Manor was built between 1874 and 1889 for Baron Ferdinand de Rothschild to entertain his guests and display his vast collection of art treasures. It houses an extraordinary assemblage of French 18th-century decorative arts. The furniture, Savonnerie carpets and Sèvres porcelain rank in importance with the Metropolitan Museum in New York and the Louvre in Paris. Out-standing are the portraits by Gainsborough and Reynolds, works by 17th-century Dutch and Flemish Masters, and a spectacular silver dinner service made for George III. Waddesdon has one of the finest Victorian gardens in Britain, renowned for its seasonal displays, colourful shrubs, giant tree ferns, parterre and restored pleasure garden. There is a rose garden, and the rococo-style aviary, newly painted and gilded,

Opening arrangements: Waddesdon Manor

Grounds	5 Mar - 20 Mar	10 - 5	M T W T F **S S**
	23 Mar - 23 Dec	10 - 5	M **T W T F S S**
	7 Jan - 26 Feb 06	10 - 5	M T W T F **S S**
House	23 Mar - 30 Oct	11 - 4	M **T W T F S S**
Part of house	16 Nov - 23 Dec	12 - 4	M **T W T F S S**
Bachelors' wing	23 Mar - 28 Oct	11 - 4	M **T W T F** S S
Shops	As grounds	10 - 5	
Manor Rest.	As grounds	10 - 5	
Stables Rest.	23 Mar - 23 Dec	10 - 5	M **T W T F S S**
Kiosks	23 Mar - 30 Oct		M **T W T F S S**

Admission by timed ticket only, inc. NT members. Open BH Mons. Last admission 1hr before closing. Sculpture in garden uncovered week before Easter, weather permitting. Bachelors' Wing: space limited and entry cannot be guaranteed. Kiosks open weather permitting. Part of house, grounds, restaurants and shops open Mon 19 Dec and Tues 20 Dec 2005

houses a splendid collection of exotic birds. The extensive wine cellars can be visited.

What's new in 2005 Displays and interpretation on Waddesdon's rich musical associations and the Drawings Collection

⭐ All visitors inc. NT members require timed tickets to enter the house, available from the ticket office. To enjoy Waddesdon to the full, visitors should allow at least 1½ hours to tour the house and another hour for the garden. Last recommended admission to house 2.30

ℹ **T** 01296 653203, 01296 653211 (Infoline), 01296 653216 (Weddings), 01296 653230 (Corporate enquiries), 01296 653247 (Mail order), 01296 653226 (Booking), 01296 658586 (Plant sales), 01296 653242 (Restaurant) **F** 01296 653237 **E** waddesdonmanor@nationaltrust.org.uk

£ **Grounds (inc. gardens, aviary, restaurants & shops)**: £4, child £2, family (2 adults & 2 children) £10. Groups £3.20, child £1.60. **House (inc. wine cellars)**: £7, child £6. Groups £5.60, child £4.80. **Bachelors' Wing**: £3, child £3. Groups £3. **Part of house (Nov/Dec)**: £4, child £2. Groups £4. To visit the house a grounds ticket must be purchased. Timed tickets to the house can be bought up to 24 hours in advance of a visit. Advance booking charge £3 per transaction. Tel. booking office Mon to Fri 10–4

For further information check our website www.nationaltrust.org.uk

🎒 Free accompanied walks around the garden inc. 'Meet the Keeper'

🎧 Adult and family audio tours

📅 Programme of events, inc. special interest days, children's activities, wine tastings, garden workshops, floodlit opening, Christmas events

🚶 Wildlife walks and trails, leaflet available

♿ Separate designated parking, 400yds. Transfer available. Drop-off point. **Building**: Ramped entrance. 4 wheelchairs. Ground floor accessible. Due to the nature of the buildings only 2 wheelchairs are admitted per floor at one time. Access to other floor via lift. Seating available. Audio visual/video. Stairlift to Prints & Drawings Rooms, alternative route to the Wine Cellars. Tel. in advance. **WCs**: Adapted WC. **Grounds**: Partly accessible, steep slopes. Accessible route map. **Shop**: Level entrance. **Refreshments**: Level entrance. Large-print menu. Stables restaurant and shop are located downhill from the house. Transfer available

🔊 Induction loop in Powerhouse

📖 Large-print guide

🎁 Gift and wine shops. Wine warehouse. Plant sales

🍽 Manor restaurant (not NT) (licensed). Children's menu. Stables restaurant (not NT) (licensed). Children's menu. Summer-house Kiosk at W end of house and Coffee Bar kiosk in shop courtyard – both open in good weather for al fresco snacks

👶 Baby-changing and feeding facilities. Front-carrying baby slings and hip-carrying infant seats for loan. Children's play area. Aviary. Children welcome under parental supervision

📺 Live interpretation. Children's quiz/trail. Adult study days. Audio-visual presentations on the Rothschilds, Waddesdon & Wine

➔ [165: SP740169] **Bus**: Arriva/Red Rose 16/7 from Aylesbury (passing close ⊠ Aylesbury). **Station**: Aylesbury 6ml; Haddenham & Thame Parkway 9ml. **Road**: Access via Waddesdon village, 6ml NW of Aylesbury on A41; M40 (westbound) exit 6 or 7 via Thame & Long Crendon or M40 (eastbound) exit 9 via Bicester

Please note: groups must book in advance with the property

🅿 Free parking

NT properties nearby
Boarstall Duck Decoy, Claydon House, Cliveden, King's Head, Stowe Landscape Gardens

Wakehurst Place

Ardingly, nr Haywards Heath, West Sussex
RH17 6TN

⊞ ❀ 🐾 🥾 🐾 🎁 🍽 1964 **(2:G7)**

Kew's 'country garden', with plants from across the world

The 200 hectares (500 acres) at Wakehurst Place include walled gardens, water gardens, a wetland conservation area, woodland, lakes and ponds. Four National Collections plus rare and exotic plants from the Himalayas and the southern hemisphere, and the Millennium Seed Bank, are among the highlights.

What's new in 2005 Exhibition area and Learning Zone in the Elizabethan mansion

⭐ **Wakehurst Place is administered and maintained by the Royal Botanic Gardens, Kew.** The Wellcome Trust Millennium Building, adjacent to Wakehurst Place, aims to house seeds from ten per cent of the world's flora by 2009, to save species from extinction in the wild. Enjoy the Millennium Seed Bank interactive public exhibition in the Orange Room and follow the journey of a seed from identification and collection, through to drying and cold storage in the massive underground vaults. The mansion in the grounds is used principally for education visits. Two rooms only (hall and former library) are open to visitors

ℹ **T** 01444 894066 (24hr information),
01444 894073 (Shop/plants),
01444 894094 (Learning),
01444 894067 (Booking),
01444 894040 (Restaurant) **F** 01444 894069
E wakehurst@kew.org

💷 £8, concessions £7. Reduced rate when arriving by public transport. Under-17s free. Friends of Kew free. Discounts for booked groups (10+). Season ticket £16 for year-round entry

Opening arrangements: Wakehurst Place			
Garden	1 Mar - 30 Oct	10 - 6	**M T W T F S S**
	31 Oct - 28 Feb 06	10 - 4:30	**M T W T F S S**
Restaurant	All year		**M T W T F S S**

Closed 24 & 25 Dec. Restaurant, shop and coffee shop open at 10. Mansion, Seed Bank and restaurant close 1 hr before garden. Sunday shop trading restricted

ℹ️ Guided tours daily, tel. office for times & availability. Booked tours on request; write to Administrator. Tours of the Loder Valley: Sat, Sun and BHols: March–Sept

🏴 Inc. regular family events all year

♿ Designated parking in main car park. **Building**: Ramped entrance. 12 wheelchairs. **WCs**: Adapted WC. **Grounds**: Partly accessible, steep slopes. Accessible route map. Some visitors may require assistance from their companion. 2 single-seater PMV, booking essential. **Shop**: Ramped entrance. **Refreshments**: Level entrance

👃 Interesting scents

🛍️ Garden and gift shop (RBG Kew Enterprises). Plant sales. Open all year

☕ Stable Restaurant (not NT) (licensed) adjacent to mansion. Children's menu. Coffee Shop (not NT) at visitor centre

🏔 Almost anywhere, inc. dedicated areas with tables

👶 Baby-changing facilities. Pushchairs and baby back-carriers admitted

▉ Suitable for school groups. Education room/centre. Live interpretation. Hands-on activities. Family guide. Children's quiz/trail. Adult study days

➔ [187: TQ339314] **Foot**: Footpath from Balcombe (5ml). **Bus**: Metrobus 81/2 Haywards Heath–Crawley, passing ⊠ Haywards Heath and Three Bridges. **Station**: Haywards Heath 6ml; E Grinstead 6½ml; Horsted Keynes (Bluebell Rly) 3¾ml. **Road**: On B2028, 1½ml N of Ardingly; S of Turners Hill

P Free parking (not NT), 400yds. Limited free parking for garden visitors only

NT properties nearby
Nymans Garden, Sheffield Park Garden, Standen

West Green House Garden

West Green, Hartley Wintney, Hampshire
RG27 8JB

[❋] [🏠] [☕] [1957] (2:D6)

Celebrated garden with an intriguing collection of follies

The delightful series of walled gardens, voted one of the UK's top 50 gardens, surrounds a charming 18th-century house. The largest features herbaceous beds with wonderful colour combinations and a superb ornamental kitchen garden. The Nymphaeum is fully restored with water steps and Italianate planting. The Lake Field and its follies and lake are now open but may, from time to time, be closed due to dampness. Restoration work is ongoing and, at the discretion of the lessee, restrictions are frequently necessary for the development and protection of the garden.

★ The property has been leased by the Trust and the house is not open to visitors. The lessee has kindly agreed to the opening of the gardens and is responsible for all arrangements and facilities (see below for access arrangements for NT members). There are limited visitor facilities.

ℹ️ **T/F** 01252 844611

£ £5. **Entry is free to NT members on Wed only and to NT groups who can book Mon & Tues only (normally closed days)**

🏴 Programme of events, inc. a season of concerts and operas

♿ **Grounds**: Partly accessible, loose gravel paths, some steps. **Shop**: Level entrance. **Refreshments**: Level entrance

🛍️ Gift shop. Plant sales

☕ Tea-room. Lunches and teas

Opening arrangements: West Green House Garden			
Garden	27 Apr - 28 Aug	11 - 4:30	M T **W T F S S**
	3 Sep - 25 Sep	11 - 4:30	M T W T F **S S**

Open BH Mons. **NB**: See £ above for arrangements for NT members

🔼 In orchard only

🧍 Pushchairs admitted

📖 Adult study days

➡️ [175: SU745564] **Bus**: Stagecoach in Hampshire 200 Basingstoke–Camberley (passing ◄► Winchfield, Blackwater and Camberley), alight Phoenix Green, 1ml. **Station**: Winchfield 2ml. **Road**: 1ml W of Hartley Wintney, 10ml NE of Basingstoke, 1ml N of A30

🅿 Free parking. Coaches must park on the gravel car park and must not let passengers alight in the lane

NT properties nearby
Basildon Park, Sandham Memorial Chapel, The Vyne

West Wycombe Park, Buckinghamshire

West Wycombe Park

West Wycombe, Buckinghamshire HP14 3AJ

 1943   **(2:E4)**

Perfectly preserved rococo landscape garden, surrounding a neo-classical mansion

The garden was created in the mid-18th century by Sir Francis Dashwood, founder of the Dilettanti Society and the Hellfire Club. The house is among the most theatrical and Italianate in England, its façades formed as classical temples. The interior has Palmyrene ceilings and decoration, with pictures, furniture and sculpture dating from the time of Sir Francis.

What's new in 2005 West Wycombe circular walks leaflet available from post office, newsagent and Hughenden estate office

⭐ The West Wycombe Caves and adjacent café are privately owned and NT members must pay admission fees. No picnics in park

ℹ️ **T** 01494 513569 (April to Aug), 01494 755573 (Hughenden estate office)

£ £5.40, child £2.70, family £13.50. **Grounds only**: £2.80, child £1.40

🚶 Tours of house on weekdays. Tours of grounds and group visits by written arrangement

♿ Separate designated parking, 150yds. **Building**: Steps to entrance. 1 wheelchair, booking essential. Ground floor accessible. Other floors not open to visitors. **WCs**: 9 steps down with handrail. **Grounds**: Fully accessible

📖 Braille guide

🐕 On leads in car park only, not in park

➡️ [175: SU828947] **Foot**: Circular walk links West Wycombe with Bradenham and Hughenden Manor. **Bus**: Arriva 340-2 High Wycombe-Stokenchurch; Red Rose 275 High Wycombe-Oxford (all pass close ◄► High Wycombe). **Station**: High Wycombe 2½ml. **Road**: 2ml W of High Wycombe. At W end of West Wycombe, S of the Oxford road (A40)

🅿 Free parking, 250yds

NT properties nearby
Hughenden Manor, West Wycombe Village

Opening arrangements: West Wycombe Park							
Grounds only	3 Apr - 31 May	2 - 6	**M T W T**	F	S	S
House/grounds	1 Jun - 31 Aug	2 - 6	**M T W T**	F	S	S
Admission by guided tour on weekdays, tours every 20 mins (approx). Last admission 45mins before closing							

Please remember – your membership card is always needed for free admission

West Wycombe Village and Hill

West Wycombe, Buckinghamshire

🏠➕🏛️⬛👥👤📷🐎 1934   (2:E4)

Chilterns village with buildings spanning several hundred years

Cottages and inns date from the 16th to 18th centuries. The hill, with its fine views, is surmounted by an Iron Age hill-fort and is part of the original landscape design of West Wycombe Park. It is now the site of a church and the Dashwood Mausoleum.

What's new in 2005 New walks leaflet

⭐ The church, mausoleum and caves do not belong to the National Trust. WCs in village

ℹ️ **T** 01494 755573 (Hughenden estate office)

🚶 Leaflets obtainable from village store (50/51 High St) and newsagent (36/37 High St): Village architechtural trail and West Wycombe, Bradenham & Hughenden circular walks

📷 Suitable for school groups

➡️ [175: SU828946] 2ml W of High Wycombe, on both sides of A40. Public transport: as for West Wycombe Park

Opening arrangements: West Wycombe Village

All year	M T W T F S S

🅿️ Free parking at top of hill and in village. Single track lane to top of hill. Height restrictions apply in village car park. Car park on hill locked at dusk

NT properties nearby
Bradenham, Hughenden Manor, West Wycombe Park

The White Cliffs of Dover

Upper Road, Langdon Cliffs, nr Dover, Kent CT16 1HJ

🏠👥🚗📷☕🍴 1968   (2:K7)

Magnificent coastal site looking out over the English Channel

The White Cliffs of Dover are internationally famous. The 'Gateway to the White Cliffs' visitor centre has spectacular views and introduces the visitor to five miles of coast and countryside through imaginative displays and interpretation. Much of the chalk downland along the clifftops is an SSSI, AONB and Heritage Coast with interesting flora and fauna, and the visitor centre is an excellent place for watching the world's busiest shipping lanes.

The 'Gateway to the White Cliffs' Visitor Centre with Dover Castle in the background, Kent

What's new in 2005 Chidren's activity packs; SeaBritain activities April–Oct

⭐ The Gateway visitor centre is sponsored by Saga Group Ltd. WC only available when centre is open

ℹ️ **T** 01304 202756 (Visitor centre), 01304 207326 (Countryside office) **F** 01304 246105 **E** whitecliffs@nationaltrust.org.uk

£ Admission free

🚶 Guided walks from White Cliffs to South Foreland Lighthouse (2ml), April–Oct

🎪 Programme of events, inc. spring plant fair, autumn apple fair

🚶 On public footpaths, 2½ml from Dover

♿ Separate designated parking, 30yds. 20 disabled spaces adjacent to visitor centre. **Building**: Ramped entrance. 2 wheelchairs, booking essential. Seating available. **WCs**: Adapted WC. **Grounds**: Partly accessible, steep slopes. **Shop**: Ramped entrance. **Refreshments**: Ramped entrance

🔖 Braille guide and large-print guide

🖼️ Range of souvenirs and gifts

☕ Coffee shop in visitor centre. Range of drinks, ice cream, snacks and light lunches to eat in or take away. Children's menu

🍴 No barbecues

👶 Baby-changing facilities. Pushchairs and baby back-carriers admitted. All-terrain pushchair for loan. 2 baby back-carriers for loan

🏫 Suitable for school groups. Education room/centre. Children's activity packs. Walking and countryside guide

🐕 Under close control at all times (stock grazing)

🚲 Cycling strictly prohibited along the White Cliffs, but National Cycle Route 1 runs through the area

➔ [138: TR336422] **Foot**: Signed pathways from the port, station and town centre. Located on the Saxon Shoreway path. **Cycle**: NCN1. **Ferry**: Signed route from Dover ferry terminal. **Bus**: Stagecoach in East Kent 90/1, 113 Dover-St Margarets (passing ➔ Dover Priory) to within ½ml. Alight at Upper Road. Sightseeing bus service from town centre, May–Sept. **Station**: Dover Priory 2½ml. **Road**: From A2/A258 Duke of York roundabout, take A258 towards town centre and follow signs. From A20 straight ahead at first 4 roundabouts and left at second set of lights. Turn right at next lights. After ½ml turn right into Upper Road and follow signs

P Parking, 100yds, £2. Charge collected at gate. Disabled badge holders £1; coaches £5; motorhomes £3. 1 year season ticket £20. Not suitable for caravans

NT properties nearby
Bockhill Farm, Kingsdown Leas, St Margaret's Leas, South Foreland Lighthouse

Opening arrangements: White Cliffs			
Visitor centre	1 Mar - 31 Oct	10 - 5	**M T W T F S S**
	1 Nov - 28 Feb 06	11 - 4	**M T W T F S S**
Car park	1 Mar - 31 Oct	8 - 6	**M T W T F S S**
	1 Nov - 28 Feb 06	8 - 5	**M T W T F S S**

Car park closed 24–25 Dec. Visitor centre closed 24–26 Dec

Winchester City Mill

Bridge Street, Winchester, Hampshire SO23 8EJ

🎟️ ♿ 📷 1929 **(2:D7)**

Working watermill

Spanning the River Itchen, this water-powered corn mill was first recorded in the Domesday survey of 1086. Rebuilt in 1744, it remained in use until the turn of the last century and has now been restored to full working order. The waterwheel and machinery turn daily throughout the season and there is something to interest everyone, including awe-inspiring mill-races, hands-on activities for children, a video presentation and displays about the river and its wildlife.

What's new in 2005 Regular flour milling demonstrations. Partnership with Hampshire & Isle of Wight Wildlife Trust with displays on the River Itchen. Monthly guided walks to nearby Winnall Moors Nature Reserve

⭐ No WC. Public WCs 20yds

Opening arrangements: Winchester City Mill

Mill									
	5 Mar - 27 Mar	11 - 5	M	T	W	T	F	S	S
	28 Mar - 10 Apr	11 - 5	M	T	W	T	F	S	S
	13 Apr - 3 Jul	11 - 5	M	T	W	T	F	S	S
	4 Jul - 23 Dec	11 - 5	M	T	W	T	F	S	S
Shop	As mill								

Open BH Mons and Good Fri. Mill open daily during
BHol week beg. 30 May

i T/F 01962 870057
E winchestercitymill@nationaltrust.org.uk

£ £3, child £1.50, family £7.50

Ï Groups by arrangement

Ö Holiday activities for children

Ġ Designated spaces at Chesil car park. Drop-
off point. **Building**: Steps to entrance. 4 steps
up to mill room. Stairs with handrail to other
floors. Seating available. Audio visual/video,
photograph album. **Shop**: Level entrance

☜ Braille guide and large-print guide. Sensory
list

Ô Well stocked gift shop

♣ Pushchairs and baby back-carriers admitted

▮ Suitable for school groups. Education
room/centre. Hands-on activities. Children's
quiz/trail

Autumn colour at Winkworth Arboretum, Surrey

ఠ Production of flour means it is no longer
possible to have dogs on the premises

➔ [185: SU487294] At foot of High Street,
beside City Bridge. **Foot**: South Downs Way,
King's Way, Itchen Way, Three Castles Path,
Clarendon Way – all pass through or terminate
at Winchester. **Bus**: From surrounding areas.
Station: Winchester 1ml

P No parking on site. Parking at Chesil car park.
Park & ride to Winchester from M3, exit 10

NT properties nearby
Hinton Ampner Garden, Mottisfont Abbey

Winkworth Arboretum

Hascombe Road, Godalming, Surrey GU8 4AD

🏵 🌲 🏠 🍽 🏞 🍵 1952   **(2:F7)**

**Tranquil hillside woodland with sweeping
views**

Established in the 20th century, this hillside
arboretum now contains over 1000 different
shrubs and trees, many of them rare. The most
impressive displays are in spring with magnolias,
bluebells and azaleas, and in autumn for
stunning colours. In the summer it is an ideal
place for family visits and a picnic.

What's new in 2005 Circular walk including
boardwalk around new wetland area (being
developed following dam restoration). Upper
lake has been restored

★ Minor engineering works from the 2004 dams
project may continue. The wetland area is in
the early stages of development and there
may be some areas of soft mud

i T 01483 208477, 01483 208265 (Shop)
F 01483 208252
E winkwortharboretum@nationaltrust.org.uk

£ £4.50, child £2, family £10. Groups £4.
Reduced rate when arriving by public
transport, cycle or on foot

Ï Guided tours (15+) £3 extra per person. All
groups must book in writing to the Head
Arborist

Ö Programme of events, inc. 'Plant of the month',
family fun day and other seasonal events

Unless indicated, last admission is always 30mins before closing time

🏃 Walks leaflet available. Tree guide listing 200 species

♿ Designated parking in main car park, 100yds. **WCs**: Adapted WC. **Grounds**: steep slopes. Accessible route map. Viewpoint accessible from car park via level paths. **Shop**: Ramped entrance with handrail. **Refreshments**: Ramped entrance with handrail. Large-print menu

👃 Interesting scents and sounds

☕ Tea-room. Children's menu

🚼 Baby-changing facilities. Pushchairs and baby back-carriers admitted

🏫 Suitable for school groups. Children's quiz/trail

🐕 On leads only

➡ [169/170/186: SU990412] **Bus**: Arriva 42/4 Guildford–Cranleigh (passing close ≋ Godalming). **Station**: Godalming 2ml. **Road**: Near Hascombe, 2ml SE of Godalming on E side of B2130

🅿 Free parking, 100yds

NT properties nearby
Clandon Park, Hindhead Commons, Oakhurst Cottage, River Wey and Dapdune Wharf, The Witley Centre

Opening arrangements: Winkworth Arboretum										
Arboretum	All year	Dawn - dusk	**M**	**T**	**W**	**T**	**F**	**S**	**S**
Shop	23 Mar - 20 Nov	11 - 5	M	**T**	**W**	**T**	**F**	**S**	**S**
	26 Nov - 18 Dec	11 - 4	M	T	W	T	**F**	**S**	**S**
	7 Jan - 19 Mar 06	11 - 4	M	T	W	T	F	**S**	**S**
Tea-room	As shop								

Shop & tea-room open BH Mons 11–5. Arboretum may be closed in bad weather (especially in high winds)

The Witley Centre

Witley, Godalming, Surrey GU8 5QA

♿🚼📷☕ 1921   (2:F7)

Countryside visitor and education centre

At the heart of Witley Common, a fascinating mix of woodland and heath, the purpose-built Centre houses a countryside exhibition and provides a venue for school groups and children's holiday activities.

ℹ **T** 01428 683207 **F** 01428 681050 **E** witleycentre@nationaltrust.org.uk

£ Admission free

🎪 Programme of events, inc. fun days and children's holiday events

🏃 Selection of walks leaflets available at shop

♿ **Building**: Level entrance. 2 wheelchairs. Ground floor accessible. Seating available. Audio visual/video. **WCs**: Adapted WC. Key available at centre. **Grounds**: Partly accessible. Accessible route. Some areas may be muddy in wet weather. **Shop**: Level entrance

👃 Braille guide. Touchable objects

🛍 Small shop with limited range of souvenirs

☕ Ice cream and soft drinks available

🪑 Picnic tables outside Centre

🚼 Pushchairs admitted

🏫 Suitable for school groups. Education room/centre. Children's quiz/trail. Learning officer available to host school visits

🐕 Under close control

🚲 Please use bridleway around commons

➡ [186: SU930410] **Bus**: Stagecoach in Hants & Surrey 70 Guildford–Midhurst, 71 Guildford–Haslemere (both passing close ≋ Godalming & passing ≋ Haslemere). **Station**: Milford 2ml. **Road**: 7ml SW of Guildford between London–Portsmouth A3 and A286 roads, 1ml SW of Milford

🅿 Free parking, 100yds

NT properties nearby
Black Down, Frensham Common, Hindhead Commons, Ludshott Common & Waggoners' Wells, Oakhurst Cottage, Winkworth Arboretum

Opening arrangements: The Witley Centre										
Centre	19 Mar - 30 Oct	11 - 5	M	T	W	T	**F**	**S**	**S**
	22 Mar - 28 Oct	11 - 4	M	**T**	**W**	**T**	F	S	S
Common	All year		**M**	**T**	**W**	**T**	**F**	**S**	**S**

Open BH Mons and Good Fri 11–5

There are special events at most Trust properties; please telephone 0870 458 4000 for details

Properties open less often

This section includes National Trust properties, often tenanted, which are open two days a week or less (plus Bank Holidays in some cases). Visits to some must be made by prior arrangement and where this applies admission prices are not shown (please ask when making contact). **Full details are on our website www.nationaltrust.org.uk or obtainable from the Membership Department, tel. 0870 458 4000.**

Boarstall Duck Decoy

Boarstall, nr Aylesbury, Buckinghamshire
HP18 9UX **(2:D3)**

Rare survival of a 17th-century decoy in working order, with a nature trail and displays for visitors.

⭐ WC not always available

ℹ️ T 01844 237488,
01280 822850 (enquiries Mon–Fri)
E boarstall@nationaltrust.org.uk

£ £2.30, child £1.10, family £5.50. Groups (6+) £1

Opening arrangements: Boarstall Duck Decoy										
19 Mar - 28 Aug	10 - 4	M	T	W	T	F	**S**	**S**
23 Mar - 31 Aug	3:30 - 6:30	M	T	**W**	T	F	S	S
Open BH Mons. Open 28/29 Jan and 25/26 Feb 2006								

Boarstall Tower

Boarstall, nr Aylesbury, Buckinghamshire
HP18 9UX **(2:D3)**

Superb 14th-century moated gatehouse and garden.

ℹ️ T 01844 239339 (Tenant),
01280 822850 (enquiries Mon–Fri)

£ £2.30, child £1.10, family £5.50

Opening arrangements: Boarstall Tower								
23 Mar - 26 Oct	3:30 - 6:30	M	T	**W**	T	F	S	S
19 Mar - 29 Oct	11 - 4	M	T	W	T	F	**S**	S
Open BH Mons								

Buckingham Chantry Chapel

Market Hill, Buckingham, Buckinghamshire **(2:D2)**

15th-century chapel, restored by Gilbert Scott in 1875.

⭐ Open daily, by appointment with the Buckingham Heritage Trust c/o Old Gaol Museum, Market Hill, Buckingham MK18 1JX (tel. 01280 823020). No WC

ℹ️ T 01280 822850 (Stowe, Mon–Fri)

Opening arrangements: Chantry Chapel							
All year	M	T	W	T	F	S	S
Open by appointment. See above							

Buscot Old Parsonage

Buscot, Faringdon, Oxfordshire SN7 8DQ **(2:C4)**

Early 18th-century riverside house with small garden.

⭐ No WC

ℹ️ T 01793 762209 (Coleshill Estate office)
E buscot@nationaltrust.org.uk

Opening arrangements: Buscot Old Parsonage								
30 Mar - 26 Oct	2 - 6	M	T	**W**	T	F	S	S
Admission by written appointment with the tenant. Please mark envelope 'NT booking'								

Dorneywood Garden

Dorneywood, Burnham, Buckinghamshire
SL1 8PY **(2:E5)**

1930s-style garden, with herbaceous borders, roses, cottage and kitchen gardens.

⭐ Garden open by written appointment only on four days a year. Write for tickets, giving at least two weeks notice, to the Secretary, Dorneywood Trust, at above address

ℹ️ T 01494 528051 (Regional office)
E dorneywood@nationaltrust.org.uk

Opening arrangements: Dorneywood Garden								
18 May	2 - 5	M	T	**W**	T	F	S	S
1 Jun	2 - 5	M	T	**W**	T	F	S	S
13 Jul	2 - 5	M	T	**W**	T	F	S	S
30 Jul	2 - 5	M	T	W	T	F	**S**	S
Admission by appointment								

The Homewood

Portsmouth Road, Esher, Surrey KT10 9JL   **(2:F6)**

20th-century Modernist house and garden, designed by Patrick Gwynne.

⭐ Limited opening planned on Fridays from 1 April to 28 October and the last Saturday of April–October. Please tel. for details (after 1 March). All visitors must first report to Claremont Landscape Garden. There is no direct access to The Homewood. No WC. Nearest WC at Claremont Landscape Garden

ℹ️ **T** 01372 471144 **F** 01372 464394
E thehomewood@nationaltrust.org.uk

Opening arrangements: The Homewood

	M	T	W	T	**F**	S	S
1 Apr - 28 Oct					**F**		

Admission by guided tour and appointment only. Tel. to book (from 1 Mar). Special tours also on last Sat of the month Apr–Oct. Visitor numbers are limited, but panoramic photographs are available to see on www.nationaltrust.org.uk/homewood

Lamb House

West Street, Rye, East Sussex TN31 7ES   **(2:I8)**

Fine brick-fronted house with walled garden, once home to novelist Henry James.

⭐ Administered and largely maintained on the Trust's behalf by a tenant. No WC

ℹ️ **T** 01372 453401 (Regional office)

💷 £2.90, child £1.40, family £7.25. Groups £2.50

Opening arrangements: Lamb House

26 Mar - 29 Oct	2 - 6	M	T	**W**	T	F	**S**	S

Monk's House

Rodmell, Lewes, East Sussex BN7 3HF   **(2:G8)**

Country retreat of the novelist Virginia Woolf, with interiors reflecting her life and times.

⭐ Administered and largely maintained on the Trust's behalf by a tenant. No WC

ℹ️ **T** 01372 453401 (Regional office)

💷 £2.90, child £1.45, family £7.25. Groups (10+): please book at least 4 weeks in advance

Opening arrangements: Monk's House

2 Apr - 29 Oct	2 - 5:30	M	T	**W**	T	F	**S**	S

Owletts

The Street, Cobham, Gravesend, Kent DA12 3AP   **(2:H5)**

Modest Charles II house with a fine staircase and kitchen garden

⭐ Owletts is occupied as a family home and is administered and maintained on the Trust's behalf by a descendant of the donor. No WC

ℹ️ **T** 01372 453401 (Regional office)

💷 £2.60, child £1.30, family £6.50. Not suitable for groups

Opening arrangements: Owletts

2 Apr - 29 Oct	2 - 5:30	M	T	**W**	**T**	F	**S**	**S**

Pitstone Windmill

Ivinghoe, Buckinghamshire   **(2:E3)**

Example of the earliest form of windmill, dating from 1627.

⭐ No WC

ℹ️ **T** 01442 851227

Opening arrangements: Pitstone Windmill

5 Jun - 28 Aug	2:30 - 6	M	T	W	T	F	S	**S**

Open BHols. Due to staffing restrictions, property may not open as publicised. Please tel. in advance

Princes Risborough Manor House

Princes Risborough, Buckinghamshire HP17 9AW   **(2:E4)**

Elegant late 17th-century house, once home to court painter Sir Peter Lely.

⭐ Hall, drawing room and staircase & front garden open to visitors

ℹ️ **T** 01494 755573

Opening arrangements: Princes Risborough Manor

23 Mar - 26 Oct	2:30 - 4:30	M	T	**W**	T	F	S	S

Only by written appointment with the lessee

For further information check our website www.nationaltrust.org.uk

Priory Cottages

1 Mill Street, Steventon, Abingdon, Oxfordshire OX13 6SP **(2:D4)**

Former monastic buildings, now converted into two houses.

⭐ No WC

ℹ️ **T** 01793 762209 (Coleshill Estate office)

Opening arrangements: Priory Cottages									
30 Mar - 28 Sep	2 - 6	M	T	**W**	T	F	S	S
Admission by written appointment with the tenant								

Quebec House

Quebec Square, Westerham, Kent TN16 1TD **(2:G6)**

Childhood home of General James Wolfe, victor of the Battle of Quebec (1759).

⭐ Administered and maintained on the Trust's behalf by a tenant

ℹ️ **T** 01732 868381 (Chartwell office)

💷 £3.20, child £1.60, family £8. Groups £2.70

Opening arrangements: Quebec House								
3 Apr - 30 Oct	2 - 5:30	M	**T**	W	T	F	S	**S**

Shalford Mill

Shalford, nr Guildford, Surrey GU4 8BS **(2:F6)**

Impressive 18th-century watermill with well-preserved machinery.

⭐ No WC

ℹ️ **T** 01483 561389 **F** 01483 531667
  E riverwey@nationaltrust.org.uk

💷 **Mill**: £2, child £1, family £5. **Booked guided tours**: . Groups £3, child £1.50. Children must be accompanied by an adult

Opening arrangements: Shalford Mill								
23 Mar - 26 Oct	11 - 5	M	T	**W**	T	F	S	S
Guided tours for groups by prior arrangement, except Wed								

St John's Jerusalem

Sutton-at-Hone, Dartford, Kent DA4 9HQ **(2:H5)**

Tranquil moated garden and 13th-century chapel of the Knights Hospitallers.

⭐ Occupied as a private residence, maintained and managed by a tenant on the Trust's behalf. Access is to the chapel and garden only. No WC

ℹ️ **T** 01732 810378 (Ightham Mote)

💷 £1, child 50p, family £2.25

Opening arrangements: St John's Jerusalem								
6 Apr - 28 Sep	2 - 6	M	T	**W**	T	F	S	S
5 Oct - 26 Oct	2 - 4	M	T	**W**	T	F	S	S

Sprivers Garden *

Horsmonden, Kent TN12 8DR **(2:H7)**

Small 18th-century style formal garden, with nearby woodland walk.

⭐ Occupied as a private residence, administered and maintained on the Trust's behalf by a tenant. No access to the house. No WC

ℹ️ **T** 01892 891081

💷 £2.20, child £1.10, family £5.50. **Woodland walk**: Free

Opening arrangements: Sprivers Garden
Open 11, 15, 19 June, 2–5.
Woodland walk (outside garden) open all year

Stoneacre

Otham, Maidstone, Kent ME15 8RS **(2:I6)**

15th-century half-timbered yeoman's house, in a harmonious setting.

⭐ Occupied as a private residence, administered and maintained on the Trust's behalf by a tenant. No WC. Not suitable for coaches

ℹ️ **T/F** 01622 862157 (Tenant)
  E stoneacrent@aol.com

💷 £2.60, child £1.30, family £6.50. Groups £2.20

Opening arrangements: Stoneacre								
19 Mar - 12 Oct	2 - 6	M	T	**W**	T	F	**S**	S
Open BH Mons. Last admission 1hr before closing								

South West South & South East
London East of England
East Midlands West Midlands
North West Yorkshire North East
Wales Northern Ireland

Many of the Trust's London properties date from the time when the countryside was still within sight of the heart of the city. Large estates such as **Osterley Park** are green lungs in the midst of suburbia, and **Sutton House** in Hackney, once part of a small village, is now ideally located for its role as a centre for the Trust's work with inner city schools.

Despite being one of the world's major conurbations, London still contains green and relatively tranquil areas. The Trust has played a major role in securing fragments of the city's once extensive common land, including **East Sheen Common** (not far from **Ham House**) and **Chislehurst Common**. Nearby at **Petts Wood** and **Hawkwood** there are attractive areas of heath, farm and woodland with fine walks. Interesting features of an ancient agricultural landscape can be seen at **Morden Hall Park** and there are woods and open grassland at **Selsdon Wood** near Croydon. At **Watermeads** on the River Wandle at Mitcham, managed as a nature reserve, there is a fascinating wetland and river environment. Keys to Watermeads can be borrowed for daily use from the Property Office at Morden Hall Park, tel. 0208 545 6850. (£10 deposit required.)

OS grid references for properties with no individual entry (OS Landranger map series numbers given in brackets)

Chislehurst Common	[177]	TQ440700
East Sheen Common	[176]	TQ197746
Hawkwood	[177]	TQ441690
Petts Wood	[177]	TQ450681
Selsdon Wood	[177]	TQ357615
Watermeads	[176]	TQ274677

Highlights for Visitors with Disabilities ...
Particularly recommended are the accessible paths through the rose garden and along the river at **Morden Hall Park**.

... and for Families
At **Osterley Park** there is lots of space to run around and play – and free 'Tracker Packs', fun family activities on various themes to do in the park.

Further Information
Please contact the Membership Department, PO Box 39, Warrington WA5 7WD. Tel. 0870 458 4000. Email: enquiries@thenationaltrust.org.uk

The Countryside and Craft Fair at Morden Hall Park, Morden

Previous page: The bay window in the drawing room at Red House, Bexleyheath

Blewcoat School Gift Shop

23 Caxton Street, Westminster, London
SW1H 0PY

🏠 🏛 1954   (2:G5)

Early 18th-century school for the poor, now the National Trust's London shop

Built in 1709 at the expense of a local brewer to provide an education for poor children and used as a school until 1926, this small and elegant building is now the National Trust London Gift Shop and Information Centre.

⭐ No WC

ℹ T/F 020 7222 2877

♿ **Building**: Steps to entrance with handrail

➡ [176: TQ295794] Near the junction of Caxton Street and Buckingham Gate. **Foot**: Thames Path within ⅞ml. **Cycle**: NCN4 ¾ml. **Bus**: Frequent local services (tel. 020 7222 1234). **Underground**: St James's Park (District & Circle Lines) 100yds. **Station**: Victoria ¼ml

🅿 No parking on site

NT properties nearby
Carlyle's House

Opening arrangements: Blewcoat School									
Shop	All Year	10 - 5:30	M	T	W	T	F	S	S
	31 Mar - 22 Dec	10 - 7	M	T	W	T	F	S	S
	19 Nov - 24 Dec	10 - 4	M	T	W	T	F	S	S
Closed BH Mons and Good Fri									

Carlyle's House

24 Cheyne Row, Chelsea, London SW3 5HL

🏠 🛡 1936   (2:F5)

Atmospheric home of the writer Thomas Carlyle and his wife Jane

Historian, social writer, ethical thinker and powerful public speaker, Thomas Carlyle lived in this 1708 Queen Anne terraced house, close to the Thames in Chelsea, from 1834 to 1881. His wife Jane is now considered one of the finest

19th-century women of letters. The Carlyles' house drew visitors from the Victorian literary world, including Dickens and George Eliot. Opened in 1895 as a literary shrine, it contains some of the Carlyles' furniture, books, pictures and personal possessions, together with portraits and memorabilia collected by devotees. Many architectural and domestic features survive, while some decorative detail has been recreated. There is a small walled garden and the surrounding streets are rich in literary and artistic associations.

ℹ T 020 7352 7087 (Custodian)
  F 020 7352 5108
  E carlyleshouse@nationaltrust.org.uk

💷 £4, child £2. Guided tours for groups outside normal hours: NT members £1, non-members £5

🎭 Booked groups welcome: Wed, Thur & Fri between 10 and 1, max. 30. Tel. for details

♿ **Building**: Steps to entrance. Ground floor has steps. Narrow hall. Many stairs to other floors. Seating available

👆 Braille guide. Sensory list

🚩 Booked school groups welcome: Wed, Thur and Fri between 10 and 1, max. 15. Tel. for details

➡ [176: TQ272777] Off Chelsea Embankment between Albert and Battersea Bridges. NT sign on corner of Cheyne Row. Or via Kings Rd and Oakley St. NT sign on corner of Upper Cheyne Row. **Foot**: Thames Path within ⅞ml. **Cycle**: NCN4. **Bus**: Frequent local services (tel. 020 7222 1234). **Underground**: Sloane Square or South Kensington (District & Circle Lines) 1ml. **Station**: Victoria 2ml

🅿 No parking on site

NT properties nearby
Blewcoat School Gift Shop, George Inn

Opening arrangements: Carlyle's House									
House	23 Mar - 28 Oct	2 - 5	M	T	W	T	F	S	S
	26 Mar - 30 Oct	11 - 5	M	T	W	T	F	S	S
Open BH Mons 11-5									

Eastbury Manor House

Eastbury Square, Barking IG11 9SN

🏠 ✳️ 🏛 ☕ 𝒊 🎞 🔔 1918   (2:G5)

Elizabethan merchant's house and gardens

An important example of a medium-sized brick-built Elizabethan manor house, the building is architecturally distinguished and well preserved, with notable early 17th-century wall paintings. Daniel Defoe described the manor in *A Tour Through the Whole Island of Great Britain* as 'where tradition says the Gunpowder Treason Plot was first contrived'. 'Bee boles' can be seen in the walled garden. The property is managed by the London Borough of Barking and Dagenham.

What's new in 2005 Drinks receptions possible in walled garden following civil weddings; Mon and Tues – adults admitted at concessionary rate; portable induction loop; temporary exhibitions on the history of the house

⭐ House open 1st & 2nd Sat of month, all year

ℹ️ **T** 020 8724 1002,
020 8724 1000 (Booking)
F 020 8724 1003
E eastburyhouse@lbbd.gov.uk
W www.barking-dagenham.gov.uk

£ £2.50, child 65p, family £5, concessions £1.25. Groups £2. Mon & Tues: all adults admitted at concessionary rate

🎭 Programme of events. 1st Sat of each month – art & craft stalls and costumed tour guides. 2nd Sat – 'Heritage Days'

♿ Parking in grounds. **Building**: Ramped entrance. 1 wheelchair. Ground floor accessible. Stairs to other floors, lift available. Access to turret is by stairs only. Seating available. **WCs**: Adapted WC. Access via lift. **Grounds**: Fully accessible. Accessible route. Some gravel paths. **Shop**: Level entrance. **Refreshments**: Ramped entrance with handrail. Ramped route to outside refreshment area in kitchen garden

📢 Induction loop in reception. Portable loop available

📖 Braille guide and large-print guide

Opening arrangements: Eastbury Manor House

House	All year	10 - 4	**M**	**T**	W	T	F	S	S
Tea-room/shop	As house	10 - 3:30							

Closed BH Mons. Last admission 45mins before closing. Closed 26, 27 Dec and 2, 3 Jan. House open 1st & 2nd Sat of month, all year

☕ Garden Tea-room (not NT) in house. In good weather, refreshments can be taken in Kitchen Garden. Hot and cold drinks, sandwiches and snacks

👶 Baby-changing facilities. Pushchairs admitted

🏫 Suitable for school groups. Education room/centre. Children's guide. Children's quiz/trail. Children's activities during school hols

🐕 On leads and only in garden

➡️ [177: TQ457838] In Eastbury Square, 10 mins walk S from Upney station (follow brown signs). **Cycle**: LCN15 ¾ml. Upney Lane local cycle route links LCN15 to property. **Bus**: TfL 287, 368 ➡ Barking–Rainham/Chadwell Heath. (Tel. 020 7222 1234).
Underground: Upney (District Line).
Station: Barking, then one stop on District Line to Upney ¼ml. **Road**: ½ml N of A13, 2ml E of A406, just off A123 Ripple Road

P Free street parking available in Eastbury Square, adjacent

NT properties nearby
Rainham Hall, Sutton House

Fenton House

Windmill Hill, Hampstead, London NW3 6RT
Visitors' entrance: Hampstead Grove

🏠 ✳️ 1952   (2:G4)

Handsome 17th-century merchant's house with walled garden

Set in the winding streets of Hampstead village, this late 17th-century house contains an outstanding collection of porcelain, 17th-century needlework pictures and Georgian furniture, and the Benton Fletcher collection of early keyboard instruments, most of which are in working order. The delightful walled garden includes fine displays of roses, an orchard and a working kitchen garden.

What's new in 2005 Bee colony in orchard producing honey for sale; autumn lecture programme

⭐ For audition to use the early keyboard instruments, apply in writing one month in advance to the Curator of Instruments, c/o Fenton House

ℹ️ **T/F** 020 7435 3471, 01494 755563 (Infoline), 01494 755572 (Box office) **E** fentonhouse@nationaltrust.org.uk

💷 £4.80, child £2.40, family £12. Groups £4. **Joint ticket with 2 Willow Road**: £6.60. **Garden only**: £1

🔧 Demonstration tours (max. 20) of instruments by the Curator, 5 May, 2 June, 15 Sept, 6 Oct: £10 (inc. NT members); 27 Oct (young persons tour): £8 child, £2 accompanying adult. 1½–2hrs. Apply to Box office

📅 Programme of events, inc. summer concerts. Send s.a.e. for details

♿ Contact in advance. Tel. for parking arrangements. **Building**: Steps to entrance, ramp available. Ground floor accessible. Many stairs with handrail to other floors. Seating available. Photograph album. **Grounds**: Partly accessible. Accessible route round upper walk and south garden

👁️ Braille guide and large-print guide. Interesting scents

👶 Front-carrying baby slings for loan

🎒 Suitable for school groups. Children's quiz/trail

➡️ [176: TQ262860] Visitors' entrance on W side of Hampstead Grove. **Bus**: Frequent local services (tel. 020 7222 1234). **Underground**: Hampstead (Northern Line) 300yds. **Station**: Hampstead Heath 1ml

🅿️ No parking on site. Not suitable for coaches

NT properties nearby
2 Willow Road, Sutton House

Opening arrangements: Fenton House

House & Garden	5 Mar - 20 Mar	2 - 5	M	T	W	T	F	**S**	**S**
	23 Mar - 28 Oct	2 - 5	M	T	**W**	**T**	**F**	S	S
	26 Mar - 30 Oct	11 - 5	M	T	W	T	F	**S**	**S**

Open BH Mons and Good Fri 11-5. Groups at other times by appointment

George Inn

The George Inn Yard, 77 Borough High Street, Southwark, London SE1 1NH

🏠 👶 🍴 🍺 1937 (2:G5)

Last remaining galleried inn in London

Famous as a coaching inn during the 17th century and mentioned by Dickens in *Little Dorrit*, the George Inn is now leased to a private company and still in use as a public house.

ℹ️ **T** 020 7407 2056

🍴 Licensed restaurant. À la carte Mon to Fri & Sat evening; tel. for reservations. Bar food daily

👶 Children admitted subject to normal licensing regulations

🐕 On leads and only in courtyard

➡️ [176: TQ326801] On E side of Borough High St, near London Bridge Station. **Cycle**: NCN4 ¼ml. **Bus**: Frequent local services (tel. 020 7222 1234). **Station**: London Bridge ≋ & Underground (Northern & Jubilee lines)

NT properties nearby
Carlyle's House, Sutton House

Opening arrangements: George Inn

All year	Licensing hrs **M T W T F S S**

Ham House

Ham Street, Ham, Richmond-upon-Thames TW10 7RS

🏠 ❄️ 🏛️ 🍴 🌳 ♿ 🍺 🔧 1948 (2:F5)

Spectacular 17th-century house with original interiors and formal garden

Ham House is unique in Europe as the most complete survival of 17th-century fashion and power. One of a series of palaces and grand houses along the banks of the Thames, it was built in 1610 and enlarged in the 1670s, when it was at the heart of Restoration court life and intrigue. It was then occupied by the same family until 1948. The formal garden is significant for its survival within the area known

Unless indicated, last admission is always 30mins before closing time

as the cradle of the English Landscape Movement. The outbuildings include an orangery, ice house, still house and dairy with cast iron 'cows legs' supporting marble slabs.

What's new in 2005 Events and exhibition celebrating the Restoration period, marking the 300th anniversary of the death of Catherine of Braganza, wife of King Charles II, for whom Ham's Queen's Apartments were created. Tel. for details

ℹ️ **T** 020 8940 1950,
020 8332 6644 (Functions inc. weddings),
020 8940 0735 (Café),
020 8948 2035 (Shop)
F 020 8332 6903
E hamhouse@nationaltrust.org.uk

💷 £7.50, child £3.75, family £18.75. **Garden only:** £3.50, child £1.75, family £8.75. Admission to garden includes outhouses and introductory video

🎫 Guided tours of house by arrangement – Wed mornings only during the open season. Guided tours of gardens 2 and 3pm Weds (dates as house). Ghost tours in Nov (booking essential)

🎪 Programme of events, inc. open-air theatre, house and ghost tours, school holiday family events, Herb Week in July, 'Putting the House to Bed' and winter programme inc. lectures, recitals and Christmas evening opening

🚶 Walks leaflet available from property. 2-hr walk on Tues 27 Dec at 11 from Ham House

♿ Contact in advance. Separate designated parking. **Building:** Steps to entrance, stairlift available (weather permitting). 3 wheelchairs. Stairs to other floors, lift available. Audio visual/video. **WCs:** Adapted WC. **Grounds:** Fully accessible, loose gravel paths. Accessible route map. Some doubling back required. 2 single-seater PMV, booking essential. **Shop:** Level entrance. **Refreshments:** Steps to entrance, ramp available

♿ Braille guide and large-print guide. Sensory list. Handling collection

🛍️ Local arts and crafts in addition to a good selection of NT items

🍽️ Orangery Café (licensed). Home-grown produce. Children's menu

The Cherry or East Garden, Ham House, Richmond

🚼 Baby-changing facilities. Front-carrying baby slings and hip-carrying infant seats for loan

🏫 Suitable for school groups. Education room/centre. Hands-on activities. Children's guide. Children's quiz/trail

➡️ [176: TQ172732] On S bank of Thames, W of A307, between Richmond and Kingston; Ham gate exit of Richmond Park, readily accessible from M3, M4 and M25. **Foot:** Thames Path passes main entrance. **Cycle:** NCN4. Or access from Twickenham via ferry.
Ferry: Seasonal foot/bike ferry across River Thames from Twickenham (towpath close to Marble Hill House – EH) to Ham. Tel. 020 8892 9620 for details. **Bus:** TfL 371 🚉 Richmond–🚉 Kingston, alight Royal Oak pub, 10 mins walk to house. 65 Ealing Broadway–Kingston, alight Ham Polo Ground, Petersham Rd, 15 mins walk down historic avenues (Tel. 020 7222 1234).
Station: Richmond 🚉 & Underground (District Line), then bus 371, taxi or walk 1½ml via Thames towpath (2ml by road); Kingston 2ml

🅿️ Free parking (not NT), 400yds

NT properties nearby
2 Willow Road, Claremont Landscape Garden, Fenton House, Morden Hall Park, Osterley Park

Opening arrangements: Ham House										
House	19 Mar - 30 Oct	1 - 5	**M**	**T**	**W**	T	F	**S**	**S**
Garden	All year	11 - 6	**M**	**T**	**W**	T	F	**S**	**S**
Café	8 Jan - 13 Mar	11 - 4	M	T	W	T	F	**S**	**S**
Shop	12 Feb - 13 Mar	11 - 4	M	T	W	T	F	**S**	**S**
Shop/Café	19 Mar - 30 Oct	11 - 5:30	**M**	**T**	**W**	T	F	**S**	**S**
Shop/Café	5 Nov - 18 Dec	11 - 4	M	T	W	T	F	**S**	**S**

Open Good Fri: house 1–5; garden 11–6. Garden: closes at dusk if earlier; closed 25, 26 Dec & 1 Jan. Special Christmas shop. Christmas lunches in Dec, some evening openings in Dec for garden/shop/café

There are special events at most Trust properties; please telephone 0870 458 4000 for details

Morden Hall Park

Morden Hall Road, Morden SM4 5JD

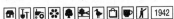 1942   (2:G5)

Open space oasis in the heart of suburbia

The parkland covers over 50ha (125 acres) with the River Wandle meandering through. The river plays an important role in the park with an old Snuff Mill, now used as an education centre, and a variety of bridges traversing it. The park has hay meadows, wetlands, a collection of old estate buildings and an impressive rose garden with over 2000 roses. The workshops now house local craftworkers. There is an independently run garden centre and a city farm.

What's new in 2005 Improved access to Snuff Mill environmental education centre, including adapted WC

[i] **T** 020 8545 6850, 020 8545 6852 (Learning), 020 8687 0881 (Shop) **F** 020 8687 0094 **E** mordenhallpark@nationaltrust.org.uk

[£] Admission free

[♥] Programme of events, inc. Craft Fair 30 April–2 May, run by Four Seasons Events (tel. 01926 812529). There is a charge for all visitors to the fair, inc. NT members

[🖈] Various walks throughout the year. Tel. for details

[♿] Designated parking in main car park, 150yds. **WCs**: Adapted WC. **Grounds**: Partly accessible. Accessible route map. Some unsurfaced paths. **Shop**: Level entrance. **Refreshments**: Level entrance

[👁] Braille guide and large-print guide. Sensory list

[🏠] NT shop. Garden centre run by Capital Gardens plc as NT tenants (tel. 020 8646 3002). Craft workshops

Opening arrangements: Morden Hall Park			
Park	All year	8 - 6	**M T W T F S S**
Shop	All year	10 - 5	**M T W T F S S**
Café	All year	10 - 5	**M T W T F S S**

Car park by café, shop and garden centre closes at 6.
Shop and café closed 25, 26 Dec & 1 Jan. Rose Garden and estate buildings area open 8–6

[♨] Riverside Café. Children's menu

[🎏] In fenced, dog-free paddock for families

[👶] Baby-changing facilities

[🏫] Suitable for school groups. Education room/centre. Full educational programme. Snuff Mill Centre for community groups and family holiday activities. Discovery Days during school hols

[🐕] On leads around buildings and rose garden; under close control elsewhere

[🚲] Park is flat and ideal for family cycling. Wandle Trail passes through

[→] [176: TQ261684] Near Morden town centre. **Foot**: Wandle Trail from Sutton or Wandsworth. **Cycle**: NCN22. Route passes through park. **Bus**: Frequent from surrounding areas (tel. 020 7222 1234). **Underground**: Morden (Northern Line) 500yds to park, 800yds to café & shop. **Tram**: Tramlink to Phipps Bridge stop, on park boundary. 10 mins from ≋ Wimbledon/Underground (District Line); also connects to ≋ Croydon. **Road**: Off A24, and A297 S of Wimbledon, N of Sutton

[P] Free parking, 25yds

NT properties nearby
Claremont Landscape Garden, Ham House

Osterley Park

Jersey Road, Isleworth TW7 4RB

[🏠][♣][🏠][♨][🎭][🔔][T] 1949   (2:F5)

Neo-classical house with Adam interiors, landscaped park and pleasure grounds

In 1761 the founders of Child's Bank commissioned Robert Adam to transform a crumbling Tudor mansion into an elegant neo-classical villa. This was their house in the country, created for entertainment and to impress friends and business associates. Today the spectacular interiors contain one of Britain's most complete examples of Adam's work. The magnificent 16th-century stables survive largely intact. The house is set in extensive park and farm land, complete with Pleasure Grounds and neo-classical garden buildings.

For further information check our website www.nationaltrust.org.uk

What's new in 2005 Mons in Aug: hands-on activities for children and families. Tues in Aug: meet some of the past inhabitants of Osterley. SeaBritain: in Sept *The New Trafalgar Despatch* calls at Osterley (commemorating events of 1805)

[i] **T** 020 8232 5050, 01494 755566 (Infoline), 020 8232 5069 (Learning), 01494 755572 (Box office), 020 8232 5062 (Shop), 020 8232 5052 (Gallery), 020 8232 5057 (Tea-room) **F** 020 8232 5080 **E** osterley@nationaltrust.org.uk

[£] **House**: £4.90, child £2.40, family £12.20. Groups £4. Reduced rate when arriving by public transport for house visitors with valid TfL travelcard. **Park & pleasure grounds**: free

[*] Booked out-of-hours 'Private View' with morning coffee Wed to Fri mornings £12 per person (inc. NT members). Minimum charge £180. Groups with own guide must book

[*] Estate guide features 2½ml waymarked trail around the park

[♿] Designated parking in main car park, 250yds. Transfer available. **Building**: Many steps to entrance. Alternative accessible entrance, stairclimber available, unsuitable for powered

Detail of the Entrance Hall, Osterley Park

or non-standard chairs, or if steps are wet. Please contact car park or info point staff on arrival. 2 wheelchairs. Seating available. Photograph album. Separate ground floor entrance to Jersey Galleries. **WCs**: Adapted WC. Close at 6pm. **Grounds**: Accessible route. PMVs available 1:30–4:30 Wed, Thur, Sat, Sun and BHols from May. 2 single-seater PMV, 1 multi-seater PMV. **Shop**: Ramped entrance. **Refreshments**: Level entrance. Large-print menu

[♿] Braille guide and large-print guide. Sensory list

[♿] The Stables Tea-room (licensed) in Tudor stableblock. Children's menu

[🏚] Picnic tables adjacent to car park

[🚼] Baby-changing facilities. Pushchairs admitted. Front-carrying baby slings and hip-carrying infant seats for loan

[📷] Suitable for school groups. Education room/centre. Live interpretation. Hands-on activities. Children's guide. Family activity packs

[🐕] On leads unless indicated, only in park

Opening arrangements: Osterley Park										
House	5 Mar - 20 Mar	1 - 4:30	M	T	W	T	F	**S**	**S**
	23 Mar - 30 Oct	1 - 4:30	M	T	**W**	**T**	**F**	**S**	**S**
Shop	5 Mar - 20 Mar	1 - 5:30	M	T	W	T	F	**S**	**S**
	23 Mar - 31 Jul	1 - 5:30	M	T	**W**	**T**	**F**	**S**	**S**
	1 Aug - 4 Sep	1 - 5:30	**M**	**T**	**W**	**T**	**F**	**S**	**S**
	7 Sep - 30 Oct	1 - 5:30	M	T	**W**	**T**	**F**	**S**	**S**
	2 Nov - 18 Dec	12 - 4	M	T	**W**	**T**	**F**	**S**	**S**
Tea-room	5 Mar - 20 Mar	11:30 - 5	M	T	W	T	F	**S**	**S**
	23 Mar - 31 Jul	11:30 - 5	M	T	**W**	**T**	**F**	**S**	**S**
	1 Aug - 4 Sep	11:30 - 5	**M**	**T**	**W**	**T**	**F**	**S**	**S**
	7 Sep - 30 Oct	11:30 - 5	M	T	**W**	**T**	**F**	**S**	**S**
	2 Nov - 18 Dec	12 - 4	M	T	**W**	**T**	**F**	**S**	**S**
Jersey Galleries	As house								
Park	All year	9 - 7:30	**M**	**T**	**W**	**T**	**F**	**S**	**S**
Pleasure Grnds	As Park								

Open BH Mons. Park & Pleasure Grounds close dusk if earlier than 7.30. On Sats house may operate guided tours only. Tel. property during week prior to visiting for details

Please note: groups must book in advance with the property

🚲 2½ml of cycle route with shared access

➔ [176: TQ146780] **Cycle**: Links to London cycle network. **Bus**: TfL H28 Hayes–Hounslow–Osterley, H91 Hounslow–Hammersmith to within ½ml. **Underground**: Osterley (Piccadilly Line), turn left on leaving station, ½ml. **Station**: Syon Lane 1½ml. **Road**: Follow brown tourist signs on A4 between Gillette Corner and Osterley underground station; M4, exit 3 then follow A312/A4 towards central London. Main gates at junction with Thornbury and Jersey Roads

🅿 Parking, 250yds, £3.50. Coach-parking free. Car park closed 25, 26 Dec

NT properties nearby
Ham House

Red House

Red House Lane, Bexleyheath DA6 8JF

🏠 ✳ 📷 ☕ 2003   (2:H5)

Home of William Morris, artist, craftsman and philosopher

Commissioned by William Morris in 1859 and designed by Philip Webb, Red House is of enormous international significance in the history of domestic architecture and garden design. The building is constructed of warm red brick, under a steep red-tiled roof, with an emphasis on natural materials and a strong Gothic influence. The garden was designed to 'clothe' the house with a series of subdivided areas which still clearly exist. Inside, the house retains many of the original features and fixed items of furniture designed by Morris and Webb, as well as wall paintings and stained glass by Burne-Jones. Originally surrounded by orchards and countryside, Red House and its garden now provide an oasis in a suburban environment.

⭐ The property was lived in as a family home for nearly 150 years, during which time many changes took place. The Trust opened Red House soon after its acquisition in 2003 so that visitors could see the property as it was when first acquired, and follow its journey as research reveals the house and garden which Morris and Webb originally created. No WC

Opening arrangements: Red House

16 Feb - 27 Feb	11 - 4:15		M	T	**W**	**T**	**F**	**S**	**S**
2 Mar - 30 Sep	11 - 5		M	T	**W**	**T**	**F**	**S**	**S**
1 Oct - 31 Dec	11 - 4:15		M	T	**W**	**T**	**F**	**S**	**S**

Admission by guided tour only, booking essential. Open BH Mons. Last tour 45 mins before closing. Closed 25/26 Dec and 1 Jan to 14 Feb 06

ℹ **T** 01494 755588 (Booking line, Mon–Fri 9:30–4), 01494 559799 (Infoline)

£ £6, child £3, family £15

♿ Limited pre-booked parking for disabled drivers. **Grounds**: Accessible route

🛍 Sales table. Limited range of items

☕ Limited refreshments available in coach house (tea and cakes)

➔ [177: TQ481750] **Station**: ➿ Bexleyheath, ¾ml. **Road**: Off A221 Bexleyheath. Visitors will be advised how to reach the property when booking

🅿 No parking on site. Parking is at Danson Park, (15 mins walk). 90p parking charge at weekends and BHols

NT properties nearby
Ightham Mote, Knole, Sutton House

Sutton House

2 & 4 Homerton High Street, Hackney, London E9 6JQ

🏠 📷 ☕ 🍴 🎧 ♿ 🛍 1938   (2:G4)

Tudor house with a fascinating history

A unique survival in London's East End, Sutton House was built in 1535 by Sir Ralph Sadleir, a rising star at the court of Henry VIII. It became home to successive merchants, Huguenot silk-weavers, Victorian schoolmistresses and Edwardian clergy, and although altered over the years, remains an essentially Tudor house. Oak-panelled rooms and carved fireplaces survive intact and an exhibition tells the history of the house and its former occupants.

ℹ **T** 020 8986 2264
  E suttonhouse@nationaltrust.org.uk

£ £2.50, child 50p, family £5.50. Groups £2

Parking in National Trust car parks is free for members

The Great Chamber, Sutton House, Hackney

☻ Programme of events, inc. Black History Month (Oct). Tel. for details

♿ Drop-off point. **Building**: Level entrance, ramp available. 1 wheelchair, booking essential. Ground floor accessible. Stairs to other floors. Seating available. Photograph album. **WCs**: Adapted WC. **Shop**: Level entrance. **Refreshments**: Level entrance

🔊 Induction loop in reception, shop

👁 Braille guide and large-print guide. Interesting scents

🍽 Brick Place Café (not NT) (licensed). Children's menu

🚼 Baby-changing facilities. Pushchairs admitted

🏫 Suitable for school groups. Education room/centre. Hands-on activities. Children's quiz/trail. Children's activity packs. Adult study days

→ [176: TQ352851] At the corner of Isabella Road and Homerton High Street.
Cycle: NCN1 1¼ml. **Underground**: Highbury & Islington (Victoria Line) then bus 30 or 277; Bethnal Green (Central Line) then bus 106 or

Opening arrangements: Sutton House

Historic rooms	21 Jan - 17 Dec	1 - 5	M	T	W	T	**F**	**S**	S
	23 Jan - 18 Dec	11:30 - 5	M	T	W	T	F	**S**	**S**
Art Gallery	19 Jan - 18 Dec	11:30 - 5	M	T	**W**	**T**	**F**	**S**	**S**
Shop	As Art Gallery								
Café-bar	As Art Gallery								

Open BH Mons 11.30–5. Closed Good Fri. Property reopens 19 Jan '06

256. (Tel. 020 7222 1234). **Station**: Hackney Central ¼ml; Hackney Downs ½ml

🅿 No parking on site. Metered parking on adjacent streets

NT properties nearby
2 Willow Road, Eastbury Manor House, Fenton House, Rainham Hall

---

2 Willow Road

Hampstead, London NW3 1TH

🏠 🚶 1994 (2:G4)

1930s Modernist house designed by Ernö Goldfinger

The architect Ernö Goldfinger designed and built the house as his family home in 1939. The central house of a terrace of three, it is one of Britain's most important examples of Modernist architecture and is filled with furniture also designed by Goldfinger. The art collection includes a number of significant British and European 20th-century works by Bridget Riley, Max Ernst and Henry Moore amongst others.

What's new in 2005 Popular walks programme extended. Late opening 1st Thurs, Apr–Oct

⭐ No WC. Local pub allows visitors to use their facilities

ℹ **T/F** 020 7435 6166, 01494 755570 (Infoline), 01494 755572 (Walks information)
E 2willowroad@nationaltrust.org.uk

£ £4.60, child £2.30, family £11.50. **Joint ticket with Fenton House**: £6.60

🚶 Walks programme runs throughout the year, covering London inc. Hampstead, the South Bank, Barbican and the City

Opening arrangements: 2 Willow Road

	5 Mar - 19 Mar	12 - 5	M	T	W	T	F	**S**	**S**
*	24 Mar - 29 Oct	12 - 5	M	T	W	**T**	**F**	**S**	**S**
	5 Nov - 26 Nov	12 - 5	M	T	W	T	F	**S**	**S**

Open Good Fri. Tours 12, 1 & 2. Tour lasts approx. 1hr. Places limited, but no booking required. Free-flow access 3–5. Introductory film shown at intervals throughout the afternoon. *Also late opening on first Thur of each month April–Oct. Evening tours at 5 & 6 and free-flow 7–9 (not open 12–5 on those days)

♿ Parking at front of house available for people requiring close access. **Building**: Level entrance. Small hallway and a cinema accessible on ground floor. Many stairs with handrail to other floors. Seating available. Audio visual/video

🔊 Induction loop in reception and Portable loop for guided tours. Subtitled introductory film and some signed tours. Email for details

♿ Braille guide and large-print guide. Braille plans. Guided tours

🎨 Children's quiz/trail

➡ [176: TQ270858] On corner of Willow Road and Downshire Hill. **Foot**: From Hampstead underground, left down High Street and first left down Flask Walk (pedestrianised). Turn right at the end into Willow Road.
Bus: Frequent local services (tel. 020 7222 1234). **Underground**: Hampstead (Northern Line) ½ml. **Station**: Hampstead Heath ¼ml

🅿 No parking on site. Limited on-street parking. East Heath Road municipal car park, 100yds, open intermittently

NT properties nearby
Fenton House

Properties open less often

This section includes National Trust properties, often tenanted, which are open two days a week or less (plus Bank Holidays in some cases). Visits to some must be made by prior arrangement and where this applies admission prices are not shown (please ask when making contact). **Full details are on our website www.nationaltrust.org.uk or obtainable from the Membership Department, tel. 0870 458 4000.**

Lindsey House

99/100 Cheyne Walk, Chelsea, London
SW10 0DQ (2:G5)
Elegant 17th-century town house.

⭐ Ground-floor entrance hall, main staircase to first floor, and front and rear gardens open on four Wednesdays in 2005

ℹ **T** 020 7447 6605 (NT London area office)

Opening arrangements: Lindsey House
Open Wed 11 May, 15 Jun, 14 Sep, 12 Oct, 2–4

Rainham Hall

The Broadway, Rainham, Havering
RM13 9YN (2:H5)
Elegant Georgian house in the Dutch style.

⭐ No WC

ℹ **T** 01708 555 360

£ £2.30, child £1.10, family £5.70

Opening arrangements: Rainham Hall									
30 Mar - 26 Oct	2 - 6	M	T	**W**	T	F	S	S

Open BH Mons. Open Sat by written appointment with tenant

'Roman' Bath

5 Strand Lane, London WC2 (2:G5)
Remains of a bath – possibly Roman.

⭐ The Bath is administered and maintained by Westminster City Council. No WC

ℹ **T** 020 7447 6605 (NT London area office), 020 7641 5263 (Westminster City Council)
F 020 7641 5215

Opening arrangements: 'Roman' Bath									
4 May - 28 Sep	1 - 5	M	T	**W**	T	F	S	S

Admission by appointment only with Westminster CC (24 hrs' notice) during office hours. Bath visible through window from pathway all year

South West South & South East
London **East of England**
East Midlands West Midlands
North West Yorkshire North East
Wales Northern Ireland

The East of England is characterised by wide expanses of open countryside and sweeping views under huge skies. Here also is a remote and beautiful coastline, studded with unspoilt fishing villages, ancient historical sites and internationally renowned nature reserves.

The North Norfolk coast is one of the most scenic areas of Britain, and is particularly important for its birdlife. At **Morston Marshes** and **Stiffkey Marshes** a range of seabirds can be seen, as well as seals at **Blakeney Point**. **Brancaster** is noted for its coastal flora and the site of the Roman fort of **Branodonum**. There are several National Trust-owned properties in the Sheringham area, including the highest point in Norfolk at **West Runton**, beautiful landscape and woodland at **Sheringham Park** and woods and heathland at **Beeston Regis Heath**. Spectacular views can be had from **Incleborough Hill**.

On the edge of Norfolk's famous Broads is **Horsey Mere**, where the Trust owns over 800ha (1900 acres) of marshland, marrams and farmland, as well as **Horsey Windpump**. In the past much of East Anglia was subject to regular flooding and drainage mills such as this were essential to maintain water levels. Another example can be seen at **Wicken Fen National Nature Reserve** in Cambridgeshire, a haven for rare wildlife and virtually the last remnant of the extensive fenland that once covered much of eastern England, with eighteen footpath routes. The imposing **Houghton Mill** near Huntingdon with its riverside meadow makes an ideal spot from which to explore the wider countryside along the River Great Ouse.

The remote character of the east coast led to the construction of the fascinating military research buildings at **Orford Ness** in Suffolk. The Ness, recently designated as a National Nature Reserve, is also an important site for breeding and overwintering birds. There are many interesting natural habitats in this area, including **Dunwich Heath**, a surviving fragment of the sandy heaths locally known as the Sandlings, and **Minsmere Beach**, adjacent to the famous bird reserve. Further south, there are pleasant walks and fine views at **Kyson Hill** near Woodbridge, and at **Pin Mill** on the River Orwell, where a wealth of sailing boats is usually present. At **Sutton Hoo** you can get close to one of the most fascinating archaeological sites in this country's history, and enjoy walks over rare lowland heath on the estuary of the River Deben. The picturesque qualities of the Essex/Suffolk border became famous through the work of John Constable, and at Bridge Cottage at **Flatford** there is an exhibition of his work and a

Blakeney Point, Norfolk.

Previous page: Ickworth House, Suffolk

The crumbling cliffs of Dunwich Heath, Suffolk

range of other facilities. Fine walks lead into the beautiful **Dedham Vale**. There are good birdwatching opportunities on the Essex coast, especially on the reserve of **Northey Island** in the Blackwater estuary (access by advance permit only from the Warden, Northey Cottage, Northey Island, Maldon, tel. 01621 853142). **Copt Hall Marshes**, near Little Wigborough, is another noted site, particularly for overwintering birds, and can be viewed from a waymarked circular route.

The ancient landscapes of East Anglia include **Danbury** and **Lingwood Commons**, a survival of the medieval manors of St Clere and Herons and a former area of common grazing, and **Blake's Wood**, an area of hornbeam and chestnut coppice, renowned in spring for its display of bluebells. **Hatfield Forest** near Bishop's Stortford is an outstanding ancient

woodland and rare surviving example of a medieval royal hunting forest, offering excellent walking. All these areas are designated SSSIs and are rich in wildlife.

The Trust is also fortunate in owning two motte-and-bailey castles: **Darrow Wood**, near Harleston in Norfolk, and **Rayleigh Mount** in Essex, recorded in the Domesday Book and providing excellent recreational space in the heart of Rayleigh town.

One of the Trust's most unusual properties in this part of England is **Whipsnade Tree Cathedral,** where different species have been planted in the form of a nave and transepts. There are many excellent walks to be had on nearby **Dunstable Downs**, which command outstanding views over the Vale of Aylesbury and along the Chiltern Ridge.

Regional Highlights for Visitors with Disabilities ...
Wicken Fen, **Sutton Hoo, Sheringham Park** and **Hatfield Forest** all have accessible pathways; **Ickworth** has a special scented walk.

...and for Families
All NT restaurants in the East of England region have special play areas for children. There are children's playgrounds at Blickling, Ickworth, Sutton Hoo and Wimpole; **Wimpole Home Farm** is a must for families with young children.

Above: Orford Ness, Suffolk
Left: Hatfield Forest, Essex

Further Information
Please contact the Membership Department, PO Box 39, Warrington WA5 7WD. Tel. 0870 458 4000. Email: enquiries@thenationaltrust.org.uk

Walks leaflets are available at the following properties: Blickling, Dunwich Heath, Felbrigg, Hatfield Forest, Ickworth, Orford Ness, Sheringham Park, West Runton, Wicken Fen and Wimpole Hall. Leaflets on walks and events are also available from the Membership Department.

OS Grid Reference

OS grid references for main properties with no individual entry (OS Landranger map series numbers given in brackets)

Beeston Regis Heath	[133] TG173418
Blake's Wood	[167] TL773067
Branodonum	[132] TF781439
Copt Hall Marshes	[168] TL981146
Danbury & Lingwood Commons	[167] TL773068
Darrow Wood	[156] TM265894
Horsey Mere	[134] TG456223
Incleborough Hill	[133] TG189423
Kyson Hill	[169] TM269477
Minsmere Beach	[156] TM476678
Morston Marshes	[132] TG010445
Northey Island	[168] TL872058
Pin Mill	[169] TM214380
Stiffkey Marshes	[133] TG956439
West Runton	[133] TG184414

Anglesey Abbey, Garden & Lode Mill

Quy Road, Lode, Cambridge, Cambridgeshire
CB5 9EJ

🏠 🏹 ❖ 🏛 💻 🎦 1966　　(3:G6)

Jacobean-style country house set in fine formal and informal gardens

The house, dating from 1600 and built on the site of a 12th-century Augustinian priory, houses a unique collection representing the tastes of one man, Huttleston Broughton, 1st Lord Fairhaven. The many paintings include notable works by Claude Lorraine, there are fine examples of furniture, silver and tapestries and one of the Trust's largest collections of clocks. It is surrounded by 40ha (98 acres) of landscape garden and arboretum with over 100 pieces of sculpture. There is all-year-round floral interest in the garden with the Winter Garden, extensive snowdrop collection in January and February, hyacinth displays in the spring, herbaceous borders and dahlia gardens in the summer and magnificent autumn foliage. There is a new woodland path to explore. The watermill has milling days on the first and third Saturday of each month – subject to water levels.

⭐ New visitor facilities being prepared for opening in May 2006. Any disruption during the building work will be kept to a minimum – business continues as usual

ℹ️ **T** 01223 810080 **F** 01223 810088
E angleseyabbey@nationaltrust.org.uk

💷 **House & garden, summer**: £7, child £3.50.
Garden, summer: £4.30, child £2.15.
Garden, winter: £3.60, child £1.80. Reduced rate when arriving by public transport or cycle. Group visits information pack

🎭 Programme of events. Send s.a.e. for details

♿ Separate designated parking. Transfer available. **Building**: Steps to entrance. Alternative accessible entrance. 5 wheelchairs, booking essential. Stairs to other floors, stairlift available. Booking essential. Seating available. Photograph album, virtual tour. **Mill**: Access to lower floor only, ramp available. **WCs**: Adapted WC. **Grounds**: Fully accessible. Accessible route map. 5 single-seater PMV, 1 multi-seater PMV, booking essential. Staff-driven multi-seater vehicle. **Shop**: Level entrance. **Refreshments**: Level entrance. Large-print menu

📢 Induction loop in reception, shop, restaurant

👁 Braille guide and large-print guide. Sensory list

🛍 NT shop. Plant sales

🍴 Licensed restaurant. Children's menu

⛱ In picnic area alongside restaurant, available subject to building work

🚼 Baby-changing facilities. Front-carrying baby slings for loan

👨‍👩‍👧 Children's quiz/trail. Adult study days. Garden activity packs – summer season

🐕 On leads and only in car park and on public footpaths, not in gardens

Cross Avenue, Anglesey Abbey Garden, Cambridgeshire

Opening arrangements: Anglesey Abbey

House	23 Mar - 30 Oct	1 - 5	M T W T F S S
Lode Mill	5 Mar - 20 Mar	11 - 3:30	M T W T F S S
	23 Mar - 30 Oct	1 - 5	M T W T F S S
	5 Nov - 18 Dec	11 - 3:30	M T W T F S S
	31 Dec - 19 Mar 06	11 - 3:30	M T W T F S S
Garden	2 Mar - 20 Mar	10:30 - 4:30	M T W T F S S
	23 Mar - 3 Jul	10:30 - 5:30	M T W T F S S
	6 Jul - 4 Sep	10:30 - 5:30	M T W T F S S
	7 Sep - 30 Oct	10:30 - 5:30	M T W T F S S
	2 Nov - 18 Dec	10:30 - 4:30	M T W T F S S
	28 Dec - 19 Mar 06	10:30 - 4:30	M T W T F S S
Restaurant	As garden		
Shop/plants	As garden		

Admission by timed ticket to house on Suns and BH Mons. Open BH Mons. **Property closed 2 Jan '06**

➜ [154: TL533622] **Foot**: Harcamlow Way from Cambridge. **Cycle**: NCN51 1¼ml.
Bus: Stagecoach in Cambridge 111, 122 from Cambridge (frequent services link 🚇 Cambridge and bus station).
Station: Cambridge 6ml. **Road**: 6ml NE of Cambridge on B1102. Signposted from A14

P Free parking

NT properties nearby
Houghton Mill, Ickworth, Wicken Fen, Wimpole Hall, Wimpole Home Farm

Blakeney National Nature Reserve

c/o The National Trust Office, Friary Farm, Cley Road, Blakeney, Holt, Norfolk NR25 7NW

 1912   (3:13)

One of the largest expanses of undeveloped coastal habitats of its type in Europe

Blakeney National Nature Reserve extends to 1097ha (2711 acres) almost all of which is within the ownership of the National Trust. It includes Blakeney Point, Blakeney Freshes, Morston and Stiffkey Marshes and supports a wide range of coastal plant communities with many nationally important species. Blakeney Point itself is a 3½ml long sand and shingle spit, noted for its colonies of breeding terns and migrant birds passing

through. Both common and grey seals can also be seen. An information centre at Morston Quay provides further details on the area.

ℹ️ **T** 01263 740241 (Office),
01263 740480 (Warden) **F** 01263 740241
E blakeneypoint@nationaltrust.org.uk

£ No landing fee. Access on foot from Cley Beach (3½ml) or by ferry from Morston and Blakeney (tidal). Restricted access to certain areas of the Point during the main bird breeding season (April to July)

🚸 For school groups and special interest groups (small charge) by arrangement

♿ Access to this site can be difficult due to the nature of the undulating terrain. The site is subject to intermittent tides. There is also a shingle ridge which has to be crossed, which is also affected by the tides. Ferry available (not NT)

🍵 Tea-room (NT-approved concession) at Morston Quay. No tea-room at Blakeney Point

🏫 Suitable for school groups

🐕 On leads only. No dogs west of Old Lifeboat House on Blakeney Point, April to Sept

➜ [133: TG000460] **Foot**: Norfolk Coast Path passes property. **Cycle**: Regional route 30 runs along ridge above the coast.
Ferry: Ferries to Blakeney Point. **Bus**: Norfolk Green Coast Hopper 36 🚇 Sheringham–Hunstanton; Sanders 45, 46/A Fakenham–Holt–Norwich. **Station**: Sheringham (U) 8ml.
Road: Morston Quay, Blakeney and Cley are all off A149 Cromer–Hunstanton road

P Parking, £2.50 (pay & display). NT members must display cards. Car parks at Blakeney Quay (administered by Blakeney Parish Council) and Morston Quay

NT properties nearby
Brancaster, Felbrigg Hall, Sheringham Park

Opening arrangements: Blakeney NNR

Reserve	All year	M T W T F S S

Tea-room and information centre at Morston Quay open according to tides and weather

---

Please see the area introductions for details of coast & countryside properties

Blickling Hall, Garden & Park

Blickling, Norwich, Norfolk NR11 6NF

🏠 🎨 ❄ 🌳 🎣 🕆 📷 🖥 🔔 📊 1942   (3:14)

Magnificent Jacobean house, garden and park

Built in the early 17th century and one of England's great Jacobean houses, Blickling is famed for its spectacular long gallery, superb plasterwork ceilings and fine collections of furniture, pictures, books and tapestries. The gardens are full of colour throughout the year and the extensive parkland features a lake and a series of beautiful woodland and lakeside walks.

⭐ An exhibition in the Harness Room outlines Blickling's World War Two connections with nearby RAF Oulton. Croquet available

ℹ️ **T** 01263 738030,
01263 731994 (Countryside Dept),
01263 738015 (Cycle hire),
01263 738050 (Learning),
0870 010 4900 (Box office),
01263 738046 (Shop),
01263 738053 (Plant sales),
01263 738045 (Restaurant)
F 01263 738035
E blickling@nationaltrust.org.uk

Opening arrangements: Blickling Hall										
House	19 Mar - 2 Oct	1 - 5	M	T	**W**	**T**	**F**	**S**	**S**
	5 Oct - 30 Oct	1 - 4	M	T	**W**	**T**	**F**	**S**	**S**
Garden	19 Mar - 31 Jul	10:15 - 5:15	M	T	**W**	**T**	**F**	**S**	**S**
	2 Aug - 4 Sep	10:15 - 5:15	M	**T**	**W**	**T**	**F**	**S**	**S**
	7 Sep - 30 Oct	10:15 - 5:15	M	T	**W**	**T**	**F**	**S**	**S**
	3 Nov - 23 Dec	11 - 4	M	T	W	**T**	**F**	**S**	**S**
	5 Jan - 18 Mar 06	11 - 4	M	T	W	**T**	**F**	**S**	**S**
Park	All year	Dawn – dusk	**M**	**T**	**W**	**T**	**F**	**S**	**S**
Plant centre	19 Mar - 30 Oct	10:15 - 5:15	M	T	**W**	**T**	**F**	**S**	**S**
Shop	As garden								
Restaurant	As garden								
Bookshop	As garden								
Art galleries	19 Mar - 30 Oct	11 - 4:30	M	T	**W**	**T**	**F**	**S**	**S**
Cycle hire	19 Mar - 30 Oct	10:15 - 5:15	M	T	W	T	F	**S**	**S**

Open BH Mons. Plant centre also open Tues in Aug. Cycle hire also available Wed–Sun during school hols March–Oct, 10.15–5.15

💷 £7.30, child £3.65, family £18.60. Groups £6.20. **Garden only**: £4.20, child £2.10. Groups £3.60. Free access to South Front, shop, restaurant, plant centre, secondhand bookshop, art exhibitions. Coarse fishing in lake; permits available at lakeside

🎟 Taster tours of house at 11.45 on most house open days (check on day for availabilty, £2 extra, inc. NT members). Garden tours at 2 on most garden open days (check on day for availability, £1 extra inc. NT members). Guided estate walks (approx. 3ml), twice a month: free. Tel. for details

🎭 Programme of events. Changing series of art exhibitions in 3 separate locations

🚶 3 waymarked walks

♿ Separate designated parking, 50yds. Steep slope from designated car park. Drop-off point. **Building**: Ramped entrance. 2 wheelchairs. Ground floor accessible. Stairs to other floors, lift available. Stairs only to basement rooms and document room. Seating available. **WCs**: Adapted WC. **Grounds**: Fully accessible. Accessible route map. 2 seated walking frames available. 3 single-seater PMV. **Shop**: Ramped entrance. **Refreshments**: Ramped entrance

👆 Braille guide and large-print guide. Touchable objects. Handling collection

🛍 NT Shop. Secondhand bookshop in Lothian Barn. Plant sales

🍴 Licensed restaurant East Wing. Children's menu

🪑 In orchard and outside visitor reception in main car park

🍼 Baby-changing and feeding facilities. Front-carrying baby slings and hip-carrying infant seats for loan. Children's play area

🏫 Suitable for school groups. Education room/centre. Hands-on activities. Family guide. Children's guide. Children's quiz/trail. Family activity packs. Education groups welcome. Workshops available

🐕 On leads at all times and only in park

🚲 Cycle hire centre in orchard picnic area. Bridleways on property give shared use for cyclists. Map available

Unless indicated, last admission is always 30mins before closing time

Aerial view of Blickling Hall, Norfolk

➜ [133: TG178286] **Foot**: Weavers' Way from near Aylsham, 2ml. Queen Anne's Walk 1½ml. **Cycle**: Permitted path alongside Bure Valley Rly, ➤ Wroxham–Aylsham. **Bus**: First Sanders X4/X50/44 Norwich–Holt (passing close ➤ Norwich), alight Aylsham 1½ml. **Station**: Aylsham (Bure Valley Rly from ➤ Hoveton & Wroxham) 1¾ml; North Walsham (U) 8ml. **Road**: 1½ml NW of Aylsham on B1354. Signposted off A140 Norwich (15ml N) to Cromer (10ml S) road

P Free parking, 300yds

NT properties nearby
Felbrigg Hall, Sheringham Park

Brancaster

Brancaster Millennium Activity Centre, Dial House, Brancaster Staithe, King's Lynn, Norfolk
PE31 8BW

 1923   (3:H3)

Large area of coastal habitat, particularly noted for birdlife

Around the village of Brancaster Staithe, the NT looks after an extensive area of saltmarsh, intertidal mud and sandflats, the site of the Roman fort of Branodonum and Scolt Head Island. The Activity Centre offers residential and day courses for schools, adults and families.

What's new in 2005 SeaBritain events throughout the year for adults and children

★ A private ferry runs from Burnham Overy Staithe (weather permitting) taking visitors to the National Nature Reserve on Scolt Head Island, managed by English Nature (EN Warden: tel. 01328 711866) and an important breeding site for four species of tern, oystercatcher and ringed plover. It is dangerous to walk over the saltmarshes and sandflats at low tide. Ferry, tel. 01485 210456

ℹ **T** 01485 210719
E brancaster@nationaltrust.org.uk

☺ Family fun weeks and activity days for children in school hols. Tel. for details

♿ **Building**: Tel. Millennium Centre for details

▦ Suitable for school groups. Education room/centre. Adult study days. The Brancaster Millennium Activity Centre offers residential courses for schools, from Key Stage 2 to A-level, with cutting-edge environmental technology. Also field studies and outdoor pursuits, inc. birdwatching, coastal processes, woodlands, saltmarshes, orienteering, sailing, kayaking and cycling. Programme for adults of day and weekend courses in craft, cookery and birdwatching

Opening arrangements: Brancaster

All year		M T W T F S S

There are special events at most Trust properties; please telephone 0870 458 4000 for details

🐕 Under control at all times on the beach; not on Scolt Head Island mid-April to mid-Aug. Dog-free area on Brancaster Beach, W of golf clubhouse May to Sept

🚲 Education centre offers group cycling activities; all staff trained in cycle group leadership. 'Start Cycling' scheme organised for groups

➔ [132: TF800450] **Foot**: Norfolk Coast Path passes property. **Cycle**: NCN1 runs along ridge above the coast. **Bus**: Norfolk Green Coast Hopper 36 ≋ Sheringham–Hunstanton. **Road**: Brancaster Staithe is halfway between Wells and Hunstanton on A149 coast road

P Parking (not NT) at golf club, charge inc. NT members. Limited parking at the Staithe

NT properties nearby
Blakeney National Nature Reserve

Coggeshall Grange Barn

Grange Hill, Coggeshall, Colchester, Essex CO6 1RE

🏠 🖾 1989 (3:H8)

13th-century monastic barn

This majestic building is one of the oldest surviving timber-framed barns in Europe and was originally part of a Cistercian monastery. It was restored in the 1980s by The Coggeshall Grange Barn Trust, Braintree DC and Essex CC, and contains a small collection of farm carts and wagons.

ℹ️ **T** 01376 562226

£ £1.80, child 90p. **Joint ticket with Paycocke's**: £3.50, child £1.80

♿ **Building**: Level entrance. Ground floor accessible. **WCs**: Adapted WC. **Grounds**: Fully accessible

🖝 Braille guide and large-print guide. Sensory list

🧍 Pushchairs and baby back-carriers admitted

🏴 Children's quiz/trail

Opening arrangements: Coggeshall Grange Barn

27 Mar - 9 Oct	2 - 5		M	T	W	T	F	S	S

Open BH Mons

➔ [168: TL848223] **Foot**: Essex Way long-distance footpath passes the barn. **Bus**: First 70 Braintree–Colchester (passing close ≋ Marks Tey). **Station**: Kelvedon 2½ml. **Road**: Signposted off A120 Coggeshall bypass; ¼ml S from centre of Coggeshall, on B1024

P Parking, 20yds. Only available during barn opening times

NT properties nearby
Bourne Mill, Copt Hall Marshes, Hatfield Forest, Paycocke's

Dunstable Downs, Countryside Centre & Whipsnade Estate

Whipsnade Road, Kensworth, Dunstable, Bedfordshire LU6 2TA

🏠 🖾 ⚓ 🗋 🍵 😕 🧍 1928 (3:F8)

Extensive area of chalk grassland and farmland

Commanding outstanding views over the Vale of Aylesbury and along the Chiltern Ridge, Whipsnade and Dunstable Downs comprise 206ha (510 acres) of grassland and farmland, where the steep slopes are rich in flora and associated fauna. This open space offers an opportunity to enjoy many forms of recreation, including walking, kite-flying and watching paragliders and gliders. The countryside centre is adjacent to the car parks on the B4541.

⭐ Dunstable Downs and the Centre are owned by Bedfordshire County Council and managed in partnership with the NT. WC not always available

Opening arrangements: Dunstable Downs

Downs	All year		M	T	W	T	F	S	S
Centre	19 Mar - 30 Oct	10 - 5	M	T	W	T	F	S	S
	1 Nov - 27 Mar 06	10 - 4	M	T	W	T	F	S	S
Shop	As Centre								
Kiosk	All year	10 - dusk	M	T	W	T	F	S	S

Countryside Centre opens weather permitting. Sun and BHols: April–Oct open until 6. School holidays open daily. Kiosk closed 25 Dec

[i] **T** 01582 608489 (Centre),
01582 873569 (Warden),
01582 873663 (Property Manager)
F 01582 671826
E dunstabledowns@nationaltrust.org.uk

[£] Admission free

[&] Designated parking in main car park, 20yds.
Building: Level entrance. Centre fully
accessible. **WCs**: Adapted WC. **Shop**: Level
entrance

[▯] Centre shop. Large range of kites available

[▯] Kiosk (NT-approved concession). Ice-cream
van. During busy periods only

[▯] No barbecues

[▯] Baby-changing facilities. Pushchairs and baby
back-carriers admitted

[▯] Suitable for school groups. Contact Centre
Manager for booking information and fees

[▯] Under close control

[▯] Public bridleway giving cyclists shared
access. Route is part of Icknield Trail

[→] [165/166: TL002189] **Bus**: Arriva 60 from
Luton, 161 from Aylesbury and Centrebus
343 from St Albans, all Suns & BHols only;
otherwise Arriva 61 Aylesbury-Luton (passing
close [≋] Luton) to within 1½ml; also Chiltern
Rambler 327, Sun May–Sept only. **Station**:
Luton 7ml. **Road**: At W end of Dunstable, 4ml
NE of Ashridge between B4540 and B4541

[P] Free parking off both B4540 and B4541, and
at Whipsnade Tree Cathedral & Whipsnade
Crossroads. Space for 1 coach only at
Dunstable (no other coach facilities)

NT properties nearby
Ascott, Ashridge Estate, Whipsnade Tree Cathedral

Dunwich Heath: Coastal Centre & Beach

Dunwich, Saxmundham, Suffolk IP17 3DJ

[▯][▯][▯][▯][▯][▯][▯] [1968]   **(3:K6)**

Coastal lowland heath, rich in wildlife

Within an AONB and offering many excellent
walks, the area is a remnant of the once

Opening arrangements: Dunwich Heath

Reserve	All year	Daylight	M	T	W	T	F	S	S
Shop	2 Mar - 27 Mar		M	T	**W**	**T**	**F**	**S**	**S**
	28 Mar - 3 Apr		**M**	**T**	**W**	**T**	**F**	**S**	**S**
	6 Apr - 10 Jul		M	T	**W**	**T**	**F**	**S**	**S**
	11 Jul - 18 Sep		**M**	**T**	**W**	**T**	**F**	**S**	**S**
	21 Sep - 23 Dec		M	T	**W**	**T**	**F**	**S**	**S**
	28 Dec - 1 Jan 06		**M**	**T**	**W**	**T**	**F**	**S**	**S**
	7 Jan - 26 Feb 06		M	T	W	T	F	**S**	**S**
Tea-room	As shop								
	Half-terms		**M**	**T**	**W**	**T**	**F**	**S**	**S**

Shop & tea-room open from 10. Closing times vary

extensive Sandlings heaths, with open tracts of
heather and gorse, shady woods, sandy cliffs
and beach. It is an important nature
conservation area and home to scarce species
like the nightjar, Dartford warbler and ant-lion.

What's new in 2005 Information centre;
guidebook

[★] Restriction on kite-flying April–July inc.
Parking restrictions may operate at times of
extreme fire risk. Cycling and horse riding on
bridleway only

[i] **T** 01728 648501 (Warden/Learning officer),
01728 648505 (Booking/shop/tea-room)
E dunwichheath@nationaltrust.org.uk

[£] Car park charge for non-members

[▯] Guided walks throughout the year and on
request for groups

[▯] Programme of events, inc. summer and
half-term hols events for families and lectures
(winter)

[▯] Good network of walks. Three waymarked
trails with map and information in guidebook

[&] Separate designated parking, 100yds.
Wheelchair-accessible transfer. Drop-off point.
Building: Level entrance. 1 wheelchair. Many
stairs to other floors. Stairlift to viewing room.
WCs: Adapted WC. **Grounds**: Partly
accessible. Accessible route map. Car park
viewing point. 2 single-seater PMV, booking
essential. Staff-driven multi-seater vehicle.
Shop: Level entrance. Shop and tea-room
mostly accessible but tight spaces.
Refreshments: Level entrance

[▯] Braille guide and large-print guide

Please note: groups must book in advance with the property

📷 Shop in Coastguard Cottages

🍴 Licensed tea-room in Coastguard Cottages. Children's menu. Kiosk outside

🚼 Pushchairs and baby back-carriers admitted. Front-carrying baby slings for loan. Children's play area

🎒 Suitable for school groups. Education room/centre. Hands-on activities. Children's quiz/trail. Family activity packs. Field Study Centre; website with electronic learning resources for schools & colleges

🐕 Under close control at all times and at some times must be on a lead. Dog-free area on beach

➡ [156: TM476685] **Foot**: Suffolk Coast and Heaths Path and Sandlings Walk. Detailed maps available. **Cycle**: On Suffolk coastal cycle route. **Station**: Darsham (U) 6ml. Current project looking into a community car link to site from station. May be available during 2005. **Road**: 1ml S of Dunwich, signposted from A12. From Westledon/Dunwich road, 1ml before Dunwich village turn right into Minsmere Road. Then 1ml to Dunwich Heath

🅿 Parking, 150yds (pay & display). NT members must display cards. Cars £2.10, coaches £25 (unless booked to use tea-room). Season tickets 6 mths £13, 1 yr £20. Coach park limited to 3 coaches

NT properties nearby
Flatford: Bridge Cottage, Orford Ness, Sutton Hoo

Elizabethan House Museum

4 South Quay, Great Yarmouth, Norfolk
NR30 2QH

 1943   (3:K5)

Museum of domestic life in a 16th-century house

In this splendid quayside house visitors can experience the lives of families who lived here from Tudor to Victorian times. Of particular interest is the Conspiracy Room, where the trial and execution of King Charles I were allegedly plotted. There are Tudor costumes to try on, and discoveries to be made through hands-on activities about 'upstairs and downstairs' Victorian life, including what it was like to work in the kitchen and scullery. Children will particularly enjoy the activity-packed rooms. There is a small but delightful walled garden.

⭐ The house is leased to Norfolk Museums and Archaeology Service

ℹ **T** 01493 855746,
01493 745526 (Learning)
F 01493 745459

£ £2.90, child £1.50, concessions £2.40. Discount for groups (10+)

🎟 Extra charge for out-of-hours tours

♿ **Building**: Level entrance. Ground floor has 1 step to kitchen and 1 step to back garden. Stairs to other floors. Seating available. Photograph album. **Shop**: Level entrance

🔊 Induction loop in reception

📖 Braille guide

🚼 Pushchairs and baby back-carriers admitted

🎒 Suitable for school groups

➡ [134: TG523073] On Great Yarmouth's historic South Quay. **Foot**: Approx. 10mins walk from railway station along North Quay onto South Quay. **Cycle**: Regional route 30 Great Yarmouth–Cromer. **Bus**: Local services, plus services from surrounding areas. **Station**: Great Yarmouth ½ml. **Road**: From A47 take town centre signs, then follow brown Historic South Quay signs. From A12 follow brown signs

🅿 No parking on site. Pay & display car park behind house, run by the Borough Council. Not reserved for visitors and spaces may not always be available

NT properties nearby
Horsey Windpump

Opening arrangements: Elizabethan House Museum			
Museum	21 Mar - 28 Oct	10 - 5	**M T W T F** S S
	26 Mar - 30 Oct	1:15 - 5	M T W T F **S S**
Shop	As museum		

Felbrigg Hall, Garden & Park

Felbrigg, Norwich, Norfolk NR11 8PR

🏠🏚✝❀🌸🦐📷🍴🍷 1969   (3:I3)

One of the finest 17th-century country houses in East Anglia

The Hall contains its original 18th-century furniture, one of the largest collections of Grand Tour paintings by a single artist, and an outstanding library. The Walled Garden has been restored and features a series of *potager* gardens, a working dovecote and the National Collection of Colchicums. The park, through which there are waymarked walks, is well known for its magnificent and aged trees. There are also walks to the church and lake and through the 200ha (500 acres) of woods.

What's new in 2005 New displays in Bookroom and in Bird Corridor

ℹ️ **T** 01263 837444,
01263 837040 (Shop),
01263 838237 (Restaurant)
F 01263 837032
E felbrigg@nationaltrust.org.uk

💷 £6.60, child £3.10, family £16.20. Groups £5.30, child £2.60. **Garden only**: £2.70. Visitors with valid bus or train tickets: £1 off entrance price to house and garden. Estate free to pedestrians and cyclists

Copper utensils in the kitchen at Felbrigg Hall, Norfolk

🗡️ Introductory tour of house at 12 noon on open days (if available) except BHols. Numbers limited (charge inc. NT members). Special guided group tours of Hall outside normal opening times; guided group tours of garden and estate walks

📅 Programme of events, inc. themed suppers monthly. Send s.a.e. for details

🚶 Waymarked walks to church, lake and woods

♿ Separate designated parking, 100yds. Drop-off point. **Building**: Level entrance. 4 wheelchairs. Ground floor has 1 step from Bird Corridor to kitchen corridor. Many stairs with handrail to other floors. Photograph album, DVD. **WCs**: Adapted WC. **Grounds**: Partly accessible, loose gravel paths. Accessible route map. All-weather path through woods. 1 single-seater PMV. **Shop**: Level entrance. **Refreshments**: Level entrance

🔊 Induction loop in reception, shop, restaurant

Opening arrangements: Felbrigg Hall										
House	19 Mar - 30 Oct	1 - 5	**M**	**T**	**W**	T	F	**S**	**S**
Gardens	19 Mar - 30 Oct	11 - 5	**M**	**T**	**W**	T	F	**S**	**S**
	21 Jul - 2 Sep	11 - 5	**M**	**T**	**W**	**T**	**F**	**S**	**S**
Shop	19 Mar - 30 Oct	10:30 - 5	**M**	**T**	**W**	T	F	**S**	**S**
	3 Nov - 18 Dec	11 - 4	M	T	W	**T**	**F**	**S**	**S**
	7 Jan - 19 Mar 06	11 - 4	M	T	W	T	F	**S**	**S**
Restaurant	As shop								
Tea-room	As shop								
Estate Walks	All year	Dawn–dusk	**M**	**T**	**W**	**T**	**F**	**S**	**S**
Bookshop	19 Mar - 30 Oct	11 - 5	**M**	**T**	**W**	T	F	**S**	**S**
	3 Nov - 18 Dec	11 - 4	M	T	W	**T**	**F**	**S**	**S**
	7 Jan - 19 Mar 06	11 - 4	M	T	W	T	F	**S**	**S**
Plant sales	As shop								
Open BH Mons 1–5									

Please remember – your membership card is always needed for free admission

Braille guide and large-print guide

NT shop. Secondhand bookshop. Plant sales

Park restaurant (licensed). Children's menu. Turret tea-room (licensed). Occasionally only Park restaurant or Turret tea-room may be open. Booking advisable for Park restaurant

Picnic tables in car park

Baby-changing facilities. Front-carrying baby slings and hip-carrying infant seats for loan

Suitable for school groups. Children's guide

On leads or under very close control in parkland when stock grazing. Under close control in woodland

Regional route 30 runs through the park

→ [133: TG193394] **Foot:** Weavers Way runs through property. **Bus:** First 780 from ≡ Sheringham, Sun June–Sept only. **Station:** Cromer (U) 2½ml; West Runton 3ml. **Road:** Nr Felbrigg village, 2ml SW of Cromer; entrance off B1436, signposted from A148 and A140

P Free parking, 100yds

NT properties nearby
Blickling Hall, Sheringham Park

Flatford: Bridge Cottage

Flatford, East Bergholt, Suffolk CO7 6UL

🔒🏱🗁👁🎭🎵 1943   (3:18)

16th-century thatched cottage

Situated just upstream from Flatford Mill, the cottage houses an exhibition on John Constable, several of whose paintings famously depict this property. There is a tea-garden, shop, information centre and boat hire, and access is possible on foot to Trust land in the beautiful Dedham Vale.

⭐ Flatford Mill, Valley Farm and Willy Lott's House are leased to the Field Studies Council which runs arts-based courses for all age groups: For information on courses tel. 01206 298283. There is no general public access to these buildings, but the Field Studies Council will arrange tours for groups

i **T** 01206 298260 **F** 01206 299193
E flatfordbridgecottage@nationaltrust.org.uk

£ **Guided walks (when available):** £2, child free. **Bridge Cottage:** Free. When tour guides not available audio tapes can be hired (£2 per tape, £5 deposit). Children must be accompanied

Guided walks of Flatford: Easter, BHols and daily May to end Sept when guides available. Booked guided walks for school and coach groups

Programme of events. Tel. for details

Separate designated parking, 50yds. **Building:** Level entrance. 1 wheelchair. Uneven floors in cottage. **WCs:** Adapted WC. **Grounds:** 1 single-seater PMV. **Shop:** Level entrance. **Refreshments:** Level entrance

Braille guide and large-print guide. Living Pictures Trust – tactile images

Licensed tea-room next to Bridge Cottage. Children's menu

Pushchairs and baby back-carriers admitted. Front-carrying baby slings for loan

Suitable for school groups

→ [168: TM077332] ½ml S of East Bergholt. **Foot:** Accessible from East Bergholt, Dedham and Manningtree. **Bus:** First/Carters 93/4 Ipswich–Colchester (passing ≡ Ipswich and close ≡ Colchester Town), alight E Bergholt, ½ml. **Station:** Manningtree 1¾ml by footpath, 3½ml by road. **Road:** On N bank of Stour, 1ml S of East Bergholt (B1070)

P Parking (not NT), 200yds (pay & display), charge inc. NT members

NT properties nearby
Dedham Vale, Thorington Hall

Opening arrangements: Flatford: Bridge Cottage										
Cottage	2 Mar - 30 Apr	11 - 5	M	T	**W**	**T**	**F**	**S**	**S**	
	1 May - 30 Sep	10 - 5:30	**M**	**T**	**W**	**T**	**F**	**S**	**S**	
	1 Oct - 30 Oct	11 - 4	**M**	**T**	**W**	**T**	**F**	**S**	**S**	
	2 Nov - 18 Dec	11 - 3:30	M	T	**W**	**T**	**F**	**S**	**S**	
	7 Jan - 26 Feb 06	11 - 3:30	M	T	W	T	F	**S**	**S**	
Shop	As cottage									
Tea-room	As cottage									
Open BH Mons										

Hatfield Forest

Takeley, nr Bishop's Stortford, Essex CM22 6NE

▓🖤🐦💺👶🏻 1924   (3:G8)

Ancient woodland – a rare surviving example of a medieval royal hunting forest

Of great historical and ecological importance, Hatfield Forest is a designated SSSI and National Nature Reserve. The pollarded hornbeams and oaks support a wide variety of wildlife and there are many excellent walks and nature trails, as well as fishing in the lake. During summer cattle graze in the forest.

What's new in 2005 The Shell House is restored and open to visitors at weekends; exhibition in Information Room by the lake, explaining history, management and wildlife of the Forest

[i] **T** 01279 874040 (Infoline),
01279 870678 (Office),
01279 870447 (Learning)
F 01279 874044
E hatfieldforest@nationaltrust.org.uk

[£] Car park charge for non-members. Riding for members of Hatfield Forest Riding Association only, tel. for details

[🎭] Programme of events, inc. Wood Fair and family events. Send s.a.e. for details

[♿] Designated parking in main car park, 60yds. Paths outside lake area can be muddy.
WCs: Adapted WC. **Grounds**: Accessible route map. 1 single-seater PMV, booking essential

[👁] Large-print guide. Sensory list

Hatfield Forest, Essex

Opening arrangements: Hatfield Forest		
All Year	Dawn – dusk	M T W T F S S
Refreshments 25 Mar - 31 Oct	10 - 4:30	M T W T F·S S
5 Nov - 26 Mar 06	10 - 3:30	M T W T F S S

Refreshments available daily in school holidays 1 Nov–31 March 10–3.30

[🍴] Lakeside Café (NT-approved concession) in lake area within forest. Children's menu

[▦] Picnic area beside lake

[👶] Baby-changing and feeding facilities. Pushchairs admitted

[▦] Suitable for school groups. Education room/centre. Children's quiz/trail. Adult study days

[🐕] On leads where cattle and sheep are grazing and around lake. Dog-free area near lake

[🚲] Several miles of grass track suitable for cycling; cyclists excluded only from area of lake and gravel pit

[→] [167: TL547203] **Foot**: Flitch Way runs along northern boundary. Three Forests Way and Forest Way pass through the forest.
Cycle: Flitch Way. **Bus**: First Village Link 7 🚌 Bishop's Stortford–🚌 Elsenham, alight Takeley Street (Green Man), then ¾ml.
Station: Stansted Airport 3ml; Bishops Stortford 4ml. **Road**: Signposted off B1256 at Takeley, E of Bishop's Stortford

[P] Parking. 25 March–31 Oct & Suns in March 10–5, cars £3.20, minibuses £6, coaches £25, school coaches £10. 1 Nov–31 March and outside normal opening times April to Oct £1, pay & display

NT properties nearby
Bourne Mill, Coggeshall Grange Barn, Danbury Common, Lingwood Common, Wimpole Hall

Please see the area introductions for details of coast & countryside properties

Horsey Windpump

Horsey, Great Yarmouth, Norfolk NR29 4EF

⚑ 🖾 🚜 🕇 🗖 💾 🗲 | 1948 | (3:K4)

Restored five-storey drainage windpump

A viewpoint affords striking views across Horsey Mere, one of the Norfolk Broads, and there is access to the beach at Horsey Gap. The Mere is internationally important for wintering wild fowl.

What's new in 2005 Improved footpaths around the Staithe

⭐ The Horsey estate was acquired by the NT in 1948 from the Buxton Family, who continue to manage the estate with nature conservation as a priority. WC not always available

ℹ️ **T** 0870 609 5388 (Regional office), 01493 393904 (open days only, tea-room manager)
E horseywindpump@nationaltrust.org.uk

£ £2, child £1. Mooring fees payable by all boat users (inc. NT members) to the Horsey Estate

🏃 For school groups and special interest groups (small charge)

🏃 Waymarked circular walks, leaflet available

♿ Separate designated parking, 50yds.
Building: Ramped entrance. Ground floor accessible. Stairs to other floors. Photograph album. **WCs**: Adapted WC.
Grounds: 400yds of accessible path leading to viewpoint overlooking Horsey Mere. Seats at regular intervals. **Refreshments**: Level entrance. Narrow doorway

👆 Braille guide and large-print guide

🏠 Small shop

🍴 Staithe Stores Tea-room close to Windpump

🏛 Suitable for school groups

🐕 Dogs on leads where cattle and sheep are grazing. Under close control elsewhere

Opening arrangements: Horsey Windpump										
Windpump	5 Mar - 27 Mar	10 - 4:30	M	T	W	T	F	**S**	**S**
	30 Mar - 30 Oct	10 - 4:30	M	**T**	**W**	**T**	**F**	**S**	**S**
Shop/tea-room	As Windpump									
Open BH Mons 10:30–4										

➔ [134: TG457223] **Bus**: First 603/4 Lowestoft–Martham (passing close 🚌 Great Yarmouth), alight W Somerton School, 1¾ml. **Station**: Acle 10ml. **Road**: 15ml N of Great Yarmouth on B1159; 4ml NE of Martham

🅿 Parking, 50yds, 50p (pay & display). Charge is per hour. Access difficult for coaches. Members can obtain free car park pass from the NT shop during opening hours

NT properties nearby
Elizabethan House Museum

Houghton Mill

Houghton, nr Huntingdon, Cambridgeshire
PE28 2AZ

⚑ 🏠 💾 🏞 | 1939 | (3:F6)

Large 18th-century timber-built watermill

The five-storey weatherboarded mill is set on an island in the Great Ouse and has intact machinery which is still operational. Milling takes place on Sundays and Bank Holiday Mondays, with the flour for sale. The riverside meadows offer marvellous walks.

What's new in 2005 Portable induction loop. Bookshop

⭐ Milling demonstrations subject to river level

ℹ️ **T** 01480 301494, 01480 466716 (Caravan Club/campsite), 01480 462413 (Tea-room) **F** 01480 469641

£ £3.20, child £1.50, family £7. Groups £2, child £1

🏃 By arrangement

Opening arrangements: Houghton Mill										
Mill	26 Mar - 1 May	1 - 5	M	T	W	T	F	**S**	**S**
	2 May - 28 Sep	1 - 5	**M**	**T**	W	T	F	**S**	**S**
	1 Oct - 30 Oct	1 - 5	M	T	W	T	F	**S**	**S**
Gallery	As Mill									
Tea room	As Mill	11 - 5							
Walks/car park	All year	9 - 6	**M**	**T**	**W**	**T**	**F**	**S**	**S**

Open BH Mons Mill 1–5; tea-room 11-5 and Good Fri 1-5. Caravan and campsite open Mar to Oct. Groups and school parties at other times by arrangement with Property Manager

Unless indicated, last admission is always 30mins before closing time

[i] Starting point for circular walks; maps available

[&] Separate designated parking, 20yds. Level tarmac surface from drop-off point to ground floor entrance. **Building**: Level entrance. Ground floor accessible. Portable ramp to bookshop available on request. Seating available. Photograph album. **WCs**: Adapted WC. **Grounds**: Fully accessible. Accessible route. Level tarmac path through mill to nearby lock. **Refreshments**: Ramped entrance

[&] Induction loop in reception

[&] Braille guide. Sensory list. Handling collection

[&] Tea-room. Delightful riverside setting

[&] Suitable for school groups. Hands-on activities. Children's guide. 'Cat & Rat' children's trail

[&] On leads, in grounds only

[&] Through riverside meadows

[→] [153: TL282720] **Foot**: Ouse Valley Way passes Mill. **Cycle**: Excellent cycling area Huntingdon/St Ives. **Bus**: Huntingdon & District 555, Whippet 1A, from Huntingdon (passing close ≞ Huntingdon). **Station**: Huntingdon 3½ml. **Road**: In village of Houghton, signposted off A1123 Huntingdon to St Ives

[P] Parking, 20yds, £1 (pay & display). No access for large coaches (drop off in village square). Members please collect pass from tea-room

NT properties nearby
Anglesey Abbey, Peckover House, Ramsey Abbey Gatehouse, Wicken Fen, Wimpole Hall

Ickworth House, Park & Garden

Ickworth, The Rotunda, Horringer, Bury St Edmunds, Suffolk IP29 5QE

 [1956] (3:H7)

Unusual Georgian house and landscape park

In 1795 the eccentric 4th Earl of Bristol created this equally eccentric house, with its central rotunda and curved corridors, to display his collections. Paintings by Titian, Gainsborough

Gainsborough's portrait painted in 1767 of Augustus John Hervey as a naval commander, and now hanging in the Drawing Room at Ickworth, Suffolk

and Velázquez and a magnificent Georgian silver collection are on display. An Italianate garden lies to the south of the house, which is set in a 'Capability' Brown park with woodland walks, vineyard, Georgian summer house, church, canal and lake.

What's new in 2005 Major building programme continues (house visitor route not affected). Access to areas of park & garden may be restricted from time to time. Tel. for details

[★] For Ickworth Hotel tel. 01284 735350

[i] **T** 01284 735270 (General enquiries), 01284 735961 (Learning/Events), 01284 769505 (Box office), 01284 735362 (Shop), 01284 735086 (Restaurant) **F** 01284 735175 **E** ickworth@nationaltrust.org.uk

[£] £6.70, child £2.50. Groups (12+) £5.70, child £2.20. **Park & garden only (inc. access to shop/restaurant)**: £3.10, child 90p

There are special events at most Trust properties; please telephone 0870 458 4000 for details

Opening arrangements: Ickworth										
House	25 Mar - 30 Sep	1 - 5	M	T	W	T	F	S	S
	1 Oct - 30 Oct	1 - 4:30	M	T	W	T	F	S	S
Garden	25 Mar - 30 Oct	10 - 5	M	T	W	T	F	S	S
	31 Oct - 23 Dec	10 - 4	M	T	W	T	F	S	S
	1 Jan - 21 Mar 06	10 - 4	M	T	W	T	F	S	S
Park	All year	7 - 7	M	T	W	T	F	S	S
Shop	25 Mar - 30 Oct	12 - 5	M	T	W	T	F	S	S
	5 Nov - 18 Dec	11 - 4	M	T	W	T	F	S	S
Restaurant	As shop								

Garden & park closed 25 Dec

🎭 Mini tours each day except Wed & Thur during open season at 12.15: £2.20 per person (inc. NT members). House admission extra. Booked guided tours and special openings of house for groups with particular interests. Also booked tours for groups of Italianate garden, woods, parkland and vineyard. Tel. for details

😃 Programme of events, inc. themed restaurant events/meals, family woodland rambles, school holiday activities

🚶 Waymarked walks in park and woodland. Lengths vary from 1¼ml to 7ml. All terrains

♿ Separate designated parking, 10yds. Outdoor wheelchair available from house. Drop-off point. **Building**: Steps to entrance, ramp available. 3 wheelchairs. Ground floor accessible. Stairs with handrail to other floors. Lift to first floor, takes small wheelchairs only. Restricted access in house for large powered vehicles. Wheelchair on each floor, for use in house only. Safety regulations permit only one wheelchair on first floor at any time. Seating available. Photograph album. **WCs**: Adapted WC. **Grounds**: Partly accessible, loose gravel paths. Accessible route map. Lady Geraldine's Walk has level gravel surface. 2 single-seater PMV. **Shop**: Many steps to entrance with handrail, stairlift available. **Refreshments**: Many steps to entrance with handrail, stairlift available

🔊 Induction loop in reception

👁 Braille guide and large-print guide. Sensory list. Handling collection

🍴 Servants' Hall Restaurant (licensed) in basement of Rotunda. Kiosk in visitor car park. Hot and cold drinks, ice cream, snacks

🏞 Picnic tables by play area and in picnic area

👶 Baby-changing and feeding facilities. Front-carrying baby slings and hip-carrying infant seats for loan. Children's play area. All-terrain pushchair available for outdoor use. Family 'trim trail' in woods

🏫 Suitable for school groups. Hands-on activities. Children's quiz/trail. Adult study days

🐕 On leads and only in park. Disposal bins in car park

🚲 Family cycle route (2½ml), various surfaces with some steep gradients; helmets and adult supervision advised. Bicycle first aid kit available

➔ [155: TL810610] **Foot**: 4½ml via footpaths from Bury St Edmunds. **Bus**: Burtons 344/5 Bury St Edmunds–Haverhill (passing close ➩ Bury St Edmunds). **Station**: Bury St Edmunds 3ml. **Road**: In Horringer, 3ml SW of Bury St Edmunds on W side of A143

🅿 Free parking, 200yds

NT properties nearby
Anglesey Abbey, Lavenham Guildhall, Melford Hall, Theatre Royal

Lavenham: The Guildhall of Corpus Christi

Market Place, Lavenham, Sudbury, Suffolk
CO10 9QZ

🏠 ❄ 📷 💷 1951 (3:I7)

Tudor building in the heart of a remarkably preserved small medieval town

This early 16th-century timber-framed building overlooks and dominates the town's market place. Inside are exhibitions on timber-framed buildings, local history, farming and industry, as well as the story of the medieval woollen cloth trade. There is an attractive walled garden with dye plants, and 19th-century lock-up and mortuary.

ℹ **T** 01787 247646, 01787 246342 (Shop), 01787 246341 (Tea-room)
E lavenhamguildhall@nationaltrust.org.uk

For further information check our website www.nationaltrust.org.uk

£ £3.25, child free. Groups £2.75, child 60p

⟨ℵ⟩ Blue-badge guided walks around Lavenham village, £2.75 (groups of 15+)

⟨&⟩ Drop-off point. **Building**: Level entrance. Ground floor accessible. Ramps available to main hall. Many stairs with handrail to other floors. Seating available. Photograph album. **WCs**: Adapted WC. Two steps down. **Grounds**: Partly accessible, some steps. **Shop**: Level entrance. **Refreshments**: Ramped entrance

⟨♪⟩ Induction loop in reception

⟨✋⟩ Braille guide. Sensory list

⟨☕⟩ Tea-room. Children's menu

⟨👶⟩ Baby back-carriers admitted. Hip-carrying infant seats for loan

⟨▦⟩ Suitable for school groups. Children's quiz/trail

→ [155: TL917494] **Foot**: 'Railway walk' links Lavenham with Long Melford. **Cycle**: South Suffolk Cycle Route A1. **Bus**: Chambers 753 Bury St Edmunds–Colchester, Mon–Sat (passes close ⊠ Sudbury); Chambers 90C Haverhill–Ipswich, Sun (passes close ⊠ Sudbury and Ipswich). **Station**: Sudbury (U) 7ml. **Road**: A1141 and B1071

P Free parking (not NT), 10yds

NT properties nearby
Ickworth, Melford Hall, Theatre Royal

Opening arrangements: Lavenham Guildhall											
Guildhall	5 Mar - 27 Mar	11 - 4	M	T	W	T	F	**S**	**S**
	2 Apr - 30 Apr	11 - 5	M	T	**W**	**T**	**F**	**S**	**S**
	1 May - 30 Oct	11 - 5	**M**	**T**	**W**	**T**	**F**	**S**	**S**
	5 Nov - 27 Nov	11 - 4	M	T	W	T	F	**S**	**S**
Shop	5 Mar - 30 Oct	As Guildhall							
	3 Nov - 22 Dec	11 - 4	M	T	W	**T**	**F**	**S**	**S**
Tea-room	5 Mar - 27 Nov	As Guildhall	M	**T**	**W**	**T**	**F**	**S**	**S**

Open BH Mons. Parts of the building may be closed occasionally for community use. Tea-room open BH Mons

Melford Hall

Long Melford, Sudbury, Suffolk CO10 9AA

⟨▦⟩ ⟨✿⟩ 1960   **(3:H7)**

Romantic turreted brick Tudor mansion

Set in the unspoilt village of Long Melford, the house has changed little externally since 1578 when Queen Elizabeth I was entertained here, and retains its original panelled banqueting hall. It has been the home of the Hyde Parker family since 1786. There are a Regency library, Victorian bedrooms, good collections of furniture and porcelain and a small display of items connected with Beatrix Potter, who was related to the family. The garden contains some spectacular specimen trees and a banqueting house, and there is an attractive walk through the park.

What's new in 2005 Tours exploring the naval traditions of the Hall; colour guidebook

i **T/F** 01787 379228, 01787 376395 (Infoline) **E** melford@nationaltrust.org.uk

£ £4.70, child £2.35, family £11.75. Groups £3.80, child £1.90

⟨𝒦⟩ By arrangement with the Property Manager

⟨▣⟩ Programme of events

⟨&⟩ Disabled drivers can park at house (10yds). Drop-off point. **Building**: Steps to entrance, ramp available. 3 wheelchairs. Ground floor accessible. Restricted access for small powered vehicles; safety regulations permit only one wheelchair on first floor at any time. Stairs to other floors, stairlift available. Seating available. **WCs**: Adapted WC. Adapted cubicle in the ladies' WC. **Grounds**: Partly accessible. Access to garden and Tudor banqueting house difficult due to steps and slopes

Opening arrangements: Melford Hall										
House/grounds	26 Mar - 1 Apr	2 - 5:30	**M**	**T**	**W**	**T**	**F**	**S**	**S**
	2 Apr - 1 May	2 - 5:30	M	T	W	T	F	**S**	**S**
	4 May - 30 Sep	2 - 5:30	M	T	**W**	**T**	**F**	**S**	**S**
	1 Oct - 30 Oct	2 - 5:30	M	T	W	T	F	**S**	**S**

Open BH Mons

Please note: groups must book in advance with the property

🔊 Induction loop in reception

👆 Braille guide and large-print guide. Sensory list

🚗 In car park area

👶 Hip-carrying infant seats for loan

🏫 Suitable for school groups. Children's quiz/trail

🐕 On leads, in car park and park walk only

➡️ [155: TL867462] **Foot**: 'Railway Walk' linking Long Melford with Lavenham, 4ml.
Bus: Beestons/Chambers/Felix various services, Mon–Sat from Sudbury; Chambers 753, Mon–Sat Bury St Edmunds–Colchester; Chambers 90C, Sun Haverhill–Ipswich (passes ⭍ Ipswich). All pass close ⭍ Sudbury. **Station**: Sudbury (U) 4ml. **Road**: In Long Melford off A134, 14ml S of Bury St Edmunds, 3ml N of Sudbury

🅿️ Free parking, 200yds. Access for coaches and other large vehicles by gated entrance 100yds north of main entrance (signed)

NT properties nearby
Flatford: Bridge Cottage, Ickworth, Lavenham Guildhall

Orford Ness National Nature Reserve

Quay Office, Orford Quay, Orford, Woodbridge, Suffolk IP12 2NU

 1993   (3:J7)

Internationally important nature reserve, with a fascinating 20th-century military history

The largest vegetated shingle spit in Europe, the Reserve contains a variety of habitats including shingle, saltmarsh, mudflat, brackish lagoons and grazing marsh. It provides an important location for breeding and passage birds as well as for the shingle flora, including a large number of nationally rare species. The Ness was a secret military test site from 1913 until the mid-1980s. Visitors follow a 5½ml route, which can be walked in total or in part (the full walk involves walking on shingle). Other walks (approx. 3mls) are open seasonally.

What's new in 2005 Display about the role of Orford Ness in the Cold War

⭐ Access around the site is on foot only, but tractor-drawn trailer tours operate 1st Sat of the month July to Sept, booking essential. Pagoda (military buildings) accessible only on guided events. No dogs or cycles

ℹ️ **T** 01394 450900, 01394 450057 (Infoline)
F 01394 450901
E orfordness@nationaltrust.org.uk

💷 **NT members**: £3.90, child £1.95. **Non-members**: £5.90, child £2.95. Under 3s free. Price inc. ferry crossing. Group pricing structure available dependent on type of visit

🗡️ Natural history, military history and general interest. Contact Warden for details

💡 Working lighthouse visit – joint NT and Trinity House event. Wildtrack Working Holidays. Tel 09704 292429 for details. Marine Conservation Society Beachwatch – coastal survey and clean up. Tel. 01394 450900 after July for details

🚶 Trail guide for sale

♿ Access involves negotiating steep and slippery steps (height influenced by tides) to embark or disembark from motor launch. Special access day for visitors with disabilities in July. Booking essential. Drop-off on Orford Quay. Car has to be returned to car park (150yds). **Building**: 1 wheelchair. **WCs**: Adapted WC. Only available with the Warden on duty. **Grounds**: Partly accessible. Accessible route map

👶 Pushchairs and baby back-carriers admitted. Access involves a boat crossing. All pushchairs etc have to be suitable to be lifted on to a boat and up and down steps

🏫 Suitable for school groups. Education room/centre. Family guide. Children's quiz/trail. Adult study days. Displays on natural history and history of the site

Opening arrangements: Orford Ness							
26 Mar - 25 Jun	M	T	W	T	F	S	S
28 Jun - 1 Oct	M	T	W	T	F	S	S
8 Oct - 29 Oct	M	T	W	T	F	S	S

The only access is by ferry from Orford Quay, with boats crossing regularly between 10 & 2 and the last ferry leaving the Ness at 5. Open throughout the year to booked groups of 12+

→ [169: TM425495 – Orford Quay] **Foot**: Suffolk Coastal Path runs via Orford Quay.
Cycle: NCN1 1ml. No cycle parking.
Ferry: Access only via ferry *Octavia*. See 'Opening arrangements' for details.
Bus: County Travel 160, 182 from Woodbridge (passing ⊞ Melton).
Station: Wickham Market 8ml. **Road**: Access from Orford Quay, Orford town 10ml E of A12 (B1094/1095), 12ml NE of Woodbridge B1152/1084

P Parking (not NT), 150yds (pay & display), charge inc. NT members. Located in Quay Street

NT properties nearby
Dunwich Heath, Kyson Hill, Sutton Hoo

Oxburgh Hall, Garden & Estate

Oxborough, King's Lynn, Norfolk PE33 9PS

🏠 ✝ ❀ 🏛 ♥ 🦡 ☂ | 1952 | (3:H5)

15th-century moated manor house

This quintessential Tudor house, with its magnificent gatehouse and accessible Priest's Hole, was built in 1482 by the Bedingfeld family, who still live here. The rooms show the development from medieval austerity to neo-Gothic Victorian comfort, and include an outstanding display of embroidery worked by Mary, Queen of Scots and Bess of Hardwick. The attractive gardens feature a French parterre,

Opening arrangements: Oxburgh Hall

House	19 Mar - 30 Oct	1 - 5	**M**	**T**	**W**	T	F	**S**	**S**
Garden	8 Jan - 13 Mar	11 - 4	M	T	W	T	F	**S**	**S**
	19 Mar - 31 Jul	11 - 5:30	**M**	**T**	**W**	T	**F**	**S**	**S**
	1 Aug - 31 Aug	11 - 5:30	**M**	**T**	**W**	**T**	**F**	**S**	**S**
	3 Sep - 30 Oct	11 - 5:30	**M**	**T**	**W**	T	**F**	**S**	**S**
	5 Nov - 18 Dec	11 - 4	M	T	W	T	F	**S - S**	
	7 Jan - 26 Feb 06	11 - 4	M	T	W	T	F	**S**	**S**
Shop	As garden	11 - 5							
Restaurant	As garden	11 - 5							

Open BH Mons 11–5 (inc. house). On Thur & Fri in Aug, only garden is open

walled orchard and kitchen garden. There are delightful woodland walks and an interesting Catholic chapel.

What's new in 2005 Historic items newly returned to the house and on display; 19th-century curtains returned to the Saloon after conservation; carpet commisioned to an historic design on the North Staircase and corridor. Photograph album showing upper rooms

ℹ️ **T** 01366 328258, 01366 327240 (Shop), 01366 328243 (Restaurant)
F 01366 328066
E oxburghhall@nationaltrust.org.uk

£ £6, child £3, family (2 adults & 2 children) £15.50. Reduced rate when arriving by cycle. Groups £5. Group visits outside normal hours £8, NT members £6. **Garden & estate only**: £3, child £1.50

🚶 Guided tours for groups of 15+ (by prior arrangement). Regular garden tours and winter woodland tours (free)

The west front, Oxburgh Hall, Norfolk

🏃 Woodland Explorer trail

♿ Designated parking in main car park, 200yds. Drop-off point. **Building**: Ramped entrance. 5 wheelchairs. Ground floor accessible. Stairs with handrail to other floors. Main exit via spiral staircase. Alternative route available. Seating available. Photograph album. **WCs**: Adapted WC. Access via ramp. **Grounds**: Partly accessible. Accessible route map. Care necessary near moat. Chapel 100yds from Hall, access via ramp. **Shop**: Level entrance. **Refreshments**: Level entrance. Large-print menu

👁 Braille guide. Sensory list

🛍 NT shop. Secondhand bookshop during season

☕ Licensed restaurant in Old Kitchen. Children's menu. Kiosk in car park, open seasonally

🎍 Picnic tables in car park

🚼 Baby-changing facilities. Front-carrying baby slings and hip-carrying infant seats for loan

🎒 Suitable for school groups. Hands-on activities. Children's guide. Children's quiz/trail. Bookable 'Oxburgh Explorer': guided and self-guided activities (KS1–3)

➜ [143: TF742012] **Station**: Downham Market 10ml. **Road**: At Oxborough, 7ml SW of Swaffham on S side of Stoke Ferry road

🅿 Free parking

NT properties nearby
Peckover House, St George's Guildhall

Paycocke's

West Street, Coggeshall, Colchester, Essex CO6 1NS

 1924   (3:H8)

Merchant's house, dating from c.1500

This fine half-timbered house is evidence of the wealth generated by the East Anglian wool trade in the 15th and 16th centuries. It contains unusually rich panelling and woodcarving. Coggeshall was also famous for its lace, examples of which are displayed inside the house. There is a very attractive cottage garden.

⭐ Groups (10+) must book in advance with the tenant. Children must be accompanied by an adult. No WC

ℹ **T/F** 01376 561305

£ £2.40, child £1.20. **Joint ticket with Coggeshall Grange Barn**: £3.50, child £1.80

♿ Drop-off point. **Building**: Step to entrance. Ground floor accessible. Stairs to other floors. Photograph album. **Grounds**: Fully accessible. Accessible route

👁 Braille guide and large-print guide

🚼 Pushchairs admitted

➜ [168: TL848225] **Bus**: First 70 Colchester–Braintree (passing ≋ Marks Tey). **Station**: Kelvedon 2½ml. **Road**: 5½ml E of Braintree. Signposted off A120. On S side of West Street, 200yds from centre of Coggeshall, on road to Braintree next to the Fleece Inn

🅿 Parking (not NT). Not suitable for coaches. Parking at Grange Barn (10 min walk) until 5

NT properties nearby
Bourne Mill, Coggeshall Grange Barn, Copt Hall Marshes, Flatford: Bridge Cottage, Hatfield Forest

Opening arrangements: Paycocke's								
27 Mar - 9 Oct	2 - 5:30	M	T	W	T	F	S	S
Open BH Mons								

Peckover House & Garden

North Brink, Wisbech, Cambridgeshire PE13 1JR

🏠 🛏 ✳ 📷 ☕ 🔔 🍴 1943   (3:G5)

Georgian brick town house with walled garden

The town house, built c.1722, is renowned for its very fine plaster and wood rococo decoration and includes displays on the Quaker banking family who owned it and the Peckover Bank. The outstanding 0.8ha (2-acre) Victorian garden includes an orangery, summer houses, roses, herbaceous borders, fernery, croquet lawn and 17th-century thatched barn, which is available for weddings and functions.

Opening arrangements: Peckover House									
House	19 Mar - 6 Nov	1 - 4	M	T	W	T	F	S	S
Garden	19 Mar - 6 Nov	12 - 5	M	T	W	T	F	S	S
Shop	As garden								
Restaurant	As garden								

Open BH Mons and Good Fri 12–5. Also 30 June and 1 July for Wisbech Rose Fair. For opening times of Octavia Hill birthplace (not NT) tel. 01945 476358

⭐ Peckover House is a town property and does not have its own car park. Please follow signs to Chapel Road car park and walk from there (250yds). Please note: visitors to Peckover will find within walking distance the birthplace of Octavia Hill, who co-founded the National Trust in 1895. House (not NT) admission £2.50, senior citizens & NT members £2, accompanied children free

ℹ️ **T/F** 01945 583463, 01945 582636 (Restaurant) **E** peckover@nationaltrust.org.uk

💷 £4.50, child £2.25, family £14. Groups £3.80. Group visits outside normal hours £6.25, NT members £3.75

🎭 Programme of events. Send s.a.e. for details

♿ Separate designated parking. Blue badge holders may park on double yellow lines. Drop-off point. **Building**: Steps to entrance. 1 wheelchair, booking essential. Seating available. Photograph album. **WCs**: Adapted WC. **Grounds**: Fully accessible, loose gravel paths. Accessible route map. 1 single-seater PMV, booking essential. **Shop**: Steps to entrance. **Refreshments**: Ramped entrance with handrail

📷 Induction loop in reception, shop

👁️ Braille guide and large-print guide. Sensory list. Handling collection

🏠 NT shop. Plant sales

☕ Restaurant (licensed) in Reed Barn (or Servants' Hall some Sats)

👶 Baby-changing facilities. Front-carrying baby slings and hip-carrying infant seats for loan

🏫 Suitable for school groups. Hands-on activities. Family guide. 'Upstairs downstairs' education package

➡️ [143: TF458097] **Foot**: From Chapel Road car park walk up passageway to left of Wisbech Arms public house, turn right by river. Peckover House is 50yds on right. **Cycle**: NCN1 ¼ml. **Bus**: First X1 ☒ Peterborough–Lowestoft; X94 and Norfolk Green 46 King's Lynn (passing close ☒ King's Lynn). **Station**: March–9½ml. **Road**: West of Wisbech town centre on N bank of River Nene (B1441)

🅿️ Free parking (not NT), 250yds

NT properties nearby
Oxburgh Hall, St George's Guildhall

Detail of the entrance front, Peckover House, Wisbech, Cambridgeshire

Please see the area introductions for details of coast & countryside properties

Ramsey Abbey Gatehouse

Abbey School, Ramsey, Huntingdon, Cambridgeshire PE17 1DH

🏠 1952   **(3:F6)**

Remains of a former Benedictine abbey

Fragments of the abbey, built on an island in the Fens, include the richly carved late 15th-century gatehouse with its ornate oriel window.

⭐ Property is on school grounds – please respect school security arrangements. No WC

ℹ️ **T** 01480 301494

£ Admission free. Donations welcome

♿ 100yds. Parking on roadside within town parking. **Building**: Steps to entrance. **Grounds**: Partly accessible, some steps

🚼 Pushchairs admitted

➔ [142: TL291851] **Bus**: Cavalier 330 from ≋ Huntingdon, 331 from Peterborough (passing close ≋ Peterborough). **Station**: Huntingdon 10ml. **Road**: At SE edge of Ramsey, at point where Chatteris road leaves B1096, 10ml SE of Peterborough

P Parking (not NT) on roadside, 100yds

NT properties nearby
Houghton Mill, Peckover House, Wicken Fen

Opening arrangements: Ramsey Abbey Gatehouse			
1 Apr - 31 Oct	10 - 5	**M T W T F S S**	

Other times by written application to Property Manager at Houghton Mill

Rayleigh Mount

Rayleigh, Essex

🔲 🔲 1923   **(3:H9)**

11th-century earthwork

This motte and bailey mound is what remains of the castle erected by Sweyn of Essex, dating from the period following the Norman invasion of 1066. Display boards explain the main points of interest.

⭐ No WC. Nearest WC in Mill Hall

ℹ️ **T** 0870 609 5388 (Regional office)

£ Admission free

♿ Stepped access to top of motte. All 3 access points have steep slopes, 1 with steps

📖 Large-print guide

➔ [178: TQ805909] 100yds from High Street, next to Mill Hall car park. **Bus**: From surrounding areas. **Station**: Rayleigh 200yds. **Road**: 6ml NW of Southend, (A129)

P Parking (not NT) (pay & display), charge inc. NT members

NT properties nearby
Blake's Wood, Danbury Common, Lingwood Common, Northey Island and South House Farm, Maldon

Opening arrangements: Rayleigh Mount			
Summer	7 - 6	**M T W T F S S**	
Winter	7 - 5	**M T W T F S S**	

Opening times may vary. Tel. Regional Office for current details

St George's Guildhall

27–29 King Street, King's Lynn, Norfolk PE30 1HA

🏠 🔲 🔲 1951   **(3:H4)**

The largest surviving English medieval guildhall

The building is now converted into an arts centre. Many interesting features survive.

ℹ️ **T** 01553 765565, 01553 779095 (Learning), 01553 764864 (Box office) **F** 01553 762141

£ Admission free

🎭 Programme of events, inc. King's Lynn Festival, performances, workshops and art exhibitions

Opening arrangements: St George's Guildhall							
Restaurant	All year		**M T W T F S**	S			

Closed Good Fri, BH Mons, 24 Dec to 1st Mon in Jan. Tel. for opening dates and times for Guildhall. The Guildhall is not usually open on days when there are performances in the theatre. Tel. box office for details

Unless indicated, last admission is always 30mins before closing time

♿ **Building**: Steps to entrance. Stairs to other floors. **Grounds**: Partly accessible. **Refreshments**: Steps to entrance

📷 Crafts, Christmas shop from mid–Nov

🍴 Riverside restaurant. Open for lunch and dinner Mon to Sat. Crofters Coffee Bar

🏫 Suitable for school groups

➔ [132: TF616202] On W side of King Street close to the Tuesday Market Place. **Cycle**: NCN1 ¼ml. **Bus**: From surrounding area. **Station**: King's Lynn ¾ml

🅿 Parking (not NT) (pay & display)

NT properties nearby
Peckover House

Shaw's Corner

Ayot St Lawrence, nr Welwyn, Hertfordshire
AL6 9BX

🏠 ✣ 📷 🎋 🧍 1944   (3:F8)

Home of famous Irish playwright G.B. Shaw

Bernard Shaw lived in this Edwardian Arts & Crafts-influenced house from 1906 until his death in 1950. The rooms remain much as he left them, with many literary and personal effects evoking the individuality and genius of this great dramatist. The kitchen and outbuildings are evocative of early 20th-century domestic life. Shaw's writing hut is hidden at the bottom of the garden, which has richly planted borders and views over the Hertfordshire countryside.

ℹ **T/F** 01438 820307, 01494 755567 (Infoline), 01438 829221 (Box office)
   E shawscorner@nationaltrust.org.uk

💷 £4, child £2, family £10. Groups £3.40, child £1.70

🧍 Introductory talks for booked groups

📅 Programme of events, inc. events for all ages, reflecting Shaw's life and interests

Opening arrangements: Shaw's Corner										
House	19 Mar - 30 Oct	1 - 5	M	T	**W**	**T**	**F**	**S**	**S**	
Garden	19 Mar - 30 Oct	12 - 5:30	M	T	**W**	**T**	**F**	**S**	**S**	
Open BH Mons										

♿ **Building**: Steps to entrance, ramp available. 2 wheelchairs. Ground floor accessible. Stairs to other floors. Seating available. Scrapbooks on life of Shaw. **WCs**: Nearest adapted WC at Wheathampstead, 2ml. **Grounds**: Partly accessible. Garden accessible for wheelchair users via Paddock Gate

🔊 Induction loop in reception

♿ Braille guide and large-print guide. Sensory list. Magnifying monocular

📷 Small selection of Shaw books on sale at reception; ice-cream and cold drinks. Plants on sale in the garden

👶 Front-carrying baby slings and hip-carrying infant seats for loan

🏫 Suitable for school groups. Family activity packs

🐕 On leads and only in car park

➔ [166: TL194167] **Cycle**: NCN12 1ml. **Bus**: Landmark 382 ⇌ St Albans– ⇌ Stevenage, Suns & BH Mons in property open season only; otherwise Centrebus 304 ⇌ St. Albans–Hitchin, alight Gustard Wood (1¼ml). **Station**: Welwyn North 4½ml; Harpenden 5ml. **Road**: In village of Ayot St Lawrence. A1(M) exit 4 or M1 exit 10. Signposted from B653 Welwyn Garden City to Luton road near Wheathamstead. Also from B656 at Codicote

🅿 Free parking, 30yds. Narrow for large vehicles

NT properties nearby
Ashridge Estate, Dunstable Downs, Pitstone Windmill

Sheringham Park

Upper Sheringham, Norfolk NR26 8TB

🏠 🌳 🚜 📷 🍴 🎋 🧍 1987   (3:I3)

Landscape park and woodland garden

Designed in 1812 by Humphry Repton, Sheringham Park is one of his most outstanding achievements. The large woodland garden is particularly famous for its spectacular show of rhododendrons and azaleas (flowering mid-May to June). There are stunning views of the coast and countryside from the viewing towers and many delightful waymarked walks through the

The Temple at Sheringham Park, Norfolk, with the house in the background

park and mature woods, including a route to the North Norfolk Railway Station (a private steam railway).

What's new in 2005 New visitor & interpretation centre opens early 2005

i **T** 01263 821429 **F** 01263 823778
E sheringhampark@nationaltrust.org.uk

£ Car park charge for non-members

♨ Tel. for details

♿ Designated parking in main car park, 60yds.
Building: Level entrance. 3 wheelchairs. Seating available. **WCs**: Adapted WC. **Grounds**: Partly accessible. Accessible route map. 2 single-seater PMV. **Shop**: Level entrance. **Refreshments**: Level entrance

⊘ Induction loop in reception

▯ Limited range of goods. Plant sales during rhododendron season

Opening arrangements: Sheringham Park			
Park	All year	Dawn – dusk	**M T W T F S S**

House: Sheringham Hall is privately occupied. April to Sept: limited access by written appointment with the leaseholder

☕ Kiosk by visitor centre. Undercover seating available

♿ Baby-changing facilities. Pushchairs admitted

▮ Suitable for school groups

🐕 On leads where stock-grazing

🚲 Cycle route restricted during rhododendron season

→ [133: TG135420] **Foot**: Norfolk Coast Path passes through property. **Cycle**: Regional route 30 1½ml S of property. Helmet/pannier lockers. **Bus**: Sanders X4,43 Norwich–Holt (passing close ≥ Norwich), alight main entrance; Norfolk Green X98 Cromer–Kings Lynn (passing ≥ Kings Lynn), alight Upper Sheringham. All pass ≥ Sheringham. **Station**: Sheringham (U) 2ml. **Road**: 2ml SW of Sheringham, 5ml W of Cromer, 6ml E of Holt. Main entrance at junction of A148 Cromer–Holt road and B1157

P Parking, £3 (pay & display). NT members must display cards. Coaches (please advise for May/June visits) £9

NT properties nearby
Beeston Regis Heath, Blickling Hall, Felbrigg Hall, West Runton

For further information check our website www.nationaltrust.org.uk

Sutton Hoo

Tranmer House, Sutton Hoo, Woodbridge, Suffolk
IP12 3DJ

 1998   (3:J7)

Anglo-Saxon royal burial site

Sutton Hoo is the site of one of the most important archaeological finds in this country's history. On a spur of land rising above the River Deben, one of several large mounds was excavated in 1939, revealing the now famous treasures, including a warrior's helmet, shield and gold ornaments in the remains of a burial chamber of a 90ft ship. The exhibition hall houses a full-size reconstruction of the chamber and tells the story of the site – described as 'page one of English history'. The burial mounds (500yds from visitor facilities) form part of the 99ha (245 acre) estate given to the National Trust by the Annie Tranmer Charitable Trust in 1998.

What's new in 2005 New exhibition in Treasury Room, 19 March–30 Oct, featuring original artefacts from the Sutton Hoo collection, on loan by kind permission of the British Museum

[i] **T** 01394 389700 (Estate office),
01394 389714 (Visitor reception),
01394 389727 (Learning),
01394 389709 (Shop),
01394 389720 (Restaurant) **F** 01394 389702

Anglo-Saxon cemetery, Sutton Hoo, Suffolk

Please note: groups must book in advance with the property

Opening arrangements: Sutton Hoo			
Exhibition Hall	5 Apr - 13 Mar	10 - 5	M T W T F **S S**
	19 Mar - 2 Oct	11 - 5	**M T W T F S S**
	5 Oct - 30 Oct	11 - 5	M T **W T F S S**
	4 Nov - 1 Jan 06	11 - 4	M T W T F **S S**
	7 Jan - 12 Mar 06	11 - 4	M T W T F **S S**
Shop	As exhibition		
Restaurant	As exhibition		

NB open daily during local half terms (Oct 11–5; Feb 11–4). Exhibition Hall, shop and restaurant closed 23–25 Dec. Burial ground and walks open daily all year round 11–5 (except for certain Thurs Nov–Feb. Tel. Estate office for details). Exhibition Hall closed 25/26 Dec & 1 Jan

£ £5, child £2.50, family (2 adults & 2 children) £12.50. Groups £4. Reduced rate when arriving by public transport, cycle or on foot. School group £2 per pupil. Different admission prices, inc. charge for NT members, on certain special event days. Tel. for details

[i] Guided tours available at set times at weekends and some weekdays, additional charge. Tel. to confirm times

Programme of events. Tel. for details or see website

Two excellent colour-coded estate walks

Separate designated parking, 20yds. Drop-off point. **Building**: Level entrance. 6 wheelchairs. **WCs**: Adapted WC. **Grounds**: Accessible route map. Burial ground tours may be difficult for visitors in wheelchairs or PMV due to undulating ground. 2 single-seater PMV, booking essential. **Shop**: Level entrance. **Refreshments**: Level entrance

Braille guide

Sells jewellery, ceramics and children's range based on Sutton Hoo artefacts

Bistro-style restaurant (licensed). Serving modern food inspired by Anglo-Saxon culinary traditions. Children's menu. Ice-cream kiosk in summer

Picnic area

Baby-changing and feeding facilities. Pushchairs admitted. Children's play area. Dressing-up box in exhibition

🏛 Suitable for school groups. Education room/ centre. Children's quiz/trail. Adult study days. Children's activities during summer holidays

🐕 On leads at all times. No entry to buildings or burial mound. Tethering rings and water bowls provided

➔ [169: TM288487] **Foot**: Entrance to Sutton Hoo 1¼ml from Melton station. **Bus**: Ipswich Buses 71/3 Ipswich–Bawdsey (passing ⇌ Melton). **Station**: Melton 1¼ml. **Road**: On B1083 Melton–Bawdsey road. Follow signs from A12 N of Woodbridge

🅿 Parking, 30yds. Car park charge (when visitor facilities and exhibition closed) £2.50. Motorcycle parking area

NT properties nearby
Dunwich Heath, Orford Ness

Theatre Royal

Westgate Street, Bury St Edmunds, Suffolk IP33 1QR

🏛 💺 🎭 | 1974 | (3:H6)

Rare and outstanding example of a late-Georgian playhouse

Built in 1819 and still in use, the theatre presents a year-round programme of professional drama, comedy, dance and music.

⭐ Managed by Bury St Edmunds Theatre Management Ltd. The Theatre is due to be closed from end of August 2005 until at least November 2006 for a major restoration

ℹ **T** 01284 769505 (Box office), 01284 755127 (Learning) **F** 01284 706035 **E** admin@theatreroyal.org

💷 Admission free. Donations welcome. Tours £2 (inc. NT members)

👤 Groups welcome until end of May 2005

Opening arrangements: Theatre Royal

	1 Jun - 31 Aug	11 - 4	M **T** W **T** F **S** S

Closed 1–2 and Sat pm. Tours 11.30 & 2.30 Tues & Thur; 11.30 Sat. Bookable in advance. Group tours welcome at other times. Individuals welcome at any time, subject to theatrical activity. Please check in advance

🦽 Drop-off point. **Building**: Ramped entrance. Stairs to other floors. **WCs**: Adapted WC

💺 Licensed bar in theatre for performances. Coffee and tea can be provided for groups if ordered in advance

🏛 Suitable for school groups

➔ [155: TL856637] **Bus**: From surrounding areas. **Station**: Bury St Edmunds ¾ml. **Road**: On Westgate Street on S side of A134 from Sudbury (one-way system)

🅿 Limited parking in Westgate Street. No parking in front of the Theatre

NT properties nearby
Ickworth, Lavenham Guildhall, Melford Hall

Whipsnade Tree Cathedral

Trustees c/o Chapel Farm, Whipsnade, Dunstable, Bedfordshire LU6 2LL

🚶 🚶 | 1960 | (3:F8)

Trees and hedges planted in the form of a medieval cathedral

Created following the First World War in 'Faith, hope and reconciliation', the Tree Cathedral covers a tranquil 3.82ha (9½ acres) and contains many tree species. Grass avenues form chancel, nave, transepts, chapels and cloisters, and there is also a dew pond.

⭐ No WC. Nearest at Dunstable Downs 1½ml

ℹ **T** 01582 872406 (Trustees), 01582 873569 (Estate office) **F** 01582 872936

💷 Admission free. Donations welcome

👤 Guided tours by arrangement

💺 The annual interdenominational service is held on 19 June at 3pm

🦽 **Grounds**: Partly accessible. Some routes difficult in bad weather

Opening arrangements: Whipsnade Tree Cathedral

Tree Cathedral	All year		M T W T F S S
Car park	All year		M T W T F S S

Car park locked at dusk

Parking in National Trust car parks is free for members

⊞ No barbecues

▦ Self-led school visits only

☒ Under close control

➔ [165/166: TL008180] **Bus**: Lutonian 43 Luton–Hemel Hempstead (passing close ⊜ Luton and close ⊜ Hemel Hempstead); also Arriva 60 from Luton, 161 from Aylesbury and Centrebus 343 from St Albans (Sun only). **Station**: Cheddington 6ml; Hemel Hempstead 8ml; Luton 8ml. **Road**: 4ml S of Dunstable, off B4540

Ⓟ Free parking. Signposted off B4540

NT properties nearby
Ascott, Ashridge Estate, Dunstable Downs

Wicken Fen National Nature Reserve

Lode Lane, Wicken, Ely, Cambridgeshire CB7 5XP

⚒ 🦆 🐕 🏠 📷 🎧 ♿ 1899   (3:G6)

Britain's oldest nature reserve

A unique fragment of the wilderness that once covered East Anglia, the Fen is a haven for birds, plants, insects and mammals alike. It can be explored by the traditional wide droves and lush green paths, including a boardwalk nature trail, giving access to several hides. The William Thorpe Visitor Centre provides a range of facilities and information about this fascinating place, which has now embarked on an ambitious expansion plan for the next 100 years.

Opening arrangements: Wicken Fen									
Reserve	All year	Dawn to dusk	M	T	W	T	F	S	S
Centre/shop	All year	10 - 5	M	T	W	T	F	S	S
Fen Cottage	27 Mar - 23 Oct	2 - 5	M	T	W	T	F	S	S
Café	1 Mar - 31 May	11 - 4	M	T	W	T	F	S	S
	1 Jun - 30 Sep	11 - 5	M	T	W	T	F	S	S
	1 Oct - 30 Oct	11 - 4	M	T	W	T	F	S	S
	1 Nov - 28 Feb 06	11 - 4	M	T	W	T	F	S	S

Open BH Mons. Reserve: closed 25 Dec. Some paths are closed in very wet weather. Visitor centre and café may occasionally be closed in winter. Fen Cottage (showing the way of life c. 1900) open BH Mons and some other days in summer

Yellow flag iris at Drainer's Dyke, Wicken Fen, Cambridgeshire

ℹ️ **T** 01353 720274
F 01353 724700
E wickenfen@nationaltrust.org.uk

£ £4.10, child £1.30. Groups (12+) £3.15. **Cottage only**: £1.55

🏃 Guided tours by arrangement

🚶 Guided walks. Audio trail. Trail guide leaflet available £1.25

♿ Separate designated parking, 20yds. **Building**: Level entrance. 2 wheelchairs. Fen Cottage: limited access by arrangement. **WCs**: Adapted WC. RADAR key available from visitor centre. **Grounds**: Partly accessible. ¾ml boardwalk route accessible for wheelchairs. **Shop**: Level entrance. **Refreshments**: Level entrance

🔊 Induction loop in reception, shop, restaurant and Wren building

👁 Large-print guide. Interesting sounds. Braille introduction to Wicken Fen

🛍 Books and gifts in visitor centre. Binoculars for hire

Please remember – your membership card is always needed for free admission

▄ Wicken Fen Café adjacent to visitor centre. Children's menu. Hot and cold drinks, and ice cream in visitor centre

▤ Picnic tables by visitor centre and in car park

▟ Baby-changing and feeding facilities. Pushchairs and baby back-carriers admitted. Children's activities in visitor centre. Family events throughout year. Boardwalk suitable for pushchairs

▣ Suitable for school groups. Education room/centre. Children's quiz/trail. Adult study days. Wren building available to hire, suitable for training courses, adult education etc

▟ On leads only

➔ [154: TL563705] **Bus**: Stagecoach in Cambridge 122 Cambridge–Ely (Sun only), A&P 117 from Ely (Thur, Sat only); otherwise Stagecoach in Cambridge X12, 122 from Cambridge, Ely & Newmarket, alight Soham Downfields, 3ml, or X7-X9 Cambridge–Ely, alight Stretham, 3½ml. All pass ▆ Ely. **Station**: Ely 9ml. **Road**: S of Wicken (A1123), 3ml W of Soham (A142), 9ml S of Ely, 17ml NE of Cambridge via A10

▣ Free parking, 120yds

NT properties nearby
Anglesey Abbey, Ickworth, Wimpole Hall, Wimpole Home Farm

Willington Dovecote & Stables

Willington, nr Bedford, Bedfordshire

▣ ▟ 1914   (3:F7)

Distinctive 16th-century stable and stone dovecote

The dovecote is lined internally with nesting boxes for over 1500 pigeons. The buildings are the remains of a historic manorial complex, and include stones probably taken from local priories during the Dissolution of the Monasteries.

★ No WC

ℹ **T** 01234 838278 (Voluntary Custodian),
01480 301494 (Property Manager)
F 01480 469641

Opening arrangements: Willington Dovecote	
1 Apr - 30 Sep	**M T W T F S S**

Admission by written appointment with the Voluntary Custodian, Mrs J. Endersby, 21 Chapel Lane, Willington MK44 3QG

£ £1

♿ **Building**: Step to entrance

➔ [153: TL107499] **Cycle**: NCN51.
Bus: Stagecoach in Bedford 171/2, 178/9 Bedford·Biggleswade (passing ▆ Bedford St JohnÕs & Biggleswade and close ▆ Sandy), alight Willington crossroads, ½ml.
Station: Bedford St JohnÕs (U), not Sun, 4ml; Sandy 4½ml; Bedford 5ml. **Road**: 4ml E of Bedford, just N of the Sandy road (A603)

▣ Free parking, 30yds

NT properties nearby
Ashridge Estate, Dunstable Downs, Stowe Landscape Gardens, Wimpole Hall, Wimpole Home Farm

Wimpole Hall

Arrington, Royston, Cambridgeshire SG8 0BW

▣ ▣ ✚ ✿ ♣ ▢ ▣ ▲ ▼ 1976   (3:G7)

Magnificent 18th-century house

Set in grand style in an extensive wooded park, the Hall has fine interiors designed by Gibbs, Flitcroft and Soane, and fascinating servants' quarters. The garden has thousands of daffodils in April and colourful parterres in July and August. The walled garden, restored to a working vegetable garden, is best seen from June to August. The park, landscaped by Bridgeman, Brown and Repton, has spectacular vistas, a Gothic folly and serpentine lakes, and offers delightful walks.

What's new in 2005 Revised opening times

ℹ **T** 01223 206000,
01223 206004 (Learning),
01223 206002 (Box office),
01223 206017 (Shop),
01223 206001 (Restaurant)
F 01223 207838
E wimpolehall@nationaltrust.org.uk

£ £6.90, child £3.40. Groups (12+) £5.90, child £2.90. **Joint ticket with Home Farm**: £10.20, child £5.50, family £26. **Garden only**: £2.70. Reduced rate when arriving by public transport or cycle

🗶 By arrangement outside normal opening hours

🖢 Programme of events, inc. concerts, craft fair, family activity days

🚶 Walks leaflet available £1

♿ Separate designated parking, 200yds. Drop-off point. **Building**: Many steps to entrance. 3 wheelchairs, booking essential. Stairs to other floors. Long main staircase between floors including basement. Stone steps up to ground floor. Seating available. **WCs**: Adapted WC. **Grounds**: Partly accessible. 3 single-seater PMV, booking essential. **Shop**: Level entrance. **Refreshments**: Ramped entrance

📷 Induction loop in reception, shop, restaurant and Hall entrance and garden ticket office

👓 Braille guide and large-print guide. Sensory list. Handling collection

🗄 NT shop, toyshop and secondhand bookshop. Plant sales

Opening arrangements: Wimpole Hall

Park	All year	Daylight	M T W T F S S
Hall	19 Mar - 31 Jul	1 - 5	M T W T F S S
	1 Aug - 31 Aug	1 - 5	M T W T F S S
	3 Sep - 30 Oct	1 - 5	M T W T F S S
	6 Nov - 27 Nov	1 - 4	M T W T F S S
Garden	1 Mar - 16 Mar	11 - 4	M T W T F S S
	19 Mar - 31 Jul	10:30 - 5	M T W T F S S
	1 Aug - 31 Aug	10:30 - 5	M T W T F S S
	3 Sep - 30 Oct	10:30 - 5	M T W T F S S
	31 Oct - 21 Dec	11 - 4	M T W T F S S
	27 Dec - 4 Jan 06	11 - 4	M T W T F S S
	7 Jan - 28 Feb 06	11 - 4	M T W T F S S
Shop	As garden		
Restaurant	As garden		
Gallery	As garden	1 - 5	
Bookshop	As Hall		

Open BH Mons (Hall 11–5) and Good Fri (Hall 1–5). The garden is open everyday during school Easter and half-term holidays. Bookshop also open winter weekends 1–4

🍴 Old Rectory Restaurant (licensed) in Old Rectory. Children's menu. Stable Kitchen in stable block

🎍 In park and picnic area

👶 Baby-changing facilities. Front-carrying baby slings and hip-carrying infant seats for loan

🚩 Suitable for school groups. Education room/centre. Live interpretation. Hands-on activities. Children's guide. Children's quiz/trail

🐕 On leads and only in park

🚲 NT permitted cycle path to main entrance from Orwell junction. on A603; connected to 20ml of public bridleways

➔ [154: TL336510] **Foot**: Wimpole Way from Cambridge, Harcamlow Way. **Bus**: Whippet 175/7 Cambridge–Biggleswade (passing close ≋ Biggleswade and Cambridge) **Station**: Shepreth 5ml. **Road**: 8ml SW of Cambridge (A603), 6ml N of Royston (A1198)

P Free parking, 200yds

NT properties nearby
Anglesey Abbey, Houghton Mill, Wicken Fen

Wimpole Home Farm

Wimpole Hall, Arrington, Royston, Cambridgeshire SG8 0BW

🐄 🐑 ♣ 🍴 🎍 1976   (3:G7)

18th-century model farm

Built by Sir John Soane in 1794 for the 3rd Earl of Hardwicke, who was passionately interested in farming and agricultural improvement, the farm is now home to a fascinating range of rare animal breeds, including sheep, goats, cattle, pigs and horses. The Great Barn contains a collection of farm implements dating back 200 years and interpretive displays.

What's new in 2005 Revised opening arrangements

ℹ **T** 01223 206000, 01223 206004 (Learning), 01223 206017 (Shop), 01223 206001 (Restaurant) **F** 01223 207838 **E** wimpolefarm@nationaltrust.org.uk

£ **NT members**: £2.80, child £1.80. **Non-members**: £5.40, child £3.40. Groups (12+) £4.40, child £2.80. **Joint ticket with Hall**: £10.20, child £5.50, family £26 (inc. NT members). Reduced rate when arriving by public transport or cycle

ℹ️ By arrangement

🎪 Programme of events, inc. spring lambing and children's events. Tel. for details

♿ Separate designated parking, 400yds. Drop-off point. **Building**: Ramped entrance. 3 wheelchairs, booking essential. Some gravel areas, concrete and grass pathways. **WCs**: Adapted WC. **Grounds**: Partly accessible. 3 single-seater PMV, booking essential. **Refreshments**: Ramped entrance

🔊 Induction loop in reception, restaurant and Farm and garden ticket office

👁️ Large-print guide. Sensory list

🍽️ Farm Kitchen. Light refreshments. Children's birthday parties catered for. Children's menu. Groups can be accepted at Wimpole Hall Restaurant

👶 Baby-changing and feeding facilities. Pushchairs and baby back-carriers admitted. Children's play area. Special children's corner; touch and feed animals

🏫 Suitable for school groups. Education room/centre. Live interpretation. Hands-on activities. Children's guide. Children's quiz/trail

➔ [154: TL336510] As Wimpole Hall

P Free parking, 400yds

NT properties nearby
Anglesey Abbey, Houghton Mill, Wicken Fen

Opening arrangements: Wimpole Home Farm										
Farm	5 Mar - 13 Mar	11 - 4	M	T	W	T	F	S	S
	19 Mar - 31 Jul	10:30 - 5	M	T	W	T	F	S	S
	1 Aug - 31 Aug	10:30 - 5	M	T	W	T	F	S	S
	3 Sep - 30 Oct	10:30 - 5	M	T	W	T	F	S	S
	5 Nov - 18 Dec	11 - 4	M	T	W	T	F	S	S
	27 Dec - 4 Jan 06	11 - 4	M	T	W	T	F	S	S
	7 Jan - 26 Feb 06	11 - 4	M	T	W	T	F	S	S
Cafétéria	As farm								

Open BH Mons and Good Fri 10:30-5. Open every day during school Easter and half-term holidays

Properties open less often

This section includes National Trust properties, often tenanted, which are open two days a week or less (plus Bank Holidays in some cases). Visits to some must be made by prior arrangement and where this applies admission prices are not shown (please ask when making contact). **Full details are on our website www.nationaltrust.org.uk or obtainable from the Membership Department, tel. 0870 458 4000.**

Bourne Mill

Bourne Road, Colchester, Essex CO2 8RT   **(3:18)**
Former fishing lodge, now a picturesque watermill

⭐ No WC. Parking limited. Not suitable for coaches. Steps to entrance, stairs to upper floors, grounds partly accessible.

ℹ️ **T** 01206 572422

£ £2, child £1. Children must be accompanied by an adult

➔ [168: TM006238] **Cycle**: NCN 1 1¼ml. **Bus**: Network Colchester 8/A/B, First 67/A from Colchester (passing ≋ Colchester) **Station**: Colchester Town ¾ml; Colchester 2ml. **Road**: 1ml S of centre of Colchester, in Bourne Road, off the Mersea Road (B1025)

Opening arrangements: Bourne Mill									
5 Jun - 26 Jun	2 - 5	M	T	W	T	F	S	**S**
3 Jul - 30 Aug	2 - 5	M	**T**	W	T	F	S	**S**

Open Easter & May BH Suns & Mons

Thorington Hall

Stoke by Nayland, Colchester, Suffolk CO6 4SS   **(3:18)**

Early 17th-century oak-framed house.

ℹ️ **T** 0870 609 5388 (Regional office)

Opening arrangements: Thorington Hall
Only by written appointment with the tenant

South West South & South East
London East of England
East Midlands West Midlands
North West Yorkshire North East
Wales Northern Ireland

The East Midlands is an area of immensely diverse scenery, ranging from the flat agricultural landscapes of southern Lincolnshire through the wooded estates of the Dukeries in Nottinghamshire to the upland drama of the Derbyshire Pennines, which lie within one of England's most famous and heavily visited national parks. The National Trust cares for over twelve per cent of the Peak District National Park and within the East Midlands there are three estates: **High Peak**, **Longshaw** and **South Peak**.

High Peak includes the **Hope Woodlands**, less wood than wild and dramatic Pennine moorland, adjoining the impressive 600-metre high **Kinder Scout** and with superb views. Nearby are the stunning valley of **Edale**, where the Trust owns several farms, and the landmark of **Mam Tor**, next to the spectacular limestone gorge of **Winnats Pass**. The **Derwent** and **Howden Moors** are important historic landscapes lying above Ladybower and Howden Reservoirs. Deeply incised by many spectacular cloughs or valleys in which run fast-flowing streams, the moors are important for upland breeding birds and stands of relict woodland.

The River Dove flowing through Dovedale, Derbyshire

On the eastern edge of the Peak District, the **Longshaw Estate** is an outstanding area of moorland, woodland and farmland, formerly a shooting estate of the Duke of Rutland. The visitor centre is situated next to the dramatic Shooting Lodge.

Mam Tor from Rushup Edge in the Derbyshire Peak District

Previous page: Lyveden New Bield, Northamptonshire

Ilam Park, Derbyshire

The South Peak Estate straddles the Derbyshire/Staffordshire border and includes **Dovedale**, famous for its limestone pinnacles and ancient ashwoods and geological features, as well as the former **Leek & Manifold Valley Light Railway**, now a surfaced track leading through dramatic limestone scenery. Nearby **Ilam Park** has a range of visitor facilities and local information and there is an information shelter at **Milldale**.

Further east are the extensive parkland, heaths and woods of **Clumber Park**, a significant area for wildlife and a remnant of the vast estates that once covered most of Nottinghamshire.

Regional Highlights for Visitors with Disabilities ...

Particularly recommended are **Clumber Park**, with excellent pathways and visitor facilities, and the **Manifold** track, which is suitable for wheelchair access.

... and for Families

The **Museum of Childhood** at **Sudbury Hall** is of special interest; at **Clumber Park** bicycles can be hired; at **Belton House** there is a **Wildlife Discovery Centre** and extensive outdoor adventure playground, and at

Woolsthorpe Manor a **Science Discovery Centre** and exhibition. Children always find much to see and do at **Tattershall Castle**.

Further Information

Please contact the Membership Department, PO Box 39, Warrington WA5 7WD.
Tel. 0870 458 4000.
Email: enquiries@thenationaltrust.org.uk

OS Grid Reference

OS grid references for main properties with no individual entry (OS Landranger map series numbers given in brackets)

Derwent Moors	[110]	SK173893
Dovedale	[119]	SK148510
Hope Woodlands	[110]	SK109914*
Kinder Scout	[110]	SK083889
Leek & Manifold	[119]	SK095561
Mam Tor	[110]	SK128836
Milldale	[119]	SK139548

*car park for access (not NT)

Belton House

Grantham, Lincolnshire NG32 2LS

 1984   **(3:E3)**

Restoration country house with magnificent interiors, gardens and park

Built in 1685-88 for 'Young' Sir John Brownlow, Belton is undoubtedly one of the finest examples of Restoration country house architecture. The stunning interiors contain exceptionally fine plasterwork and wood-carving, as well as important collections of paintings, furniture, tapestries and silver. The grounds include 14ha (36 acres) of gardens, the Lakeside Walk, a magnificent landscaped park and the largest children's adventure playground in Lincolnshire.

What's new in 2005 Stableyard Coffee House. Opening of newly refurbished Blue Bedroom

[i] **T** 01476 566116, 01476 572292 (Wardens), 01476 576551 (House Manager), 01476 561541 (Gardeners), 01476 577290 (Learning), 01476 576347 (Shop), 01476 569453 (Restaurant) **F** 01476 579071 **E** belton@nationaltrust.org.uk

[£] £6.80, child £3.40, family £16. Groups £5.20, child £2.60. **Family – grounds only (available in Aug only)**: £12.50. 'Hidden England' passport scheme: with a stamped passport, one person can obtain free admission when a full price ticket is purchased from other properties in the 'Hidden England' group

Opening arrangements: Belton House									
House	23 Mar - 30 Oct	12:30 - 5	M	T	**W**	**T**	**F**	**S**	**S**
Garden	23 Mar - 30 Oct	11 - 5:30	M	T	**W**	**T**	**F**	**S**	**S**
	4 Nov - 18 Dec	12 - 4	M	T	W	T	**F**	**S**	**S**
Shop	23 Mar - 30 Oct	11 - 5:15	M	T	**W**	**T**	**F**	**S**	**S**
	4 Nov - 18 Dec	12 - 4	M	T	W	T	**F**	**S**	**S**
Restaurant	As shop								
Shop/restaurant	7 Jan - 26 Feb 06	12 - 4	M	T	W	T	F	**S**	**S**

Open BH Mons. Property closes at 4:30 on 16 July. Grounds open 10.30 on open days throughout Aug. Pedestrian access to park only **does not** provide access to house, garden and adventure playground. Park may be closed occasionally for special events. Bellmount Woods: daily, access from separate car park

[K] Guided tours in house 11.30 and 12 on open days during Aug. Guided tours for groups, outside normal hours only, by arrangement

[theatre] Programme of events, inc. open-air concert, family day

[walk] Park leaflet available

[access] Separate designated parking, 20yds. Limited parking – please contact gatekeeper on arrival. Drop-off point. **Building**: Many steps to entrance. 2 wheelchairs. Seating available. Photograph album, virtual tour. **WCs**: Adapted WC. **Grounds**: Partly accessible, loose gravel paths. Accessible route map. 1 single-seater PMV. **Shop**: Ramped entrance with handrail. **Refreshments**: Level entrance

[loop] Induction loop in shop, restaurant, guided tour

[braille] Braille guide and large-print guide. Sensory list. Handling collection

[restaurant] The Stables Restaurant (licensed). Main meals 12–2; last service 15 mins before closing. Children's menu. Ice-cream kiosk in adventure playground, weekends and school holidays 2–5. Stableyard Coffee House in stableyard, weather permitting (opening beginning of May): weekends in high season and school holidays 12–5

[picnic] In car park and adventure playground

[baby] Baby-changing and feeding facilities. Pushchairs admitted. Front-carrying baby slings and hip-carrying infant seats for loan. Children's play area. Activity room in house; Wildlife Discovery Centre; extensive outdoor adventure playground with under-6s 'corral'; miniature train rides in summer

[school] Suitable for school groups. Education room/centre. Live interpretation. Hands-on activities. Family guide. Children's quiz/trail. Family activity packs. Adult study days

[dog] On leads and only in parkland

[→] [130: SK930395] **Bus**: Road Car 1 Grantham–Lincoln; MassReliance 609 Grantham–Sleaford (both pass close [rail] Grantham). **Station**: Grantham 3ml. **Road**: 3ml NE of Grantham on A607 Grantham–Lincoln road, easily reached and signposted from A1

Please see the area introductions for details of coast & countryside properties

P Free parking, 250yds

NT properties nearby
Tattershall Castle, Woolsthorpe Manor, The Workhouse, Southwell

---

Calke Abbey

Ticknall, Derby, Derbyshire DE73 1LE

🏠 🏠 ✝ 👟 ✿ ♣ 📷 📹 🎭 🍷 1985   (3:C4)

Vivid example of a great house in decline, with extraordinary contents, historic park and restored garden

This baroque mansion, built 1701–4 and set in a stunning landscape park, has become famous as a graphic illustration of the English country house in decline. Little restored, the house contains the spectacular natural history collection of the Harpur Crewe family, as well as a magnificent 18th-century state bed and interiors that are essentially unchanged since the 1880s. The open parkland is managed for its nature conservation value and the attractive grounds feature a beautiful walled garden, including a flower garden, physic garden and Auricula Theatre and an interesting collection of garden buildings.

What's new in 2005 Park designated as a National Nature Reserve

⭐ All visitors (inc. NT members) require a house and garden (or garden only) ticket from the ticket office. At busy times these will be timed tickets. Delays in entry to house are possible at BHols. The house, church and garden are closed on Sat 13 Aug for annual concert. One-way system operates in the park; access only via Ticknall entrance

Opening arrangements: Calke Abbey										
House	26 Mar - 30 Oct	1 - 5:30	**M**	**T**	**W**	T	F	**S**	**S**	
Gdn & church	26 Mar - 30 Oct	11 - 5:30	**M**	**T**	**W**	T	F	**S**	**S**	
Restaurant	26 Mar - 30 Oct	10:30 - 5	**M**	**T**	**W**	T	F	**S**	**S**	
	5 Nov - 27 Nov	11 - 4	M	T	W	T	F	**S**	**S**	
	28 Nov - 18 Dec	11 - 4	**M**	**T**	**W**	T	F	**S**	**S**	
	7 Jan - 19 Mar 06	11 - 4	M	T	W	T	F	**S**	**S**	
Shop	As restaurant	10:30 - 5:30								

Admission by timed ticket. Ticket office opens 11.
Park: Open most days until 9 or dusk if earlier

ℹ️ **T** 01332 863822, 01332 862665 (Warden), 01332 864813 (Learning), 01332 865699 (Shop), 01332 864803 (Restaurant) **F** 01332 865272 **E** calkeabbey@nationaltrust.org.uk

£ £6.30, child £3.10, family £15.70. Groups £5.30, child £2.60. **Garden only**: £3.80, child £1.90, family £9.50

🎭 Morning guided tours for groups (but not Sun or BH weekends). Tours last approx. 1hr 20min (extra charge inc. NT members)

🚶 Park guide available

♿ Separate designated parking, 500yds. Volunteer-driven vehicle operates between car park/ticket office and house/garden. Passengers required to transfer from wheelchairs to vehicle at pickup points. **Building**: Level entrance. Access to 3 showrooms on ground floor. 5 wheelchairs. Stairs to other floors. Audio visual/video, photograph album. **WCs**: Adapted WC. **Grounds**: Partly accessible. Accessible route map. Grass and gravel paths to garden and church. **Park**: Parts are accessible. Some visitors may require assistance from their companion. **Shop**: Level entrance. **Refreshments**: Level entrance

🔊 Induction loop in reception

👐 Braille guide. Sensory list

☕ Licensed restaurant. Children's menu. Kiosk open on busy afternoons

🅰 In park

🚼 Baby-changing facilities. Pushchairs admitted. Front-carrying baby slings and hip-carrying infant seats for loan. Children's play area (for under 8s)

🏫 Suitable for school groups. Education room/centre. Live interpretation. Children's guide. Children's quiz/trail. Family activity packs

🐕 On leads and only in park; no shaded parking

➔ [128: SK367226] **Bus**: Arriva 69/A, Derby–Swadlincote (passing close ≋ Derby), alight Ticknall, then 1½ml walk through park to house. **Station**: Derby 9½ml; Burton-on-Trent 10ml. **Road**: 10ml S of Derby, on A514 at Ticknall between Swadlincote and Melbourne. Access from M42/A42 exit 13 and A50 Derby South

Unless indicated, last admission is always 30mins before closing time

P Parking, £3.20 (refunded on admission to house & garden when open). Height of arch at Middle Lodge 3.6m

NT properties nearby
Kedleston Hall, Staunton Harold Church, Sudbury Hall

Canons Ashby House

Canons Ashby, Daventry, Northamptonshire
NN11 3SD

🏠 ✚ ✲ 🍴 ♿ 🛍 📷 1981 **(3:D7)**

Tranquil Elizabethan manor house set in beautiful gardens

The home of the Dryden family since its construction, Canons Ashby has survived more or less unaltered since c.1710. The intimate and atmospheric interior contains wall paintings and Jacobean plasterwork of the highest quality. There are also a formal garden with colourful herbaceous borders, an orchard featuring varieties of fruit trees from the 16th century and a surprisingly grand church – all that remains of the Augustinian priory from which the house takes its name.

What's new in 2005 Home paddock being restored to wildflower meadow

The south front, Canons Ashby House, Northamptonshire

i **T** 01327 861900, 01327 860044 (Infoline),
01327 861904 (Shop),
01327 861905 (Tea-room)
F 01327 861909
E canonsashby@nationaltrust.org.uk

£ £5.80, child £2.90, family £14.50. Groups £4.80, child £2.50. **Garden only**: £2. Donation box for church

🎓 Guided house tours for booked school groups only

🎭 Programme of events. Tel. for details

♿ Separate designated parking, 20yds. **Building**: Many steps to entrance. 2 wheelchairs. Ground floor has 3 steps to Winter Parlour and 1 step to Book Room. Many stairs with handrail to other floors. Seating available. Virtual tour. **WCs**: Adapted WC. **Grounds**: Partly accessible. Grounds have 4 steps and terraces. **Shop**: Level entrance. **Refreshments**: Steps to entrance. Ramp to tea-room garden

👐 Braille guide and large-print guide. Interesting scents

🛍 NT Shop. Secondhand bookshop. Plant sales

🍴 Cottage Garden Tea-Room. Light lunches. Children's menu

🅿 Picnic facilities in car park only

Opening arrangements: Canons Ashby

			M	T	W	T	F	S	S
House	23 Mar - 28 Sep	1 - 5:30	M	T	W	T	F	S	S
	1 Oct - 2 Nov	1 - 4:30	M	T	W	T	F	S	S
Gardens	23 Mar - 28 Sep	11 - 5:30	M	T	W	T	F	S	S
	1 Oct - 2 Nov	11 - 4:30	M	T	W	T	F	S	S
	5 Nov - 18 Dec	12 - 4	M	T	W	T	F	S	S
Shop/tea-room	23 Mar - 28 Sep	12 - 5	M	T	W	T	F	S	S
	1 Oct - 2 Nov	12 - 4:30	M	T	W	T	F	S	S
	5 Nov - 18 Dec	12 - 4	M	T	W	T	F	S	S
Park & church	23 Mar - 28 Sep	11 - 5:30	M	T	W	T	F	S	S
	1 Oct - 2 Nov	11 - 4:30	M	T	W	T	F	S	S
	5 Nov - 18 Dec	12 - 4	M	T	W	T	F	S	S

Open Good Fri 1–5:30. Closes dusk if earlier

🚼 Baby-changing facilities. Pushchairs and baby back-carriers admitted. Front-carrying baby slings for loan

🎒 Suitable for school groups. Children's quiz/trail

🐕 On leads and only in Home Paddock and car park

➔ [152: SP577506] **Cycle**: NCN70.
Bus: Occasional Sun services from Northampton. **Station**: Banbury 10ml.
Road: Easy access from either M40, exit 11 or M1, exit 16. From M1, take A45 (Daventry) and at Weedon crossroads turn left onto A5; 3ml S turn right onto unclassified road through Litchborough and Adstone. From M40 at Banbury, take A422 (Buckingham) and after 2ml turn left onto B4525; after 3ml turn left onto unclassified road signposted to property

P Free parking, 200yds

NT properties nearby
Farnborough Hall, Stowe Landscape Gardens, Upton House

Clumber Park

The Estate Office, Clumber Park, Worksop, Nottinghamshire S80 3AZ

🎒➕❄️♣️♨️🏠🛒🎡🐕🍴 1946   **(3:D2)**

Vast area of parkland and woods

The park comprises over 1500ha (3800 acres), including peaceful woods, open heath and rolling farmland, with a superb serpentine lake at its heart and the longest avenue of lime trees in Europe. Part of Nottinghamshire's famed 'Dukeries', Clumber was formerly home to the Dukes of Newcastle. The house was demolished in 1938, but many fascinating features of the estate remain, including an outstanding Gothic Revival Chapel and walled kitchen garden with spectacular glass houses, growing old varieties of vegetables.

⭐ Park closed 9 July & 20 Aug (concert days) and 25 Dec

ℹ️ **T** 01909 476592,
01909 544917 (Infoline),
01909 544911 (Cycle hire),
01909 544918 (Learning),
01909 511061 (Box office),
01909 544912 (Shop),
01909 544914 (Plant sales),
01909 544915 (Restaurant)
F 01909 500721
E clumberpark@nationaltrust.org.uk

£ Admission free. **Vehicle entry charge**: £4 per car; £5.20 car + caravan, minibus, car + trailer; coaches free. **Walled kitchen garden**: £1, child free. Orienteering by arrangement (orienteering packs £1.95). Horse riding by permit only, £7 day permit or £55 annual season ticket. Coarse fishing: 16 June to 14 March; 7am to dusk; £4 day ticket or £50 annual season ticket

Opening arrangements: Clumber Park

			M	T	W	T	F	S	S
Park	All year	Daylight	M	T	W	T	F	S	S
Kitchen garden	26 Mar - 30 Oct	10 - 6	M	T	W	T	F	S	S
	28 Mar - 28 Oct	10 - 5:30	M	T	W	T	F	S	S
Plant sales	As kitchen gdn								
Shop/restnt	26 Mar - 30 Oct	10 - 6	M	T	W	T	F	S	S
	28 Mar - 28 Oct	10 - 5:30	M	T	W	T	F	S	S
	31 Oct - 26 Mar 06	10 - 4	M	T	W	T	F	S	S

Main facilities open BH Mons, closed 25/26 Dec. Chapel open as shop but closed 12 Jan–25 March 2006 for cleaning. Cycle hire and Information point open as shop except Nov–March, when open weekends and school holidays only. 183-berth caravan site run by Caravan Club; open to non-members (tel. 01909 484758). Camp site run by Camping & Caravanning Club of Great Britain: April to Sept, limited spaces, booking advisable (tel. 01909 482303). Plant sales open occasional weekends up to 18 Dec (weather permitting)

For further information check our website www.nationaltrust.org.uk

Nineteenth-century glasshouses in the Walled Kitchen Garden, Clumber Park, Nottinghamshire

By arrangement

Programme of events, inc. open-air concerts and theatre; Country Show. Leaflet available from Estate office

Separate designated parking, 200yds. **Building**: Ramped entrance to chapel and walled garden. 5 wheelchairs. **WCs**: Adapted WC. **Grounds**: Partly accessible. Accessible route map. Ramped access from conservatory to garden. Cycle hire: Trikes, tandems and adapted cycle. 2 single-seater PMV, booking essential. **Shop**: Ramped entrance. **Refreshments**: Ramped entrance

Braille guide and large-print guide. Sensory list. Handling collection

NT shop. Plant sales

Clocktower Restaurant (licensed). Children's menu during school holidays. Muniment Room and Duke's Study within Clocktower Restaurant available for private hire weekends only

Baby-changing and feeding facilities. Pushchairs and baby back-carriers admitted. Cycles with child carriers or buggies available; parkland ideal for family activities

Suitable for school groups. Education room/centre. Hands-on activities. Children's guide. Children's quiz/trail. Family activity packs. Adult study days

Welcome in park. Must be on leads in Pleasure Ground and grazing enclosures

Cycle hire available April to Sept, daily; Oct to March, Sat & Sun and school holidays. Times: opens 10, variable closing. £5.20 for 2hrs, ID essential. Free helmet hire. Tandems, child seats, trailer bikes and trikes available. Waymarked cycle routes. Cycle orienteering

→ [120: SK625745 – 626746] **Cycle**: NCN6. **Bus**: Stagecoach in Bassetlaw F1 from Heanor & Hucknall, F2 from Nottingham. First 150/1 from Rotherham. All Sun only; otherwise Stagecoach 33 Worksop–Nottingham (passing close ≋ Worksop), alight Carburton, ¾ml. **Station**: Worksop 4½ml; Retford 6½ml. **Road**: 4½ml SE of Worksop, 6½ml SW of Retford, 1ml from A1/A57, 11ml from M1 exit 30

P Parking, 200yds

NT properties nearby
Hardwick Hall, Mr Straw's House, The Workhouse, Southwell

Please note: groups must book in advance with the property

Hardwick Hall

Doe Lea, Chesterfield, Derbyshire S44 5QJ

🏛 ⓗ ✿ ♣ ⬇ 🗀 ☕ 🎭 ⚗ 🔔 ▲ 1959   (3:D2)

One of Britain's greatest and most complete Elizabethan houses

Like a huge glass lantern, Hardwick dominates the surrounding area – a magnificent statement of the wealth and authority of its builder, Bess of Hardwick. Designed by Robert Smythson, the house is remarkable for being almost unchanged since Bess lived here, giving a rare insight into the formality of courtly life of the Elizabethan age. There are outstanding collections of 16th-century embroidery, tapestries, furniture and portraits. Walled courtyards enclose fine gardens, orchards and a herb garden, and the surrounding country park contains rare breeds of cattle and sheep. In the grounds are the remains of Hardwick Old Hall, which Bess continued to use after her new house was built.

What's new in 2005 New museum rooms in Hall, including Tobit Table Carpet. 'Bess' exhibition in Butler's Pantry. New south border planting in garden

⭐ The ruins of Hardwick Old Hall in the grounds are administered by English Heritage (01246 850431)

ℹ️ **T** 01246 850430,
01246 858400 (Office),
01246 851787 (Park Centre),

Opening arrangements: Hardwick Hall

			M	T	W	T	F	S	S
Hall	23 Mar - 30 Oct	12 - 4:30	M	T	**W**	**T**	**F**	**S**	**S**
Garden	23 Mar - 30 Oct	11 - 5:30	M	T	**W**	**T**	**F**	**S**	**S**
Parkland gates	All year	8 - 6	**M**	**T**	**W**	**T**	**F**	**S**	**S**
Old Hall (EH)	23 Mar - 30 Oct	10 - 6	M	**W**	**T**		**S**	**S**	
Shop	23 Mar - 30 Oct	11 - 5	M	T	**W**	**T**	F	**S**	**S**
Restaurant	As shop								
Stone Centre	23 Mar - 30 Oct	11 - 4	M	T	**W**	**T**	F	**S**	**S**

Open BH Mons and Good Fri 12–4:30. Parkland gates close 5.30 in winter

01246 858411 (Group/Education visits),
01246 858407 (Shop),
01246 858406 (Restaurant)
F 01246 858424
E hardwickhall@nationaltrust.org.uk

💷 **House & garden**: £7.20, child £3.60, family £18. Groups £6.20. **Garden only**: £3.90, child £1.95, family £9.75. **Joint ticket for Old and New Halls (NT/EH)**: £9.70, child £4.85, family £24.25. Children under 15 must be accompanied by an adult

🚶 Tours of stonemasons' yard and Centre Wed/Thur pm, £1 (inc. NT members)

♿ Designated parking in main car park, 50yds. Drop-off point. **Building**: Ramped entrance. 3 wheelchairs, booking essential. Ground floor accessible. Stairs with handrail to other floors. Seating available. Photograph album, virtual tour. **WCs**: Adapted WC. **Grounds**: Fully accessible. Accessible route map. **Shop**: Many steps to entrance with handrail, ramp available. **Refreshments**: Steps to entrance, ramp available. Booking essential

Hardwick Hall, Derbyshire

Ⓑ Braille guide and large-print guide. Sensory list. Handling collection. Staff trained to assist hard of hearing and visually-impaired visitors

Ⓟ Licensed restaurant. Children's menu

Ⓐ In designated area and parkland

Ⓚ Baby-changing facilities. Front-carrying baby slings and hip-carrying infant seats for loan. Reins for loan

Ⓢ Suitable for school groups. Children's quiz/trail. Visits to Hall, gardens, Park Centre and Stone Centre. Resource packs

Ⓚ On leads and only in park and car park

➔ [120: SK463638] **Foot**: Rowthorne trail; Teversal trail. **Bus**: Cosy Coaches C1 from ≋ Chesterfield to Hall (Sun, June–Aug only); otherwise Stagecoach Express 737, 747 Sheffield/Chesterfield–Nottingham, alight Glapwell 'Young Vanish', 1½ml. **Station**: Chesterfield 8ml. **Road**: 6½ml W of Mansfield, 9½ml SE of Chesterfield; approach from M1 (exit 29) via A6175. **Note**: A one-way traffic system operates in the park; access only via Stainsby Mill entrance (leave M1, exit 29, follow brown signs), exit only via Hardwick Inn. Park gates shut 6 in summer, 5.30 in winter

Ⓟ Parking, 100yds, £2. Country park car park £1.20 for non-members (season ticket £10)

NT properties nearby
Clumber Park, Kedleston Hall, Stainsby Mill, Mr Straw's House, The Workhouse, Southwell

---

High Peak Estate

High Peak Estate Office, Edale End, Hope Valley, Derbyshire S33 6RF

Ⓜ Ⓣ Ⓔ Ⓚ Ⓚ | 1936 | (3:C2)

Vast area of outstanding walking country

The High Peak stretches from the heather-clad moors of Park Hall to the gritstone of Derwent Edge, and from the peat bogs of Bleaklow to the limestone crags of Winnats Pass. The wild Pennine moorlands are of international importance for their populations of breeding birds, including golden plover, merlin and red grouse. Sites of particular interest include Mam Tor, with its spectacular views, landslip and prehistoric settlement; Odin Mine, one of the oldest lead mines in Derbyshire; and the unspoilt valley of Snake Pass. Kinder Scout, where the Mass Trespass of 1932 took place, is the highest point for fifty miles around. The Trust also owns several farms in the beautiful Edale valley. A major woodland restoration project (in partnership with the Forestry Commission) is underway in the recently acquired Alport valley.

What's new in 2005 Recently refurbished information shelters at Edale and Dalehead

ⓘ **T** 01433 670368 **F** 01433 670397
E highpeakestate@nationaltrust.org.uk

Ⓔ Programme of events. Tel. for details

Ⓓ Contact in advance

Ⓢ Suitable for school groups. Live interpretation. Hands-on activities. Children's guide. Wide range of leaflets available

➔ [110: SK100855] **Foot**: Pennine Way passes through property. **Bus**: Bowers 403 New Mills–Castleton to within 1ml of South Head Farm, Suns only, April–Oct only. Frequent services to Castleton from surrounding areas; also Stagecoach 260 Castleton–Edale, weekends only. **Station**: Edale is 1½ml from Dale Head, 2ml from Lee Barn and 3ml from Edale End; Chinley is 3ml from South Head Farm; Hope is 3ml from Edale End. **Road**: Estate covers area N & S of A57 on Sheffield side of Snake Top, E of Hayfield and W of Castleton

Ⓟ Many free car parks (not NT) in area. Also pay & display (not NT) at Edale, Castleton, Bowden Bridge and Hayfield. NT pay & display at Mam Nick (SK123833)

NT properties nearby
Longshaw Estate, Lyme Park

Opening arrangements: High Peak Estate	
All year	M T W T F S S
Open and unrestricted access for walkers all year to moorland, subject to occasional management closures (advertised locally). Access to farmland is via public rights of way and permitted paths. Five information shelters open all year: Lee Barn (110:SK096855) on Pennine Way near Jacob's Ladder; Dalehead (110: SK101843) in Edale; South Head Farm (SK060854) at Kinder; Edale End (SK161864) between Edale and Hope; Grindle Barns above Ladybower Reservoir (SK189895)	

Please remember – your membership card is always needed for free admission

Ilam Park

Ilam, Ashbourne, Derbyshire DE6 2AZ

❀ ♣ ♨ 🏠 💷 🎭 [1934]   (3:C3)

Beautiful area of open park and woodland

Ilam Park runs along both banks of the River Manifold, with spectacular views towards Dovedale. What remains of Ilam Hall is a youth hostel and NT visitor centre, tea-room and shop. A small garden has been created on the site of the old Italian Garden situated below the stableblock.

ℹ️ **T** 01335 350503 (Estate office),
01335 350310 (Caravan site booking office),
01335 350245 (Visitor centre),
01335 350549 (Learning) **F** 01335 350511
E ilampark@nationaltrust.org.uk

💷 Admission free

🏃 Guided walks around the estate and hands-on activities may be booked by groups; contact Learning Officer

🚶 Walks information available from visitor centre/shop

♿ Contact in advance. Designated parking in main car park, 75yds. Drop-off point in stableyard to rear of hall. Vehicle drop-off point and some parking possible in front of shop by arrangement. Tel. visitor centre.
Building: Access to all facilities over uneven cobbled surface. 1 wheelchair. Seating available. **WCs**: Adapted WC.
Grounds: Partly accessible, steep slopes, some steps, undulating terrain. Areas of the park are accessible on hard surfaces. Upgrading of access is ongoing. **Shop**: Step to entrance, ramp available.
Refreshments: Many steps to entrance with handrail. Large-print and braille menu. Uneven paths and steps, alternative arrangements are available, enquire in shop

👁 Braille guide and large-print guide. Interesting sounds

☕ Manifold Tea-Room. Children's menu

🏕 Informal picnics allowed. No open fires/barbecues

👶 Baby-changing and feeding facilities. Pushchairs and baby back-carriers admitted

Opening arrangements: Ilam Park										
Park	All year		**M**	**T**	**W**	**T**	**F**	**S**	**S**	
Shop	8 Jan - 27 Mar	11 - 4	M	T	W	T	F	**S**	**S**	
	28 Mar - 30 Oct	11 - 5	**M**	**T**	W	T	**F**	**S**	**S**	
	5 Nov - 18 Dec	11 - 4	M	T	W	T	F	**S**	**S**	
	7 Jan - 25 Mar 06	11 - 4	M	T	W	T	F	**S**	**S**	
Tea-room	8 Jan - 27 Mar	11 - 4	M	T	W	T	F	**S**	**S**	
	2 Apr - 22 May	11 - 5	M	T	W	T	F	**S**	**S**	
	23 May - 30 Oct	11 - 5	**M**	**T**	W	T	**F**	**S**	**S**	
	5 Nov - 18 Dec	11 - 4	M	T	W	T	F	**S**	**S**	
	7 Jan - 25 Mar 06	11 - 4	M	T	W	T	F	**S**	**S**	

Hall is let to YHA and not open. **Note**: Small caravan site run by NT (basic facilities) open to Caravan Club/NT members March to Oct (tel. caravan site booking office)

🏫 Suitable for school groups. Education room/centre. Hands-on activities. Family guide. Children's quiz/trail. Adult study days. Visitor centre has exhibition on Ilam and South Peak Estate. Small events throughout year, contact Learning Officer. When not in use by pre-booked groups, Learning and Discovery Centre open to visitors to browse for information and for children's activities

🐕 On leads only

➡️ [119: SK132507] 4½ml NW of Ashbourne. **Cycle**: NCN68 2ml. **Bus**: Wornington 443 from Ashbourne, Thur & Sat only, with connections from Derby; TM Travel 202 from Derby, Sun only; otherwise Bowers 442 Buxton–Ashbourne, alight Thorpe, 2ml

🅿️ Parking, 75yds (pay & display)

NT properties nearby
Biddulph Grange Garden, Dovedale, Hamps & Manifold Valley, Kedleston Hall, Longshaw Estate, Sudbury Hall and Museum of Childhood

Kedleston Hall

Derby, Derbyshire DE22 5JH

🏛 ✝ ❀ ♣ 🏠 💷 🎧 🔔 🍴 [1987]   (3:C3)

Neo-classical mansion with Adam interiors, landscape gardens and park

Kedleston was built between 1759 and 1765 for the Curzon family, who have lived in the area since the 12th century. The house boasts the most complete and least-altered sequence of Robert Adam interiors in England, with the magnificent state rooms retaining their great collections of paintings and original furniture. The Eastern Museum houses a remarkable range of objects collected by Lord Curzon when Viceroy of India (1899-1905). The gardens have been restored in part to an 18th-century 'pleasure ground' and the surrounding park, also designed by Adam, includes a fine bridge, fishing pavilion and series of lakes and cascades. All Saints' Church (in the ownership of the Churches Conservation Trust) is the only survivor of the medieval village of Kedleston and contains a collection of monuments and memorials to the Curzons.

[i] **T** 01332 842191,
01332 842338 (Head Warden),
01332 843405 (Shop),
01332 843404 (Restaurant) **F** 01332 841972
E kedlestonhall@nationaltrust.org.uk

[£] £6.30, child £3, family £15.50. Groups £5.20, child £2.60. **Park & garden only**: £2.80, child £1.40, family £7. Reduced rate when arriving by public transport, cycle or on foot. (Park & garden ticket refundable against tickets for house). Winter admission for park only £2.70 per vehicle

[𝟙] Introductory talks from 18th-century housekeeper. Guided walks around park, stables, fishing room and gardens, tel. for dates and times

North front, Kedleston Hall, Derbyshire

Opening arrangements: Kedleston Hall										
House	19 Mar - 31 Oct	12 - 4:30	M	T	W	T	F	S	S
Garden	19 Mar - 31 Oct	10 - 6	M	T	W	T	F	S	S
Park	19 Mar - 31 Oct	10 - 6	M	T	W	T	F	S	S
	1 Nov - 31 Mar 06	10 - 4	M	T	W	T	F	S	S
Shop	19 Mar - 31 Oct	11:30 - 5:30	M	T	W	T	F	S	S
	5 Nov - 26 Mar 06	12 - 4	M	T	W	T	F	S	S
Restaurant	19 Mar - 31 Oct	11 - 5	M	T	W	T	F	S	S
	5 Nov - 26 Mar 06	12 - 4	M	T	W	T	F	S	S
Church	19 Mar - 31 Oct	11 - 5	M	T	W	T	F	S	S

Open Good Fri. Park: occasional day restrictions may apply in Dec 2005 and Jan 2006. Closed 25/26 Dec

[🎪] Programme of events, inc. open-air concert, antiques fairs, working craft fair, garden fête, numerous family activities. Leaflet available

[🚶] Wilderness Walk and Long/Short Walk plus unrestricted access to rest of park

[♿] Designated parking in main car park, 55yds. 3 spaces for disabled drivers adjacent to Hall. Available by permit from main ticket point. Drop-off point. **Building**: Many steps to entrance. Alternative accessible entrance. 4 wheelchairs. Shop and restaurant fully accessible (transfer required from PMV to manual wheelchair). Many stairs to other floors, stairclimber available. Booking essential. Seating available. **WCs**: Adapted WC. **Grounds**: Accessible route map. Stability of ground currently prevents use of PMVs. This is under review, please contact property. 1 single-seater PMV, booking essential. **Shop**: Level entrance. **Refreshments**: Level entrance

[🔊] Induction loop in reception, shop, restaurant

[👓] Braille guide and large-print guide. Sensory list

[🛍] NT shop, includes limited quantities of plants grown in peat-free compost

[🍽] Licensed restaurant. Children's menu

[▭] In the park only

[🚼] Baby-changing facilities. Hip-carrying infant seats for loan

[🏫] Suitable for school groups. Live interpretation. Hands-on activities. Children's guide. Children's quiz/trail. Family activity packs

[🐕] On leads and only in park (but not on Long/Short Walk)

Please see the area introductions for details of coast & countryside properties

Cycling permitted on parkland roads

→ [128: SK312403] **Bus**: Arriva 109 ⊠ Derby–Ashbourne calls at Hall on Sun, otherwise alight the Smithy, then 1ml. **Station**: Duffield (U) 3½ml; Derby 5½ml. **Road**: All traffic should aim for Markeaton roundabout where A52 intersects with A38. Follow brown signs to first exit from A38 (N) and then along Kedleston Road

P Free parking, 200yds. Non-members must pay relevant admission fee to property in order to use car park

NT properties nearby
Calke Abbey, Ilam Park, Sudbury Hall and Museum of Childhood

Longshaw Estate

Sheffield, Derbyshire S11 7TZ

 1931 **(3:C2)**

Wide expanse of moorland, woods and farmland within the Peak District National Park

The estate provides excellent walking country with dramatic views, only ten miles south-west of the centre of Sheffield.

What's new in 2005 Children's/family activity leaflet

i **T** 01433 631708 (Visitor centre),
01433 631757 (Wardens' office),
01433 670368 (Learning)
F 01433 630629
E longshaw@nationaltrust.org.uk

Heather blooming on the Longshaw Estate, Derbyshire

£ Admission free

Walks and leaflets from visitor centre. Groups may book guided walks; contact Wardens' office

Programme of events, inc. school holiday family activities and other events throughout the year. Tel. Learning Officer for details

Contact in advance. Separate designated parking, 10yds. Drop-off point. **Building**: Ramped entrance. **WCs**: Adapted WC. **Grounds**: Partly accessible, areas accessible on hard surfaces. Variable terrain beyond visitor centre. Accessible route map. Some visitors may require assistance from their companion. **Shop**: Ramped entrance. **Refreshments**: Ramped entrance. Tea-room and shop step has 1in high lip

NT shop in visitor centre. Christmas tree sales in main car park in Dec, tel. Wardens' office for details

Tea-room at visitor centre. Children's menu

Informal picnics allowed. No open fires/barbecues

Baby-changing facilities. Pushchairs and baby back-carriers admitted

Suitable for school groups

On leads only, not in visitor centre

Opening arrangements: Longshaw Estate										
Estate	All year		M	T	W	T	F	S	S
Visitor centre	8 Jan - 20 Mar	10:30 - 5	M	T	W	T	**F**	**S**	**S**
	21 Mar - 3 Apr	10:30 - 5	**M**	**T**	**W**	**T**	**F**	**S**	**S**
	6 Apr - 24 Jul	10:30 - 5	M	**T**	**W**	**T**	**F**	**S**	**S**
	25 Jul - 4 Sep	10:30 - 5	**M**	**T**	**W**	**T**	**F**	**S**	**S**
	7 Sep - 30 Oct	10:30 - 5	M	**T**	**W**	**T**	**F**	**S**	**S**
	5 Nov - 18 Dec	10:30 - 5	M	T	W	T	F	**S**	**S**
	7 Jan - 26 Feb 06	10:30 - 5	M	T	W	T	**F**	**S**	**S**
Shop	As visitor centre								

Open BH Mons. Closes dusk if earlier than 5. Lodge is not open

Unless indicated, last admission is always 30mins before closing time

→ [110/119: SK266800] **Bus**: First 240 Sheffield–
Bakewell (passing ≷ Grindleford); 272
Sheffield–Castleton (passing ≷ Hathersage). All
pass close ≷ Sheffield. **Station**: Grindleford (U)
2ml. **Road**: 7½ml from Sheffield, next to A625
Sheffield–Hathersage road; Woodcroft car park
is off B6055, 200yds S of junction with A625

P Parking, £1 (pay & display). NT members must
display cards. Car parks for estate at Haywood
[110/119: SK256778] and Wooden Pole
[110/119: SK267790] and Woodcroft [110/119:
SK267802]. Car parks not accessible to
coaches, which should park on roadsides

NT properties nearby
Hardwick Hall, High Peak Estate, Ilam Park,
Stainsby Mill

Lyveden New Bield

nr Oundle, Peterborough, Northamptonshire
PE8 5AT

🏠 ✝ ❀ ♿ 📷 🎞 👁 ⊤ 1922   (3:F6)

**Intriguing Elizabethan lodge and moated
garden**

Begun in 1595 by Sir Thomas Tresham to
symbolise his Catholic faith, Lyveden remains
incomplete and virtually unaltered since work
stopped on his death in 1605. The building has
fascinating architectural detail and the water
garden, with its terraces and spiral mounds,
remains one of the oldest surviving layouts in
Britain. There are miles of footpaths through the
surrounding open countryside and nearby
Rockingham Forest.

What's new in 2005 Accompanied children free;
400th Anniversary

⭐ As featured in BBC series *Hidden Gardens*;
see www.nationaltrust.org.uk/lyveden. WC
not always available

Opening arrangements: Lyveden New Bield										
31 Mar - 31 Jul	10:30 - 5	M	T	**W**	**T**	**F**	**S**	**S**
1 Aug - 31 Aug	10:30 - 5	**M**	**T**	**W**	**T**	**F**	S	S
1 Sep - 30 Oct	10:30 - 5	M	T	**W**	**T**	**F**	S	S
5 Nov - 27 Nov	10:30 - 4	M	T	W	T	F	**S**	**S**
4 Feb - 27 Mar 06	10:30 - 4	M	T	W	T	F	**S**	**S**
Open BH Mons and Good Fri 10:30–5								

ⓘ **T** 01832 205358
E lyvedennewbield@nationaltrust.org.uk

£ £3.50, child free

🚶 Tours for groups by arrangement

♿ Separate designated parking, 40yds.
Building: Steps to entrance. Low entrance.
Grounds: Partly accessible, grass paths,
uneven paths

👓 Braille guide

🎁 Small selection of gifts and ice cream sales

👶 Pushchairs and baby back-carriers admitted

🏫 Suitable for school groups. Family guide

🐕 On leads only

→ [141: SP983853] **Bus**: Stagecoach in
Northants X4 Northampton–Peterborough
(passing close ≷ Peterborough); alight Lower
Benefield, 2ml by bridlepath; 8 Kettering
Corby, alight Brigstock, 2½ml. Both pass close
≷ Kettering. **Station**: Kettering 10ml.
Road: 4ml SW of Oundle via A427, 3ml E of
Brigstock, leading off A6116

P Main parking ½ml from property. Limited
parking at property for less able visitors

NT properties nearby
Canons Ashby, Houghton Mill

The Old Manor

Norbury, Ashbourne, Derbyshire DE6 2ED

🏠 ❀ 🚶 1987   (3:C3)

Low stone-built medieval hall

Built between the 13th and 15th centuries, the
hall's architectural features include a rare king
post, medieval fireplace, a Tudor door and some
17th-century Flemish glass. The delightful
gardens include a parterre herb garden.

ⓘ **T** 01283 585337 (Sudbury Hall)

Opening arrangements: The Old Manor							
2 Apr - 29 Oct	M	T	**W**	T	F	**S**	S

Property is tenanted and visits are strictly by
appointment only by letter to Mrs J. Raine at the Old
Manor, or fax to 01335 324280, a minimum of 7 days
in advance. Visitors will be guided around the hall and
gardens

There are special events at most Trust properties; please telephone 0870 458 4000 for details

£ £2, child £1

⅘ Very limited parking by the church.
Building: Many steps to entrance with
handrail. The hall has two flights of stairs to
access. **WCs**: Adapted WC. **Grounds**: Partly
accessible. The gardens have one small flight
of steps

⍟ Braille guide and large-print guide. Interesting
scents

⫟ Baby back-carriers admitted

⚏ Suitable for school groups

➔ [128: SK125424] 4ml from Ashbourne; 9ml
from Sudbury Hall. **Foot**: Norbury Village is
clearly signposted from A515. 2½ml walk to
Norbury Church. **Bus**: Arriva Midlands 409
Uttoxeter–Ashbourne (passing close ⊟
Uttoxeter), alight Ellastone, ¾ml.
Station: Uttoxeter (U) 7½ml

P No designated car park. Coaches must drop
passengers at top of drive

NT properties nearby
Ilam Park, Kedleston Hall, Sudbury Hall and
Museum of Childhood

Priest's House

Easton on the Hill, nr Stamford, Northamptonshire

⌂ 1966   **(3:F5)**

Small pre-Reformation stone building

Of interest for its architecture, the house also
contains a small museum illustrating past village
life.

★ No WC

i **T** 01909 486411 (Regional office)

£ Admission free. Donation of 50p requested

⅘ **Building**: Level entrance. Ground floor
accessible. Access to other floors via stone
spiral staircase

Opening arrangements: Priest's House

Unmanned. Names of keyholders on property
noticeboard. Appointments for groups may be made
through local representative Mr Paul Way, 39 Church
St, Easton on the Hill, Stamford PE9 3LL

➔ [141: TF009045] **Bus**: Blands/Searle/Transline
180, 303, 313 from Stamford (passing close
⊟ Stamford), alight Easton, ½ml.
Station: Stamford 2ml. **Road**: Approx. 2ml
SW of Stamford off A43

P No parking on site. Not suitable for coaches

NT properties nearby
Lyveden New Bield, Woolsthorpe Manor

Stainsby Mill: Hardwick Estate

Doe Lea, Chesterfield, Derbyshire S44 5QJ

⌘ 🏠 1976   **(3:D2)**

**Remarkably complete water-powered flour
mill**

With newly reconstructed 1849-50 machinery,
the mill is still in good working order. Flour is
ground regularly and for sale throughout the
season.

★ No WC. Available at Hardwick Hall car park

i **T** 01246 850430 (Hardwick Hall)
F 01246 858424
E stainsbymill@nationaltrust.org.uk

£ £2.50, child £1.25, family £6.25. Children
under 15 must be accompanied by an adult

🛈 On request at the mill. For private out-of-
hours tours contact Property Administrator at
Hardwick Hall

🏳 National Mills Day

⅘ **Building**: Many steps to entrance. Very steep
access. Ground floor accessible. Stairs with
handrail to other floors. Seating available.
WCs: Adapted WC. **Grounds**: Partly
accessible. Steep steps to upper area

⍟ Braille guide and large-print guide. Touchable
objects and interesting sounds. Handling
collection

Opening arrangements: Stainsby Mill

23 Mar - 30 Jun	11 - 4:30	M	T	**W**	**T**	F	**S**	**S**
1 Jul - 31 Aug	11 - 4:30	M	T	**W**	**T**	F	**S**	**S**
1 Sep - 30 Oct	11 - 4:30	M	T	**W**	**T**	F	**S**	**S**

Open BH Mons and Good Fri. Open 26 Dec & 1 Jan
2006

For further information check our website www.nationaltrust.org.uk

⬛ NT shop at Hardwick Hall. Flour and souvenirs sold at mill

⬛ Refreshments available at Hardwick Hall

⬛ Pushchairs admitted

⬛ Suitable for school groups. Live interpretation. Children's quiz/trail

⬛ On leads and only in park

➡ [120: SK455653] **Foot**: Rowthorne Trail and Teversal Trail nearby. **Bus**: As for Hardwick Hall but, except for the C1, alight Heath, then 1ml. **Station**: Chesterfield 7ml. **Road**: From M1 exit 29 take A6175 signposted to Clay Cross, then first left and left again to Stainsby Mill

P Free parking. Limited car/coach parking area

NT properties nearby
Clumber Park, Hardwick Hall, Kedleston Hall, Mr Straw's House, The Workhouse, Southwell

---

Staunton Harold Church

Staunton Harold, Ashby-de-la-Zouch, Leicestershire LE65 1RW

⬛⬛ 1954   (3:C4)

Imposing church built in 1653, with fine panelled interior

Set in attractive parkland, this is one of the few churches built between the outbreak of the English Civil War and the restoration of the monarchy, representing an open act of defiance to Cromwell's Puritan regime by its creator, Sir Robert Shirley. The interior retains its original 17th-century cushions, carved woodwork and painted ceilings.

⭐ A one-way system operates on the estate; coaches follow alternative brown sign route. WCs (not·NT) 500yds

ⓘ **T** 01332 863822 (Calke Abbey)
F 01332 865272
E stauntonharold@nationaltrust.org.uk

Opening arrangements: Staunton Harold Church									
1 Apr - 25 Sep	1:30 - 4:30	M	T	**W**	**T**	**F**	**S**	**S**
1 Oct - 30 Oct	1:30 - 4:30	M	T	W	T	F	**S**	**S**

Closes at dusk if earlier than 4.30

£ Admission free. Donations of £1 requested: collection box

⬛ Parking behind Hall, 150yds (not NT). **Building**: Step to entrance, ramp available

⬛ Refreshments available at Ferrers Centre and garden centre nearby

⬛ Pushchairs admitted

⬛ Suitable for school groups

➡ [128: SK380209] **Cycle**: NCN6 2½ml. **Bus**: Arriva 68/9 Derby–Swadlincote (passing close ≋ Derby), alight Melbourne, 3½ml or Ticknall via Calke Park, 3ml. **Road**: 5ml NE of Ashby-de-la-Zouch, W of B587. Access from M42/A42, exit 13

P Free parking (not NT) at garden centre, 150yds. Entrance indicated by brown signs – anvil symbol. Additional parking next to rear of the Hall (by courtesy of the owner)

NT properties nearby
Calke Abbey, Kedleston Hall, Sudbury Hall

Mr Straw's House

7 Blyth Grove, Worksop, Nottinghamshire S81 0JG

⬛⬛ 1990   (3:D2)

Fascinating 1920s tradesman's home

This modest semi-detached Edwardian house was the family home of well-to-do grocers William and Florence Straw from 1923. It is remarkable because the Straws' two sons preserved it almost unaltered till it came to the National Trust in 1990. The interior with its 1920s wallpaper, heavy Victorian furniture and household objects provides a rare glimpse into interwar middle-class life. There are displays of family costume, letters and photos and a typical suburban garden.

What's new in 2005 Exhibition and events to celebrate 100 years since the house was built

⭐ Blyth Grove is a private road; there is no access without advance booking. There is a car park with picnic area for visitors opposite the house. On arrival please go to reception at 5 Blyth Grove

Please note: groups must book in advance with the property

→ [120: SK592802] **Cycle**: NCN6 ¾ml.
Bus: From surrounding areas.
Station: Worksop ½ml. **Road**: In Worksop,
follow signs to Bassetlaw General Hospital.
House signposted from Blyth Road (B6045)

P Free parking, 30yds

NT properties nearby
Clumber Park, Hardwick Hall, Stainsby Mill, The
Workhouse, Southwell

The family living room in Mr Straw's House, Worksop,
Nottinghamshire

i **T** 01909 482380
E mrstrawshouse@nationaltrust.org.uk

£ £4.60, child £2.30, family £11.50

Booked morning and evening guided tours for
groups (max. 24) by arrangement (extra
charge, inc. NT members, £1 for morning and
£2.50 evening)

Programme of events. Send s.a.e. for details

Designated parking in main car park, 30yds.
Building: Many steps to entrance. Stairs to
other floors. Small scale of the property
enables staff to cater individually for specific
needs. Very narrow corridors, very limited
turning space

Subtitled video

Braille guide. Sensory list. Handling collection

In car park area

Suitable for school groups. Children's quiz/trail

Opening arrangements: Mr Straw's House									
19 Mar - 29 Oct	11 - 4:30	M	**T**	**W**	**T**	**F**	**S**	S

Admission by timed ticket only for all visitors (inc. NT
members), **which must be booked in advance.** All
bookings by tel. or letter (with s.a.e.) to Property
Manager. On quiet days a same-day tel. call is often
sufficient. Closed Good Fri. Due to its location in
residential area, property is closed on BHols as a
courtesy to neighbours

Sudbury Hall

Sudbury, Ashbourne, Derbyshire DE6 5HT

🏛 ✳ 🖻 🖤 🔔 🍷 1967   (3:C4)

**Late 17th-century house with sumptuous
interiors**

The decoration includes woodcarving by
Grinling Gibbons, superb plasterwork and
painted murals and ceilings by Louis Laguerre,
and there is a fine collection of portraits. The
Great Staircase is one of the most elaborate of
its kind in an English house. Several rooms
featured in the BBC's *Pride and Prejudice.*

What's new in 2005 'Taster' tours weekly
throughout season

⭐ Owing to low light levels, visitors wishing to
study the Hall's plasterwork or paintings in
detail should avoid dull days and late
afternoons towards end of season

i **T** 01283 585337, 01283 585305 (Infoline),
01283 585022 (Learning)
F 01283 585139
E sudburyhall@nationaltrust.org.uk

£ £5, child £2, family £11.50. Groups £4.25,
child £1.50. **Joint ticket for Hall &
Museum**: £9, child £4.50, family £20.
Garden only: £1, child 50p, family £2.50.
Reduced rate when arriving by public
transport or cycle

Opening arrangements: Sudbury Hall									
Hall	6 Mar - 30 Oct	1 - 5	M	T	**W**	**T**	**F**	**S**	**S**
Grounds	6 Mar - 30 Oct	11 - 6	M	T	**W**	**T**	**F**	**S**	**S**
Tea-room	6 Mar - 30 Oct	11:30 - 5	M	T	**W**	**T**	**F**	**S**	**S**
Shop	6 Mar - 30 Oct	12:30 - 5	M	T	**W**	**T**	**F**	**S**	**S**
Open BH Mons. Closes dusk if earlier									

Parking in National Trust car parks is free for members

🎭 Guided and specialist tours of Hall; 'Behind the Scenes' tours; evening and morning tours by prior arrangement; for details contact Property Manager

🎭 Programme of events, inc. family activities every weekend and school holidays

♿ Designated parking in main car park. Transfer available. Drop-off point. **Building**: Many steps to entrance. 1 wheelchair. Ground floor has 2 steps. Many stairs to other floors. Seating available. Photograph album. **WCs**: Adapted WC. **Grounds**: Partly accessible, loose gravel paths. Mainly level, only top terrace accessible. **Shop**: Level entrance. Shop small with limited turning space. **Refreshments**: Level entrance

👆 Braille guide and large-print guide. Sensory list

📷 Wide range of products, specialising in children's goods

🍽 The Coach House tea-room (licensed). Children's menu

🚗 In the car park and in the grounds

🚼 Baby-changing and feeding facilities. Front-carrying baby slings and hip-carrying infant seats, reins and indoor buggies for loan

🏫 Suitable for school groups. Education room/centre. Live interpretation. Hands-on activities. Children's guide. Children's quiz/trail. Adult study days

🐕 In car park only

🚲 Tea-room registered with CTC

➡ [128: SK158322] **Cycle**: Cycleway from Uttoxeter to Doveridge, then road to property. **Bus**: Arriva 1 Burton on Trent–Uttoxeter (passing ≋ Tutbury & Hatton and close ≋ Burton on Trent). **Station**: Tutbury & Hatton (U) 5ml. **Road**: 6ml E of Uttoxeter at junction of A50 Derby–Stoke and A515 Ashbourne

🅿 Free parking, 500yds

NT properties nearby
Calke Abbey, Ilam Park, Kedleston Hall, The Old Manor

The Great Hall, Sudbury Hall, Derbyshire

Sudbury Hall – The National Trust Museum of Childhood

As Sudbury Hall, Ashbourne, Derbyshire DE6 5HT

🏛 📷 🍽 🍸 [1967] (3:C4)

Museum showing aspects of the life of children over the past 200 years

Housed in the 19th-century service wing of Sudbury Hall, the Museum contains fascinating displays about children from the 18th century onwards. There are chimney climbs for adventurous 'sweep-sized' youngsters, a Victorian schoolroom and a fine collection of toys, games and dolls.

What's new in 2005 August: includes family activities in connection with SeaBritain 2005

ℹ **T** 01283 585337,
01283 585305 (Infoline),
01283 585022 (Learning)
F 01283 585139
E museumofchildhood@nationaltrust.org.uk

Please remember – your membership card is always needed for free admission

Opening arrangements: Museum of Childhood

			M T W T F S S
Museum	6 Mar - 30 Oct	1 - 5	M T **W T F S S**
	3 Dec - 11 Dec	11 - 4	M T W T F **S S**
Tea-room	6 Mar - 30 Oct	11:30 - 5	M **T W T F S S**
	3 Dec - 11 Dec	11 - 4	M T W T F **S S**
Shop	6 Mar - 30 Oct	12:30 - 5	M **T W T F S S**
	3 Dec - 11 Dec	11 - 4	M T W T F **S S**

Open BH Mons. Closes dusk if earlier

£ £5.50, child £3.50, family £12.50. Groups £4.70, child £2.10. **Joint ticket for Hall & Museum**: £9, child £4.50, family £20. Reduced rate when arriving by public transport or cycle

Special Christmas openings with family activities, Santa's grotto, seasonal fare and gifts 3 & 4 Dec and 10 & 11 Dec 11–4 (last entry 3:30). Programme of events, inc. family activities every weekend and school hols

Designated parking in main car park, 500yds. Transfer available. Drop-off point. **Building**: Level entrance. Many stairs with handrail to other floors. Small steps to day nursery and night nursery. **WCs**: Adapted WC. **Grounds**: Partly accessible. Entrance to museum over cobbles. **Refreshments**: Level entrance

Sensory list

The Coach House tea-room (licensed). Children's menu

In the car park and in the grounds

Baby-changing and feeding facilities. Pushchairs and baby back-carriers admitted. Front-carrying baby slings and hip-carrying infant seats for loan

Suitable for school groups. Education room/centre. Live interpretation. Hands-on activities. Children's quiz/trail

In car park only on leads

→ [128: SK158322] As for Sudbury Hall. **Cycle**: Tea-room registered with CTC

P Free parking. 500 yds

NT properties nearby
Calke Abbey, Ilam Park, Kedleston Hall, The Old Manor

Tattershall Castle

Tattershall, Lincoln, Lincolnshire LN4 4LR

🔲 🏠 🗄 🍽 🎧 🎭 🔔 1925 (3:F3)

Dramatic 15th-century red-brick tower, with six floors to explore

This vast fortified and moated tower was built for Ralph Cromwell, Lord Treasurer of England from 1433 to 1443. The building was restored by Lord Curzon between 1911 and 1914 and contains four great chambers with enormous Gothic fireplaces, tapestries and brick vaulting. There are spectacular views across the Fens from the battlements and a guardhouse with museum room.

i **T** 01526 342543,
01526 348821 (Shop)
E tattershallcastle@nationaltrust.org.uk

£ £3.70, child £1.90, family £9.30. Groups £3.20, child £1.60. Free audio guide

Leaflet on walk around Tattershall village available from shop

Separate designated parking, 50yds. **Building**: Ramped entrance. Some visitors may require assistance. Many stairs to other floors. Photograph album. **WCs**: Adapted WC. **Grounds**: Steep gravel paths. **Shop**: Level entrance

Induction loop in shop

Braille guide. Sensory list

Hot and cold drinks and ice cream available in shop. Sitting area in exhibition room above shop

In grounds

Baby-changing facilities. Pushchairs and baby back-carriers admitted

Opening arrangements: Tattershall Castle

			M T W T F S S
Castle	5 Mar - 20 Mar	12 - 4	M T W T F **S S**
	26 Mar - 28 Sep	11 - 5:30	**M T W** T F **S S**
	1 Oct - 2 Nov	11 - 4	**M T W** T F **S S**
	5 Nov - 11 Dec	12 - 4	M T W T F **S S**
Shop	As castle		

Open Good Fri 11–5:30. Last audio guide issued 1¼ hrs before closing each day

230

Tattershall Castle, Lincolnshire

🎭 Suitable for school groups. Education room/centre. Live interpretation. Hands-on activities. Children's guide. Children's quiz/trail

🐕 On leads and only in car park; no shaded parking; dog hooks in shade by entrance to grounds

➔ [122: TF211575] **Cycle**: Hull to Harwich cycle route passes within 1ml. **Bus**: Brylaine 5 Lincoln–Boston (passing close ➥ Lincoln and Boston). **Station**: Ruskington (U) 10ml. **Road**: On S side of A153, 15ml NE of Sleaford; 10ml SW of Horncastle

🅿 Free parking, 150yds. Coaches must reverse into parking area

NT properties nearby
Belton House, Gunby Hall, Monksthorpe Chapel, Whitegates Cottage

Ulverscroft Nature Reserve

nr Loughborough, Leicestershire

🌿 1945 (3:D5)

Reserve in the care of the Leicestershire and Rutland Wildlife Trust

Part of the ancient forest of Charnwood, Ulverscroft is especially beautiful in spring during the bluebell season.

⭐ No WC

ℹ **T** 01909 486411 (Regional office)

£ Admission free

➔ [129: SK493118] 6ml SW of Loughborough. **Bus**: Arriva 117–9, 217/8 Leicester–Swadlincote (passing close ➥ Leicester). **Station**: Barrow upon Soar 7ml, Loughborough 7½ml

🅿 Roadside parking only

NT properties nearby
Calke Abbey, Staunton Harold Church

Opening arrangements: Ulverscroft Reserve
Access by permit only from The Secretary, Leicestershire & Rutland Wildlife Trust, Brocks Hill Environment Centre, Washbrook Lane, Oadby, Leics LE2 5JJ. Tel. 0116 2720444

Winster Market House

Main Street, Winster, nr Matlock, Derbyshire

🏠 1906 (3:C3)

Late 17th- or early 18th-century market house

The restored building is a reminder of when cheese and cattle fairs were a prominent feature of local life. The Trust's first acquisition in the Peak District, it now houses an information room, with recently created interpretation panels and scale model of Winster village.

⭐ No WC. Public WC in side street nearby

ℹ **T** 01335 350503 (Estate office)

£ Admission free

♿ **Building**: Many steps to entrance with handrail

👆 Braille guide

🎭 Suitable for school groups

➔ [119: SK241606] **Cycle**: NCN67 3ml. **Bus**: Hulley's 172 Matlock–Bakewell (passing close ➥ Matlock). **Station**: Matlock (U) 4ml. **Road**: 4ml W of Matlock on S side of B5057 in main street of Winster

🅿 No parking on site. Not suitable for coaches

NT properties nearby
Dovedale, Hardwick Hall, Ilam Park, Kedleston Hall, Longshaw Estate

Opening arrangements: Winster Market House
21 Mar - 30 Oct   Times vary **M T W T F S S**

Please see the area introductions for details of coast & countryside properties

Woolsthorpe Manor

23 Newton Way, Woolsthorpe-by-Colsterworth, nr Grantham, Lincolnshire NG33 5NR

🏠 🚿 ♣ 💼 🎋 1943   (3:E4)

Small 17th-century manor house, birthplace and family home of Sir Isaac Newton

Newton formulated some of his major works here during the Plague years (1665–67). An early edition of his *Principia* is on display and the orchard includes a descendant of the famous apple tree. Newton's ideas can be explored in the hands-on Science Discovery Centre. Visitors can see the restored Wet Kitchen in the house, and outside there are orchards, paddocks and farm buildings, with rare breed Lincoln Longwool sheep and hens.

What's new in 2005 New events and children's quiz. Costumed guides on some weekends

⭐ Entrance to the property is on Water Lane

ℹ️ T 01476 860338,
01476 862823 (Learning)
F 01476 862826
E woolsthorpemanor@nationaltrust.org.uk

£ £4.20, child £2.10, family £10.50, family (one adult) £6.30

🏃 Tours of house and Science Discovery Centre for booked groups throughout year, by arrangement with Property Manager

🎭 Programme of events, inc. summer events for families. Tel. for details

🚶 Village walk from property. Leaflets available at ticket desk

♿ Drop-off point close to Manor entrance. **Building**: Step to entrance, ramp available. 1 wheelchair, booking essential. Stairs to other floors. Seating available. **WCs**: Adapted WC. Approached via sloping farm yard. **Grounds**: Partly accessible. Sloping farm yard accessible, although surface is rough. Access to orchard difficult. **Shop**: Very low step up from car park. **Refreshments and Science Centre**: Level entrance

👁️ Braille guide and large-print guide. Sensory list. Handling collection

Opening arrangements: Woolsthorpe Manor										
House	5 Mar - 27 Mar	1 - 5	M	T	W	T	F	**S**	**S**
	1 Apr - 30 Sep	1 - 5	M	T	**W**	**T**	**F**	**S**	**S**
	1 Oct - 30 Oct	1 - 5	M	T	W	T	F	**S**	**S**

Admission by timed ticket to house during busy periods, particularly at weekends and BHols. Open BH Mons and Good Fri 1–5

💼 Coffee shop in Science Centre. Limited selection of refreshments

🚼 Baby-changing facilities

🏫 Suitable for school groups. Education room/centre. Hands-on activities. Family guide. Children's quiz/trail. Costumed guides by arrangement

🐕 On leads and only in car park

➔ [130: SK924244] **Bus**: MassReliance 606/8 Grantham–South Witham (passing close 🚉 Grantham). **Station**: Grantham 7ml. **Road**: 7ml S of Grantham, ½ml NW of Colsterworth, 1ml W of A1 (not to be confused with Woolsthorpe near Belvoir). Leave A1 at Colsterworth roundabout via B676, at second crossroads turn right, then first left into Water Lane for car park

P Free parking, 50yds. Groups must book in advance as parking for coaches is limited

NT properties nearby
Belton House, Tattershall Castle

The Wet Kitchen, Woolsthorpe Manor, Lincolnshire

The Workhouse, Southwell

Upton Road, Southwell, Nottinghamshire
NG25 0PT

🔥 🎧 2002 (3:E3)

19th-century institution for paupers

The Workhouse survives as the least altered example of its kind in existence today. Visitors can explore the segregated rooms and stairways as well as the master's quarters to discover the thought-provoking story of the 'welfare' system, created by the New Poor Law of 1834. The audio guide, based on archive records, brings the 19th-century inhabitants back to life in the empty rooms. Interactive displays address the issue of poverty through the years and across the country, while children's games illuminate the life of people who once inhabited the Workhouse.

What's new in 2005 Working gardens

⭐ An advance booking service by telephone is available at no extra charge. Visitors are advised to book at peak times, ie weekends and BHols. Groups welcome but please book in advance. Limited refreshments on site; food available in local villages

ℹ️ **T** 01636 817250
F 01636 817251
E theworkhouse@nationaltrust.org.uk

💷 £4.60, child £2.30, family £11.50. Groups £3.90, child £2.30. Reduced rate when arriving by public transport, cycle or on foot. Introductory video, displays and audio guide included

🧍 Tours held throughout the season (also available for private groups). Tel. for details

📅 Programme of events, inc. changing arts and social issues exhibitions. Every month: 1st Sun – Rag doll-making workshops; 3rd Sun – Living History day. Tel. for details

♿ Contact in advance. Separate designated parking, 200yds. Drop-off point.
Building: Ramped entrance. 5 wheelchairs. Not suitable for motorised wheelchairs. Stairs

Opening arrangements: The Workhouse									
21 Mar - 31 Jul	12 - 5	**M**	T	**W**	**T**	**F**	**S**	**S**
1 Aug - 30 Aug	11 - 5	**M**	T	**W**	**T**	**F**	**S**	**S**
1 Sep - 30 Oct	12 - 5	**M**	T	**W**	**T**	**F**	**S**	**S**

Open BH Mons and Good Fri 11–5. Last admission 1hr before closing

to other floors. Manual wheelchairs available on other floors. Seating available. Audio visual/video, photograph album, virtual tour. **WCs**: Adapted WC. **Grounds**: loose gravel paths. Accessible route

🔊 Induction loop in reception, audioguide. Film subtitles on request. Printed script of audio guide available

👁 Braille guide and large-print guide. Handling collection

🪑 On grassed area to the front of the property

👶 Baby-changing facilities. Pushchairs admitted. Hip-carrying infant seats for loan. 'Master's Punishment' game available to play

🏫 Suitable for school groups. Education room/centre. Live interpretation. Hands-on activities. Children's quiz/trail. Adult study days. Study room available for private use, by prior appointment, for researching family history, workhouse history and social services

🐕 On leads in the grounds only

➡️ [120: SK712543] **Foot**: Robin Hood trail goes past the Workhouse. **Cycle**: National Byway (Heritage Cycle Route). **Bus**: Nottingham City Transport 100/1, 201 ⊞ Newark North Gate–Nottingham; Stagecoach in Mansfield 29/A Newark–Mansfield (passing ⊞ Fiskerton). All pass ⊞ Newark Castle. **Station**: Fiskerton (U) 2ml, Newark North Gate 7½ml. **Road**: 13ml from Nottingham on A612 and 8ml from Newark on A617 and A612

🅿️ Free parking, 200yds

NT properties nearby
Belton House, Clumber Park, Mr Straw's House, Tattershall Castle, Woolsthorpe Manor

There are special events at most Trust properties; please telephone 0870 458 4000 for details

Properties open less often

This section includes National Trust properties, often tenanted, which are open two days a week or less (plus Bank Holidays in some cases). Visits to some must be made by prior arrangement and where this applies admission prices are not shown (please ask when making contact). **Full details are on our website www.nationaltrust.org.uk or obtainable from the Membership Department, tel. 0870 458 4000.**

Grantham House

Castlegate, Grantham, Lincolnshire
NG31 6SS   **(3:E4)**

Handsome town house, with architectural features from various eras and walled riverside garden.

⭐ No WC

[i] **T** 01909 486411 (Regional office)

Opening arrangements: Grantham House										
Ground floor	6 Apr - 28 Sep	2 - 5	M	T	**W**	T	F	S	S

Admission by written appointment only with the tenant, Major-General Sir Brian Wyldbore-Smith

Gunby Hall

Gunby, nr Spilsby, Lincolnshire PE23 5SS   **(3:G2)**

Fine red-brick house, dating from 1700, with Victorian walled gardens.

[i] **T** 01909 486411 (Regional office)

[£] £4.20, child £2.10, family £10.50. **Garden only**: £3, child £1.50, family £7.50

Opening arrangements: Gunby Hall										
House	30 Mar - 28 Sep	2 - 6	M	T	**W**	T	F	S	S
Garden	30 Mar - 29 Sep	2 - 6	M	T	**W**	T	F	S	S

Only ground floor and basement are shown. House & garden also open Tues, Thur and Fri by written appointment only with Mr J. D. Wrisdale at above address

Gunby Hall Estate: Monksthorpe Chapel

Monksthorpe, nr Spilsby, Lincolnshire
PE23 5PP   **(3:G2)**

Remote late 17th-century Baptist chapel.

[i] **T** 01909 486411 (Regional office)

Opening arrangements: Monksthorpe Chapel										
Chapel	30 Mar - 29 Sep	2 - 5	M	T	**W**	T	F	S	S

Access by key collected from Gunby Hall – £10 returnable deposit required. Chapel open and stewarded on some Sats: 9 April, 14 May, 11 June, 9 July (craft event), 13 Aug, 10 Sept 1–5. Services on Sats 23 April, 28 May, 11 June, 23 July, 27 Aug, 1 Oct (Harvest Service), 10 Dec (Carol Service)

Gunby Hall Estate: Whitegates Cottage

Mill Lane, Bratoft, nr Spilsby, Lincolnshire
PE24 5BU   **(3:G2)**

Small thatched cottage with mud and stud walls, dating from c.1770.

⭐ **Please note: Limited access for 2005 season due to structural repairs**. No WC. WCs at Gunby Hall

[i] **T** 01909 486411 (Regional office)

Opening arrangements: Whitegates Cottage										
	30 Mar - 28 Sep	2 - 6	M	T	**W**	T	F	S	S

Admission by written appointment with NT East Midlands regional office

South West South & South East
London East of England
East Midlands **West Midlands**
North West Yorkshire North East
Wales Northern Ireland

The West Midlands is an intriguing mix of urban areas and delightful unspoilt countryside of much variety and charm. There are surprisingly extensive areas of open moorland and hills, as well as picturesque villages, grand country houses and some notable gardens.

The area's key upland properties lie to the west – the **Clent Hills** in Worcestershire, splendid country for walkers with an easy-access trail from Nimmings Wood car park and café to the viewing platform near the summit of the hill with breathtaking views in all directions, and Shropshire's **Long Mynd**. The Long Mynd is an area of upland heath and a Site of Special Scientific Interest. Excellent access is possible via **Carding Mill Valley**. The Trust owns eight miles of nearby **Wenlock Edge**, a geologically interesting wooded escarpment near the village of Much Wenlock. The borderland of England and Wales runs south from here into the green rolling countryside of Herefordshire, where excellent walking is possible. The Trust cares for nearly 2000ha (5000 acres) of parkland and countryside in the county, including the Brockhampton Estate with its ancient woodland, traditionally managed farmland and glorious views across the undulating landscape.

The Malvern Hills, Worcestershire

Kinver Edge in South Staffordshire is an area of beautiful woodland and rare lowland heath, offering dramatic views across the surrounding counties. Further north in Staffordshire the Trust is restoring an important stretch of lowland heath at **Downs Banks**, near Stone, and cares for 126ha (300 acres) of woodland with delightful wooded trails at **Hawksmoor**.

The Long Mynd, Shropshire

Previous page: The tailor's shop in the Back to Backs, Birmingham

West Midlands Countryside

OS Grid Reference

Regional Highlights for Visitors with Disabilities ...

The **Brockhampton Estate** has a nature trail with touchable sculptures (the trail may not suit all visitors, so please tel. property for details); the Birmingham **Back to Backs**; the Sensory Garden at **Charlecote Park**.

...and for Families

Regular family events take place throughout the region. **Dudmaston** has a children's activity room in the house, as does **Attingham Park**, which also has one in the park. Many properties, including Attingham Park, **Berrington Hall** and the **Long Mynd** at Carding Mill Valley, have 'Tracker Packs' with activities for families and children – and there are play areas at Attingham Park and Berrington Hall. Charlecote Park has an orienteering course and **Shugborough** a working historic farm. Children can take part in trails and quizzes at all the mansions in the region.

Further Information

Please contact the Membership Department, PO Box 39, Warrington WA5 7WD. Tel. 0870 458 4000. Email: enquiries@thenationaltrust.org.uk

OS grid references for main properties with no individual entry (OS Landranger map series numbers given in brackets)

Clent Hills	[139]	SO932803
Croft Ambrey	[137]	SO449656
Downs Banks	[127]	SJ902370
Hawksmoor	[128]	SK035445
Long Mynd	[137]	SO430940
Wenlock Edge	[138]	SO595988

The Clent Hills, Worcestershire

Attingham Park

Shrewsbury, Shropshire SY4 4TP

🏛 🌳 📷 ☕ 🚶 1947   (4:H4)

Elegant 18th-century mansion with Regency interiors and deer park

One of the great houses of the Midlands, Attingham Park was built in 1785 for the 1st Lord Berwick to the design of George Steuart and has a picture gallery by John Nash. The magnificent rooms contain collections of ambassadorial silver, Italian furniture and Grand Tour paintings. The park, landscaped by Repton, has attractive walks along the River Tern and a play area and environmental centre for children. Home Farm, run by NT tenants, is one of Britain's few completely organic open farms.

The Boudoir, Attingham Park, Shropshire

What's new in 2005 New activity in children's play area

ℹ️ **T** 01743 708162, 01743 708123 (Infoline), 01743 709243 (Home Farm tenant), 01743 708196 (Learning), 01743 708177 (Shop), 01743 708176 (Tea-room)
F 01743 708155
E attingham@nationaltrust.org.uk

💷 £5.80, child £2.90, family £14. Groups £4.90.
Park & grounds only: £3, child £1.50, family £7.50. Free entry to house and grounds when arriving by cycle

🛈 Free costumed introductory talks and guided tours of the house available from 12 on house open days, except BH Mons. Out-of-hours tours available for booked groups at 11; £6 per head (inc. NT members)

🌱 Annual spring plant fair

Opening arrangements: Attingham Park										
House	4 Mar - 30 Oct	12 - 5	**M**	**T**	W	T	**F**	**S**	**S**
Deer park	1 Mar - 30 Oct	10 - 8	**M**	**T**	**W**	**T**	**F**	**S**	**S**
	5 Nov - 26 Feb 06	10 - 5	M	T	W	T	F	**S**	**S**
Shop	4 Mar - 30 Oct	11:30 - 5	**M**	**T**	W	T	**F**	**S**	**S**
Tea-room	4 Mar - 30 Oct	11:30 - 5	**M**	**T**	W	T	**F**	**S**	**S**
	5 Nov - 26 Mar 06	11:30 - 4	M	T	W	T	F	**S**	**S**

Open BH Mons 11–5. Last admission 1hr before closing. Closed 25 Dec. On house open days (Fri–Tues), 12–1 guided tours only

♿ Separate designated parking, 20yds. Transfer available. **Building**: Many steps to entrance with handrail. Alternative accessible entrance, ask staff to open. 3 wheelchairs. Ground floor accessible. Many stairs with handrail to other floors. **WCs**: Adapted WC.
Grounds: Accessible route map. 2 single-seater PMV. **Shop**: Ramped entrance with handrail. **Refreshments**: Steps to entrance. Seating available on tea-room lawn

👁 Braille guide and large-print guide. Sensory list. Handling collection

📷 NT shop. Plant sales

☕ Licensed tea-room in West Pavilion. Children's menu. Kiosk in stableyard

🎞 Picnic sites near play area. Picnics not permitted in deer park

👶 Baby-changing and feeding facilities. Front-carrying baby slings and hip-carrying infant seats for loan. Children's play area. Family activity room in the house. Children's house quiz

🏫 Suitable for school groups. Education room/centre. Live interpretation. Hands-on activities. Children's quiz/trail. Family activity packs. Environmental discovery room in the park. Teacher's pack. Joint visits to Home Farm available

🐕 On leads in immediate vicinity of house and in deer park. Waste bins and gloves available

Please see the area introductions for details of coast & countryside properties

➜ [126: SJ550099] **Cycle**: NCN81. Leaflet on cycling from Shrewsbury station to Attingham available. **Bus**: Arriva 81, 96 Shrewsbury–Telford (passing close ⊠ Shrewsbury & Telford Central). **Station**: Shrewsbury 5ml. **Road**: 4ml SE of Shrewsbury, on N side of B4380 in Atcham village

P Free parking

NT properties nearby
Benthall Hall, Dudmaston, Morville Hall, Moseley Old Hall, Powis Castle, Sunnycroft

Opening arrangements: Baddesley Clinton			M	T	W	T	F	S	S
House	2 Mar - 30 Apr	1:30 - 5	M	T	**W**	**T**	**F**	**S**	**S**
	1 May - 30 Sep	1:30 - 5:30	M	T	**W**	**T**	**F**	**S**	**S**
	1 Oct - 6 Nov	1:30 - 5	M	T	**W**	**T**	**F**	**S**	**S**
Grounds	2 Mar - 30 Apr	12 - 5	M	T	**W**	**T**	**F**	**S**	**S**
	1 May - 30 Sep	12 - 5:30	M	T	**W**	**T**	**F**	**S**	**S**
	1 Oct - 6 Nov	12 - 5	M	T	**W**	**T**	**F**	**S**	**S**
	9 Nov - 11 Dec	12 - 4:30	M	T	**W**	**T**	**F**	**S**	**S**
Shop	As grounds								
Restaurant	As grounds								

Admission by timed ticket to house; visitors may then stay until house closes if they wish. Open BH Mons

Baddesley Clinton

Rising Lane, Baddesley Clinton Village, Knowle, Solihull, Warwickshire B93 0DQ

🏠 ✚ ✿ ♣ ⌂ ☕ 🎭 ⚲ ☂ 1980   (4:K6)

Picturesque medieval moated manor house and garden

This atmospheric house dates from the 15th century and has changed little since 1634. The interiors reflect the house's heyday in the Elizabethan era, when it was a haven for persecuted Catholics – there are no fewer than three priest-holes. There is a delightful garden with stewponds, a lake walk and nature walk.

What's new in 2005 Vegetable garden

ⓘ **T** 01564 783294,
01564 787906 (Visitor reception),
01564 787907 (Shop),
01564 787908/787909 (Restaurant)
F 01564 782706
E baddesleyclinton@nationaltrust.org.uk

£ £6.60, child £3.30, family £16.50. Groups £5.60, group visits outside normal hours £11.20. **Grounds only (inc. access to restaurant & shop)**: £3.30, child £1.65. **Combined ticket to both Baddesley Clinton and Packwood House**: £9.60, child £4.80, family £24. Groups £8.20. **Combined ticket for gardens only**: £4.80, child £2.40

⚲ Wed, Thur evenings by appointment. Supper can be included

♿ Separate designated parking, 10yds. **Building**: Level entrance. 4 wheelchairs. Ground floor accessible. Many stairs with handrail to other floors. Seating available. Photograph album. **WCs**: Adapted WC. **Grounds**: Fully accessible. Accessible route. **Shop**: Step to entrance. **Refreshments**: Steps to entrance with handrail, ramp available

🔊 Induction loop in reception and in restaurant for lectures

👁 Braille guide. Sensory list

Baddesley Clinton, Warwickshire

[🏠] NT shop. Plant sales

[🍴] The Barn Restaurant (licensed). Children's menu

[🍽] In designated area with tables near entrance

[👶] Baby-changing facilities. Front-carrying baby slings and hip-carrying infant seats for loan

[🎒] Suitable for school groups. Children's guide. Children's quiz/trail. Family activity packs

[🐕] On leads and only in car park (reasonable walks nearby)

[🚲] 1½ml public bridleway giving shared access for cyclists

[→] [139: SP199723] **Foot**: Heart of England Way passes close. **Station**: Lapworth (U), 2ml; Birmingham International 9ml. **Road**: ¾ml W of A4141 Warwick–Birmingham road, at Chadwick End, 7½ml NW of Warwick, 6ml S of M42 exit 5; 15ml SE of central Birmingham

[P] Free parking, 50yds. Coaches welcome by written arrangement

NT properties nearby
Birmingham Back to Backs, Charlecote Park, Clent Hills, Hanbury Hall, Packwood House

---

Benthall Hall

Broseley, Shropshire TF12 5RX

[🏛][✝][✿] 1958   (4:I5)

Handsome 16th-century house and restored garden

Situated on a plateau above the gorge of the River Severn, this fine stone house has mullioned and transomed windows and a stunning interior with carved oak staircase, decorated plaster ceilings and oak panelling. There is an intimate and carefully restored plantsman's garden, old kitchen garden and interesting Restoration church.

Opening arrangements: Benthall Hall										
House	27 Mar - 28 Mar	2 - 5:30	**M**	T	W	T	F	S	**S**
	29 Mar - 29 Jun	2 - 5:30	**M**	**T**	**W**	T	F	S	S
	3 Jul - 28 Sep	2 - 5:30	**M**	**T**	**W**	T	F	S	**S**
Garden	27 Mar - 29 Jun	2 - 5:30	**M**	**T**	**W**	T	F	S	S
	3 Jul - 28 Sep	2 - 5:30	**M**	**T**	**W**	T	F	S	**S**
Open BHSuns and Mons									

[★] Benthall Hall is the home of Edward & Sally Benthall

[i] **T** 01952 882159
   E benthall@nationaltrust.org.uk

[£] £4.20, child £2.10. **Garden only**: £2.60, child £1.30. Group tours outside normal hours £5, NT members £2.50

[🎫] For groups, by appointment only

[⛪] Church services alternate Suns; visitors welcome

[♿] Drop-off point. **Building**: Ramped entrance. Ground floor has steps. Stairs to other floors. **WCs**: Adapted WC. **Grounds**: Partly accessible, slopes. Some visitors may require assistance from their companion

[👓] Braille guide and large-print guide

[🚼] Pushchairs admitted

[🎒] Children's quiz/trail

[→] [127: SJ658025] **Bus**: Arriva 9, 39, 99 Telford/Wellington–Bridgnorth, alight Broseley, 1ml (pass close [≋] Telford Central). **Station**: Telford Central 7½ml. **Road**: 1ml NW of Broseley (B4375), 4ml NE of Much Wenlock, 1ml SW of Ironbridge

[P] Free parking, 100yds. Only one coach at a time

NT properties nearby
Attingham Park, Dudmaston, Kinver Edge, Morville Hall, Moseley Old Hall, Sunnycroft, Wightwick Manor

---

Berrington Hall

nr Leominster, Herefordshire HR6 0DW

[🏛][✿][🏠][🍴][♿][☕] 1957   (4:H6)

Neo-classical mansion with fine interiors, set in landscaped grounds

Beautifully sited above a wide valley with sweeping views to the Brecon Beacons, this elegant Henry Holland house was built in the late 18th century and is set in parkland designed by 'Capability' Brown. The rather austere external appearance belies a surprisingly delicate interior, with beautifully decorated ceilings and a spectacular staircase hall. There are good collections of furniture and paintings,

---

There are special events at most Trust properties; please telephone 0870 458 4000 for details

Thomas Luny's depiction of the Battle of Martinique, 1780, one of a pair of paintings celebrating the naval victories of Admiral Lord Rodney. These hang in the dining room of Berrington Hall, Herefordshire

as well as a nursery, Victorian laundry and Georgian dairy. One room has a display of costumes from the collection of Charles Paget Wade. The attractive walled garden contains a historic collection of local apple trees.

What's new in 2005 Potting shed with exhibition of horticultural implements (opening early summer)

⭐ Not all of the costume collection is displayed, but can be viewed by appointment. Please write to the property or tel. Costume Curator

ℹ️ **T** 01568 615721, 01568 613720 (Wade Costume Collection Curator), 01568 610529 (Shop), 01568 610134 (Restaurant) **F** 01568 613263 **E** berrington@nationaltrust.org.uk

💷 £5, child £2.50, family £12.50. Groups £4.20. **Grounds only**: £3.50. **Joint ticket with Croft Castle**: £6.50

🎭 At weekends. Other times by arrangement

🚶 Park walk open July to Dec

♿ Separate designated parking. Space for 4 disabled drivers at house. **Building**: Many steps to entrance with handrail. 2 wheelchairs. Photograph album, virtual tour. **WCs**: Adapted WC. **Grounds**: Partly accessible, loose gravel paths. Accessible route map. 1 single-seater PMV, booking essential. **Shop**: Ramped entrance. **Refreshments**: Many steps to entrance with handrail

♨️ Braille guide. Sensory list

🛍️ NT shop. Plant sales

🍽️ Licensed restaurant. Tea-room

🎪 Picnic tables in car park and in children's play area

🚼 Baby-changing facilities. Front-carrying baby slings and hip-carrying infant seats for loan. Children's play area. Pet sheep and peacocks

🎒 Suitable for school groups. Hands-on activities. Children's quiz/trail. Family activity packs. Adult study days. Outdoor orienteering course, eye spy sheet

➔ [137: SO510637] **Bus**: Lugg Valley/R & B 492 Ludlow–Hereford (passing close ▣ Ludlow & Leominster), alight Luston, 2ml. **Station**: Leominster (U) 4ml. **Road**: 3ml N of Leominster, 7ml S of Ludlow on W side of A49

Opening arrangements: Berrington Hall										
House	5 Mar - 20 Mar	1 - 4:30	M	T	W	T	F	S	S
	21 Mar - 30 Oct	1 - 4:30	M	T	W	T	F	S	S
Garden	5 Mar - 20 Mar	12 - 5	M	T	W	T	F	S	S
	21 Mar - 30 Oct	12 - 5	M	T	W	T	F	S	S
	5 Nov - 18 Dec	12 - 4:30	M	T	W	T	F	S	S
Park walk	2 Jul - 30 Oct	12 - 5	M	T	W	T	F	S	S
	5 Nov - 18 Dec	12 - 4:30	M	T	W	T	F	S	S
Shop	As garden								
Restaurant	As garden								
Open Good Fri. Between 5 Mar & 30 Oct house access 12–1 is by guided tour only										

P Free parking, 30yds. Coaches: entry and exit via Luston/Eye Lane. Tight turn. No entry or exit directly from/to A49. Local area map on request

NT properties nearby
Brockhampton Estate, Croft Castle, The Weir

Biddulph Grange Garden

Grange Road, Biddulph, Staffordshire ST8 7SD

❖ ⬚ 🖳 1988   (4:J2)

A rare and exciting survival of a high Victorian garden

Designed in the mid-19th century by James Bateman to display specimens from his extensive and wide-ranging plant collection, the garden is set out in a series of connected 'compartments'. Visitors are taken on a journey of discovery through tunnels and pathways to individual gardens inspired by countries around the world – from the tranquility of a Chinese garden or an Egyptian Court to a formal Italian garden.

i **T** 01782 517999 **F** 01782 510624
E biddulphgrange@nationaltrust.org.uk

£ **19 March to 30 Oct**: £5, child £2.50, family £12.50. Groups £4.20. **5 Nov to 18 Dec**: £2, child £1, family £5. Voucher available for reduced entry to Little Moreton Hall when purchasing full-price adult ticket at Biddulph Grange Garden

𝕂 Booked guided tours in groups of 10+, at 10 on Wed, Thur & Fri; £7 per person (inc. NT members)

🎪 Programme of events. Send s.a.e. for details

♿ **Grounds**: Contact in advance. Limited accessibility. Many steps, undulating terrain, tunnels and stepping stones throughout the garden. Some visitors may require assistance from their companion. **Shop**: Steps to entrance. **Refreshments**: Many steps to entrance. 6 steps from car park to terrace

📖 Braille guide

🛒 NT shop. Plant sales

🍽 Tea-room. Children's menu

🅰 In car park area only, picnic tables opposite entrance steps

---

Opening arrangements: Biddulph Grange Garden

Garden	19 Mar - 30 Oct	11 - 6	M T W T F S S
	23 Mar - 28 Oct	12 - 6	M T **W T F** S S
	5 Nov - 18 Dec	11 - 3	M T W T F S S
Shop	As garden		
Tea-room	As garden		

Open BH Mons 11–5:30. Closes dusk if earlier. Tea-room: last orders 5 or half hour before garden closes

🧑 Access for pushchairs is difficult

🧩 Children's quiz/trail

🐕 On leads and only in car park

➔ [118: SJ895591] **Bus**: Bakers 99 from Congleton (passing ➤ Congleton). **Station**: Congleton 2½ml. **Road**: ½ml N of Biddulph, 3½ml SE of Congleton, 7ml N of Stoke-on-Trent. Access from A527 (Tunstall–Congleton road). Entrance on Grange Road

P Free parking, 50yds

NT properties nearby
Little Moreton Hall

Birmingham Back to Backs

50-54 Inge Street/55-63 Hurst Street, Birmingham, West Midlands B5 4TE

🏠 ⬚ 𝕂 2004   (4:J5)

Carefully restored 19th-century courtyard of working people's houses

Birmingham's last surviving court of back to back housing has now been fully restored by the Birmingham Conservation Trust and the National Trust. Thousands of houses like these were built, literally back to back, around courtyards, for the rapidly increasing population of Britain's expanding industrial towns. The story of the site

Opening arrangements: Back to Backs

| | 1 Mar - 26 Feb 06 | 10 - 5 | M **T W T F S S** |

Admission by timed ticket and guided tour only. Open BH Mons but closed on Tues following BH Mons. Please tel. booking line in advance if planning to visit before 2pm during school terms, as property may be in use by a school group. Closed 25 & 26 Dec & 1 Jan

---

Please note: groups must book in advance with the property

is told through the experiences of the people who lived and worked here. Visitors move through four different periods, from 1840 to the 1970s. The design of each interior reflects the varied cultures, religions and professions of the families who made their homes here.

⭐ **Visiting the Back to Backs is by guided tour only**. Capacity is limited, so advance booking is advised. Tel. booking line for details

ℹ️ **T** 0121 666 7671 (Booking line)
E backtobacks@nationaltrust.org.uk

💷 £4, child £2, family £12

♿ Drop-off point. **Building**: Ramped entrance. Virtual tour. **WCs**: Adapted WC

👁️ Braille guide and large-print guide. Touchable objects

🔊 Induction loops

📕 Suitable for school groups. Education room/centre. Live interpretation. Hands-on activities

➡️ [139: SP071861] In the centre of Birmingham next to the Hippodrome Theatre, within easy walking distance of bus and railway stations. **Station**: Birmingham New Street ¼ml

🅿️ No parking on site

NT properties nearby
Baddesley Clinton, Clent Hills, Hanbury Hall, Kinver Edge, Moseley Old Hall, Packwood House, Wightwick Manor

Brockhampton Estate

Greenfields, Bringsty, Worcestershire WR6 5TB

 1946   (4:17)

Traditionally farmed estate and medieval manor house

This 688ha (1700-acre) estate was bequeathed to the National Trust in 1946 and still maintains traditional farms and extensive areas of woodland, including ancient oak and beech. Visitors can enjoy a variety of walks through park and woodland, which combine to form a rich habitat for wildlife such as the dormouse, buzzard and raven. A stone-flagged trail leads to the Lawn Pool and provides some access for

Lower Brockhampton House, Worcestershire

those with disabilities. At the heart of the estate lies Lower Brockhampton House, a late 14th-century moated manor house with a beautiful timber-framed gatehouse and interesting ruined chapel.

What's new in 2005 Nursery Rhyme trail; wildflower meadow; local crafts and produce from The Granary at Lower Brockhampton

ℹ️ **T** 01885 482077 (Estate office),
01885 488099 (Lower Brockhampton)
F 01885 482151
E brockhampton@nationaltrust.org.uk

💷 **House**: £3.60, child £1.80, family £8.50. Groups £3

🐴 Farm tours by arrangement

🎪 Events programme throughout the year. Tel. Lower Brockhampton for details

🚶 Guided walks throughout the year and by arrangement. Woodland and park walks from estate car park. Leaflets available

Opening arrangements: Brockhampton Estate											
Estate	All year		Daylight	**M**	**T**	**W**	**T**	**F**	**S**	**S**
House	5 Mar - 20 Mar		12 - 4	M	T	W	T	F	**S**	**S**
	23 Mar - 2 Oct		12 - 5	M	T	**W**	**T**	**F**	**S**	**S**
	5 Oct - 30 Oct		12 - 4	M	T	**W**	**T**	**F**	**S**	**S**
Tea-room	As house									
Open BH Mons and Good Fri 12–5. Tea-room closes 30 mins after house										

♿ Separate designated parking. **Building**: Step to entrance, ramp available. Ground floor accessible. Stairs to other floors. Seating available. Chapel ruins accessible.
WCs: Adapted WC. None available at Lower Brockhampton. **Grounds**: Partly accessible. Parkland can have uneven, muddy surfaces.
Shop: Step to entrance, ramp available.
Refreshments: Level entrance

👁 Braille guide. Sensory list

📷 Selection of produce and crafts. Plant sales

🍽 Old Apple Store Tea-room in estate car park

🚶 Pushchairs admitted

🏫 Suitable for school groups. Education room/centre. Hands-on activities. Children's quiz/trail

🐕 Only in woods and, on leads, in parkland

→ [149: SO682546] **Bus**: First Bromyard Omnibus 419/420 Worcester–Hereford (passing ❁ Worcester Foregate Street & close ❁ Hereford). **Road**: 2ml E of Bromyard on Worcester road (A44); house reached by a narrow road through 1½ml of woods and parkland

P Parking, £2 (pay & display). Coaches should contact property on arrival. Road to Lower Brockhampton House is steep with tight corners. Parking fee is for estate car park. Parking at Lower Brockhampton is free; not suitable for large vehicles

NT properties nearby
Berrington Hall, Croft Castle, The Greyfriars, The Weir

Carding Mill Valley

Chalet Pavilion, Carding Mill Valley, Church Stretton, Shropshire SY6 6JG

♿ 🍽 📷 🏖 🚶 🍹 1979   **(4:H5)**

Extensive area of historic upland heath

The area includes part of the great ridge, the Long Mynd, with stunning views across the Shropshire and Cheshire plains and Black Mountains. This is excellent walking country with much of interest to the naturalist; the

Opening arrangements: Carding Mill Valley

			M T W T F S S
Heathland	All year		**M T W T F S S**
Tea-room	21 Mar - 30 Oct	11 - 5	**M T W T F S S**
	5 Nov - 26 Mar 06	11 - 4	M T W T F **S S**
Shop	21 Mar - 30 Oct	11 - 5	**M T W T F S S**

Tea-room and shop close dusk if earlier. Closed 8 June, 19–26 Dec. Open daily 27 Dec–1 Jan 2006 (weather dependent), 14–18 Feb 2006 (half term). WC open 9–7 summer; 9–4 winter

Chalet Pavilion in Carding Mill Valley offers information about the area, as well as a tea-room and shop.

What's new in 2005 Many events of interest to walkers, families and others

🛈 **T** 01694 723068,
01694 722631 (Shop/tea-room/Events),
01694 724536 (Learning)
E cardingmill@nationaltrust.org.uk

🚶 Guided walks in summer

🏷 Holiday activities, Wed & Fri 11–2

♿ Separate designated parking. Drop-off point. **WCs**: Adapted WC. **Shop**: Level entrance.
Refreshments: Level entrance

📷 NT shop. Plant sales

🍽 Chalet Pavilion. Children's menu

🚶 Baby-changing facilities. Pushchairs admitted. Family room with activities for children in Pavilion

🏫 Suitable for school groups. Education room/centre. Live interpretation. Children's quiz/trail. Family activity packs. Adult study days

🐕 Must be under control

🚲 Off-road routes in valley, on bridle paths only

→ [137: SO443945] **Bus**: Arriva/Whittlebus 435 Shrewsbury–Ludlow, alight Church Stretton, ½ml. NT shuttle bus service at weekends and BHols (Easter–Oct) connects Carding Mill Valley with Church Stretton station and other shuttles to Stiperstones, Discovery Centre and Bishops Castle. **Station**: Church Stretton (U) 1m. **Road**: 15ml S of Shrewsbury, W of Church Stretton valley and A49; approached from Church Stretton and, on W side, from Ratlinghope or Asterton

Please remember – your membership card is always needed for free admission

P Parking, 50yds (pay & display). NT members must display cards. Open daily all year. Parking £3 (March-Oct), £2 (Nov-Feb), minibus £5, coach £10

NT properties nearby
Attingham Park, Berrington Hall, Croft Castle, Powis Castle, Wenlock Edge, Wilderhope Manor

---

Charlecote Park

Warwick, Warwickshire CV35 9ER

🏠 ➡ ✂ ♣ 🗓 💻 ♿ 🍴 1946 (4:K7)

Superb Tudor house and landscaped deer park

The home of the Lucy family for over 700 years, the mellow brickwork and great chimneys of Charlecote seem to sum up the very essence of Tudor England. There are strong associations with both Queen Elizabeth and Shakespeare, who knew the house well – he is alleged to have been caught poaching the estate deer. The rich early Victorian interior contains many important objects from Beckford's Fonthill Abbey and, outside, the balustraded formal garden opens onto a fine deer park landscaped by 'Capability' Brown. Visitors can see a video film of life at Charlecote Park in the Victorian period.

i **T** 01789 470277, 07788 658495 (Events), 01789 472812 (Shop), 01789 470448 (Restaurant) **F** 01789 470544 **E** charlecote.park@nationaltrust.org.uk

The west front, Charlecote Park, Warwickshire

£ £6.60, child £3.30, family £16. Groups £5.60. **Grounds only**: £3.30, child £1.65. Reduced rate when arriving by public transport, cycle or on foot. Croquet set available £2.50 per hour (deposit required)

🛈 Evening guided tours for booked groups May to Sept: Tues 7.30–9.30 (£7.40 inc. NT members; minimum charge £150)

🎭 Programme of events. Send s.a.e. for details

♿ Separate designated parking, 200yds. Transfer available. Drop-off point.
Building: Ramped entrance. 5 wheelchairs. Ground floor accessible. Stairs to other floors. Seating available. Photograph album.
WCs: Adapted WC. **Grounds**: Accessible route. **Shop**: Steps to entrance with handrail. Alternative entrance, please ask.
Refreshments: Ramped entrance

👁 Braille guide and large-print guide. Sensory list

🛍 Shop located beyond Victorian kitchens

🍴 The Orangery (licensed). Children's menu

🅿 In the park only

👶 Baby-changing facilities. Front-carrying baby slings and hip-carrying infant seats for loan. Children's play area

🏫 Suitable for school groups. Education room/centre. Live interpretation. Children's guide. Children's quiz/trail. Adult study days. Children's activities during school holidays

Opening arrangements: Charlecote Park

			M	T	W	T	F	S	S
House	5 Mar - 30 Sep	12 - 5	M	T	W	T	F	S	S
	1 Oct - 30 Oct	12 - 4:30	M	T	W	T	F	S	S
Park & Gardens	5 Mar - 30 Oct	10:30 - 6	M	T	W	T	F	S	S
	5 Nov - 18 Dec	11 - 4	M	T	W	T	F	S	S
Garden	5 Mar - 30 Oct	10:30 - 5:30	M	T	W	T	F	S	S
	5 Nov - 18 Dec	11 - 4	M	T	W	T	F	S	S
Shop	As garden								
Restaurant	5 Mar - 30 Oct	10:30 - 5	M	T	W	T	F	S	S
	5 Nov - 18 Dec	11 - 4	M	T	W	T	F	S	S

Also open Weds following BHols and Weds in July and Aug

➔ [151: SP263564] **Bus**: Stagecoach in Warwickshire 18, X18 Coventry–Stratford-upon-Avon (passing ⇌ Leamington Spa). **Station**: Stratford-upon-Avon, 5½ml; Warwick 6ml; Leamington Spa 8ml. **Road**: 1ml W of Wellesbourne, 5ml E of Stratford-upon-Avon, 6ml S of Warwick on N side of B4086

P Free parking, 300yds

NT properties nearby
Baddesley Clinton, Coughton Court, Hidcote Manor Garden, Packwood House, Upton House

---

Coughton Court

nr Alcester, Warwickshire B49 5JA

 1946   **(4:K6)**

Tudor house and gardens in period style

Coughton Court is one of England's finest Tudor houses. Home of the Throckmorton family since 1409, the house has fine collections of furniture, porcelain and family portraits, and a fascinating exhibition on the Gunpowder Plot of 1605. The family has created and developed the grounds over the past 12 years so they are now totally in keeping with the period setting. Highlights include the walled garden and labyrinth, spectacular displays of roses, hot and cool herbaceous border, bog garden and river walk.

What's new in 2005 Daffodil garden featuring American Throckmorton varieties. 400th anniversary of the Gunpowder Plot – related events throughout the season

★ The Throckmorton family manage and live at Coughton Court. National Trust members are admitted to the house and garden free of charge (except the walled garden) on production of their membership card

ℹ **T** 01789 400777, 01789 762435 (Infoline), 01789 400702 (Booking), 01789 763301 (Shop) **F** 01789 765544 **E** office@throckmortons.co.uk

£ £8.60, child £4.30, family £28.75, family (2 adults & 2 children) £24.80. Groups £7.50. **Garden only**: £5.90, child £2.95, family £19.50, family £17. Groups £5.15. Walled garden (created by the family) £2.50 for NT members (inc. in admission price for non-members). For group prices there must be 15+ non-NT members

🎓 Out-of-hours guided tours of the house and/or gardens by appointment. No group rate or membership concessions for out-of-hours visits

🎪 Programme of events, inc. Easter egg hunt, Rose Festival, children's days in summer, Christmas carols, events based on various aspects of life in a historic house. See www.coughtoncourt.co.uk

🚶 Riverside walk and bluebell wood in season

♿ Separate designated parking, 120yds. Drop-off point. **Building**: Ramped entrance. 3 wheelchairs. Stairs to other floors. Audio visual/video, photograph album. **WCs**: Adapted WC. **Grounds**: Partly accessible, loose gravel paths, hoggin paths. Accessible route map. **Shop**: Ramped entrance. **Refreshments**: Level entrance

Opening arrangements: Coughton Court

House	5 Mar - 27 Mar	11:30 - 5	M	T	W	T	F	S	S
	1 Apr - 30 Jun	11:30 - 5	M	T	W	T	F	S	S
	1 Jul - 31 Aug	11:30 - 5	M	T	W	T	F	S	S
	1 Sep - 30 Sep	11:30 - 5	M	T	W	T	F	S	S
	1 Oct - 30 Oct	11:30 - 5	M	T	W	T	F	S	S
Gardens	As house	11 - 5:30							
Walled garden	As house	11:30 - 4:30							
Shop	As house	11 - 5:30							
Restaurant	As house	11 - 5:30							

Admission by timed ticket on very busy days. Open BH Mons & Tues 11–5 (House). Closed Sats 18 June & 16 July. The house may shut mid-afternoon occasionally on Sat. Tel. infoline for details

Please see the area introductions for details of coast & countryside properties

Braille guide. Interesting scents

All items selected by the Throckmorton family. Plants for sale cultivated by the family's gardeners

Coach House Café (not NT) (licensed). Children's menu. Tudor Restaurant (not NT) (licensed). Children's menu

Only in the car park

Baby-changing and feeding facilities. Front-carrying baby slings for loan. Children's play area

Suitable for school groups. Family guide. Children's guide. Children's quiz/trail. 'House and history' and 'Gunpowder Plot' videos

On leads and only in car park

→ [150: SP080604] **Cycle**: NCN5 ½ml. **Bus**: First 246/7 Redditch–Evesham (passing ≊ Redditch & close ≊ Evesham); Stagecoach in Warwickshire 25/6 from Stratford-upon-Avon (passing close ≊ Stratford-upon-Avon). **Station**: Redditch 6ml. **Road**: 2ml N of Alcester on A435

P Parking, 150yds, £1, charge inc. NT members

NT properties nearby
Baddesley Clinton, Charlecote Park, Hidcote Manor Garden, Packwood House, Upton House

Croft Castle

nr Leominster, Herefordshire HR6 9PW

🔨 ✚ 🏰 ❖ ♣ 🍺 1957 (4:H6)

Castellated manor house set in extensive parkland

Croft Castle is an imposing country house containing fine Georgian interiors and furniture, and with family connections dating back to the Norman Conquest. There are restored walled gardens and a park with a magnificent avenue of ancient Spanish chestnuts and panoramas across the once turbulent border country. The Iron Age hill-fort at nearby Croft Ambrey commands views over 14 of the old counties.

i **T** 01568 780246, 01568 780141 (Infoline)
  F 01568 780462
  E croftcastle@nationaltrust.org.uk

Croft Castle, Herefordshire

£ £4.60, child £2.30, family £11.50. Groups £4, group visits outside normal hours £8.20. **Garden**: £3.20. **Joint ticket with Berrington Hall**: £6.50

Programme of events. Tel. for details

Occasional guided walks

♿ Separate designated parking, 20yds. Drop-off point. **Building**: Ramped entrance. 2 wheelchairs. Ground floor has steps. Stairs to other floors. **WCs**: Adapted WC. **Grounds**: Accessible route. **Refreshments**: Level entrance. Large-print menu

Braille guide

Opening arrangements: Croft Castle										
House	5 Mar - 13 Mar	1 - 5	M	T	W	T	F	**S**	**S**
	19 Mar - 25 Sep	1 - 5	M	T	**W**	**T**	**F**	**S**	**S**
	1 Oct - 30 Oct	1 - 5	M	T	W	T	F	**S**	**S**
Gardens	5 Mar - 20 Mar	12 - 5	M	T	W	T	F	**S**	**S**
	23 Mar - 25 Sep	12 - 5	M	T	**W**	**T**	**F**	**S**	**S**
	1 Oct - 30 Oct	12 - 5	M	T	W	T	F	**S**	**S**
Tea-room	As gardens								
Park	All year		**M**	**T**	**W**	**T**	**F**	**S**	**S**
Open BH Mons									

Unless indicated, last admission is always 30mins before closing time

📹 Carpenter's Shop Tea-Room

🎍 In picnic area

👶 Hip-carrying infant seats for loan

🎪 Suitable for school groups. Children's quiz/trail. Family activity packs

🐕 On leads and only in parkland

➔ [137: SO455655] **Bus**: Lugg Valley Primrose/R & B/Whittlebus 492 Ludlow–Hereford (passing close ➿ Ludlow & Leominster), alight Gorbett Bank, 2¼ml. **Station**: Leominster (U) 7ml. **Road**: 5ml NW of Leominster, 9ml SW of Ludlow; approach from B4362, turning N at Cock Gate between Bircher and Mortimer's Cross; signposted from Ludlow–Leominster road (A49) and from A4110 at Mortimer's Cross

P Parking, 100yds, £2.50. Coaches £12

NT properties nearby
Berrington Hall, Brockhampton Estate, The Weir

Croome Park

NT Estate Office, The Builders' Yard, High Green, Severn Stoke, Worcestershire WR8 9JS

✚ ❇ ♣ ♨ 📹 [1996]   **(4:J7)**

Magnificent landscape park being restored to its former glory

Croome was 'Capability' Brown's first complete landscape, making his reputation and establishing a new style of garden design which became universally adopted over the next fifty years. The elegant park buildings and other structures are mostly by Robert Adam and James Wyatt. There are miles of walks through lakeside gardens, shrubberies and open parkland.

Opening arrangements: Croome Park									
Park	4 Mar - 29 May	10 - 5:30	M	T	**W**	**T**	**F**	**S**	**S**
	30 May - 4 Sep	10 - 5:30	**M**	**T**	**W**	**T**	**F**	**S**	**S**
	7 Sep - 30 Oct	10 - 5:30	M	T	**W**	**T**	**F**	**S**	**S**
	2 Nov - 18 Dec	10 - 4	M	T	**W**	**T**	**F**	**S**	**S**
Croome Church	As park								

Open BH Mons. Croome Church open in association with the Churches Conservation Trust which owns it. Tel. Estate Office for out-of-hours openings

What's new in 2005 Continued restoration of the Pleasure Ground and park including tree replanting and opening of the church shrubbery

⭐ The Trust acquired 270ha (670 acres) of the park in 1996 with substantial grant aid from the Heritage Lottery Fund. It has embarked on a 10-year restoration plan, including dredging the water features, clearance and replanting of the gardens and parkland. Royal & SunAlliance is making a major financial contribution towards the cost

ℹ **T** 01905 371006 **F** 01905 371090 **E** croomepark@nationaltrust.org.uk

£ £3.70, child £1.80, family £9. Groups £3

🎫 Out-of-hours booked guided tours for groups of 10 or more: £5 (inc. NT members)

🎭 Programme of events. Send s.a.e. for details

🚶 Walks available. Ask at reception

♿ Contact in advance. Ask at reception for parking closer to the lake. **WCs**: Adapted WC. **Grounds**: Some paths steep and uneven

👓 Braille guide and large-print guide

📹 Ice cream available at visitor reception

🎍 Picnic tables at top of park. Picnic area in wilderness walk

👶 Pushchairs and baby back-carriers admitted

🎪 Children's quiz/trail

🐕 On leads only in Pleasure Ground; under close control in wider parkland

➔ [150: SO878448] **Bus**: First/Aston's Coaches 372–4 Worcester–Upton-upon-Severn, alight Severn Stoke, then 2ml. **Station**: Pershore 7ml. **Road**: 8ml S of Worcester and E of A38 and M5, 6ml W of Pershore, and B4084. Signposted from A38 and B4084

P Parking, £2 (refunded on admission)

NT properties nearby
Brockhampton Estate, The Greyfriars, Hanbury Hall

There are special events at most Trust properties; please telephone 0870 458 4000 for details

Dudmaston

Quatt, nr Bridgnorth, Shropshire WV15 6QN

🎡 ❄ ♣ 🎣 📕 📗 1978　　　　　　(4:I5)

Late 17th-century mansion with art collection, lakeside garden and estate

The house with its intimate family rooms contains fine furniture and Dutch flower paintings, as well as one of Britain's most important public collections of contemporary art in a country house setting. The delightful gardens are a mass of colour in spring and visitors can enjoy walks in the Dingle, a wooded valley, or the popular 'Big Pool' walk. There are also estate walks to and from Hampton Loade. Dudmaston is the home of Colonel and Mrs Hamilton-Russell.

ℹ️ **T** 01746 780866
F 01746 780744
E dudmaston@nationaltrust.org.uk

£ £4.75, child £2.40, family £11. Groups £3.75.
Garden only: £3.50, child £1.50, family £8.
Groups £2.75

🚶 Garden: free tours Mon pm (except BH Mons)

🎪 Programme of events, inc. Christmas events. Send s.a.e. for details

🚶 Walks leaflet available. Please send s.a.e.

♿ Designated parking in main car park.
Building: Ramped entrance. 3 wheelchairs. Ground floor accessible. Stairs to other floors. Seating available. **WCs**: Adapted WC.
Grounds: Partly accessible. Accessible route map. Steep slopes and terraces, access may be difficult for PMVs. Some visitors may require assistance from their companion. 1 single-seater PMV. **Shop**: Ramped entrance.
Refreshments: Level entrance

👓 Braille guide and large-print guide

🏠 NT shop. Plant sales

📗 Tea-room in orchard car park. Light lunches.
Note: tea-room is open to the general public and not restricted to visitors to house or garden. Children's menu. Ice-cream kiosk

🅰 In orchard car park

👶 Baby-changing facilities. Front-carrying baby slings and hip-carrying infant seats for loan. Log pile to play on

Opening arrangements: Dudmaston										
House	27 Mar - 28 Sep	2 - 5:30	M	**T**	**W**	T	F	S	**S**
Garden	27 Mar - 28 Sep	12 - 6	**M**	**T**	**W**	T	F	S	**S**
Shop	27 Mar - 28 Sep	1 - 5:30	M	**T**	**W**	T	F	S	**S**
Tea-room	27 Mar - 28 Sep	11:30 - 5:30	**M**	**T**	**W**	T	F	S	**S**

Open BH Mons. St Andrew's Church, Quatt open at same times as house

🏫 Suitable for school groups. Children's quiz/trail. Lecture lunches – tel. for details. Children's activity room

🐕 Everywhere except house and gardens immediately surrounding house. Must be on leads and keep to existing footpaths. Shady area in car park

➡️ [138: SO746887] **Foot**: NT walks from Hampton Loade car park to the property.
Ferry: From Severn Valley Railway via river ferry and walk from Hampton Loade.
Bus: Choice Travel 297 Bridgnorth–Kidderminster (passing close ⊠ Kidderminster). **Station**: Hampton Loade (Severn Valley Rly) 1½ml; Kidderminster 10ml.
Road: 4ml SE of Bridgnorth on A442

🅿️ Orchard car park, 100yds. Also parking in Hampton Loade (pay & display)

NT properties nearby
Attingham Park, Benthall Hall, Berrington Hall, Kinver Edge, Sunnycroft, Wightwick Manor

The Fleece Inn

Bretforton, nr Evesham, Worcestershire WR11 5JE

🏠 🍴 📗 🎪 1978　　　　　　(4:J7)

Medieval building, still in use as a village inn

A black-and-white half-timbered house, which originally sheltered a farmer and his stock under the same roof, The Fleece first became a licensed house in 1848.

⭐ As a result of serious fire damage in February 2004, the Inn is undergoing major restoration work. Meanwhile a temporary pub has been opened in the barn, which will continue to host events. Full reopening is scheduled for late spring 2005

For further information check our website www.nationaltrust.org.uk

Opening arrangements: The Fleece Inn

All year	11 - 11	**M**	**T**	**W**	**T**	**F**	**S**	S
All year	12 - 10:30	M	T	W	T	F	S	**S**

Closed weekdays 3–6pm from mid Sept–mid June

[i] **T** 01386 831173
E fleeceinn@nationaltrust.org.uk

[🍽] Food available lunchtime and evening

[→] [150: SP093437] **Bus**: First 554, 954 from Evesham. **Station**: Evesham 3ml. **Road**: 4ml E of Evesham, on B4035

[P] Parking (not NT). Parking in village square only

NT properties nearby
Croome Park, Dover's Hill, Hidcote Manor Garden, Middle Littleton Tithe Barn, Snowshill Manor

---

The Greyfriars

Friar Street, Worcester, Worcestershire WR1 2LZ

[🏠][✳][⛶][👹] 1966   (4:J7)

15th-century merchant's house in Worcester city centre

This fine timber-framed merchant's house was built in 1480 next to the Franciscan friary. Rescued from demolition and carefully restored, the panelled interior contains interesting textiles and furnishings. An archway leads through to the delightful walled garden.

What's new in 2005 Children's activity room

[★] No WC. WC at Corn Market 200yds
[i] **T** 01905 23571
E greyfriars@nationaltrust.org.uk
[£] £3.40, child £1.70, family £8. Groups £2.75
[🔑] Guided tours for booked groups available
[♿] **Building**: Steps to entrance. Stairs to other floors. Photograph album

Opening arrangements: The Greyfriars

2 Mar - 2 Jul	1 - 5	M	T	**W**	**T**	**F**	**S**	S
3 Jul - 28 Aug	1 - 5	M	T	**W**	**T**	**F**	**S**	**S**
31 Aug - 17 Dec	1 - 5	M	T	**W**	**T**	**F**	**S**	S

Admission by timed ticket on Sats & BHols. Open BH Mons 1–5. Closes dusk if earlier

[◀◀] Braille guide

[▦] Suitable for school groups. Hands-on activities. Children's guide

[→] [150: SO852546] In centre of Worcester on Friar Street. **Bus**: From surrounding areas. **Station**: Worcester Foregate Street ½ml

[P] No parking on site. Public car park in Friar Street

NT properties nearby
Brockhampton Estate, Croome Park, Hanbury Hall

Hanbury Hall

School Road, Droitwich, Worcestershire WR9 7EA

[🏠][🐾][✳][♣][📷][💷][♿][⛶] 1953   (4:J6)

Early 18th-century country house, garden and parkland

Completed in 1701, this homely William & Mary-style house is famed for its fine painted ceilings and staircase, and has other fascinating features including an orangery, ice house, pavilions and working mushroom house. The stunning 8ha (20-acre) garden, recreated in keeping with the period of the house, is surrounded by 160ha (395 acres) of parkland, with beautiful views over the surrounding countryside. The tercentenary exhibition in the Long Gallery interprets the social, family, garden and architectural history.

What's new in 2005 Circular park walk

Opening arrangements: Hanbury Hall

House	5 Mar - 20 Mar	1 - 5	M	T	W	T	F	**S**	**S**
	21 Mar - 31 Oct	1 - 5	**M**	**T**	**W**	T	F	**S**	**S**
House tours	5 Mar - 30 Oct	11 - 1	M	T	W	T	F	**S**	**S**
Garden	5 Mar - 20 Mar	11 - 5:30	M	T	W	T	F	**S**	**S**
	21 Mar - 31 Oct	11 - 5:30	**M**	**T**	**W**	T	F	**S**	**S**
Shop	5 Mar - 20 Mar	11 - 5	M	T	W	T	F	**S**	**S**
	21 Mar - 31 Oct	11 - 5	**M**	**T**	**W**	T	F	**S**	**S**
Tea-room	As shop								

Admission by timed ticket on Suns & BHols. Open Good Fri. Closes dusk if earlier. Sat & Sun 11–1 access to house by guided tour only. **House and garden closed on 11, 12 & 13 March for Homes & Garden Exhibition. Event admission charge applies to NT members**

Please note: groups must book in advance with the property

The west front of Hanbury Hall, Worcestershire

⭐ Recreated 18th-century crown bowling green available for visitors to play on during normal opening hours. Private groups may book it at other times. Property available for wedding ceremonies, receptions and private hire

ℹ️ **T** 01527 821214,
01527 821459 (Shop)
F 01527 821251
E hanburyhall@nationaltrust.org.uk

💷 £5.70, child £2.80, family £13.50. Groups £4.80. **Garden only**: £3.70, child £1.90, family £8.70

🚶 Guided tours 11–1 Sat & Sun throughout season. Private guided tours for booked groups by arrangement

🎭 Programme of events. Send s.a.e. for details

♿ Designated parking in main car park, 150yds. Transfer available. Drop-off point.
Building: Ramped entrance. 2 wheelchairs. Stairs to other floors. Photograph album.
WCs: Adapted WC. **Grounds**: Partly accessible, loose gravel paths. 1 single-seater PMV. **Shop**: Step to entrance. Access across cobbled area. **Refreshments**: Steps to entrance. Level access possible from house

🔊 Induction loop in reception

👁 Braille guide and large-print guide. Sensory list

🛍 NT shop. Plant sales

🍽 Tea-room. Serving light lunches and refreshments. Group bookings by arrangement. Children's menu

🏞 Picnic tables in car park

🚼 Baby-changing facilities. Pushchairs admitted. Hip-carrying infant seats for loan

🏫 Suitable for school groups. Children's quiz/trail

🐕 On leads in park on footpaths, not in garden

➡️ [150: SO943637] **Bus**: First 144 Worcester–Birmingham (passing close ⌑ Droitwich Spa), alight Wychbold, 2½ml. **Station**: Droitwich Spa 4ml. **Road**: From M5 exit 5 follow A38 to Droitwich. From Droitwich 4½ml along B4090

🅿️ Free parking, 150yds

NT properties nearby
Clent Hills, Coughton Court, Croome Park, The Greyfriars

Hawford Dovecote

Hawford, Worcestershire

🏠 1973 (4:J6)

16th-century dovecote

The recently restored half-timbered dovecote is what remains of a former monastic grange.

⭐ No WC

ℹ️ **T** 01743 708100 (Regional office)
E hawforddovecote@nationaltrust.org.uk

Opening arrangements: Hawford Dovecote									
1 Apr - 31 Oct	9 - 6	**M**	**T**	**W**	**T**	**F**	**S**	**S**

Closed Good Fri. Closes sunset if earlier. Other times by appointment with regional office

Parking in National Trust car parks is free for members

£ £1

& **Building**: Level entrance

➔ [150: SO846607] **Bus**: First 303
Worcester–Kidderminster (passing ≋
Worcester Foregate Street & Kidderminster),
alight Hawford Lodge, ¼ml.
Station: Worcester Foregate Street 3ml;
Worcester Shrub Hill 3½ml. **Road**: 3ml N of
Worcester, ½ml E of A449

P Parking on roadside, 50yds. Not suitable for
coaches. Access is on foot via the drive of the
adjoining house

NT properties nearby
The Greyfriars, Hanbury Hall, Wichenford
Dovecote

Kinver Edge

The Warden's Lodge, Comber Road, Kinver, nr
Stourbridge, Staffordshire DY7 6HU

🏠 ⟨T⟩ 🏋 1917   (4:I5)

**High sandstone ridge with fascinating rock
houses**

The ridge is covered in woodland and heath and
offers dramatic views across surrounding counties
and miles of walking country. The famous Holy
Austin rock houses, which were inhabited until the
1950s, have now been restored and are open to
visitors at selected times.

★ WC on Comber Road adjacent to warden's
lodge

i **T** 01384 872418 (Edge),
01384 872553 (Rock houses booking)
E kinveredge@nationaltrust.org.uk

£ **Lower rock houses**: 50p, child 25p. Kinver
Edge: free

Opening arrangements: Kinver Edge											
Kinver Edge	All year		M	T	W	T	F	S	S
House grounds	1 Apr - 30 Sep	9 - 7	M	T	W	T	F	S	S
	1 Oct - 31 Mar 06	9 - 4	M	T	W	T	F	S	S
Upper terrace	2 Apr - 29 Mar 06	2 - 4	M	T	W	T	F	S	S
Lwr rock houses	5 Mar - 27 Nov	2 - 4	M	T	W	T	F	S	S
Open BH Mons. Lower rock houses open for guided tours at other times throughout the year, by arrangement with Custodian										

𝐊 Lower rock houses: by prior arrangement with
Custodian (min. 10 people). Please tel.

𝐀 Walks leaflet for sale from machine by
Warden's lodge

& **Building**: Seating available.
Grounds: Accessible route from car park to
lower rock houses

▦ Suitable for school groups

🐾 On leads within grounds of rock houses

➔ [138: SO836836] **Bus**: Hansons 228, Pete's
227 ≋ Stourbridge–Kinver.
Station: Stourbridge Town 5ml. **Road**: 5ml W
of Stourbridge, 6ml N of Kidderminster. 2½ml
off A458

NT properties nearby
Clent Hills, Dudmaston

Kinwarton Dovecote

Kinwarton, nr Alcester, Warwickshire

🏠 1958   (4:K7)

Circular 14th-century dovecote

The building still houses doves and retains its
potence, an unusual pivoted ladder from which
access is possible to the nesting boxes.

★ No WC

i **T** 01743 708100 (Regional office)

£ £1

& **Building**: Step to entrance

➔ [150: SP106585] **Cycle**: NCN5. **Bus**:
Stagecoach in Warwickshire 25 from Stratford-
upon-Avon; otherwise as for Coughton Court,
but alight Alcester, 1½ml . **Station**: Wilmcote
(U), 5ml; Wootton Wawen (U), not Sun, 5ml.
Road: 1½ml NE of Alcester, just S of B4089

P Parking (not NT)

NT properties nearby
Charlecote Park, Coughton Court, Hanbury Hall

Opening arrangements: Kinwarton Dovecote									
1 Apr - 31 Oct	9 - 6	M	T	W	T	F	S	S
Closed Good Fri. Closes dusk if earlier. Other times by appointment with regional office									

Please remember – your membership card is always needed for free admission

Letocetum Roman Baths Site & Museum

Watling Street, Wall, nr Lichfield, Staffordshire
WS14 0AW

 1934 **(4:K5)**

Excavated Roman bathhouse and site museum

Letocetum was an important staging post on the Roman military road to North Wales. Foundations of a *mansio* (Roman inn) and bathhouse can be seen, and many of the excavated finds are displayed in the museum.

⭐ Letocetum is in the guardianship of English Heritage

ℹ **T** 01543 480768 (Visitor reception), 0121 625 6820 (EH Regional office/Booking)

£ £2.60, child £1.30, concessions £2. Groups (11+) £2.15. NT members admitted free but pay a small charge on EH special events days. 2005 prices to be confirmed by EH

♿ **Building**: Many steps to entrance. Ground floor accessible. Audio interpretation. Steps to Roman site. Museum on ground floor. **Grounds**: Partly accessible, uneven paths. Some visitors may require assistance from their companion. **Shop**: Many steps to entrance

👆 Touchable objects

🚼 Pushchairs and baby back-carriers admitted

🏫 Suitable for school groups

🐕 On leads only

➡ [139: SK099067] **Cycle**: NCN5 2¼ml. **Station**: Shenstone 1½ml. **Road**: On N side of A5 at Wall, near Lichfield

🅿 Free parking (not NT), 50yds. Not suitable for coaches. Limited spaces

NT properties nearby
Moseley Old Hall, Shugborough

Opening arrangements: Wall Roman Site		
1 Apr - 31 May	10 - 5	**M T W T F S S**
1 Jun - 31 Aug	10 - 6	**M T W T F S S**
1 Sep - 31 Oct	10 - 5	**M T W T F S S**
Closes dusk if earlier. Closed 1–2pm. 2005 opening times may be subject to slight changes. Tel. for confirmation		

Middle Littleton Tithe Barn

Middle Littleton, Evesham, Worcestershire

🏠 1975 **(4:K7)**

13th-century tithe barn, one of the largest and finest in the country

⭐ No WC

ℹ **T** 01905 371006
E middlelittleton@nationaltrust.org.uk

£ £1. Not suitable for groups

♿ **Building**: Step to entrance. Ground floor accessible. Uneven floors

🅰 On grass forecourt only

🚼 Pushchairs and baby back-carriers admitted

➡ [150: SP080471] **Bus**: First 246/7 Evesham–Redditch (passing close ≋ Evesham), alight Middle Littleton School Lane, ½ml. **Station**: Honeybourne (U) 3½ml; Evesham 4½ml. **Road**: 3ml NE of Evesham, E of B4085

🅿 Parking (pay & display). Not suitable for coaches

NT properties nearby
Charlecote Park, Croome Park, The Fleece Inn, Hidcote Manor Garden, Snowshill Manor

Opening arrangements: Middle Littleton		
1 Apr - 4 Nov	2 - 5	**M T W T F S S**
Directions for access on barn door		

Moseley Old Hall

Moseley Old Hall Lane, Fordhouses, Wolverhampton, Staffordshire WV10 7HY

🏠🏠✚✿🏠💷🐕 1962 **(4:J5)**

Elizabethan house, famous for its association with Charles II

The richly panelled walls of Moseley Old Hall conceal ingenious secret hiding places, designed for Catholic priests. One of these cramped priest holes saved Charles II when he hid here after the Battle of Worcester in 1651 and the bed where he slept is on view. An exhibition in the barn retells the story of the King's dramatic escape from Cromwell's troops. The house underwent various alterations in the 19th century. The garden, recreated in 17th-century style with a formal knot garden, arbour and nut walk, has appropriate varieties of herbs and plants.

[i] **T** 01902 782808
E moseleyoldhall@nationaltrust.org.uk

[£] £4.80, child £2.40, family £12. Groups (15+) £4.10, group visits outside normal hours £5.40

[𝑖] Optional free guided tours; last guided tour 3.30. Tel. for details of out-of-hours tours

[🎭] Programme of events. Send s.a.e. for details

[♿] Separate designated parking, 10yds.
Building: Level entrance. Alternative accessible entrance. 1 wheelchair. Ground floor accessible. Stairs to other floors. Seating available. **WCs**: Adapted WC. **Grounds**: Fully accessible. **Shop**: Level entrance. **Refreshments**: Level entrance. Main seating is on first floor - 6 seats on ground floor

[👐] Braille guide and large-print guide. Sensory list. Handling collection

[🛍] NT shop. Plants for sale, mainly herbs

[☕] Tea-room on first floor of 18th-century barn. 2 tables at ground floor level. Children's menu

[🎪] Picnic tables provided

[👶] Baby-changing facilities. Baby back-carriers admitted. Front-carrying baby slings and hip-carrying infant seats for loan

The knot garden glimpsed from Moseley Old Hall, Staffordshire

[🏫] Suitable for school groups. Live interpretation. Hands-on activities. Children's guide. Children's quiz/trail

[➔] [127: SJ932044] **Bus**: Arriva Midlands 870–2 Wolverhampton–Cannock, alight Bognop Road, ¾ml; Travel West Midlands 613 from Wolverhampton, then 1¼ml (all pass close ≋ Wolverhampton). **Station**: Wolverhampton 4ml. **Road**: 4ml N of Wolverhampton; S of M54 between A449 and A460; traffic from N on M6 leave motorway at exit 11, then A460; traffic from S on M6 & M54 take exit 1; coaches must approach via A460 to avoid low bridge

[P] Free parking, 50yds. Narrow lanes, tight corners, full instructions and sketch map issued with group booking form. Coach parking by lane side

NT properties nearby
Benthall Hall, Letocetum, Shugborough, Sunnycroft, Wightwick Manor

Opening arrangements: Moseley Old Hall										
Hall	19 Mar - 30 Oct	1 - 5	M	T	W	T	F	S	S
	6 Nov - 20 Nov	1 - 4	M	T	W	T	F	S	S
Tea-room	19 Mar - 30 Oct	12 - 5	M	T	W	T	F	S	S
	6 Nov - 20 Nov	12 - 4	M	T	W	T	F	S	S
Garden	As tea-room								
Exhibition	As tea-room								
Shop	As tea-room								

Open BH Mons (11–5) and following Tues (1–5). Tea-room & garden open 12–5. Sun 6 March pre-season preview: ground floor of house, tea-room, shop and garden open 12–4, £2, child £1. 6 Nov–18 Dec: Sun – guided tours only. Christmas events, tel. for details

Packwood House

Lapworth, Solihull, Warwickshire B94 6AT

[🏠][❄][🌺][📷][🎭] 1941   **(4:K6)**

A much-restored Tudor house, garden with notable topiary and park

The house, originally 16th-century, is a fascinating 20th-century evocation of domestic Tudor architecture. Created by Graham Baron Ash, its interiors were restored during the period

Opening arrangements: Packwood House										
House	2 Mar - 6 Nov	12 - 4:30	M	T	W	T	F	S	S
Garden	2 Mar - 30 Apr	11 - 4:30	M	T	W	T	F	S	S
	1 May - 30 Sep	11 - 5:30	M	T	W	T	F	S	S
	1 Oct - 6 Nov	11 - 4:30	M	T	W	T	F	S	S
Park *	All year		**M**	**T**	**W**	**T**	**F**	**S**	**S**
Shop	As garden								
Admission by timed ticket to house at busy times. Open BH Mons										

between the World Wars and contain a fine collection of 16th-century textiles and furniture. The gardens have renowned herbaceous borders and a famous collection of yews.

What's new in 2005 Reinstatement of flower beds and paths in the Carolean Garden

[i] **T** 01564 783294,
01564 787924 (Visitor reception),
01564 787925 (Shop) **F** 01564 782706
E packwood@nationaltrust.org.uk

[£] £6, child £3, family £15. Groups £5.10, group visits outside normal hours £10.20. **Garden only**: £3, child £1.50. **Combined ticket to Packwood House and Baddesley Clinton**: £9.60, child £4.80, family £24. Groups £8.20. **Combined ticket for gardens only**: £4.80, child £2.40

[🎭] Out-of-hours tours by written arrangement

[🚶] Lakeside walk

[♿] Designated parking in main car park, 70yds. Drop-off point. **Building**: Steps to entrance. Alternative accessible entrance. 2 wheelchairs. Great Hall can be viewed from Long Gallery doorway. Many stairs with handrail to other floors. Seating available. Photograph album. **WCs**: Adapted WC. **Grounds**: Fully accessible. **Shop**: Steps to entrance with handrail

[👁] Braille guide. Sensory list

[🛍] NT shop. Plant sales

[☕] Cold drinks and ice cream sold in the shop. Vending machine offering hot drinks and soup near visitor reception

[🪑] In designated area with tables near car park

[👶] Baby-changing facilities. Front-carrying baby slings and hip-carrying infant seats for loan

[🎒] Suitable for school groups. Children's guide. Children's quiz/trail

[🐕] On leads and only in car park (reasonable walks nearby)

[→] [139: SP174723] **Bus**: Stratford Blue X20 Birmingham–Stratford-upon-Avon, alight Hockley.Heath, 1¾ml. **Station**: Lapworth (U) 1½ml; Birmingham International 8ml. **Road**: 2ml E of Hockley Heath (on A3400), 11ml SE of central Birmingham

[P] Free parking, 70yds. Coaches welcome by written arrangement

NT properties nearby
Baddesley Clinton, Birmingham Back to Backs, Charlecote Park, Clent Hills, Hanbury Hall

Shugborough

Milford, nr Stafford, Staffordshire ST17 0XB

[🏛][🐕][♿][🔥][✳][♣][🛍][☕][🎧][🔔][🪑][T][1966] (4:J4)

Complete historic estate, with late 17th-century mansion, 19th-century model farm and servants' quarters

Seat of the Earls of Lichfield, the house at Shugborough was enlarged c.1750 and again at the turn of the 19th century and contains interesting collections of china, silver, paintings and furniture. Extensive servants' quarters include a working kitchen and laundry and nearby a brewery. In the parkland is the model farm (1805) with working watermill, kitchens and dairy, and rare breeds of farm animal. Eight major monuments adorn the wider landscape.

What's new in 2005 SeaBritain events. See website for details. New virtual tour and audio tour

Opening arrangements: Shugborough										
House & farm	19 Mar - 31 Oct *	11 - 5	**M**	**T**	**W**	**T**	**F**	**S**	**S**
Servant' quarters	As house								
Parkland/gdns	As house								
Tea-room	As house								
Shop	19 Mar - 25 Sep	11 - 5	**M**	**T**	**W**	**T**	**F**	**S**	**S**
	26 Sep - 23 Dec	11 - 4	**M**	**T**	**W**	**T**	**F**	**S**	**S**
Opening times may vary when special events held. Tel. or see website to check										

The west front, Shugborough Hall, Staffordshire

★ Shugborough is financed and administered by Staffordshire County Council. NT members are offered a greatly reduced price all sites ticket, entitling them to refund of car parking charge. Otherwise house is free, but in this case NT members pay to park. Admission charges and opening arrangements may vary when special events are held

ℹ **T** 01889 881388, 01889 882122 (Shop) **F** 01889 881323 **E** shugborough.promotions@staffordshire.gov.uk

£ **NT members** (free entry to house only): £3, family (2 adults & 2 children) £10. **All sites ticket**: £5, family £15. **Non-members/day visitors**: £8, child £5, family £20, concessions £5. Farm only tickets available. Visitors may return to visit sites not seen on day of ticket purchase

🏋 Wide range of tours and activities for adult groups. Tailor-made itineraries

📅 Programme of events, inc. open-air concerts and themed activities, Christmas evenings and craft festivals

🚶 Walks and trails suitable for all abilities

♿ Separate designated parking, 100yds. Drop-off point. **Building**: Many steps to entrance, stairclimber available. 6 wheelchairs. Stairs to other floors. Audio visual/video, photograph album. **WCs**: Adapted WC. **Grounds**: Accessible route. 5 single-seater PMV. **Shop**: Level entrance. **Refreshments**: Ramped entrance with handrail

👁 Braille guide and large-print guide. Sensory list

☕ Lady Walk Tea-room (not NT) (licensed) at main site. Children's menu. Granary Tea-room (not NT) at farm. Kiosk (not NT) at main site. Orangery available for groups. Dinners available for booked groups

🏕 Picnic sites at main and farm car parks

👶 Baby-changing and feeding facilities. Hip-carrying infant seats for loan. Children's play area. Farm gives children chance to see domestic and rare breeds of animal and poultry. Games gallery in corn mill. Pushchairs admitted to farm

🏫 Suitable for school groups. Education room/centre. Live interpretation. Hands-on activities. Children's guide. Children's quiz/trail

There are special events at most Trust properties; please telephone 0870 458 4000 for details

On leads and only in parkland and gardens

→ [127: SJ992225] **Foot**: Pedestrian access from E, from the canal/Great Haywood side of the Estate. Estate walks link to towpaths along Trent & Mersey Canal and Staffs & Worcs Canal and to Cannock Chase trails. Lies on Staffordshire Way. **Bus**: Arriva 825 ⬗ Stafford–Tamworth (passing close ⬗ Lichfield City). **Station**: Rugeley Town 5ml; Rugeley Trent Valley 5ml; Stafford 6ml. **Road**: Signposted from M6 exit 13; 6ml E of Stafford on A513; entrance at Milford.

P Parking, £3 (pay & display), charge inc. NT members. Refunded on purchase of all sites ticket

NT properties nearby
Attingham Park, Biddulph Grange Garden, Little Moreton Hall, Moseley Old Hall

---

Upton House

nr Banbury, Warwickshire OX15 6HT

 1948 (4:K7)

Late 17th-century house with significant art collections and superb terraced gardens

The house, built in 1695 of mellow local stone, was purchased and remodelled 1927–29 by Walter Samuel, 2nd Viscount Bearsted, Chairman of Shell 1921–46 and son of the founder of that company. Upton contains his outstanding collection of English and continental Old Master paintings including works by Hogarth, Stubbs, Guardi, Canaletto, Brueghel and El Greco; tapestries; French porcelain; Chelsea figures and 18th-century furniture. There is an exhibition of paintings and publicity posters commissioned by Shell during Viscount Bearsted's chairmanship; also Lady Bearsted's restored Art Deco bathroom. The garden is very fine, with terraces, herbaceous borders, kitchen garden, ornamental pools and an interesting 1930s water garden, together with the National Collection of Asters.

What's new in 2005 Opening in mid 2005: visitor reception centre, WCs next to house, cycle racks and newly restored Bog Cottage, available as a holiday let

★ Property closed to visitors on 6 July until 2

i **T** 01295 670266 (Property office),
01295 671124 (Shop),
01295 671112 (Restaurant)
E uptonhouse@nationaltrust.org.uk

£ £6.80, child £3.50, family £16. Groups (15+) £5.40. **Garden only (inc. restaurant & shop) 19 Mar–30 Oct**: £4, child £2. Groups £3.20. **Garden only 5 Nov–18 Dec**: £2, child £1

🕴 Free taster tours. Tel. for details. Guided tours out-of-hours by written arrangement. Refreshments can be included

📅 Programme of events, inc. fine arts study tours, jazz concerts, conservation displays, garden tours, workshops and lecture lunches. Tel. for details

♿ Designated parking in main car park, 350yds. Wheelchair-accessible transfer. Drop-off point. **Building**: Many steps to entrance. Alternative accessible entrance, door to open – bell available to summon assistance if required. 1 wheelchair. Ground floor accessible. Stairs to other floors. Seating available. Photograph album. **WCs**: Adapted WC. **Grounds**: Partly accessible, some steps, terraces. Accessible route map. Volunteer-driven buggy provides access to lower part of garden on request (not adapted for wheelchairs). **Shop**: Ramped entrance. **Refreshments**: Steps to entrance, ramp available. Large-print menu. Alternative route avoiding steps

👁 Braille guide. Sensory list

🏠 NT shop. Plants and garden produce on sale (when available) in the garden

Opening arrangements: Upton House									
House	19 Mar - 2 Nov	1 - 5	**M**	**T**	**W**	T	F	**S**	**S**
Garden	19 Mar - 30 Oct	11 - 5	M	T	W	T	F	**S**	**S**
	21 Mar - 2 Nov	12 - 5	**M**	**T**	**W**	T	F	S	S
	5 Nov - 18 Dec	12 - 4	M	T	W	T	F	**S**	**S**
Shop	19 Mar - 2 Nov	1 - 5:15	**M**	**T**	**W**	T	F	**S**	**S**
	5 Nov - 18 Dec	12 - 4	M	T	W	T	F	**S**	**S**
Restaurant	As garden								

Admission by timed ticket on BHols but visitors may then stay until 5 if they wish. Open Good Fri: house & shop 1–5, garden & restaurant 11–5. Guided tours available weekends in Nov & Dec. Property opens at 2 on Wed 6 July. No lunchtime menu on this day

⚑ Pavilion Restaurant (licensed). Outdoor seating available. Children's menu

⌂ Picnic area in visitors' car park

⚹ Baby-changing and feeding facilities. Front-carrying baby slings and hip-carrying infant seats for loan

▣ Children's quiz/trail. Adult study days

⚐ Dogs welcome on leads, only in car park. Limited shade available. Water available

➔ [151: SP371461] **Foot**: Footpath SM177 runs adjacent to property, Centenary Way ½ml, Macmillan Way 1ml. **Cycle**: NCN5 5ml. Oxfordshire Cycle Way 1½ml. **Bus**: Johnson's 270 from Banbury. **Station**: Banbury 7ml. **Road**: On A422, 7ml N of Banbury, 12ml SE of Stratford-upon-Avon. Signed from exit 12 of M40

ⓟ Free parking, 350yds. Parking is on grass with hard-standing for coaches

NT properties nearby
Canons Ashby, Charlecote Park, Chastleton House, Farnborough Hall, Hidcote Manor Garden

The Dry Banks in the garden of Upton House, Warwickshire

The Weir

Swainshill, nr Hereford, Herefordshire HR4 7QF

❇ ⌂ 1959 (4:H7)

Informal 1920s riverside garden with fine views

A tranquil garden of 4ha (10 acres) on a steep slope above a bend in the River Wye, The Weir is most spectacular in spring with drifts of snowdrops, daffodils and narcissi. In summer the sheltered setting provides the perfect habitat for butterflies, bees, dragonflies and damselflies. The bird population is prolific and varied. The many vantage points provide spectacular views of the Wye valley and the Herefordshire countryside.

ⓘ **T** 01981 590509
E theweir@nationaltrust.org.uk

£ £3.60, child £1.80, family £8.50

⚲ Guided tours by arrangement

♿ **Grounds**: Partly accessible, loose gravel paths, steep slopes, some steps, narrow paths

⚹ Baby-changing facilities. Pushchairs and baby back-carriers admitted

⚐ On leads and only in car park

➔ [149: SO438418] **Bus**: Yeoman's Canyon 446 from Hereford; otherwise First 71 Hereford–Credenhill (both passing close ⮀ Hereford), then 1½ml. **Station**: Hereford 5ml. **Road**: 5ml W of Hereford on A438

ⓟ Free parking. Not suitable for coaches

NT properties nearby
Berrington Hall, Brockhampton Estate, Croft Castle, Cwmmau Farmhouse

Opening arrangements: The Weir									
28 Feb - 3 Apr	11 - 4	**M**	**T**	**W**	**T**	**F**	**S**	**S**	
6 Apr - 30 Oct	11 - 5	M	**T**	**W**	**T**	**F**	**S**	**S**	
21 Jan - 29 Jan 06	11 - 4	M	T	W	T	F	**S**	**S**	
1 Feb - 26 Feb 06	11 - 4	M	T	**W**	**T**	**F**	**S**	**S**	
Open BH Mons									

Please note: groups must book in advance with the property

The night nursery, Wightwick Manor, West Midlands

Wichenford Dovecote

Wichenford, Worcestershire

🎭 1965   (4:I7)

17th-century half-timbered black-and-white dovecote

⭐ No WC

ℹ️ **T** 01743 708100 (Regional office)
   E wichenforddovecote@nationaltrust.org.uk

£ £1

🚪 **Building**: Steps to entrance

➔ [150: SO788598] **Bus**: First 310/1/3 from Worcester (passing close ⮕ Worcester Foregate Street), alight Wichenford, ½ml.
Station: Worcester Foregate Street 7ml; Worcester Shrub Hill 7½ml. **Road**: 5½ml NW of Worcester, N of B4204

🅿️ Free parking, 50yds

NT properties nearby
The Greyfriars, Hanbury Hall, Hawford Dovecote

Opening arrangements: Wichenford Dovecote									
1 Apr - 31 Oct	9 - 6	**M**	**T**	**W**	**T**	**F**	**S**	**S**	

Closed Good Fri. Open other times by appointment with NT West Midlands regional office

Wightwick Manor

Wightwick Bank, Wolverhampton, West Midlands WV6 8EE

🏛️ ✳️ 🏠 🍽️ 🖼️ 🍵 1937   (4:J5)

Victorian manor house with William Morris interiors and colourful garden

Wightwick Manor is one of only a few surviving examples of a house built and furnished under the influence of the Arts & Crafts Movement. The many original William Morris wallpapers and fabrics, Pre-Raphaelite paintings, Kempe glass and de Morgan ware help conjure up the spirit of the time. An attractive 7ha (17-acre) garden reflects the style and character of the house.

ℹ️ **T** 01902 761400,
   01902 760100 (Booking, Thu & Fri only),
   01902 760101 (Learning),
   01902 760102 (Shop), 01902 760107 (Tea-room) **F** 01902 764663
   E wightwickmanor@nationaltrust.org.uk

£ £6.30, child £3.20, family £15.50. Groups £5.30, child £2.65, group visits outside normal hours £8. **Garden only**: £3.20, child free

🎭 Booked groups Tues, Wed, Fri. Thur & Sat in spring and autumn. Evening groups by arrangement

💬 Inc. servants tours, upstairs tours and art study days. Tel. for details

🚪 Contact in advance. Separate designated parking. **Building**: Level entrance. Ground

Parking in National Trust car parks is free for members

floor has 2 steps in hall. Seating available. Photograph album. **WCs**: Adapted WC. **Grounds**: Partly accessible, slopes, some steps. Accessible route map. Some visitors may require assistance from their companion. **Shop**: Step to entrance. **Refreshments**: Level entrance. Large-print and braille menu. Space restricted

🔊 Induction loop in reception

👓 Braille guide and large-print guide. Touchable objects

🏺 Pottery (not NT) open as shop. **Note**: William Morris shop, tea-room and pottery open to the general public, not just visitors to house and garden. Plant sales at certain times of year

☕ Tea-room. Limited seating. Children's menu

👶 Baby-changing facilities. Hip-carrying infant seats for loan

🎭 Suitable for school groups. Live interpretation. Hands-on activities. Children's quiz/trail. Adult study days. Family activity days during Aug

🐕 On leads and only in garden

➔ [139: SO869985] **Bus**: Arriva 890 Wolverhampton-Bridgnorth; Midland Choice 516 Wolverhampton–Pattingham (both pass close ≥ Wolverhampton). **Station**: Wolverhampton 3ml. **Road**: 3ml W of Wolverhampton, up Wightwick Bank (off A454 beside Mermaid Inn)

🅿 Free parking, 120yds. Located at bottom of Wightwick Bank (please do not park in Elmsdale opposite the property)

NT properties nearby
Benthall Hall, Dudmaston, Moseley Old Hall

Opening arrangements: Wightwick Manor										
House	3 Mar - 24 Dec	12:30 - 5	M	T	**W**	T	**F**	S	**S**	
Garden	2 Mar - 24 Dec	11 - 6	M	T	**W**	T	**F**	S	**S**	
Tea-room	2 Mar - 24 Dec	11 - 5	M	T	**W**	T	**F**	S	**S**	
Shop	2 Mar - 24 Dec	12 - 5	M	T	**W**	T	**F**	S	**S**	

Admission by timed ticket and guided tour only, available from 11 at visitor reception. Open BH Mons. First Thur & Sat of each month: no guided tours – free-flow through house. House open BH Suns & Mons for ground floor only, 12.30–5. Also house openings for families Weds in Aug, 12.30–5. Many of the contents are fragile and some rooms cannot always be shown, so tours vary

Attingham Park Estate: Cronkhill

Atcham, Shrewsbury, Shropshire SY5 6JP**(4:H4/5)**

First and best-known example of John Nash's Italianate villa designs, built in 1805.

⭐ Visitors are reminded that the contents of the property belong to the tenants and should not be touched

ℹ **T** 01743 708123 (Infoline)

£ £2, child £1

Opening arrangements: Cronkhill
Open Sun 10 Apr, Wed 13 Apr, Wed 1 June, Sun 7 Aug, Wed 10 Aug, Sun 9 Oct: 11–5

Cwmmau Farmhouse

Brilley, Whitney-on-Wye, Herefordshire HR3 6JP **(4:G7)**

Superb early 17th-century farmhouse

⭐ Open ten afternoons a year. At other times the farmhouse is available as holiday accommodation (tel: 0870 458 4411 for NT Holiday Cottages information)

ℹ **T** 01981 590509

£ £3.20, child £1.60, family £7

Opening arrangements: Cwmmau Farmhouse								
25 Mar - 28 Mar	2 - 5	M	T	W	T	**F**	**S**	**S**
28 May - 30 May	2 - 5	M	T	W	T	**F**	**S**	**S**
27 Aug - 29 Aug	2 - 5	**M**	T	W	T	**F**	**S**	**S**

The staircase hall at Sunnycroft, Wellington, Shropshire

Farnborough Hall

Farnborough, Banbury, Warwickshire
OX17 1DU   **(4:L7)**

Stone-built house with exceptional 18th-century decoration and superb landscaped garden.

⭐ Farnborough Hall is occupied and administered by the Holbech family

ℹ️ 01295 690002 (Infoline)

💷 **House, garden & terrace walk**: £4, child £2, family £11. **Terrace walk only**: £2

Opening arrangements: Farnborough Hall										
House & garden	2 Apr - 28 Sep	2 - 5:30	M	T	**W**	T	F	**S**	S
	1 May - 2 May	2 - 5:30	**M**	T	W	T	F	**S**	**S**
Terrace walk open same days as house. Strong shoes advisable										

Morville Hall

nr Bridgnorth, Shropshire WV16 5NB   **(4:I5)**

Stone-built house of Elizabethan origin

ℹ️ **T** 01746 780838 (Estate office)
   E morvillehall@nationaltrust.org.uk

💷 Admission free

Opening arrangements: Morville Hall
By written appointment only with the tenants, Dr & Mrs C. Douglas

Sunnycroft

200 Holyhead Road, Wellington, Telford,
Shropshire TF1 2DR   **(4:I4)**

Remarkably complete late-Victorian gentleman's suburban villa, outbuildings and grounds.

⭐ Planning permission for a visitor car park has been applied for. It is hoped a car park will be available from early summer. Tel. for details

ℹ️ **T** 01952 242884

💷 £4.40, child £2.20. **Garden only**: £2.30. Out-of-hours tours £5, inc. NT members

Opening arrangements: Sunnycroft									
20 Mar - 30 Oct	1 - 5	**M**	T	W	T	F	S	**S**
Admission by timed ticket (advance booking not possible) and guided tour only, except BH Mons. Last admission 1hr before closing									

Town Walls Tower

Shrewsbury, Shropshire SY1 1TN   **(4:H4)**

Shrewsbury's last remaining watchtower, built in the 14th century.

⭐ No WC

ℹ️ **T** 01743 708162 (Attingham Park)
   F 01743 708155

Opening arrangements: Town Walls Tower
By written appointment only with the tenant, Mr A. A. Hector, Tower House, 26a Town Walls, Shrewsbury SY1 1TN

Wilderhope Manor

Longville, Much Wenlock, Shropshire
TF13 6EG   **(4:H5)**

Elizabethan gabled manor house, unfurnished but with fine interior architectural features.

⭐ The Manor is used as a Youth Hostel so access to some occupied rooms may be restricted

ℹ️ **T** 0870 770 6090 (Hostel Warden YHA)

💷 £1

Opening arrangements: Wilderhope Manor									
3 Apr - 28 Sep	2 - 4:30	M	T	W	**W**	T	F	**S**	S
2 Oct - 26 Mar 06	2 - 4:30	M	T	W	T	F	S	**S**

South West South & South East
London East of England
East Midlands West Midlands
North West Yorkshire North East
Wales Northern Ireland

The North West of England has some of Britain's most impressive scenery, as well as some fascinating industrial heritage. In the north, the dramatic grandeur of the Lake District offers great opportunities for outdoor recreation. To the south, the urban centres of Manchester and Liverpool are surrounded by unspoilt countryside.

The National Trust looks after around one quarter of the Lake District National Park, including England's highest mountain, **Scafell Pike,** her deepest lake, **Wastwater**, and over 90 farms. Almost all the central fell area and major valley heads are owned or leased by the Trust, together with 24 lakes and tarns. Beatrix Potter (otherwise known as Mrs Heelis) acquired houses and cottages to protect the landscape and gave 1600ha (4000 acres), a total of 15 farms in the Lake District, to the Trust on her death in 1943. The acquisition of this great estate – piece by piece over 100 years, since the purchase of **Brandlehow Park** on the shore of Derwentwater in 1902 – is one of the Trust's greatest achievements. In fact the Lake District makes up almost one quarter of the Trust's

The stone circle at Castlerigg, Derwentwater, Cumbria

entire holding across England, Wales and Northern Ireland.

The Trust cares for many other sites in Cumbria in addition to the Lake District properties which have individual entries in this Handbook. These include the tiny 16th-century **Keld Chapel** near Shap (access at all times; key in village, see notice on chapel door), in the

Previous page: Low Tilberthwaite farm and cottages near Little Langdale, Cumbria
Below: Fold Head Farm, Watendlath in Borrowdale, Cumbria

north **Wetheral Woods**, along the River Eden near Carlisle, and on the south-west coast near Barrow, **Sandscale Haws**, a superb dune system and nature reserve.

Arnside Knott in Cumbria and the Silverdale properties of **Eaves and Waterslack Woods** in Lancashire, are home to a wide variety of wild flowers and butterflies, with fine views over limestone countryside. Near Kendal is **Holme Park Fell,** an important example of limestone pavement. Further south the Trust has begun to protect the coastline at **Heysham**, with its small, ruined Saxon chapel and unique rock-cut graves.

In east Lancashire the **Stubbins Estate** and **Holcombe Moor**, north of Manchester, are noted for their moorland bird species. Equally important for wildlife are the sand dunes and pinewoods at **Formby**, and the ancient woodland of **Stocktons Wood**, part of the landscape surrounding **Speke Hall** on Merseyside.

Across the Mersey, the Wirral peninsula has a 12-mile long country park, several parts of which are owned by the Trust. **Caldy Hill** gives spectacular views across the mouth of the River Dee, home to wildfowl and waders. At **Thurstaston Common** there is a rare surviving fragment of acid heathland, rich in insect life. To the south east lies **Helsby Hill**, from the summit of which there are breathtaking views over the Mersey and the mountains of North Wales. Several of the Trust's beauty spots in this region are very near the great industrial conurbations of Liverpool and Manchester, for example the wooded sandstone escarpment of **Alderley Edge,** which provides spectacular views across the Cheshire Plains.

The River Cocker in Buttermere Valley, Cumbria

Sandscale Haws in Cumbria, looking out over the dunes towards the hills of the southern Lake District

The south of the area runs towards the Welsh border and comprises beautiful mixed woodland, heathland and fields, with excellent walking opportunities. **Bickerton Hill** lies at the southern tip of the Peckforton Hills, a wooded ridge crossed by a 30-mile-long footpath, the Sandstone Trail, which passes a variety of dwellings from black-and-white cottages to prehistoric hill-forts.

Regional highlights for Visitors with Disabilities

Wheelchair access to **Tarn Hows**, **Friar's Crag** at Derwentwater, **White Moss Common** at Grasmere and at **Claife**, near Hawkshead, among many others. There is adapted holiday accommodation at Restharrow on the shores of Windermere and at Acorn Bank Garden (tel: 0870 458 4411 for details).

Derwentwater, Cumbria

...and for Families

Most of our properties are great for families - especially recommended are :
Fell Foot Park, Lyme Park, Dunham Massey, Speke Hall, Formby, Quarry Bank Mill, Beatrix Potter Gallery, Wordsworth House, Tarn Hows and **Steam Yacht** *Gondola* on Coniston Water.

Further information

Please contact the Membership Department, PO Box 39, Warrington, WA5 7WD. Tel: 0870 458 4000. Email: enquiries@thenationaltrust.org.uk.

Leaflets on National Trust campsites, bed and breakfast, 'Wildlife, Wild Places' and events are available from local NT information centres or the NT North West regional office (see page 387). Please send a s.a.e. if requesting these by post.

OS Grid Reference

OS grid references for main properties with no individual entry (OS Landranger map series numbers given in brackets)

Arnside Knott	[97] SD456775
Bickerton Hill	[117] SJ504529
Brandelhow Park	[97] NY250205
Caldy Hill	[108] SJ224855
Castlerigg Circle	[89] NY292236
Eaves & Waterslack Woods	[97] SD465758
Heald Brow	[97] SD467742
Helsby Hill	[117] SJ492754
Heysham	[97] SD419618
Jack Scout	[90] SD459737
Keld Chapel	[90] NY554145
Sandscale Haws	[96] SD200756
Scafell Pike	[89/90] NY214069
Stubbins Estate	[109] SD781183
Stocktons Wood	[108] SJ422828
Tarn Hows	[96] SD328998
Thurstaston Common	[108] SJ244853
Wetheral Woods	[86] NY470553
White Moss Common	[90] NY347064

Car Parks in the Lake District

The National Trust is an independent charity which protects about one quarter of the Lake District National Park. All income from National Trust pay a display car parks supports landscape conservation work in the valleys where the car parks are located

Lanthwaite Wood	NY 149 215
Buttermere	NY 172 173
Honister Pass	NY 225 135
Seatoller	NY 246 137
Rosthwaite	NY 257 148
Bowderstone	NY 254 167
Watendlath	NY 276 164
Kettlewell	NY 269 196
Great Wood	NY 272 213
Aira Force	NY 401 201
Glencoyne Bay	NY 387 188
Wasdale Head	NY 182 074
Old Dungeon Ghyll	NY 285 062
Stickle Ghyll	NY 295 064
Elterwater	NY 329 047
Silverthwaite	NY 342 037
White Moss Common	NY 348 066
Tarn Hows	SD 326 995
Ash Landing	SD 388 955
Sandscale Haws	SD 199 758
Blea Tarn	NY 296 044
Harrowslack	SD 388 960
Red Nab	SD 385 995

Acorn Bank Garden & Watermill

Temple Sowerby, nr Penrith, Cumbria CA10 1SP

❄ 🛠 ❖ 🏠 💼 1950   (6:E7)

Delightful sheltered garden, renowned for its herbs and orchards growing old English fruit varieties

Ancient oaks and high enclosing walls keep the extremes of the Cumbrian climate out of the garden, resulting in a spectacular display of shrubs, roses and herbaceous borders. Orchards contain a variety of traditional fruit trees and the famous herb garden is the largest collection of medicinal and culinary plants in the north of England. A circular woodland walk runs along Crowdundle Beck to the partially restored Acorn Bank watermill, which is open to visitors. The house is not open to the public, though parts of it are available as holiday cottages.

What's new in 2005 Change in opening days

ℹ️ 017683 61893 (Shop),
017683 66826 (Tea-room)
F 017683 66824
E acornbank@nationaltrust.org.uk

💷 £3, child £1.50, family £7.50. Groups £2.50

🎗 Programme of events, inc. Newt Watch in June, Apple Day in Oct

🚶 Through woodland, beside beck and pond, to the watermill

♿ Separate designated parking, 50yds.
Building: Level access only available to upper information room. 2 wheelchairs. Narrow outside staircase to lower mill rooms. Seating available. Photograph album. **WCs**: Adapted WC. **Grounds**: Partly accessible, loose gravel paths, grass paths, undulating terrain. Accessible route map. **Shop:** Level entrance. **Refreshments**: Ramped entrance. Large-print menu

📖 Braille guide and large-print guide. Sensory list

🛍 NT shop. Plant sales

☕ Restaurant. Children's menu

Opening arrangements: Acorn Bank Garden										
Woodland walks	5 Mar - 13 Mar	11 - 4	M	T	W	T	F	**S**	**S**
	19 Mar - 30 Oct	10 - 5	M	T	**W**	**T**	**F**	**S**	**S**
Garden	19 Mar - 30 Oct	10 - 5	M	T	**W**	**T**	**F**	**S**	**S**
Shop	As garden								
Tea-room	5 Mar - 13 Mar	11 - 4	M	T	W	T	F	**S**	**S**
	19 Mar - 30 Oct	11 - 4:30	M	T	**W**	**T**	**F**	**S**	**S**

Open BH Mons 10–5

🏞 Picnic area near car park

👶 Baby-changing facilities. Pushchairs and baby back-carriers admitted

🎒 Suitable for school groups. Children's guide. Adult study days

🐕 On leads on woodland walk

➡️ [91: NY612281] **Cycle**: NCN7 6ml.
Bus: Stagecoach in Cumbria Grand Prix 563 Penrith–Kirkby Stephen, to within 1ml (passes close ➡ Penrith & ➡ Appleby).
Station: Langwathby (U) 5ml; Penrith 6ml.
Road: Just N of Temple Sowerby, 6ml E of Penrith on A66

P Free parking, 80yds

NT properties nearby
Ullswater and Aira Force

An angelica seed-head in the herb garden at Acorn Bank, Cumbria

Alderley Edge

c/o Cheshire Countryside Office, Nether Alderley, Macclesfield, Cheshire SK10 4UB

 1946 **(5:D8)**

Dramatic red sandstone escarpment, with impressive views

Alderley Edge is designated an SSSI for its geological interest. It has a long history of copper mining, going back to prehistoric and Roman times. The mines are open twice a year, organised by the Derbyshire Caving Club. There are views across Cheshire and the Peak District and numerous paths through the oak and beech woodlands, including a link to Hare Hill.

[i] **T** 01625 584412,
0161 928 0075 (NT Altrincham office)
F 01625 587555

[⚐] Walks to Hare Hill 1½ml and Nether Alderley Mill 2ml

[⚐] One path quite level and accessible for wheelchairs. Some visitors may require assistance. **WCs**: Adapted WC

[⚐] Tea-room (not NT)

[⚐] Suitable for school groups

[⚐] Dogs under close control; on leads in fields

[→] [118: SJ860776] **Bus**: Bakers 287 Wilmslow–Macclesfield passing 🚉 Alderley Edge. **Station**: Alderley Edge 1½ml. **Road**: 1½ml east of Alderley village on B5087 Macclesfield road

[P] Parking (pay & display). NT members must display cards. Closed 25 Dec. Locked at dusk; hours displayed on gate

NT properties nearby
Hare Hill, Nether Alderley Mill, Quarry Bank Mill and Styal Estate

Opening arrangements: Alderley Edge									
All year	8 - 6:30	**M**	**T**	**W**	**T**	**F**	**S**	**S**	
Tea-room	10 - 5	M	T	W	T	F	**S**	**S**	

Closes dusk if earlier than 6:30pm. Tea-room also open BHols

Beatrix Potter Gallery

Main Street, Hawkshead, Cumbria LA22 0NS

[🏠] 1944 **(6:D8)**

Gallery showing original book illustrations by Beatrix Potter

The exhibition of original sketches and watercolours painted by Beatrix Potter for her children's stories changes annually. Also on display are artefacts and information relating to her life and work beyond the 'Tales'. The 17th-century building, the model for Tabitha Twitchit's shop, was once the office of Beatrix's husband, William Heelis. The interior remains substantially unaltered since his day, giving an interesting insight into an Edwardian law office.

What's new in 2005 Exhibition will feature *The Tale of Mrs Tiggy-Winkle* and *The Tale of the Pie and the Patty-Pan*, celebrating their 100th birthdays. Also an emphasis on Hill Top, the house purchased by Beatrix Potter in 1905. Occasional story reading for families

[★] The annual exhibition shows a selection of the NT's Beatrix Potter collection. No WC. WC 200yds away, in town car park

[i] **T** 015394 36355 (shop)
F 015394 36187
E beatrixpottergallery@nationaltrust.org.uk

[£] £3.50, child £1.70, family £8.70. Discount available to Hill Top ticket holders (not applicable to groups)

[⚐] Easter trail

[⚐] 2 local walks leaflets

[⚐] Designated parking in main car park, 200yds. **Building**: Exhibition housed in old property entered from street, step to narrow entrance. Level access to 3 rooms on ground floor. Illustrations are upstairs, objects relating to Beatrix Potter downstairs. Many stairs with handrail to other floors. Seating available. **Shop**: Level entrance. Steps to upper floor

[⚐] Braille guide. Touchable objects

[⚐] 50yds away in The Square. Main NT supplier of Herdwick sheep products

[⚐] Suitable for school groups. Children's quiz/trail

Please see the area introductions for details of coast & countryside properties

Opening arrangements: Beatrix Potter Gallery

Gallery	19 Mar - 30 Oct	10:30 - 4:30	M	T	W	T	F	S	S
	2 & 3 Jun	10:30 - 4:30	M	T	W	**T**	**F**	S	S
	27 & 28 Oct	10:30 - 4:30	M	T	W	**T**	**F**	S	S
	18 Feb - 26 Feb 06	10:30 - 4:30	**M**	**T**	**W**	**T**	**F**	**S**	**S**
Shop	5 Mar - 13 Mar	10 - 4	M	T	W	T	F	**S**	**S**
	19 Mar - 30 Oct	10:30 - 4:30	**M**	**T**	**W**	**T**	**F**	**S**	**S**
	5 Nov - 18 Dec	10:30 - 4	M	T	W	T	F	**S**	**S**
	19 Dec - 23 Dec	10:30 - 4	**M**	**T**	**W**	**T**	**F**	S	S
	18 Feb - 26 Feb 06	10:30 - 4	**M**	**T**	**W**	**T**	**F**	**S**	**S**

Admission by timed ticket issued on arrival to all visitors. Open Good Fri

→ [96: SD352982] In Main Street, Hawkshead village, next to Red Lion pub.
Bus: Stagecoach in Cumbria 505 ☒ Windermere–Coniston; Cross Lakes Shuttle from Bowness (Apr–Oct) tel. 015394 45161.
Station: Windermere 6½ml via ferry.
Road: B5286 from Ambleside (4ml); B5285 from Coniston (5ml)

P Parking (not NT), 200yds (pay & display)

NT properties nearby
Fell Foot Park, Hawkshead, Hill Top, *Gondola*, Stagshaw Garden, Tarn Hows, Townend

---

Borrowdale

Bowe Barn, Borrowdale Road, Keswick, Cumbria CA12 5UP

🏠🛗🌳♿🏛💷🎋🚶🐕 1902   (6:D7)

Spectacular and varied landscape around Derwentwater

This is the location of the Trust's first acquisition in the Lake District, Brandelhow Woods, on the lakeshore. Total NT protection in the area today covers 11,806ha (29,173 acres), including eleven farms, half of Derwentwater (including the main islands), the hamlet of Watendlath and sites with literary or historical interest such as the Bowder Stone, Friar's Crag, Ashness Bridge

Opening arrangements: Borrowdale

		M	T	W	T	F	S	S
All year		**M**	**T**	**W**	**T**	**F**	**S**	**S**
Shop/info centre 26 Mar - 30 Oct	10 - 5	**M**	**T**	**W**	**T**	**F**	**S**	**S**

Shop/information centre closes later on summer evenings, tel. for details

and Castlerigg Stone Circle, a free-standing megalithic monument of 38 stones near Keswick.

What's new in 2005 Access to the buildings at Force Crag Mine on two days (provisionally 5 Aug and 9 Sept). Further dates may be added. Admission through pre-booked tours only. This was the last working mineral mine in the Lake District, extracting zinc and barytes. Buildings and machinery have been restored to allow visitors to see the processes and to experience the working conditions of this remote site. No access into the mine itself. Tel. for details

i **T** 017687 73780 (Shop/info), 017687 74649 (Property office & fax)
E borrowdale@nationaltrust.org.uk

⚲ Guided walks; see Events leaflet (obtainable from NW regional office)

☺ Programme of events. Tel. for details

♿ Several sites and paths are accessible. Access to Friar's Crag, Bowder Stone, Crow Park, Calf Close Bay, Castlerigg Stone Circle and shore of Derwentwater at Brandelhow.
WCs: Adapted WC. **Shop**: Step to entrance

🛍 Shop and information centre at Keswick lakeside

☕ Tea-rooms (not NT) at Caffle House, Watendlath; at the Flock-In, Rosthwaite; at Ashness Farm, nr Ashness Bridge; at Knotts View, Stonethwaite; and at Seathwaite – properties owned, but not managed, by NT

🏫 Suitable for school groups. Farm tours available

→ [90: NY266228 – Keswick Lakeside information centre] **Cycle**: NCN71. (C2C).
Ferry: Derwentwater launch service to various NT properties around lake, tel. 017687 72263. **Bus**: To information centre: Stagecoach in Cumbria X4/5 ☒ Penrith–Workington, 555/6 Lancaster–Keswick (pass close ☒ Lancaster, Kendal & Workington).
Road: B5289 runs S from Keswick along Borrowdale

P Six pay & display car parks in valley (NT members free at NT car parks only)

NT properties nearby
Derwent Island House, Wordsworth House

Unless indicated, last admission is always 30mins before closing time

Buttermere and Ennerdale

c/o Block 16, Leconfield Industrial Estate, Cleator Moor, Cumbria CA25 5QB

🏛 ♨ 👤 🗻 🧍 🐕 1935   **(6:C7)**

Tranquil area of dramatic fells, farms and woodland, encompassing three lakes

This area of 3588ha (8866 acres) of fell and commonland includes the lakes of Buttermere, Crummock and Loweswater, seven farms and woodland, as well as lakeshore access to Ennerdale Water. The famous Pillar Rock can be found in the high fells to the south, and there are extensive prehistoric settlements on the fells south of Ennerdale. Fishing and boats are available on Buttermere, Crummock Water and Loweswater.

⭐ WC in Buttermere village (not NT)

ℹ **T/F** 019468 61235, 01900 85267 (Warden)
E buttermere@nationaltrust.org.uk

📋 Programme of events

♿ 2ml route along SW side of Buttermere lake; some short steep gradients and uneven surfaces. Adapted gate by car park at Lanthwaite Woods leads to short route on firm gravel to Crummock Water

🎒 Suitable for school groups. Education room /centre. Hands-on activities. Adult study days

➡ [89: NY180150 – Buttermere] 8ml S of Cockermouth. **Bus**: Services from 🚃 Penrith, Whitehaven, 🚃 St Bees & Keswick and Cockermouth, inc. Honister Rambler and Ennerdale Rambler

Crummock Water in Buttermere, Cumbria

Opening arrangements: Buttermere and Ennerdale	
All year	**M T W T F S S**

🅿 Parking at Honister Pass, Buttermere village, Lanthwaite Wood and Crummock Water (pay & display). NT members must display cards

NT properties nearby
Wordsworth House

Cartmel Priory Gatehouse

The Square, Cartmel, Grange-over-Sands, Cumbria LA11 6QB

🏠 📷 1946   **(6:D9)**

14th-century gatehouse of medieval priory

Apart from the church, the gatehouse is all that is left of a 12th-century Augustinian priory, which was later strengthened following devastating raids by Robert the Bruce. The Dissolution of the Monasteries put an end to the priory in the mid-16th century. The gatehouse later served as a grammar school from 1624 to 1790. It is managed by the Cartmel Village Society as a village heritage centre, with an exhibition catering for all ages depicting the history of the building, Cartmel village and the Cartmel peninsula.

⭐ This property is managed by the Cartmel Village Society. No WC

ℹ **T** 015395 36874 (Gatehouse),
01524 701178 (Property Manager)

💷 £2, child 50p. Donations welcome from NT members

Opening arrangements: Cartmel Priory Gatehouse

25 Mar - 30 Oct	10 - 4	M T **W T F S S**
Winter	10 - 4	M T W T F **S S**

Open BH Mons. Closed on Cartmel Race Days, even if BH Mon

🎭 Guided tours by arrangement

🎪 Occasional specialist heritage events

🚶 Heritage walk around the historic village centre, leaflet available

♿ Drop-off point. **Building**: Steps to entrance. Stairs to other floors. Book showing main elements of CD-ROM and reference books in reception. **Shop**: Steps to entrance

📷 Small area in reception

🏫 Suitable for school groups. Hands-on activities. Family guide. Children's quiz/trail

➡ [96: SD378788] In the Square in village centre. **Cycle**: No cycle parking. **Bus**: D&H 532 ➩ Grange-over-Sands–Cartmel. **Station**: Cark (U) 2ml

P Parking (not NT) Some free parking in village centre, also car park, 100yds, 50p

NT properties nearby
Fell Foot Park, Sizergh Castle & Garden

Coniston & Tarn Hows

Boon Crag, Coniston, Cumbria LA21 8AQ

🏚️🦯♿🚶🌾 1930   (6:D8)

Landscape of fell, meadow and woodland around Coniston Water

The area looked after by the Trust covers some 2695ha (6660 acres) and includes twelve farms, the well-known Tarn Hows beauty spot with its magnificent views of the mountains, and Little Langdale, which shows several signs of early settlement, including the Thingmount (a Norse meeting place) by Fell Foot Farm. There is access to the lakeshore of Coniston Water.

⭐ No WC

ℹ️ **T** 015394 41197 (Property Manager), 015394 41172 (Warden) **F** 015394 41197 **E** coniston@nationaltrust.org.uk

🎭 Guided walks available

♿ Separate designated parking. Short route on firm gravel path from car park to a good view point over the tarn

🏫 Suitable for school groups. Audio guide to Tarn Hows

🚲 Cycle tracks along Coniston lakeshore (west), Yewdale and in woodland south of Tarn Hows

➡ [89/90: NY290040 – Blea Tarn] Little Langdale valley starts 4ml N of Coniston village

P Car parks, pay & display, not suitable for coaches. Located at Tarn Hows and Blea Tarn

NT properties nearby
Beatrix Potter Gallery, Hill Top, *Gondola*

Opening arrangements: Coniston & Tarn Hows

All year	**M T W T F S S**

Dunham Massey

Altrincham, Cheshire WA14 4SJ

🏛️🏠✝🍴♣🌼📷💷🍽 1976   (5:D8)

Country estate including mansion with important collections and 'below stairs' areas, impressive garden and deer park

An early Georgian house built around a Tudor core, Dunham Massey was extensively reworked in the early years of the 20th century. The result is one of Britain's most sumptuous Edwardian interiors, housing exceptional collections of 18th-century walnut furniture, paintings and Huguenot silver, as well as extensive servants' quarters. Here is one of the North West's great plantsman's gardens with richly planted borders and majestic trees, as well as an orangery, Victorian bark-house and

Opening arrangements: Dunham Massey

House	19 Mar - 30 Oct	12 - 5	**M T W** T F **S S**
Garden	19 Mar - 30 Oct	11 - 5:30	**M T W T F S S**
Park	19 Mar - 30 Oct	9 - 7:30	**M T W T F S S**
	31 Oct - 31 Mar 06	9 - 5	**M T W T F S S**
Restaurant	19 Mar - 30 Oct	10:30 - 5	**M T W T F S S**
	31 Oct - 31 Mar 06	10:30 - 4	**M T W T F S S**
Shop	As restaurant		
Mill	19 Mar - 30 Oct	12 - 4	**M T W** T F **S S**

House open Good Fri and BH Sun & Mon 11–5.
Restaurant closed 25 Dec. Shop closed 25/26 Dec

well-house. The ancient deer park contains a series of beautiful avenues and ponds and a Jacobean mill, originally used for grinding corn but refitted as a sawmill *c*.1860 and now restored to working order.

What's new in 2005 The magnificent 17th-century state bed is being conserved – elements on display for the first time in 100 years

The early 17th-century mill on the Dunham Massey estate, Cheshire

[i] **T** 0161 941 1025, 0161 928 4351 (Infoline), 0161 941 4986 (Learning), 0161 928 6820 (Shop), 0161 941 2815 (Restaurant) **F** 0161 929 7508 **E** dunhammassey@nationaltrust.org.uk

[£] **House & garden**: £6.50, child £3.25, family £16.25. Groups £5. **House or garden only**: £4.50, child £2.25. Reduced rate when arriving by public transport

[🏃] Optional guided tours of house most afternoons and garden tours Mon and Wed at no extra charge. Booked evening tours of house and garden – charge applies

[🎭] Programme of events. Send s.a.e. for details

[🚶] Guided deer park walks Mon, Wed, Fri throughout the year at 1.30. Free walks leaflet

[♿] Designated parking in main car park, 200yds. Transfer available. Drop-off point. **Building**: Many steps to entrance. 4 wheelchairs. 4 steps at front entrance to house. Steps to saloon and great hall. Many stairs with handrail to other floors. Seating available. Photograph album. **WCs**: Adapted WC. **Grounds**: Accessible route. 2 single-seater PMV, booking essential. **Shop**: Level entrance. **Refreshments**: Steps to entrance with handrail, lift available

[♨] Braille guide and large-print guide. Sensory list

[🛍] NT shop. Plant sales in garden

[🍴] Stables Restaurant (licensed) on first floor of old stables. Open for corporate and private bookings outside normal hours, parties only. Children's menu. Kiosk in car park

[⛺] Extensive picnic area. Picnics not permitted in deer park

[👶] Baby-changing facilities. Front-carrying baby slings and hip-carrying infant seats for loan

[🏫] Suitable for school groups. Education room/centre. Live interpretation. Hands-on activities. Children's quiz/trail. Family activity packs. Family tours. Family activities during school holidays

[🐕] Good walks around estate, but must be on leads in deer park at all times

[🚲] No cycling in deer park

[→] [109: SJ735874] **Foot**: Close to Trans-Pennine Trail and Bridgewater Canal. **Cycle**: NCN62 1ml. **Bus**: Big House Bus from ≋ Altrincham Interchange, Sun April–Sept only; otherwise Arriva/Warrington Transport 38 ≋ Altrincham Interchange–Warrington. **Station**: Altrincham 3ml; Hale 3ml. **Road**: 3ml SW of Altrincham off A56: M6 exit 19; M56 exit 7

[P] Parking, 200yds. Park visitors £3.80 car, £1 motorbike, £10 coach/minibus, refundable on purchase of adult house and garden ticket. Coaches bringing booked groups park free. Shuttle service operates between car park and visitor facilities 19 Mar–30 Oct

NT properties nearby
Hare Hill, Lyme Park, Nether Alderley Mill, Quarry Bank Mill and Styal Estate, Tatton Park

Please note: groups must book in advance with the property

Fell Foot Park

Newby Bridge, Ulverston, Cumbria LA12 8NN

🔱 🏛 ♿ 🌲 ⏰ 1948   **(6:D8)**

Country park beside Lake Windermere

This Victorian park, restored to its former glory, offers substantial access to the lakeshore of Windermere, where there are leisure facilities in season. Fine picnic areas and rowing boat hire make this property particularly suitable for families. Spring and early summer bring impressive displays of daffodils, followed by rhododendrons, and there are magnificent views of the Lakeland fells.

⭐ No launching or landing of speedboats or jet-skis

ℹ️ **T** 015395 31273, 015395 39924 (Shop), 015395 39922 (Tea-room) **F** 015395 39926 **E** fellfootpark@nationaltrust.org.uk

£ Admission free. Donations welcome

📅 Programme of events. Tel. for details

♿ Transfer available. Drop-off point. **WCs**: Adapted WC. **Grounds**: Partly accessible, loose gravel paths, steep slopes, grass paths, undulating terrain. Staff driven vehicles are available everyday during the season, 11am–4pm. 3 multi-seater PMV. **Shop**: Ramped entrance. **Refreshments**: Level entrance

🍴 Licensed tea-room at lake shore. Trusty the Hedgehog lunch boxes

Fell Foot Park at the south end of Windermere, Cumbria

Opening arrangements: Fell Foot Park										
Park	All year	9 - 5	**M**	**T**	**W**	**T**	**F**	**S**	**S**
Shop	19 Mar - 30 Oct	11 - 5	**M**	**T**	**W**	**T**	**F**	**S**	**S**
Tea-room	As shop									

Site closed 25 & 26 Dec. Closes dusk if earlier. Facilities, eg rowing boat hire (buoyancy aids available), 29 March to 30 Oct: daily 11–4 (last boat), must be returned by 4.30

🚼 Pushchairs and baby back-carriers admitted. Children's play area

🏫 Suitable for school groups. Hands-on activities. Children's quiz/trail. Family activity packs. 100 bird and bat boxes around the park relay live pictures to wildlife room

🐕 On leads only

➜ [96/97: SD381869] **Ferry**: Seasonal ferry links Fell Foot to Lakeside (southern terminus of main Windermere cruise ferries). **Bus**: Stagecoach in Cumbria 618 Ambleside–Barrow-in-Furness (connections from ➌ Windermere). **Station**: Grange-over-Sands 6ml; Windermere 8ml. **Road**: At the extreme S end of Lake Windermere on E shore, entrance from A592

🅿️ Parking (pay & display). NT members must display cards. Members' season tickets obtainable from most NT outlets in Cumbria. Access difficult for coaches, which must book in advance

NT properties nearby
Sizergh Castle & Garden

The foreshore at Formby, Merseyside

Formby

Victoria Road, Freshfield, Formby, Liverpool
L37 1LJ

 1967   (5:B7)

Large area of beach, sand dunes and pine woods

This wonderful stretch of unspoilt coastline set between the sea and Formby town offers miles of walks through the woods and dunes. There are interesting plants and birds to be found, and this is one of the last places in England where visitors may catch a glimpse of the rare red squirrel.

What's new in 2005 Programme of walks and events for SeaBritain 2005 – see NT website

★ Major work to create a new car park is planned for winter 2005/06

i **T** 01704 878591 (Countryside office), 01704 874949 (Learning Tel/Fax) **F** 01704 835378 **E** formby@nationaltrust.org.uk

🏃 Contact Learning Officer to book

🎦 Programme of events. Send s.a.e. for details

🏃 Send s.a.e. for details

♿ **WCs**: Adapted WC. RADAR key at entrance kiosk. **Grounds**: Partly accessible. Accessible route map. Beach access difficult due to steep sand dunes

👓 Braille guide

🥤 Ice cream and soft drinks available

Opening arrangements: Formby

	All year	Dawn – dusk	M	T	W	T	F	S	S

Closed 25 Dec. Property will be closed for 1 or 2 days early/mid May for resurfacing work

🏕 Three picnic areas. No barbecues

🚼 Baby-changing facilities

▥ Suitable for school groups. Children's quiz/trail. Children's red squirrel booklet 50p

🐕 On leads around the squirrel walk

➔ [108: SD275080] **Cycle**: NCN62 3ml. **Bus**: Cumfy Coaches 160/1/4/5, 🚆 Formby–BR Freshfield, to within ½ml. **Station**: Freshfield 1ml. **Road**: 15ml N of Liverpool, 2ml W of Formby, 2ml off A565. 6ml S of Southport

P Parking, £3.20. Coaches £15. Beach overflow car park closes 5.30, April–Oct. All beach car parks close 4.30, Nov–March. Note width restriction 3 metres

NT properties nearby
59 Rodney Street, 20 Forthlin Road, Mendips, Rufford Old Hall, Speke Hall

---

20 Forthlin Road, Allerton

Liverpool L24 1YP

🏠 🎧 1995   (5:C8)

Former home of the McCartney family

This 1950s terraced house is where the Beatles met, rehearsed and wrote many of their earliest songs. Displays include contemporary photographs by Michael McCartney and early

---

Please remember – your membership card is always needed for free admission

Beatles memorabilia. The audio tour features contributions from both Michael and Sir Paul McCartney.

⭐ **There is no direct access by car or on foot**. Visits are by combined minibus tour only with Mendips, the childhood home of John Lennon. Any photography inside 20 Forthlin Road or duplication of audio tour material is strictly prohibited. You will be asked to deposit all handbags, cameras and recording equipment at the entrance to the house. No WC

ℹ️ **T** 0870 900 0256 (Infoline for Speke Hall, Forthlin Road & Mendips),
0151 708 8574 (to book morning tours),
0151 427 7231 (to book afternoon tours)
E 20forthlinroad@nationaltrust.org.uk

💷 **Joint ticket Forthlin Road & Mendips**: £12, child £1. **NT members (to cover minibus)**: £6, child £1

♿ **Building**: Step to entrance. Ground floor accessible. Stairs with handrail to other floors. Seating available. Audio visual/video, photograph album. **WCs**: Adapted WC

♒ Braille guide

📷 At nearby Speke Hall

🏪 At nearby Speke Hall

🎒 Suitable for school groups. Maximum group size 15

➔ [108: SJ403862] Access is via minibus from Liverpool city centre or Speke Hall

🅿️ No parking on site. Not suitable for coaches

NT properties nearby
59 Rodney Street, Formby, Mendips, Rufford Old Hall, Speke Hall

Opening arrangements: 20 Forthlin Road							
19 Mar - 30 Oct	M	T	W	T	F	S	S

Admission by guided tour only, 4 tours depart on days open to the public. Open BH Mons (booking essential). To guarantee a place on a tour visitors are advised to book in advance. Tours depart by minibus from the city centre in the morning and Speke Hall in the afternoon. Tel. infoline to check times and pick-up points

Gawthorpe Hall

Padiham, nr Burnley, Lancashire BB12 8UA

🏠 ♣ 🏠 🍽️ 🔔 ⌐ 1972 **(5:D6)**

Elizabethan house with rich interiors and an important textile collection

This imposing house, set in tranquil grounds in the heart of urban Lancashire, resembles the great Hardwick Hall and is very probably by the same architect, Robert Smythson. In the middle of the 19th century Sir Charles Barry was commissioned to restore the house, thereby creating the opulent interiors we see today. The Long Gallery is hung with portraits of society figures from the 17th century, some of the paintings being on loan from the National Portrait Gallery. Several rooms display part of the unparalleled international collection of needlework, lace and costume assembled by the last family member to live here, Rachel Kay-Shuttleworth. The wooded park and riverside location offer good summer walks.

⭐ Gawthorpe Hall is financed and administered by Lancashire County Council. The Great Barn, an unusual aisled threshing barn with a cathedral-like atmosphere, is available for private hire and registered for weddings.

ℹ️ **T** 01282 771004,
01282 770353 (Shop),
01282 779346 (Tea-room)
F 01282 770178/776663
E gawthorpehall@nationaltrust.org.uk

💷 £3, concessions £1.50. Child free when accompanied by an adult. Prices subject to confirmation in March 2005. Garden free

🎭 Group evening guided tours and special activities available

🎪 Programme of events. Tel. for details

🚶 Two walks leaflets, one riverside and one historic

Opening arrangements: Gawthorpe Hall									
Hall	25 Mar - 31 Mar	1 - 5	M	T	W	T	F	S	S
	2 Apr - 2 Nov	1 - 5	M	T	W	T	F	S	S
Garden	All year	10 - 6	M	T	W	T	F	S	S
Tea-room	As hall	12:30 - 5							
Open BH Mons									

♿ Drop-off point. **Building**: Steps to entrance. Steps from dining room. Stairs to other floors. Photograph album. **WCs**: Adapted WC. **Grounds**: Partly accessible. Level route from car park to lawn. Gradient route through trees. **Shop**: Level entrance. **Refreshments**: Level entrance. 2 steps to picnic benches

⏱ Braille guide

📷 Run by volunteers. Opening times vary

☖ Coach House Tea-Room in the Courtyard

⛶ Three picnic benches

🚸 Baby-changing facilities

■ Suitable for school groups. Live interpretation. Hands-on activities. Children's quiz/trail. Adult study days. Urdu interpretation of RBKS textile collection

🐾 In grounds only and under close control

→ [103: SD806340] **Foot**: Pleasant walk by the River Calder from Padiham, ½ml; on route of Brontë Way public footpath. **Bus**: Frequent services from Burnley. All pass close  Burnley Barracks & Burnley Manchester Road. **Station**: Rose Grove (U) 2ml. **Road**: On E outskirts of Padiham; ¾ml drive to house on N of A671; M65 exit 8 towards Clitheroe, then signposted from second traffic light junction to Padiham

P Free parking, 150yds. Tight access to site. Tight turning facilities

NT properties nearby
East Riddlesden Hall, Rufford Old Hall, Stubbins Estate & Holcombe Moor

---

Gondola

NT *Gondola* Bookings Office, The Hollens, Grasmere, Cumbria LA22 9QZ

📷 ☗ ⛶ 1980   **(6:D8)**

Rebuilt Victorian steam-powered yacht on Coniston Water

The original steam yacht *Gondola* was first launched in 1859 and now, completely rebuilt by the Trust, gives passengers the chance to sail in her sumptuous, upholstered saloons. This is the perfect way to view Coniston's spectacular scenery.

What's new in 2005 25th anniversary of *Gondola's* relaunch on Coniston Water – series of events to celebrate throughout the season. See **www.nationaltrust.org.uk/gondola**

★ All sailings are weather permitting. No WC on board, nearest WC at Coniston Pier

ⓘ **T** 015394 41288 (Gondola Pier), 015394 35599 (Booking)
F 015394 41962 (Gondola Pier)
E gondola@nationaltrust.org.uk

£ **Round trip:** Ticket prices and timetable on application and published locally. No reduction for NT members as *Gondola* is an enterprise and not held solely for preservation. Groups and private charters by prior arrangement; tel. in office hours. Discount vouchers available for Ruskin Museum, Brantwood House and Windermere Steamboat Museum. *Gondola* passengers can disembark at Brantwood House

♿ Ramped gangway and steps to *Gondola*. Contact in advance. Separate designated parking, 50yds. **WCs**: Adapted WC

⏱ Braille guide

📷 Guidebook and *Gondola* souvenirs available on board

⛶ Outside saloons only

🚸 Pushchairs and baby back-carriers admitted

■ Suitable for school groups

🐾 Outside saloons. Free

→ [96: SD307970] Sails from Coniston Pier, (½ml from Coniston village). **Cycle**: No cycle parking. **Bus**: Stagecoach in Cumbria 505 from  Windermere. **Station**: Foxfield (U), not Sun, 10ml; Windermere 10ml via vehicle ferry. **Road**: A593 from Ambleside. Pier is at end of Lake Road, turn immediately left after petrol station if travelling S from centre of Coniston village

Opening arrangements: *Gondola*							
23 Mar - 30 Oct	M	T	W	T	F	S	S

Steam yacht *Gondola* sails from Coniston Pier daily, weather permitting. Last sailing at 4. The National Trust reserves the right to cancel sailings and special charters in the event of high winds. Piers at Coniston and Brantwood (not NT)

Please see the area introductions for details of coast & countryside properties

P Parking (not NT) at Coniston Pier, 50yds. 2 free coach parking spaces for booked groups

NT properties nearby
Beatrix Potter Gallery, Hill Top, Tarn Hows

Grasmere and Great Langdale

High Close, Loughrigg, Ambleside, Cumbria LA22 9HH

❄🏊📷🏠🚶🐕 1925 (6:D8)

Picturesque and varied landscape with Wordsworth connections

The area of 4925ha (12,170 acres) with ten farms includes the protection of the famous Langdale Pikes. It also encompasses the popular White Moss Common, the glaciated valley of Mickleden, a Victorian garden at High Close and dramatic Dungeon Ghyll, as well as the bed of Grasmere lake and part of Rydal Water.

★ There is a spectacularly located NT campsite at Great Langdale, open all year [NY288057], charge (inc. NT members): visit **www.langdalecampsite.org.uk**

i T 015394 37663,
015394 37668 (Langdale campsite)
F 015394 37131
E grasmere@nationaltrust.org.uk

♿ Separate designated parking. Located in lower White Moss car park, beside A591 Ambleside–Grasmere. **Building**: Ramped entrance to Grasmere information centre. **WCs**: Adapted WC

📷 Shop at campsite

▉ Suitable for school groups

🚲 Good cycling on quiet roads and bridleways

➔ [89/90: NY290060] Great Langdale valley starts 4ml W of Ambleside. **Bus**: To Grasmere information centre: Stagecoach in Cumbria 555/6, 599 from ▆ Windermere. To Langdale

Opening arrangements: Grasmere			
Countryside	All year		**M T W T F S S**
Campsite	All year		**M T W T F S S**

Campsite: Stagecoach in Cumbria 516 from Ambleside. **Station**: Windermere 8ml

P Parking (pay & display). NT members must display cards. Five car parks in the two valleys, but none in Grasmere village

NT properties nearby
Stagshaw Garden, Townend

Hare Hill

Over Alderley, Macclesfield, Cheshire SK10 4QB

❄🌳 1978 (5:E8)

Charming wooded and walled garden

This woodland garden, especially spectacular in early summer, includes azaleas, rhododendrons, hollies and hostas. At its heart is a delightful walled area with a pergola and wire sculptures. The surrounding parkland has attractive walks, including a link path to Alderley Edge (2ml).

★ Car park closes at 5

i T 0161 928 0075 (NT Altrincham office),
01625 584412 (Countryside office),
01625 828981 (Gardener)
F 01625 587555 (Countryside Office)

£ £2.70, child £1.25. Groups either by written appointment c/o Garden Lodge, Oak Road, Over Alderley, Macclesfield SK10 4QB, or tel. Gardener

🚶 To Alderley Edge 2ml

♿ **Grounds**: Partly accessible. Level access to walled garden

♿ Braille guide. Interesting scents

🏞 Near lake

🐕 Not in garden. On leads at all times on estate

➔ [118: SJ875765] **Bus**: Bakers 287 Wilmslow–Macclesfield (passing ▆ Alderley Edge), to within ¾ml. **Station**: Alderley Edge

Opening arrangements: Hare Hill			
25 Mar - 8 May	10 - 5		M T **W T** F **S S**
9 May - 29 May	10 - 5		**M T W T F S S**
1 Jun - 30 Oct	10 - 5		M T **W T** F **S S**

Open BH Mons & Good Fri. Last admission 1hr before closing

Unless indicated, last admission is always 30mins before closing time

2½ml; Prestbury 2½ml. **Road**: Between Alderley Edge and Macclesfield (B5087). Turn off N on to Prestbury Road, continue ¾ml. Hare Hill entrance on the left

P Parking, £1.50 (refunded on admission)

NT properties nearby
Alderley Edge, Dunham Massey, Lyme Park, Nether Alderley Mill, Quarry Bank Mill and Styal Estate, Tatton Park

Hawkshead and Claife

c/o Hill Top, Near Sawrey, Ambleside, Cumbria LA22 0LF

🔲🔲🔲🔲🔲🔲 1929   **(6:D8)**

Classic Lakeland village

The village, home to the Beatrix Potter Gallery, is surrounded by beautiful scenery, much of which is owned by the Trust. This includes four miles of access along Windermere lakeshore from Ash Landing to Low Wray Bay. Claife Woodlands and the low-lying small farms between Hawkshead and Lake Windermere are typical of the area. Just north of the village is the Courthouse, which dates from the 15th century and is all that remains of the village manorial buildings (once held by Furness Abbey). Claife Station, on the west bank of Windermere, is a late 18th-century viewing station with glimpses of the lake. At Wray Castle there is limited access to the grounds and occasional access to the castle, tel. property office for details.

⭐ There is a NT campsite in a superb location on the lakeshore at Low Wray [NY372012], open Easter to end Oct; charge (inc. NT members): tel. for details

ℹ️ T 015394 36269,
015394 44746/46534 (Wardens),
015394 32810 (Low Wray campsite),
015394 36471 (Shop) F 015394 36811
E hawkshead@nationaltrust.org.uk

Opening arrangements: Hawkshead										
Countryside	All year		M	T	W	T	F	S	S
Courthouse	19 Mar - 30 Oct	11 - 4	M	T	W	T	F	S	S

Hawkshead Courthouse: access by key from NT shop, The Square, Hawkshead; free admission, but no parking facilities. Approx. 1½ml walk from village

🏇 Guided walks available

♿ Level route on lakeshore of Windermere from Red Nab car park [SD385995]. Tel. for details. Access to the Courthouse up grassy slope, then short flight of steps with one handrail. **Shop**: Level entrance. Steps to upper floor

📷 See Beatrix Potter Gallery

🎒 Suitable for school groups

🚲 Lakeshore track for mountain bikes from Harrowslack (SD388960) to St Margaret's Church (NY374006) along Windermere lakeshore (west)

➡️ [96/97: SD352982] Hawkshead is 6ml SW of Ambleside. **Foot**: Off-road path from Windermere ferry to Sawrey; many footpaths in the area. **Ferry**: Windermere ferry. **Bus**: Stagecoach in Cumbria 505
🚂 Windermere–Coniston. Cross Lakes Shuttle from Bowness, April–Oct. Tel. 015394 45161 for details. **Station**: Windermere 6ml via vehicle ferry

P Pay & display car parks at Ash Landing (close to ferry) and Harrowslack; free car parks at Red Nab and Wray Castle. All close to Lake Windermere. Pay & display car parks (not NT) in Hawkshead village

NT properties nearby
Beatrix Potter Gallery, Fell Foot Park, Hill Top, *Gondola*, Tarn Hows

Hill Top

Near Sawrey, Hawkshead, Ambleside, Cumbria LA22 0LF

🏠⚜️📷 1944   **(6:D8)**

Delightful small 17th-century house where Beatrix Potter wrote many of her famous children's stories

Many of the enchanting illustrations for Beatrix Potter's little tales were inspired by Hill Top. It remains as she left it and in each room can be found something that appears in one of her books. The cottage garden contains the same pleasing mix of flowers, herbs, fruit and vegetables as grown by Beatrix. A selection of the original illustrations is displayed at the Beatrix Potter Gallery nearby.

There are special events at most Trust properties; please telephone 0870 458 4000 for details

What's new in 2005 Centenary of Beatrix Potter's purchase of Hill Top; tel. for more information

⭐ Hill Top is a small house and a timed entry system is operated to avoid overcrowding and to protect the fragile interior. This is a popular property, and visitors sometimes have to wait to enter. We regret that occasionally some visitors may not gain entry at all. School holidays are particularly busy so, if at all possible, come at the beginning or end of the season and enjoy a slightly quieter visit

ℹ️ **T** 015394 36269 **F** 015394 36811
E hilltop@nationaltrust.org.uk

£ £5, child £2, family £12. Discount available to Beatrix Potter Gallery ticket holders (not applicable for groups). Ticket office is in car park. Entry to shop and garden free on Thur & Fri when house closed. All tour groups must book

🐾 Occasional Beatrix Potter-themed guided walks in surrounding countryside with NT Warden

🚶 Walks on nearby Windermere lake shore – leaflet available

♿ Contact in advance. **Building**: Level entrance. Level access to 2 rooms downstairs. Many stairs with handrail to other floors. Seating available. Photograph album. **Grounds**: Partly accessible, some steps. **Shop**: Steps to entrance

♨️ Braille guide and large-print guide. Touchable objects

📷 Specialises in Beatrix Potter-related items; mail order available all year

Opening arrangements: Hill Top										
House	19 Mar - 30 Oct	10:30 - 4:30	**M**	**T**	**W**	T	F	**S**	**S**
	2 Jun - 3 Jun	10:30 - 4:30	M	T	W	**T**	**F**	S	S
	4 Aug - 25 Aug	10:30 - 4:30	M	T	W	**T**	**F**	S	S
	27 Oct - 28 Oct	10:30 - 4:30	M	T	W	**T**	**F**	S	S
Shop/garden	5 Mar - 13 Mar	10 - 4	M	T	W	T	F	**S**	**S**
	19 Mar - 30 Oct	10:30 - 5	**M**	**T**	**W**	T	F	**S**	**S**
	24 Mar - 28 Oct	10 - 5	M	T	W	**T**	**F**	S	S
	5 Nov - 18 Dec	10 - 4	M	T	W	T	F	**S**	**S**
	19 Dec - 23 Dec	10 - 4	**M**	**T**	**W**	**T**	**F**	S	S
	18 Feb - 26 Feb 06	10 - 4	**M**	**T**	**W**	**T**	**F**	**S**	**S**

Admission by timed ticket for all visitors. Open Good Fri

🍴 Bar lunches and evening meals at the Tower Bank Arms (NT-owned and let to tenant) nearby, during licensing hours. Tea-rooms in village

➡️ [96/97: SD370955] 2ml S of Hawkshead, in hamlet of Near Sawrey; 3ml from Bowness via ferry. **Foot**: Off-road path from ferry (2ml), marked. **Bus**: Stagecoach in Cumbria 505 ⇌ Windermere–Coniston. **Station**: Windermere 4½ml via vehicle ferry. **Road**: B5286 and B5285 from Ambleside (6ml), B5285 from Coniston (7ml)

P Free parking, 200yds. A large number of coaches and minibuses come to Hill Top, but the roads are busy and narrow, with few convenient parking or turning areas. Coaches will be advised of the various arrangements available when booking. Visitors may need to wait to park during summer holidays

NT properties nearby
Beatrix Potter Gallery, Fell Foot Park, Hawkshead, *Gondola*, Tarn Hows, Townend

---

Little Moreton Hall

Congleton, Cheshire CW12 4SD

🏛️ ✛ ✿ 🏠 📷 🍴 1938 (5:E9)

Moated manor house – the 'icon' of English Tudor domestic architecture

This is Britain's most famous and arguably finest timber-framed manor house. The drunkenly reeling south front, topped by a spectacular long gallery, opens onto a cobbled courtyard and the main body of the Hall. Magnificent wall paintings and a notable knot garden are of special interest.

ℹ️ **T** 01260 272018
E littlemoretonhall@nationaltrust.org.uk

Opening arrangements: Little Moreton Hall									
House	5 Mar - 6 Nov	11:30 - 5	M	T	**W**	**T**	**F**	**S**	**S**
	12 Nov - 18 Dec	11:30 - 4	M	T	W	T	F	**S**	**S**
Shop	As house								
Restaurant	As house								

Open BH Mons. Closes dusk if earlier. Access in Dec restricted to ground floor, garden, shop and restaurant. Special openings at other times for booked groups

For further information check our website www.nationaltrust.org.uk

£ £5.25, child £2.50, family £12.50. Groups £4.50, group visits outside normal hours £10. **Special openings (inc. NT members)**: £10. Voucher available for reduced entry to Biddulph Grange Garden when purchasing full-price adult ticket at Little Moreton Hall. **3–18 Dec**: children free

ℹ️ Optional free guided tours daily (Wed–Sun) 5 March–27 Nov

📅 Programme of events, inc. open-air theatre and regular events during normal opening hours. Chapel service Suns between 6 March & 6 Nov

♿ Designated parking in main car park, 100yds. **Building**: Level entrance. 3 wheelchairs, booking essential. Entrance and exit through great hall only. Stairs to other floors. Seating available. Photograph album. **WCs**: Adapted WC. **Grounds**: Fully accessible, some cobbles. Accessible route map. **Shop**: Level entrance. **Refreshments**: Level entrance. Large-print menu

👁 Braille guide and large-print guide. Sensory list. Handling collection

🏠 NT shop. Plant sales (herbs)

🍽 Licensed restaurant. Children's menu. Cold drinks available from shop

🍴 At car park and front lawn only

👶 Baby-changing facilities. Front-carrying baby slings and hip-carrying infant seats for loan

🏫 Suitable for school groups. Education room/centre. Live interpretation. Hands-on activities. Children's guide. Children's quiz/trail

🐕 On leads and only in car park

➡️ [118: SJ832589] **Bus**: Bakers 77 Congleton–Hanley (passing close ≆ Kidsgrove & Congleton), alight Brownlow Heath, 1½ml. **Station**: Kidsgrove 3ml; Congleton 4¼ml. **Road**: 4ml SW of Congleton, on E side of A34

P Parking, 100yds, £5 (refunded on admission). Open 11–6

NT properties nearby
Biddulph Grange Garden

Lyme Park

Disley, Stockport, Cheshire SK12 2NX

🏠 ♣ ♠ 🏠 🍽 🍸 1947 (5:E8)

Great estate with lavishly decorated house and fine gardens

Originally a Tudor house, Lyme was transformed by the Venetian architect Leoni into an Italianate palace. Some of the Elizabethan interiors survive and contrast dramatically with later rooms. The state rooms are adorned with Mortlake tapestries, Grinling Gibbons woodcarvings and an important collection of English clocks. The 6.8ha (17-acre) Victorian garden boasts impressive bedding schemes, a sunken parterre, an Edwardian rose garden, Jekyll-style herbaceous borders, reflection lake, a ravine garden and Wyatt conservatory. The garden is surrounded by a medieval deer park of almost 566ha (1400 acres) of moorland, woodland and parkland, containing an early 18th-century hunting tower (The Cage). Lyme appeared as 'Pemberley' in the BBC's adaptation of Jane Austen's novel *Pride and Prejudice*.

⭐ Lyme Park is owned and managed by the NT and partly financed by Stockport Metropolitan Borough Council

Opening arrangements: Lyme Park										
House	21 Mar - 30 Oct	1 - 5	M	T	W	T	F	S	S
Park	1 Apr - 31 Oct	8 - 8:30	M	T	W	T	F	S	S
	1 Nov - 31 Mar 06	8 - 6	M	T	W	T	F	S	S
Garden	5 Mar - 20 Mar	12 - 3	M	T	W	T	F	S	S
	21 Mar - 30 Oct	11 - 5	M	T	W	T	F	S	S
	5 Nov - 18 Dec	12 - 3	M	T	W	T	F	S	S
Shop	21 Mar - 30 Oct	11 - 5	M	T	W	T	F	S	S
	5 Nov - 18 Dec	12 - 4	M	T	W	T	F	S	S
	27 Dec - 1 Jan 06	12 - 4	M	T	W	T	F	S	S
	7 Jan - 19 Mar 06	12 - 4	M	T	W	T	F	S	S
Restaurant	21 Mar - 30 Oct	11 - 5	M	T	W	T	F	S	S
Coffee shop	21 Mar - 30 Oct	10:30 - 5	M	T	W	T	F	S	S
	5 Nov - 18 Dec	11 - 4	M	T	W	T	F	S	S
	27 Dec - 1 Jan 06	11 - 4	M	T	W	T	F	S	S
	7 Jan - 19 Mar 06	11 - 4	M	T	W	T	F	S	S

Open BH Mons and Good Fri 11–5. The Cage: April to Oct on 2nd and 4th weekends of each month. Paddock Cottage (17th-century hunting lodge): April to Oct on 1st & 3rd weekends of month, 1–4

Please note: groups must book in advance with the property

ⓘ **T** 01663 762023, 01663 766492 (Infoline), 01663 761406 (Learning), 01663 761413 (Shop) **F** 01663 765035 **E** lymepark@nationaltrust.org.uk

£ **House & Garden**: £6.20, child £3.10, family £15. **House only**: £4.50, child £2.30. **Garden only**: £3, child £1.50. **The Cage**: £1, child free

🎫 Taster tours of house at noon on open days. Guided tours of house, garden & park on some days, limited places. Enquire at information centre on arrival. House & garden tours by arrangement outside normal opening hours

😃 Programme of events

🚶 Walks leaflets in information centre

♿ Contact in advance. Separate designated parking. Enquire at admissions kiosk. Minibus (with small step) from main car park to house on days house is open. Drop-off point. **Building**: Many steps to entrance with handrail. Alternative accessible entrance. 4 wheelchairs. Stairs to other floors. Photograph album. **WCs**: Adapted WC. **Grounds**: Partly accessible, steep slopes, some steps. **Shop**: Level entrance. **Refreshments**: Steps to entrance with handrail, ramp available

📻 Induction loop in reception, shop, restaurant

👆 Braille guide

🏪 Shops in workshop courtyard and house courtyard

☕ Ale Cellar restaurant (licensed) in house. Children's menu. Park Coffee Shop in workshop courtyard. Children's menu. Ice-cream kiosk in main car park

🎋 Picnic tables in park

👶 Baby-changing and feeding facilities. Front-carrying baby slings and hip-carrying infant seats for loan. Children's play area. Bottle-warming facilities

🏫 Suitable for school groups. Education room/centre. Live interpretation. Children's guide. Children's quiz/trail. Family activity packs

🐕 Under close control and only in park. Limited shaded parking, dog hooks and water bowls in workshop courtyard

The Bright Gallery, Lyme Park, Cheshire

🚲 Off-road cycling on the 'Knott'

➡️ [109: SJ965825] **Foot**: Northern end of Gritstone Trail; paths to Macclesfield Canal, Poynton Marina 1ml and Peak Forest Canal 2¼ml. **Bus**: Arriva 60 from Macclesfield (passing close ≷ New Mills Central and Disley); otherwise Stagecoach 361 Stockport–Glossop, Trent 199 Buxton–Manchester Airport, both to park entrance. **Station**: Disley, ½ml from park entrance. NT courtesy bus from park admission kiosk to house for pedestrians on days house is open, tel. property for details. **Road**: Entrance on A6, 6½ml SE of Stockport (M60 exit 1), 12ml NW of Buxton (house and car park 1ml from entrance)

🅿️ Parking, £4. (£2 motorbike) refunded on purchase of adult house & garden ticket. £6 coach/minibus. Coaches bringing booked groups admitted free to Park

NT properties nearby
Alderley Edge, Dunham Massey, Hare Hill, High Peak Estate, Nether Alderley Mill, Quarry Bank Mill and Styal Estate

Parking in National Trust car parks is free for members

Mendips

Woolton, Liverpool

 | 2002 | (5:C8)

Childhood home of John Lennon

John Lennon lived at Mendips with his Aunt Mimi and Uncle George. This was where his passion for music began and where some of his early songs were written. The house evokes the time he spent here during his formative years.

What's new in 2005 Extracts from recorded interviews with former student lodgers

⭐ **There is no direct access by car or on foot**. Visits are by combined minibus tour only with 20 Forthlin Road, the childhood home of Paul McCartney. Any photography inside Mendips or duplication of audio tour material is strictly prohibited. You will be asked to deposit all handbags, cameras and recording equipment at the entrance to the house. No WC

ℹ️ **T** 0870 900 0256 (Infoline for Speke Hall, 20 Forthlin Road & Mendips), 0151 708 8574 (Booking line for morning tours), 0151 427 7231 (Booking line for afternoon tours)

£ **Joint ticket Forthlin Road & Mendips**: £12, child £1. **NT Members (to cover minibus)**: £6, child £1 (inc. NT members)

♿ **Building**: Steps to entrance. Ground floor accessible. Stairs to other floors. Seating available. Photograph album. **WCs**: Adapted WC

🍴 At nearby Speke Hall

🛍️ At nearby Speke Hall

👶 Pushchairs admitted

🏫 Suitable for school groups. Max. group size 15

Opening arrangements: Mendips								
19 Mar - 30 Oct		M	T	**W**	**T**	**F**	**S**	**S**

Admission by guided tour only, 4 tours depart on days open to the public. To guarantee a place on a tour visitors are advised to book in advance. Tours depart by minibus from city centre in the morning and Speke Hall in the afternoon. Tel. infoline to check times and pick-up points. Open BH Mons (booking essential)

➡️ [108: SJ422855] Access is via minibus from Liverpool city centre or Speke Hall

🅿️ No parking on site. Not suitable for coaches

NT properties nearby
59 Rodney Street, Formby, 20 Forthlin Road, Rufford Old Hall, Speke Hall

Nether Alderley Mill

Congleton Road, Nether Alderley, Macclesfield, Cheshire SK10 4TW

🏚️ 🔧 🍴 | 1950 | (5:E8)

15th-century mill beside a tranquil mill pool

With its heavy oak framework, low beams and floors connected by wooden ladders, set beneath an enormous sloping stone roof, this charmingly rustic mill is one of only four virtually complete corn mills in Cheshire.

What's new in 2005 Static display of mill machinery while survey work undertaken. Tours available

⭐ No WC

ℹ️ **T** 01625 584412 (Countryside office), 01625 527468 (Quarry Bank Mill reception) **E** netheralderleymill@nationaltrust.org.uk

£ £2.50, child £1.20, family £8

♿ **Building**: Steps to entrance. Stairs to other floors. Restricted headroom in places

🏫 Suitable for school groups

➡️ [118: SJ844763] **Bus**: Arriva 130 Manchester–Macclesfield (passing ≋ Alderley Edge). **Station**: Alderley Edge 2ml. **Road**: 1½ml S of Alderley Edge, on E side of A34

🅿️ Free parking. Space for one coach at a time, booking essential

NT properties nearby
Alderley Edge, Dunham Massey, Hare Hill, Quarry Bank Mill and Styal Estate, Tatton Park

Opening arrangements: Nether Alderley Mill								
1 Apr - 30 Oct	1 - 5	M	T	**W**	**T**	**F**	S	**S**

Open BH Mons

Please remember – your membership card is always needed for free admission

Quarry Bank Mill and Styal Estate

Styal, Wilmslow, Cheshire SK9 4LA

�</🔨🛗🍴🏠🍷🅿️♨️T 1939 **(5:D8)**

One of Britain's greatest industrial heritage sites, including complete working cotton mill

Quarry Bank Mill and Styal Estate once belonged to the wealthy Greg family who founded the Mill and gave the property to the National Trust. The water-powered Georgian mill still produces cotton calico, sold in the Mill Shop. Hands-on exhibits and demonstrations show how traditional spinning and weaving was transformed through the ingenuity of early textile engineers. The most powerful working waterwheel in Europe and two mill engines help to bring the past to life through sight, sound and smell. At the Apprentice House you can discover what 'home life' was like for the pauper children who worked in the Mill in the 1830s by exploring the dormitories, kitchen, schoolroom, parlour and attic. The adjoining garden contains traditional varieties of vegetables, fruit and herbs, as well as geese and hens. Visitors should allow at least 1½ hours to visit the Mill. Guided tours of the House take about 45 minutes. Styal Village was built by the Gregs to house the mill workers and is still a thriving

community. There are two chapels, the school, allotment gardens and cottages. The village and the estate of farmland and woodland walks along the River Bollin provide a delightful contrast to the grandeur of the Mill.

What's new in 2005 Greg Room refurbished to include Greg family portrait of 1765 (on long term loan)

⭐ A popular venue for educational visits, particularly on weekday mornings

ℹ️ **T** 01625 527468,
01625 415199 (Warden),
01625 445888 (Learning),
01625 445847 (Shop),
01625 445846 (Restaurant)
F 01625 539267
E quarrybankmill.reception@nationaltrust.org.uk

£ **Mill and Apprentice House**: £8, child £4.70, family £18. Groups (20+) £4.70. **Mill only**: £5.50, child £3.70, family £15. Groups £3.70. Discounted combined rail, bus and entry tickets from within Greater Manchester

🎫 Available for booked groups from 10.30 except BH Mons; plus evening opening 14 July. Guided tours of Mill at weekends at 2 all year, no extra charge for Mill ticket holders. Tours of Apprentice House: availability strictly limited during school term times

🎭 Programme of events. Tel. for details

🚶 Guided walk of woodlands and village every second Sun in month at 2, plus other specialist guided walks. Leaflet available

♿ Designated parking in main car park, 200yds. Transfer available. Drop-off point.
Building: Many steps to entrance with handrail. Chair lift available. 2 wheelchairs. Lift to function rooms or stairs with handrails. Mill: 3 floors accessible by ramps or chairlift. Restricted access for wheelchairs to Mill, particularly battery operated. Apprentice House: level access to ground floor.
WCs: Adapted WC. **Grounds**: Accessible route. **Shop**: Many steps to entrance with handrail, stairlift available.
Refreshments: Level entrance

🔊 Induction loop in Workshop only

♿ Braille guide and large-print guide. Sensory list

Opening arrangements: Quarry Bank Mill										
Mill	19 Mar - 30 Sep	10:30 - 5:30	M	T	W	T	F	S	S
	1 Oct - 18 Mar 06	10:30 - 5	M	T	W	T	F	S	S
Apprentice Hse	19 Mar - 30 Sep	See below	M	T	W	T	F	S	S
	1 Oct - 18 Mar 06	See below	M	T	W	T	F	S	S
Estate	All year	Daylight hours	M	T	W	T	F	S	S
Shop	As Mill								
Restaurant	19 Mar - 30 Sep	10:30 - 5	M	T	W	T	F	S	S
	4 Oct - 17 Mar 06	10:30 - 4	M	T	W	T	F	S	S
	1 Oct - 18 Mar 06	10:30 - 4:30	M	T	W	T	F	S	S

Open BH Mons. Mill: last admission 1½ hrs before closing. Mill open on school hol Mons in winter. Apprentice House open 2-4.30 weekdays, 11-4.30 weekends & school hols (Mar-Sep); 2-3.30 weekdays, 11-3.30 weekends and school hols (Oct-Mar). Admission to Apprentice House by timed ticket only, available from Mill on arrival. Apprentice House closed for conservation cleaning 12 – 23 Dec. Site closed 24 & 25 Dec

For general and membership enquiries, please telephone 0870 458 4000

 Selling goods made from cloth woven in the Mill and wide range of gifts and souvenirs. Mail order catalogue for Styal Calico available

🍽 Mill Restaurant (licensed) off Mill yard. Children's menu during school holidays. Mill Pantry Kiosk. Snacks and ice cream

🏠 Picnics on the Mill meadow

👶 Baby-changing and feeding facilities. Baby back-carriers admitted. Front-carrying baby slings and hip-carrying infant seats for loan. Children's play area

📖 Suitable for school groups. Education room/centre. Live interpretation. Hands-on activities. Children's quiz/trail. Adult study days

🐕 Under close control on estate. Must be on lead in Mill yard

🚲 No cycling in the woods

➡ [109: SJ835835] **Bus**: Styal Shuttle 200/1 ⊞ Manchester Airport–Wilmslow. **Station**: Styal, ½ml (not Sun); Manchester Airport 2ml; Wilmslow 2½ml. **Road**: 1½ml N of Wilmslow off B5166, 2½ml from M56, exit 5, 10ml S of Manchester. Heritage signs from A34 and M56

🅿 Parking, 200yds, £2.60. Coaches under 12ft high can drop off/collect from Mill yard by arrangement

NT properties nearby
Dunham Massey, Lyme Park, Nether Alderley Mill, Tatton Park

---

59 Rodney Street

The E. Chambré Hardman Studio, House & Photographic Collection, Liverpool L1 9EX

🏛 🖼 | 2003 | (5:B8)

Georgian terraced house – the studio and home of the photographer E. Chambré Hardman

Situated just below the Anglican Cathedral in the centre of Liverpool is this fascinating house, home between 1947 and 1988 to Edward Chambré Hardman and his wife Margaret. The house contains an extensive collection of photographs, the studio where most were taken,

Chambré Hardman's darkroom at 59 Rodney Street, Liverpool

the darkroom where they were developed and printed, the business records and the rooms complete with all their contents and ephemera of daily life. The subject matter of the photographs – portraits of the people in Liverpool, their city and the landscapes of the surrounding countryside – provide a record of a more prosperous time when Liverpool was the gateway to the British Empire and the world. Parallel to this is the quality of Hardman's work and his standing as a pictorial photographer.

⭐ Admission by timed ticket and guided tour only, to avoid overcrowding and to preserve the fragile contents. No photography allowed inside property

ℹ **T** 0151 709 6107 (Custodian), 0151 709 6261 (Booking)
E 59rodneystreet@nationaltrust.org.uk

£ £4.50, child £1.25, family £10

Opening arrangements: 59 Rodney Street		M	T	W	T	F	S	S
19 Mar - 30 Oct	11 - 4:15	M	T	**W**	**T**	**F**	**S**	**S**
5 Nov - 4 Dec	10 - 3:15	M	T	W	T	F	**S**	**S**

Admission by timed ticket only, inc. NT members. Open BH Mons. Visitors are advised to book in advance by tel. or email to Custodian. Tickets on the day subject to availability

Please see the area introductions for details of coast & countryside properties

🎓 Booked morning tours for groups (max. 6) by arrangement (extra charge inc. NT members £1.50)

♿ Separate designated parking, 50yds. Parking in Pilgrim St, behind Rodney St.
Building: Steps to entrance. Alternative accessible entrance. 3 steep staircases to other floors. Photograph album.
WCs: Adapted WC. **Shop**: Level entrance

👁 Braille guide and large-print guide

📷 Limited range of photographic prints available

👶 Pushchairs admitted

🏫 Suitable for school groups

➜ [108: SJ355895] Short walk north of Liverpool city centre. Rodney St is off Hardman St and Upper Duke St. **Foot**: City centre ½ml.
Ferry: Mersey Ferry 1ml. **Bus**: Frequent from surrounding areas. **Underground**: Liverpool Central ½ml. **Station**: Lime St ½ml

🅿 No parking on site. Off-site parking most days near Anglican Cathedral (pay & display). Slater St NCP. Limited parking Rodney St and Pilgrim St (pay & display)

NT properties nearby
Formby, 20 Forthlin Road, Mendips, Rufford Old Hall, Speke Hall

---

Rufford Old Hall

Rufford, nr Ormskirk, Lancashire L40 1SG

 1936   (5:C6)

One of Lancashire's finest 16th-century buildings

The spectacular Great Hall has an intricately carved 'moveable' wooden screen and dramatic hammer-beam roof. Evidence suggests that Shakespeare performed in this hall for the owner, Sir Thomas Hesketh, whose family owned Rufford for over 400 years. The house contains fine collections of 16th- and 17th-century oak furniture, arms, armour and tapestries. The grounds are laid out in late-Victorian style and feature a herbaceous border, orchard, topiary, sculpture and a woodland walk.

⭐ An admission charge may be applicable to NT members for special events. Please tel. for details

ℹ **T** 01704 821254 (Property office),
01704 823812 (Weddings/Events),
01704 823815 (Learning),
01704 823816/7 (Restaurant)
F 01704 823823
E ruffordoldhall@nationaltrust.org.uk

💷 £4.70, child £2.20, family £11.50. Groups £2.90, child £1.10. **Garden only**: £2.60, child £1.20

🎓 For groups, by arrangement

🎭 Programme of events, inc. indoor and outdoor plays and concerts, Victorian Christmas fair

♿ Designated parking in main car park, 20yds. **Building**: Level entrance. 2 wheelchairs. Steps from Great Hall to other areas. Seating available. Audio visual/video, photograph album. **WCs**: Adapted WC. **Grounds**: Fully accessible, some cobbles. Accessible route map. Some visitors may require assistance from their companion. **Shop**: Level entrance. **Refreshments**: Level entrance

👁 Braille guide and large-print guide. Sensory list

☕ The Old Kitchen Restaurant (licensed). Winter opening and Christmas dinners, tel. for details. Children's menu

🧺 Picnic tables in grounds

👶 Baby-changing facilities. Front-carrying baby slings for loan. Bottle-warming service. Early learning toys

🏫 Suitable for school groups. Education room/centre. Hands-on activities. Children's guide. Children's quiz/trail. Adult study days

🐕 On leads and only in grounds, not in formal gardens. Fresh water and bowl available; tether rings in front of shop

Opening arrangements: Rufford Old Hall										
House	19 Mar - 30 Oct	1 - 5	**M**	**T**	**W**	T	F	**S**	**S**
Garden	19 Mar - 30 Oct	11 - 5:30	**M**	**T**	**W**	T	F	**S**	**S**
Shop	19 Mar - 30 Oct	11 - 5	**M**	**T**	**W**	T	F	**S**	**S**
Restaurant	As shop								

Open Good Fri. Winter opening of shop and restaurant: tel. for details. Christmas gifts and lunches available Nov & Dec. Also open 6 Mar (Mother's Day) and 13 Mar

Unless indicated, last admission is always 30mins before closing time

Rufford Old Hall,
Lancashire

→ [108: SD462161] **Foot**: Adjoins towpath of Rufford extension of Leeds–Liverpool Canal. **Bus**: Arriva 303, Stagecoach in Lancashire 101 Preston–Ormskirk; Stagecoach in Lancashire 347 Southport–Chorley. **Station**: Rufford (U), not Sun, ½ml; Burscough Bridge 2½ml. **Road**: 7ml N of Ormskirk, in village of Rufford on E side of A59. From M6 exit 27, follow signs for Rufford

P Free parking, 10yds. Car park can be very busy on summer days. Limited coach parking

NT properties nearby
Formby, Gawthorpe Hall, Speke Hall

Sizergh Castle & Garden

Sizergh, nr Kendal, Cumbria LA8 8AE

🏠 🏛 ✿ 🍴 🐾 📷 📺 👤 1950   (6:E8)

Medieval house extended in Elizabethan times, with handsome gardens

Originally built in the Middle Ages by the Strickland family, who still live here, this imposing house has an exceptional series of oak-panelled rooms culminating in the Inlaid Chamber. Portraits, fine furniture and ceramics accumulated over centuries by the family are shown alongside their recent photographs. The garden includes two lakes and a superb rock garden. All this is set in a 638ha (1600-acre) estate crossed by public footpaths, providing

short walks from the castle to dramatic viewpoints over Morecambe Bay and the Lake District fells.

i **T** 015395 60951
E sizergh@nationaltrust.org.uk

£ £5.80, child £2.90, family £14.50. Groups £4.80. **Garden only**: £3.50, child £1.70

🏃 For booked groups only (book 21 days in advance). Tel. for details

🚶 Country walks on estate. Leaflets available from shop

♿ Separate designated parking, 250yds. Drop-off point. **Building**: Level entrance. 2 wheelchairs. Many stairs to other floors. Seating available. Photograph album, reproduction of Inlaid Chamber panelling in lower hall. **WCs**: Adapted WC. **Grounds**: Partly accessible, loose gravel paths, steep slopes. Accessible route map. 2 single-seater PMV. **Shop**: Ramped entrance. **Refreshments**: Steps to entrance with handrail, ramp available. Large-print menu. Tea-room is inside castle

👁 Braille guide and large-print guide. Sensory list

🛍 NT shop. Peat-free plants grown on the estate

Opening arrangements: Sizergh Castle & Garden										
Castle	23 Mar - 30 Oct	1:30 - 5:30	M	T	W	T	F	S	S
Garden	23 Mar - 30 Oct	12:30 - 5:30	M	T	W	T	F	S	S
Tea-room	As castle									
Shop	As garden									

There are special events at most Trust properties; please telephone 0870 458 4000 for details

◼ Tea-room in castle (queues likely)

◼ Tables available

◼ Baby-changing facilities. Hip-carrying infant seats for loan

◼ Suitable for school groups. Children's guide. Children's quiz/trail. Adult study days

◼ On public footpaths only, not in garden

→ [97: SD498878] 3½ml S of Kendal.
Cycle: NCN6 1¼ml. Regional route 20 passes main gate. **Bus**: Stagecoach in Cumbria 555/6 Keswick–Lancaster (passing close ▣ Lancaster); 552 Kendal–Arnside (passing ▣ Arnside). All pass ▣ Kendal.
Station: Oxenholme 3ml; Kendal (U) 3½ml.
Road: M6 exit 36 then A590 towards Kendal, take Barrow-in-Furness turning and follow brown signs. From Lake District take A591 S then A590 towards Barrow-in-Furness

▣ Parking, 250yds. Car park available only when property is open

NT properties nearby
Arnside Knott, Fell Foot Park, Townend

Speke Hall, Garden & Estate

The Walk, Liverpool L24 1XD

◼◼◼◼◼◼◼ 1944   **(5:C8)**

Tudor half-timbered house with rich interiors and fine gardens

The atmospheric interior of this rambling house spans many periods. Originally built in 1530, its Great Hall and priest hole date from Tudor times, while the Oak Parlour and smaller rooms, some with William Morris wallpapers, show the Victorian desire for privacy and comfort. There is also fine Jacobean plasterwork and intricately carved furniture. A fully equipped Victorian kitchen and servants' hall enable visitors to see 'behind the scenes'. The restored garden has spring bulbs, a rose garden, summer border and stream garden, and there are woodland walks and magnificent views of the Mersey basin and North Wales hills from The Bund, a high bank. Home Farm, a 5-minute walk from Speke Hall, is a model Victorian farm building, restored and part-adapted to provide a restaurant, shop and visitor facilities, and offers estate walks, children's play area and orchard.

What's new in 2005 Restored stationary farm engine operating on selected days of the week

★ Speke Hall is administered and financed by the National Trust with the help of a grant through the National Museums Liverpool

ℹ **T** 0151 427 7231, 08457 585702 (Infoline), 0151 728 5847 (Learning)
F 0151 427 9860
E spekehall@nationaltrust.org.uk

💷 £6.25, child £3.50, family £19. Groups £5.50, child £3. **Grounds & Home Farm only**: £3.25, child £1.75, family £10. Reduced rate when arriving by public transport, cycle or on foot

◼ Tudor tours by costumed guides when house open. Group tours of gardens and estate by arrangement

◼ Programme of events. Many free with admission ticket

◼ Walks on The Bund and elsewhere on the estate. Leaflet guide. Family estate trail available at reception

◼ Separate designated parking, 150yds. Drop-off point. **Building**: Level entrance. 4 wheelchairs, booking essential. Stairs to other floors. Photograph album. **WCs**: Adapted WC. **Grounds**: Accessible route map. Multi-seater transfer from Home Farm to mansion. **Shop**: Level entrance. **Refreshments**: Level entrance. Large-print menu

Opening arrangements: Speke Hall										
House	19 Mar - 30 Oct	1 - 5:30	M	T	**W**	**T**	**F**	**S**	**S**
	5 Nov - 4 Dec	1 - 4:30	M	T	W	T	**F**	**S**	**S**
Grounds	19 Mar - 30 Oct	11 - 5:30	**M**	**T**	**W**	**T**	**F**	**S**	**S**
	31 Oct - 18 Mar 06	11-Dusk	**M**	**T**	**W**	**T**	**F**	**S**	**S**
Home Farm	19 Mar - 17 Jul	11 - 5	M	**T**	**W**	**T**	**F**	**S**	**S**
	19 Jul - 4 Sep	11 - 5	M	**T**	**W**	**T**	**F**	**S**	**S**
	7 Sep - 30 Oct	11 - 5	M	**T**	**W**	**T**	**F**	**S**	**S**
	5 Nov - 4 Dec	11 - 4:30	M	T	W	T	**F**	**S**	**S**
Restaurant	As Home Farm									
Shop	As Home Farm									

Open BH Mons. Grounds (garden and estate) closed 24–26 Dec, 31 Dec, 1 Jan

⚐ Braille guide. Sensory list. Handling collection. Booking required

🗂 Located at Home Farm

🍽 Home Farm Restaurant. Children's menu

🅰 Designated picnic and family area adjacent to Home Farm

🚼 Baby-changing facilities. Front-carrying baby slings and hip-carrying infant seats for loan. Children's play area

▦ Suitable for school groups. Education room/centre. Live interpretation. Hands-on activities. Children's guide. Children's quiz/trail

🐾 On leads around woodland and estate walks

→ [108: SJ419825] **Cycle**: NCN62 1¾ml. **Bus**: Arriva 80, 180 ≋ Liverpool Lime Street–Liverpool Airport (passing ≋ Garston) or 82 ≋ Liverpool Lime Street–Speke, both to within ½ml. **Station**: Garston 2ml; Hunt's Cross 2ml. **Road**: On N bank of the Mersey, 1ml off A561 on W side of Liverpool Airport. Follow airport signs from M62 exit 6, A5300; M56 exit 12

P Free parking, 100yds

NT properties nearby
59 Rodney Street, Formby, 20 Forthlin Road, Mendips, Rufford Old Hall

---

Stagshaw Garden

Ambleside, Cumbria LA22 0HE

❖ 1957   (6:D8)

Steep woodland garden, noted for its flowering shrubs

The garden was created by the late Cubby Acland, Regional Agent for the Trust. It contains a fine collection of shrubs, including rhododendrons, azaleas and camellias. Adjacent to the garden are **Skelghyll Woods**, which offer delightful walks and access to the fells beyond.

Opening arrangements: Stagshaw Garden		
1 Apr - 30 Jun	10 - 6:30	M T W T F S S

July to end Oct: by appointment, send s.a.e. to Property Office, St Catherine's, Patterdale Road, Windermere LA23 1NH

★ No WC

i **T/F** 015394 46027
  E stagshaw@nationaltrust.org.uk

£ £2. Payment by honesty box at entrance

♿ **Grounds**: Partly accessible, steep slopes, narrow paths. Some visitors may require assistance from their companion

⚐ Interesting scents

🚼 Difficult for pushchairs

→ [90: NY380029] **Ferry**: Landing at Waterhead ½ml. **Bus**: Stagecoach in Cumbria 555/6, 599 from ≋ Windermere. **Station**: Windermere 4ml. **Road**: ½ml S of Ambleside on A591

P Parking. Very limited; access dangerous due to poor visibility; further pay & display parking for cars and coaches (not NT) ½ml at Waterhead

NT properties nearby
Ambleside Roman Fort, Bridge House, Townend, Windermere

Tatton Park

Knutsford, Cheshire WA16 6QN

🏠 🐾 🅱 ❖ 🍽 🗂 🍴 🔔 ⊤ 1960   (5:D8)

Magnificent estate with mansion, grand garden, deer park, farm and Tudor Old Hall

This is one of the most complete historic estates open to visitors. The early 19th-century Wyatt house sits amid a landscaped deer park and is opulently decorated, providing a fine setting for the Egerton family's collections of pictures, books, china, glass, silver and specially commissioned Gillow furniture. The theme of Victorian grandeur extends into the garden, with fernery, orangery, Tower garden, pinetum and Italian and Japanese gardens. The restored Walled Garden includes a kitchen garden and magnificent glasshouses, where traditional methods of gardening are used. Other features include the Tudor Old Hall, a working 1930s farm, a children's play area and speciality shops.

★ Tatton Park is financed, administered and maintained by Cheshire County Council. Without this commitment the Trust would not

Please note: groups must book in advance with the property

Opening arrangements: Tatton Park

House	19 Mar - 2 Oct	1 - 5	M	T	W	T	F	S	S
Gardens	19 Mar - 2 Oct	10 - 6	M	T	W	T	F	S	S
	4 Oct - 31 Mar 06	11 - 4	M	T	W	T	F	S	S
Tudor Old Hall	19 Mar - 2 Oct	12 - 5	M	T	W	T	F	S	S
Park	19 Mar - 2 Oct	10 - 7	M	T	W	T	F	S	S
	4 Oct - 31 Mar 06	11 - 5	M	T	W	T	F	S	S
Farm	19 Mar - 2 Oct	12 - 5	M	T	W	T	F	S	S
	8 Oct - 26 Mar 06	11 - 4	M	T	W	T	F	S	S
Restaurant	19 Mar - 2 Oct	10 - 6	M	T	W	T	F	S	S
	4 Oct - 31 Mar 06	11 - 4	M	T	W	T	F	S	S
Shops	19 Mar - 2 Oct	10:30 - 5	M	T	W	T	F	S	S
	4 Oct - 31 Mar 06	11 - 4	M	T	W	T	F	S	S

Open BH Mons. Last admission 1hr before closing. House: special opening Oct half-term & Christmas events in Dec. Guided tours Tues to Sun 12 and 12.15 by timed ticket (available from garden shop from 10.30) on first-come first-served basis. Limited number of tickets per tour. Tudor Old Hall: guided tours only, hourly Sat & Sun and Oct half-term (except Mon). Farm: Open Oct half-term and Feb half-term (except Mons)

have been able to acquire this property. Members have free admission to the house and gardens only, except during special events, and half-price entry to the Tudor Old Hall and farm. Members must pay car entry charges, and full admission to any special events, such as the RHS Flower Show on 20–24 July

i **T** 01625 534400, 01625 534435 (Infoline), 01625 534428 (Booking), 01625 534421 (Restaurant) **F** 01625 534403 **E** tatton@cheshire.gov.uk

£ **Mansion**: £3, child £2, family £8. Groups (12+) £2.40, child £1.60. **Gardens**: £3, child £2, family £8. Groups £2.40, child £1.60. **Farm**: £3, child £2, family £8. Groups £2.40, child £1.60. **Old Hall**: £3, child £2, family £8. Groups £2.40, child £1.60. NT members free to house (except guided tours) and gardens, but must pay (reduced rate) for entry to Tudor Old Hall and farm. Saver tickets available

Guided tours of mansion and Tudor Old Hall. Tours of the Japanese Garden available on selected days

Programme of events, inc. RHS Flower Show and Hallé concert

Walks leaflets available in shops – some waymarked walks

Designated parking in main car park. Limited spaces. Drop-off point. **Building**: Alternative accessible entrance, please ask staff for assistance. 3 wheelchairs. Stairs to other floors, stairclimber available. Photograph album. **WCs**: Adapted WC. **Grounds**: Partly accessible, loose gravel paths, slopes, some steps. Accessible route map. Some visitors may require assistance from their companion. 9 single-seater PMV. **Shop**: Level entrance. **Refreshments**: Level entrance

Sign interpreter and lip speaker by arrangement

Braille guide and large-print guide. Sensory list

Tatton Gifts (not NT), Housekeeper's Store selling estate and local food produce. Garden shop selling plants, produce and gifts

Stables Restaurant (not NT) (licensed) in stableyard. Serves hot and cold food throughout the day from quality local ingredients. Children's menu

In parkland

Baby-changing facilities. Children's play area

Suitable for school groups. Education room/centre. Children's quiz/trail. Adult study days. Living history

On leads at farm and under close control in park, not in gardens

Cycle tracks

→ [109/118: SJ745815] **Cycle**: Cheshire Cycleway passes property. **Bus**: Big House Bus from Altrincham Interchange, Sun April–Sept only; Bakers 27 from Macclesfield (passing close Macclesfield) June–Oct only; otherwise from surrounding areas to Knutsford, then 2ml. **Station**: Knutsford 2½ml. **Road**: 2ml N of Knutsford, 4ml S of Altrincham, 5ml from M6, exit 19; 3ml from M56, exit 7, well signposted on A556; entrance on Ashley Road, 1½ml NE of junction A5034 with A50

P Parking, £4, charge inc. NT members

NT properties nearby
Alderley Edge, Dunham Massey, Little Moreton Hall, Lyme Park, Quarry Bank Mill and Styal Estate

Parking in National Trust car parks is free for members

Townend

Troutbeck, Windermere, Cumbria LA23 1LB

 1948 (6:E8)

Fine example of Lake District vernacular architecture

Largely 17th-century, the solid stone and slate house is an exceptional survival. It belonged to a wealthy 'statesman' farming family and contains carved woodwork, books, papers, furniture and fascinating domestic implements from the past, largely accumulated by the Browne family who lived here from 1626 to 1943. A real fire burns in the 'down house' most days, lending a homely atmosphere.

i **T** 015394 32628 (Custodian)
 F 015394 32628
 E townend@nationaltrust.org.uk

£ £3.40, child £1.70, family £8.50

Building: Steps to entrance

Sensory list

Children's quiz/trail

➔ [90: NY407023] 3ml SE of Ambleside at S end of Troutbeck village. **Bus**: Stagecoach in Cumbria 555/6, 599 from ➤ Windermere, alight Troutbeck Bridge, then 1½ml. **Station**: Windermere 2½ml

Townend at Troutbeck, Cumbria

Opening arrangements: Townend								
23 Mar - 30 Oct	1 - 5	M	T	**W**	**T**	**F**	**S**	**S**
Open BH Mons. Closes dusk if earlier								

P Free parking. Coaches must apply to Cumbria County Council (Legal Services) for permission to use a restricted road if visiting Townend. Tel. property or NT NW regional office for guidance. Minibuses can access Townend, and this may be a preferable option for groups

NT properties nearby
Ambleside Roman Fort, Stagshaw Garden

Ullswater and Aira Force

Tower Buildings, Watermillock, Penrith, Cumbria CA11 0JS

1906 (6:E7)

Beautiful lake winding through a glaciated valley, and an impressive waterfall

Dramatic walks around Aira Force waterfall, renowned in Victorian times as a beauty spot, provide one of the highlights of the Trust's ownership in the valley. This totals 5242ha (13,000 acres) of fell and woodland, and four farms (including Glencoyne, the largest). There is access to parts of Brotherswater and Ullswater, site of Wordsworth's famous daffodils.

i **T** 017684 82067, 017684 82467 (Warden)
 F 017684 82802
 E ullswater@nationaltrust.org.uk

Walks leaflet available

Access to Victorian glade and Aira Green on the shore of Ullswater but not to waterfall. **WCs**: Adapted WC. **Refreshments**: Ramped entrance

Tea–room (not NT) at Aira Force. Tel. 017684 82881. Tea–room (not NT) at Side Farm, Patterdale. Tel. 017684 82337 (walkers only, no parking)

Steps and slopes to waterfall at Aira Force, difficult for pushchairs

Suitable for school groups

Opening arrangements: Ullswater and Aira Force							
All year	M	T	W	T	F	S	S

➡ [90: NY401203 – Aira Force] 7ml S of Penrith. **Cycle**: NCN71 2ml. **Bus**: Stagecoach in Cumbria 108 ☒ Penrith–Patterdale. **Station**: Penrith 10ml

🅿 Parking. Two pay & display car parks at Aira Force and Glencoyne Bay. NT members must display cards. Coaches by arrangement

NT properties nearby
Acorn Bank Garden, Townend

Wasdale, Eskdale and Duddon

The Lodge, Wasdale Hall, Wasdale, Cumbria CA20 1ET

🏛🍴🚻🏃🎞🏃🐕 1929   (6:D8)

Vast area of open country from wild Wasdale to the River Duddon estuary

In Wasdale the Trust owns England's highest mountain, Scafell Pike, and deepest lake, Wastwater, which has impressive scree slopes. Almost the whole of the surrounding mountains are NT-owned, including Great Gable and the famous historic wall patterns at the valley head. Lower down the valley is the wooded and tranquil Nether Wasdale Estate. Over 7000ha (17,000 acres) and eleven farms are protected in neighbouring Eskdale, with extensive areas of fell, six farms and Hardknott Roman Fort. In the beautiful Duddon valley the Trust cares for almost 3000ha (7400 acres) and nine farms.

⭐ The stunningly located NT campsite at Wasdale Head (with WC for the less able and shop) is open Easter to end Oct (and Nov to Easter 2006 with limited facilities) [NY183076]; charge (inc. NT members): tel. or visit www.wasdalecampsite.org.uk for details

ℹ **T** 019467 26064 (Property Office), 019467 26110 (Warden, Wasdale), 01229 716552 (Warden, Duddon & Eskdale), 019467 26220 (Campsite) **F** 019467 26115 **E** wasdale@nationaltrust.org.uk

🎦 Suitable for school groups

Opening arrangements: Wasdale
| All year | M T W T F S S |

➡ [NY152055] Wasdale – Wastwater: 5ml E of A595 Cumbrian coast road from Barrow to Whitehaven, turning at Gosforth. Also from Santon Bridge. Eskdale [NY177013] – Boot: 6ml E of A595, turning at Eskdale Green. Also from Santon Bridge. Duddon [NY196932] – Ulpha: 3ml N of A595, turning at Duddon Bridge near Broughton-in-Furness. **Station**: Drigg 8ml; Dalegarth (Ravenglass & Eskdale Rly) ¼ml from Eskdale; Foxfield 8ml from Duddon; Seascale 8ml from Wasdale

🅿 Parking (pay & display). At Wasdale Head

NT properties nearby
Dalton Castle, Sandscale Haws

Windermere and Troutbeck (including Bridge House)

St Catherine's, Patterdale Road, Windermere, Cumbria LA23 1NH

🏠🏛🍴🚻🏃🐕 1927   (6:E8)

Fine varied walking country around popular Lake Windermere

This property includes the beautiful and secluded head of the Troutbeck valley, as well as several sites next to Windermere and six farms. One of these, Troutbeck Park, was once owned by Beatrix Potter and was her largest farm. Ambleside Roman Fort, tiny Bridge House in Ambleside and Cockshott Point on the lake at Bowness-on-Windermere are all popular places to visit. Footpaths lead from Ambleside over Wansfell to the Troutbeck Valley and offer high-level views and contrasting valley landscapes. A Community Education Officer is based at the property and educational group visits and other activities can be arranged.

⭐ No WC

ℹ **T/F** 015394 46027, 015394 32617 (Bridge House), 015394 46402 (Learning) **E** windermere@nationaltrust.org.uk

🛡 Programme of events, inc. annual Out-and-About events

For general and membership enquiries, please telephone 0870 458 4000

Opening arrangements: Windermere										
	All year		**M**	**T**	**W**	**T**	**F**	**S**	**S**	
Bridge House	25 Mar - 31 Oct	10 - 5	**M**	**T**	**W**	**T**	**F**	**S**	**S**	

♿ Contact in advance. **Grounds**: Partly accessible. Accessible route

⚑ At Bridge House, Ambleside

■ Suitable for school groups. Education room/centre. Hands-on activities. Adult study days

→ [90: NY407023 – Townend] **Bus**: Stagecoach in Cumbria 555/6, 599 from 🚉 Windermere, alight Troutbeck Bridge, then 1½ml walk. **Station**: Windermere 2½ml. **Road**: Troutbeck is signposted E of A591 Windermere to Ambleside road

P Car parks (not NT)

NT properties nearby
Fell Foot Park, Stagshaw Garden, Townend

Wordsworth House

Main Street, Cockermouth, Cumbria CA13 9RX

⚑ ❊ ⚑ ♔ 1938   **(6:C6)**

Fine Georgian town house, the birthplace and childhood home of William Wordsworth

Wordsworth House provides an opportunity to experience something of the Wordsworths' life in 1770s Cockermouth. Following painstaking research the house has recently been transformed using historic and reproduction items to give a picture of the home in which young William and his sister Dorothy grew up. Visitors are welcome to touch and use items in the 'working rooms' of the house including the fascinating Georgian kitchen. As in any home, there are different activities going on in the house each day and sometimes special events. Costumed interpreters provide an insight into the daily life of the family and their servants. Visitors can enjoy the rare example of a northern Georgian townhouse garden and the Terrace walk where William and Dorothy loved to play. The visitor reception area and the Discovery Room with its interactive touchscreens and written material provide a chance for the whole family to find out more about the house and the early life and inspiration of one of the greatest poets in the English language.

What's new in 2005 Events and 'hands-on' activities. Tel. for details

ⓘ **T** 01900 820882 (Opening times and prices), 01900 824805 (Other enquiries), 01900 820880 (Shop) **F** 01900 820883 **E** wordsworthhouse@nationaltrust.org.uk

£ £4.50, child £2.50, family (2 adults & 2 children) £13. Groups £3.50, child £1.50. Reduced rate when arriving by public transport. Additional charges may apply for some living history activities for groups out of hours. Reciprocal discount ticket available from Wordsworth House allows visitors to enjoy Dove Cottage and Rydal Mount (nr Grasmere, not NT) at reduced prices

🗺 Introductory talks for groups – book in advance. Out-of-hours tours Tues, Wed, Thur am only

♿ Very limited parking on Low Sand Lane, adjacent to house. Drop-off point. **Building**: Access to ground floor of house via lift, located in visitor reception. Ground floor accessible. No access to other floors except Discovery Room. Photograph album, computer. **WCs**: Adapted WC. **Grounds**: Partly accessible. Accessible route. Level gravel paths for access except for terrace. **Shop**: Level entrance

💬 Braille guide and large-print guide. Touchable objects, interesting scents and sounds. Handling collection

😬 Refreshments available at nearby cafés

🚼 Baby-changing and feeding facilities. Front-carrying baby slings and hip-carrying infant seats for loan

■ Suitable for school groups. Education room/centre. Live interpretation. Hands-on activities. Children's guide. Adult study days. Daily activities for families, including costumes to try on, and toys in the children's bedroom to play with

Opening arrangements: Wordsworth House										
House	21 Mar - 29 Oct	11 - 4:30	**M**	**T**	**W**	**T**	**F**	**S**	S	
Shop	9 Mar - 24 Dec	10 - 5	**M**	**T**	**W**	**T**	**F**	**S**	S	
	4 Jan - 28 Jan 06	10 - 4	M	**T**	**W**	**T**	**F**	**S**	S	

Admission by timed ticket available from visitor reception. Tel. for opening details. Education groups: 21 Mar–29 Oct: Tues, Wed & Thur 9.30–11 and at other times by arrangement. Booking essential

Please see the area introductions for details of coast & countryside properties

On leads, in garden only

➡ [89: NY118307] **Cycle**: NCN71 (C2C) 7ml.
Bus: Stagecoach in Cumbria X4/5
⊞ Penrith–Workington, Benson/Hobson/
Reay's 35/6 Workington–Cockermouth. All
pass close ⊞ Workington. **Station**: Maryport
6½ml. **Road**: Just off A66, in Cockermouth
town centre

P No parking on site. Parking in town centre car
parks. Long stay car park (not NT) 300yds on
Wakefield Road, walk back over footbridge to
house

NT properties nearby
Buttermere and Ennerdale

Children in
Georgian
costume at
Wordsworth
House,
Cockermouth,
Cumbria

Properties open less often

This section includes National Trust
properties, often tenanted, which are open
two days a week or less (plus Bank
Holidays in some cases). Visits to some
must be made by prior arrangement and
where this applies admission prices are not
shown (please ask when making contact).
**Full details are on our website
www.nationaltrust.org.uk
or obtainable from the Membership
Department, tel. 0870 458 4000.**

Dalton Castle

Market Place, Dalton-in-Furness, Cumbria
LA15 8AX   (**6:D9**)

14th-century tower with display on the painter
George Romney.

⭐ Opened on behalf of the Trust by the Friends
of Dalton Castle

ℹ **T** 01524 701178 (Property office)
F 01524 701178
E daltoncastle@nationaltrust.org.uk

Opening arrangements: Dalton Castle		
26 Mar - 24 Sep	2 - 5	M T W T F **S** S

Derwent Island House

Derwent Island, Lake Road, Keswick,
Cumbria CA12 5DJ   (**6:D7**)

Intriguing 18th-century house on an idyllic
wooded island in Derwentwater.

⭐ Open on five days of the year only. No WC

ℹ **T** 015394 35599 (Regional office),
017687 73780 (Shop/info centre at Keswick)
E borrowdale@nationaltrust.org.uk

Opening arrangements: Derwent Island House
Admission by timed ticket. The house is privately let, but parts are open to the public by booked timed ticket on: Wed 8 June, Sun 26 June, Sun 24 July, Sun 21 Aug, Wed 31 Aug. For booking form send s.a.e. to: The National Trust (Derwent Island Bookings), The Hollens, Grasmere, Ambleside, Cumbria LA22 9QZ

Dunham Massey: White Cottage

Park Lane, Little Bollington, Altrincham,
Cheshire WA14 4TJ   (**5:D8**)

Recently restored timber-framed cottage, built
c.1500.

⭐ All visits must be booked through the NT
Altrincham office, tel. 0161 928 0075 Mon to
Fri 9–5

Opening arrangements: White Cottage		
3 Apr - 30 Oct	2 - 5	M T W T F S **S**
NB: open last Sun of each month only		

Unless indicated, last admission is always 30mins before closing time

South West South & South East
London East of England
East Midlands West Midlands
North West **Yorkshire** North East
Wales Northern Ireland

Yorkshire is world renowned for the beauty and scale of its scenery and many of the county's most outstanding stretches of coast and countryside are in the care of the National Trust. The **Malham Tarn Estate** and **Upper Wharfedale** protect some of the finest upland landscapes in the Yorkshire Dales, with limestone pavements, waterfalls, and flower-rich hay meadows criss-crossed with stone walls and studded with traditional field barns. This is magnificent walking country with dramatic and varied scenery. At the gateway to Swaledale, on the edge of Richmond, lie **Hudswell Woods**, an area of semi-natural ancient woodland adjacent to the River Swale, reputedly England's fastest flowing river.

There is further wild and open country due east at **Scarthwood Moor**, from where there are fine views over the Pennines. Further east is the delightful valley of **Farndale**, famed for its dramatic springtime display of wild daffodils.

The Trust also owns **Bridestones**, **Crosscliff** and **Blakey Topping**, within the North York Moors National Park, as well as the bent pinnacle of **Roseberry Topping**, used as a beacon station at the time of the Armada and

The Peak Alum Works at Ravenscar, North Yorkshire, looking towards the North Sea

again when Napoleon threatened invasion.

The spine of the Pennine chain runs through the south west of the area, and at **Hardcastle Crags**, near Hebden Bridge, there are waymarked trails and a rich variety of birdlife.

Near Huddersfield lies the **Marsden Moor Estate**, with many interesting archaeological remains and much wildlife interest, including significant numbers of breeding moorland birds. This whole area rewards exploration on foot. There are also good walking opportunities at the strange and fantastic geological formations of **Brimham Rocks** near Pateley Bridge, set in open moorland overlooking Nidderdale.

The Trust cares for twelve miles of Yorkshire's wild and rugged coastline, including **Newbiggin Cliffs**, where razor-bills and guillemots nest, and **Cayton Bay** and **Hayburn Wyke** near Scarborough. These areas of wooded valley and cliffs are notable for their abundance of wild flowers. Further north, Trust land at **Runswick** and **Port Mulgrave** is best viewed from the Cleveland Way long-distance footpath. At the **Old Coastguard Station** in Robin Hood's Bay and the Trust's **Coastal Centre, Ravenscar** there are fascinating insights into the local wildlife and geology, while the **Peak Alum Works** explain the alum industry and history of this early industrial site.

Hardcastle Crags, West Yorkshire

Previous page: Cowbar Nab at Staithes, North Yorkshire, the birthplace in 1728 of Captain Cook

Brimham Rocks, North Yorkshire

Regional Highlights for Visitors with Disabilities ...

Special arrangements can be made at **Malham Tarn** and **Brimham Rocks** for visitors with disabilities (tel. the properties for details).

...and for Families
The Old Coastguard Station and **Coastal Centre** at **Ravenscar** have rockpool aquariums; **Townhead Barn** at Malham has hands-on displays for children.

Further Information
Please contact the Membership Department, PO Box 39, Warrington WA5 7WD.
Tel. 0870 458 4000.
Email: enquiries@thenationaltrust.org.uk

Farm buildings near Cray, Upper Wharfedale, North Yorkshire

OS Grid Reference

OS grid references for main properties with no individual entry (OS Landranger map series numbers given in brackets)

Cayton Bay	[101] TA063850
Farndale	[94] SE654994
Hayburn Wyke	[101] TA010970
Hudswell Woods	[92] NZ153005
Newbiggin Cliffs	[93] TA827105
Peak Alum Works	[94] NZ973024
Port Mulgrave	[94] NZ796175
Runswick	[94] NZ808165
Scarthwood Moor	[94] SE465995

Beningbrough Hall & Gardens

Beningbrough, York, North Yorkshire YO30 1DD

🏠 🐾 ♣ 🗄 💼 🚶 🔔 ⚓ 🍷 1958   **(5:G4)**

18th-century mansion with fine interiors and walled garden

York's 'country house and garden', this imposing Georgian mansion was built in 1716 and contains one of the most impressive baroque interiors in England. Exceptional wood carving, an unusual central corridor running the full length of the house and over 100 portraits on loan from the National Portrait Gallery can be seen. There is also a fully equipped Victorian laundry, delightful walled garden and interesting sculptures in wood.

⭐ Most rooms have no electric light. Visitors wishing to make a close study of the interior and portraits should avoid dull days early and late in the season. A series of building and development works will at times affect the external appearance of the house in 2005

ℹ️ **T** 01904 470666, 01904 470082 (Shop), 01904 470513 (Restaurant) **F** 01904 470002 **E** beningbrough@nationaltrust.org.uk

💷 £6.30, child £3.20, family £14.50. Groups £5.70, child £2.90. **Garden, laundry, potting shed & exhibitions only**: £5.30, child £2.70, family £13. Groups £4.70, child £2.35. Reduced rate when arriving by cycle

🚶 Garden walks most weekends

💮 Programme of events. Tel. for details

♿ Separate designated parking, 20yds. Drop-off point. **Building**: Many steps to entrance with handrail. Alternative accessible entrance. Level entrance to reception building. 3 wheelchairs. Ground floor accessible. Stairs with handrail to other floors. Wheelchairs available on all floors. Seating available. **WCs**: Adapted WC. Approach to WC is over a short cobbled footpath (15m). **Grounds**: Fully accessible, hard gravel paths, some cobbles. Accessible route. **Shop**: Level entrance. **Refreshments**: Level entrance

👁️ Braille guide. Sensory list

Opening arrangements: Beningbrough Hall										
House	5 Mar - 26 Jun	12 - 5	M	T	W	T	F	S	S
	27 Jun - 28 Aug	12 - 5	M	T	W	T	F	S	S
	29 Aug - 30 Oct	12 - 5	M	T	W	T	F	S	S
Grounds	As house	11 - 5:30							
Shop	As house	11 - 5:30							
Restaurant	As house	11 - 5							

Open Good Fri. Limited opening Feb 05 half-term. Tel. for details

🗄 NT shop. Plant sales

💼 Licensed restaurant. Lunches 12-2. Gluten-free and vegan lunch options available, 30 mins notice required. Children's portions and lunch boxes. Kiosk in the garden open on busy days

🖼 In walled garden

🚼 Baby-changing facilities. Front-carrying baby slings and hip-carrying infant seats for loan. Wilderness play area

🏫 Suitable for school groups. Education room/centre. Children's quiz/trail. Family activity packs. Live interpretation in the laundry (tel. for dates)

🚴 2ml of NT permitted cycle path through parkland. NT-Sustrans leaflet available

The enfilade viewed from the State Dressing Room at Beningbrough Hall, North Yorkshire

Please see the area introductions for details of coast & countryside properties

➡ [105: SE516586] **Cycle**: NCN65.
Bus: Stephensons/Hutchinson 31 ⊠
York–Easingwold. **Station**: York 8ml.
Road: 8ml NW of York, 2ml W of Shipton,
2ml SE of Linton-on-Ouse (A19)

🅿 Free parking, 100yds. Coaches must come
via A19 and use coach entrance. No coach
access from the west via Aldwark toll bridge

NT properties nearby
Fountains Abbey & Studley Royal, Nunnington
Hall, Rievaulx Terrace & Temples, Treasurer's
House

Bridestones, Crosscliff and Blakey Topping

Smout House, Bransdale, Fadmoor, York, North
Yorkshire YO62 7JL

�' 🕈 🖋 🚶 1944   **(5:I3)**

Moorland nature reserve

The Bridestones and Crosscliff Estate covers an
area of 488ha (1205 acres) and is a mixture of
farmland, open moorland and woodland.
Bridestones Moor, named after its peculiar rock
formations created from sandstone laid down
under the sea during the Jurassic period, is a
SSSI and nature reserve with typical moorland
vegetation, including three species of heather,
an ancient woodland estimated to date from the
end of the last Ice Age, and herb-rich meadows.
The Bridestones Nature Trail is approximately
1½ml long and leads visitors through a range of
habitats. Blakey Topping at the northern end of
Crosscliff Moor is the result of massive erosion
by glacial meltwater and today gives a superb
360-degree view from its summit.

★ WC at Staindale Lake car park

ℹ **T** 01751 431693, 01751 460396 (Warden)
F 01751 430169
E bridestones@nationaltrust.org.uk

💷 Admission free. Donations welcome. Access
by car is via Forest Enterprise's Forest Drive:
toll payable (inc. NT members)

Opening arrangements: Bridestones		
All year		M T W T F S S

🖵 Programme of events. Tel. for details

♿ Designated parking in main car park.
WCs: Adapted WC. **Grounds**: The
Bridestones accessible via 400yds 1:10 track.
Valley bottom accessible along rough track

🛇 No barbecues

🎒 Suitable for school groups. Hands-on
activities. Adult study days

🐕 On leads

🚲 No cycles in Nature Reserve

➡ [94: SE877906] In North York Moors National
Park. **Foot**: From Hole of Horcum via Old
Wives' Way. **Cycle**: along Forest Drive.
Bus: To Bridestones: Moorsbus from
Thornton le Dale (connections from York and
Scarborough), Sun, May–Oct and daily in
Aug; otherwise Yorkshire Coastline 840
Leeds–Whitby (passing ⊠ York) to within
2¼ml. To Blakey Topping: Yorkshire Coastliner
as above, but to within 1¼ml. **Road**: 3½ml
along Dalby Forest Drive (toll payable) which
starts 2½ml N of Thornton-le-Dale NE of
Pickering

🅿 Free parking (not NT) at Hole of Horcum for
Blakey Topping, 100yds. Further parking at
Staindale Lake or Crosscliff Viewpoint

NT properties nearby
Nunnington Hall, Ormesby Hall, Rievaulx Terrace &
Temples, Yorkshire Coast

Brimham Rocks

Summerbridge, Harrogate, North Yorkshire
HG3 4DW

�' 🏠 🖶 🛇 🖵 🚶 1970   **(5:F4)**

Dramatic moorland rock formations

At a height of nearly 300m, Brimham Rocks
enjoy spectacular views over the surrounding
countryside. Set within the Nidderdale Area of
Outstanding Natural Beauty, this fascinating
moorland is filled with strange and fantastic rock
formations and is rich in wildlife.

★ The property can be extremely busy in July
and August

Unless indicated, last admission is always 30mins before closing time

Opening arrangements: Brimham Rocks										
	All year	8 – dusk	M	T	W	T	F	S	S
Shop/	12 Mar - 22 May	11 - 5	M	T	W	T	F	S	S
exhibition	28 May - 30 Sep	11 - 5	M	T	W	T	F	S	S
& kiosk	1 Oct - 30 Oct	11 - 5	M	T	W	T	F	S	S
.	6 Nov - 18 Dec	11–dusk	M	T	W	T	F	S	S

Facilities may close in bad weather. Shop, kiosk and exhibition room open daily during local school holidays, also BHols, 26 Dec & 1 Jan, weather permitting

i **T** 01423 780688 (Office), 01423 780768 (Warden) **F** 01423 781020 **E** brimhamrocks@nationaltrust.org.uk

Drop-off point. Building: Steps to entrance. 1 wheelchair, booking essential. Many stairs with handrail to other floors. **WCs**: Adapted WC. **Grounds**: Partly accessible. Surfaced path from car park to main rocks. Slopes and rough surfaces. Some visitors may require assistance from their companion. **Shop**: Steps to entrance

Braille guide and large-print guide. Touchable objects

Kiosk near Brimham House. Serves light refreshments

Baby-changing facilities

Suitable for school groups. Exhibition

Under strict control at all times and on leads during April, May & June (ground-nesting birds)

→ [99: SE206650] 10ml SW of Ripon. **Foot**: Nidderdale Way passes through. **Bus**: Keighley & District 802 Bradford–Leyburn (Sun, June–Oct only); otherwise Harrogate & District 24 Harrogate–Pateley Bridge, alight Summerbridge, 2ml. **Road**: 11ml NW of Harrogate off B6165, 10ml SW of Ripon, 4ml E of Pateley Bridge off B6265

P Parking (pay & display). £3 up to 4 hrs, £4 over 4 hrs; motorcycle free; minibus £7 all day; coach £12 all day; members' season ticket available from property to display in car. Pay machines only accept coins. Coaches cannot be accepted on busy days

NT properties nearby
Fountains Abbey & Studley Royal

East Riddlesden Hall

Bradford Road, Keighley, West Yorkshire
BD20 5EL

⬛ ⬛ ✳ ⬛ ⬛ ⬛ ⬛ ⬛ | 1934 | (5:F5)

Intimate 17th-century manor house with oak-framed barns and a lovely garden

The house has distinctive architectural features and is set in mature grounds with beech trees and a large duck pond. The interior has a wonderful ambience, furnished with textiles, Yorkshire oak furniture and pewter, together with fine examples of 17th-century embroidery. There is also a handling collection for visitors to discover. The ruined façade of the Starkie wing, covered in clematis, honeysuckle and roses, provides a dramatic backdrop to the garden. Wild flowers, perennials, lavender and a fragrant herb border provide a changing carpet of colour throughout the year, whilst the orchard garden contrasts with the more formal borders.

What's new in 2005 17th-century Great Barn open. Evening tours and supper available (min. 20 people). Tel. for details

i **T** 01535 607075 (Property office), 01535 646231 (Weddings/Functions), 01909 511061 (Box office) **F** 01535 691462 **E** eastriddlesden@nationaltrust.org.uk

£ £4, child £2, family £10. Groups £3.50, child £1.80. £1 off admission when arriving via Keighley & District Transport buses

Costumed interpreters July and Aug – Sun, Mon, Tues

Programme of events, inc. Spring Fair, outdoor concerts, children's events, textile exhibitions, craft fair. Tel. for details

Opening arrangements: East Riddlesden Hall										
House	19 Mar - 29 Jun	12 - 5	M	T	W	T	F	S	S
	2 Jul - 31 Aug	12 - 5	M	T	W	T	F	S	S
	3 Sep - 30 Oct	12 - 5	M	T	W	T	F	S	S
Shop/tea-room	19 Mar - 30 Oct	As house							
	5 Nov - 18 Dec	12 - 4	M	T	W	T	F	S	S

Open BH Mons and Good Fri. Open additional days in school holidays. Shop & tea-room open (pre-booked lunches) 6 March (Mother's Day) 12–5

There are special events at most Trust properties; please telephone 0870 458 4000 for details

♿ Designated parking in main car park, 100yds. 3 spaces. Drop-off point. **Building**: Steps to entrance. Alternative accessible entrance, ramp available. 2 wheelchairs. Ground floor accessible. Many stairs with handrail to other floors. Seating available. Photograph album. **WCs**: Adapted WC. **Grounds**: Fully accessible. Accessible route. Portable ramps. Garden directories. **Shop**: Steps to entrance. **Refreshments**: Many steps to entrance with handrail. Large-print menu. 1 table can be made available on ground floor

🦯 Braille guide and large-print guide. Sensory list. Handling collection

🛍 NT shop. Plant sales

🍽 Tea-room on first floor of Bothy. Children's menu

🏞 Tables in lower field area

👶 Baby-changing facilities. Front-carrying baby slings for loan. Children's play area. Grass maze

🏫 Suitable for school groups. Education room/centre. Live interpretation. Hands-on activities. Children's guide. Children's quiz/trail. Adult study days

🐕 On leads and only in grounds, not garden area

➡ [104: SE079421] **Bus**: Frequent services from 🚌 Bradford Interchange, Bingley, Keighley, Leeds. **Station**: Keighley 1½ml. **Road**: 1ml NE of Keighley on S side of the Bradford Road in Riddlesden, close to Leeds & Liverpool Canal. A629 relief road from Shipley and Skipton signed for East Riddlesden Hall

🅿 Free parking, 100yds. Coach parking for two coaches. Narrow entrance to property. No double-decker coaches

NT properties nearby
Fountains Abbey & Studley Royal, Gawthorpe Hall, Hardcastle Crags, Malham Tarn Estate

Fountains Abbey & Studley Royal Water Garden

Fountains, Ripon, North Yorkshire HG4 3DY

🏠 🪑 ✝ 🧆 🔆 ♣ 🛍 🍽 🏞 🚸 🍴 1983 (5:F4)

Cistercian abbey, Georgian water garden and medieval deer park

One of the most remarkable places in Europe, this World Heritage Site comprises the spectacular ruin of a 12th-century Cistercian abbey and monastic watermill, an Elizabethan mansion (two rooms open to visitors) and one of the best surviving examples of a Georgian water garden. Elegant ornamental lakes, canals, temples and cascades provide a succession of dramatic eye-catching vistas. The Victorian St Mary's Church gives a majestic focus to the medieval deer park, home to 500 deer and a wealth of flora and fauna.

What's new in 2005 Minibus service from Ripon to Studley Royal Water Garden and Fountains visitor centre: June–Oct, Mon–Sat from 10.30. Tel 01423 526655 for details

⭐ The National Trust works in partnership with English Heritage to care for this site. EH maintains the Abbey (which is owned by the NT) and owns St Mary's Church (managed by the NT)

Opening arrangements: Fountains Abbey										
Abbey/garden	1 Mar - 31 Oct	10 - 5	**M T W T F S S**
	1 Nov - 28 Feb 06	10 - 4	**M T W T** F **S S**
Deer park	All year	Dawn – dusk	**M T W T F S S**
St Mary's	25 Mar - 30 Sep	1 - 5	**M T W T F S S**
Mill	1 Mar - 31 Oct	10 - 5	**M T W T F S S**
	1 Nov - 28 Feb 06	10 - 4	**M T W T** F **S S**
Shop	1 Mar - 31 Oct	10 - 6	**M T W T F S S**
	1 Nov - 28 Feb 06	10 - 4	**M T W T** F **S S**
Restaurant	As shop		

Closed 24, 25 Dec. Also open Fri in Feb. Abbey, Mill, Fountains Hall & water garden: close dusk if earlier. Floodlighting: 9 Sept–15 Oct. Abbey is floodlit on Fri & Sat evenings until 10 (last admission 9). Visitor centre shop closes dusk if earlier. Restaurant closes 30 mins before last admissions. Lakeside shop: limited opening, enquire at property. Lakeside tea-room: open during local school holidays & weekends: opens 10, closes ½ hr before last admission to garden

For further information check our website www.nationaltrust.org.uk

Fountains Abbey, North Yorkshire

[i] **T** 01765 608888,
01765 643196/8 (Functions/weddings),
01765 643197 (Group bookings),
01765 643167 (Learning),
01765 643199 (Box office),
01765 601004 (Shop),
01765 601003 (Restaurant),
01765 604246 (Tea-room) **F** 01765 601002
E fountainsenquiries@nationaltrust.org.uk

[£] £5.50, child £3, family £15. Groups (15–30)
£5, child £2.50. Groups (31+) £4.50, children
£2.20. EH members free. Visitor centre, deer
park, St Mary's Church: free

[🎭] Free volunteer-led guided tours of Abbey and
water garden April to Oct plus extended tours
of complete estate throughout the year.
Floodlit tours of Abbey: 9 Sept to 14 Oct
every Fri 7.45pm & 8.15pm. Specialist guides
for booked groups (£1 per person)

[🎭] Programme of events, inc. open-air
Shakespeare, concerts and Christmas
entertainment; details from box office.
Extensive programme of wildlife and historical
tours, music events and family activities

[🚶] Walks activity leaflets on request

[♿] Designated parking in main car park. Some
areas of Abbey and water garden
inaccessible. Designated parking at visitor

centre and at Westgate entrance. Transfer
available. Drop-off point. **Building**: 6
wheelchairs, booking essential. Level access
into Abbey and Mill. Many steps with handrails
to Fountains Hall. Ramp into St Mary's
Church. **WCs**: Adapted WC. **Grounds**: steep
slopes, some cobbles. Accessible route map.
Main areas on level ground. Upper footpaths
restricted preventing full circular tour. 2 single-
seater PMV, booking essential.
Shop: Ramped entrance with handrail.
Refreshments: Level entrance

[👂] Induction loop in Fountains Abbey Mill

[👆] Braille guide and large-print guide. Sensory list

[🛍️] 2 shops, at visitor centre and at entrance to
water garden

[☕] Licensed restaurant at visitor centre.
Children's menu. Licensed tea-room at
entrance to water garden. Kiosk at Fountains
Mill. Ice cream and beverages. Limited
opening

[👶] Baby-changing and feeding facilities.
Pushchairs and baby back-carriers admitted.
Programme of children's activities in school
holidays

[🏫] Suitable for school groups. Education
room/centre. Hands-on activities. Family
guide. Children's quiz/trail. Adult study days

Please note: groups must book in advance with the property

🐕 On short leads only. Enclosed dog walk/toilet at visitor centre

♿ Cycling allowed through the deer park and on bridle paths around the property

➡ [99: SE271683] **Cycle**: Signed on-road cycle loop. **Bus**: Reliance 812 from ⊠ York, with connections from ⊠ Harrogate on Harrogate & District 36, Sun, June–Oct only; Keighley & District 802 from Bradford and Leeds, Sun, June–Oct only; otherwise Abbots 145 from Ripon (with connections from ⊠ Harrogate) Thur & Sat only. Minibus service from Ripon (see What's New in 2005). **Road**: 4ml W of Ripon off B6265 to Pateley Bridge, signposted from A1, 10ml N of Harrogate (A61)

P Free parking. Deer park £2 (pay & display; NT members free – members' season ticket to display in car available from property). **Note**: Charges may be reduced if access to estate is restricted because of events

NT properties nearby
Beningbrough Hall, Brimham Rocks, East Riddlesden Hall

Hardcastle Crags

Estate Office, Hollin Hall, Crimsworth Dean, Hebden Bridge, West Yorkshire HX7 7AP

 1950 (5:E6)

Beautiful wooded valley with natural and industrial history interest

The landscape encompasses deep rocky ravines, tumbling streams and oak, beech and pine woods. Halfway up the valley loom the Crags – stacks of millstone grit. The area is famous as the home of the hairy wood ant, which lives here in huge anthills. Waymarked walks lead through the valley and link with footpaths and the Pennine Way. Gibson Mill, an 18th-century former cotton mill, is at the heart of the property.

⭐ Visitors are encouraged to come on foot, by cycle or public tansport. During busy times limited car-parking leads to heavy congestion. WC (30yds from main car park) is council-maintained; from Oct to March open weekends & BHols only

i **T** 01422 844518 **F** 01422 841026
E hardcastlecrags@nationaltrust.org.uk

𝑋 Guided walks throughout the year. Send s.a.e. for details. Also for booked groups; contact Warden. Orienteering course bookable

📋 Programme of events. Send s.a.e. for details

♿ Designated parking in main car park. 2 designated parking spaces, unmarked 100yds from main car park. Permit for parking directly at Gibson Mill can be arranged.
Grounds: Partly accessible, loose gravel paths, steep slopes, uneven paths, undulating terrain

BSL Interpreter at all events and guided walks

Braille guide. Sensory list

Suitable for school groups

Under control at all times

➡ [103: SD988291] **Foot**: Access on foot via riverside walk from Hebden Bridge. Pennine Bridleway passes property. **Bus**: Hebden Bridger H from ⊠ Hebden Bridge. **Station**: Hebden Bridge 2ml. **Road**: At end of Midgehole Road, 1½ml NE of Hebden Bridge off the A6033 Keighley road

P Parking (pay & display). Midweek £2.50, weekend £3; motorcycle 60p; minibus £5 (members' season ticket available from property to display in car)

NT properties nearby
East Riddlesden Hall, Gawthorpe Hall, Marsden Moor Estate

Opening arrangements: Hardcastle Crags							
All year	M	T	W	T	F	S	S

Maister House

160 High Street, Hull, East Yorkshire HU1 1NL

🏠 1966 (5:J6)

18th-century merchant's house

Rebuilt in 1743 during Hull's heyday as an affluent trading centre, this house is a typical but rare survivor of a contemporary merchant's residence. The restrained exterior belies the spectacular plasterwork staircase inside. The house is now let as offices.

There are special events at most Trust properties; please telephone 0870 458 4000 for details

⭐ Staircase and entrance hall only on show. No WC

ℹ️ **T** 01482 324114,
01723 870423 (Yorkshire Coast estate office)
F 01482 227003

💷 Admission free. Donations welcome

♿ **Building**: Many steps to entrance

➔ [107: TA102287] In Hull city centre.
Cycle: NCN65. **Bus**: Local services to within 100yds. **Station**: Hull ¾ml

🅿️ No parking on site. Not suitable for coaches

NT properties nearby
Treasurer's House, Yorkshire Coast

Opening arrangements: Maister House										
House	All year	10-4	**M**	**T**	**W**	**T**	**F**	S	S
Closed BHols									

Malham Tarn Estate

Yorkshire Dales Estate Office, Waterhouses, Settle, North Yorkshire BD24 9PT

🎖️🔌👤 1946   (5:E4)

High moorland landscape with dramatic limestone features

This outstanding area of upland limestone country consists of six farms, some with flower-rich hay meadows, limestone pavements and a National Nature Reserve around Malham Tarn, where there is a bird hide. In Malham village visitors can see an exhibition about farming in the Dales.

ℹ️ **T/F** 01729 830416
E malhamtarn@nationaltrust.org.uk

👤 Guided walks programme

♿ **Grounds**: Partly accessible. Section of accessible boardwalk at Malham Tarn Nature Reserve

Opening arrangements: Malham Tarn Estate									
Estate	All year		**M**	**T**	**W**	**T**	**F**	**S**	**S**
Townhead Barn	9 Jan - 3 Apr	10-4	M	T	W	T	F	S	**S**
	9 Apr - 30 Oct	10-4	M	**T**	**W**	**T**	**F**	S	**S**
	6 Nov - 18 Dec	10-4	M	T	W	T	F	S	**S**
	8 Jan - 26 Mar 06	10-4	M	T	W	T	F	S	**S**

📺 Exhibition in Townhead Barn, Malham

🚲 Off-road cycling permitted on bridleways

➔ [98: SD890660] Estate extends from Malham village, 19ml NW of Skipton, N past Malham Tarn. **Foot**: 6ml of Pennine Way & ⅔ml of Pennine Bridleway on property. **Bus**: Pennine 210, Arriva Yorkshire 804 from ➤ Skipton, with 804 also from Wakefield on Sat & Sun, April–Oct. **Station**: Settle 7ml

🅿️ Parking (not NT) in Malham village (pay & display)

NT properties nearby
Brimham Rocks, East Riddlesden Hall, Fountains Abbey & Studley Royal, Upper Wharfedale

Marsden Moor Estate

Estate Office, The Old Goods Yard, Station Road, Marsden, Huddersfield, West Yorkshire HD7 6DH

🏛️🔌🎖️👤🏕️👤 1955   (5:E7)

Huge area of peak and moorland

The estate, covering nearly 2429ha (5685 acres) of unenclosed common moorland and almost surrounding the village of Marsden, takes in the northern part of the Peak District National Park, with valleys, reservoirs, peaks and crags, as well as archaeological remains dating from pre-Roman times to the great engineering structures of the canal and railway ages. The landscape supports large numbers of moorland birds such as the golden plover, red grouse, curlew and diminutive twite. The estate is a designated SSSI and forms part of an international Special Protection Area and is a candidate Special Area of Conservation. At the NT estate office is the 'Welcome to Marsden' exhibition, giving a good insight into the area.

⭐ Public WC in Marsden village

ℹ️ **T** 01484 847016
F 01484 847071
E marsdenmoor@nationaltrust.org.uk

👤 Send s.a.e. to estate office for events and guided walks leaflet, a pocket guide to Marsden including 6 self-guided walks and a heritage trail covering Tunnel End and Marsden village

Please remember – your membership card is always needed for free admission

Walkers on Buckstones Moss in the north of the Marsden Moor Estate, West Yorkshire

---

Building: The 'Welcome to Marsden' exhibition is level and accessible.
Grounds: Partly accessible, some accessible paths

Plant sales at events and some weekends at estate office

Suitable for school groups

On leads at all times

2 bridleways cross the property. Also possible to undertake circular rides using these together with quiet roads

→ [109: SE025100 – 160110] **Foot**: Kirklees Way and Pennine Way pass through the property. Huddersfield Narrow Canal towpath nearby. **Bus**: First 350, 352, 365 from Huddersfield. **Station**: Marsden (adjacent to estate office). **Road**: Estate covers area around Marsden village, between A640 and A635

P Free parking areas around the estate, inc. in Marsden village (not NT) and at Buckstones and Wessenden Head (NT)

NT properties nearby
East Riddlesden Hall, Hardcastle Crags, Lyme Park, Nostell Priory

Opening arrangements: Marsden Moor Estate									
Estate	All year		M	T	W	T	F	S	S
Exhibition	All year	9 - 5	M	T	W	T	F	S	S

Mount Grace Priory

Staddle Bridge, Northallerton, North Yorkshire
DL6 3JG

✝ 📷 🎭 🧑 1953 (5:G3)

Ruin of a 14th-century Carthusian priory

This is England's most important Carthusian ruin. The individual cells reflect the hermit-like isolation of the monks; a reconstruction enables visitors to see the austere and simple furnishings. There is a small herb garden.

★ The priory is financed, administered and maintained by English Heritage. Please contact property before your visit to check details

i **T** 01609 883494

£ £3.50, child £1.80, family £8.80, concessions £2.60. Groups (11+) £2.70. NT members free, except for special events

Drop-off point. **Building**: Ramped entrance. Stairs to other floors. Seating available. **WCs**: Adapted WC. **Shop**: Level entrance

Opening arrangements: Mount Grace Priory									
Priory	25 Mar - 30 Sep	10 - 6	M	T	W	T	F	S	S
	1 Oct - 31 Mar 06	10 - 4	M	T	W	T	F	S	S
Shop	As Priory								
Closed 24 – 26 Dec & 1 Jan									

For general and membership enquiries, please telephone 0870 458 4000

🍴 Shop. Herbs for sale May to Aug

🍽 Hot and cold drinks and biscuits from shop (EH)

🚼 Baby-changing facilities. Pushchairs and baby back-carriers admitted

🎭 Suitable for school groups. Children's quiz/trail. Family activity packs

➔ [99: SE449985] **Foot**: Cleveland Way within $\frac{2}{3}$ml. **Cycle**: NCN65 2$\frac{1}{2}$ml. **Bus**: Abbott 80, 89 ⊞ Northallerton–Stokesley, alight Priory Road End, $\frac{1}{4}$ml. **Station**: Northallerton 6ml. **Road**: 6ml NE of Northallerton, $\frac{1}{2}$ml E of A19 and $\frac{1}{2}$ml S of its junction with A172

🅿 Free parking

NT properties nearby
Nunnington Hall, Ormesby Hall, Rievaulx Terrace & Temples

Nostell Priory

Doncaster Road, Nostell, nr Wakefield, West Yorkshire WF4 1QE

 **1954**   **(5:G6)**

18th-century architectural masterpiece with Adam interiors, fine collections and landscape park

Nostell Priory was built by James Paine on the site of a medieval priory for Sir Rowland Winn, 4th Baronet, in 1733. Later Robert Adam was commissioned to complete the state rooms which are among the finest examples of his interiors. The Priory houses one of England's best collections of Chippendale furniture, designed especially for the house by the great cabinetmaker. Other treasures include an outstanding art collection with works by Pieter Brueghel the Younger and Angelica Kauffmann, the remarkable 18th-century doll's house with its original fittings and Chippendale-style furniture, and the John Harrison long-case clock with its extremely rare movement made of wood. In the grounds are delightful lakeside walks with a stunning collection of rhododendrons and azaleas in late spring.

What's new in 2005 More of the historic parkland open. Family croquet, giant chess set. Weekdays: 'Object of the week', 'Every picture

tells a story' and 'Treasures from the library'. Cabinets and commodes open on Sat, June, July and Aug

ℹ️ **T** 01924 863892,
01924 866830 (Group booking),
0845 4504545 (Weddings/functions),
01924 866833 (Learning),
01924 866830 (Box office),
01924 866845 (Shop),
01924 865021 (Tea-room)
F 01924 866846
E nostellpriory@nationaltrust.org.uk

💷 £6, child £3, family £15. Groups (20+) £5.50, group visits outside normal hours £10.
Garden only: £3.50, child £1.50

🗝 Tours for groups by prior arrangement: 'You rang m'Lord'; 'Meet the head gardener'

😃 Programme of events, inc. craft and country fairs, open-air theatre and jazz and other musical spectaculars. Send s.a.e. for details

♿ Separate designated parking, 100yds. Drop-off point. **Building**: Level entrance. 3 wheelchairs, booking essential. Stairs to other floors, lift available. **WCs**: Adapted WC. **Grounds**: Partly accessible. Accessible route map. 1 single-seater PMV, booking essential. **Shop**: Level entrance. **Refreshments**: Level entrance

👆 Braille guide. Sensory list

🍴 NT shop. Plant sales

🍽 Stables Tea-room. Serving lunches and refreshments. Children's menu

Opening arrangements: Nostell Priory										
House	19 Mar - 6 Nov	1 - 5	M	T	**W**	**T**	**F**	**S**	**S**
	3 Dec - 11 Dec	12 - 4	**M**	**T**	**W**	**T**	**F**	**S**	**S**
Grounds	5 Mar - 20 Mar	11 - 5	M	T	W	T	F	**S**	**S**
	23 Mar - 6 Nov	11 - 6	M	**T**	**W**	**T**	**F**	**S**	**S**
	3 Dec - 11 Dec	11 - 4:30	**M**	**T**	**W**	**T**	**F**	**S**	**S**
Shop	5 Mar - 20 Mar	11 - 4	M	T	W	T	F	**S**	**S**
	25 Mar - 6 Nov	11 - 5:30	M	**T**	**W**	**T**	**F**	**S**	**S**
	3 Dec - 11 Dec	11 - 4:30	**M**	**T**	**W**	**T**	**F**	**S**	**S**
Tea-room	As shop								
Park	5 Mar - 6 Nov	9 - 7	**M**	**T**	**W**	**T**	**F**	**S**	**S**
	7 Nov - 4 Mar	9 - 5	**M**	**T**	**W**	**T**	**F**	**S**	**S**

Open BH Mons House 1–5; gardens, shop & tea-room 11–5.30. Rose garden may be closed on occasions for private functions

Please see the area introductions for details of coast & countryside properties

Detail of the Top Hall, Nostell Priory, West Yorkshire

Nunnington Hall

Nunnington, nr York, North Yorkshire YO62 5UY

🏠 ✛ 🗄 💷 🥤 1953 (5:H4)

Picturesque Yorkshire manor house with organic garden

The sheltered walled garden on the bank of the River Rye, with its delightful mixed borders, orchards of traditional fruit varieties and spring-flowering meadows, complements this mellow 17th-century manor house. From the magnificent oak-panelled hall, three staircases lead to the family rooms, the nursery, the haunted room and the attics, with their fascinating Carlisle collection of miniature rooms fully furnished to reflect different periods. Nunnington is also noted for its changing programme of temporary exhibitions and 100 per cent organic management of the garden.

🛈 **T** 01439 748283
F 01439 748284
E nunningtonhall@nationaltrust.org.uk

💷 £5, child £2.50, family £12.50. Groups £4.50.
Garden only: £2.50, child free

🚶 By arrangement

♿ Limited parking. Drop-off point.
Building: Step to entrance. Alternative accessible entrance, ask for assistance. 2 wheelchairs. Ground floor largely accessible. Stairs with handrail to other floors. Seating available. Photograph album. **WCs**: Adapted WC. **Grounds**: Partly accessible, loose gravel paths, slopes, grass paths. **Shop**: Step to entrance. **Refreshments**: Level entrance

👁 Braille guide. Interesting scents and sounds

🏞 Picnics welcome in car park and vista parkland in front of house

👶 Baby-changing and feeding facilities. Front-carrying baby slings and hip-carrying infant seats for loan. Children's play area. Family area in tea-room

🏫 Suitable for school groups. Education room/centre. Children's quiz/trail. Family activity packs

🐕 On leads on walks around vista, not in garden

➜ [111: SE407172] **Cycle**: NCN67 3ml.
Bus: Arriva 485, 496/8 Wakefield–Doncaster; Yorkshire Traction 244/5 Barnsley–Pontefract.
Station: Fitzwilliam 1½ml. **Road**: On A638 5ml SE of Wakefield towards Doncaster

🅿 Parking, £2. Refunded on purchase of adult house & garden ticket

NT properties nearby
Clumber Park, Marsden Moor Estate, Mr Straw's House

Opening arrangements: Nunnington Hall									
House	12 Mar - 30 Apr	1:30 - 5	M	T	**W**	**T**	**F**	**S**	**S**
	1 May - 30 May	1:30 - 5:30	M	T	**W**	**T**	**F**	**S**	**S**
	31 May - 31 Aug	1:30 - 5:30	M	**T**	**W**	**T**	**F**	**S**	**S**
	1 Sep - 30 Sep	1:30 - 5:30	M	T	**W**	**T**	**F**	**S**	**S**
	1 Oct - 30 Oct	1:30 - 5	M	T	**W**	**T**	**F**	**S**	**S**
Garden	As house	Opens 12:30							
Restaurant	As house	Opens 12:30							
Shop	As house	As house							
Open BH Mons									

Unless indicated, last admission is always 30mins before closing time

The south front, Nunnington Hall, North Yorkshire

📷 NT shop. Plant sales

🍽 Restaurant within historic building. Children's menu

🌳 Tables in tea garden

👶 Baby-changing and feeding facilities. Hip-carrying infant seats for loan. Toddler reins for loan

🔲 Suitable for school groups. Children's guide. Children's quiz/trail. Children's activity packs. Adult study days

🐕 On leads and only in car park; shaded parking

➡ [100: SE670795] **Bus**: Hutchinson 195 Hovingham–Helmsley with connections from 🚂 Malton on Stephensons 194. 'Moorsbus' from Helmsley. **Road**: In Ryedale, 4½ml SE of Helmsley (A170) Helmsley–Pickering road; 1½ml N of B1257 Malton–Helmsley road; 21ml N of York, B1363. Nunnington Hall is 7½ml SE of the NT Rievaulx Terrace and Temples

🅿 Free parking, 50yds. Not suitable for trailer caravans

NT properties nearby
Bridestones, Ormesby Hall, Rievaulx Terrace & Temples

Ormesby Hall

Ormesby, Middlesbrough TS7 9AS

🏠🐾✂🍀📷🍽🌳🧍🍸 1962   (5:G2)

Mid-18th-century Palladian mansion

Ormesby Hall is notable for its fine plasterwork and carved wood decoration. The Victorian laundry and kitchen with scullery and game larder are especially interesting, and there is a beautiful stable block (let to the Cleveland Mounted Police). A large model railway exhibition is on show. There is also an attractive garden and holly walk.

What's new in 2005 Change in opening days

ℹ️ **T** 01642 324188, 01642 328906 (Learning), 01642 328908 (Shop), 01642 328907 (Tea-room) **F** 01642 300937
E ormesbyhall@nationaltrust.org.uk

£ £4.10, child £2, family £10.50. Groups £3.50. **Garden, railway & exhibitions only**: £2.90; child £1.30

Opening arrangements: Ormesby Hall											
House	25 Mar - 31 Oct	1:30 - 5	M	T	W	T		F	S	S
Shop/tea-room	As house	12:30 - 5	M	T	W	T		F	S	S

There are special events at most Trust properties; please telephone 0870 458 4000 for details

🎭 Programme of events. Tel. for details

♿ Separate designated parking, 15yds. Drop-off point. **Building**: Ramped entrance. 2 wheelchairs. Photograph album. **WCs**: Adapted WC. **Grounds**: Accessible route. **Shop**: Steps to entrance. **Refreshments**: Ramped entrance

👁 Large-print guide. Sensory list

☕ Tea-room. Children's menu

👶 Baby-changing facilities. Front-carrying baby slings for loan

🔳 Suitable for school groups. Education room/centre. Children's quiz/trail. Family activity packs

🐕 On leads in park only

➡ [93: NZ530167] **Cycle**: NCN65 2¼ml. **Bus**: From Middlesbrough (passing close ➤ Middlesbrough). **Station**: Marton (U) 1½ml; Middlesbrough 3ml. **Road**: 3ml SE of Middlesbrough, W of A171. From A19 take A174 to A172. Follow signs for Ormesby Hall. Car entrance on Ladgate Lane (B1380)

🅿 Free parking, 100yds

NT properties nearby
Mount Grace Priory, Nunnington Hall, Rievaulx Terrace & Temples, Roseberry Topping, Washington Old Hall

The Great Kitchen, Ormesby Hall, Middlesbrough

Rievaulx Terrace & Temples

Rievaulx, Helmsley, North Yorkshire YO62 5LJ

🔳🎭🏋🏠☕🎋🚶 1972 (5:G3)

One of Yorkshire's finest 18th-century landscape gardens

The ½mile-long grass terrace and adjoining woodland offer vistas over Rievaulx Abbey (English Heritage) to Ryedale and the Hambleton Hills. There is an abundance of wild flowers in spring. The two mid-18th-century temples include the Ionic Temple, intended as a banqueting house with elaborate ceiling paintings and fine 18th-century furniture.

⭐ No access to Rievaulx Abbey from Terrace

ℹ **T** 01439 798340/01439 748283, 01439 798340 (Shop) **F** 01439 748284 **E** nunningtonhall@nationaltrust.org.uk

💷 £3.80, child £2, family £9.60. Groups £3.20

🚶 By arrangement

🎭 Programme of events. For details contact Nunnington Hall

♿ Separate designated parking, 5yds. Drop-off point. **Building**: Steps to entrance. Alternative accessible entrance. **Grounds**: Partly accessible, some steps. Accessible route map. Benches available. 2 single-seater PMV, booking essential. **Shop**: Step to entrance, ramp available

👁 Braille guide

🏠 NT shop. Plant sales

☕ Ice cream, coffee/tea machine and cold drinks

👶 Baby-changing facilities. Pushchairs and baby back-carriers admitted

🔳 Suitable for school groups. Children's activity packs

Opening arrangements: Rievaulx										
	12 Mar - 30 Sep	10:30 - 6	**M**	**T**	**W**	**T**	**F**	**S**	**S**	
	1 Oct - 30 Oct	10:30 - 5	**M**	**T**	**W**	**T**	**F**	**S**	**S**	
Shop	As property									

Last admission 1hr before closing. Ionic Temple closed 1–2pm

The Ionic Temple at Rievaulx Terrace, North Yorkshire

🐕 On leads only

➡ [100: SE579848] **Foot**: Cleveland Way within ⅔ml. **Bus**: 'Moorsbus' from Helmsley (connections from ⊠ Scarborough) Sun, May–Oct plus daily in Aug; York Country C12 from York (Sun, May–Oct only); otherwise Scarborough & District 128 from Scarborough or Stephensons 31/X from ⊠ York, alight Helmsley, then 2½ml. **Road**: 2½ml NW of Helmsley on B1257

🅿 Free parking, 100yds. Unsuitable for trailer caravans. Cars park beside visitor centre, coaches a short walk away. Tight corners and no turning space beyond coach park

NT properties nearby
Bridestones, Nunnington Hall, Ormesby Hall

Roseberry Topping

Newton-under-Roseberry, North Yorkshire

🚻 ♿ 🏠 🚶 🐕 1985   (5:G2)

Distinctive hill with fine views across Yorkshire

The peculiar shape of this hill is due to a geological fault and a mining collapse early in the 20th century. From the summit at 320m there is a magnificent 360-degree view, which on a clear day allows the visitor to see as far as Teeside in one direction and the Yorkshire Dales in another. Newton and Cliff Ridge Woods skirt the northern edge of the property and Cliff Rigg quarry still retains evidence of the extraction of whinstone, once used for road-building. The area is rich in wildlife, particularly moorland birds. A spur of the Cleveland Way National Trail runs up to the summit.

⭐ Address for correspondence: Peakside, Ravenscar, Scarborough, North Yorkshire YO13 0NE. WC at Ayton car park

ℹ **T** 01947 841386,
01723 870423 (Yorkshire Coast estate office),
07879 417797 (Warden mobile)
E roseberrytopping@nationaltrust.org.uk

🎭 Programme of events. Tel. for details

♿ **WCs**: Adapted WC

➡ [93: NZ575126] **Foot**: Cleveland Way passes property. **Bus**: Arriva North East 81, 781 Redcar–Stokesley, alight Newton-under-Roseberry, then ½ml. **Station**: Great Ayton 1½ml. **Road**: 1ml from Gt Ayton next to Newton-under-Roseberry on A173 Gt Ayton–Guisborough

🅿 Free parking (not NT) at Newton-under-Roseberry

NT properties nearby
Bridestones Moor, Nunnington Hall, Ormesby Hall, Rievaulx Terrace & Temples, Souter Lighthouse, Yorkshire Coast

Opening arrangements: Roseberry Topping		
All year		M T W T F S S

Please note: groups must book in advance with the property

Treasurer's House

Minster Yard, York, North Yorkshire YO1 7JL

🏛 ✿ 💷 🎭 ♿ 🅃 1930   **(5:G5)**

Elegant town house dating from medieval times

Originally home to the treasurers of York Minster and built over a Roman road, the house is not all that it seems. Nestled behind the Minster, its size, splendour and contents are a constant surprise to visitors – as are the famous ghost stories. The house was carefully restored between 1897 and 1930 by one remarkable man, wealthy local industrialist Frank Green, with rooms presented in a variety of historic styles.

What's new in 2005 Tea-room: extended opening in November and December for shoppers' lunches and themed food events. Tel. for details. Herb garden open on selected days for events and plant sales

ⓘ **T** 01904 624247
  F 01904 647372
  E treasurershouse@nationaltrust.org.uk

💷 **House**: £4.80, child £2.40, family £12. Groups £4, child £2. **House & cellar**: £6.80, child £3.60. Groups £6, child £3.20. **Cellar (NT members)**: £2, child £1.20. **Garden/tea-room/gallery**: Free. (Large groups welcome but need to divide so not more than 15 touring the house at a time)

🕴 Garden; ghost cellar tours daily except Friday (charge, inc. NT members)

♿ Drop-off point. **Building**: Steps to entrance. Stairs to other floors. Seating available. Audio tour, Subtitled video of ghost cellar and story. **WCs**: Adapted WC. **Grounds**: Accessible route. **Refreshments**: Many steps to entrance with handrail. Large-print menu

📢 Induction loop in Audio tour guide

👁 Braille guide and large-print guide. Sensory list

🏠 York NT town shop 2 mins walk away

💷 Licensed tea-room. All food freshly prepared and baked on premises inc. traditional Yorkshire recipes. Children's menu

Opening arrangements: Treasurer's House

House/garden	16 Mar - 31 Oct	11 - 4:30	**M T W T** F **S S**

Tea-room/gallery open as house. Ghost cellar open daily as house, by guided tour only (timed tickets)

👶 Baby-changing and feeding facilities. Hip-carrying infant seats for loan. Interactive exhibition area for children. Storage for pushchairs

📷 Suitable for school groups. Children's guide. Children's quiz/trail. Exhibition/video

🐕 On leads and only in garden

➡ [105: SE604523] In city centre adjacent to Minster (N side, at rear) . **Cycle**: NCN65 $\frac{1}{3}$ml. Close to city cycle routes. **Bus**: From surrounding areas. **Station**: York $\frac{1}{2}$ml

🅿 No parking on site. Public car park nearby in Lord Mayor's Walk. Park & ride service from city outskirts

NT properties nearby
Beningbrough Hall, Nunnington Hall

Treasurer's House, York

Parking in National Trust car parks is free for members

Upper Wharfedale

Yorkshire Dales Estate Office, Waterhouses, Settle, North Yorkshire BD24 9PT

🖼️🚻 1989   (5:E4)

Area of classic Yorkshire Dales countryside

Amongst these 2470ha (6100 acres) of the Upper Wharfe valley north of Kettlewell, the Trust owns nine farms and the hamlets of Yockenthwaite and Cray. The landscape incorporates dry-stone walls and barns, important flower-rich hay meadows, valleyside woodland and blanket bog.

ℹ️ **T/F** 01729 830416,
01756 760283 (Warden)
E upperwharfedale@nationaltrust.org.uk

🎒 Guided walks programme

📺 Exhibition in Townhead Barn, Buckden

➜ [98: SD935765] Upper Wharfedale extends from Kettlewell village (12ml N of Skipton) N to Beckermonds and Cray. **Bus**: Pride of the Dales 72 ➡️ Skipton–Buckden; Arriva Yorkshire/Keighley & District 800/5/6 from Leeds and ➡️ Ilkley (Sun, Apr–Oct)

🅿️ Parking (not NT) in Kettlewell and Buckden (pay & display)

Opening arrangements: Upper Wharfedale										
Estate	All year		M	T	W	T	F	S	S
Townhead Barn	9 Jan - 27 Mar	10 - 4	M	T	W	T	F	S	S
	28 Mar - 29 Sep	10 - 4	M	T	W	T	F	S	S
	2 Oct - 18 Dec	10 - 4	M	T	W	T	F	S	S
	8 Jan - 26 Mar 06	10 - 4	M	T	W	T	F	S	S

NT properties nearby

Brimham Rocks, East Riddlesden Hall, Fountains Abbey & Studley Royal, Malham Tarn Estate

Yorkshire Coast

Peakside, Ravenscar, Scarborough, North Yorkshire YO13 0NE

🚾🖼️🏛️🏠🎁🎭🎒🐾 1976   (5:I2)

Varied coastal area with natural history and industrial archaeology interest

This group of coastal properties extends over 40ml from Saltburn in the north to Filey in the south, centred around Robin Hood's Bay. The Cleveland Way National Trail follows the clifftop and gives splendid views. A wide range of habitats – meadow, woodland, coastal heath and cliff grassland – provides sanctuary to many forms of wildlife, from orchids to nesting birds. The area is rich in industrial archaeology and the

Robin Hood's Bay looking towards Ravenscar, North Yorkshire

Please remember – your membership card is always needed for free admission

remains of the alum industry and jet and ironstone mining can be seen. The Old Coastguard Station in Robin Hood's Bay, an exciting exhibition and education centre, is run in partnership with the North York Moors National Park Authority. It shows how the elements have shaped this part of the coastline.

[i] **T** 01723 870423 (Office),
01947 885900 (Old Coastguard Station),
01723 870138 (Ravenscar Coastal Centre)
F 01723 870423
E yorkshirecoast–nationaltrust.org.uk

[𝕏] Guided walks

[&] **Old Coastguard Station**: Steps to entrance. Ground floor fully accessible. Access to other floors via lift. **Ravenscar Coastal Centre**: Steps to shop entrance. **WCs**: Adapted WC

[👁] Sensory list

[🏠] Shops in Old Coastguard Station and Ravenscar Coastal Centre

[▥] Suitable for school groups. Education room/centre. Hands-on activities

[→] [94: NZ980025] **Foot**: Cleveland Way passes through property. **Bus**: Scarborough & District 16 from Scarborough, Tues, Thur, Sat only: otherwise Arriva North East 93/A Scarborough–Whitby to within 3ml. **Station**: Scarborough 10ml. **Road**: Coastal Centre in Ravenscar village, signposted off A171 Scarborough–Whitby. Old Coastguard Station in Robin Hood's Bay

[P] Parking (not NT) (pay & display), charge inc. NT members

NT properties nearby
Bridestones, Nunnington Hall, Ormesby Hall, Rievaulx Terrace & Temples

Opening arrangements: Yorkshire Coast										
All year			**M**	**T**	**W**	**T**	**F**	**S**	**S**	
Coastguard Stn	5 Mar - 29 May	10 - 5	M	T	W	T	F	**S**	**S**	
	31 May - 2 Oct	10 - 5	M	**T**	**W**	**T**	**F**	**S**	**S**	
	8 Oct - 30 Oct	10 - 5	M	T	W	T	F	**S**	**S**	
	5 Nov - 26 Feb 06	11 - 4	M	T	W	T	F	**S**	**S**	
Ravenscar	26 Mar - 29 May	10 - 5	M	T	W	T	F	**S**	**S**	
	30 May - 2 Oct	10 - 5	**M**	**T**	**W**	**T**	**F**	**S**	**S**	

Open BH Mons and Good Fri. Old Coastguard Station and Ravenscar Coastal Centre also open daily in local school holidays

Properties open less often

This section includes National Trust properties, often tenanted, which are open two days a week or less (plus Bank Holidays in some cases). Visits to some must be made by prior arrangement and where this applies admission prices are not shown (please ask when making contact). **Full details are on our website www.nationaltrust.org.uk or obtainable from the Membership Department, tel. 0870 458 4000.**

Braithwaite Hall

East Witton, Leyburn, North Yorkshire
DL8 4SY   (5:F3)
17th-century farmhouse with fine original features.

[⭐] No WC
[i] **T** 01969 640287

Opening arrangements: Braithwaite Hall
1st & 3rd Wed April–Sept, 2–5. Tel. the tenant, Mrs Duffus, in advance

Goddards Garden

27 Tadcaster Road, York, North Yorkshire
YO24 1GG   (5:H5)
Formal garden with a variety of features, designed in 1927.

[⭐] Open first Sun in May and Sept
[i] **T** 01904 702021
[£] £2, child £1

Opening arrangements: Goddards Garden
Open Sun 1 May, 4 Sep, 2–5

Moulton Hall

Moulton, Richmond, North Yorkshire
DL10 6QH   (5:F2)
17th-century manor house with fine carved staircase.

[i] **T** 01325 377227

Opening arrangements: Moulton Hall
By arrangement with the tenant, Viscount Eccles

For general and membership enquiries, please telephone 0870 458 4000

South West South & South East
London East of England
East Midlands West Midlands
North West Yorkshire **North East**
Wales Northern Ireland

The beach at Horden on the Durham coast

England's far north-eastern counties of Northumberland, Durham and Tyne & Wear offer magnificent scenery, with wide open stretches of unspoilt moorland and upland pasture, and a long and dramatic coastline, arguably one of the finest in Britain.

In the south of the area, near Horden in Co. Durham, lie two denes, **Warren House Gill** and **Foxholes Dene**. Connected by a narrow coastal strip, this piece of coast marks the 500th mile acquired through the Trust's Neptune Coastline Campaign. Just north of Easington is **Beacon Hill**, the highest point on the Durham coast and famed for its spectacular views; access is via **Hawthorn Dene**. Inland are beautiful woodland walks along the River Wear at **Moorhouse Woods**, just north of Durham City, and along the banks of the Derwent at the village of **Ebchester**. **Penshaw Monument**, an unroofed Doric temple, was built in 1844 to commemorate the 1st Earl of Durham, and is visible for miles around.

Meanwhile, the spectacular coastline continues north to the dramatic **Souter Lighthouse**, the famous seabird colony on **Marsden Rock** and on to **Druridge Bay**, where the Trust owns a mile of coast backed by golden sand dunes and grassland. From **Craster**, Trust ownership runs for five miles, including the brooding ruins of **Dunstanburgh Castle**, **Embleton Links** and **Low Newton-by-Sea**, where **Newton Pool** provides a habitat for many water birds. There are 18th-century lime kilns at **Beadnell Harbour**, from where the road hugs the coast north to Bamburgh, passing **St Aidan's Dunes**, rich in dune grassland plants. There is a Trust information centre and shop at **Seahouses**, from where boats cross to the **Farne Islands**.

Northumberland's hinterland is as stunning as its coastline. There are magnificent walks around **Allen Banks** and **Staward Gorge**, and the nearby **Bellister Estate**. Both **Ros Castle** and the **Hadrian's Wall Estate** offer breathtaking views. Ancient history abounds here – some of England's best preserved Roman remains can be seen at **Housesteads Fort**, and in the Kyloe Hills is **St Cuthbert's Cave**, in which the saint's body is said to have rested on its way from Lindisfarne to Durham. Also closely associated with Northumberland is St Ninian, who is linked with **Lady's Well** on the edge of the Cheviot Hills.

Hadrian's Wall, Northumberland

North East

Regional Highlights for Visitors with Disabilities ...

Newton Pool has a boarded walkway and adapted bird hide. **Cragside** has a lift to the first floor for visitors in wheelchairs. **Wallington** offers a leaflet showing the gradients of all its paths. **Souter Lighthouse** has a closed-circuit television and remote camera so that people unable to climb the lighthouse stairs can still enjoy the view from the top.

...and for Families

There are miles of beautiful beaches along the Northumberland coast. At **Souter Lighthouse** children can handle flags, have a go at morse code and use the CCTV remote camera. Inland at **Wallington** young visitors can enjoy the adventure playground in the West Woods. **Cragside** too has an adventure playground and Nelly's labyrinth, a wild maze to explore.

Further Information

Please contact the Membership Department, PO Box 39, Warrington WA5 7WD.
Tel. 0870 458 4000.
Email: enquiries@thenationaltrust.org.uk

OS grid references for main properties with no individual entry (OS Landranger map series numbers given in brackets)

Beacon Hill & Hawthorn Dene	[88] NZ254460
Beadnell Lime Kilns	[75] NU237286
Bellister Estate	[86] NY697626
Druridge Bay	[81] NZ276961
Ebchester	[88] NZ100551
Embleton Links	[75] NU243235
Horden Beach	[88] NZ454409
Lady's Well	[81] NT953029
Marsden Rock	[88] NZ388665
Moorhouse Woods	[88] NZ305460
Newton Pool	[75] NU243240
Penshaw Monument	[88] NZ333544
Ros Castle	[75] NU081253
St Aidan's Dunes	[75] NU211327
St Cuthbert's Cave	[75] NU059352
Warren House Gill & Foxholes Dene	[88] NZ444427

Allen Banks & Staward Gorge·

Bardon Mill, Hexham, Northumberland NE47 7BU

🏛🐿🔺🧍🎍🗡 1942   (6:F5)

Wooded ravine of the River Allen

This extensive area of hill and river scenery, including the 41ha (101-acre) SSSI of Stawardpeel Woods, has many miles of waymarked walks through ornamental and ancient woodland. On a high promontory within Staward Wood are the remains of a medieval pele tower and at Allen Banks is a reconstructed Victorian summer house.

[i] **T** 01434 344218
   E allenbanks@nationaltrust.org.uk

[£] Admission free

[𝑿] Groups by request

[ⱥ] Free map and guide

[♿] **WCs**: Adapted WC. **Grounds**: Partly accessible. Gorge, rough terrain. Access route to picnic area in car park

[🚼] Baby-changing facilities

[🎒] Suitable for school groups. Family guide. Children's quiz/trail

[➔] [86: NY798640] **Cycle**: NCN72 2½ml.
   Bus: Arriva Northumbria/Stagecoach in Cumbria 85, 685 Carlisle–Newcastle upon Tyne, to within ½ml. **Station**: Bardon Mill 1½ ml. **Road**: 3ml W of Haydon Bridge, ½ml S of A69, near meeting point of Tyne and Allen rivers

[P] Parking (pay & display). NT members must display cards. Cars £1 half day, £2 full day. Can accommodate two coaches at a time. 3.3m (11ft) height restriction on approach road. Coaches £5 half day, £10 full day (NT Educational Group members free). All coaches must book

NT properties nearby
Hadrian's Wall

Opening arrangements: Allen Banks										
All year	Dawn – dusk	**M**	**T**	**W**	**T**	**F**	**S**	**S**		

Cherryburn

Station Bank, Mickley, nr Stocksfield, Northumberland NE43 7DD

🏠🐿🔧🔥✳🗂☕ 1991   (6:G5)

Cottage and farmhouse, the birthplace of Thomas Bewick

Thomas Bewick (1753–1828), Northumberland's greatest artist, wood engraver and naturalist, was born in the cottage here. The nearby 19th-century farmhouse, the later home of the Bewick family, houses an exhibition on Bewick's life and work and a small shop selling books, gifts and prints from his original wood engravings. Occasional printing demonstrations take place in the adjoining barn. There are splendid views over the Tyne valley. The south bank of the River Tyne, where Bewick spent much of his childhood, is a short walk away.

[i] **T** 01661 843276
   E cherryburn@nationaltrust.org.uk

[£] £3.50, child £1.75. Groups (20+) £3, child £1.50

[🎭] Programme of events, inc. May Day celebration, Bewick whistling competition, traditional Northumbrian music, song or dance every Sun throughout the season, concerts, lecture evenings and press room demonstrations. Also available to groups. Tel. for details

[♿] Contact in advance. Designated parking in main car park, 100yds. Drop-off point 20yds. Gravel car park and drive. Cobbled farmyard. **Building**: Level entrance. Ground floor has 3 steps and 2 steps to rear exit. **WCs**: Adapted WC. **Grounds**: loose gravel paths. Some visitors may require assistance from their companion. **Shop**: Steps to entrance with handrail

Opening arrangements: Cherryburn										
Public opening	18 Mar - 30 Oct	11 - 5	**M**	T	**W**	**T**	**F**	**S**	**S**	
Booked groups	18 Mar - 31 Oct	10 - 12	**M**	**T**	**W**	**T**	**F**	S	S	
	22 Mar - 26 Oct	1 - 3	M	**T**	**W**	T	F	S	S	
	1 Nov - 29 Mar 06	10 - 12	**M**	**T**	**W**	**T**	**F**	**S**	**S**	
	1 Nov - 29 Mar 06	1 - 3	**M**	**T**	**W**	**T**	**F**	**S**	**S**	
Shop	As house									

Shop open at other times by arrangement, tel. for details

Please see the area introductions for details of coast & countryside properties

♿ Braille guide. Sensory list

🏠 Shop situated in farmhouse. Send s.a.e. for mail order Bewick print price list. Small selection of plants grown by Cherryburn volunteers, summer months only

☕ Tea, coffee and soft drinks available

🀆 On picnic lawn

🚼 Children's play area. Farmyard animals usually include donkeys, poultry and lambs

🏫 Suitable for school groups. Family guide. Children's quiz/trail. Occasional hands-on activities

➜ [88: NZ075627] Close to S bank of River Tyne. **Bus**: Arriva Northumbria 602 Newcastle–Hexham (passes ⊞ Newcastle). alight Mickley Square ¼ml. **Station**: Stocksfield (U) 1½ml or Prudhoe (U) 1½ml. **Road**: 11ml W of Newcastle, 11ml E of Hexham; ¼ml N of Mickley Square (leave A695 at Mickley Square onto Riding Terrace leading to Station Bank)

🅿 Free parking, 100yds

NT properties nearby
George Stephenson's Birthplace, Gibside

Cragside House perched on a rocky crag above the Debdon valley. Northumberland

---

Cragside House, Gardens & Estate

Rothbury, Morpeth, Northumberland NE65 7PX

🏠🀆⚒✳🔔📷🏠☕🀆🚼 1977   **(6:G3)**

Extraordinary Victorian house – the wonder of its age – set in dramatic and varied gardens

The revolutionary home of Lord Armstrong, Victorian inventor and landscape genius, was a wonder of its age. Built on a rocky crag high above the Debdon Burn, Cragside is crammed with ingenious gadgets and was the first house in the world lit by hydroelectricity. Even the variety and scale of Cragside's gardens are incredible. Surrounding the house on all sides is one of the largest 'hand-made' rock gardens in Europe. In the Pinetum below, England's tallest Douglas Fir soars above other woodland giants. Across the valley, the Orchard House still produces many varieties of fresh fruit. Today Armstrong's amazing creation can be explored on foot or by car and provides one of the last shelters for the endangered red squirrel. The lakeside walks, adventure play area and labyrinth all appeal especially to families.

⭐ Visitors may find the uneven ground, steep footpaths and distances between various parts of the property difficult. Stout footwear advisable. Possible closure of house from end of September 2005 for rest of year for renewal of essential services. Please tel. before visiting or see website. Estate, gardens and all other facilities open as usual. Civil engineering work on estate's water systems may cause some disruption to access throughout the year. Pedestrians and vehicles share the same route in places, so please be vigilant

ℹ **T** 01669 620333/620150,
Ext 4 (Infoline),
Ext 7 (Learning),
01669 622020 (Shop),
01669 622040 (Restaurant)
F 01669 620066
E cragside@nationaltrust.org.uk

💷 **House, gardens & estate**: £8.50, child £4, family £20. Groups £7. **Gardens & estate only**: £5.70, child £2.60, family £14. Groups £4.70. **Gardens & estate only 2 Nov–18 Dec**:

Unless indicated, last admission is always 30mins before closing time

Opening arrangements: Cragside										
House	22 Mar - 25 Sep	1 - 5:30	M	**T**	**W**	**T**	**F**	**S**	**S**
Gdns/estate	22 Mar - 30 Oct	10:30 - 7*	M	**T**	**W**	**T**	**F**	**S**	**S**
	2 Nov - 18 Dec	11 - 4*	M	T	**W**	**T**	**F**	**S**	**S**
Shop	22 Mar - 30 Oct	10:30 - 5:30	M	**T**	**W**	**T**	**F**	**S**	**S**
	2 Nov - 18 Dec	11 - 4	M	T	**W**	**T**	**F**	**S**	**S**
Restaurant	22 Mar - 30 Oct	10:30 - 5:30	M	**T**	**W**	**T**	**F**	**S**	**S**
	2 Nov - 18 Dec	11 - 4	M	T	**W**	**T**	**F**	**S**	**S**

Open BH Mons. Please note that on some BHols the property can be congested. Last admission to house 1 hr before closing. Gardens and estate last admission 5 (Mar–Oct), 3 (Nov–Dec); last serving in restaurant 5 (March–Oct). *Close dusk if earlier

£2.80, child £1.30, family £7. Groups £2.30. Admission free 2 Nov –18 Dec when spending over £10 in restaurant or shop

🛡 Programme of events. Send s.a.e. for details

🚶 Self-guided walks leaflet available

♿ Contact in advance. Designated parking in main car park. 100yds uphill from entrance. House: Drop-off point on gravel forecourt. Ask house staff for nearest parking after 1pm. Visitor centre: Drop-off point. 3 spaces 10yds from entrance. **Building**: Ramped entrance. 2 wheelchairs, booking essential. Ground floor accessible. Stairs with handrail to other floors, lift available. Access to 3 bedrooms and Morning Room. Seating available. Photograph album. **WCs**: Adapted WC. WC at Crozier car park not fully adapted. **Grounds**: Partly accessible, loose gravel paths, steep slopes, undulating terrain. Accessible route. Paths can be waterlogged. **Shop**: Level entrance. **Refreshments**: Level entrance. Large-print menu

🔊 Induction loop in reception, shop, restaurant

👁 Braille guide and large-print guide. Touchable objects

🍴 Stables Restaurant (licensed) in visitor centre. Hot meals served 12–2. Children's menu. Kiosk in Crozier car park. Mainly weekends and school hols, weather permitting

🚼 Baby-changing facilities. Front-carrying baby slings and hip-carrying infant seats for loan. Children's play area. Pushchairs and baby back carriers admitted except in house

🎒 Suitable for school groups. Education room/centre. Children's quiz/trail

🐕 On leads and only on estate

➜ [81: NU073022] **Bus**: Arriva 508 from ⊠ Newcastle, Sun only, Jun–Oct; otherwise Northumbria Mini Coaches Arriva Northumbria 516 Morpeth–Thropton (all passing ⊠ Morpeth) with connections from Newcastle (passing Tyne & Wear Metro Haymarket), alight Reivers Well Gate, ¾ml to house. **Road**: 13ml SW of Alnwick (B6341) and 15ml NW of Morpeth on Wooler road (A697), turn left on to B6341 at Moorhouse Crossroads, entrance 1ml N of Rothbury; bus passengers enter by Reivers Well Gate from Morpeth Road (B6344)

🅿 Free parking. Coach park 350yds from house. Coaches cannot tour estate as drive is too narrow in places

NT properties nearby
Wallington

Dunstanburgh Castle

Craster, Alnwick, Northumberland

🖼 ⛩ 🏠 🚶 1961 (6:H3)

Massive ruined castle in an impressive coastal setting

A magnificent ruin dominating a lonely stretch of Northumberland's beautiful coastline, Dunstanburgh must be reached on foot along paths following the rocky shore.

⭐ The castle is managed by English Heritage

ℹ **T** 01665 576231 (Custodian)

£ £2.50, child £1.30 (may change from 1 April)

🏠 Small shop for postcards and souvenirs

🎒 Suitable for school groups. Free school visits; book through EH tel. 0191 269 1200

🐕 On leads only

Opening arrangements: Dunstanburgh Castle									
1 Apr - 30 Sep	10 - 6	**M**	**T**	**W**	**T**	**F**	**S**	**S**
1 Oct - 30 Oct	10 - 4	**M**	**T**	**W**	**T**	**F**	**S**	**S**
2 Nov - 31 Mar 06	10 - 4	**M**	T	W	**T**	**F**	**S**	**S**

Opening dates and times from 1 April subject to confirmation by EH. Tel. Custodian for details

There are special events at most Trust properties; please telephone 0870 458 4000 for details

Dunstanburgh Castle from Embleton Beach, Northumberland

➡️ [75: NU258220] 9ml NE of Alnwick, approached from Craster to the S or Embleton to the N (on foot only).
Cycle: NCN1 ¾ml. **Bus**: Arriva Northumbria 401, 501 Alnwick–Belford with connections from ≣ Berwick-upon-Tweed & Newcastle (passing Tyne & Wear Metro Haymarket), alight Craster, 1½ml. **Station**: Chathill (U), not Sun, 5ml from Embleton, 7ml from castle; Alnmouth, 7ml from Craster, 8¼ml from castle

🅿 Parking (not NT). Car parks at Craster and Embleton, 1½ml (no coaches at Embleton)

NT properties nearby
Embleton Links, Farne Islands, Lindisfarne Castle

Farne Islands

Northumberland

✚ 🏛 ✦ 🛍 | 1925 | (6:H2)

Rocky islands, habitat for seals and many species of seabird

One of Europe's most important seabird sanctuaries, the islands are home to more than 20 different species, including puffins, eider ducks and four species of tern. Many of the birds are extremely confiding and visitors can enjoy close views. There is also a large colony of seals. St Cuthbert died on Inner Farne in 687 and the chapel built in his memory can be visited.

⭐ WC on Inner Farne only

ℹ️ **T** 01665 720651, 01665 721099 (Infoline)

💷 **25 Mar-30 Apr & 1 Aug-30 Sep**: £4, child £2. **1 May–31 Jul**: £5, child £2.50. **Groups**: 1 May–31 July no adult group reduction. Booked school groups £2.50 per island. At other times adults £4, booked school groups £2 per island. Admission fees do not include boatmen's charges. Boat tickets may be bought from boatmen in Seahouses harbour and island tickets from Warden on landing. No landing in bad weather. To enquire about landing contact the Property Manager: The Sheiling, 8 St Aidan's, Seahouses, Northumberland NE68 7SR

♿ Only Inner Farne is accessible. Tidal conditions in harbour can make access to boats (not NT) difficult. Contact in advance. **WCs**: Adapted WC

👁 Braille guide

🛍 Information centre and shop at 16 Main Street, Seahouses

📷 Suitable for school groups

➡️ [75: NU230370] 2–5ml off the Northumberland coast, opposite Bamburgh: trips every day from Seahouses harbour, weather permitting.
Cycle: NCN1 ¾ml. from Seahouses harbour.
Bus: As for Dunstanburgh Castle, but alight Seahouses. **Station**: Chathill (U), not Sun, 4ml

Opening arrangements: Farne Islands			
Both Islands	25 Mar - 30 Apr	10:30 - 6	**M T W T F S S**
Staple	1 May - 31 Jul	10:30 - 1:30	**M T W T F S S**
Inner Farne	1 May - 31 Jul	1:30 - 5	**M T W T F S S**
Both Islands	1 Aug - 30 Sep	10:30 - 6	**M T W T F S S**
Centre/shop	24 Mar - 30 Jun	10 - 5	**M T W T F S S**
	1 Jul - 31 Aug	10 - 5:30	**M T W T F S S**
	1 Sep - 30 Sep	10 - 5	**M T W T F S S**
	1 Oct - 31 Oct	11 - 4	**M T W T F S S**
	3 Nov - 24 Dec	11 - 4	M T **W T F S S**
	4 Jan - 1 Apr 06	11 - 4	M T **W T F S S**

Only Inner Farne and Staple Islands can be visited. Visitors to Inner Farne in June should wear hats! Information centre/shop open half-term hols 10–5

Visitors on the Farne Islands, Northumberland

P Parking (not NT) in Seahouses, opposite harbour (pay & display)

NT properties nearby
Dunstanburgh Castle, Lindisfarne Castle, Northumberland Coast

---

George Stephenson's Birthplace

Wylam, Northumberland NE41 8BP

🏠 🛗 ♿ 🚻 🍴 🖼 1949   **(6:G5)**

Birthplace of the world famous railway engineer

This small stone tenement was built c.1760 to accommodate mining families. The furnishings reflect the year of Stephenson's birth here (1781), his whole family living in the one room.

⭐ Portaloo only

ℹ️ **T** 01661 853457
   F 01661 843276

💷 £1, child 50p

♿ ½ml from car park along cinder path.
   Building: Step to entrance.
   Refreshments: Ramped entrance

🍴 Tea-room

🚼 Pushchairs admitted

Opening arrangements: Stephenson's Birthplace		
18 Mar - 30 Oct	12 - 5	M T W **T F S S**
Open BH Mons		

Please note: groups must book in advance with the property

🔲 Suitable for school groups. Children's quiz/trail

➡️ [88: NZ126650] **Foot**: Access on foot (and cycle) through country park, ½ml E of Wylam. **Cycle**: NCN72. Easy (flat) ride beside River Tyne (approx. 5ml). **Bus**: Go North East 684 Newcastle–Ovington, alight Wylam, 1ml. **Station**: Wylam (U) ½ml. **Road**: 8ml W of Newcastle, 1½ml S of A69 at Wylam

P Parking (not NT) by war memorial in Wylam village, ½ml (pay & display).

NT properties nearby
Cherryburn, Gibside

Gibside

nr Rowlands Gill, Burnopfield, Newcastle upon Tyne NE16 6BG

🚻 🛗 🌳 ♿ 🏠 🖼 👫 🍴 1974   **(6:G5)**

Large wooded riverside estate

One of the North's finest landscapes, much of which is SSSI, Gibside is a 'forest garden' currently under restoration, embracing many miles of walks through woodland and beside the River Derwent. There are several outstanding buildings, including a Palladian chapel, Column of Liberty, and others awaiting or undergoing restoration. The estate is the former home of the Queen Mother's family, the Bowes-Lyons.

What's new in 2005 First stage of greenhouse restoration complete in spring; stables fully restored as working stables and education centre in summer

Opening arrangements: Gibside

Grounds	7 Mar - 23 Oct	10 - 6	**M T W T F S S**
	24 Oct - 5 Mar 06	10 - 4	**M T W T F S S**
Chapel	7 Mar - 23 Oct	11 - 4:30	**M T W T F S S**
Stables	1 Jul - 23 Oct	11 - 4:30	**M T W T F S S**
	24 Oct - 5 Mar 06	11 - 4	**M T W T F S S**
Shop/tea-room	7 Mar - 23 Oct	11 - 5	**M T W T F S S**
	24 Oct - 5 Mar 06	11 - 4	**M T W T F S S**

Open BH Mons. Closed 20–26 Dec and 30 Dec–1 Jan. Last admission 7 March–23 Oct 4.30; 24 Oct–5 March 3.30. Shop & tea-room open at 10 weekends. Last entry to tea-room 15 mins before closing

ℹ️ **T** 01207 541820, 01207 541829 (Shop), 01207 541828 (Tea-room) **F** 01207 541830 **E** gibside@nationaltrust.org.uk

💷 £3.50, child £2, family £10, family (one adult) £7. Groups £3

🛈 Evening guided tours by arrangement: tour and light refreshments

🎭 Programme of events. Weddings (Church of England ceremonies only)

♿ Separate designated parking, 100yds. **Building**: Steps to Chapel. Photos in information centre. **WCs**: Adapted WC. **Grounds**: Partly accessible, steep slopes. Accessible route map. 1 single-seater PMV, booking essential. **Shop**: Ramped entrance with handrail. **Refreshments**: Ramped entrance with handrail

📖 Braille guide and large-print guide. Sensory list

🍴 Tea-room beside car park. Children's menu

Visitors walking along the Avenue towards the Chapel at Gibside, Newcastle upon Tyne

🚼 Baby-changing facilities. Pushchairs and baby back-carriers admitted. Children's play area

🏫 Suitable for school groups. Children's quiz/trail. Family activity packs. Adult study days from mid-summer

🐕 On leads and only in the grounds. Disposal bins provided

➡️ [88: NZ172583] **Foot**: ½ml from Derwent Walk, footpath/cycle track linking Swalwell and Consett. **Cycle**: NCN14 ½ml. **Bus**: Go North East 45, 46/A, 47/A from Newcastle, (passing ≈ Newcastle and ≈ Metro Centre). On all, alight Rowlands Gill, ½ml. **Station**: Blaydon (U) 5ml. **Road**: 6ml SW of Gateshead, 20ml NW of Durham; entrance on B6314 between Burnopfield and Rowlands Gill; from A1 take exit north of Metro Centre and follow brown signs.

🅿️ Free parking. Limited coach parking

NT properties nearby
Cherryburn, George Stephenson's Birthplace, Souter Lighthouse, Washington Old Hall

Hadrian's Wall & Housesteads Fort

Bardon Mill, Hexham, Northumberland NE47 6NN

🏛️ 🐾 📷 🎭 1930   (6:F5)

Roman wall snaking across dramatic countryside

One of Rome's most northerly outposts, the Wall was built around AD 122 when the Roman Empire was at its height. It remains amongst Britain's most impressive ruins. There were sixteen permanent bases along the Wall, of which Housesteads Fort is one of the best-preserved, conjuring up an evocative picture of Roman military life.

Opening arrangements: Hadrian's Wall

Museum/fort	1 Apr - 30 Sep	10 - 6	**M T W T F S S**
	1 Oct - 31 Mar 06	10 - 4	**M T W T F S S**
Shop	As Museum		

Closed 24–26 Dec & 1 Jan. Opening times subject to confirmation by English Heritage. Tel. Custodian for details

Parking in National Trust car parks is free for members

⭐ The Trust owns approx. 6 miles of the Wall, running west from Housesteads Fort to Cawfields Quarry, and over 1000ha (2471 acres) of farmland. Access to the Wall and the public rights of way is from car parks operated by the Northumberland National Park Authority at Housesteads, Steel Rigg and Cawfields. Housesteads Fort is owned by the National Trust, and maintained and managed by English Heritage

ℹ️ **T** 01434 344363 (EH Custodian), 01434 344525 (Shop)

£ **Museum/Fort**: £3.10, child £1.60, concessions £2.30. Free to NT and EH members. Hadrian's Wall, NT information centre and shop free

♿ Steep slope from car and coach park to fort and EH museum. On request at NT info centre, cars can be taken up to museum, 100yds from fort. **Building**: Ramped entrance. **WCs**: Adapted WC. **Grounds**: Partly accessible. Uneven paths at Housesteads. Ramped access to Wall at Steel Rigg, 75yds from car park through rough field

📖 Braille guide

🏪 Shop/info centre at Housesteads car park

🍽️ Kiosk. Picnic tables outside information centre; seating inside. Children's lunch pack available

🚼 Baby-changing facilities

🏫 Suitable for school groups. Education room/centre. Children's guide

🐕 On leads only (sheep and ground-nesting birds)

➡️ [87: NY790688] **Foot**: 6ml of Hadrian's Wall Path & Pennine Way on property. **Bus**: Stagecoach in Cumbria AD122 Hadrian's Wall service, May-Oct only, ➎ Hexham–Carlisle (passing ➎ Haltwhistle). **Station**: Bardon Mill (U) 4ml. **Road**: 6ml NE of Haltwhistle, ½ml N of B6318; best access from car parks at Housesteads, Cawfields and Steel Rigg

🅿️ Parking (not NT) (pay & display), charge inc. NT members. Car and coach parks (operated by National Park Authority) at Housesteads (½ml walk to the Fort), Steel Rigg and at Cawfields at the western end

NT properties nearby
Allen Banks, Bellister Estate

Holy Jesus Hospital

City Road, Newcastle upon Tyne NE1 2AS

 (6:H5)

An extraordinary mix of architecture from over seven centuries of Newcastle upon Tyne's history

The Holy Jesus Hospital survives amid 1960s city centre developments, displaying features from all periods of its 700-year existence. There are remains of the 14th-century Augustinian friary, 16th-century fortifications connected with the Council of the North, a 17th-century almshouse built for the Freemen of the City and a 19th-century soup kitchen. The National Trust's Inner City Project is now based here, working to provide opportunities for modern inner-city dwellers to gain access to and enjoy the countryside on their doorstep. An exhibition room is open to visitors and guided tours of the whole site are offered once a month.

What's new in 2005 SeaBritain event during Tall Ships Race

⭐ Holy Jesus Hospital is owned by Newcastle City Council and leased to the NT as the base for its Inner City Project. The building and arrangements for visiting are managed by the NT

ℹ️ **T** 0191 255 7610
F 0191 232 4562
E innercityproject@nationaltrust.org.uk

£ **Exhibition room**: £1. **Sat opening (inc. guided tour)**: £2

🕐 1st Saturday of every month (except Jan) or by arrangement

♿ Visitors in wheelchairs from the city centre should use subway from Pilgrim Street to All Saints. No level access from roundabout. Separate designated parking. Drop-off point. **Building**: Level entrance. Alternative accessible entrance. Ground floor accessible. Stairs to other floors, lift available. Stairs to tower. Seating available. **WCs**: Adapted WC

🚼 Pushchairs and baby back-carriers admitted

🏫 Exhibition on the history of the site

Please remember – your membership card is always needed for free admission

Opening arrangements: Holy Jesus Hospital			
Exhibition	All year	12 - 4	**M T W T F** S S
Tours	(see below)	10 - 4	M T W T F **S** S

Closed BH Mons and Good Fri. Guided tours by timed ticket take place first Sat of every month except Jan, 10-4

➡️ [88: NZ253642] In centre of Newcastle upon Tyne. **Cycle**: Close to riverside routes. **Bus**: Close to city centre bus station. **Underground**: Tyne & Wear Metro–Manors, ¼ml. **Station**: Newcastle ½ml. **Road**: Close to Tyne Bridge and A167

🅿️ No parking on site. City centre car parks nearby; pay & display 30 yds

NT properties nearby
Cherryburn, George Stephenson's Birthplace, Gibside, The Leas & Marsden Rock, Souter Lighthouse, Washington Old Hall

Lindisfarne Castle

Holy Island, Berwick-upon-Tweed,
Northumberland TD15 2SH

🏛️🔦✿🏰🔔 1944   **(6:G1)**

Romantic 16th-century castle with spectacular views, transformed by Lutyens into an Edwardian holiday home

Dramatically perched on a rocky crag and accessible over a causeway at low tide only, the island castle presents an exciting and alluring aspect. Originally a Tudor fort, it was converted into a private house in 1903 by the young Edwin Lutyens. The small rooms are full of intimate decoration and design, with windows looking down upon the charming walled garden planned by Gertrude Jekyll.

⭐ Holy Island can only be reached by vehicle or on foot via a 3ml causeway, which is closed from 2 hours before high tide until 3 hours after. Tide tables are printed in local newspapers, on Northumberland CC website and displayed at the causeway. To avoid disappointment check safe crossing times before making a long/special journey. No large bags, pushchairs or rucksacks inside castle, please. Emergency WC only; otherwise nearest WC in village 1ml from castle

ℹ️ **T** 01289 389244, 01289 389253 (Shop)
F 01289 389909
E lindisfarne@nationaltrust.org.uk

💷 £5, child £2.50, family (2 adults & accompanying children under 18) £12.50. **Garden only**: £1, child free. Guided group visits outside normal hours £6, NT members £4

🚶 By arrangement

♿ Separate designated parking, 1500yds. Parking available on council road leading up to Castle. Transfer available. Drop-off point. **Building**: 200yd steep cobbled path to admission point. Ground floor has low doorways. Steep cobbled ramp and flight of 15 steps leading to ground level and lower battery. Some rope handrails. Many stairs with handrail to other floors. Seating available. **WCs**: Emergency WC on lower battery. **Grounds**: Partly accessible. Sloping farm field to Gertrude Jekyll garden. **Shop**: Steps to entrance with handrail

👁️ Braille guide and large-print guide. Sensory list

The dining room in Lindisfarne Castle, Northumberland

Opening arrangements: Lindisfarne Castle

Castle	12 Feb - 20 Feb	Times vary	**M T W T F S S**
	12 Mar - 30 Oct	Times vary	M **T W T F S S**
Garden	All year	10–dusk	**M T W T F S S**

Open BH Mons (inc. Scottish BHols). Lindisfarne is a tidal island accessed via a 3ml causeway at low tide. Therefore the castle opening times vary depending on the tides. On open days the castle will open for $4\frac{1}{2}$ hrs, which will always include 12-3. It will open either 10.30-3 or 12-4.30. To obtain a copy of the tide tables and detailed opening times send s.a.e to Lindisfarne Castle stating which month you wish to visit

🏠 In Main Street, Holy Island village. Tel. 01289 389253

👶 Baby-changing and feeding facilities. Front-carrying baby slings and hip-carrying infant seats for loan

🎒 Suitable for school groups. Family guide. Children's quiz/trail

🐕 On leads in field only

➔ [75: NU136417] **Cycle**: NCN1. Coast & Castles cycle route. **Bus**: Travelsure 477 from 🚉 Berwick-upon-Tweed. Times vary with tides, with connecting buses at Beal to and from Newcastle. Also island minibus service from Holy Island car park to castle. **Station**: Berwick-upon-Tweed 10ml from causeway. **Road**: On Holy Island, 6ml E of A1 across causeway

🅿 Parking (not NT), 1800yds (pay & display)

NT properties nearby
Farne Islands

Souter Lighthouse

Coast Road, Whitburn, Sunderland, Tyne & Wear
SR6 7NH

 1990   (6:15)

Striking Victorian lighthouse

Now boldly painted in red and white hoops, Souter lighthouse opened in 1871 and was the first to use alternating electric current, the most advanced lighthouse technology of its day. The engine room, light tower and keeper's living quarters are all on view, and there is a video, model and information display. A ground-floor

closed-circuit TV shows views from the top for those unable to climb. The Compass Room contains hands-on exhibits for all visitors, covering storms at sea, communication from ship to shore, pirates and smugglers, lighthouse life, lighting the seas and shipwreck. Immediately to the north is The Leas, $2\frac{1}{2}$ miles of beach, cliff and grassland with spectacular views, flora and fauna, and to the south, Whitburn Coastal Park, with coastal walks to the Whitburn Point Local Nature Reserve.

What's new in 2005 SeaBritain events throughout the year – send s.a.e. for details or see website

ℹ **T** 0191 529 3161, 01670 773966 (Infoline), 0191 529 3452 (Head Warden), 01670 773939 (Box office) **F** 0191 529 0902 **E** souter@nationaltrust.org.uk

£ £3.80, child £2.30, family £10. Groups (10+) £3.30, child £2. Entry to shop and tea-room free

🧍 For booked groups

🎭 Programme of events, inc. Spring Plant Fair, Festival of the Sea, themed evenings, Christmas lunches and talks. Send s.a.e. for details

🧍 Rockpool rambles and coastal walks

♿ Level access from main car park. Drop-off point. **Building**: Ramped entrance. 1 wheelchair. 1 step to Victorian keeper's cottage on ground floor. Stairs to other floors. Seating available. Photograph album, CCTV shows views from the top. **WCs**: Adapted WC. **Grounds**: Fully accessible. Accessible coast route from north to south of property. **Shop**: Level entrance. **Refreshments**: Ramped entrance. Large-print and braille menu. Range of home-made food answering dietary requirements where possible

🤟 Sign interpreter by arrangement. Induction loop in reception, shop and Video room

Opening arrangements: Souter Lighthouse

Lighthouse	19 Mar - 6 Nov	11 - 5	**M T W T** F **S S**
Tea-room/shop	As lighthouse		

Open Good Fri. Week of local Feb half-term: open every day except Fri

Please see the area introductions for details of coast & countryside properties

Souter Lighthouse, Tyne & Wear

☞ Braille guide and large-print guide. Sensory list. Handling collection

🍵 Tea-room. Home-made food includes seasonal vegetables and fruit grown in lighthouse grounds. Children's menu. Paint Store Pantry in Foghorn Field, within lighthouse grounds. Open weekends throughout season and other days, weather permitting. Children's menu

👶 Baby-changing facilities. Pushchairs admitted. Hip-carrying infant seats for loan. Children's play area. Families welcome but for safety reasons back-carriers are not permitted inside. At busy times it may not be possible to allow small children up steep tower staircase

▓ Suitable for school groups. Education room/centre. Hands-on activities. Children's quiz/trail. Family activity packs. Interpretation panels along coastal path, describing The Leas and Whitburn Coastal Park

🐕 On leads and only in grounds

➡ [88: NZ408641] **Foot**: South Tyneside Heritage Trail; 'Walking Works Wonders' local trail. **Cycle**: NCN1. Cycle route adjacent to property. **Bus**: Stagecoach in South Shields E1 � Sunderland–South Shields (passes 🚉 Sunderland & Tyne & Wear Metro South Shields). **Station**: East Boldon (Tyne & Wear Metro) 3ml. **Road**: 2½ml S of South Shields and 5ml N of Sunderland on A183 coast road

🅿 Free parking, 100yds

NT properties nearby
Gibside, Penshaw Monument, Washington Old Hall

Wallington

Cambo, Morpeth, Northumberland NE61 4AR

🏰 🐦 ✿ ♿ ♨ 🏠 😮 🎭 ♀ ▲ | 1941 | **(6:G4)**

Magnificent mansion with fine interiors and collections, set in extensive gardens and parkland

Dating from 1688, the house was home to many generations of the Blackett and Trevelyan families, who all left their mark. The restrained Palladian exterior gives way to the magnificent rococo plasterwork of the interior, which houses fine ceramics, paintings, needlework and a

Opening arrangements: Wallington										
House	23 Mar - 4 Sep	1 - 5:30	**M**	T	**W**	**T**	**F**	**S**	**S**
	5 Sep - 30 Oct	1 - 4:30	**M**	T	**W**	**T**	**F**	**S**	**S**
Walled garden	1 Apr - 30 Sep	10 - 7	**M**	**T**	**W**	**T**	**F**	**S**	**S**
	1 Oct - 31 Oct	10 - 6	**M**	**T**	**W**	**T**	**F**	**S**	**S**
	1 Nov - 31 Mar 06	10 - 4	**M**	**T**	**W**	**T**	**F**	**S**	**S**
Shop	2 Mar - 29 May	10:30 - 5:30	**M**	T	**W**	**T**	**F**	**S**	**S**
	30 May - 4 Sep	10:30 - 5:30	**M**	**T**	**W**	**T**	**F**	**S**	**S**
	5 Sep - 30 Oct	10:30 - 4:30	**M**	T	**W**	**T**	**F**	**S**	**S**
	2 Nov - 12 Feb 06	10:30 - 4:30	M	T	**W**	**T**	**F**	**S**	**S**
	13 Feb - 27 Mar	10:30 - 5:30	**M**	T	**W**	**T**	**F**	**S**	**S**
Restaurant	As shop									
Farm shop	1 Apr - 24 Dec	10:30 - 5	**M**	**T**	**W**	**T**	**F**	**S**	**S**
	28 Dec - 31 Mar 06	10:30 - 4	**M**	**T**	**W**	**T**	**F**	**S**	**S**
Grounds	All year	Dawn-dusk	**M**	**T**	**W**	**T**	**F**	**S**	**S**

Last admission 1hr before closing. Last admission to restaurant 30 mins before closing. Shop and restaurant closed 20 Dec–13 Jan inc. Farm Shop (outside the turnstile) closed 25–27 Dec & 1–2 Jan 06. Gardens open all year except 25 Dec

Unless indicated, last admission is always 30mins before closing time

collection of dolls' houses. The Central Hall was decorated to look like an Italian courtyard, heavily influenced by the Pre-Raphaelites, with a series of scenes of Northumbrian history by William Bell Scott. The original formality of Sir Walter Blackett's 18th-century landscape, influenced by 'Capability' Brown, who went to school in the estate village, underlies the present surroundings which offer walks through a variety of lawns, shrubberies, lakes and woodland, enlivened with buildings, sculpture, water features and a wildlife hide. The beautiful walled garden has varied collections of plants and an abundant conservatory. Longer estate walks encompass wooded valleys and high moorland.

What's new in 2005 The second stage of the redecoration scheme begun in 2004 continues the major refurbishment of the house

★ The gardens and estate remain open throughout the year, as does the Farm Shop, opened in 2002, in support of the estate's farm tenants and other regional suppliers

[i] **T** 01670 773600, 01670 773967 (Infoline), 01670 773619 (Farm Shop), 01670 773602 (Learning), 01670 773939 (Box office), 01670 773611 (Shop), 01670 773610 (Restaurant) **F** 01670 774420 **E** wallington@nationaltrust.org.uk

[£] **House, garden & grounds**: £7.30, child £3.65, family £18.25. Groups £6.50. **Garden & grounds only**: £5.20, child £2.60, family £13. Groups £4.60

[↑] Available outside normal opening hours. Contact Events and Education Co-ordinator

[♿] Separate designated parking, 200yds. Parking adjacent to ticket office and at walled garden (obtain pass from ticket office). Drop-off point by arrangement. **Building**: Steps to entrance, ramp available. 3 wheelchairs. Lift to other floors. Seating available. **WCs**: Adapted WC. **Grounds**: Accessible route map. 1 single-seater PMV, booking essential. **Shop**: Level entrance. **Refreshments**: Many steps to entrance with handrail. Access to downstairs self-service restaurant on request when not open

[✿] Interesting scents

[🛍] NT shop. Plant sales

[🍽] Restaurant. May be limited off-season. Children's menu

[🎌] In grassed courtyard and grounds

[👶] Baby-changing facilities. Front-carrying baby slings and hip-carrying infant seats for loan. Children's play area

[▦] Suitable for school groups. Hands-on activities. Children's quiz/trail

West front, Wallington, Northumberland

On leads in grounds and walled garden

→ [81: NZ030843] **Bus**: Northumbria Mini Coaches 419 from Morpeth, Wed, Fri, Sat only (passing close ⁂ Morpeth); Arriva Northumbria 508 from ⁂ Newcastle, Sun, June–Oct only; otherwise National Express from Newcastle (passing close ⁂ Newcastle), alight Capheaton Road End, 2ml. **Road**: 12ml W of Morpeth (B6343), 6ml NW of Belsay (A696), take B6342 to Cambo

P Free parking

NT properties nearby
Cragside

Washington Old Hall

The Avenue, Washington Village, Washington, Tyne & Wear NE38 7LE

🏯 ⁂ 🏠 🍷 ♨ ⧗ 1956   (6:H5)

Manor house associated with the family of George Washington

Washington Old Hall is a delightful stone-built 17th-century manor house, which incorporates parts of the original medieval home of George Washington's direct ancestors. It is from here that the family surname of Washington was derived. There are displays on George Washington, and the recent history of the Hall. There is also a fine collection of oil paintings, delftware and heavily carved oak furniture, giving an authentic impression of gentry life following the turbulence of the English Civil War. The tranquil Jacobean garden leads to the Nuttery, a wildflower nut orchard.

ℹ **T** 0191 416 6879
   F 0191 419 2065
   E washington.oldhall@nationaltrust.org.uk

£ £3.80, child £2.30, family £10. Groups £3.30, child £2

🎟 Introductory talks for pre-booked group visits

Opening arrangements: Washington Old Hall									
House	25 Mar - 30 Oct	11 - 5	**M**	**T**	**W**	T	F	S	**S**
Garden	As house	10 - 5							
Tea-room	As house	11 - 4							
Open Good Fri									

Programme of events, inc. 4 July Independence Day celebrations. Lunchtime lectures. Tel. for details

Contact in advance. Parking available beside Old Hall. **Building**: Many steps to entrance with handrail. Alternative accessible entrance. 1 wheelchair. Ground floor accessible. Stairs with handrail to other floors. Seating available. Photograph album. **WCs**: Adapted WC. **Grounds**: Partly accessible. Accessible route. **Shop**: Access by alternative entrance to building. **Refreshments**: Many steps to entrance with handrail. Refreshments can be served on ground floor or in garden

Induction loop in Liberty room, where subtitled video is played

Large-print guide. Sensory list. Handling collection

Souvenir desk in entrance hall

Tea-room (not NT) on first floor. Serving light refreshments (run by Friends of Washington Old Hall)

In the Nuttery, rugs for loan

Hip-carrying infant seats for loan. Pushchairs admitted (ground floor only)

Suitable for school groups. Education room/centre. Children's quiz/trail

On leads in garden only

→ [88: NZ312566] In Washington Village next to church on the hill. **Cycle**: NCN7 1ml. **Bus**: Go North East 194, 291-2 from Tyne & Wear Metro Heworth, 185/6, X85 from ⁂ Sunderland. **Station**: Heworth (Tyne & Wear Metro) 4ml; Newcastle 7ml. **Road**: 7ml S of Newcastle, 5ml from The Angel of the North. From A1 or A19 follow signs onto the A1231, then to Washington Village. **Note**: Local District road signs are being changed during 2005; this may affect signage to Old Hall (District 4)

P Free parking in small car park beside Old Hall. Otherwise unrestricted parking on The Avenue. Coaches must park on The Avenue

NT properties nearby
Gibside, The Leas & Marsden Rock, Penshaw Monument, Souter Lighthouse

---

For further information check our website www.nationaltrust.org.uk

South West South & South East
London East of England
East Midlands West Midlands
North West Yorkshire North East
Wales Northern Ireland

Mae'r wybodaeth sydd yn y llawlyfr hwn am feddiannau'r Ymddiriedolaeth Genedlaethol yng Nghymru ar gael yn Gymraeg o Swyddfa'r Ymddiriedolaeth Genedlaethol, Sgwar y Drindod, Llandudno LL30 2DE, ffôn 01492 860123.

Wales is famous for its spectacular coastline, rugged mountain scenery and lush green valleys. With three national parks and thousands of hectares designated as Areas of Outstanding Natural Beauty, visitors do not have to travel far to reach beautiful open countryside offering many recreational opportunities. The National Trust plays an active role in protecting and managing this countryside and owns 133 miles of the Welsh coastline. In fact, the first property ever given to the Trust was in Wales, at **Dinas Oleu** above Barmouth on the Cardigan Bay coast, bequeathed in 1895.

The **Gower Peninsula**, near Swansea, was the first place in Britain to be given AONB status and offers a diversity of habitats, including stunning beaches and walks with breathtaking views. The Trust's Neptune Coastline Campaign has helped to purchase beautiful areas of scenery around the headland on the Taf/Tywi estuary, and also further west at **Ragwen Point** in Carmarthenshire, from where there are views

back towards Gower and along the coast to Caldy Island.

In Pembrokeshire, the 186-mile Coast Path starts at Amroth and runs through several areas owned by the Trust, including the **Colby Estate & Woodland Garden**, from where there are dramatic views of Devon and Carmarthen Bay. To the west lies the fascinating **Stackpole Estate**, which includes **Barafundle Bay**, the beach at **Broadhaven South** and the delightful freshwater lily ponds at **Bosherston**.

Further west, the Trust owns 15½ miles of the coastline of **St Bride's Bay**, including the former **Deer Park** at **Marloes** and the tiny harbour of **Martin's Haven**. Nearby **Marloes Sands** offer wonderful walks. This part of the coast is excellent for wildlife, with ravens, choughs and grey seals to be seen, as well as a wide variety of interesting plants and insects.

The city of **St David's**, dedicated to the patron saint of Wales, is situated in an area of spectacular geology, with rocky outcrops and coastal plateaux, much of which is Trust-owned. The spectacular coastline and wonderful views continue northwards to Ceredigion, where the beaches at **Mwnt** and **Penbryn** are especially popular. From the dramatic coast at **Mynachdy'r Graig** the whole sweep of Cardigan Bay can be admired.

Rhossili beach, Gower, Swansea

Previous page: The gardener's bothy at Powis Castle, Powys

Behind the coast lies a fascinating hinterland of green meadows, rivers and rolling hills. Much of this countryside is unspoilt and ideal for a relaxing holiday. At the heart of this area of Carmarthenshire lies **Dinefwr Castle and Park** near Llandeilo, the historic seat of the former Welsh princes of South Wales and an ancient deer park of much wildlife interest. Nearby is **Paxton's Tower**, an early 19th-century folly dedicated to Lord Nelson, from which there are fine views of the Towy Valley.

Mid and South East Wales holds some of the country's most spectacular scenery, including the Brecon Beacons National Park and the Wye Valley AONB. Within the National Park the Trust owns 3500ha (9000 acres), including **Cribyn, Corn Du,** and **Pen-y-Fan** (the highest point in southern Britain), and also, fringing the Beacons, a number of valley heads where traditional hill farms and woodlands give way to heather moorland. Further west can be found **Henrhyd Falls,** South Wales' highest waterfall and farms in the Neath valley with wonderfully rich and unspoilt hay meadows.

East of the Beacons is the conical summit of **Sugar Loaf** mountain, overlooking the market town of Abergavenny and commanding stunning panoramic views across the Usk valley. Nearby, the **Skirrid Fawr,** known locally as the

The limestone cliffs at Stackpole Head, Pembrokeshire

holy mountain, offers both woodland and upland walks.

North of the National Park can be found the **Begwns**, a 523ha (1300-acre) hilltop common with dramatic views. Further north is **Abergwesyn Common**. Stretching $12\frac{1}{2}$ miles from Llanwrthwl in the east to the Nant Irfon gorge in the west, it offers a huge area of very remote and wild walking country for the adventurous.

Lanlay Meadows near Peterstone Supe Ely is an area of lowland haymeadow and pasture bordering the river Ely. Rich in wildlife, it is a treat to walk through in early summer. At **Clytha** estate near Raglan, a classic 18th-century parkland landscape, there are signed walks around the perimieter and along the river Usk. (The house and castle are not open to the public.)

Snowdonia, in North Wales, is justly famous for its epic upland landscapes, including **Hafod y Llan** on the southern flank of Snowdon, acquired following a successful public appeal in 1998. The Watkin Path, one of the main routes up Snowdon, runs the length of the entire estate. Hafod y Llan is one of the seven properties that surround the picturesque village of Beddgelert with its riverside walk to the romantic Gelert's Grave. Near the village lies the miniature Victorian estate of **Craflwyn**, where

Paxton's Tower, Dyfed, built in 1811 as a memorial to Lord Nelson

The beach at Porthor, Gwynedd

visitors can learn about the estate's restoration by following a family trail.

The Trust owns eleven of the main mountain peaks in Snowdonia, including **Tryfan** (part of the Carneddau property), where the first successful Everest climbers trained. The **Carneddau** and **Ysbyty Estate**, together covering over 15,000ha (37,000 acres), contain some of the most exciting scenery of all and include **Cwm Idwal**, a nature reserve famous for its flora. South west of Betws-y-coed is **Tŷ Mawr** in the charming little valley of Wybrnant, which offers many delightful walks. In the south of the Snowdonia National Park at **Cregennan** there are splendid walks amidst hill farms and upland lakes, with fine views towards **Cadair Idris** and over Cardigan Bay. The **Dolmelynllyn Estate** near Dolgellau contains one of Wales's most impressive waterfalls, **Rhaeadr Ddu**, which can be reached by footpath from Ganllwyd, as well as sheepwalks on **Y Llethr**, the highest peak in the Rhinog Mountains. This whole area is full of wildlife interest and is particularly noted for its late summer and autumn colours.

The north-west arm of Wales – the beautiful Llŷn Peninsula – is noted for its spectacular coastal scenery. Through successful coastline campaigns, it has been possible for the Trust to acquire and protect such wonderful places as **Porthdinllaen**, a charming fishing village, the famous 'whistling sands' of **Porthor**, and **Traeth Llanbedrog**, popular for its safe bathing and colourful beach huts.

The National Trust owns large sections of the rugged and remote coast of Anglesey, including **Porth Dafarch**, a beach and headland near Holyhead. Also on Anglesey is the restored thatched cottage of **Swtan**, which although

owned by the Trust is managed by the local community. (Visitors, including NT members, are charged a small fee.)

Another Anglesey highlight is the lagoon at **Cemlyn**, internationally famous for its colonies of breeding terns, and managed as a nature reserve in conjunction with the North Wales Wildlife Trust.

Highlights in Wales for Visitors with Disabilities ...

There is a wheelchair-accessible footpath to Gelert's Grave, and many excellent paths on the **Stackpole Estate**, including a lakeside route with two accessible bird hides and a level woodland route suitable for unaccompanied wheelchair users; (tel. 01646 661359 for a leaflet). **Erddig Country Park** at Felin Puleston offers good pathways, suitable for unaccompanied

Porthdinllaen on the Llŷn Peninsula, Gwynedd

Hafod y Llan farm with the backdrop of Snowdonia

wheelchair users, leading through woodland and along the River Clywedog; tel. 01978 355314 for details. At **Dinefwr** there is a boardwalk through Bog Wood to the lake. On the Gower peninsula at **Rhossili** an accessible path leads to the old coastguard lookout. Accessible picnic sites can be found on the **Dolmelynllyn Estate** at Ganllwyd, at **Glan Faenol** on the Menai Strait and at **Porthdinllaen** on Llŷn. An accessible path leads to a viewing terrace and beach café at **Porthor** (Whistling Sands) on Llŷn.

...and for Families

Particularly recommended are the beaches at **Broadhaven**, **Porthdinllaen**, **Llanbedrog** and **Porthor**, as well as **Rhossili**, where shipwrecks become visible at low tide, and **Mwnt**, from where dolphins can often be seen.

Further Information

Please contact the NT Office for Wales in Llandudno, tel. 01492 860123.

OS Grid Reference

OS grid references for main properties with no individual entry (OS Landranger map series numbers given in brackets)

Abergwesyn Common	[147]	SN841551
Barafundle Bay	[158]	SR992958
The Begwns	[148]	SO163442
Bosherston	[158]	SR976938
Broadhaven	[151]	SR976937
Carneddau	[115]	SH649604
Cemlyn	[114]	SH336932
Clytha	[161]	SO367091
Corn Du	[160]	SO008214
Craflwyn	[115]	SH600490
Cregennan	[124]	SH660140
Cribyn	[160]	SO024213
Cwm Idwal	[115]	SH647603
Dinas Oleu	[124]	SH615158
Dolmelynllyn Estate	[124]	SH728243
Gelli Iago	[115]	SH640481
Glan Faenol	[115]	SH534698
Gower	[159]	SS420900
Hafod y Llan	[115]	SH627507
Henrhyd Falls	[160]	SN855121
Lanlay Meadows	[170]	ST075760
Llanbedrog Beach	[123]	SH330315
Marloes Deer Park	[157]	SM758091
Marloes Sands	[157]	SM770085
Martin's Haven	[157]	SM758091
Mwnt	[145]	SN190520
Mynachdy'r Graig	[135]	SN563742
Paxton's Tower	[159]	SN541191
Pen-y-Fan	[160]	SO013215
Penbryn	[145]	SN295519
Porthclais Harbour	[157]	SM740241
Porth Dafarch	[114]	SH234200
Porthdinllaen	[123]	SH278415
Porthor	[123]	SH166298
Ragwen Point	[158]	SN220070
Skirrid Fawr	[161]	SO330180
Stackpole Quay	[158]	SR992958
Sugar Loaf	[161]	SO268167
Swtan	[114]	SH301892
Ysbyty Estate	[115]	SH842488

Aberconwy House

Castle Street, Conwy LL32 8AY

🏠 🗄 𝑖 [1934]   (4:F2)

14th-century merchant's house

This is the only medieval merchant's house in Conwy to have survived the turbulent history of the walled town over nearly six centuries. Furnished rooms and an audio-visual presentation show daily life from different periods in its history.

What's new in 2005 Guidebook for House and Conwy Suspension Bridge

⭐ The house has limited electric lighting and is therefore dark on dull days. No WC

ℹ️ **T** 01492 592246 (House and shop)
   F 01492 564818

£ £2.60, child £1.30, family £6.50. Groups £2.10, child £1

🎭 Various musical events. Tel. for details

♿ **Building**: Many steps to entrance. Alternative accessible entrance, via internal staircase from shop. Stairs to other floors. Seating available. **Shop**: (in basement) is accessible via 3 steps from High Street pavement

📱 Sensory list

🏛 Suitable for school groups. Family guide. Children's quiz/trail

➡️ [115: SH781777] At junction of Castle Street and High Street. **Cycle**: NCN5. **Bus**: From surrounding areas. **Station**: Conwy 300yds

P No parking on site

NT properties nearby
Bodnant Garden, Conwy Suspension Bridge, Penrhyn Castle

Opening arrangements: Aberconwy House										
House	18 Mar - 30 Oct	11 - 5	M	T	W	T	F	S	S
Shop	1 Mar - 31 Mar	10 - 5	M	T	W	T	F	S	S
	1 Apr - 31 Oct	10 - 5:30	M	T	W	T	F	S	S
	1 Nov - 31 Dec	10 - 5	M	T	W	T	F	S	S
	5 Jan - 26 Feb 06	10 - 5	M	T	W	T	F	S	S
Shop closed 25, 26 Dec									

Aberdulais Falls

Aberdulais, nr Neath, Neath & Port Talbot SA10 8EU

🌊 🏊 🗄 🛒 🎧 🎥 🎭 [1981]   (4:F9)

Famous waterfalls and fascinating industrial site

For over 400 years the falls provided the energy to drive the wheels of industry, from the manufacture of copper in 1584 to the later tinplate works. It has also been visited by famous artists, such as Turner in 1796. The site today houses a unique hydroelectric scheme which has been developed to harness the waters of the River Dulais. The Turbine House provides access to an interactive computer, fish pass, observation window and display panels. Special lifts have been installed to allow disabled visitors access to the upper levels, which afford excellent views of the Falls. The waterwheel is the largest currently used in Europe to generate electricity, which makes Aberdulais Falls self-sufficient in environmentally friendly energy.

⭐ The operation of the fish pass, waterwheel and turbine is subject to water levels and maintenance. Site may be closed for major alterations from 4 Sept. Tel. for details

ℹ️ **T** 01639 636674
   F 01639 645069
   E aberdulais@nationaltrust.org.uk

£ £3.20, child £1.60, family £8. Groups £2.40, child £1.20. Children must be accompanied by an adult

𝑖 Guided tours in July and Aug; groups at other times by arrangement. Audio tours available

Opening arrangements: Aberdulais Falls										
Falls	4 Mar - 3 Apr	11 - 4	M	T	W	T	**F**	**S**	**S**
	4 Apr - 28 Oct	10 - 5	**M**	**T**	**W**	**T**	**F**	S	S
	9 Apr - 30 Oct	11 - 6	M	T	W	T	**F**	**S**	**S**
	4 Nov - 18 Dec	11 - 4	M	T	W	T	**F**	**S**	**S**
	19 Dec - 21 Dec	11 - 4	**M**	**T**	**W**	T	F	S	S
Christmas shop	2 Dec - 21 Dec	As Falls							
Open BH Mons and Good Fri 11–6. Please check after Aug 05 for opening times as property will be undergoing refurbishment									

Please see the area introductions for details of coast & countryside properties

Aberdulais Falls, near Neath, Neath & Port Talbot

➔ [170: SS772995] **Foot**: via Neath-Aberdulais Canal footpath. **Cycle**: NCN47 passes property. Access near B&Q Neath to Neath Canal towpath and Aberdulais Canal Basin. **Bus**: First 158 Swansea–Banwen, 154/8, 161 from Neath; Stagecoach in South Wales X75 Swansea–Merthyr Tydfil. All pass close ⇌ Neath. **Station**: Neath 3ml. **Road**: On A4109, 3ml NE of Neath. 4ml from M4 exit 43 at Llandarcy, take A465 signposted Vale of Neath

P Free parking. On-road parking for coaches and cars on A4109 outside property entrance; coaches must check in advance as parking limited

NT properties nearby
Henrhyd Falls

♿ Separate designated parking, 30yds. Designated bay outside property. Drop-off point. **Building**: Level entrance. 2 wheelchairs. Ground floor accessible. Stairs to other floors, lift available. Lifts provide access to interactive display and fish pass observation window. Seating available. Audio visual/video. **WCs**: Adapted WC. **Grounds**: Fully accessible. **Shop**: Steps to entrance, ramp available. **Refreshments**: Ramped entrance

☕ Tea-room. The Friends of Aberdulais Falls serve light refreshments in the Old Works Library and Victorian schoolroom on public holidays and daily throughout the summer; other times by arrangement

👶 Baby-changing facilities. Pushchairs and baby back-carriers admitted

▦ Suitable for school groups. Education room/centre. Children's guide. Children's quiz/trail

🐕 On leads only

Bodnant Garden

Tal-y-Cafn, Colwyn Bay, Conwy LL28 5RE

🏠 ❖ 🏚 ☕ 1949   (4:F2)

World-famous garden noted for its botanical collections

One of the world's most spectacular gardens, Bodnant is situated above the River Conwy, with stunning views across Snowdonia. Begun in 1875, Bodnant is the creation of four generations of Aberconways and features huge Italianate terraces and formal lawns on its upper level, with a wooded valley, stream and wild garden below. There are dramatic colours throughout the season, with fine collections of rhododendrons, magnolias and camellias and the spectacular laburnum arch, a 55yd tunnel of golden blooms, from mid-May to early June.

★ The garden and Pavilion Tea-room are managed on behalf of the Trust by the Hon. Michael McLaren QC

ℹ **T** 01492 650460, 01492 650758 (Tea-room)
F 01492 650448
E office@bodnantgarden.co.uk

Opening arrangements: Bodnant Garden										
Garden	12 Mar - 30 Oct	10 - 5	**M**	**T**	**W**	**T**	**F**	**S**	**S**
Plant centre	All Year	10 - 5	**M**	**T**	**W**	**T**	**F**	**S**	**S**
Tea-room	As garden	11 - 5							

Unless indicated, last admission is always 30mins before closing time

£ £5.50, child £2.75. Groups (20+) £5. RHS members free

♿ Designated parking in main car park, 50yds. **WCs**: Adapted WC. **Grounds**: steep slopes, many steps. Accessible route map. Some visitors may require assistance from their companion. **Shop**: Ramped entrance. **Refreshments**: Ramped entrance

👁 Braille guide. Interesting scents

📷 Shop (not NT). Plant sales. Tel. 01492 650731

🍴 Bodnant Pavilion Tea-room in car park

🚻 In car park only

🚼 Baby-changing facilities. Pushchairs and baby back-carriers admitted. Front-carrying baby slings for loan

🐕 On leads in car park only

➔ [115/116: SH801723] **Bus**: Arriva/Alpine 25 from Llandudno (passing ☰ Llandudno Junction). **Station**: Tal-y-Cafn (U) 1½ml. **Road**: 8ml S of Llandudno and Colwyn Bay off A470, entrance ½ml along the Eglwysbach road. Signposted from A55, exit 19

P Free parking, 50yds

NT properties nearby
Aberconwy House, Conwy Suspension Bridge, Tŷ Mawr Wybrnant

Chirk Castle

Chirk, Wrexham LL14 5AF

🕍➕✥♿🏠🍴🚼👶🐕⏱ 1981   (4:G3)

Magnificent 14th-century fortress of the Welsh Marches

Completed in 1310, Chirk's rather austere exterior belies the comfortable and elegant state rooms inside, with elaborate plasterwork, superb Adam-style furniture, tapestries and portraits. Features from different eras include the medieval tower and dungeon and 18th-century Servants' Hall. In the formal garden are clipped yews, roses and climbers on the castle wall. Further on the garden is more informal, with a thatched 'Hawk House' and rock garden. The shrub garden has a small pool and rare varieties of trees and shrubs. A terrace with stunning views leads to a classical pavilion and

Opening arrangements: Chirk Castle										
Castle	18 Mar - 30 Sep	12 - 5	M	T	**W**	**T**	**F**	**S**	**S**
	1 Oct - 30 Oct	12 - 4	M	T	**W**	**T**	**F**	**S**	**S**
Garden	18 Mar - 30 Sep	11 - 6	M	T	**W**	**T**	**F**	**S**	**S**
	1 Oct - 30 Oct	11 - 5	M	T	**W**	**T**	**F**	**S**	**S**
Tea-room	18 Mar - 30 Sep	11 - 5	M	T	**W**	**T**	**F**	**S**	**S**
	1 Oct - 30 Oct	11 - 4	M	T	**W**	**T**	**F**	**S**	**S**
Shop	As castle								

Open BH Mons. Last admission to garden 1hr before closing. Last admission to state rooms ½hr before closing

17th-century lime tree avenue. The 18th-century parkland contains many mature trees and elaborate gates, made in 1719 by the Davies brothers. After 400 years of occupation, the house is still lived in by the Myddelton family.

What's new in 2005 2ml circular estate walk; library exhibition

ℹ **T** 01691 777701,
01691 776310 (Learning),
01691 776309 (Box office),
01691 776306 (Shop),
01691 776304 (Tea-room)
F 01691 774706
E chirkcastle@nationaltrust.org.uk

£ £6.40, child £3.20, family £15.80. Groups £5, child £2.50. **Garden only**: £4, child £2, family £10. Groups £3.20, child £1.60

🔑 Connoisseurs' tour by arrangement (min. 15), Wed–Fri am only

😊 Programme of events, inc. family fun days and snowdrop walks. Send s.a.e. for details

♿ Designated parking in main car park. Wheelchair-accessible transfer. Drop-off point. **Building**: Many steps to entrance, stairlift available. 3 wheelchairs, booking essential. Ground floor accessible. Many stairs with handrail to other floors. Access restricted to one wheelchair user at any one time on first floor. Seating available. Photograph album. **WCs**: Adapted WC. **Grounds**: Partly accessible, loose gravel paths. Some visitors may require assistance from their companion. **Shop**: Many steps to entrance with handrail. **Refreshments**: Level entrance. Large-print menu

📱 Induction loop in reception, shop and mobile unit for house

There are special events at most Trust properties; please telephone 0870 458 4000 for details

The east front of Chirk Castle, Wrexham

Braille guide. Sensory list

NT shop. Plant sales

Licensed tea-room in castle courtyard. Children's menu only during school hols and weekends. Kiosk at Home Farm

Picnics in car park and picnic area only

Baby-changing and feeding facilities. Front-carrying baby slings and hip-carrying infant seats for loan. Children's play area

Suitable for school groups. Education room/centre. Hands-on activities. Children's guide. Children's quiz/trail. Adult study days

On leads and only in car park and on estate walks

[126: SJ275388] **Foot**: Offa's Dyke Path passes property. **Bus**: Arriva 2/A Wrexham–Oswestry. **Station**: Chirk (U) $\frac{1}{4}$ml to gates, 2ml to castle. **Road**: Entrance 1ml off A5, 2ml W of Chirk village; 7ml S of Wrexham, signposted off A483

P Free parking, 200yds. Short, steep hill between car park and castle

NT properties nearby
Erddig, Powis Castle

Cilgerran Castle

nr Cardigan, Pembrokeshire SA43 2SF

[1938]   (4:C7)

Striking 13th-century ruined castle

The remains of the castle are perched overlooking the spectacular Teifi Gorge and have inspired many artists, including Turner.

★ Cilgerran Castle is in the guardianship of Cadw: Welsh Historic Monuments

i **T** 01239 615007

£ £2.50, child £2, family £7, students £1.50. (Prices may increase from April '05)

[145: SN195431] **Bus**: Midway 430 from Cardigan; otherwise First 460/1 Carmarthen–Cardigan, alight Llechryd, 1$\frac{3}{4}$ml by footpath. **Road**: On rock above left bank of the Teifi, 3ml SE of Cardigan, 1$\frac{1}{2}$ml E of A478

Opening arrangements: Cilgerran Castle										
Castle	1 Apr - 26 Oct	9:30 - 6:30	**M**	**T**	**W**	**T**	**F**	**S**	**S**
	27 Oct - 31 Mar 06	9:30 - 4	**M**	**T**	**W**	**T**	**F**	**S**	**S**
Tel. after 31 March to confirm opening dates & prices									

For further information check our website www.nationaltrust.org.uk

Colby Woodland Garden

Amroth, Narberth, Pembrokeshire SA67 8PP

❀ 🌳 ⛲ 🏛 ⎙ 💷 🚶 1980 (4:C8)

Beautiful woodland garden with year-round interest

The 3¼ha (8-acre) garden has a fine display of colour in spring, with rhododendrons, magnolias, azaleas and camellias, underplanted with bluebells. Later highlights are the summer hydrangeas and autumn foliage. Open and wooded pathways through the valley offer lovely walks.

What's new in 2005 Replanting near monkey puzzle tree in West Wood; water feature

⭐ The early 19th-century house is not open; Mr & Mrs A Scourfield Lewis kindly allow access to the walled garden during opening hours

ℹ️ **T/F** 01834 811885, 01834 814200 (Gallery), 01834 814163 (Tea-room)

💷 £3.60, child £1.80, family £9. Groups £3, child £1.50. Coaches welcome. Open evenings by arrangement

🎭 Programme of events, inc. guided walks and lunch with Gardener-in-charge in the season, evening entertainment, family fun days

♿ Drop-off point. **WCs**: Adapted WC. **Grounds**: Partly accessible. Some visitors may require assistance from their companion. **Shop**: Level entrance. Steep access path from car park. **Refreshments**: Ramped entrance

🏛 Gallery displaying work of Pembrokeshire artists and craftspeople

💷 Tea-room (not NT). Children's menu

🅿 In car park

🚼 Baby-changing facilities. Pushchairs admitted

🏫 Suitable for school groups. Children's quiz/trail. Family activity packs

Opening arrangements: Colby Woodland Garden										
Woodland gdn	18 Mar - 30 Oct	10 - 5	**M**	**T**	**W**	**T**	**F**	**S**	**S**
Walled gdn	18 Mar - 30 Oct	11 - 5	**M**	**T**	**W**	**T**	**F**	**S**	**S**
Shop/gallery	As Wood. Gdn									
Tea-room	As Wood. Gdn	10 - 4:30								

Please note: groups must book in advance with the property

Rhododendrons in Colby Woodland Garden, Pembrokeshire

🐕 On leads, but not in walled garden

➔ [158: SN155080] **Foot**: from beach via public footpath in Amroth (beside Amroth Arms). **Bus**: Silcox/First 350/1 from Tenby (passing ☒ Kilgetty). **Station**: Kilgetty (U) 2½ml. **Road**: 1½ml inland from Amroth beside Carmarthen Bay. Follow brown signs from A477 Tenby–Carmarthen road or off coast road at Amroth Castle

🅿 Free parking, 100yds. Contact property for route map for coaches and cars

NT properties nearby
Stackpole Estate, Tudor Merchant's House

Conwy Suspension Bridge

Conwy LL32 8LD

🏠 ⛴ 🐕 1965 (4:F2)

Elegant suspension bridge and toll-keeper's house

Designed and built by Thomas Telford, the bridge was completed in 1826. It replaced the ferry, which was previously the only means of

Opening arrangements: Conwy Suspension Bridge		
18 Mar - 30 Oct	11 - 5	**M T W T F S S**

crossing the river. The house has been restored and furnished as it would have been a century ago.

What's new in 2005 Guidebook for Bridge and Aberconwy House

⭐ No WC

ℹ️ **T** 01492 573282 **F** 01492 564818

£ £1.40, child 70p, family £3.50

♿ Limited parking available during day by adjoining bridge. **Building**: Level entrance. Ground floor accessible. **Grounds**: Steps to lower terraces

🎦 At Lower Terrace only

📖 Suitable for school groups. Family guide

➡️ [115: SH785775] 100yds from town centre, adjacent to Conwy Castle. **Cycle**: NCN5. **Bus**: From surrounding areas. **Station**: Conwy ¼ml; Llandudno Junction ½ml

🅿️ No parking on site

NT properties nearby
Aberconwy House, Bodnant Garden, Penrhyn Castle

Dinefwr

Llandeilo, Carmarthenshire SA19 6RT

 1990 (4:E8)

18th-century landscape park, enclosing a medieval deer park

Dinefwr is home to more than 100 fallow deer and a small herd of Dinefwr White Park Cattle. A number of scenic walks include access to Dinefwr Castle, with fine views across the Towy valley. There is also a wooded boardwalk, particularly suitable for families and wheelchair users. Newton House, built in 1660, but now with a Victorian façade and a fountain garden, is at the heart of the site. The tea-room here looks out over the deer park. Showrooms and exhibition rooms are open to visitors, including an exhibition in the basement on the history of Dinefwr.

What's new in 2005 Exhibition in Old Slaughterhouse about the Dinefwr Estate, its flora and fauna. New park tours by tractor and trailer

⭐ Some rooms in the house may be closed after 1 Sept, due to renovation work. Tel. for details

ℹ️ **T** 01558 823947 **F** 01558 825925
E dinefwr@nationaltrust.org.uk

£ £3.80, child £1.90, family £9. Groups £3.
Park only: £2.60, child £1.30, family £6.30. Groups £2.10

🎪 Guided tours of Newton House and the deer park by arrangement in advance at a small additional charge. Badger watches can be booked

♿ Drop-off point. **Building**: Ramped entrance. 2 wheelchairs, booking essential. Steep steps to basement. Virtual tour. **WCs**: Adapted WC. **Grounds**: Partly accessible. Accessible route. Long level boardwalk to mill pond. **Refreshments**: Ramped entrance. Large-print menu

♒ Braille guide. Sensory list

☕ Tea-room (not NT). Children's menu

🚼 Baby-changing and feeding facilities. Pushchairs admitted

📖 Suitable for school groups. Education room/centre. Children's quiz/trail

🐕 On leads and only in outer park

➡️ [159: SN625225] **Bus**: From surrounding areas to Llandeilo, then 1ml. **Station**: Llandeilo 1½ml. **Road**: On W outskirts of Llandeilo A40(T); from Swansea take M4 to Pont Abraham, then A48(T) to Cross Hands and A476 to Llandeilo; entrance by police station

🅿️ Parking, 50yds. Narrow access

NT properties nearby
Aberdeunant, Dolaucothi Gold Mines, Paxton's Tower

Opening arrangements: Dinefwr			
House/park	18 Mar - 30 Oct	11 - 5	**M** T W **T F S S**

Last admission 45mins before closing. Park open every day during school hols. On Tues & Wed the house is available for pre-arranged conferences

Parking in National Trust car parks is free for members

Dolaucothi Gold Mines

Pumsaint, Llanwrda, Carmarthenshire SA19 8RR

🏛️ ⚓ 🎫 🏠 ♿ 👤 🚶 1941 (4:E7)

Gold mines in use from Roman times to the 20th century

These unique gold mines are set amid wooded hillsides overlooking the beautiful Cothi Valley. The Romans who exploited the site almost 2000 years ago left behind a complex of pits, channels, adits and tanks. Mining resumed in the 19th century and continued through the 20th century, reaching a peak in 1938. Guided tours take visitors through the Roman and the more recent underground workings. The main mine yard contains a collection of 1930s mining machinery, an exhibition about the history of gold and gold mining, video and interpretation. Gold-panning gives visitors the opportunity to experience the frustrations of the search for gold. Other attractions include waymarked walks, cycle hire and an Information Centre in Pumsaint. There is fishing and accommodation on the estate, including a 35-pitch touring caravan site.

Dolaucothi Gold Mines, Carmarthenshire

What's new in 2005 Working trains on mine floor. New level tour of mine yard suitable for less mobile

⭐ Stout footwear essential for underground tours

ℹ️ **T** 01558 650177, 01558 825146 (Infoline), 01558 650707 (Estate office), 01558 650359 (Shop) **F** 01558 650707 **E** dolaucothi@nationaltrust.org.uk

💷 **Site**: £3.20, child £1.60, family £8. Groups £2.60, child £1.30. **Underground tour (additional charge)**: £3.80, child £1.90, family £9.50. Groups £3, child £1.50. **Underground tour (NT members)**: £3.60, child £1.80, family £9

♿ Drop-off point. **Building**: Ramped entrance. Audio visual/video. Access to part of mine is possible, must be booked in advance. Access to Roman and Victorian Mines via 70 steps. **Shop**: Ramped entrance. **Refreshments**: Ramped entrance.

📖 Braille guide

🏺 Welsh gold for sale (including by mail order)

☕ Tea-room

🅿️ In picnic areas

👶 Baby-changing and feeding facilities. Pushchairs admitted. Children's parties (booking essential)

🏫 Suitable for school groups. Education room/centre. Children's quiz/trail

🐕 On leads only, and not on tours

🚲 2½ml of NT permitted cycle route; guided cycle tours by NT staff in summer

Opening arrangements: Dolaucothi Gold Mines									
Mines	18 Mar - 30 Oct	10 - 5	**M**	**T**	**W**	**T**	**F**	**S**	**S**
Shop	18 Mar - 30 Oct	10 - 5	**M**	**T**	**W**	**T**	**F**	**S**	**S**
	10 Nov - 18 Dec	11 - 4	M	**T**	**W**	**T**	**F**	**S**	**S**
Tea-room	18 Mar - 30 Oct	10 - 5	**M**	**T**	**W**	**T**	**F**	**S**	**S**

Groups can be booked at other times. Pumsaint Information Centre and estate walks open all year. Underground tours last about 1hr and involve hillside walking, so stout footwear is essential; helmets with lights are provided. These tours are unsuitable for visitors with poor mobility. Smaller children will be allowed on the tours only at the discretion of the property staff. Please tel. for advice

→ [146: SN660400] **Bus**: Castle Garage 289 from Lampeter. **Station**: Llanwrda (U), 8ml. **Road**: Between Lampeter and Llanwrda on A482

P Free parking

NT properties nearby
Aberdeunant, Dinefwr, Llanerchaeron

Erddig

Wrexham LL13 0YT

 1973   (4:G3)

Atmospheric house and estate, vividly evoking its family and servants

Erddig is one of the most fascinating houses in Britain, not least because of the unusually close relationship that existed between the family of the house and their servants. The beautiful and extensive range of outbuildings includes kitchen, laundry, bakehouse, stables, sawmill, smithy and joiner's shop, while the stunning state rooms display most of their original 18th- and 19th-century furniture and furnishings, including some exquisite Chinese wallpaper. The large walled garden has been restored to its 18th-century formal design and has a Victorian parterre and yew walk. It also contains the National Collection of Ivies. There is an extensive park with woodland walks. Horse-drawn carriage rides are available.

What's new in 2005 Children's garden trail

★ Most rooms have no electric light; visitors wishing to make a close study of pictures and textiles should avoid dull days. The Small Chinese Room is open Wed and Sat on application

i **T** 01978 355314, 01978 315151 (Infoline), 01978 315156 (Learning), 01978 315183 (Shop), 01978 315184 (Restaurant) **F** 01978 313333 **E** erddig@nationaltrust.org.uk

£ £7.40, child £3.70, family £18.40. Groups £6, child £3. **Garden & outbuildings only**: £3.80, child £1.90, family £9.20. Groups £3, child £1.50

Garden tours (groups 20+) by arrangement with Head Gardener. House tours by arrangement with House Manager

Programme of events

3 different walks

Contact in advance. Designated parking in main car park, 75yds. Drop-off point. **Building**: Ramped entrance. Access across rough gravel. 3 wheelchairs. Ground floor accessible. Stairs to other floors. Audio visual/video, photograph album, model of house on lower ground floor. **WCs**: Adapted WC. **Shop**: Level entrance. **Refreshments**: Steps to entrance with handrail, lift available. Access restricted to 3 wheelchair users at any one time. Parlour accessible to all visitors

Induction loop in audio-visual room

Braille guide. Sensory list

NT shop. Plant sales. Secondhand bookshop. Christmas opening

Licensed restaurant. Children's menu. Tea-room. Parlour for drinks and ice cream at weekends

In the car park

Baby-changing facilities. Front-carrying baby slings and hip-carrying infant seats for loan

Suitable for school groups. Education room/centre. Hands-on activities. Children's guide. Children's quiz/trail

On leads and only in car park and country park

Bridleway crosses estate giving cyclists shared access

Opening arrangements: Erddig											
House	19 Mar - 28 Sep	12 - 5	M	T	W	T	F	S	S
	1 Oct - 30 Oct	12 - 4	M	T	W	T	F	S	S
Garden	19 Mar - 29 Jun	11 - 6	M	T	W	T	F	S	S
	2 Jul - 31 Aug	10 - 6	M	T	W	T	F	S	S
	3 Sep - 28 Sep	11 - 6	M	T	W	T	F	S	S
	1 Oct - 30 Oct	11 - 5	M	T	W	T	F	S	S
	5 Nov - 18 Dec	11 - 4	M	T	W	T	F	S	S
Shop/plants	19 Mar - 28 Sep	11 - 5:30	M	T	W	T	F	S	S
	1 Oct - 18 Dec	As garden							
Restaurant	19 Mar - 30 Oct	11 - 5:15	M	T	W	T	F	S	S
	5 Nov - 18 Dec	11 - 4	M	T	W	T	F	S	S
Open Good Fri. Last admission 1hr before closing									

→ [117: SJ326482] **Station**: Wrexham Central (U) 1½ml, Wrexham General 2ml via Erddig Rd & footpath. **Road**: 2ml S of Wrexham, signposted A525 Whitchurch road, or A483/A5152 Oswestry road

P Free parking, 200yds. Passing bays on access drive

NT properties nearby
Chirk Castle

The Kymin

Monmouth, Monmouthshire NP25 3SE

🏠 ✸ 💪 🎋 1902   **(4:H8)**

Landmark hill topped by two interesting Georgian buildings

Set in 4ha (9 acres) of woods and pleasure grounds, this property encompasses a small two-storey circular banqueting house and naval temple, a monument dedicated to the glories of the British Navy. Nelson visited the site in 1802. The grounds afford spectacular views of the surrounding countryside.

⭐ A croquet set is available for hire. No WC

ℹ️ **T/F** 01600 719241

£ **Round House**: £2, child £1, family £5. Groups £1.60. **Grounds**: Free

The Naval Monument on The Kymin, Monmouthshire

Opening arrangements: The Kymin

Round House	25 Mar - 27 Mar	11 - 4	M	T	W	T	**F**	**S**	**S**
	28 Mar - 24 Oct	11 - 4	**M**	T	W	T	F	**S**	**S**
Temple/grounds	All year		**M**	**T**	**W**	**T**	**F**	**S**	**S**
Round House: last entry 3.45									

♿ Separate designated parking, 5yds. Drop-off point. **Building**: Step to entrance with handrail, ramp available. Alternative accessible entrance, via ramps through kitchen. Many stairs with handrail to other floors. Seating available. Interpretation panel on ground floor. **Grounds**: Pleasure grounds are mostly lawns

🎒 Children's quiz/trail

🐕 In grounds only

→ [162: SO528125] **Foot**: Offa's Dyke Path runs through the property. **Bus**: Glyn Williams/H&H 60 from Newport (passing close ⊞ Newport), Stagecoach in S Wales/Welcome 69 from Chepstow (passing close ⊞ Chepstow), Glyn Williams/Welcome 83 from Abergavenny (passing close ⊞ Abergavenny), Duke's 416 from Hereford. On all, alight Monmouth, then 1½ml (very steep). **Road**: 1ml E of Monmouth and signposted off A4136

P Free parking, 300yds. Not suitable for coaches. Steep narrow road with hairpin bends from junction with A4136

NT properties nearby
Skenfrith Castle, Skirrid Fawr, Westbury Court Garden

Llanerchaeron

Ciliau Aeron, nr Aberaeron, Ceredigion SA48 8DG

🏠 🏠 🛏️ ✸ 🌳 📷 💷 1989   **(4:E6)**

18th-century Welsh gentry estate

Set in the beautiful Dyffryn Aeron, the estate survived virtually unaltered into the 20th century and was bequeathed to the National Trust by J. P. Ponsonby Lewes in 1989. The house was designed by John Nash in 1794–96 and is the most complete example of his early work. Llanerchaeron was a self-sufficient estate – evident in the dairy, laundry, brewery and salting house of the service courtyard, as well as the

Please see the area introductions for details of coast & countryside properties

The bakehouse at Llanerchaeron, Ceredigion

Home Farm buildings, from the stables to the threshing barns. Today it is a working organic farm and the two restored walled gardens also produce home-grown fruit, vegetables and herbs. There are extensive walks around the estate and parkland.

What's new in 2005 Opportunity to see the continuing restoration of farm buildings and lake. 'Abermydyr' – a recently restored estate cottage available for weekly lets is an ideal base for exploring the Aeron valley

[i] **T** 01545 570200, 01558 825147 (Infoline)
F 01545 571759
E llanerchaeron@nationaltrust.org.uk

[£] £5.20, child £2.60, family £12.60. Groups £4.20, child £2.10. **Home Farm & garden only**: £4.20, child £2.10. Reduced rate when arriving by public transport, cycle or on foot (on 'all sites' ticket)

[T] Guided tours of the garden and Home Farm start 1.30 every Thur, June to end of Sept. Additional £1, inc. NT members

Opening arrangements: Llanerchaeron									
House	18 Mar - 30 Oct	11:30 - 4:30	M	T	W	T	F	S	S
Farm/garden	18 Mar - 30 Oct	11 - 5	M	T	W	T	F	S	S
Open BH Mons. Car park closes at 5:30									

[🎭] Programme of events. Send s.a.e. for details

[🚶] Five walks leaflets (50p each)

[♿] Designated parking in main car park. Drop-off point. **Building**: Ramped entrance. Alternative accessible entrance. 1 wheelchair, booking essential. Ground floor accessible. Stairs to other floors. Information panels and album. Limited seating available for emergency use. **WCs**: Adapted WC. **Grounds**: Fully accessible. **Shop**: Level entrance. **Refreshments**: Level entrance

[👆] Braille guide

[🛍] Small shop area in the visitor building selling local produce and Llanerchaeron farm produce and plants as available

[🍴] Tea-room (NT-approved concession) in visitor building. Light lunches and teas – using local produce

[🏕] In picnic areas

[👶] Baby-changing and feeding facilities. Hip-carrying infant seats for loan

[🏫] Suitable for school groups. Education room/centre. Children's quiz/trail. Adult study days

[🐕] On leads and only in parkland fields

[→] [146: SN480602] **Foot**: 2½ml foot/cycle track from Aberaeron to property along old railway track. **Bus**: Arriva Cymru 540 [≡] Aberystwyth–Lampeter. **Road**: 2½ml E of Aberaeron off A482

[P] Free parking, 50yds

NT properties nearby
Dinefwr, Dolaucothi Gold Mines, Mwnt, Penbryn

Penrhyn Castle

Bangor, Gwynedd LL57 4HN

[🏰][✝][⬆][✳][📷][💷][☂][1951]   **(4:E2)**

19th-century fantasy castle with spectacular contents and grounds

This enormous neo-Norman castle sits between Snowdonia and the Menai Strait. Built by Thomas Hopper between 1820 and 1845 for the wealthy Pennant family, who made their fortune from Jamaican sugar and Welsh slate, the castle

Unless indicated, last admission is always 30mins before closing time

is crammed with fascinating things such as a one-ton slate bed made for Queen Victoria. Hopper also designed its interior with elaborate carvings, plasterwork and mock-Norman furniture. The castle contains an outstanding collection of paintings. The Victorian kitchen and other servants' rooms, including scullery, larders and chef's sitting room, have been restored to reveal the preparations for the banquet for the Prince of Wales' visit in 1894. The stable block houses an industrial railway museum, a model railway museum and a superb dolls' museum displaying a large collection of 19th- and 20th-century dolls. The 18.2ha (45 acres) of grounds include parkland, an extensive exotic tree and shrub collection and a Victorian walled garden.

i T 01248 353084, 01248 371337 (Infoline)
F 01248 371281
E penrhyncastle@nationaltrust.org.uk

£ £7, child £3.50, family £17.50. Groups £5.50.
Garden and stable block exhibitions only:
£5, child £2.50

🎓 Specialist guided tours by arrangement

🎧 £1 adult's and child's, in English and Welsh

🎪 Programme of events. Tel. for details

♿ Separate designated parking, 200yds. Alternative arrangements can be made on request. Drop-off point. **Building**: Ramped entrance. 3 wheelchairs. 1st floor of castle is inaccessible. Photograph album. **Stable block**: Fully accessible. Lift to 1st-floor gallery and museums. **WCs**: Adapted WC. **Grounds**: 1 multi-seater PMV, booking essential. **Shop**: Ramped entrance. **Refreshments**: Level entrance

The Lamp Room, Penrhyn Castle, Gwynedd

♒ Braille guide and large-print guide. Sensory list

☕ Licensed tea-room. Children's menu. Gallery coffee shop

🧺 Picnics welcome except in walled garden

🚼 Baby-changing and feeding facilities. Front-carrying baby slings for loan. Children's play area. Model railway museum and dolls' museum

🏛 Suitable for school groups. Education room/centre. Hands-on activities. Children's guide. Children's quiz/trail. Adult study days

🐕 On leads and only in grounds

➔ [115: SH602720] **Cycle**: NCN5 1¼ml. **Bus**: Arriva 5/X Caernarfon–Llandudno; Silver Star 6, Arriva 7 Bangor–Bethesda; 66 Bangor–Gerlan. All pass close ≠ Bangor and end of drive to Castle. **Station**: Bangor 3ml. **Road**: 1ml E of Bangor, at Llandygai on A5122. Signposted from junction 11 of A55 and A5

P Free parking. 200 & 500yds

NT properties nearby
Glan Faenol, Plas Newydd

Opening arrangements: Penrhyn Castle										
Castle	23 Mar - 30 Jun	12 - 5	M	T	W	T	F	S	S
	1 Jul - 31 Aug	11 - 5	M	T	W	T	F	S	S
	1 Sep - 31 Oct	12 - 5	M	T	W	T	F	S	S
Grounds	23 Mar - 30 Jun	11 - 5	M	T	W	T	F	S	S
and tea-room	1 Jul - 31 Aug	10 - 5	M	T	W	T	F	S	S
	1 Sep - 31 Oct	11 - 5	M	T	W	T	F	S	S
Shop	23 Mar - 31 Oct	11 - 5	M	T	W	T	F	S	S
Museums	23 Mar - 31 Oct	11 - 5	M	T	W	T	F	S	S

Victorian kitchen: as castle but last admission 4.45. Last audio tour 4. Castle and grounds: last admission 4:30.

There are special events at most Trust properties; please telephone 0870 458 4000 for details

Plas Newydd

Llanfairpwll, Anglesey LL61 6DQ

 1976 (4:E2)

Home of the Marquess of Anglesey, with spectacular views of Snowdonia

Set amidst breathtakingly beautiful scenery on the banks of the Menai Strait, this elegant house was redesigned by James Wyatt in the 18th century and is an interesting mixture of classical and Gothic. The comfortable interior, restyled in the 1930s, is famous for its association with Rex Whistler, whose largest painting is here. There is also an exhibition about his work. A military museum contains campaign relics of the 1st Marquess of Anglesey, who commanded the cavalry at the Battle of Waterloo. There is a fine spring garden and Australasian arboretum with an understorey of shrubs and wild flowers, as well as a summer terrace and, later, massed hydrangeas and autumn colour. A woodland walk gives access to a marine walk on the Menai Strait.

What's new in 2005 Licensed for civil weddings

⭐ Historical cruises – boat trips on the Menai Strait – operate from the property, weather and tide permitting (additional charge). Tel. for details

ℹ️ **T** 01248 714795, 01248 715272 (Infoline), 01248 716848 (Shop/tea-room)
F 01248 713673
E plasnewydd@nationaltrust.org.uk

£ £5, child £2.50, family £12. Groups £4.50.
Garden only: £3, child £1.50

🔑 Connoisseurs' and garden tours by arrangement

🎭 Programme of events. Send s.a.e. for details

Opening arrangements: Plas Newydd										
House	19 Mar - 2 Nov	12 - 5	M	T	W	T	F	S	S
Garden	19 Mar - 2 Nov	11 - 5:30	M	T	W	T	F	S	S
Walks	As garden									
Shop	19 Mar - 2 Nov	10:30 - 5:30	M	T	W	T	F	S	S
	5 Nov - 18 Dec	11 - 4	M	T	W	T	F	S	S
Tea-room	As shop									

Open Good Fri. Rhododendron garden open 19 Mar – early Jun, 11–5.30

🚶 Woodland & marine walk (leaflet available)

♿ Designated parking in main car park, 400yds. Minibus and shuttle service to house and garden. Drop-off point. **Building**: Steps to entrance, ramp available. 3 wheelchairs, booking essential. Ground floor accessible. Seating available. Photograph album. **WCs**: Adapted WC. **Grounds**: Partly accessible. Accessible route. Staff-driven multi-seater vehicle. **Shop**: Level entrance. **Refreshments**: Level entrance

👓 Braille guide and large-print guide. Touchable objects and interesting scents

☕ Licensed tea-room. Home-cooked food with a regional and historical theme using local produce whenever possible. Seasonal menu in Nov & Dec. Children's menu

🧺 In picnic area near car park

👶 Baby-changing and feeding facilities. Front-carrying baby slings for loan. Children's play area

🎒 Suitable for school groups. Family guide. Children's quiz/trail

➡️ [114/115: SH521696] **Cycle**: NCN8 ¼ml.
Bus: Arriva 42 from Bangor (passing ⇄ Bangor & Llanfairpwll). **Station**: Llanfairpwll (U), no practical Sun service, 1¾ml. **Road**: 2ml SW of Llanfairpwll A55 junctions 7 and 8a, or A4080 to Brynsiencyn; turn off A5 at W end of Britannia Bridge

🅿️ Free parking, 400yds

NT properties nearby
Penrhyn Castle

Plas yn Rhiw

Rhiw, Pwllheli, Gwynedd LL53 8AB

🏠 1952 (4:D4)

Small manor house with ornamental garden and wonderful views

The house was rescued from neglect and lovingly restored by the three Keating sisters, who bought it in 1938. The views from the delightful grounds and garden across Cardigan Bay are among the most spectacular in Britain. The house is 16th century with Georgian

Opening arrangements: Plas yn Rhiw										
House	18 Mar - 30 May	12 - 5	M	T	W	T	F	S	S
	1 Jun - 30 Sep	12 - 5	M	T	W	T	F	S	S
	1 Oct - 23 Oct	12 - 4	M	T	W	T	F	S	S
	24 Oct - 30 Oct	12 - 4	M	T	W	T	F	S	S
Shop	As house								

Garden and snowdrop wood open occasionally at weekends in Jan & Feb; tel. for details

additions, and the garden contains many interesting flowering trees and shrubs, with beds framed by box hedges and grass paths. Brilliant displays of snowdrops and bluebells can be found in the wood above the house at the appropriate season.

[i] **T/F** 01758 780219, 01758 780267 (Shop)
E plasynrhiw@nationaltrust.org.uk

[£] **House & garden**: £3.40, child £1.70, family £8.50. Groups £2.80, child £1.40. **Garden only**: £2.20, child £1.10, family £5.50. Groups £1.70. **Garden & snowdrop wood** (see above) : £2.20, child £1.10, family £5.50

[K] Advance notice is required; booked groups £1.40 per person extra (inc. NT members)

[&] Drop-off point. **Building**: Level entrance. step from main entrance to hall. Seating available. Photograph album. **WCs**: Adapted WC. **Grounds**: some steps, narrow paths. **Shop**: Level entrance

[braille] Braille guide. Interesting scents

[A] In garden meadow

[baby] Baby-changing facilities

[school] Suitable for school groups

[dog] On leads and only on the woodland walk

[→] [123: SH237282] **Bus**: Arriva 17B, Nefyn 8B from Pwllheli (passing [rail] Pwllheli) to Rhiw village, 1ml from property. **Road**: 16ml from Pwllheli. Approach road changed due to landslip. Follow A499 and B4413 from Pwllheli. At Botwnnog, follow signs to Plas yn Rhiw along narrow lanes past Rhiw village. Entrance at bottom of steep hill.

[P] Free parking, 80yds

NT properties nearby
Llanbedrog Beach, Porthdinllaen, Porthor

Powis Castle & Garden

Welshpool, Powys SY21 8RF

[icons] 1952   (4:G5)

Medieval castle rising dramatically above the celebrated garden

The world-famous garden, overhung with enormous clipped yews, shelters rare and tender plants. Laid out under the influence of Italian and French styles, it retains its original lead statues, an orangery and an aviary on the terraces. In the 18th century an informal woodland wilderness was created on the opposite ridge. High on a rock above the terraces, the castle, originally built c.1200, began life as a fortress of the Welsh Princes of Powys and commands magnificent views toward England. Remodelled and embellished over more than 400 years, it reflects the changing needs and ambitions of the Herbert family, each generation adding to the magnificent collection of paintings, sculpture, furniture and tapestries. A superb collection of treasures from India is displayed in the Clive Museum. Edward, the son of Robert Clive, the conqueror of India, married Lady Henrietta Herbert in 1784, uniting the Powis & Clive Estates.

What's new in 2005 Major conservation work ongoing in State Bedroom, giving occasional opportunities to see work in progress

[★] All visitors (inc. NT members) need to obtain a ticket from visitor reception in the main car park on arrival. A timed ticket system for the castle may be in operation. Please note: dogs cannot be walked in the park which does not belong to the NT

[i] **T** 01938 551929, 01938 551944 (Infoline), 01938 551928 (Shop), 01938 551926 (Plant sales), 01938 551927 (Restaurant) **F** 01938 554336 **E** powiscastle@nationaltrust.org.uk

[£] £8.80, child £4.40, family £22. Groups £7.80. **Garden only**: £6.20, child £3.10, family £15.20. Groups £5.20

[K] Guided tours of castle and/or garden by prior arrangement (additional charge)

Please note: groups must book in advance with the property

♿ Contact in advance. Separate designated parking. Drop-off point. **Building**: Many steps to entrance. Very steep staircase to Castle and Clive Museum. Seating available. Photograph album. **WCs**: Adapted WC. **Grounds**: Partly accessible. Accessible route map. Partly terraced with steps in some areas. No access for PMVs in garden due to very steep terraces. Wheelchair for garden use must be pre-booked. **Shop**: Level entrance. **Refreshments**: Level entrance

♿ Braille guide. Sensory list

♿ NT shop. Plant sales

♿ Licensed restaurant. Children's menu

♿ Baby-changing and feeding facilities. Front-carrying baby slings for loan. Limited routes around terraced garden for pushchairs

♿ Suitable for school groups. Children's guide. Children's quiz/trail

➚ [126: SJ216064] **Foot**: 1ml walk from Park Lane, off Broad St in Welshpool. **Bus**: Arriva 71 Oswestry–Welshpool; D75 Shrewsbury–Llanidloes, alight High Street, 1ml. **Station**: Welshpool 1¾ml from town on footpath. **Road**: 1ml S of Welshpool; pedestrian access from High Street (A490); vehicle route signed from main road to Newtown (A483); enter by first drive gate on right

□ **P** Free parking. All groups (15+) must book in advance and call at visitor reception on arrival

NT properties nearby
Attingham Park, Chirk Castle, Erddig

Opening arrangements: Powis Castle										
Castle/museum	21 Mar - 4 Apr	1 - 5	**M**	T	W	**T**	**F**	**S**	**S**
	7 Apr - 28 Apr	1 - 4	**M**	T	W	**T**	**F**	**S**	**S**
	29 Apr - 4 Sep	1 - 5	**M**	T	W	**T**	**F**	**S**	**S**
	5 Sep - 30 Oct	1 - 4	**M**	T	W	**T**	**F**	**S**	**S**
Coach house	As castle	Opens 11	**M**	T	W	**T**	**F**	**S**	**S**
Garden	As castle	Opens 11	**M**	T	W	**T**	**F**	**S**	**S**
Shop	As castle	Opens 11	**M**	T	W	**T**	**F**	**S**	**S**
Restaurant	As castle	Opens 11	**M**	T	W	**T**	**F**	**S**	**S**

Admission by timed ticket on busy days. Last admission 45mins before closing. Coach house opens 11, closes same time as castle. Garden opens 11, closes at at 6 when castle closes at 5, or at 5.30 when castle closes at 4. Shop & restaurant open 11, close 30mins before garden. Christmas shop, 11–4, and lunches: Fri, Sat & Sun, 4 Nov–18 Dec

Rhossili Visitor Centre

Coastguard Cottages, Rhossili, Gower SA3 1PR

♿ ♿ ♿ ♿ 1933   **(4:D9)**

Visitor centre in area of spectacular countryside and coast with lovely beaches

The Trust owns and protects much land on the beautiful Gower Peninsula. The visitor centre is situated near to the Warren, the Down, Worm's Head, Rhossili beach and coastal cliffs, and provides information about the area. There is also an exhibition and shop.

★ No WC. Nearest WC at Rhossili car park

ⓘ **T** 01792 390707
E rhossili@nationaltrust.org.uk

♿ Drop-off point. **Building**: Ramped entrance. Exhibition on first floor. Seating available. Photograph album, Book available in shop of main information/walk with warden from NT website. **WCs**: Adapted WC. RADAR key in shop. **Grounds**: Grounds have slopes and a variety of path surfaces. **Shop**: Ramped entrance

♿ Braille guide and large-print guide

♿ Suitable for school groups. Hands-on activities

♿ Must be under control and on leads at lambing time; not in visitor centre

➚ [159: SS418883] **Bus**: Pullman 114/8/9 from Swansea (passing close ⚫ Swansea). **Road**: SW tip of Gower Peninsula, approached from Swansea via A4118 and then B4247

□ **P** Parking (not NT)

NT properties nearby
Aberdulais Falls, Dinefwr

Opening arrangements: Rhossili Visitor Centre									
Centre/shop	8 Jan - 20 Mar	11 - 4	M	T	W	T	**F**	**S**	**S**
	22 Mar - 5 Nov	10:30 - 5:30	**M**	**T**	**W**	**T**	**F**	**S**	**S**
	6 Nov - 23 Dec	11 -4	M	T	**W**	**T**	**F**	**S**	**S**

St David's Visitor Centre & Shop

Captains House, High Street, St David's,
Haverfordwest, Pembrokeshire SA62 6SD

 1974   **(4:B8)**

Visitor centre on the beautiful Pembrokeshire coast

The National Trust owns and protects much of the picturesque St David's Head and surrounding coastline. The visitor centre is situated in the centre of St David's, Wales' smallest historic city, opposite The Cross (owned by the NT). Using interactive technology the centre offers a complete guide to the National Trust in Pembrokeshire, its properties, beaches and walks.

★ No WC

i T/F 01437 720385

🏃 Local walks leaflets avaialble

⅃ **Building**: Steps to entrance

➡ [115: SM753253] In the centre of St David's.
Foot: Pembrokeshire Coast Path within 1ml.
Bus: Richards 411 from ≋ Haverfordwest;
coastal shuttle buses operate in summer

P No parking on site

NT properties nearby
Porthclais Harbour, St David's Head

Opening arrangements: St David's										
Centre/shop	3 Jan - 19 Mar	10 - 4	M	T	W	T	F	S	S
	21 Mar - 30 Oct	10 - 5:30	M	T	W	T	F	S	S
	21 Mar - 30 Oct	10 - 4:30	M	T	W	T	F	S	S
	31 Oct - 31 Dec	10 - 4:30	M	T	W	T	F	S	S
	31 Oct - 31 Dec	10 - 3	M	T	W	T	F	S	S

Closed 25–26 Dec

Segontium

Caernarfon, Gwynedd

🏛 🎋 1937   **(4:E2)**

Remains of a Roman fort

The fort was built to defend the Roman Empire against rebellious tribes and later plundered to provide stone for Edward I's castle at Caernarfon. There is a museum containing relics found on-site (not NT).

★ Segontium is in the guardianship of Cadw: Welsh Historic Monuments. The museum is not NT and is managed by a local trust on behalf of the National Museums and Galleries of Wales, c/o Institute Building, Pavilion Hill, Caernarfon, Gwynedd LL55 1AS. WC not always available

i T 01286 675625 (Museum, not NT)

£ Admission free. There may be a charge for the museum (inc. NT members)

⅃ **Grounds**: Partly accessible, slopes. Some visitors may require assistance from their companion

🚸 Pushchairs and baby back-carriers admitted

▦ Occasional educational activities – contact museum directly for details

➡ [115: SH485624] **Cycle**: NCN8 ½ml. **Bus**: From surrounding areas to Caernarfon (KMP 95, S4 and Arvonia 93 pass museum, on others ½ml walk to fort). **Station**: Bangor 9ml. **Road**: On Beddgelert road, A4085, on SE outskirts of Caernarfon, 500yds from town centre

P No parking on site

NT properties nearby
Glan Faenol, Penrhyn Castle, Plas Newydd, Plas yn Rhiw

Opening arrangements: Segontium										
Site	All year	10:30 - 4:30	M	T	W	T	F	S	S

Open BH Mons. Opening times may vary, please tel. for details. Closed 24–26 Dec & 1 Jan 06. Museum (not NT) open 12:30–4:30, Tues–Sun. See website: www.segontium.org.uk

Skenfrith Castle

Skenfrith, nr Abergavenny, Monmouthshire

🏰 1936   **(4:H8)**

Remains of an early 13th-century fortress

The castle was built beside the River Monnow to command one of the main routes between England and Wales, at a time when the two nations were involved in a long drawn-out conflict following the Norman Conquest. A keep and the curtain wall with towers have survived.

Please remember – your membership card is always needed for free admission

⭐ Skenfrith Castle is in the guardianship of Cadw: Welsh Historic Monuments

ℹ️ **T** 01874 625515

£ Admission free

♿ **Building**: Many steps to entrance with handrail. **Grounds**: Fully accessible

➔ [161: SO456203] **Cycle**: Local 'Four Castles' cycle trail starts at nearby Abergavenny castle. **Road**: 6ml NW of Monmouth, 12ml NE of Abergavenny, on N side of the Ross road (B4521)

P Free parking (not NT)

NT properties nearby
The Kymin, Skirrid Fawr, Sugar Loaf, Westbury Court Garden

Opening arrangements: Skenfrith Castle

Castle	All year	Dawn – dusk	M	T	W	T	F	S	S

Stackpole Estate

Old Home Farm Yard, Stackpole, nr Pembroke, Pembrokeshire SA71 5DQ

🏛️✳️♦️🏋️🎨👟🍽️🅿️🎋 (4:C9)

Beautiful and varied stretch of the Pembrokeshire coast

This extensive estate includes eight miles of cliff, headlands, beaches and sand dunes, freshwater lakes bordered by trees, sheltered bays and mature woodlands. The Bosherton Lakes and Stackpole Warren are part of Stackpole National Nature Reserve, managed by the National Trust in partnership with the Countryside Council for Wales. Eight species of bat live in the out-buildings of the former mansion of Stackpole Court, demolished in 1963 – an exhibition about which is displayed in the old game larder. There is an excellent bathing beach at Broadhaven South, and also at Barafundle Bay which is accessed from Stackpole Quay by means of a walk along the cliff path, followed by a steep descent down to the beach.

ℹ️ **T/F** 01646 661359 (Estate Office),
01646 661464 (Learning),
01646 672058 (Tea-room)
E stackpole@nationaltrust.org.uk

£ Admission free. Donations welcome

🚶 Guided walks (see Pembrokeshire Coast National Park *Coast to Coast* newspaper).

🚶 19ml of footpaths. Map leaflets available

♿ Many facilities for disabled visitors. Contact property for information leaflet

🔊 Listening post in boathouse hide

🍽️ Boathouse Tea-room (NT-approved concession) (licensed) at Stackpole Quay

🎒 Suitable for school groups. Education room/centre. Residential Centre – Stackpole for Outdoor Learning

➔ [158: SR992958 – (Stackpole Quay); SR977938 (Broadhaven South); SR968947 (Bosherton Lily Ponds)]. **Foot**: Via Pembrokeshire Coast Path. **Bus**: Silcox 387 Summer Coastal Cruiser from Pembroke (May-Sep only). **Station**: Pembroke 5ml. **Road**: 6ml S of Pembroke. On B4319 from Pembroke to Stackpole and Bosherton (various entry points onto estate)

P 3 car parks – 1 free (Bosherton Lily Ponds), 2 paying, £2 per car (NT members display card) at Stackpole Quay and Broadhaven South (Apr-Sept). Access via narrow roads with passing places

NT properties nearby
Tudor Merchant's House

Opening arrangements: Stackpole Estate

	All year	M	T	W	T	F	S	S

Tudor Merchant's House

Quay Hill, Tenby, Pembrokeshire SA70 7BX

🏠 [1937] (4:C9)

Late 15th-century town house

Located near the harbour in this historic walled town, the house is characteristic of the area at the time when Tenby was a thriving trading port. On the ground floor at the rear of the house is a fine example of a 'Flemish' round chimney, and the original scarfed roof-trusses survive. The remains of early seccos can be seen on three interior walls and the house is furnished to recreate family life from the Tudor period onwards. There is access to the small herb garden, weather permitting.

What's new in 2005 Display of pottery shards found after excavation of 500-year-old latrine tower

⭐ No WC

ℹ️ **T/F** 01834 842279

💷 £2.20, child £1.10, family £5.50. Groups £1.80, child 90p

♿ **Building**: Steps to entrance. Stairs to other floors. Photograph album

📖 Braille guide

👶 Hip-carrying infant seats for loan

🏫 Suitable for school groups. Hands-on activities. Children's quiz/trail

➔ [158: SN135004] In the centre of Tenby off Tudor Square. **Foot**: Pembrokeshire Coast Path within ⅜ml. **Bus**: From surrounding areas. **Station**: Tenby 700yds

🅿️ Parking (not NT). Limited parking on town streets. Town is pedestrianised throughout July & Aug when parking is in pay & display car parks only or via park & ride

NT properties nearby
Colby Woodland Garden, Stackpole Estate

Opening arrangements: Tudor Merchant's House									
House	18 Mar - 30 Oct	11 - 5	**M**	**T**	**W**	**T**	**F**	S	S

Tŷ Isaf

Beddgelert, Gwynedd LL55 4YA

🏠♿📷 1985   (4:E3)

17th-century cottage

The cottage, formerly known as Bwthyn Llywelyn, is the oldest house in the picturesque village of Beddgelert, situated within the Snowdonia National Park, near the spectacular Aberglaslyn Pass. It houses a 'plot to plate' exhibition on the area's local foods, and its recently restored 19th-century kitchen contains information on the diet of 200 years ago. There are superb walks in the area, including a 1¼ml

circular wheelchair route along the riverbank and past the legendary Gelert's grave.

What's new in 2005 Waymarked family trails at nearby Craflwyn and farm trail at Hafod y Llan

⭐ No WC. Nearest WC 90yds down lane behind cottage

ℹ️ **T** 01766 510129,
01766 510120 (Warden/Learning Officer),
01766 510131 (Property Manager)
F 01766 890663

💷 Admission free

🚶 Leaflet and walks booklet available

♿ **Building**: Ramped entrance. **WCs**: Adapted WC

📖 Braille guide

🪑 Picnic site on riverside path 100yds

👶 Pushchairs admitted

🏫 Live interpretation. Hands-on activities. Children's quiz/trail. Educational visits can be arranged at nearby Craflwyn

🐕 Must be on lead April–May

➔ [115: SH590481] **Cycle**: NCN8 6ml. **Bus**: KMP S4 from Caernarfon (with connections from 🚃 Bangor), Express 97/A from Porthmadog (passes close 🚃 Porthmadog). **Station**: Penrhyndeudraeth (U) or Porthmadog (U) both 6ml. **Road**: At centre of village beside old bridge, at junction of A498 and A4085. Beddgelert is well signposted from A5 and A487

🅿️ Parking (not NT), 200yds (pay & display), charge inc. NT members. Also NT pay & display car park 2ml away at Nantmor (free to NT members)

NT properties nearby
Craflwyn, Hafod y Llan

Opening arrangements: Tŷ Isaf									
Cottage	25 Mar - 30 Oct	1 - 4	M	T	**W**	**T**	**F**	**S**	**S**
Open BH Mons. Times shown may be extended, tel. for details									

Please see the area introductions for details of coast & countryside properties

Tŷ Mawr Wybrnant

Penmachno, Betws-y-Coed, Conwy LL25 0HJ

🏠 ♿ 🎋 🐚 1951   (4:F3)

Traditional stone-built upland farmhouse

Situated in the beautiful and secluded Wybrnant Valley, Tŷ Mawr was the birthplace of Bishop William Morgan, first translator of the entire Bible into Welsh. The house has been restored to its probable 16th-/17th-century appearance and includes a display of Welsh and other bibles and an exhibition room. A footpath leads from the house through woodland and the surrounding fields, which are traditionally managed.

⭐ No access for coaches. 33-seater minibuses welcome. Tel. to arrange access

ℹ️ **T** 01690 760213 **F** 01690 710678

£ £2.60, child £1.30, family £6.30. Groups £2.10, child £1

🎭 The Custodian offers live interpretation of Tŷ Mawr to all visitors

🚶 Leaflet available, featuring interesting walks around Tŷ Mawr and on Ysbyty Estate

♿ Separate designated parking, 20yds. Car park adjoining property off council maintained road. **Building**: Level entrance. Ground floor has uneven floors, slate flagstones. Steep wooden staircase with roped handrail to other floor. Interpretation panels within exhibition room. Seating in exhibition room. **WCs**: Adapted WC. **Grounds**: Partly accessible, uneven paths

🚼 Pushchairs admitted

🎒 Suitable for school groups. Live interpretation. Children's guide. Children's quiz/trail. Exhibition room

🐕 Under close control

🚲 Newly constructed cycle path around the Penmachno area

➡️ [115: SH770524] **Bus**: Jones 64 Llanrwst–Cwm Penmachno (passing ⊕ Betws-y-Coed), alight Penmachno, then 2ml.

Opening arrangements: Tŷ Mawr Wybrnant									
House	20 Mar - 30 Sep	12 - 5	M	T	W	**T**	**F**	**S**	**S**
	1 Oct - 30 Oct	12 - 4	M	T	W	**T**	**F**	**S**	**S**

Station: Pont-y-pant (U) 1½ml. **Road**: At the head of the Wybrnant Valley. From A5 3ml S of Betws-y-Coed, take B4406 to Penmachno. House is 2½ml NW of Penmachno by forest road

P Free parking, 500yds

NT properties nearby
Aberconwy House, Bodnant Garden, Ysbyty Estate

Properties open less often

This section includes National Trust properties, often tenanted, which are open two days a week or less (plus Bank Holidays in some cases). Visits to some must be made by prior arrangement and where this applies admission prices are not shown (please ask when making contact). **Full details are on our website www.nationaltrust.org.uk or obtainable from the Membership Department, tel. 0870 458 4000.**

Aberdeunant

Taliaris, Llandeilo, Carmarthenshire
SA19 6DL   (4:E8)

Traditional Carmarthenshire farmhouse in an unspoilt setting.

⭐ As the property is extremely small, visitor access is limited to no more than 6 people at a time. The property is administered and maintained on the Trust's behalf by a resident tenant. The gegin fawr (farm kitchen) and one bedroom are shown to visitors. No WC

ℹ️ **T/F** 01558 650177

Opening arrangements: Aberdeunant
Admission by guided tour and appointment only. Tours take place April to Sept: first Sat & Sun of each month 12-5. Tel. to book

Ty'n-y-Coed Uchaf

Penmachno, Betws-y-Coed, Conwy LL24 0PS
Closed in 2005. Tel. 01492 860233 (NT Wales office) for further information.

Unless indicated, last admission is always 30mins before closing time

South West South & South East
London East of England
East Midlands West Midlands
North West Yorkshire North East
Wales **Northern Ireland**

Northern Ireland is famed worldwide for its outstanding natural beauty. The spectacular and varied coastline, rolling green scenery and evocative mountains, interspersed with areas of wetland and open water, combine to produce a uniquely attractive landscape.

The only World Heritage Site in Northern Ireland, the **Giant's Causeway** needs no introduction, but it is only one part of the beautiful 14-mile **North Antrim Cliff Path**. The path runs from the Causeway, past the ruins of **Dunseverick Castle**, through the majestic sweep of **Whitepark Bay** (car park charge at weekends, BHols and Public Hols May to August), with its sandy beach and backdrop of white chalk cliffs, to the tiny stack of basalt rock, **Carrick-a-Rede**. At **Larrybane** there are good views of seabird colonies, of **Rathlin Island** and, in good weather, the west coast of Scotland. The distinctive headland of **Fair Head** rises 190m and gives dramatic views of nearby **Murlough Bay** and, on a clear day, the Western Isles of Scotland. This is beautiful walking country and full of wildlife, but much of the land is grazed by livestock so dogs must be on leads at all times.

To the south east is **Cushleake Mountain**, an exceptional example of raised blanket peat bog and home to rare plants and birds, and the delightful coastal village of **Cushendun**, where there are cottages designed by Clough Williams-Ellis, the architect of Portmeirion in Wales. On the island of Rathlin the Trust has opened way-marked paths at **Ballyconagan**, a traditional farm which has remained unchanged for centuries. And at the Trust's **Manor House** on the island visitors can enjoy comfortable guesthouse accommodation and excellent cuisine in tranquil surroundings (tel. 028 2076 3964 to book).

The dramatic north coast of Counties Londonderry and Antrim includes **Portstewart Strand**, a 2-mile-long stretch of historic duneland and sandy beach (basic visitor facilities are open here from March to September daily: 10–6, October at weekends: 10–5; car parking £4.50, minibus £12.50. Dogs must be kept on leads during summer months. Tel. 028 7083 6396). Nearby, at the mouth of the River Bann, are the **Barmouth** and **Grangemore Dunes**, a wildlife sanctuary with observation hide. At the tiny village of **Glenoe** near Larne is a spectacular waterfall, while the footpath along **Skernaghan Point** on the northern tip of Islandmagee leads to the open headland, cliffs, coves and beautiful beaches.

Many of the properties owned by the Trust in Northern Ireland are important for their wildlife

Strangford Lough, County Down. On the left is the fifteenth-century Audley's Castle on the Castle Ward estate

Previous page: Building sandcastles, Whitepark Bay, County Antrim

A boat on Lough Erne, part of the Crom Estate in Co. Fermanagh where the National Trust has seven holiday cottages

interest, offering a wide range of opportunities to enjoy unspoilt habitats and fascinating flora and fauna. **Murlough National Nature Reserve**, near Newcastle, was Ireland's first nature reserve (open from May to mid-September daily: 10–6; car £2, minibus £5; tel. 028 4375 1467). The oldest sand dunes here are at least 5000 years old and the soil ranges from lime-rich to acid, supporting a wide variety of plants, which in turn provide nesting sites for birds in spring. Nearby are the beautiful Mourne Mountains, where the Trust protects **Slieve Donard**, Ulster's highest peak, and from the foot of which there is a path connecting with the **Mourne Coastal Path**. Further south, at the mouth of Carlingford Lough, are **Blockhouse and Green Islands**, important breeding locations for terns and leased to the RSPB.

Strangford Lough is one of Europe's most important wildlife sites. In order to protect this habitat and the interesting birds and animals it supports, the Trust operates a Wildlife Scheme embracing the entire foreshore of the Lough, as well as some fifty islands. Depending on the season, visitors may see vast flocks of wintering wildfowl and nesting birds. Seals, otters and other marine animals can also be seen, as well as interesting flowers. The **Strangford Lough Wildlife Centre** (tel. 028 4488 1411) is located in the grounds of the **Castle Ward Estate** and provides exhibitions, leaflets and other information.

The County Down coastline has much to offer the walker and naturalist, with rocky shore and heathland at **Ballymacormick Point** and wildfowl, wading birds and gulls at **Orlock Point**. Offshore is **Lighthouse Island**, which has a bird observatory and can be visited by arrangement with Mr Neville McKee, 67 Temple Rise, Templepatrick, Co. Down (tel. 028 9443 3068). On the outer arm of the Ards Peninsula is the picturesque former fishing village of **Kearney** (Information Centre and WCs open from 13 March to end September daily: 10–6; 2 to 10 Oct w/ends only: 1–5pm), where the Trust owns thirteen houses and from where there are attractive walks to the beach at **Knockinelder**.

In the Belfast area, to the south and west of the city, are hidden winding woodland paths at **Collin Glen** and **Minnowburn**, and waterfalls at **Lisnabreeny**. The Trust has acquired heathland-rich **Divis Mountain** and the **Black Mountain**, which can be seen towering above west Belfast. During the early part of 2005 a major restoration project will begin to secure access to the mountains.

In the west, the lush valleys and pastures of County Fermanagh provide a splendid setting for **Florence Court** and **Castle Coole**, as well as for the spectacular woodland and wetlands of the **Crom Estate** around Lough Erne.

Under the National Trust **Ulster Gardens Scheme** a number of private gardens are generously opened to the public in order to provide income for Trust gardens in Northern Ireland. For the 2005 programme please tel. 028 9751 0721.

Highlights in Northern Ireland for Visitors with Disabilities ...
Murlough National Nature Reserve offers a boarded walkway to the dunes and beach (strong pusher needed), with wheelchair and adapted WC available in summer; at the **Giant's Causeway** a bus service runs to the Causeway stones, equipped with a hoist for wheelchairs; there is also easy access to the shop and tea-room; at **Carrick-a-Rede** there is a special viewing platform for disabled visitors; a path of nearly a mile around **Florence Court** allows wheelchair access.

The beach at Loughan Bay, County Antrim

...and for Families

A hands-on demonstration of 19th-century linen production at **Wellbrook Beetling Mill** is very popular with all ages, as is watching spades being made at **Patterson's Spade Mill**.

The beach at **Portstewart Strand** is an ideal place for a family day out, with its wardening service and dedicated children's play areas. **Strangford Lough Wildlife Centre** at **Castle Ward** has a theatre showing wildlife films and information, and around the Lough there are many observation points for watching wildlife. Children will love the spectacular new adventure play parks at Castle Ward and Springhill. Many other properties also have children's play areas and activities, and most run a programme of family events. Tel. the properties for details.

Further Information

Please contact the NT Office for Northern Ireland, tel. 028 9751 0721 or visit **www.ntni.org.uk**. You can obtain copies of free leaflets or details about hiring Trust venues for private functions, corporate events or weddings, and information on holiday cottages.

For information about public transport throughout Northern Ireland tel. 028 9066 6630.

The euro is accepted by the Trust's Northern Ireland properties (daily exchange rate adopted).

Please note that on special event days properties may be required to close for a short period of time whilst setting up.

OS Grid Reference

OS NI grid references for properties with no individual entry

Ballymacormick Point	J525837
Ballyconagan	D146520
Barmouth & Grangemore Dunes	C782365
Black Mountain	J294748
Blockhouse & Green Islands	J254097
Carrick-a-Rede/ Larrybane	D062450
Collin Glen	J270720
Cushendun	D248327
Cushleake Mountain	D228364
Divis Mountain	J281755
Dunseverick Castle	C987445
Fair Head/ Murlough Bay	D185430
Glenoe	J397967
Kearney & Knockinelder	J650517
Lighthouse Island	J596858
Lisnabreeny	J367703
Loughan Bay	D243375
Minnowburn	J325684
Murlough Nature Reserve	J410350
Orlock Point	J539838
Portstewart Strand	C720360
Skernaghan Point	J437036
Slieve Donard/Mourne Coastal Path	J389269
Strangford Lough	J574498
Whitepark Bay	D023440

The Argory

144 Derrycaw Road, Moy, Dungannon,
Co. Armagh BT71 6NA

🏠 🏚 ✳ ♨ 🏛 ♿ 👗 🖼 ⛲ 🍴 ⛲ 1979   (7:C7)

Atmospheric Irish gentry house of the 1820s

This handsome house is unchanged since 1900.
The cluttered interiors evoke the Bond family's
Edwardian taste and interests, and include a
barrel organ that is played for musical house
tours. Horse carriages, a harness room, the
acetylene gas plant and a laundry are in the
imposing stable yard. The beautiful estate offers
garden, woodland and riverside walks for all
ages, with superb spring bulbs.

⭐ The house has no electric light. Visitors
wishing to make a close study of the interior
and paintings should avoid dull days early and
late in the season

ℹ️ **T** 028 8778 4753,
028 8778 9484 (Learning)
F 028 8778 9598
E argory@nationaltrust.org.uk

💷 £4.50, child £2.40, family £11.40. Groups
£4.10, group visits outside normal hours £5

The staircase hall, The Argory, County Armagh

Opening arrangements: The Argory

House	19 Mar - 20 Mar	1 - 6	M T W T F S S
	25 Mar - 1 Apr	1 - 6	M T W T F S S
	2 Apr - 29 May	1 - 6	M T W T F S S
	1 Jun - 31 Aug	1 - 6	M T W T F S S
	3 Sep - 25 Sep	1 - 6	M T W T F S S
	1 Oct - 9 Oct	1 - 5	M T W T F S S
Shop	As house	1 - 5:30	
Tea-room	As house	2 - 5	
Grounds	1 May - 30 Sep	10 - 7	M T W T F S S
	1 Oct - 30 Apr	10 - 4	M T W T F S S

Admission by guided tour. Open BH Mons and all
other public hols in N Ireland **inc. 17 March**. Please
note house and grounds open at 2pm on special event
days. **Tea-room open until 6 at weekends**

🎭 Programme of events, inc. craft fairs, walks,
musical tours and family days

♿ Drop-off point. **Building**: Ramped entrance.
2 wheelchairs. Ground floor accessible.
Seating available. Photograph album.
WCs: Adapted WC. **Grounds**: Accessible
route map. **Shop**: Step to entrance.
Refreshments: Step to entrance

🦻 Induction loop in reception. Hearing helper
system available

👓 Braille guide. Sensory list. Handling collection

☕ Tea-room

👶 Baby-changing facilities. Hip-carrying infant
seats for loan. Children's play area

🏫 Suitable for school groups. Education
room/centre. Live interpretation. Hands-on
activities. Children's quiz/trail. Adult study
days

🐕 On leads and only in grounds and garden

➔ [H418640] **Cycle**: NCN95 7ml.
Bus: Ulsterbus 67 Portadown–Dungannon
(both pass close ≢ Portadown), alight
Charlemont, 2½ml walk. **Road**: 4ml from
Charlemont, 3ml from M1, exit 13 or 14
(signposted). NB: coaches must use exit 13;
weight restrictions at Bond's Bridge

🅿 Parking, 100yds, £2.50

NT properties nearby
Ardress House, Derrymore House

Carrick-a-Rede

c/o 119a Whitepark Road, Ballintoy, Co. Antrim
BT54 6LS

🏰 📷 1967   (7:D3)

**Rock island connected to the cliffs by a rope
bridge**

On the North Antrim Coast Road, just east of
Ballintoy, is one of Northern Ireland's best-loved
attractions: the Carrick-a-Rede rope bridge.
Traditionally salmon fishermen have erected this
precarious bridge to the island over a 30m-deep
and 20m-wide chasm. Those bold enough to
cross are rewarded with fantastic views and
wildlife.

⭐ Suitable outdoor footwear recommended

ℹ️ **T** 028 2073 1582 (North Antrim office),
028 2076 9839 (Warden) **F** 028 2073 2963
E carrickarede@nationaltrust.org.uk

💷 **Rope Bridge**: £2.20, child £1.20, family
£5.60. Groups £1.70

🧑 Available for groups (min.10) by arrangement.
Tel. for details

♿ Footpath surface and car park strip have been
improved to Millennium mile standard for first
300yds (as far as view point). Designated
spaces provided alongside access strip
between visitor centre and main path. 1
manual wheelchair. **WCs**: Adapted WC.
Grounds: Partly accessible. Accessible route
map. Level access for 1400yds, then a
platform with telescopes to view bridge.
Refreshments: Ramped entrance

☕ Tea-room (not NT)

🪑 Picnic table available

👶 Baby-changing facilities. Baby back-carriers
admitted. Pushchairs not permitted over rope
bridge

The rope bridge across to Carrick-a-Rede, County
Antrim

🪧 Suitable for school groups. NT interpretation
panels on display in tea-room

🐕 On leads, not permitted to cross rope bridge

➡️ [D062450] **Foot**: On North Antrim Coastal
Path,10ml from Giant's Causeway, ½ml from
Ballintoy village and 1½ml from Ballintoy
Church on Harbour Rd. **Cycle**: NCN93 5ml.
Bus: Ulsterbus 172, 177. Causeway Rambler
bus (Ulsterbus 376) between Bushmills and
Carrick-a-Rede operates in summer; or
Ulsterbus 252 is a circular route via the Antrim
Glens from Belfast. Both stop at Carrick-a-
Rede. **Road**: On B15, 7ml E of Bushmills, 5ml
W of Ballycastle. Giant's Causeway 6ml

🅿️ Free parking. Access all year

NT properties nearby
Cushendun, Giant's Causeway, Whitepark Bay

Opening arrangements: Carrick-a-Rede			
Rope bridge	12 Mar - 12 Jun	10 - 6	**M T W T F S S**
	13 Jun - 31 Aug	10 - 7	**M T W T F S S**
	1 Sep - 9 Oct	10 - 6	**M T W T F S S**
Bridge open weather permitting. Last crossing 45 mins before closing. Access to North Antrim Coastal Path all year			

Castle Coole

Enniskillen, Co. Fermanagh BT74 6JY

🏰 🚗 🍴 🏠 📷 🧑 🌳 🧍 🔔 ▲ 🍽️ 1951   (7:A7)

**Magnificent 18th-century mansion and
landscape park**

One of the finest neo-classical houses in Ireland,
Castle Coole was designed by James Wyatt for
the 1st Earl of Belmore and completed in 1798.
The interior was created by some of the leading
craftsmen of the day. The state rooms with their
sumptuous Regency furnishings include the
bedroom prepared for a visit by George IV in
1821 and the elegant hall, where evening

Please see the area introductions for details of coast & countryside properties

concerts are often held. Nearby are the servants' quarters and tunnel, stable yard and ice house. The surrounding wooded landscape park sloping down to Lough Coole is ideal for long walks.

[i] **T** 028 6632 2690
F 028 6632 5665
E castlecoole@nationaltrust.org.uk

[£] £4.20, child £2.10, family £10.50. Groups £3.50, group visits outside normal hours £4.50

[☺] Programme of events, inc. musical evenings and guided walks

[♿] Separate designated parking. Drop-off point. **Building**: Steps to entrance, ramp available. 1 wheelchair. Photograph album. **WCs**: Adapted WC. **Grounds**: loose gravel paths. Accessible route map. **Shop**: Ramped entrance

[♨] Large-print guide. Sensory list

[♨] Tea-room (NT-approved concession) in Tallow House

[♟] Baby-changing facilities. Baby back-carriers admitted. Front-carrying baby slings for loan. Children's play area

[▮] Suitable for school groups

[🐾] On leads and only in grounds

[→] [H378788] **Cycle**: NCN91. Property entrance lies on the Kingfisher Trail, Ireland's first long-distance trail covering approx. 300 miles. **Bus**: Ulsterbus 95, Enniskillen–Clones (connections from Belfast). **Road**: 1½ml SE of Enniskillen on Belfast–Enniskillen road (A4)

[P] Free parking, 150yds

NT properties nearby
Crom Estate, Florence Court

Castle Ward

Strangford, Downpatrick, Co. Down BT30 7LS

[🏠][🐦][🔧][🔥][✿][♨][🥾][🚜][↑][🍴][♨][🎫][🧒][♿]

[🍸] 1953   (7:F7)

Interesting 18th-century mansion, famed for its mixture of architectural styles

Castle Ward's 300ha (750-acre) walled estate is in a stunning location overlooking Strangford Lough. The mid-Georgian mansion is an architectural curiosity of its time, built inside and out in two distinct styles, Classical and Gothic. The Victorian laundry, playroom, cornmill, leadmine and sawmill give the full flavour of how the estate worked. The grounds encompass woodland and lough-side paths and horse trails, formal gardens, Old Castle Ward, Temple Water and the Strangford Lough Wildlife Centre. There are many spaces available for private hire, a caravan site and a holiday cottage.

What's new in 2005 Artists-in-residence programme: local and international artists working in a traditional cottage with studio; adventure playground in woodland area

[i] **T** 028 4488 1204,
028 4488 1543 (Learning)
F 028 4488 1729
E castleward@nationaltrust.org.uk

Opening arrangements: Castle Coole										
House	12 Mar - 20 Mar	12 - 6	M	T	W	T	F	S	S
	25 Mar - 1 Apr	12 - 6	M	T	W	T	F	S	S
	2 Apr - 29 May	12 - 6	M	T	W	T	F	S	S
	30 May - 30 Jun	12 - 6	M	T	W	T	F	S	S
	1 Jul - 31 Aug	12 - 6	M	T	W	T	F	S	S
	3 Sep - 25 Sep	12 - 6	M	T	W	T	F	S	S
	1 Oct - 9 Oct	1 - 5	M	T	W	T	F	S	S
Grounds	1 Apr - 30 Sep	10 - 8	M	T	W	T	F	S	S
	1 Oct - 31 Mar 06	10 - 4	M	T	W	T	F	S	S

Admission by guided tour. Open BH Mons and all other public hols in N Ireland **inc. 17 March**. Last admission 1hr before closing. Tel. property for shop and tea-room opening arrangements

Opening arrangements: Castle Ward										
House &	12 Mar - 20 Mar	1 - 6	M	T	W	T	F	S	S
wildlife centre	25 Mar - 1 Apr	1 - 6	M	T	W	T	F	S	S
	2 Apr - 30 Apr	1 - 6	M	T	W	T	F	S	S
	1 May - 30 May	1 - 6	M	T	W	T	F	S	S
	1 Jun - 31 Aug	1 - 6	M	T	W	T	F	S	S
	3 Sep - 30 Oct	1 - 6	M	T	W	T	F	S	S
Grounds	1 May - 30 Sep	10 - 8	M	T	W	T	F	S	S
	3 Oct - 30 Apr 06	10 - 4	M	T	W	T	F	S	S

Admission by guided tour. Open BH Mons and all other public hols in N Ireland **inc. 17 March**. Last house tour starts at 5. Tel. property for shop and tea-room opening arrangements

Unless indicated, last admission is always 30mins before closing time

£ **House, grounds & wildlife centre**: £5.30, child £2.40, family £13. Groups £4.20, group visits outside normal hours £5.50. **Grounds & wildlife centre only**: £3.70, child £1.70, family £9.10. Groups £2.70

♥ Programme of events, inc. jazz, opera, musical recitals, open-air concert, craft fairs, lecture series

♿ Separate designated parking, 50yds. Drop-off point. **Building**: Many steps to entrance with handrail, ramp available. Alternative accessible entrance, still has a few steps, ramp available. 2 wheelchairs, booking essential. Ground floor accessible. Seating available. Photograph album. Basement and tunnel not accessible to wheelchair users. **WCs**: Adapted WC. **Grounds**: Partly accessible, some steps. Accessible route map. Staff-driven multi-seater vehicle. **Shop**: Level entrance. **Refreshments**: Level entrance. Large-print menu

🔖 Sign interpreter by arrangement

👆 Braille guide. Touchable objects and interesting scents

🍵 Tea-room in stableyard. Children's menu

🔲 Picnic tables beside lough

🧑‍🍼 Baby-changing and feeding facilities. Hip-carrying infant seats for loan. Children's play area. Victorian pastime centre; toys & dressing up

🏫 Suitable for school groups. Education room/centre. Live interpretation. Hands-on activities. Family guide. Children's quiz/trail. Children's activity packs. Adult study days

🐕 On leads and only in grounds

➔ [J752494] **Foot**: On Lecale Way. **Ferry**: From Portaferry. **Bus**: Ulsterbus 16E Downpatrick–Strangford, with connections from Belfast (passing close 🚆 Belfast Great Victoria Street); bus stop at gates. Ulsterbus Lecale Rambler (Sat, Sun only) in summer. **Road**: 7ml NE of Downpatrick, 1½ml W of Strangford village on A25, on S shore of Strangford Lough, entrance by Ballyculter Lodge

P Free parking, 250yds

NT properties nearby
Mount Stewart, Murlough National Nature Reserve, Rowallane Garden

The Gothic Boudoir, Castle Ward, County Down

Crom Estate

Upper Lough Erne, Newtownbutler,
Co. Fermanagh BT92 8AP

🔲🔲🔲🔲🔲🔲🔲🔲🔲 1987   (7:A8)

Romantic and tranquil landscape of islands, woodland and historical ruins

Set on the shores of Upper Lough Erne, Crom is one of Ireland's most important nature conservation areas with many rare species. There are nature trails, a programme of guided walks, boats for hire, a jetty for overnight boats, coarse angling, comfortable holiday cottages, campsite, a wildlife exhibition and rooms for private hire.

What's new in 2005 Licensed for civil weddings

⭐ The 19th-century castle is private and not open to the public. WC available only when visitor centre open. Showers available for campsite users

There are special events at most Trust properties; please telephone 0870 458 4000 for details

i **T/F** 028 6773 8118,
0870 458 4422 (Holiday cottage bookings)
E crom@nationaltrust.org.uk

£ **Grounds & visitor centre – car or boat**:
£4.70. **Minibus**: £13. **Coach**: £16.70.
Motorbike: £2. Campsite charge: £10 per
tent per night

By special arrangement

Programme of events, inc. family days, bat
nights

Guided walks to discover wildlife and social
history

Separate designated parking, 100yds.
Building: Ramped entrance. 1 wheelchair,
booking essential. **WCs**: Adapted WC.
Grounds: Accessible route. Access route to
Old Castle area. 1 single-seater PMV, booking
essential. **Shop**: Level entrance.
Refreshments: Level entrance

Braille guide. Sensory list

Tea-room in visitor centre

Baby-changing facilities. Pushchairs and baby
back-carriers admitted. Hip-carrying infant
seats for loan. Children's play area

Suitable for school groups. Family activity packs

On leads only

2ml of NCN91 designated as the Kingfisher
Trail runs through the property

→ [H455655 – 361245, 381232] **Cycle**: NCN91.
Ferry from Derryvore Church must be booked
24 hrs in advance, tel. for details.

The Castle (not NT) and boat house, Crom Estate,
County Fermanagh

Bus: Ulsterbus 95 Enniskillen–Clones
(connections from Belfast), alight
Newtownbutler, 3ml. **Road**: 3ml W of
Newtownbutler, on Newtownbutler–Crom
road, or follow signs from Lisnaskea. Crom is
next to the Shannon–Erne waterway. Public
jetty at visitor centre

P Parking, 100yds

NT properties nearby
Castle Coole, Florence Court

Opening arrangements: Crom Estate										
Grounds	12 Mar - 30 Jun	10 - 6	M	T	W	T	F	S	S
	1 Jul - 31 Aug	10 - 8	M	T	W	T	F	S	S
	1 Sep - 30 Sep	10 - 6	M	T	W	T	F	S	S
	1 Oct - 30 Oct	12 - 6	M	T	W	T	F	S	S
Visitor centre	12 Mar - 20 Mar	10 - 6	M	T	W	T	F	S	S
	25 Mar - 1 Apr	10 - 6	M	T	W	T	F	S	S
	2 Apr - 24 Apr	10 - 6	M	T	W	T	F	S	S
	25 Apr - 30 Sep	10 - 6	M	T	W	T	F	S	S
	1 Oct - 9 Oct	1 - 5	M	T	W	T	F	S	S

Open BH Mons and all other public hols in N Ireland
inc. **17 March. All Suns: grounds and visitor centre
open 12–6**. Tel. property for shop and tea-room
opening arrangements

Crown Liquor Saloon

46 Great Victoria Street, Belfast, Co. Antrim
BT2 7BA

[🏠] [🍷] 1978 (7:E6)

The most famous pub in Belfast

The Crown Liquor Saloon is one of the finest
examples of a High Victorian public house in
existence, with rich ornamentation, gas lighting
and snugs still intact.

i **T** 028 9027 9901

£ Admission free

→ [J336736] **Cycle**: NCN9 ½ml. **Bus**: Located
opposite Europa Buscentre.
Station: Opposite Great Victoria Street

Opening arrangements: Crown Liquor Saloon		
All year	11:30 - 11	**M T W T F S** S
All year	12:30 - 10	M T W T F S **S**

P Street parking only

NT properties nearby
Mount Stewart, Patterson's Spade Mill, Rowallane Garden

Derrymore House

Bessbrook, Newry, Co. Armagh BT35 7EF

🏠 🚶 🔼 🚶 1953   **(7:D8)**

Late 18th-century thatched house in gentrified vernacular style

The house is typical of the informal thatched retreats, or *cottages ornées*, boasted by many estates in the 18th century. It was built in a picturesque setting by Isaac Corry, who represented Newry in the Irish House of Commons for thirty years from 1776.

⭐ Portaloo in car park only

ℹ️ **T** 028 8778 4753 (The Argory)
F 028 8778 9598
E derrymore@nationaltrust.org.uk

💷 **House tour**: £3, child £1.50, family £7.50. Groups £2.20, group visits outside normal hours £4

♿ Separate designated parking, 30yds.
Building: Step to entrance.
Grounds: Accessible route. Some visitors may require assistance from their companion

🚼 Pushchairs admitted

🐕 On leads and only in grounds

🚲 NCN9 passes through estate

➡️ [J056280] **Cycle**: NCN9. **Bus**: Ulsterbus 42, 44, 341C from Newry (passing close ⊞ Newry). **Station**: Newry 2ml. **Road**: On A25 off the Newry–Camlough road at Bessbrook, 1½ml from Newry

Opening arrangements: Derrymore House									
House	5 May - 27 Aug	2 - 5:30	M	T W	**T**	**F**	**S**	S
Grounds	1 May - 30 Sep	10 - 7	**M**	**T**	**W**	**T**	**F**	**S**	**S**
	1 Oct - 30 Apr	10 - 4	**M**	**T**	**W**	**T**	**F**	**S**	**S**
Admission by guided tour									

P Free parking, 30yds

NT properties nearby
Ardress House, The Argory

Downhill Estate & Mussenden Temple

North Derry Office, Hezlett Farm, 107 Sea Road, Castlerock, Co. Londonderry BT51 4TW

🏠 🔼 🔼 ❖ 🍴 🚜 🎋 👤 ▲ 🔼 1949   **(7:C4)**

Landscaped estate in a dramatic coastal setting

Set on a wild and rugged headland with fabulous clifftop walks and views over Ireland's north coast is the Downhill Estate, laid out in the late 18th century by the eccentric Earl and Bishop, Frederick Hervey. The estate includes ruins, a mausoleum, beautiful gardens and the renowned Mussenden Temple perched on the cliff edge. The Temple is licensed for weddings.

What's new in 2005 Family activity packs (from Lion's Gate car park. Deposit required)

⭐ WC available when Temple open (situated at Lion's Gate car park). Other WC 1ml east at promenade, Castlerock village

ℹ️ **T/F** 028 7084 8728,
028 2073 1582 (Learning)
E downhillcastle@nationaltrust.org.uk

💷 **Grounds & Temple – Motorbike**: £2.30.
Car: £3.70. **Minibus**: £7.40. Charges apply when Temple open

🎪 Programme of events, inc. midsummer concerts (10 & 11 June), Sheepdog Trials 2 July

Opening arrangements: Downhill Estate									
Temple	12 Mar - 20 Mar	11 - 6	M	T W	T	F	**S**	**S**
	25 Mar - 1 Apr	11 - 6	**M**	**T**	**W**	**T**	**F**	**S**	**S**
	2 Apr - 29 May	11 - 6	M	T W	T	F	**S**	**S**
	1 Jun - 30 Jun	11 - 6	**M**	**T**	**W**	**T**	**F**	**S**	**S**
	1 Jul - 31 Aug	11 - 7:30	**M**	**T**	**W**	**T**	**F**	**S**	**S**
	3 Sep - 25 Sep	11 - 6	M	T W	T	F	**S**	**S**
	1 Oct - 30 Oct	11 - 5	M	T W	T	F	**S**	**S**
Grounds	All year	Dawn-dusk	**M**	**T**	**W**	**T**	**F**	**S**	**S**
Open BH Mons and all other public hols in N Ireland inc. **17 March**									

Please note: groups must book in advance with the property

♿ Wheelchair access to Downhill ruins and Temple via stoned laneway, key needed for last gate (opened on request when Temple is open). Contact in advance. **Building**: Level entrance. **WCs**: Adapted WC. On request, car access to WCs possible when warden on duty (Temple opening hours). **Grounds**: Accessible route map

♟ Baby-changing facilities. Pushchairs admitted

▮ Suitable for school groups. Family guide. Children's quiz/trail. Family activity packs

✢ On leads only

→ [C757357] **Cycle**: NCN93 borders property. **Ferry**: Magilligan–Greencastle Ferry (8ml). **Bus**: Ulsterbus 134 Coleraine–Londonderry. **Station**: Castlerock ½ml. **Road**: 1ml W of Castlerock and 5ml W of Coleraine on A2 Coleraine–Downhill coast road

♲ Parking at Lion's Gate where information, WCs and picnic tables are provided, £3.70. Not suitable for 50-seater coaches. Or parking at Bishop's Gate entrance, ½ml from Temple

NT properties nearby
Carrick-a-Rede, Giant's Causeway, Hezlett House, Portstewart Strand

---

Florence Court

Enniskillen, Co. Fermanagh BT92 1DB

▫▫▫▫▫▫▫▫▫▫▫ 1954   (7:A7)

Fine 18th-century house and estate

Florence Court is set against the stunning backdrop of the Cuilcagh Mountains. It was the home of the Earls of Enniskillen and is one of the most important houses in Ulster. Now, with many original contents returned, it is a popular attraction for all ages. The tour includes the exquisite rococo decoration, fine Irish furniture and service quarters. There are extensive walks in the grounds, a sawmill and walled garden.

What's new in 2005 Licensed for civil weddings

ⓘ **T** 028 6634 8249, 028 6634 8873 (Learning), 028 6634 8788 (Shop)
F 028 6634 8873
E florencecourt@nationaltrust.org.uk

£ **House tour**: £4, child £2, family £10. Groups £3.50, group visits outside normal hours £4.50. **Grounds**: car £3, minibus £15, coach £20, motorbike £1.50

✣ Living History tours, Suns in July & Aug

⚗ Programme of events, inc. concerts, family days and country fairs

♿ Separate designated parking. Drop-off point. **Building**: Steps to entrance, ramp available. 2 wheelchairs. Photograph album. **WCs**: Adapted WC. **Grounds**: Accessible route map. 1 single-seater PMV. **Shop**: Level entrance. **Refreshments**: Level entrance

☞ Braille guide and large-print guide

☎ Stables Restaurant (not NT) in stable yard

♟ Baby-changing facilities. Baby back-carriers admitted. Front-carrying baby slings for loan. Children's play area

▮ Suitable for school groups. Education room/centre. Live interpretation. Hands-on activities. Children's quiz/trail

✢ On leads and only in garden and grounds

→ [H175344] **Cycle**: NCN91. Property entrance lies on Kingfisher Trail. **Bus**: Ulsterbus 192 Enniskillen–Swanlinbar, alight Creamery Cross, 2ml walk. **Road**: 8ml SW of Enniskillen via A4 Sligo road and A32 Swanlinbar road, 4ml from Marble Arch Caves

♲ Parking, 200yds

NT properties nearby
Castle Coole, Crom Estate

Opening arrangements: Florence Court										
House	12 Mar - 20 Mar	12 - 6	M	T	W	T	F	S	S
	25 Mar - 1 Apr	12 - 6	**M**	**T**	**W**	**T**	**F**	**S**	**S**
	2 Apr - 29 May	12 - 6	M	T	W	T	F	**S**	**S**
	30 May - 30 Jun	1 - 6	**M**	T	**W**	**T**	F	S	S
	4 Jun - 26 Jun	12 - 6	M	T	W	T	F	**S**	**S**
	1 Jul - 31 Aug	12 - 6	**M**	**T**	**W**	**T**	**F**	**S**	**S**
	3 Sep - 25 Sep	12 - 6	M	T	W	T	F	**S**	**S**
	1 Oct - 9 Oct	1 - 5	M	T	W	T	F	**S**	**S**
Grounds	1 Apr - 30 Sep	10 - 8	**M**	**T**	**W**	**T**	**F**	**S**	**S**
	1 Oct - 31 Mar 06	10 - 4	**M**	**T**	**W**	**T**	**F**	**S**	**S**

Admission by guided tour to house. Open BH Mons and all other public hols in N Ireland **inc. 17 March**. Last admission 1hr before closing. Tel. property for shop and restaurant opening arrangements

Giant's Causeway

c/o 44a Causeway Road, Bushmills, Co. Antrim
BT57 8SU

 1962 **(7:D3)**

Famous geological phenomenon on the North Antrim coast

The Giant's Causeway, renowned for its polygonal columns of layered basalt, is the only World Heritage Site in Northern Ireland. Resulting from a volcanic eruption 60 million years ago, this is the focal point of a designated Area of Outstanding Natural Beauty and has attracted visitors for centuries. It harbours a wealth of local and natural history that can be enjoyed from the North Antrim Coastal Path.

★ Car park and information centre are owned and operated by Moyle District Council

ℹ **T** 028 2073 1582 (N Antrim office),
028 2073 1855 (Moyle Visitor Centre),
028 2073 2972 (Shop),
028 2073 2282 (Tea-room)
F 028 2073 2963
E giantscauseway@nationaltrust.org.uk

£ Admission free. Donations welcome

Giant's Causeway, County Antrim

Opening arrangements: Giant's Causeway

Stones/coast	All year				M T W T F S S

Visitor facilities closed 25 Dec & 1 Jan. Shop open March–mid Dec daily; mid Dec–Feb, tel. for opening arrangements. Tea-room open mid March–mid Nov daily. Tel. for opening times

🛈 Guided tours by arrangement for groups, 10+. Tel. N. Antrim office for details

🎪 Programme of events, inc. boat trips, fun trails, painting classes

🚶 Sensible outdoor footwear recommended

♿ Designated parking in main car park.
Building: Ramped entrance. 1 wheelchair. Seating available. **WCs**: Adapted WC.
Grounds: Partly accessible, steep slopes. Accessible route map. **Shop**: Ramped entrance. **Refreshments**: Ramped entrance

🍵 Tea-room. Children's menu

🧺 Picnic tables adjacent to car park

👶 Baby-changing facilities. Pushchairs and baby back-carriers admitted

🏫 Suitable for school groups. Education room/centre

🐕 On leads

➔ [C952452] **Foot**: Path from Portballintrae alongside steam railway. Accessible also via Causeway Coast Cliff path from Carrick-a-Rede (10ml), Whitepark Bay (7ml) and Dunseverick Castle (4½ml). **Cycle**: NCN93.
Bus: Ulsterbus 172, 177. Causeway Coaster minibus from visitor centre to stones (NT members free). Causeway Rambler bus (Ulsterbus 376) between Bushmills and Carrick-a-Rede operates in summer; Ulsterbus 252 is a circular route via the Antrim Glens from Belfast. Both stop at the Causeway. **Station**: Coleraine 10ml or Portrush 8ml. Giant's Causeway & Bushmills Steam Railway, 200yds. Tel. 028 2073 2844.
Road: On B146 Causeway–Dunseverick road 2ml from Bushmills

P Parking (not NT), 100yds, charge inc. NT members

NT properties nearby
Carrick-a-Rede, Hezlett House, Portstewart Strand, Whitepark Bay

Please remember – your membership card is always needed for free admission

Gray's Printing Press

49 Main Street, Strabane, Co. Tyrone BT82 8AU

🐌 🎭 🎨 🛡 1966   (7:B5)

18th-century printing press

It was here that John Dunlap, the printer of the American Declaration of Independence, and James Wilson, grandfather of President Woodrow Wilson, learnt their trade. There is a collection of 19th-century hand-printing machines, and an audio-visual display. The former stationer's shop is now a local museum run by Strabane District Council.

[i] **T** 028 718 80055, 028 867 48210 (Learning)
F 028 867 48210

[£] £2.70, child £1.60, family £7. Groups £2.20, group visits outside normal hours £3.50

[♿] **Building**: Level entrance. Ground floor accessible. Many stairs to other floors. Seating available. Audio visual/video.
WCs: Adapted WC. **Grounds**: Fully accessible

[👆] Touchable objects

[▦] Suitable for school groups

[➔] [H345977] **Cycle**: NCN92. **Bus**: Ulsterbus Express 273 Belfast–Derry City, alight Strabane centre; few mins walk.
Road: Situated close to the Omagh Road on the main street in the centre of Strabane

[P] Parking (not NT), 100yds (pay & display)

NT properties nearby
Downhill Estate & Mussenden Temple, Springhill, Wellbrook Beetling Mill

Opening arrangements: Gray's Printing Press										
Press	2 Apr - 28 May	2 - 5	M	T	W	T	F	**S**	**S**
	1 Jun - 30 Jun	2 - 5	M	**T**	**W**	**T**	**F**	**S**	S
	1 Jul - 31 Aug	11 - 5	M	**T**	**W**	**T**	**F**	**S**	S
	1 Sep - 30 Sep	2 - 5	M	T	W	T	F	**S**	**S**

Admission by guided tour. Last admission 45mins before closing

Hezlett House

107 Sea Road, Castlerock, Coleraine, Co. Londonderry BT51 4TW

🏠 ❄ 1976   (7:C4)

17th-century thatched house and farmyard

One of the few buildings in Northern Ireland surviving from before the 18th century, the house has an interesting cruck-truss roof construction and is simply furnished in late Victorian style. There is a small museum of farm implements.

[★] WC not always available. Other WC 1ml E at promenade, Castlerock village

[i] **T/F** 028 7084 8728
E hezletthouse@nationaltrust.org.uk

[£] £3.70, child £2.20, family £9.60. Groups £3.10, group visits outside normal hours £4.50

[🎓] Groups must book in advance (max.10 in house at any one time)

[♿] Separate designated parking, 10yds.
Building: Level entrance. Portable ramps available to enter 2 ground-floor rooms (ask for assistance). Outbuildings accessible.
WCs: Adapted WC. **Grounds**: Partly accessible

[🅰] Tables in car park

[👶] Baby-changing facilities. Baby back-carriers admitted

[▦] Suitable for school groups. Family guide

[🐕] On leads and only in garden

[➔] [C772349] **Cycle**: NCN93. **Bus**: Ulsterbus 134 Coleraine–Londonderry, alight crossroads, few mins walk.
Station: Castlerock ¾ml. **Road**: 4ml W of Coleraine on Coleraine–Downhill coast road, A2. Beside Castlerock turn-off cross roads

[P] Free parking, 100yds

NT properties nearby
Downhill Estate & Mussenden Temple, Giant's Causeway, Portstewart Strand

Opening arrangements: Hezlett House										
	4 Jun - 26 Jun	1 - 5	M	T	W	T	F	**S**	**S**
	1 Jul - 31 Aug	1 - 5	**M**	T	**W**	**T**	**F**	**S**	**S**

Admission by guided tour

Mount Stewart House, Garden & Temple of the Winds

Portaferry Road, Newtownards, Co. Down
BT22 2AD

🏠 🏚 ✽ 🗔 🍴 🚶 🚻 🔔 🍽 | 1976 | **(7:F6)**

Neo-classical house and celebrated gardens

The famous gardens at Mount Stewart were planted in the 1920s by Edith, Lady Londonderry and have been nominated a World Heritage Site. The magnificent series of outdoor 'rooms' and vibrant parterres contain many rare plants that thrive in the mild climate of the Ards Peninsula. There are dramatic views over Strangford Lough from the Temple of the Winds. The house tour includes world-famous paintings and stories about the prominent political figures to whom the Londonderry family played host.

What's new in 2005 Licensed for civil weddings; children's house tours Sat & Sun, July & Aug; hearing loop system for house tours

ℹ️ **T** 028 4278 8387,
 028 4278 8830 (Learning),
 028 4278 7805 (Shop),
 028 4278 7807 (Restaurant)
 F 028 4278 8569
 E mountstewart@nationaltrust.org.uk

£ **House & gardens**: £5.45, child £2.70, family £13.60. Groups £4.80, group visits outside normal hours £6. **Gardens only**: £4.40, child £2.30, family £11.10. Groups £4.10

🎭 Programme of events, inc. drama, music and craft events, Easter egg trails, half-term holiday clubs, garden and craft fair

🚶 Varied programme of garden and house walks

♿ Separate designated parking, 100yds. Drop-off point. **Building**: Level entrance. 2 wheelchairs, booking essential. Stairs to other floors. Photograph album. **WCs**: Adapted WC. **Grounds**: Accessible route map. 2 single-seater PMV, booking essential. **Shop**: Level entrance. **Refreshments**: Level entrance

👁 Braille guide. Sensory list

Opening arrangements: Mount Stewart			
Lakeside Gdns	1 Apr - 30 Apr	10 - 6	**M T W T F S S**
	1 May - 30 Sep	10 - 8	**M T W T F S S**
	1 Oct - 31 Oct	10 - 6	**M T W T F S S**
	1 Nov - 31 Mar 06	10 - 4	**M T W T F S S**
Formal Gardens	5 Mar - 27 Mar	10 - 4	M T W T F **S S**
	1 Apr - 30 Apr	10 - 6	**M T W T F S S**
	1 May - 30 Sep	10 - 8	**M T W T F S S**
	1 Oct - 31 Oct	10 - 6	**M T W T F S S**
House	12 Mar - 20 Mar	12 - 6	M T W T F **S S**
	25 Mar - 1 Apr	12 - 6	**M T W T F S S**
	2 Apr - 1 May	12 - 6	M T W T F **S S**
	7 May - 26 Jun	12 - 6	M T W T F **S S**
	2 May - 1 Jul	1 - 6	**M** T **W T F** S S
	2 Jul - 31 Aug	12 - 6	**M T W T F S S**
	1 Sep - 30 Sep	12 - 6	**M** T **W T F S S**
	1 Oct - 30 Oct	12 - 6	M T W T F **S S**
Temple	3 Apr - 30 Oct	2 - 5	M T W T F S **S**

Admission by guided tour to house. Open BH Mons and all other public hols in N Ireland **inc. 17 March.** Lakeside gardens closed 25 Dec. Tel. property for shop and restaurant opening arrangements

🛍 NT shop selling quality local gifts. Plant sales

🍴 Bay Restaurant (licensed). Serving main and light meals using finest local ingredients. Catering available outside normal hours by arrangement. Children's menu

🚼 Baby-changing facilities

🏫 Suitable for school groups. Education room/centre. Live interpretation. Hands-on activities. Children's quiz/trail. Family activity packs. Winter trails for children

🐕 On leads and in grounds and garden only

➔ [J553695] **Bus**: Ulsterbus 10 Belfast–Portaferry bus stop at gates. **Station**: Bangor 10ml. **Road**: 15ml SE of Belfast on Newtownards–Portaferry road, A20, 5ml SE of Newtownards

🅿 Free parking, 100yds

NT properties nearby
Castle Ward, Patterson's Spade Mill, Rowallane Garden

Please see the area introductions for details of coast & countryside properties

Patterson's Spade Mill

751 Antrim Road, Templepatrick, Co. Antrim
BT39 0AP

🔲🗶🔟🎨🎨🐕🍸 1991 (7:E6)

The last working water-driven spade mill in daily use in the British Isles

Visitors can hear and smell the grit on a guided tour of traditional spade-making and find out about the history and culture of the humble turf and garden spade. You can purchase one of only 200 tailor-made spades made by hand each year.

ℹ️ **T/F** 028 9443 3619

💷 £3.80, child £2.20, family £9.80. Groups £3, group visits outside normal hours £5

😃 Programme of events, inc. Farming in the 40s, Pets Day & Harvest Day

♿ Separate designated parking, 50yds. Drop-off point. **Building**: Ramped entrance. 1 wheelchair. Ground floor accessible. Seating available. Audio visual/video. **WCs**: Adapted WC. **Grounds**: Fully accessible

👁️ Sensory list. Handling collection

🏪 No shop but spades for sale

🚼 Pushchairs and baby back-carriers admitted

🏫 Suitable for school groups. Live interpretation. Hands-on activities. Children's guide

➡️ [J263856] **Bus**: Ulsterbus 110 & 120, bus stop at gates. **Station**: Antrim 8ml. **Road**: 2ml NE of Templepatrick on Antrim–Belfast road, A6; M2 exit 4

🅿️ Free parking, 50yds

NT properties nearby
Mount Stewart, Rowallane Garden, Springhill

Opening arrangements: Patterson's Spade Mill										
Mill	13 Mar - 20 Mar	2 - 6	M	T	W	T	F	S	**S**
	25 Mar - 1 Apr	2 - 6	**M**	**T**	**W**	**T**	**F**	**S**	**S**
	2 Apr - 29 May	2 - 6	M	T	W	T	F	**S**	**S**
	1 Jun - 31 Aug	2 - 6	**M**		**W**	**T**	**F**	**S**	**S**
	3 Sep - 9 Oct	2 - 6	M	T	W	T	F	**S**	**S**

Admission by guided tour. Open BH Mons and all other public hols in N Ireland **inc. 17 March**. Last admission 1hr before closing

Rowallane Garden

Saintfield, Ballynahinch, Co. Down BT24 7LH

✳️🍽️🅿️🚶 1956 (7:E7)

Beautiful informal garden of trees and shrubs, with plants from around the world

Much of the garden retains the natural landscape of the surrounding area, into which many exotic species have been introduced. There are spectacular displays of azaleas and rhododendrons and a notable rock garden with primulas, alpines and heathers. The walled garden has mixed borders which include the National Collection of Penstemons; there are also several areas managed as wildflower meadows.

ℹ️ **T** 028 9751 0131 **F** 028 9751 1242 **E** rowallane@nationaltrust.org.uk

💷 £3.70, child £1.70, family £9.10. Groups £2.80, group visits outside normal hours £3.50

🦯 Available on request

😃 Programme of events, inc. Easter trail, garden workshops, fairs and musical events

♿ Separate designated parking. **Building**: 2 wheelchairs. **WCs**: Adapted WC. **Grounds**: Partly accessible, undulating terrain. **Refreshments**: Level entrance

🏪 Plant sales. Spring and summer only

☕ Tea-room

🚼 Pushchairs admitted

🏫 Children's quiz/trail

🐕 On leads only

➡️ [J412581] **Foot**: 15 mins from Saintfield village centre. **Bus**: Ulsterbus 15 Belfast–Downpatrick (passing 🚉 Belfast Great Victoria Street). **Road**: 11ml SE of Belfast, 1ml S of Saintfield, on road to Downpatrick (A7)

🅿️ Free parking

NT properties nearby
Castle Ward, Mount Stewart, Patterson's Spade Mill

Opening arrangements: Rowallane Garden									
Gardens	16 Apr - 18 Sep	10 - 8	**M**	**T**	**W**	**T**	**F**	**S**	**S**
	19 Sep - 14 Apr 06	10 - 4	**M**	**T**	**W**	**T**	**F**	**S**	**S**

Open daily all year except 25–26 Dec and 1 Jan. Tel. for tea-room opening times

Unless indicated, last admission is always 30mins before closing time

Springhill

20 Springhill Road, Moneymore, Magherafelt,
Co. Londonderry BT45 7NQ

🏠 🐾 ✿ 🗎 🍵 🕴 🔔 ⊤ 1957   (7:C6)

**Pretty 17th-century 'Plantation' home with a
significant costume collection**

The tour of this atmospheric house takes in the
exceptional library, Conyngham family furniture,
gun room, nursery, resident ghost and, housed in
the laundry, the unusual and colourful costume
exhibition, which has some fine 18th- to 20th-
century pieces. There are walled gardens,
waymarked paths through the parkland, a
caravan site and beautiful barn for hire.

What's new in 2005 Adventure trail play park

ℹ️ **T/F** 028 8674 8210,
028 8674 7927 (Museum Curator),
028 8674 8215 (Learning)
E springhill@nationaltrust.org.uk

£ £4.10, child £2.20, family £10.40. Groups
£3.70, group visits outside normal hours £5

🎭 Out-of-hours tours for groups only

📅 Programme of events, inc. special tours and
family days

♿ Drop-off point. **Building**: Many steps to
entrance with handrail. Alternative accessible
entrance. 1 wheelchair. Ground floor accessible.
Stairs to other floors. Seating available.
Photograph album. **WCs**: Adapted WC.

Entrance front, Springhill, County Londonderry

Opening arrangements: Springhill

House			
12 Mar - 20 Mar	12 - 6	M T W T F **S S**
25 Mar - 1 Apr	12 - 6	**M T W T F S S**
2 Apr - 26 Jun	12 - 6	M T W T F **S S**
1 Jul - 31 Aug	12 - 6	**M T W T F S S**
3 Sep - 25 Sep	12 - 6	M T W T F **S S**
1 Oct - 9 Oct	12 - 5	M T W T F **S S**

Admission by guided tour to house. Open BH Mons
and all other public hols in N Ireland **inc. 17 March.**
Last admission 1hr before closing. Tel. property for
shop and tea-room opening arrangements

Grounds: Fully accessible. **Shop**: Many steps
to entrance with handrail. **Refreshments**:
Many steps to entrance with handrail

♿ Braille guide. Sensory list. Handling collection

🛍️ NT shop. Plant sales

🍵 Tea-room in servants' hall. Light refreshments

🏕️ Picnic areas in garden and woodland

👶 Baby-changing facilities. Pushchairs and baby
back-carriers admitted. Children's play area

🎒 Suitable for school groups. Education
room/centre. Live interpretation. Hands-on
activities. Children's quiz/trail. Adult study
days. Children's costumes and activities
available on request

🐕 On leads and only in grounds

➡️ [H866828] **Bus**: Ulsterbus 210 & 110
Belfast–Cookstown, alight Moneymore village,
1ml. **Road**: 1ml from Moneymore on
Moneymore–Coagh road, B18

Entrance front, Springhill, County Londonderry

P Free parking, 50yds

NT properties nearby
Gray's Printing Press, Wellbrook Beetling Mill

Wellbrook Beetling Mill

20 Wellbrook Road, Corkhill, Cookstown, Co. Tyrone BT80 9RY

⊠🛠♨🏠🚹🎞🚹 1968   (7:C6)

Working water-powered mill used in the manufacture of linen

Beetling was the final stage in the production of linen, an industry of major importance in 19th-century Ireland. The mill has its original hammer machinery, used to beat a sheen into the cloth, and 'hands-on' demonstrations of the process are popular with children. The mill is situated in an attractive glen through which there are many good walks.

[i] **T/F** 028 8674 8210
   E springhill@nationaltrust.org.uk

[£] £3, child £1.70, family £7.70. Groups £2.50, group visits outside normal hours £3.50

[♥] Programme of events, inc. flax sowing and pulling days; Living History days

[♿] Drop-off point. **Building**: Level entrance. Ground floor has steps. Many stairs with handrail to other floors. Guide available to talk to visitors. **WCs**: Adapted WC. Entrance ramp. **Grounds**: Partly accessible, 1 accessible route, 1 route has steps and narrow paths. **Shop**: Level entrance

[👁] Sensory list. Handling collection

Opening arrangements: Wellbrook Beetling Mill				
Mill	12 Mar - 20 Mar	1 - 6	M T W **T** F **S S**	
	25 Mar - 1 Apr	1 - 6	**M T W T F S S**	
	2 Apr - 26 Jun	1 - 6	M T W T F **S S**	
	1 Jul - 31 Aug	1 - 6	**M T W T F S S**	
	3 Sep - 25 Sep	1 - 6	M T W T F **S S**	
	1 Oct - 9 Oct	1 - 5	M T W T F **S S**	

Admission by guided tour. Open BH Mons and all other public hols in N Ireland **inc. 17 March**. Last admission 1hr before closing. Tel property for shop opening arrangements

[🚼] Pushchairs and baby back-carriers admitted

[🏫] Suitable for school groups. Live interpretation. Hands-on activities

[🐕] On leads and in grounds only

→ [H750792] **Cycle**: NCN95. **Bus**: Ulsterbus 90 from Cookstown, with connections from Belfast. ½ml walk to mill. **Road**: 4ml W of Cookstown, ½ml off Cookstown–Omagh road (A505): from Cookstown turn right at Kildress Parish Church or follow Orritor Road (A53) to avoid town centre

P Free parking, 10yds

NT properties nearby
Gray's Printing Press, Springhill

Properties open less often

This section includes National Trust properties, often tenanted, which are open two days a week or less (plus Bank Holidays in some cases). Visits to some must be made by prior arrangement and where this applies admission prices are not shown (please ask when making contact). **Full details are on our website www.nationaltrust.org.uk or obtainable from the Membership Department, tel. 0870 458 4000.**

Ardress House

64 Ardress Road, Annaghmore, Portadown, Co. Armagh BT62 1SQ   (7:D7)

17th-century house with elegant 18th-century decoration and a traditional farmyard.

[i] **T** 028 8778 4753 (The Argory)
   F 028 3885 1236
   E ardress@nationaltrust.org.uk

[£] £3.30, child £1.70, family £8.30. Groups £3, group visits outside normal hours £5

Opening arrangements: Ardress House			
House	19 Mar - 25 Sep	2 - 6	M T W T F **S S**

Admission by guided tour. Open BH Mons and all other public hols in N Ireland **inc. 17 March**. Grounds ('My Lady's Mile') open daily all year, dawn to dusk

- Membership of the National Trust allows you free parking in Trust car parks and free entry to most Trust properties open to the public during normal opening times and under normal opening arrangements, **provided you can present a valid membership card.**

- **Please check that you have your card with you before you set out on your journey. We very much regret that you cannot be admitted free of charge without it, nor can admission charges be refunded subsequently.**

- Membership cards are **not transferable**.

- If your card is lost or stolen, please contact the Membership Department (address on p.386), tel. 0870 458 4000.

- A replacement card can be quickly sent to a temporary address if you are on holiday. Voluntary donations to cover the administrative costs of a replacement card are always welcome.

- Free entry is not guaranteed; additional charges may be made for the following:
  - when a special event is in progress at a property
  - when a property is opened specially for a National Gardens Scheme open day
  - where the management of a property is not under the National Trust's direct control, eg Tatton Park, Cheshire
  - where special attractions are not an integral part of the property, eg Steam Yacht *Gondola* in Cumbria, Wimpole Hall Home Farm in Cambridgeshire, Dunster Watermill in Somerset, the model farm and museum at Shugborough in Staffordshire and the Old Hall and farm at Tatton Park in Cheshire
  - where special access conditions apply, eg 20 Forthlin Road or Mendips in Liverpool, where access is only by minibus from Speke Hall and Liverpool city centre, and **all** visitors (including Trust members) pay a fare for the minibus journey

- The National Trust encourages educational use of its properties. Education Group Membership is open to all non-profit-making educational groups whose members are in full-time education. Subscription rates are banded according to the number of pupils on roll. Tel. 0870 458 4000 for further details.

- Individual life members of the National Trust who enrolled as such before 1968 have cards which admit one person only. Members wishing to exchange these for 'admit two' cards, i.e. to include the guest

Japanese Garden, Tatton Park, Cheshire

Please remember – your membership card is always needed for free admission

How you can support the National Trust in the USA
Join the Royal Oak Foundation

More than 40,000 Americans belong to the Royal Oak Foundation, the National Trust's membership affiliate in the USA. A not-for-profit organisation, the Royal Oak Foundation helps the National Trust through the generous tax-deductible support of members and friends by making grants towards its work. Member benefits include the National Trust Handbook, three editions of *The National Trust Magazine*, the quarterly Royal Oak Newsletter, and free admission to properties of the National Trust and of the National Trust for Scotland.

Royal Oak sponsors lectures, tours and events in both the US and the UK, designed to inform Americans of the Trust's work, on topics related to architecture, gardens and collections.

For further information please write, call, fax or email
**The Royal Oak Foundation, 26 Broadway, Suite 950,
New York, NY 10004, USA**
tel **001 212 480 2889**, fax **001 212 785 7234**
email **general@royal-oak.org** website **www.royal-oak.org**

facility, or those wishing to change from one category of life membership to another, should contact the Membership Department for the scale of charges.

- Entry to properties owned by the Trust but maintained and administered by English Heritage or Cadw (Welsh Historic Monuments) is free to members of the Trust, English Heritage and Cadw.

- Members of the National Trust are also admitted free of charge to properties of the National Trust for Scotland, a separate charity with similar responsibilities. NTS properties include the famous Inverewe Garden, Bannockburn, Culloden and Robert Adam's masterpiece, Culzean Castle. Full details are contained in *The National Trust for Scotland Guide to Properties* (priced £5, inc. p.&p.), which can be obtained by contacting the NTS Customer Service Centre, tel. 0131 243 9300. Information is also available on the Internet at **www.nts.org.uk**

- Reciprocal visiting arrangements also exist with certain overseas National Trusts, including Australia, New Zealand, Barbados, Bermuda, Canada, Jersey, Guernsey and the Manx Museum and National Trust on the

Isle of Man. During 2005 all National Trust members will receive a 50% discount on entry to properties belonging to the Italian National Trust (FAI). For a full list, contact our Membership Department.

- National Trust members visiting properties owned by the National Trust for Scotland or overseas Trusts are only eligible for free entry **on presentation of a valid membership card**.

Become a member today

Your subscription goes directly to support the Trust's work caring for much-loved countryside and coast, historic houses and gardens.

Benefits include:

- free admission to most of the properties listed in this Handbook

- three mailings a year which include a free copy of this Handbook, three editions of the full colour *National Trust Magazine* (available also on tape) and two editions of your regional newsletter

See the Application for membership form on page 374 for details of how to join.

For further information check our website www.nationaltrust.org.uk

Application for membership

To: The National Trust, FREEPOST NAT9775, Warrington WA5 7BR

Twelve-month membership

☐ **Individual: £38**
and, for each additional member living at the same address, £25.50.
One card for each member.
Pensioner rate available to those who have held membership for at least five years, aged 60+ and retired. Available on request. Tel. 0870 458 4000 for details.

☐ **Family group: £68.50**
for two adults, living at the same address, and their children or grandchildren under 18. Please give names and dates of birth for all children. Two cards cover the family.

☐ **Family one adult: £52**
for one adult and his/her children under 18, living at the same address. Please give names and dates of birth for all children. One card covers the family.

☐ **Child: £17.50**
Must be under 13 at time of joining. Please give date of birth.

Rates valid until 28 February 2006.

☐ **Young person: £17.50**
Must be 13 to 25 at time of joining. Please give date of birth.

☐ **Education group membership:**
See page 372. Tel. 0870 458 4000 for further details.

Life membership

☐ **Individual: £912**
(£608 if aged 60 or over and retired).
One card admits the named member and a guest.

☐ **Joint: £1102**
for lifetime partners (£722 if either partner is aged 60 or over and retired). Two cards, each admitting the named member.

☐ **Family joint: £1254**
for two adults, living at the same address, and their children or grandchildren under 18. Please give names and dates of birth for all children. Two cards cover the family.

SOURCE 048441M1		Date	
Full address			
Postcode		Tel.	
I am happy to be contacted by email. My email address is			

Title	First name	Surname	Date of birth	Value £

Credit/debit card/direct debit payments can be made by telephoning 0870 458 4000 (Minicom 0870 240 3207) in office hours, 7 days a week

Immediate membership can be obtained by joining at a National Trust property, shop or countryside information point

You can join online at **www.nationaltrust.org.uk/join**

Amount attached: £

Cheque/postal order
Delete as appropriate

Please allow up to 21 days for receipt of your membership card and new member's pack

This section of the Handbook provides a range of information that will help you make the most of your visits to our properties. Please also see the questions and answers on pp.382 and 383 as these contain important information.

£ Admission fees and opening arrangements

Members of the National Trust are admitted free to virtually all properties (see Special Information about National Trust Membership, p.372). Each property entry shows the normal adult admission fee. This includes VAT and is liable to change if the VAT rate is altered.

Children: under 5s are free. Children aged 5–16 pay half the adult price, unless stated. 17s and over pay the adult price. Children not accompanied by an adult are admitted at the Trust's discretion. Most properties offer discounted family tickets (covering 2 adults and up to 3 children, unless stated otherwise in the property entry).

Concessions: as a registered charity which has to raise all its own funds, the National Trust cannot afford to offer concessions on admission fees.

Education groups: many properties offer educational facilities and programmes. Teachers are urged to make a free preliminary visit by prior arrangement with the property. Education Group Membership is highly recommended (see p.372 for more details).

Group visits: all groups are required to book in advance and confirm the booking in writing. Some properties have limited access for groups so early booking is recommended. Most properties offer a discount for booked groups of 15 or more. (The standard minimum group size is 15. Any variations are stated in the individual property entries). The discount may not apply on certain days, eg at weekends or Bank Holidays. For full information on group visits to National Trust properties tel. the Travel Trade Office at NT Central Office (see p.386), or visit **www.nationaltrust.org.uk/groups**

National Gardens Scheme days: each year many of the National Trust's gardens are opened on extra days in support of the National Gardens Scheme. National Trust members may have to pay for entry on these days, when money raised is donated by NGS to support nurses' and garden charities, including National Trust gardens (primarily for the provision of apprenticeships). The National Trust acknowledges with gratitude the generous and continuing support of the National Gardens Scheme Charitable Trust.

Busy properties: properties can be extremely popular at Bank Holidays and summer weekends. At some houses and gardens timed tickets may be issued to smooth the flow of people entering (but not to limit the duration of a visit), and all visitors (including NT members) are required to use these tickets. This system aims to create better viewing conditions for visitors and to minimise wear-and-tear on historic interiors or gardens. On very rare occasions entry may not be possible on that day. If you are planning a long journey, please telephone the property in advance. At a few places special considerations apply and booking is essential, eg Red House, Mr Straw's House.

Anything new? see *What's new in 2005* in property entries for details of exciting changes, from special events to newly opened features.

The Well Court, Snowshill Manor, Gloucestershire

For further information check our website www.nationaltrust.org.uk

WCs

There is always one available, either at the property, when open, or nearby, unless the property entry specifically indicates 'no WC'.

Events

National Trust properties offer events and activities throughout 2005. Our varied programmes include spring snowdrop days, countryside walks, family Easter trails, garden tours and fairs, with outdoor theatre and summer concerts to suit every taste. Living history days and 'behind the scenes' tours provide an insight into the past and modern-day residents of our properties, whilst Hallowe'en fun and Christmas festivities round off the year. For more details ask for a regional events leaflet from the Membership Department or visit **www.nationaltrust.org.uk/events**.

Facilities for young families

The National Trust welcomes families. Family tickets are offered at most properties, parking is made easy, and many places provide baby-feeding and baby-changing areas, sometimes in purpose-designed parent and baby rooms. Our restaurants have high chairs, children's menus, colouring sheets and, at some properties, play areas. Staff are happy to advise you about what is on offer.

In historic buildings, visitors with smaller babies are welcome to use front slings, which are often also available on loan, and hip-carrying infant seats or reins for toddlers can also be borrowed at some places. There are usually arrangements for storing prams or pushchairs at the entrance, as it is not possible to take these into fragile interiors. Some houses are able to admit baby back-carriers at all times; others may admit them on quiet days mid-week, at the discretion of staff. We realise that the restriction on back-carriers, prams and pushchairs may be awkward for those with older and/or heavier children, and as access arrangements vary at each property, we suggest that you telephone in advance to check whether there are any restrictions that will affect you.

Learning and Discovery – for families, for schools, for everyone

The National Trust launched its new Vision for Learning in 2004, and is committed to learning and to providing experiences which are inspiring, stimulating and fun. Within the Trust, and in our work with others, we value learning for its own sake as well as the equality of opportunity that it brings.

Our properties welcome visits from schools, colleges, universities and other groups. Many of them have an on-site learning officer and programme of learning activities. For more information email **learning@nationaltrust.org.uk** or visit **www.nationaltrust.org.uk/learning**.

Over 60 National Trust properties have children's guidebooks – and many more have trails, quiz sheets and other activities for young visitors. 'Tracker packs' are available at some houses and gardens, providing activities for the whole family as they explore the property. Trusty the Hedgehog, the Trust's children's character, appears at events across the country and has his own website, **www.trusty.org**.

At **www.nationaltrust.org.uk/events**, you can search by date or location for things to do especially suitable for children and families. Many more activities are arranged than may be listed, especially during weekends, bank holidays and school holidays, so do call individual properties for information. The Membership Department can send you appropriate regional events leaflets. Tel. 0870 458 4000 or email **enquiries@thenationaltrust.org.uk**.

The National Trust Theatre stages participatory performances for all ages at a range of properties. For further information, please call 020 8986 0242 or email **theatre@nationaltrust.org.uk**.

Getting involved: volunteer with us

We could not continue to care for our rich architectural heritage, countryside and coastline without the help of our 40,000 volunteers.

Why not get actively involved and share your experience of the National Trust through volunteering with us? As well as making a

Visitors at Ightham Mote, Kent

valuable contribution, you can make new friends, learn a new skill, and most importantly, enjoy the experience! Whether your interests are in practical countryside conservation, helping in our houses and gardens, or providing professional and technical support, there are opportunities for everyone.

Groups can get involved, as well as individuals. You could join one of our many Volunteer and Friends groups which undertake practical conservation work at properties in their area, or get your company involved by joining our innovative employee volunteering programme. We also work with youth and community groups who undertake projects nationwide.

To find out more, tel. 0870 609 5383, email **volunteers@nationaltrust.org.uk**, or visit **www.nationaltrust.org.uk/volunteers**.

Voluntary Talks Service

The National Trust has a group of enthusiastic and knowledgeable volunteer speakers. They are available to give illustrated talks to groups of all sizes. Talks cover many different aspects of the Trust's work, from the Neptune Coastline Campaign to garden history, conservation, individual properties and regional round-ups. Talks can also be tailored to meet your group's particular interests. To find out more, contact the Talks Service Co-ordinator at your local National Trust regional office (see p.386).

How to get there

Each property entry includes the appropriate OS Landranger (or OSNI) series map number and grid reference, an indication of its location and how to get there.

Travelling on foot, by bike, bus, train or boat to National Trust properties can be an enjoyable and environmentally friendly way of visiting. In support of sustainable transport options the Trust publishes *Green Transport News* regularly during the year; this can be obtained from the Membership Department (see p.386) or visit **www.nationaltrust.org.uk/greentransport**

Details of access by public transport are given throughout the Handbook (correct as at October 2004), but due to limited space and the changing nature of this information, no indication of frequency of services is given, so please check times and routes before setting out. The National Trust is grateful to Barry Doe, a life member, for this travel information. If you have suggestions to make please contact him at: 25 Newmorton Road, Moordown, Bournemouth, Dorset BH9 3NU (tel. 01202 528707; fax. 01202 519914; email info@barrydoe.co.uk).

Individual property entries include the following information:

Foot: Pedestrian access from, eg, the nearest town or railway station, and details of routes passing through or nearby.

Cycle: Unless stated otherwise, most properties now have cycle parking on site or nearby. The nearest National Cycle Network (NCN) routes are given, shown as, eg: NCN4 2ml (denoting that the property is two miles from NCN route number 4). For further information on NCN routes or for maps, contact Sustrans on 0117 929 0888 or visit **www.sustrans.org.uk**

Ferry: Some properties are best reached – or indeed can only be reached – by boat.

Bus: 'Passing ≡' indicates that the bus service passes the station entrance or approach road, and 'Passing close ≡' indicates that a walk is necessary.

Unless otherwise stated, bus services pass the property (although there may be a walk from

For further information check our website www.nationaltrust.org.uk

the bus-stop). **Bus information is available for England, Wales and Scotland by ringing a single number charged at national rates: 0870 608 2608. For Northern Ireland** information (bus and train), tel. **028 9066 6630.**

Station/London Underground: The railway station name is followed by the distance from the property. Unstaffed stations are indicated by station name followed by (U). **Information on train times and routes is available from National Rail Enquiries on 08457 48 49 50 (local rate), or www.nationalrail.co.uk.** Some properties are within a few miles of a railway station, as shown, but do not always have good bus links to bridge the gap. At **www.traintaxi.co.uk** taxi and private hire operators for all Britain's railway stations are listed.

Road: Brief description of location and appropriate road numbers. **If you are taking your car please be aware that visitors use car parks at National Trust properties entirely at their own risk, and are advised to secure their cars and not to leave any valuable items in them during their visit.**

Cycling

The Trust actively promotes cycling as a means of reaching its properties, and is working closely with organisations such as Sustrans with this in mind. The National Cycle Network covers over 5000 miles and, combined with existing bridleways, quiet roads and greenways, provides many opportunities for visitors to enjoy cycling to their favourite places (See p.377 for Sustrans contact details).

Under each individual property entry, where relevant, the bicycle symbol gives information about opportunities for cycling at the property itself. For example, Clumber Park in Nottinghamshire has an excellent cycle hire facility with waymarked routes suitable for both novice and experienced riders and cyclo-orienteering courses. For more information see **www.nationaltrust.org.uk/cycle**

Walking

There is no better way of appreciating the immense variety of places cared for by the National Trust than by exploring on foot. The Trust welcomes the new rights of access on foot for open-air recreation on registered commons and open country and is a major provider of this land. The Trust also welcomes freedom to roam over unenclosed land and woods. The extent of these access opportunities can best be found on Ordnance Survey Explorer maps. Long-distance routes, including thirteen designated as National Trails, link many Trust properties. For further information, contact the Countryside Agency on 0870 120 6466 or visit **www.nationaltrail.co.uk**. See also **www.nationaltrust.org.uk/openaccess** for information about the new rights of access.

There are also hundreds of guided walks and publications offered by the Trust aimed at walkers of all ages, including children, parents with pushchairs and people with disabilities.

Walking in moorland on the Longshaw Estate in the Peak District, Derbyshire

⌨ Dogs

Dogs assisting visitors with disabilities are welcome inside Trust houses, gardens, restaurants and shops.

The dog symbol is used in property entries to indicate those places where dogs are welcome in the grounds or specified areas only (not in houses, gardens, restaurants and shops). If a property does not feature the dog symbol, dogs are not allowed at all.

The Trust endeavours to provide facilities for dogs such as water for drinking bowls, advice on suitable areas where dogs may be exercised and a shady parking space in car parks (though dogs should not be left alone in cars). These facilities vary from property to property and according to how busy it may be on a particular day. The primary responsibility for the welfare of dogs remains, of course, with their owners.

Dogs are welcome at most countryside properties, where they should be kept under close control at all times. Please observe local notices on the need to keep dogs on leads, particularly at sensitive times of year, eg during the breeding season for ground-nesting birds, at lambing time or when deer are calving. When the new countryside access rights come into force dogs should be kept on a short lead on access land between 1 March and 31 July, and at any other time in the vicinity of livestock.

In some areas the Trust has found it necessary to introduce restrictions, usually seasonal, and particularly on beaches, due to conflicts with other users. Where access for dogs has been restricted, the Trust attempts to identify suitable alternative locations nearby. A list of where restrictions apply is included in a leaflet: see below.

Many local authorities implement legislation on dog fouling and this can include Trust property. Where the law applies, it is an offence not to clear up dog waste. Failure to do so could result in a fine of up to £1000. Dog waste bins are only installed at very heavily used sites. If bins are not provided, please dispose of the waste thoughtfully.

For a free leaflet, *Beaches with Dog-Free Areas*, please send a first class stamp to the Membership Department (see p.386), or visit **www.nationaltrust.org.uk/dogs**

♿ Visitors with disabilities

We welcome visitors with disabilities to all our properties; we also welcome assistance dogs. The necessary companion of a disabled visitor is admitted free of charge, while the normal charge applies to the disabled visitor.

Most properties have a good degree of access and, where provided, adapted WCs are mentioned in the individual property entries. Self-drive and volunteer-driven powered vehicles are available at some larger gardens and parks. Wherever possible, the Trust admits to its buildings users of powered wheelchairs and similar small vehicles. This is subject to the physical limitations of the individual building and any other temporary constraints which may apply on the day. Please telephone the property in advance to check.

Most of our properties offer Braille and large-print guides, and we are developing sensory information. The *Information for Visitors with Disabilities* booklet, which includes information about opportunities to experience our properties with a variety of senses, can be viewed on **www.nationaltrust.org.uk**, and is available from the Membership Department. Tel. 0870 458 4000 or write to FREEPOST NAT9775, Warrington, WA5 7BR. This booklet is also available in large print and on tape.

The National Trust Magazine is available free on tape, as are several regional newsletters. If you wish to receive these regularly please contact the **Access for All** Office at our Swindon address – see p.386. (Email: **accessforall@nationaltrust.org.uk**).

🛍 Shopping and eating

The Trust's shops, restaurants, tea-rooms and holiday cottages are all managed by National Trust Enterprises. The profit they generate goes to support the work of the National Trust, and in 2003/2004 contributed over £16 million to funds.

New products and gift ideas are introduced month by month, some of them suggested by our own supporters. Every purchase makes a vital contribution to the Trust's work.

Shops: Many Trust properties have shops offering a wide range of related merchandise, much of which is exclusive to the National Trust.

These shops are indicated in relevant property entries by the shop symbol and their times given in the 'Opening arrangements' table. Many are open for Christmas shopping. The Trust also operates a number of shops in towns and cities throughout the country, which are open during normal trading hours (see below). And we now offer many National Trust gifts for sale online at **www.nationaltrust-shop.co.uk**

The National Trust Home Collection: National Trust Enterprises collaborates with leading British designers and manufacturers to create inspiring collections based on the Trust's historical properties, land and archives. Partners include Farrow & Ball heritage paints, Zoffany furnishings and wallpaper, Bylaw and Duresta furniture, Brintons carpets, Mark Wilkinson kitchens, Hypnos beds and Stevensons of Norwich. You can also join the National Trust Wine Club and take advantage of regular offers. For further details tel. 01373 828761 for a brochure or visit **www.nationaltrust.org.uk/homecollection**

Restaurants and tea-rooms: The National Trust operates over 140 tea-rooms and restaurants. They are usually located in very special old buildings including castles, lighthouses, stables, and even hot-houses! We aim to offer a welcoming atmosphere, value for money and traditional home cooking, with many properties featuring menus with an historical theme. Tea-rooms and restaurants are often open at times of year when houses and gardens are closed and many offer special programmes of events, such as lecture lunches, as well as festive meals in the run-up to Christmas.

Weddings and functions

These symbols at the top of entries in this Handbook indicate that the property is licensed for civil weddings and/or available for functions. For information on weddings, corporate and private functions and parties at National Trust properties, contact the property, the Membership Department on 0870 458 4000 or visit **www.nationaltrust.org.uk/hiring**

Town shops: opening times vary so please telephone for details if you are making a special journey.

Bath Marshall Wade's House, Abbey Churchyard BA1 1LY (tel. 01225 460249)

Bluewater Shopping Centre Unit U128B Upper Guild Hall, Greenhithe, Kent DA9 9ST (tel. 01322 423826)

Cambridge 9 King's Parade CB2 1SJ (tel. 01223 311894)

Canterbury 24 Burgate CT1 2HA (tel. 01227 457120)

Cirencester Tourist Information Centre, Cornhall, Market Place GL7 2NW (tel. 01285 654180)

Conwy Aberconwy House, Castle Street LL32 8AY (tel. 01492 592246)

Dartmouth 8 The Quay TQ6 9PS (tel. 01803 833694)

Hexham 25/26 Market Place NE46 3PB (tel. 01434 607654)

Kendal K Village, Lound Rd LA9 7DA (tel. 01539 736190)

London Blewcoat School, 23 Caxton St, Victoria SW1H 0PY (tel. 020 7222 2877)

Monmouth 5 Church St NP25 3BX (tel. 01600 713270)

St David's Visitor Centre & Shop, Captain's House, High St SA62 6SD (tel. 01437 720385)

Salisbury 41 High St SP1 2PB (tel. 01722 331884)

Seahouses Information Centre & Shop, 16 Main St NE68 7RQ (tel. 01665 721099)

Sidmouth Old Fore St EX10 8LS (tel. 01395 578107)

Stratford-upon-Avon 45 Wood St CV37 6JG (tel. 01789 262197)

Street Clark's Village, Farm Road BA16 0BB (tel. 01458 440578)

Swindon – Heelis Café & Shop, (opening summer 2005) Kemble Drive SN2 2NA (tel. 0870 242 6620)

Truro 9 River St TR1 2SQ (tel. 01872 241464)

Wells 16 Market Place BA5 2RB (tel. 01749 677735)

York – Shop & Tea-room, 32 Goodramgate YO1 7LG (tel. 01904 659050: shop 01904 659282: tea-room)

Your safety

We aim to provide a safe and healthy environment for visitors to our properties, and we take measures to ensure that the work of our staff, volunteers and contractors does not in any way jeopardise visitors' safety or health. You can help us by:

- observing all notices and signs during your visit;
- following any instructions and advice given by Trust staff;
- ensuring that children are properly supervised at all times;
- wearing appropriate clothing and footwear at countryside properties and in gardens.

At all our properties the responsibility for the safety of visitors should be seen as one that is shared between the Trust and the individual visitor. The Trust takes reasonable measures to minimise risks in ways that are compatible with our conservation objectives – but not necessarily to eliminate all risks. This is especially the case at our coastal and countryside properties. As the landscape becomes more rugged and remote, the balance of responsibility between the landowner and the visitor changes. There will be fewer safety measures and warning signs, and visitors will need to rely more on their own skills, knowledge, equipment and preparation. You can help to ensure your own safety by:

- taking note of weather conditions and forecasts and being properly equipped for changes in the weather;
- making sure you are properly prepared, equipped and clothed for the terrain and the activity in which you are participating;
- giving notice of your intended route and estimated time of return;
- making sure you have the necessary skills and fitness for the location and activity, and being aware of your own limitations.

National Trust Books

The National Trust publishes a wide range of books that promote its work and the great variety of properties in its care. These superbly illustrated books make excellent presents, as well as memorable souvenirs of visits. We have over 70 exciting titles to choose from. You can buy these at National Trust shops, at good bookshops worldwide, or by mail order from: Antique Collectors' Club, Sandy Lane, Old Martlesham, Woodbridge, Suffolk, IP12 4SD, tel. 01394 389950, fax 01394 389999.

Marvel at the wonderful landscapes and beautiful houses featured in *History and Landscape*, the only comprehensive guide to the properties in the care of the National Trust. With lavish illustrations and a foreword by HRH The Prince of Wales, this is an absolute essential for anyone interested in the treasures of Britain. Or take a culinary tour of Great Britain in *Farmhouse Cookery* and *Fish: Recipes from a Busy Island*; with mouthwatering recipes these books celebrate regional, traditional and contemporary cooking,

For a catalogue containing details of all our books, please call or write to the Membership Department. Copies of guidebooks to National Trust properties can be obtained from Heelis, Swindon (central office). See p.386 for contact details.

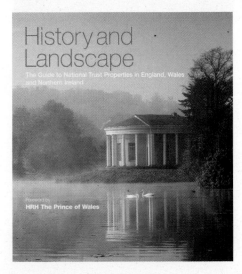

Your questions answered

These are some of the questions most commonly asked by visitors. If you need any further information regarding a visit you are planning, please telephone the relevant property or 0870 458 4000. At properties you can obtain free copies of our leaflets – 'A Future for the Past – Caring for country house collections' and 'Detect and Protect! – Looking after historic collections' (aimed at visitors of all ages). These outline the Trust's conservation policies and housekeeping practices.

Where can I take photographs?

We welcome amateur photography out-of-doors at our properties. We regret that photography is not permitted indoors when houses are open to visitors. The use of mobile phones with built-in cameras is also not permitted indoors.

However, at most properties special arrangements can be made for interested amateurs (as well as voluntary National Trust speakers, research students and academics) to take interior photographs by appointment outside normal opening hours.

Edward Chambré Hardman, whose photographic studio can be visited at 59 Rodney Street, Liverpool

Requests to arrange a mutually convenient appointment must be made in writing to the property concerned. Not all properties are able to offer this facility and those that do may make an admission charge (including NT members).

All requests for commercial photography must be channelled through the Broadcast Media Liaison Officer at our London Central Office, tel. 0870 609 5380.

Why is it dark inside some houses?

To prevent deterioration of light-sensitive contents, especially textiles and watercolours, light levels are regularly monitored and carefully controlled using blinds and sun-curtains. We recommend that visitors allow time for their eyes to adapt to darker conditions in rooms where light levels are reduced to preserve vulnerable material.

Some historic houses offer special tours during the winter months, when house staff demonstrate traditional housekeeping practices. They explain why National Trust conservation policies require low light levels inside houses and closure to visitors during the winter. These 'Putting the House to Bed' events are advertised in the local press and in regional newsletters, or details can be obtained from the Membership Department (see p.386), or **www.nationaltrust.org.uk/events**

Where can I picnic?

Many properties welcome picnics; some have a designated picnic area, a few cannot accommodate them (in which case the 'suitable for picnics' symbol 🎍 is not included in the property entry). Fires and barbecues are generally not allowed. If you are planning a picnic at a Trust property for the first time, please telephone in advance to check.

Where can I sit down?

Seats for visitors' use are provided at various points in all the Trust's historic houses and gardens. Visitors who wish to sit down should feel free to use the identified seats, or ask a room steward or member of staff if seating is not immediately obvious.

Please remember – your membership card is always needed for free admission

Picnic ware at Tyntesfield,
North Somerset

Is there somewhere to leave large or bulky bags?

At some properties visitors will be asked to leave behind large items of hand luggage while they make their visit. This is to avoid accidental damage and to improve security. This restriction includes rucksacks, large handbags, carrier bags, bulky shoulder bags and camera/camcorder bags. These can be left safely at the entrance to any house where the restriction applies (principally historic houses with vulnerable contents, fragile decorative surfaces or narrow visitor routes). See the *Facilities for young families* section on p.376 for additional information on back-carriers and pushchairs.

What types of footwear are restricted?

Any heel which covers an area smaller than a postage stamp can cause irreparable damage to floors, carpets and rush matting. We regret, therefore, that sharp-heeled shoes are not permitted. Plastic slippers are provided for visitors with unsuitable or muddy footwear, or alternative footwear is available for purchase.

Please remember that ridged soles trap grit and gravel, which scratch fine floors. Boot-scrapers and brushes are readily available. Overshoes may be provided at properties with vulnerable floors.

May I use my mobile telephone?

The use of mobile telephones can interfere with the correct operation of sensitive electronic environmental monitoring equipment, and so visitors are asked to switch them off when entering houses and other buildings where such equipment is likely to be fitted. Please also show consideration when using mobile phones in gardens and other enclosed open spaces where ringing may cause disturbance to the quiet enjoyment of others.

What about smoking?

Smoking is not permitted inside Trust houses, restaurants or shops. Smoking is also discouraged in gardens, since the scent of flowers is such an important part of visitors' enjoyment.

For further information check our website www.nationaltrust.org.uk

The National Trust has far more to offer than just a great day out. There are also some really unusual holiday ideas and choices available, both in this country and overseas.

The National Trust Holiday Cottages
Choose from over 320 unique cottages, houses and apartments, all in outstanding locations. The Trust's own portfolio of holiday homes is without rival in England, Wales and Northern Ireland. It includes a manor house in Cornwall, a lighthouse keeper's cottage on the cliff tops in Devon, converted barns in north Norfolk and Yorkshire, a turret apartment in Warwickshire and many more intriguing buildings. For a brochure call 0870 458 4411, quoting ref. NT HBK. To book or check availability tel. 0870 458 4422 or visit **www.nationaltrustcottages.co.uk**

The National Trust European Self-Catering Collection
Cottages in the Provençal countryside, beautifully renovated apartments in the Chianti hills of Tuscany, farmhouses in the meadows of Switzerland, a restored mill in southern Spain – these are just a few of the highlights of this new overseas self-catering programme, operated for the Trust by Inntravel, one of the country's leading specialist travel companies.

For more information call 01653 617790, email **nationaltrust@inntravel.co.uk** or visit **www.nationaltrust.org.uk/europeancottages**

The National Trust Travel and Cruise Collections
This is an extensive and expanding range of escorted tours and cruises operated for the Trust by leading group tour operator, Page & Moy. The programme has been designed with the interests of Trust members and supporters in mind, so whether you are fascinated by historic houses, both at home and overseas, like to explore great cities or simply enjoy travelling in Europe or further afield, there will be a holiday for you. There is also a range of exclusive National Trust ocean and river cruises. Page & Moy makes a financial contribution to the Trust for every holiday booked and so far over £1.7 million has been raised. Call the brochure line 0870 010 6434, quoting ref. N00040, or visit **www.nationaltrust.org.uk/travel**

The National Trust Active Holiday Collection
Discover the most beautiful regions of Europe, staying in welcoming authentic country inns and small hotels. The 2005 programme includes relaxed walking and cycling holidays, operated for the Trust by leading activity tour operator, Inntravel. The carefully planned routes are full of interest for independent travellers or for small parties, all with a range of inclusive travel options. Inntravel makes a financial contribution to the Trust for every holiday booked. For a brochure call 01653 627999, quoting ref. NT HBK, or visit **www.nationaltrust.org.uk/activeholidays**

Derwentwater, Cumbria

Please remember – your membership card is always needed for free admission

The National Trust Hotel Reservation Service

A huge range of hotels throughout Britain is on offer through this service, operated for the Trust by leading short break operator, Superbreak. The wide choice of locations, many close to National Trust properties, makes them ideal as a base from which to visit that house or garden you've always wanted to see. Superbreak makes a financial contribution to the Trust for every short break booked. Call the brochure line 0870 600 1818, quoting ref. NT HBK, or visit **www.nationaltrust.org.uk/superbreak** and book online.

The National Trust Working Holidays

The Trust's Working Holidays programme has been running for nearly 40 years. The holidays provide a great opportunity to make new friends, socialise and work together in a team, to achieve a worthwhile objective and make a significant difference to the preservation of our coast and countryside. Activities range from hedge laying or dry stone walling to archaeological digs or dragonfly identification. For those of you who like your home comforts, we have introduced a new category of premium holidays with en-suite accommodation and meals cooked for you. Each holiday is run by Trust staff and trained leaders, so experience is not necessary – just plenty of energy and enthusiasm! There is a wide range for all ages from 16 upwards. Call 0870 429 2428 or email **workingholidays@nationaltrust.org.uk** for a brochure, or book online at **www.nationaltrust.org.uk/workingholidays**

Bed and Breakfast on National Trust Farms, Camping and Caravan Sites

There are plenty of opportunities to enjoy some of the best of our countryside and coastal areas by staying with National Trust tenant farmers or at one of our camping and caravan sites.

For brochures please call our Membership Department (see p.386) or visit **www.nationaltrust.org.uk/holidays**

Data Protection Charter

We would like to make your involvement with the National Trust more enjoyable and there are many ways in which you can support our charitable work.

We will write to you from time to time about aspects of the National Trust's work and about offers from National Trust Enterprises, our wholly owned trading company. This runs our retail operations, restaurants and holiday cottages and all of its profits are donated by Gift Aid to the National Trust. If you have become a member of the National Trust you may also receive information from our Members' Centres and Associations.

We may also contact you about products and services, such as the National Trust Travel Collection, which are offered by carefully selected companies and which will benefit the work of the National Trust.

If you would prefer not to be contacted about products and services offered by such companies, or by Members' Centres and Associations, or if you would rather we did not contact you about our work or offers from National Trust Enterprises – or any combination of the above - please advise our Membership Department (see below), quoting your membership number if you have one. You can call, email or write, to suit you.

You should also contact the Membership Department if you have any general enquiries about data protection: tel. 0870 458 4000, email **enquiries@thenationaltrust.org.uk** or write to The National Trust, Membership Department, PO Box 39, Warrington WA5 7WD.

The National Trust adheres to Visit Britain's Visitors' Charter for Attractions.

We are very willing to answer questions and receive comments from members and visitors. Please speak to a member of staff in the first instance. Many properties provide their own comment cards and boxes which visitors are most welcome to use. All comments will be noted, and action taken where necessary, but it is not possible to answer every comment or suggestion individually.

Enquiries by telephone, email or in writing should be made to the Trust's Membership Department (see 1 below), open seven days a week (9–5.30 weekdays, 9–4 weekends and Bank Holidays). Detailed property enquiries, eg accessibility for wheelchairs, should be made to the individual property. Business callers should contact the appropriate regional office by telephone (0870 numbers are national rates), listed below. You can also obtain information from our website, **www.nationaltrust.org.uk**

1. National Trust Membership Department,
PO Box 39, Warrington WA5 7WD
Tel: 0870 458 4000 Fax: 0870 609 0345
Minicom: 0870 240 3207
email **enquiries@thenationaltrust.org.uk** for all general enquiries, including membership and requests for information

2. Central Office *From August 2005*:
**The National Trust
& National Trust (Enterprises) Ltd**
Heelis, Kemble Drive, Swindon,
Wiltshire SN2 2NA
Tel: 0870 242 6620
(National Trust guidebooks obtainable from the shop)

Until August 2005:
London Office
36 Queen Anne's Gate, London SW1H 9AS
Tel: 0870 609 5380 Fax: 020 7222 5097
(National Trust guidebooks obtainable from reception)

Swindon Office
Rowan House, Kembrey Park,
Swindon, Wiltshire SN2 8YL
Tel: 0870 242 6620 Fax: 01793 496813

Conservation Directorate
33 Sheep Street, Cirencester,
Gloucestershire GL7 1RQ
Tel: 0870 609 5382

National Trust Enterprises
The Stable Block, Heywood House,
Westbury, Wiltshire BA13 4NA
Tel: 01373 828602 for enquiries relating to shops & restaurants

3. National Trust Holiday Cottages
Tel: 0870 458 4411 for brochures
Tel: 0870 458 4422 for reservations

4. National Trust Regional Offices in England
Devon & Cornwall
(Devon)
Killerton House, Broadclyst, Exeter EX5 3LE
Tel: 01392 881691 Fax: 01392 881954

(Cornwall)
Lanhydrock, Bodmin PL30 4DE
Tel: 01208 74281 Fax: 01208 77887

Wessex
*(Bristol/Bath, Dorset, Gloucestershire,
Somerset & Wiltshire)*
Eastleigh Court, Bishopstrow, Warminster,
Wiltshire BA12 9HW
Tel: 01985 843600 Fax: 01985 843624

Thames & Solent *(Berkshire,
Buckinghamshire, Hampshire, part of
Hertfordshire, Isle of Wight, Greater London &
Oxfordshire)* Hughenden Manor, High
Wycombe, Bucks HP14 4LA
Tel: 01494 528051 Fax: 01494 463310

South East
(East Sussex, Kent, Surrey & West Sussex)
Polesden Lacey, Dorking, Surrey RH5 6BD
Tel: 01372 453401 Fax: 01372 452023

East of England
*(Bedfordshire, Cambridgeshire, Essex, part of
Hertfordshire, Norfolk & Suffolk)*
Westley Bottom, Bury St Edmunds,
Suffolk IP33 3WD
Tel: 0870 609 5388 Fax: 01284 736006

Please remember – your membership card is always needed for free admission

East Midlands (*Derbyshire, Leicestershire, S. Lincolnshire, Northamptonshire, Nottinghamshire & Rutland*) Clumber Park Stableyard, Worksop, Notts S80 3BE
Tel: 01909 486411 Fax: 01909 486377

West Midlands (*Birmingham, Herefordshire, Shropshire, Staffordshire, Warwickshire & Worcestershire*)
Attingham Park, Shrewsbury, Shropshire SY4 4TP
Tel: 01743 708100 Fax: 01743 708150

North West (*Cumbria & Lancashire*)
The Hollens, Grasmere, Ambleside, Cumbria LA22 9QZ
Tel: 015394 35599 Fax: 015394 35353

(*Cheshire, Greater Manchester & Merseyside*)
16 Market Street, Altrincham, Cheshire WA14 1PH
Tel: 0161 928 0075 Fax: 0161 929 6810

Yorkshire & North East
(*Yorkshire, Teesside, N. Lincolnshire*)
Goddards, 27 Tadcaster Road, York YO24 1GG
Tel: 01904 702021 Fax: 01904 771970

(*Co. Durham, Newcastle & Tyneside, Northumberland*)
Scots' Gap, Northumberland NE61 4EG
Tel: 01670 774691 Fax: 01670 774317

5. National Trust Office for Wales
Trinity Square, Llandudno LL30 2DE
Tel: 01492 860123 Fax: 01492 860233

6. National Trust Office for Northern Ireland
Rowallane House, Saintfield, Ballynahinch, Co. Down BT24 7LH
Tel: 028 9751 0721 Fax: 028 9751 1242

7. National Trust for Scotland
Wemyss House, 28 Charlotte Square, Edinburgh EH2 4ET
Tel: 0131 243 9300

8. National Trust Theatre,
Sutton House, 2 & 4 Homerton High Street, Hackney, London E9 6JQ
Tel: 020 8986 0242

The National Trust Online

You can find information about all the properties in this Handbook on our website at **www.nationaltrust.org.uk** Online property information is updated on a daily basis, so you can always find out about current news or forthcoming events. Most properties also show additional information about their history and features, to help you decide where you want to visit and to make the most of your day.

The website offers lots of other services, including information about volunteering and learning opportunities, hiring a venue for corporate or private functions, events and regional news. We have more than 250,000 visitors to the website a month, so if you haven't visited yet, take a look! We also have a dedicated holiday cottages website at **www.nationaltrustcottages.co.uk** and online gift shop at **www.nationaltrust-shop.co.uk**

For monthly up-to-the minute National Trust news, events information, details of things to do and places to visit, updates on our work and suggestions of how you might help or get involved, sign up for your free email newsletter.

All you have to do is register at **www.nationaltrust.org.uk/email**

This Handbook contains email addresses for those properties which can be contacted direct. General email enquiries should be sent to **enquiries@thenationaltrust.org.uk**

As a charity we rely greatly upon additional support, beyond membership fees, to help us to protect and manage the coastline, countryside, historic buildings and gardens in our care. You can help us in several ways, such as volunteering (see p.376), making a donation or considering a gift to the National Trust in your Will.

● Donations

The Trust organises several programmes to give donors the opportunity to see at first hand the work they support, such as the Benefactor and Patron programmes, which include special 'behind-the-scenes' events. You can help us by donating to our appeals such as the Neptune Coastline Campaign, Tyntesfield or other projects of special significance to you, or by buying raffle tickets at our properties.

For further information or to make a donation, please contact the Fundraising Office at our Swindon Central Office (see p.386).

● Legacies

Any legacy, no matter what size, provides a vital source of income for the Trust. It is our second largest income source after membership subscription fees and without it the Trust could not survive. Also, legacies are NOT spent on administrative costs but go directly to help fund major restoration works, to acquire new properties or to benefit any other area of the Trust's work which a legator may wish to specify.

If you would like further information about making a gift in your will to the National Trust or to request a copy of our free booklet, please tel. 0870 458 4000 or visit **www.nationaltrust.org.uk/legacies**

Join a group

Members of the National Trust can make the most of their membership by joining their local members' group. Known as associations, or in some areas as centres or clubs, there are around 200 groups across England, Wales and Northern Ireland, as well as in Belgium and Germany. Run by members, associations are independent of but affiliated to the Trust.

Associations make membership more enjoyable by organising a year-round programme of talks, rambles, visits and holidays, as well as social and fundraising events. Many members also act as voluntary speakers for the National Trust or volunteer at properties in an enormous range of roles, from stewarding in historic houses and gardens to marshalling at events. New members are always welcome, and many especially appreciate the chance to make friends with

A local centre member helping at a spring plant fair at Petworth House, West Sussex

people who share their interest in heritage and conservation. Last year associations raised more than £750,000 to support the Trust. Since the first group was founded in Manchester in 1948, associations have raised more than £15 million.

For details of your nearest group tel. 0870 458 4000 or visit **www.nationaltrust.org.uk/associations**

Please remember – your membership card is always needed for free admission

Index of properties by county

Properties with no individual entries are shown in italics

Bath & NE Somerset
Bath Assembly Rooms 39
Bath Skyline 30, 87
Prior Park Landscape Garden 87

Bedfordshire
Dunstable Downs *181*, 187
Whipsnade Estate 187
Whipsnade Tree Cathedral *181*, 205
Willington Dovecote & Stables 207

Berkshire
Ankerwycke 145
Ashdown House 112
Basildon Park 113
Finchampstead Ridges 109
The Holies 114
Lardon Chase 114
Lough Down 114
Pinkney's Green 110
Weathercock Hill 112

Birmingham
Back to Backs *237*, 242

Bristol
Blaise Hamlet 39
Leigh Woods 31
Westbury College Gatehouse 105

Buckinghamshire
Ascott 112
Boarstall Duck Decoy 163
Boarstall Tower 163
Bradenham Village *109*, 118
Buckingham Chantry Chapel 163
Claydon House 125
Cliveden 126
Coombe Hill 109, 110
Dorneywood Garden 163
Hughenden Manor 131
King's Head 133
Long Crendon Courthouse 136

Pitstone Windmill 164
Princes Risborough Manor House 164
Stowe Landscape Gardens 151
Waddesdon Manor 155
West Wycombe Park 158
West Wycombe Village and Hill *109*, 159

Cambridgeshire
Anglesey Abbey 183
Houghton Mill *180*, 193
Lode Mill 183
Peckover House & Garden 199
Ramsey Abbey Gatehouse 201
Wicken Fen National Nature Reserve *180*, *182*, 206
Wimpole Hall *182*, 207
Wimpole Home Farm *182*, 208

Cheshire
Alderley Edge *265*, 268
Bickerton Hill 265
Dunham Massey *266*, 271
Hare Hill 277
Helsby Hill 265
Little Moreton Hall 279
Lyme Park *266*, 280
Nether Alderley Mill 282
Quarry Bank Mill *266*, 283
Styal Estate 283
Tatton Park 288
White Cottage 293

Cornwall
Antony 33
Bedruthan Steps 45
Bodigga Cliff 31
Boscastle *28*, 40
Botallack Count House 76
Cape Cornwall 28
Carnewas 45
Chapel Porth 28
Cornish Mines & Engines 52
Cotehele *28*, 53
Cotehele Mill 54
Crackington Haven 28
The Dodman 28
Ethy 28
Glendurgan Garden 60

The Godolphin Estate *28, 31*, 61
Godrevy *28*, 62
The Gribbin 28
Gunwalloe *28*, 86
Holywell Bay 28
The Kelseys 28
Kynance Cove *28*, 76
Lanhydrock *28*, *31*, 74
Lawrence House 75
Levant Mine & Beam Engine 76
The Lizard 76
Lizard Point 28
Lizard Wireless Station 77
Loe Pool *28*, 86
Logan Rock 28
Marconi Centre 77
Nare Head 28, 31
North Cliffs 28
Penberth 28
Penrose Estate 86
Pentire 28
Porthcurno 28
The Rumps 28
St Anthony Head *31*, 88
St Michael's Mount 89
Tintagel Old Post Office 96
Trelissick Garden 98
Trengwainton Garden 99
Trerice 100
Valency Valley 28
Zennor Head 28

Cumbria
Acorn Bank Garden & Watermill 267
Aira Force 290
Arnside Knott 265
Beatrix Potter Gallery *266*, 268
Borrowdale 269
Brandlehow Park 264
Bridge House 291
Buttermere 270
Cartmel Priory Gatehouse 270
Castlerigg Stone Circle 269
Claife *265*, 278
Coniston 271
Dalton Castle 293
Derwent Island House 293
Duddon 291

Ennerdale 270
Eskdale 291
Fell Foot Park 266, 273
Friar's Crag 265
Gondola 266, 276
Grasmere 277
Great Langdale 277
Hawkshead 278
Heald Brow 266
Hill Top 278
Holme Park Fell 265
Keld Chapel 264
Sandscale Haws 265
Scafell Pike 264
Sizergh Castle & Garden 286
Skelghyll Woods 288
Stagshaw Garden 288
Tarn Hows 265, 266, 271
Townend 290
Troutbeck 291
Ullswater 290
Wasdale 291
Wastwater 264
Wetheral Woods 265
White Moss Common 265
Windermere 291
Wordsworth House 266, 292

Derbyshire
Calke Abbey 215
Derwent Moor 212
Dovedale 213
Edale 212
Hardwick Hall 219
High Peak Estate 212, 220
Hope Woodlands 212
Howden Moor 212
Ilam Park 213, 221
Kedleston Hall 221
Kinder Scout 212
Longshaw Estate 212, 223
Mam Tor 212
Milldale 213
Museum of Childhood,
    Sudbury Hall 213, 228
The Old Manor 224
South Peak 212
Stainsby Mill 225
Sudbury Hall 213, 227
Winnats Pass 212
Winster Market House 230

Devon
A La Ronde 33
Abbotsham 28
Arlington Court 34
Ashclyst Forest 32

Baggy Point 28
Bolt Tail 28
Bradley 40
Branscombe – Old Bakery,
    Manor Mill & Forge 28, 41
Brownsham 28
Buckland Abbey 43
Buck's Mills 28
Budlake Old Post Office Room
    69
Castle Drogo 29, 45
The Church House,
    Widecombe in the Moor 47
Clyston Mill 69
Coleton Fishacre 49
Compton Castle 50
Countisbury 28
Damage Cliffs 32
Dewerstone 29
East Titchberry 28
Finch Foundry 59
Fingle Bridge 29
Foreland Point 28
Gammon Head 28
Greenway 63
Heddon Valley Shop 31, 65
Hembury Woods 29
Hentor 29
Holne Woods 29
Killerton 67
Kingswear 28
Knightshayes Court 72
Little Dartmouth 28
Loughwood Meeting House
    78
Lundy 79
Lydford Gorge 79
Marker's Cottage 70
Morte Point 28
The Old Mill 84
Overbeck's Museum & Garden
    28, 85
Parke Estate 29
Plym Bridge Woods 29, 31
Portledge 28
Portlemouth Down 28
Prawle Point 28
Salcombe Hill 28, 31
Saltram 89
Shute Barton 105
Soar Mill Cove 28
South Hole 28
Starehole Bay 28
Steps Bridge 29
Trowlesworthy Warren 29
Watersmeet House 28, 102
Wheal Coates 28

Whiddon Deer Park 29
Willings Walls 29
Woody Bay 28

Dorset
Badbury Rings 71
Brownsea Island 42
Burton Bradstock 31
Cerne Giant 29
Clouds Hill 48
Cogden Beach 29
Coney's Castle 29
Corfe Castle 29, 51
Dancing Ledge 29
Fontmell Down Estate 29
Golden Cap 29
Hardy Monument 104
Hardy's Cottage 64
Hartland Moor 28, 29, 31
Hod Hill 29
Kingston Lacy 31, 70
Lamberts Castle 29
Langdon Hill Wood 31
Max Gate 81
Melbury Beacon 29
Melbury Down 29
Pilsdon Pen 29
Spyway Farm 29
Stonebarrow Hill 31
Studland Beach & Nature
    Reserve 29, 31, 95
Turnworth Down 29
White Mill 105

County Durham
Beacon Hill 316
Ebchester 316
Foxholes Dene 316
Hawthorn Dene 316
Horden Beach 316
Moorhouse Woods 316
Penshaw Monument 316
Warren House Gill 316

East Sussex:
see Sussex

East Yorkshire:
see Yorkshire

Essex
Blake's Wood 181
Bourne Mill 209
Coggeshall Grange Barn 187
Copt Hall Marshes 181
Danbury Common 181
Dedham Vale 181

Hatfield Forest *181, 182*, 192
Lingwood Common *181*
Northey Island *181*
Paycocke's 199
Rayleigh Mount *181*, 201

Gloucestershire

Arlington Row 30
Ashleworth Tithe Barn 35
Chedworth Roman Villa 47
Dover's Hill 30, 31
Dyrham Park *31*, 57
Ebworth Estate 30
Hailes Abbey 64
Haresfield Beacon 30, 31
Hidcote Manor Garden 65
Horton Court 104
Little Fleece Bookshop 105
Lodge Park 77
Minchinhampton Common 30
Newark Park 84
Rodborough Common 30
Sherborne Estate 77
Snowshill Manor 91
Westbury Court Garden 102
Woodchester Park 104

Hampshire

Bramshaw Commons 109
Curbridge Nature Reserve 109
Hale Purlieu 109
Hinton Ampner Garden 130
Ibsley Common 109
Ludshott Common 109
Mottisfont Abbey Garden,
    House & Estate 136
Rockford Common 109
Sandham Memorial Chapel
    145
Selborne Hill & Common 109
Speltham Down 109
*Stockbridge Common Down &
    Marsh 109*
The Vyne 154
Waggoners Wells 109
West Green House Garden
    157
Winchester City Mill 160

Herefordshire

Berrington Hall *237*, 240
Brockhampton Estate *237*,
    243
Croft Ambrey 237
Croft Castle 247
Cwmmau Farmhouse 260
The Weir 258

Hertfordshire

Ashridge Estate *109*, 113
Shaw's Corner 202

Isle of Wight

Afton 108
Bembridge Windmill *108,* 116
Brighstone Shop & Museum
    119
Brook 108
Compton 108
Culver 108
Mottistone Manor Garden *108*,
    137
The Needles Old Battery *109*,
    138
Old Town Hall, Newtown *109*,
    140
St Catherine's 108
St Helen's Duver 110
Tennyson Down 109
Ventnor 108

Kent

Chartwell 120
Chiddingstone 108
Coldrum Long Barrow 108
Emmetts Garden 127
Ightham Mote 132
Knole 134
Old Soar Manor 140
Owletts 164
Quebec House 165
Royal Military Canal 108
St John's Jerusalem 165
Scotney Castle Garden &
    Estate 146
Sissinghurst Castle Garden
    148
Smallhythe Place 149
South Foreland Lighthouse
    108, 149
Sprivers Garden 165
Stoneacre 165
Toys Hill 108
The White Cliffs of Dover *108*,
    110, 159

Lancashire

*Eaves & Waterslack Woods
    265*
Gawthorpe Hall 275
Heysham 265
Holcombe Moor 265
Jack Scout 266
Rufford Old Hall 285
Stubbins Estate 265

Leicestershire

Staunton Harold Church 226
Ulverscroft Nature Reserve 230

Lincolnshire

Belton House 213, 214
Grantham House 233
Gunby Hall 233
Monksthorpe Chapel 233
Tattershall Castle *213*, 229
Whitegates Cottage 233
Woolsthorpe Manor 213, 231

Liverpool/Merseyside
(inc. Sefton)

Caldy Hill 265
Formby *265, 266*, 274
20 Forthlin Road 274
Mendips 282
59 Rodney Street 284
Speke Hall, Garden & Estate
    265, 266, 287
Stocktons Wood 265
Thurstaston Common 265

London Boroughs:

Barking & Dagenham
Eastbury Manor House 170
Bexley
Red House 175
Bromley
Chislehurst Common 168
Petts Wood 168
Hawkwood 168
Camden
Fenton House 170
2 Willow Road 176
Croydon
Selsdon Wood 168
Hackney
Sutton House *168*, 175
Havering
Rainham Hall 177
Hounslow
Osterley Park *168*, 173
Kensington & Chelsea
Carlyle's House 169
Lindsey House 177
Merton
Morden Hall Park *168*, 173
Watermeads 168
Richmond
East Sheen Common 168
Ham House *168*, 171
Southwark
George Inn 171

Westminster
Blewcoat School Gift Shop
169
'Roman' Bath 177

Middlesbrough/Teeside
Ormesby Hall 308

Newcastle/Tyne & Wear
Gibside 322
Holy Jesus Hospital 324
Marsden Rock 316
Souter Lighthouse 316, 317,
326
Washington Old Hall 329

Norfolk
Beeston Regis Heath 180
Blakeney National Nature
Reserve 184
Blakeney Point 180
Blickling Hall, Garden & Park
185
Brancaster 180, 186
Branodonum 180
Darrow Wood 181
Elizabethan House Museum
189
Felbrigg Hall, Garden & Park
190
Horsey Mere 180
Horsey Windpump 180, 193
Incleborough Hill 180
Morston Marshes 180
Oxburgh Hall, Garden & Estate
198
St George's Guildhall 201
Sheringham Park 180, 182,
202
Stiffkey Marshes 180
West Runton 180

Northamptonshire
Canons Ashby House 216
Lyveden New Bield 224
Priest's House 225

Northumberland
Allen Banks 316, 318
Beadnell Harbour 316
Bellister Estate 316
Cherryburn 318
Cragside House, Gardens &
Estate 317, 319
Craster 316
Druridge Bay 316
Dunstanburgh Castle 316, 320

Embleton Links 316
Farne Islands 316, 321
George Stephenson's
Birthplace 322
Hadrian's Wall 316, 323
Housesteads Fort 316, 323
Lady's Well 316
Lindisfarne Castle 325
Low Newton-by-Sea 316
Newton Pool 316, 317
Ros Castle 316
St Aidan's Dunes 316
St Cuthbert's Cave 316
Seahouses 316
Staward Gorge 316, 318
Wallington 317, 327

North Yorkshire:
see Yorkshire

Nottinghamshire
Clumber Park 213, 217
Mr Straw's House 226
The Workhouse, Southwell
232

Oxfordshire
Alfred's Castle 112
Badbury Hill 109
Buscot Old Parsonage 163
Buscot Estate 109, 119
Buscot Park 120
Buscot Weir 109
Chastleton House 122
Coleshill Estate 109, 119
Dragon Hill 110
Great Coxwell Barn 128
Greys Court 128
Priory Cottages 165
Uffington Castle 110
Watlington Hill 109
White Horse Hill 109

Shropshire
Attingham Park 237, 238
Benthall Hall 240
Carding Mill Valley 236, 244
Cronkhill 260
Dudmaston 237, 249
Long Mynd 236, 237
Morville Hall 261
Sunnycroft 261
Town Walls Tower 261
Wenlock Edge 236
Wilderhope Manor 261

Somerset
Barrington Court 38
Beacon Hill 30
Bicknoller Hill 30
Blackdown Hills 30
Brean Down 30, 41
Clevedon Court 48
Coleridge Cottage 49
Collard Hill 30
Crook Peak 30
Dunster Castle 56
Dunster Working Watermill 57
Fyne Court 59
Glastonbury Tor 30, 60
Holnicote Estate 30, 67
King John's Hunting Lodge
70
Lytes Cary Manor 80
Middle Hope 30
Montacute House 82
North Hill 31
Priest's House 87
Sand Point 30
Selworthy 67
Shute Shelve Hill 30
Stembridge Tower Mill 105
Stoke-sub-Hamdon Priory 92
Tintinhull Garden 97
Treasurer's House 97
Tyntesfield 101
Walton Hill 30
Wavering Down 30
Webbers Post 31
Wellington Monument 30
West Pennard Court Barn 105

Staffordshire
Biddulph Grange Garden 242
Downs Banks 236
Hawksmoor 236
Kinver Edge 236, 252
Leek & Manifold Valley 213
Letocetum (Wall) Roman Site
253
Moseley Old Hall 253
Shugborough 237, 255

Suffolk
Dunwich Heath 180, 188
Flatford: Bridge Cottage 180,
191
Ickworth House, Park &
Garden 182, 194
Kyson Hill 180
Lavenham: Guildhall 195
Melford Hall 196
Minsmere Beach 180

Orford Ness National Nature
  Reserve *180*, 197
Pin Mill 180
Sutton Hoo *180*, *182*, 204
Theatre Royal 205
Thorington Hall 209

Surrey
Box Hill 109, *110*, 117
Clandon Park 123
Claremont Landscape Garden
  124
Dapdune Wharf *109*, *110*, 143
The Devil's Punch Bowl Café
  109, 130
Frensham Common 109
Hatchlands Park 129
Headley Common 110
Hindhead Commons *109*, 130
The Homewood 164
Leith Hill 109, *110*, 135
Oakhurst Cottage 140
Polesden Lacey *110*, 142
Reigate Hill 109
River Wey & Godalming
  Navigations *109*, 143
Runnymede 145
Shalford Mill 165
Winkworth Arboretum 161
The Witley Centre *109*, *110*,
  162

Sussex:
**(East Sussex and West
Sussex)**
Alfriston Clergy House 111
Bateman's 115
Birling Gap 108
Black Down 109
Bodiam Castle *110*, 116
Chyngton Farm 108
Cissbury Ring 108
Crowlink 108
Devil's Dyke 108, 110
East Head 108
Frog Firle Farm 108
Harting Down 108
Lamb House 164
Monk's House 164
Nymans Garden 139
Petworth House & Park 141
Seven Sisters 108, 110
Sheffield Park Garden 147
Slindon Estate 108
Standen 150
Uppark 153
Wakehurst Place 156

Warwickshire
Baddesley Clinton 239
Charlecote Park *237*, 245
Coughton Court 246
Farnborough Hall 261
Kinwarton Dovecote 252
Packwood House 254
Upton House 257

West Midlands
Wightwick Manor 259

West Sussex:
see Sussex

West Yorkshire:
see Yorkshire

Wiltshire
Avebury *29*, 36
Avebury Manor & Garden 37
Cherhill Down 29
Cley Hill 29
The Courts Garden 55
Dinton Park 86
Figsbury Ring 29
Fox Talbot Museum 73
Great Chalfield Manor 62
Lacock Abbey & Village 73
Little Clarendon 105
Mompesson House 81
Pepperbox Hill 30
Philipps House 86
Stonehenge Historic
  Landscape *29*, 92
Stourhead 93
Westwood Manor 103
Win Green Hill 30

Worcestershire
Bredon Barn 42
Clent Hills 236
Croome Park 248
The Fleece Inn 249
The Greyfriars 250
Hanbury Hall 250
Hawford Dovecote 251
Middle Littleton Tithe Barn 253
Wichenford Dovecote 259

Yorkshire
**(East Yorkshire, North
Yorkshire inc.
Middlesbrough, West
Yorkshire and York)**
Beningbrough Hall & Gardens
  298

Blakey Topping 296, 299
Braithwaite Hall 313
Bridestones Moor *296*, 299
Brimham Rocks *296*, 297, 299
Cayton Bay 296
Crosscliff Moor *296*, 299
East Riddlesden Hall 300
Farndale 296
Fountains Abbey 301
Goddards Garden 313
Hardcastle Crags *296*, 303
Hayburn Wyke 296
Hudswell Woods 296
Maister House 303
Malham Tarn Estate *296*, *297*,
  304
Marsden Moor Estate *296*,
  304
Moulton Hall 313
Mount Grace Priory 305
Newbiggin Cliffs 296
Nostell Priory 306
Nunnington Hall 307
Old Coastguard Station 296,
  297
Ormesby Hall 308
Peak Alum Works 296
Port Mulgrave 296
Ravenscar Coastal Centre
  296, *297*, 313
Rievaulx Terrace & Temples
  309
Roseberry Topping *296*, 310
Runswick Bay 296
Scarthwood Moor 296
Studley Royal Water Garden
  301
Townhead Barn 297
Treasurer's House 311
Upper Wharfedale *296*, 312
Yorkshire Coast 312

Wales

Anglesey
Cemlyn 334
Plas Newydd 347
Porth Dafarch 334
Swtan 334

Carmarthenshire
Aberdeunant 353
Dinefwr *333*, *335*, 341
Dolaucothi Gold Mines 342
Newton House 341
Paxton's Tower 333

Ceredigion
Llanerchaeron 344
Mwnt 332, 335
Mynachdy'r Graig 332
Penbryn 332

Conwy
Aberconwy House 336
Bodnant Garden 337
Conwy Suspension Bridge 340
Tŷ Mawr Wybrnant 334, 353
Ty'n-y-Coed Uchaf 353

West Glamorgan
Lanlay Meadows 333

Gwynedd
Bwythyn Llywelyn see Tŷ Isaf 352
Cadair Idris 334
Carneddau 334
Craflwyn 333
Cregennan 334
Dinas Oleu 332
Dolmelynllyn Estate 334, 335
Gelli Iago 335
Glan Faenol 335
Hafod y Llan 333
Llanbedrog Beach 334, 335
Penrhyn Castle 345
Plas yn Rhiw 347
Porthdinllaen 334, 335
Porthor 334, 335
Rhaeadr Ddu 334
Segontium 350
Tryfan 334
Tŷ Isaf 352
Y Llethr 334
Ysbyty Estate 334

Monmouthshire
Clytha 333
Cwm Idwal 334
The Kymin 344
Skenfrith Castle 350
Skirrid Fawr 333
Sugar Loaf 333

Neath & Port Talbot
Aberdulais Falls 336

Pembrokeshire
Barafundle Bay 332
Bosherston 332
Broadhaven 332, 335
Cilgerran Castle 339

Colby Woodland Garden *332, 340*
Marloes Deer Park & Sands 332
Martin's Haven 332
Porthclais Harbour 335
Ragwen Point 332
St Bride's Bay 332
St David's Visitor Centre & Shop *332*, 350
Stackpole Estate *332, 334,* 351
Tudor Merchant's House 351

Powys
Abergwesyn Common 333
The Begwns 333
Brecon Beacons 333
Corn Du 333
Cribyn 333
Henrhyd Falls 333
Pen-y-Fan 333
Powis Castle & Garden 348

Swansea
Gower Peninsula 332
Rhossili Visitor Centre *335,* 349

Wrexham
Chirk Castle 338
Erddig *334,* 343

Northern Ireland

Co. Antrim
Ballyconagan 356
Carrick-a-Rede *356, 357,* 360
Cushendun 356
Cushleake Mountain 356
Dunseverick Castle 356
Fair Head 356
Giant's Causeway *356, 357,* 366
Glenoe 356
Larrybane 356
Loughan Bay 358
The Manor House, Rathlin Island 356
Murlough Bay 356
North Antrim Cliff Path 356
Patterson's Spade Mill *358,* 369
Skernaghan Point 356
Whitepark Bay 356

Co. Armagh
Ardress House 371
The Argory 359
Derrymore House 364

Belfast
The Black Mountain 357
Collin Glen 357
Crown Liquor Saloon 363
Divis Mountain 357
Lisnabreeny 357
Minnowburn 357

Co. Down
Ballymacormick Point 357
Blockhouse Island 357
Castle Ward 357, *358,* 361
Green Island 357
Kearney 357
Knockinelder 357
Lighthouse Island 357
Mount Stewart House, Garden & Temple of the Winds 368
Mourne Coastal Path 357
Murlough National Nature Reserve 357
Orlock Point 357
Rowallane Garden 369
Slieve Donard 357
Strangford Lough Wildlife Centre 357, 358

Co. Fermanagh
Castle Coole *357,* 360
Crom Estate *357,* 362
Florence Court *357,* 365

Co. Londonderry
Barmouth 356
Downhill Estate 364
Grangemore Dunes 356
Hezlett House 367
Mussenden Temple 364
Portstewart Strand 356, 358
Springhill 370

Co. Tyrone
Gray's Printing Press 367
Wellbrook Beetling Mill *358,* 371

Properties with no individual entries are shown in italics

A La Ronde 33
Abbotsham 28
Aberconwy House 336
Aberdeunant 353
Aberdulais Falls 336
Abergwesyn Common 333
Acorn Bank Garden &
  Watermill 267
Afton 108
Aira Force 290
Alderley Edge *265*, 268
Alfred's Castle 112
Alfriston Clergy House 111
Allen Banks *316*, 318
Anglesey Abbey 183
Ankerwycke 145
Antony 33
Ardress House 371
The Argory 359
Arlington Court 34
Arlington Row 30
Arnside Knott 265
Ascott 112
Ashclyst Forest 32
Ashdown House 112
Ashleworth Tithe Barn 35
Ashridge Estate *109*, 113
Associations and Centres
  388
Attingham Park *237*, 238
Avebury *29*, 36
Avebury Manor & Garden 37

Badbury Hill 109
Badbury Rings 71
Baddesley Clinton 239
Baggy Point 28
Ballyconagan 356
Ballymacormick Point 357
Barafundle Bay 332
Barmouth 356
Barrington Court 38
Basildon Park 113
Bateman's 115
Bath Assembly Rooms 39
Bath Skyline 30, 87
Beacon Hill (Durham) 316
Beacon Hill (Somerset) 30
Beadnell Harbour 316

Beatrix Potter Gallery *266*,
  268
Bedruthan Steps 45
Beeston Regis Heath 180
The Begwns 333
Bellister Estate 316
Belton House 213, 214
Bembridge Windmill *108*, 116
Beningbrough Hall & Gardens
  298
Benthall Hall 240
Berrington Hall 237, 240
Bickerton Hill 265
Bicknoller Hill 30
Biddulph Grange Garden 242
Birling Gap 108
Birmingham Back to Backs
  237, 242
Black Down 109
The Black Mountain 357
Blackdown Hills 30
Blaise Hamlet 39
Blake's Wood 181
Blakeney National Nature
  Reserve 184
Blakeney Point 180
Blakey Topping 296, 299
Blewcoat School Gift Shop
  169
Blickling Hall, Garden & Park
  185
Blockhouse Island 357
Boarstall Duck Decoy 163
Boarstall Tower 163
Bodiam Castle *110*, 116
Bodigga Cliff 31
Bodnant Garden 337
Bolt Tail 28
Books 381
Borrowdale 269
Boscastle *28*, 40
Bosherston 332
Botallack Count House 76
Bourne Mill 209
Box Hill *109*, *110*, 117
Bradenham Village *109*, 118
Bradley 40
Braithwaite Hall 313
Bramshaw Commons 109

Brancaster *180*, 186
Brandlehow Park 264
Branodonum 180
Branscombe – Old Bakery,
  Manor Mill & Forge *28*, 41
Brean Down *30*, 41
Brecon Beacons 333
Bredon Barn 42
Bridestones Moor *296*, 299
Bridge House 291
Brighstone Shop & Museum
  119
Brimham Rocks *296*, *297*,
  299
Broadhaven 332, 335
Brockhampton Estate *237*,
  243
Brook 108
Brownsea Island 42
Brownsham 28
Buckingham Chantry Chapel
  163
Buckland Abbey 43
Buck's Mills 28
Budlake Old Post Office
  Room 69
Burton Bradstock 31
Buscot Estate 109, 119
Buscot Old Parsonage 163
Buscot Park 120
Buscot Weir 109
Buttermere 270
Bwythyn Llywelyn see Tŷ Isaf
  352

Cadair Idris 334
Caldy Hill 265
Calke Abbey 215
Canons Ashby House 216
Cape Cornwall 28
Carding Mill Valley *236*, 244
Carlyle's House 169
Carneddau 334
Carnewas 45
Carrick-a-Rede *356*, *357*,
  360
Cartmel Priory Gatehouse
  270
Castle Coole *357*, 360

Castle Drogo *29*, 45
Castle Ward *357*, *358*, 361
Castlerigg Stone Circle 269
Cayton Bay 296
Cemlyn 334
Cerne Giant 29
Chapel Porth 28
Charlecote Park *237*, 245
Chartwell 120
Chastleton House 122
Chedworth Roman Villa 47
Cherhill Down 29
Cherryburn 318
Chiddingstone 108
Chirk Castle 338
Chislehurst Common 168
The Church House,
   Widecombe in the Moor
   47
Churchill, Winston 120
Chyngton Farm 108
Cilgerran Castle 339
Cissbury Ring 108
Claife *265*, 278
Clandon Park 123
Claremont Landscape
   Garden 124
Claydon House 125
Clent Hills 236
Clevedon Court 48
Cley Hill 29
Cliveden 126
Clouds Hill 48
Clumber Park *213*, 217
Clyston Mill 69
Clytha 333
Cogden Beach 29
Coggeshall Grange Barn 187
Colby Woodland Garden
   332, 340
Coldrum Long Barrow 108
Coleridge Cottage 49
Coleshill Estate 109, 119
Coleton Fishacre 49
Collard Hill 30
Collin Glen 357
Compton 108
Compton Castle 50
Coney's Castle 29
Coniston 271
Constable, John 191
Conwy Suspension Bridge
   340
Coombe Hill 109, 110

Copt Hall Marshes 181
Corfe Castle *29*, 51
Corn Du 333
Cornish Mines & Engines 52
Cotehele *28*, 53
Cotehele Mill 54
Coughton Court 246
Countisbury 28
The Courts Garden 55
Crackington Haven 28
Craflwyn 333
Cragside House, Gardens &
   Estate *317*, 319
Craster 316
Cregennan 334
Cribyn 333
Croft Ambrey 237
Croft Castle 247
Crom Estate *357*, 362
Cronkhill 260
Crook Peak 30
Croome Park 248
Crosscliff Moor 296, 299
Crowlink 108
Crown Liquor Saloon 363
Culver 108
*Curbridge Nature Reserve
   109*
Cushendun 356
Cushleake Mountain 356
Cwm Idwal 334
Cwmmau Farmhouse 260
Cycling 378

Dalton Castle 293
Damage Cliffs 32
Danbury Common 181
Dancing Ledge 29
Dapdune Wharf *109*, *110*,
   143
Darrow Wood 181
Dedham Vale 181
Derrymore House 364
Derwent Island House 293
Derwent Moor 212
Devil's Dyke 108, 110
The Devil's Punch Bowl Café
   109, 130
Dewerstone 29
Dinas Oleu 332
Dinefwr *333*, *335*, 341
Dinton Park 86
Disabilities 379
Divis Mountain 357

The Dodman 28
Dogs 379
Dolaucothi Gold Mines 342
Dolmelynllyn Estate 334, 335
Donations 388
Dorneywood Garden 163
Dovedale 213
Dover's Hill 30, 31
Downhill Estate 364
Downs Banks 236
Dragon Hill 110
Druridge Bay 316
Duddon 291
Dudmaston *237*, 249
Dunham Massey *266*, 271
Dunseverick Castle 356
Dunstable Downs *181*, 187
Dunstanburgh Castle *316*,
   320
Dunster Castle 56
Dunster Working Watermill 57
Dunwich Heath *180*, 188.
Dyrham Park *31*, 57

East Head 108
East Riddlesden Hall 300
East Sheen Common 168
East Titchberry 28
Eastbury Manor House 170
*Eaves & Waterslack Woods
   265*
Ebchester 316
Ebworth Estate 30
Edale 212
Education 372, 375, 376
Elizabethan House Museum
   189
Embleton Links 316
Emmetts Garden 127
Ennerdale 270
Erddig *334*, 343
Eskdale 291
Ethy 28
Events 376

Fair Head 356
Families 375
Farnborough Hall 261
Farndale 296
Farne Islands *316*, 321
Felbrigg Hall, Garden & Park
   190
Fell Foot Park *266*, 273
Fenton House 170

Figsbury Ring 29
Finch Foundry 59
Finchampstead Ridges 109
Fingle Bridge 29
Flatford: Bridge Cottage 180, 191
The Fleece Inn 249
Florence Court 357, 365
Fontmell Down Estate 29
Foreland Point 28
Formby 265, 266, 274
20 Forthlin Road, Allerton 274
Fountains Abbey 301
Fox Talbot Museum 73
Foxholes Dene 316
Frensham Common 109
Friar's Crag 265
Frog Firle Farm 108
Functions 380
Fyne Court 59

Gammon Head 28
Gawthorpe Hall 275
Gelli lago 335
George Inn 171
George Stephenson's Birthplace 322
Giant's Causeway 356, 357, 366
Gibside 322
Glan Faenol 335
Glastonbury Tor 30, 60
Glendurgan Garden 60
Glenoe 356
Goddards Garden 313
The Godolphin Estate 28, 31, 61
Godrevy 28, 62
Golden Cap 29
Gondola 266, 276
Gower Peninsula 332
Grangemore Dunes 356
Grantham House 233
Grasmere 277
Gray's Printing Press 367
Great Chalfield Manor 62
Great Coxwell Barn 128
Great Langdale 277
Green Island 357
Greenway 63
The Greyfriars 250
Greys Court 128
The Gribbin 28

Group visits 375
Gunby Hall 233
Gunwalloe 28, 86

Hadrian's Wall 316, 323
Hafod y Llan 333
Hailes Abbey 64
Hale Purlieu 109
Ham House 168, 171
Hanbury Hall 250
Hardcastle Crags 296, 303
Hardman, E. Chambré 284
Hardwick Hall 219
Hardy Monument 104
Hardy, Thomas 64, 81
Hardy's Cottage 64
Hare Hill 277
Haresfield Beacon 30, 31
Harting Down 108
Hartland Moor 28, 29, 31
Hatchlands Park 129
Hatfield Forest 181, 182, 192
Hawford Dovecote 251
Hawkshead 278
Hawksmoor 236
Hawkwood 168
Hawthorn Dene 316
Hayburn Wyke 296
Headley Common 110
Heald Brow 266
Heddon Valley Shop 31, 65
Heelis 10, 380, 386
Helsby Hill 265
Hembury Woods 29
Henrhyd Falls 333
Hentor 29
Heysham 265
Hezlett House 367
Hidcote Manor Garden 65
High Peak Estate 212, 220
Hill Top 278
Hindhead Commons 109, 130
Hinton Ampner Garden 130
Hod Hill 29
Holcombe Moor 265
Holidays 384
The Holies 114
Holme Park Fell 265
Holne Woods 29
Holnicote Estate 30, 67
Holy Jesus Hospital 324
Holywell Bay 28
The Homewood 164

Hope Woodlands 212
Horden Beach 316
Horsey Mere 180
Horsey Windpump 180, 193
Horton Court 104
Houghton Mill 180, 193
Housesteads Fort 316, 323
Howden Moor 212
Hudswell Woods 296
Hughenden Manor 131

Ibsley Common 109
Ickworth House, Park & Garden 182, 194
Ightham Mote 132
Ilam Park 213, 221
Incleborough Hill 180

Jack Scout 266
James, Henry 164

Kearney 357
Kedleston Hall 221
Keld Chapel 264
The Kelseys 28
Killerton 67
Kinder Scout 212
King John's Hunting Lodge 70
King's Head 133
Kingston Lacy 31, 70
Kingswear 28
Kinver Edge 236, 252
Kinwarton Dovecote 252
Kipling, Rudyard 115
Knightshayes Court 72
Knockinelder 357
Knole 134
The Kymin 344
Kynance Cove 28, 76
Kyson Hill 180

Lacock Abbey & Village 73
Lady's Well 316
Lamb House 164
Lamberts Castle 29
Langdon Hill Wood 31
Lanhydrock 28, 31, 74
Lanlay Meadows 333
Lardon Chase 114
Larrybane 356
Lavenham: Guildhall 195
Lawrence House 75
Lawrence T.E. 48

Learning 372, 375, 376
Leek & Manifold Valley 213
Legacies 388
Leigh Woods 31
Leith Hill 109, 110, 135
Lennon, John 282
Letocetum Roman Baths Site & Museum 253
Levant Mine & Beam Engine 76
Lighthouse Island 357
Lindisfarne Castle 325
Lindsey House 177
Lingwood Common 181
Lisnabreeny 357
Little Clarendon 105
Little Dartmouth 28
Little Fleece Bookshop 105
Little Moreton Hall 279
The Lizard 76
Lizard Point 28
Lizard Wireless Station 77
Llanbedrog Beach 334, 335
Llanerchaeron 344
Lode Mill 183
Lodge Park 77
Loe Pool 28, 86
Logan Rock 28
Long Crendon Courthouse 136
Long Mynd 236, 237
Longshaw Estate 212, 223
Lough Down 114
Loughan Bay 358
Loughwood Meeting House 78
Low Newton-by-Sea 316
Ludshott Common 109
Lundy 79
Lydford Gorge 79
Lyme Park 266, 280
Lytes Cary Manor 80
Lyveden New Bield 224

Maister House 303
Malham Tarn Estate 296, 297, 304
Mam Tor 212
The Manor House, Rathlin Island 356
Marconi Centre 77
Marker's Cottage 70
Marloes Deer Park & Sands 332

Marsden Moor Estate 296, 304
Marsden Rock 316
Martin's Haven 332
Max Gate 81
McCartney, Paul 274
Melbury Beacon 29
Melbury Down 29
Melford Hall 196
Membership 372
Mendips 282
Middle Hope 30
Middle Littleton Tithe Barn 253
Milldale 213
Minchinhampton Common 30
Minnowburn 357
Minsmere Beach 180
Mompesson House 81
Monk's House 164
Monksthorpe Chapel 233
Montacute House 82
Moorhouse Woods 316
Morden Hall Park 168, 173
Morris, William 175
Morston Marshes 180
Morte Point 28
Morville Hall 261
Moseley Old Hall 253
Mottisfont Abbey Garden, House & Estate 136
Mottistone Manor Garden 108, 137
Moulton Hall 313
Mount Grace Priory 305
Mount Stewart House, Garden & Temple of the Winds 368
Mourne Coastal Path 357
Murlough Bay 356
Murlough National Nature Reserve 357
Museum of Childhood, Sudbury Hall 213, 228
Mussenden Temple 364
Mwnt 332, 335
Mynachdy'r Graig 332

Nare Head 28, 31
National Gardens Scheme 375
National Trust for Scotland 373, 387

The Needles Old Battery 109, 138
Nether Alderley Mill 282
Newark Park 84
Newbiggin Cliffs 296
Newton House 341
Newton Pool 316, 317
Newton, Isaac 231
North Antrim Cliff Path 356
North Cliffs 28
North Hill 31
Northey Island 181
Nostell Priory 306
Nunnington Hall 307
Nymans Garden 139

Oakhurst Cottage 140
Old Coastguard Station 296, 297
The Old Manor 224
The Old Mill 84
Old Soar Manor 140
Old Town Hall, Newtown 109, 140
Orford Ness National Nature Reserve 180, 197
Orlock Point 357
Ormesby Hall 308
Osterley Park 168, 173
Overbeck's Museum & Garden 28, 85
Owletts 164
Oxburgh Hall, Garden & Estate 198

Packwood House 254
Parke Estate 29
Patterson's Spade Mill 358, 369
Paxton's Tower 333
Paycocke's 199
Peak Alum Works 296
Peckover House & Garden 199
Pen-y-Fan 333
Penberth 28
Penbryn 332
Penrhyn Castle 345
Penrose Estate 86
Penshaw Monument 316
Pentire 28
Pepperbox Hill 30
Petts Wood 168
Petworth House & Park 141

Philipps House 86
Photography 382
Pilsdon Pen 29
Pin Mill 180
Pinkney's Green 110
Pitstone Windmill 164
Plas Newydd 347
Plas yn Rhiw 347
Plym Bridge Woods 29, 31
Polesden Lacey 110, 142
Port Mulgrave 296
Porth Dafarch 334
Porthclais Harbour 335
Porthcurno 28
Porthdinllaen 334, 335
Porthor 334, 335
Portledge 28
Portlemouth Down 28
Portstewart Strand 356,
    358
Potter, Beatrix 268, 278
Powis Castle & Garden 348
Prawle Point 28
Priest's House, Easton 225
Priest's House, Muchelney
    87
Princes Risborough Manor
    House 164
Prior Park Landscape Garden
    87
Priory Cottages 165
Public Transport 377

Quarry Bank Mill 266, 283
Quebec House 165

Ragwen Point 332
Rainham Hall 177
Ramsey Abbey Gatehouse
    201
Ravenscar Coastal Centre
    296, 297, 313
Rayleigh Mount 181, 201
Red House 175
Reigate Hill 109
Restaurants and tea-rooms
    380
Rhaeadr Ddu 334
Rhossili Visitor Centre 335,
    349
Rievaulx Terrace & Temples
    309
River Wey & Godalming
    Navigations 109, 143

Rockford Common 109
Rodborough Common 30
59 Rodney Street 284
'Roman' Bath 177
Ros Castle 316
Roseberry Topping 296, 310
Rowallane Garden 369
Royal Military Canal 108
Royal Oak Foundation 373
Rufford Old Hall 285
The Rumps 28
Runnymede 145
Runswick Bay 296

St Aidan's Dunes 316
St Anthony Head 31, 88
St Bride's Bay 332
St Catherine's 108
St Cuthbert's Cave 316
St David's Visitor Centre &
    Shop 332, 350
St George's Guildhall 201
St Helen's Duver 110
St John's Jerusalem 165
St Michael's Mount 89
Salcombe Hill 28, 31
Saltram 89
Sand Point 30
Sandham Memorial Chapel
    145
Sandscale Haws 265
Scafell Pike 264
Scarthwood Moor 296
Scotney Castle Garden &
    Estate 146
Seahouses 316
Segontium 350
Selborne Hill and Common
    109
Selsdon Wood 168
Selworthy 67
Seven Sisters 108, 110
Shalford Mill 165
Shaw's Corner 202
Sheffield Park Garden 147
Sherborne Estate 77
Sheringham Park 180, 182,
    202
Shopping 379
Shugborough 237, 255
Shute Barton 105
Shute Shelve Hill 30
Sissinghurst Castle Garden
    148

Sizergh Castle & Garden 286
Skelghyll Woods 288
Skenfrith Castle 350
Skernaghan Point 356
Skirrid Fawr 333
Slieve Donard 357
Slindon Estate 108
Smallhythe Place 149
Snowshill Manor 91
Soar Mill Cove 28
Souter Lighthouse 316, 317,
    326
South Foreland Lighthouse
    108, 149
South Hole 28
South Peak 212
Speke Hall, Garden & Estate
    265, 266, 287
Speltham Down 109
Spencer, Stanley 145
Springhill 370
Sprivers Garden 165
Spyway Farm 29
Stackpole Estate 332, 334,
    351
Stagshaw Garden 288
Stainsby Mill 225
Standen 150
Starehole Bay 28
Staunton Harold Church 226
Staward Gorge 316, 318
Stembridge Tower Mill 105
Steps Bridge 29
Stiffkey Marshes 180
Stockbridge Common Down
    & Marsh 109
Stocktons Wood 265
Stoke-sub-Hamdon Priory
    92
Stoneacre 165
Stonebarrow Hill 31
Stonehenge Historic
    Landscape 29, 92
Stourhead 93
Stowe Landscape Gardens
    151
Strangford Lough Wildlife
    Centre 357, 358
Mr Straw's House 226
Stubbins Estate 265
Studland Beach & Nature
    Reserve 29, 31, 95
Studley Royal Water Garden
    301

Styal Estate 283
Sudbury Hall *213*, 227
Sugar Loaf 333
Sunnycroft 261
Sutton Hoo *180*, *182*, 204
Sutton House *168*, 175
Swtan 334

Talks Service 377
Tarn Hows *265*, *266*, 271
Tattershall Castle *213*, 229
Tatton Park 288
Tennyson Down 109
Terry, Ellen 149
Theatre Royal 205
Thorington Hall 209
Thurstaston Common 265
Tintagel Old Post Office 96
Tintinhull Garden 97
Town Walls Tower 261
Townend 290
Townhead Barn 297
Toys Hill 108
Treasurer's House, Martock 97
Treasurer's House, York 311
Trelissick Garden 98
Trengwainton Garden 99
Trerice 100
Troutbeck 291
Trowlesworthy Warren 29
Tryfan 334
Tudor Merchant's House 351
Turnworth Down 29
Tŷ Isaf 352
Tŷ Mawr Wybrnant *334*, 353
Ty'n-y-Coed Uchaf 353
Tyntesfield 101

Uffington Castle 110
Ullswater 290
Ulster Gardens Scheme 357
Ulverscroft Nature Reserve 230
Uppark 153
Upper Wharfedale *296*, 312
Upton House 257

Valency Valley 28
Ventnor 108
Volunteering 376
The Vyne 154

Waddesdon Manor 155
Waggoners Wells 109
Wakehurst Place 156
Walking 378
Wall Roman Site (Letocetum) 253
Wallington *317*, 327
Walton Hill 30
Warren House Gill 316
Wasdale 291
Washington Old Hall 329
Wastwater 264
Watermeads 168
Watersmeet House *28*, 102
Watlington Hill 109
Wavering Down 30
Weathercock Hill 112
Webbers Post 31
Weddings 380
The Weir 258
Wellbrook Beetling Mill *358*, 371
Wellington Monument 30
Wenlock Edge 236
West Green House Garden 157
West Pennard Court Barn 105
West Runton 180
West Wycombe Park 158
West Wycombe Village and Hill *109*, 159
Westbury College Gatehouse 105
Westbury Court Garden 102
Westwood Manor 103
Wetheral Woods 265
Wheal Coates 28
Whiddon Deer Park 29
Whipsnade Estate 187
Whipsnade Tree Cathedral *181*, 205

The White Cliffs of Dover *108*, *110*, 159
White Cottage 293
White Horse Hill 109
White Mill 105
White Moss Common 265
Whitegates Cottage 233
Whitepark Bay 356
Wichenford Dovecote 259
Wicken Fen National Nature Reserve *180*, *182*, 206
Wightwick Manor 259
Wilderhope Manor 261
Willings Walls 29
Willington Dovecote & Stables 207
2 Willow Road 176
Wimpole Hall *182*, 207
Wimpole Home Farm *182*, 208
Win Green Hill 30
Winchester City Mill 160
Windermere 291
Winkworth Arboretum 161
Winnats Pass 212
Winster Market House 230
The Witley Centre 109, *110*, 162
Wolfe, General James 165
Woodchester Park 104
Woody Bay 28
Woolf, Virginia 164
Woolsthorpe Manor 213, 231
Wordsworth House *266*, 292
The Workhouse, Southwell 232

Y Llethr 334
Yorkshire Coast 312
Ysbyty Estate 334

Zennor Head 28